PER BESKOW

REX GLORIAE

PER BESKOW

REX GLORIAE

*The Kingship of Christ
in the Early Church*

WIPF & STOCK · Eugene, Oregon

Translated by
ERIC J. SHARPE

On the cover:
TRADITIO LEGIS FROM THE SARCOPHAGUS
OF JUNIUS BASSUS, ROME

Wipf and Stock Publishers
199 W 8th Ave, Suite 3
Eugene, OR 97401

Rex Gloriae
The Kingship of Christ in the Early Church
By Beskow, Per and Sharpe, Eric J.
Copyright©1962 by Beskow, Per
ISBN 13: 978-1-62564-641-5
Publication date 2/12/2014
Previously published by Almqvist & Wiksells, 1962

CHRISTUS VINCIT

CHRISTUS REGNAT

CHRISTUS IMPERAT

CONTENTS

Foreword 9

Part I. The Problem

1. The Kingship of Christ in the Fourth Century 11

Part II. The Kingship of Christ in New Testament Messianism and its Development in the post-Apostolic Age

2. Royal Terminology in the New Testament and the Apostolic Fathers 33
3. The Testimonia Tradition 74
4. The Apocalyptic Literature 123
5. Liturgy and Hierarchy 157
6. Christ the King and the Pagan Emperor 173

Part III. The Kingship of Christ in pre-Constantinian Speculative Systems

7. The Logos as King 187
8. The Incarnate Christ as King in Alexandrian Theology . . . 212
9. The Antiochene Tradition 231
10. The Political Thought of the Pseudo-Clementines 242

Part IV. The Kingship of Christ in the Arian Conflict

Introduction 259
11. Eusebius and the Arians 261
12. The Nicene Theologians and the Kingship of Christ 276
13. Pantocrator and Hypsistos 295
14. Christ the King and the Christian Emperor 313

Bibliography 331
Index of Authors 364
Index of Passages 368

FOREWORD

The object of this book is more limited than its title may at first sight seem to indicate. It is intended to be an account of the way in which the New Testament representation of Christ in royal categories lived on during the pre-Constantinian period; how it became enriched by its confrontation with Hellenistic culture; and how this development, in the course of the doctrinal disputes of the 4th century, gave rise to that conception of Christ as King which dominated the theology of the Byzantine period and the Middle Ages in the West. It would have been impossible, in a work of this kind, to have given an exhaustive account of every aspect of the problem, and I have therefore imposed considerable restrictions, particularly upon the religio-historical background. The sacral kingship, for example, is such a huge subject that to trace its connexions with early Christology would require a large number of specialist studies. I hope, however, that this book will suggest areas of wider study, and provide the requisite points of departure for further research. I have also been compelled to leave the Gnostic material virtually untouched, largely because Gnosticism does not seem to have contributed to the Christology of the Byzantine Church.

Since most of the Old Testament quotations in this book are taken from the LXX, I have followed its system of numbering. The numbering of the Hebrew text is as a rule given in parentheses.

Per Beskow

Uppsala, March 22nd, 1962

PART I

The Problem

1. THE KINGSHIP OF CHRIST IN THE FOURTH CENTURY

In recent years scholars have demonstrated the primary importance of the concept of Christ as King during the period subsequent to the victory of Christianity in the Roman Empire; it has also been shown how it reached its zenith under the rule of Theodosius and Honorius (ca. A.D. 380–420). The concept as such recurs frequently in sermons, iconography and the liturgies, and it has often been pointed out that the Church drew freely upon the imperial ideology of post-Constantinian Rome for its imagery.[1] Art historians have paid particular attention to this complex of ideas; the influence of imperial art on Christian iconography during and after the 4th century has proved to be a most fruitful field of research.[2]

---

[1] For the outward form of the imperial ideology in the late Roman Empire the following works are of primary importance: R. DELBRÜCK, *Die Consulardiptychen*, SSK 2 (1929). IDEM, *Das spätantike Kaiserornat*, Die Antike 8 (1932), pp. 1–21. IDEM, *Spätantike Kaiserportraits*, SSK 8 (1933). A. ALFÖLDI, *Die Ausgestaltung des monarchischen Zeremoniells am römischen Kaiserhofe*, RM 49 (1934), pp. 1–118. IDEM, *Insignien und Tracht der römischen Kaiser*, RM 50 (1935), pp. 1–171. O. TREITINGER, *Die oströmische Kaiser- und Reichsidee nach ihrer Gestaltung im höfischen Zeremoniell* (1939). Further, we may refer to two invaluable works on the Emperor cult which have appeared during recent years, viz. L. CERFAUX & J. TONDRIAU, *Un concurrent du christianisme*, Bibl. de théol. 3.5 (1957), and F. TAEGER, *Charisma* 1–2 (1957–60).

[2] Of the comprehensive literature on this subject, the following works are especially worth mentioning: W. J. A. VISSER, *Die Entwicklung des Christusbildes in Literatur und Kunst in der frühchristlichen und frühbyzantinischen Zeit* (1934). A. GRABAR, *L'Empereur dans l'art byzantin*, PFLS 75 (1936). J. KOLLWITZ, *Christus als Lehrer und die Gesetzesübergabe an Petrus in der konstantinischen Kunst Roms*,

Christ is seldom or never portrayed as King in pre-Constantinian Christian art: on Roman sarcophagi or in the catacomb paintings; what we find instead is Christ the Good Shepherd, Christ the Miracle-worker, or Christ the Philosopher in conversation with his disciples. But by the middle of the 4th century—or a little earlier—attempts were being made to stress the majestic aspect of the figure of Christ. In exactly the same way as the Roman Emperor had been represented as *cosmocrator*, Christ is now represented as the cosmic ruler, enthroned on the vault of heaven.[1] His hand is raised in the same gesture of power as Sol Invictus—already adopted as an attribute of Caesar[2]— and he is portrayed in conformity with imperial iconography in the act of bestowing his law on St. Peter (or St. Paul), or of granting the crown of victory to the martyrs.[3] The Heavenly King is surrounded by a court of apostles and martyrs, who face him, their hands raised in a gesture of acclamation, or offering him their crowns.[4]

From the point of view of the history of art, the *Majestas* figure has developed out of the 3rd century representation of Christ the Philosopher. The low chair is raised, and placed on a platform, *suggestus*; it is ornamented in a manner not unlike that of the imperial throne; the fingers, formerly fixed in a rhetorical gesture, are now held in Sol Invictus' gesture of power; the philosopher's scroll has become the

---

RQ 44 (1936), pp. 45–66. IDEM, *Oströmische Plastik der theodosianischen Zeit*, SSK 12 (1941). IDEM, *Das Bild von Christus dem König in Kunst und Liturgie der christlichen Frühzeit*, ThGl 1 (1947), pp. 95–117. IDEM, art. *Christus Basileus*, RAC 2 (1951–54), col. 1257–1262. F. VAN DER MEER, *Maiestas Domini*, StAntCr 13 (1938). H. P. L'ORANGE, *Kejseren på himmeltronen* (1949). IDEM, *Studies in the Iconography of Cosmic Kingship in the Ancient World*, Inst. f. sammenl. kulturforskn. A. 23 (1953). C. IHM, *Die Programme der christlichen Apsismalerei*, FKCA 4 (1960).

[1] On the Galerius arch in Saloniki the two *augusti* are represented as enthroned upon the *Coelus*; Constantine is also said to have been depicted in the same way after his death, Eusebius, Vita Const. 4.69. See KOLLWITZ, *Christus als Lehrer*, p. 56. The motif appears in its Christianized form on Roman sarcophagi shortly after the middle of the 4th century (the sarcophagus of Junius Bassus and Lat. 174).

[2] H. P. L'ORANGE, *Sol invictus imperator*, SO 14 (1935), pp. 86–114. IDEM, *Studies*, pp. 139 ff.

[3] There is here no reason to go into the wide and continuing discussion about the origin and meaning of the *traditio legis*. A good survey of the problems is given by W. N. SCHUMACHER, "*Dominus legem dat*", RQ 54 (1959), pp. 1–39. On the victor's wreath, see below, p. 16, n. 6.

[4] GRABAR, *L'Empereur*, pp. 202 and 205. IHM, *Programme*, pp. 19 f.

Divine law given to Peter.¹ Where the rhetorical gesture has been retained it is reinterpreted as a blessing, *benedictio latina*. However, during the 4th century neither Christ the Philosopher nor Christ the King are portrayed so clearly as to be unmistakably the one or the other, and it is often difficult, when considering certain representations, to decide which of the two aspects is the more prominent.

The influence of imperial iconography is not limited to the actual figure of Christ. A large number of attributes drawn from imperial art came into general use during the 4th century as independent Christian symbols: the Constantinian *labarum*; the "empty" throne, *etimasia*, decorated with symbols of Christ; the victor's wreath; the trophy—all these symbols recur frequently during the period.² Similarly the Christian church, *basilica*, incorporates elements derived from the imperial audience halls: the altar, like the imperial throne, is placed under a canopy, *ciborium*, and is surrounded by curtains, *vela*, emphasizing its sacred and separate character.³

The origin of the Christian basilica has been the subject of a particularly extensive discussion, in which an important role has been played by the question of the Kingship of Christ.⁴ Four of the suggested theories have been considerably influenced by this motif in connexion with the growth of the Christian basilica:

1) The basilica can be traced back to the palace architecture of Imperial Rome.⁵ This theory is accepted in certain circles, but con-

---

[1] F. GERKE, *Die christlichen Sarkophage der vorkonstantinischen Zeit*, SSK 11 (1940), pp. 226 ff. L'ORANGE, *Studies*, pp. 139 ff.

[2] For the throne in early Christian art, see C. O. NORDSTRÖM, *Ravennastudien*, Figura 4 (1953), pp. 46 ff. For the wreath and the trophy, see below, p. 16, n. 6.

[3] On the problem of the canopy-altar, see ALFÖLDI, *Insignien*, pp. 130 f. G. EGGER, *Der Altarbaldachin*, Christl. Kunstbl. 1953, pp. 77 ff. (unavailable to the author). On the altar veils, see KOLLWITZ, *Das Bild*, pp. 105 f. TREITINGER, *Reichsidee*, pp. 40 ff. C. SCHNEIDER, *Studien zum Ursprung liturgischer Einzelheiten östlicher Liturgien* 1 (καταπέτασμα), Kyrios 1 (1936), pp. 57–73.

[4] The best survey of the present state of this discussion (with an extensive bibliography) is given by C. DELVOYE, *Recherches récentes sur les origines de la basilique paléochrétienne*, AIPh 14 (1954–57), pp. 205–228.

[5] DELVOYE, *op. cit.*, pp. 216 ff. J. KOLLWITZ in BZ 42 (1942), pp. 273–276, cf. below, p. 21, n. 4. E. DYGGVE, *Dødekult, Kejserkult og Basilika*, SSO 192 (1943). IDEM, *Fra evangeliekirke til magtkirke*, KÅ 58 (1958), pp. 11–52. E. LANGLOTZ, art. *Basilika*, RAC 1 (1941–50), col. 1225–1249. IDEM, *Der architektonische Ursprung der christlichen Basilika*, Festschr. f. H. Jantzen (1951), pp. 30–36. W. SESTON, *Le culte impérial et les origines de la basilique chrétienne*, Bull. Soc. Nat. des Antiqu. de

tains no special theological implications. It does however form the fundation of the three following theories.

2) The basilica developed in response to the demands of the Christian liturgy, which was in turn influenced by imperial ceremonial.[1] This theory is without doubt correct when applied to some of the later stages in the history of the development of the basilica, but gives rise to distinct problems if we attempt to explain the basilica's *origins* in this way. This applies e.g. to Egger's hypothesis that the transept of the basilica developed from imperial ceremonial. Recent excavations under the Lateran basilica have shown a transept to have been part of the original construction from 313. At this early date we can hardly assume there to have been imperial influence on Christian liturgy.

These two theories are based on the history of architecture, and thus have to do with the Kingship of Christ only indirectly; the two other theories connect the basilica direct with Christ the *basileus*. They have furthermore given rise to much wider discussion than the first pair.

3) During the 4th century the basilica was thought to be an image of the heavenly Jerusalem, or the throne-room of God or Christ.[2]

4) The term basilica has to do with the idea of Christ as *basileus*.[3]

France (1948–49), pp. 200–201. IDEM, *Le culte impérial, le culte des morts et les origines de la basilique latine chrétienne*, REL 27 (1949), pp. 82–83. A. STANGE, *Das frühchristliche Kirchengebäude als Bild des Himmels* (1950). W. SAS-ZALOZIECKY, *Westrom oder Ostrom*, JÖBG 2 (1952), pp. 150–152. J. B. WARD PERKINS, *Constantine and the Origin of the Christian Basilica*, PBSR 22 (1954), pp. 69–90.

[1] ALFÖLDI, *Ausgestaltung*, passim. IDEM, *Insignien*, passim. SAS-ZALOZIECKY, op. cit. DELVOYE, op. cit., p. 217. G. EGGER, *Römischer Kaiserkult und konstantinischer Kirchenbau*, JAIW 43 (1958), pp. 20–132. Cf. the critical review by O. NUSSBAUM, JbAC 2 (1959), pp. 146–148.

[2] L. KITSCHELT, *Die frühchristliche Basilika als Darstellung des himmlischen Jerusalems*, Münch. Beitr. z. Kunstgesch. 3 (1938)—(unavailable to the author). Cf. the critical review by KOLLWITZ in BZ 42 (1942), pp. 273–276. SESTON, *Le culte impérial, le culte des morts*. STANGE, *Kirchengebäude*, cf. the critical review by KOLLWITZ in BZ 47 (1954), pp. 169–171. LANGLOTZ, *Ursprung*. A. VON GERKAN, *Die profane und die christliche Basilika*, RQ 48 (1953), pp. 128–146. S. LANG, *A few Suggestions toward a New Solution of the Origin of the Early Christian Basilica*, RivAC 30 (1954), pp. 189–208. G. BANDMANN, *Mittelalterlicher Architektur als Bedeutungsträger* (1951), pp. 89 f. accepts KITSCHELT's hypothesis but with some reservations.

[3] L. VOELKL, *Die konstantinischen Kirchenbauten nach Eusebius*, RivAC 29 (1953), pp. 49–66, 187–206. IDEM, *Die konstantinischen Kirchenbauten nach den literarischen Quellen des Okzidents*, RivAC 30 (1954), pp. 99–136, especially pp. 105 ff. LANG, *Suggestions*. A criticism of this hypothesis is given by A. M. SCHNEIDER, *Die*

We shall discuss both these theories in the following pages, in the context of the general problem of how the Kingship of Christ was envisaged during the Constantinian period.[1]

This artistic and architectural development may be paralleled in the ceremonial of the Church. Candles and incense are brought before the Gospel or the image of Christ as they were once brought before the image of Caesar.[2] We know from the proceedings of a number of Councils that a particular stage in the proceedings the Gospel was placed on a throne, symbolizing the presence of Christ the King.[3] There developed a rich ceremonial, on the pattern of that connected with the Emperor, around the bishop as the representative of Christ; the design of the bishop's throne was based on that of the imperial throne; his vestments and insignia resemble those of high civic dignitaries.[4] The liturgy takes on more and more of the character of court ceremonial —before the invisible, but present, King of Glory.

This development is also reflected in the literature of the Theodosian period and after, particularly in the most outstanding preacher of the time, St. John Chrysostom.[5] Sermons frequently describe Christ as the Heavenly King, enthroned in a palace gleaming with gold and precious stones; the angels form his body-guard and the martyrs his *philoi*; he is the supreme commander of the *militia christiania*; he presides over the imperial games of life, like Caesar in his circus, and crowns the victor. The "royal" motif has a particular eucharistic significance in the Antiochene tradition, in St. John Chrysostom, Theodore of Mopsuestia and Narses: the Eucharist is compared to a royal audience, constant emphasis being placed on the fear and trembling in which

---

altchristlichen Bischofs- und Gemeindekirchen und ihre Benennung, GN 1952. 7, pp. 153–161, and VON GERKAN, *Basilika*.

[1] Cf. J. A. JUNGMANN, *Missarum Sollemnia* (1948), pp. 51 f.

[2] KOLLWITZ, *Plastik*, p. 148. IDEM, *Das Bild*, p. 104. C. SCHNEIDER, *Studien zum Ursprung liturgischer Einzelheiten östlicher Liturgien* 2 (θυμιάματα), Kyrios 3 (1938), pp. 149–190.

[3] KOLLWITZ, *Plastik*, p. 149. IDEM, *Das Bild*, p. 107. GRABAR, *L'Empereur*, p. 199.

[4] For the bishop's throne, see E. STOMMEL, *Die bischöfliche Kathedra im christlichen Altertum*, MThZ 3 (1952), pp. 17–32. IDEM, *Bischofsstuhl und Hoher Thron*, JbAC 1 (1958), pp. 52–78. H. U. INSTINSKY, *Bischofsstuhl und Kaiserthron* (1955). Cf. the criticism of INSTINSKY's ideas in STOMMEL, *Bischofsstuhl*. For the other episcopal insignia, see TH. KLAUSER, *Der Ursprung der bischöflichen Insignien und Ehrenrechte*, Bonner Rektoratsrede 11.12.1948 (1949).

[5] Examples in KOLLWITZ *Plastik*, pp. 145 ff.

the faithful ought to approach the King, present in the bread and the wine.¹

As early as in the NT we find a striking degree of resemblance between the epithets applied to Christ and the titles bestowed upon the Roman Emperor;² this parallelism lived on in the post-Apostolic age. But the ecclestial literature of the 4th century, and the liturgies in particular, witness to a considerable amount of borrowing from the imperial ideology and hence to a new and characteristic accent in Christology.³

Certain of the military titles and attributes of the Roman Emperor were also taken over by the Church. Christ is depicted in the NT and in the pre-Constantinian Church as *victor, triumphator* and *imperator*; the faithful are described as his soldiers and the martyrs as sharing his victory.⁴ This terminology occurs most frequently in the Acts of the Martyrs, but also exercised a distinct influence on the developing Christian Latin, where concepts like *statio* and *sacramentum* were taken from the language of the Roman army.⁵ Again, this terminology becomes more common during the 4th century. Christian art, too, began at this time to make use of military symbols, such as the trophy and the laurel wreath; the Cross is the sign of Christ's victory and the wreath the martyr's prize, reserved for those who have proved victorious in the race of life.⁶

---

[1] J. QUASTEN, *Mysterium tremendum*, in Vom christlichen Mysterium ... zum Gedächtnis von O. Casel (1951), pp. 61–75. From the Homilies of Narses some examples are quoted by G. WIDENGREN, *Religionens värld*, 2nd ed. (1953), p. 248, which belong in this context. Cf. JUNGMANN, *Missarum Sollemnia*, pp. 47 ff. On the φόβος-motif in Byzantine conception of the liturgy, cf. also examples in G. ANRICH, *Das antike Mysterienwesen in seinem Einfluss auf das Christentum* (1894), pp. 218 ff.

[2] G. A. DEISSMANN, *Licht vom Osten*, 4th ed. (1923), pp. 298 ff. See further below, p. 36.

[3] KOLLWITZ, *Plastik*, pp. 145 ff. IDEM, *Das Bild*, pp. 96 ff. W. DÜRIG, *Pietas liturgica* (1958), pp. 170 ff.

[4] A. VON HARNACK, *Militia Christi* (1905), *passim*. E. PETERSON, *Christus als Imperator*, PThT (1951), pp. 149–164. IDEM, *Zeuge der Wahrheit*, PThT, pp. 165–224. Cf. also S. W. J. TEEUWEN, *Sprachlicher Bedeutungswandel bei Tertullian*, StGKA 14.1 (1926).

[5] HARNACK, *op. cit.*, pp. 33 ff. IDEM, *Mission und Ausbreitung des Christentums* 1 (1906), pp. 348 ff. J. DE GHELLINCK, *Pour l'histoire du mot "sacramentum"*, SSL Études et doc. 3 (1924). Cf. also A. A. T. EHRHARDT, *Christian Baptism and Roman Law*, in Festschrift G. Kisch (1955), pp. 147–166.

[6] J. GAGÉ, Σταυρὸς νικοποιός, RhPhR 13 (1933), pp. 370–400. GRABAR, *L'Empereur*, pp. 237 ff. KOLLWITZ, *Plastik*, pp. 150 ff. IDEM, *Das Bild*, p. 97. J. VOGT,

We must note that the concept of Christ as King appears in different areas at different periods. From a purely literary and terminological point of view, Christ is described in royal terms as early as in the NT, and in the post-Apostolic age up to the time of Constantine, although the motif is not dominant. But it is difficult to demonstrate its occurrence in iconography before the time of Constantine; there have been attempts to trace the *Majestas* figure in the catacomb paintings and on sarcophagi, but all such attempts must be regarded as failures—or at least dubious in the extreme.[1] To judge from the evidence, the motif did not gain a foothold in the liturgy and ceremonial until an even later date.

This lack of unanimity has proved something of a stumbling-block for scholars wishing to determine the precise point at which the concept gained general acceptance. Results achieved have varied enormously, depending on the kind of material which has been used: some say the victory of Constantine, others the accession of Theodosius— not to mention the many dates in between, and those scholars who would date the break-through to the time of the Tetrarchy or even earlier. The most important theories can however be summarized under three headings:

1. The motif came into use during the years immediately following the victory of Constantine. It is an expression of the self-consciousness

---

Berichte über Kreuzeserscheinungen aus dem 4. Jahrh. nach Chr., Mélange Grégoire 1 (1949), pp. 593–606. C. CECCHELLI, *Il trionfo della croce* (1954). For the crown of victory as a Christian symbol, see K. BAUS, *Der Kranz in Antike und Christentum*, Theophaneia 2 (1940). TH. KLAUSER, *Aurum coronarium*, RM 59 (1944), pp. 129–153. K. WESSEL, *Kranzgold und Lebenskronen* AA 65–66 (1950–51), pp. 103–114. E. H. KANTOROWICZ, *Kaiser Friedrich II. und das Königsbild des Hellenismus*, in Varia Variorum, Festgabe für K. Reinhardt (1952), p. 182 and n. 73 f. See also GRABAR, *op. cit.*, pp. 202, 230 ff., and KOLLWITZ, *Das Bild*, p. 104.

[1] The two most important hypotheses of this kind, viz. those of VON SYBEL and WESSEL, are dealt with in special excursus to this chapter. It may be of interest in this context to draw attention to ROOSVAL's unfortunate attempt to date the Junius Bassus sarcophagus to the latter half of the 3rd century. See J. ROOSVAL, *Junius Bassus' sarkofag och dess datering*, in Arkeologiska studier tillägnade HKH Kronprins Gustaf Adolf, Stockholm 1932, pp. 273–287, and IDEM, *Petrus- och Moses-gruppen bland Roms sarkofager*, in Konsthist. Tidskr. 1 (1932), pp. 77–88. ROOSVAL's dating won little support, and is now considered to have been disproved by GERKE, *Ist der Sarkophag des Junius Bassus umzudatieren?* in RivAC 10 (1933), pp. 105–118. It is generally considered that the sarcophagus originated in 358 or 359.

and triumph felt by all Christans at that time; the persecutions were over, and the future of Christianity as the privileged religion of the Roman Empire seemed assured. In the victory of the Church was seen the victory of Christ. During the persecutions the Church had confessed Christ as leader and King; now, after a period of political revolution and under a new regime, what had previously been an illegal battle-cry had become the call of a victorious ideology. At the same time the Church was compelled to adapt her picture of Christ to meet the needs of a flood of converts, who wanted a powerful and victorious Lord, not a crucified God.[1]

This theory has been expressed in extreme form by Gerke, who is of the opinion that the contrast between pre-Constantinian and Constantinian Christian art is based on profound ideological differences.[2] He expresses this contrast in a number of antitheses: the pre-Constantinian period is a time of trouble for the Church; the Constantinian a time of political security. Before Constantine Christian thought is dominated by Christian philosophy, the concept of immortality, which developed out of the individual Christian's longing for salvation. Here the stage is held by the conflict between death and salvation, But the later period sees the rise of other concepts: instead of symbolism and philosophy, the writing of history; instead of the abstract "shepherd" symbol, Christ the King in all his glory. The symbol of salvation is replaced by that of typology.

Although Gerke claims to be able to demonstrate this development from the art of the periods in question, his construction is nevertheless ideologically misleading. The pre-Constantinian Church was not distinguished by its supra-historical views, or by Hellenistic notions of immortality. Its God was not remote and transcendent; it was recognized even before the 4th century—even in Alexandrian theology—that God had revealed himself in history through Christ. Throughout

---

[1] See the account in C. RICHTSTAETTER, *Christusfrömmigkeit in ihrer historischen Entfaltung* (Köln 1949), pp. 36 ff. and its authoritative criticism in BAUS, *Das Nachwirken*, pp. 37 ff. The theory has been criticized from the point of view of iconography in GRABAR, *L'Empereur*, p. 193. GRABAR states that Christian triumphal art depicts, not the victory of the Christians, but of Christ. He considers the borrowing which took place from imperial triumphal art to be connected rather with the court theologians' view of Caesar as an earthly image of the heavenly monarch. On this view see further text, point 2.

[2] F. GERKE, *Ideengeschichte der ältesten christlichen Kunst*, ZKG 59 (1940), pp. 1–102. IDEM, *Der Trierer Agricius-Sarkophag* (1949), pp. 29 f.

the early Church there is the consciousness that the OT contains *typoi* of the coming salvation in Christ; this is no more prominent during the 4th century than it was earlier. Gerke's work is, consciously or unconsciously, dependent upon a view of the history of religions which has been superseded.[1]

The theory that faith in Christ as King was dependent on the victory of the Church, a theory which seems to have been most common in older literature, has been favoured particularly by historians of art, who have attempted to show that the Christian basilica received its name from Christ the *basileus*, and that it was built as the throne-room of God or Christ.[2] This is supported by Eusebius' famous speech at the consecration of the basilica at Tyre, probably in the year 314 (HE X.4).[3] Here the theme of the victory of Constantine and Licinius is combined with that of the Lordship of God and Christ. God is described with a mass of OT quotations, particularly from the Psalter, which describe him as a mighty King, who establishes and removes the kings of the earth according to his will (X.4.5–9). He has crushed his opponents and enemies and has raised up his friends, so that both emperors now confess him as the only God, confess Christ the Son of God as King of all creation, and write his beneficent deeds in Rome herself with royal letters (X.4.15–16). The speech continues with a panegyric of Christ the King which is worth reproducing *in extenso*. Of particular interest is the Hellenistic–Roman king–emperor ideal which forms the basis of the analogy:

> For what king ever attained to so much virtue as to fill the ears and tongues of all mankind upon earth with his name? What king, when he had laid down laws so good and wise, was powerful enough to cause them to be published from the ends of the earth and to the bounds of the whole world in the hearing of all mankind? Who abolished the barbarous and uncivilized nations by his civilized and most humane laws? Who, when warred on by all men for whole ages, gave such proof of superhuman might as to flourish daily and remain young throughout his entire life? Who began, which now lies not hidden in some obscure corner of the earth but extends wherever the sun shines? Who so defended his soldiers with the weapons of piety that

---

[1] An example of this supra-historical interpretation is C. SCHNEIDER, *Geistesgeschichte des antiken Christentums* 1–2 (1954). Cf. the sharp criticism by E. STOMMEL in JbAC 1 (1958), pp. 119–129.

[2] VOELKL, *Kirchenbauten* (in RivAC 29), pp. 191 ff. LANG, *Suggestions*, pp. 195 f. Cf. the opinion of STANGE, who considers that the basilica was the throne-room of God, but not of Christ, before the Theodosian era; see below, p. 25 f.

[3] GCS Eus. 2.2.862 ff. See VOELKL, *op. cit.*, pp. 191 ff.

their souls proved harder than adamant when they contended with their adversaries? Which of the kings exercises so great a sway, takes the field after death, triumphs over enemies, and fills every place and district and city, both Greek and barbarian, with votive offerings of his royal houses and divine temples, such as the fair ornaments and offerings that we see in this temple? Truly venerable and great are these things, worthy of amazement and wonder, and in themselves clear proofs of the sovereignty of our Saviour: for even now he spoke, and they were made; he commanded, and they were created: for what could resist the will of the universal King and Ruler and the Word of God himself? (X.4.17-20).[1]

Eusebius is here carrying on a rhetorical tradition common in the early Church, but he fills it with new content. It was usual in pre-Constantinian Christian literature to point to the rapid and extensive spread of the Christian faith as a proof of its Divine character. Constant emphasis was placed on the way in which the Gospel had been transmitted to all peoples, to Greeks and barbarians, and to all sorts and conditions of men.[2] It is possible that tradition in its turn is dependent upon the Jewish interpretation of history: at all events, there is a tendency in late Hellenistic Judaism to look upon the diaspora not as a misfortune and a Divine punishment, but as a proof of the Divine commission of Judaism.[3] The Christian Church looked upon itself as the new Israel, the third people, called to gather in both Jews and Gentiles. There was from the very beginning a consciousness of a political commission—a commission to form a nation. The world had been created for the sake of the Church; the victory of Christ had laid the world at his feet; and the task of the Church was to share both in his post-Resurrection rule and in the coming judgment.[4]

The theme that Christ had crushed the opposition of his enemies and placed the kings of the earth beneath his feet is occasionally encountered in pre-Constantinian Christian literature. It need hardly be said that this is not primarily intended to be descriptive of a historical situation; it is rather a confession of the Lordship of Christ after his

---

[1] GCS Eus. 2.2.868 f.

[2] von Harnack, *Mission* 2, pp. 1-16 contains a collection of examples, which provide excellent illustrations of this fact. See especially the following examples quoted by von Harnack: St. Justin, Dial. 117. Clemens of Alexandria, Strom. VI 18.167. Tertullian, Apolog. 37.4 f.; Adv. Jud. 7.6 f. Origenes, De princ. IV 1.1 f.; Comm. on Matt., Comm. ser. 39.

[3] M. Simon, *Verus Israel* (1948), pp. 64 ff.

[4] von Harnack, *op. cit.*, 1, ch. 7 (Die Botschaft von dem neuen Volk und dem dritten Geschlecht), pp. 206-234.

victory—leaving aside the fact that these ideas were stimulated by the undeniable successes of the Church at certain times during the pre-Constantinian period.[1]

What is new in Eusebius' address is to be seen largely in the new religious and political situation. He sees the Kingdom of Christ coming to occupy a more prominent position in the world, since both Constantine and Licinius have attributed their victories to the help of Christ.[2] Christ is the real ruler of the Roman Empire, and hence of the whole world. Eusebius' address in this respect gives a remarkably clear picture of the new situation in which the Church is now placed.[3]

It is also likely that what Eusebius is saying here is representative of common tendency, and that the Kingdom of Christ is a more prominent conception than formerly. Nevertheless, what we find in the earliest documents from the Constantinian period is no more than a point of departure for future developments.[4]

---

[1] Origenes, Hom. on Josh. 9.10, GCS Orig. 2.100: "Convenerunt reges terrae, senatus populusque et principes Romani, ut expugnarent nomen Jesu et Israel simul, decreverunt enim legibus suis ut non sint Christiani. Omnis civitas, omnis ordo Christianorum nomen impugnat. Sed ... principes vel potestates istae contrariae ut non Christianorum genus latius ac profusius propagetur obtinere non valebunt. Confidimus autem quia solum non nos poterunt obtinere visibiles inimici et adversarii nostri verum etiam velociter Jesu domine nostro vincente contereretur satanae sub pedibus servorum eius. Illo etenim duce semper vincent milites sui." VON HARNACK, op. cit., 2, p. 10. N.b. also the classical conception of Christians as the soldiers of Christ, an idea which also occurs in Eusebius' consecration speech. The progress of the Church among the governing classes and at the imperial court is mentioned by Eusebius, HE VIII. 1.1 ff., GCS Eus. 2.2.736 ff.

[2] Lactantius, De mort. persec. 48.11, CSEL 27.2.233. Eusebius, HE IX. 9.12, GCS Eus. 2.2.832.

[3] It is not easy to understand why VOELKL (Kirchenbauten in RivAC 29, pp. 191 f.) considers the consecration speech as an expression of Eusebius' double role of Nicene theologian and Constantinian court theologian. Both belong to a much later period in Eusebius' life—if Eusebius can be called a Nicene theologian at all. Furthermore, his speech is not an isolated phenomenon in his ecclesiastical history; the same ideas recur on a number of occasions elsewhere. Of particular significance is HE I 3.19, GCS Eus. 2.1.36 ff.: "It is a great and convincing proof of his incorporeal and divine unction that he alone of all those who have ever existed is even to the present day called Christ by all men throughout the world, and is confessed and witnessed to under this name, and is commemorated both by Greeks and Barbarians, and even to this day is honoured as a King by his followers throughout the world ..."

[4] The theory that the oldest Christian basilicas, those from the time of Constantine, were designed as throne-rooms for Christ the King, has been sharply criticized

2. The concept derives its real importance from the Christological development after the Council of Nicaea; both Athanasian orthodoxy and Arian court theology must therefore be taken into consideration as contributory factors. The actual turning-point must thus be placed at some time before or around the death of Constantine in 337.

This estimate is confirmed by Roman iconography; we have no images of Christ which date from the time of Constantine and which can be regarded with certainty as being *Majestas* representations.[1] Not before the years around the death of Constantine do we encounter the first examples of Christian adaptations of imperial symbols: a group of passion sarcophagi, with the Cross in the centre, crowned by the Constantinian *labarum* in a laurel wreath, and surrounded by the sun and moon, symbolizing the cosmic dimensions of salvation.[2]

(see above p. 14). This is even more true of the statement that the Christian basilica derived its name from the idea that God or Christ was regarded as King. At this time "basilica" seems to have been the common name for a rectangular building with columns inside; it could also be used of other, larger buildings. In neither case is there a normal train of thought leading from basilica to *basileus*. The original meaning of the word seems to have declined altogether during the Constantinian period. Further, Eusebius' speech contains a rhetorical play on words, in which the basilica (βασίλειος οἶκος) is made into a palace for the victorious King of the world. A. M. SCHNEIDER's idea (*Bischofs- und Gemeindekirchen*, p. 161) that Eusebius' expression βασίλειος οἶκος in the consecration speech (X. 4.20, 42 and 63) was used as a technical term for the court basilica, *basilica forensis*, is based on a misunderstanding of X.4.20. SCHNEIDER understands it as meaning that it is *Constantine* who is said to have had built (court) basilicas and temples (=churches) after his victory; the first stage took place in the towns in which he did not reside, and where he thus had no need of a palace. But as is clear from the above quotation from the speech, it is *Christ* whom Eusebius calls the master-builder; the houses built by the King cannot be other than churches.

We cannot consider in this context the connexion between the Constantinian basilica and the palace architecture, or Constantine's ambition to create a Christian monumental architecture. See above, p. 13 f.

[1] The information in *Liber Pontificalis* (Duchesne 1, p. 172) that Constantine gave the Lateran Church a *fastidium* bearing a picture of Christ enthroned between four angels (accepted by GRABAR, L'Empereur, p. 196), can hardly be accounted accurate since the theme is otherwise entirely unknown from this period. See KOLLWITZ, *Christus als Lehrer*, p. 54, n. 43. The reliability of *Liber Pontificalis* as a historical source-book is subject to serious doubts. On the sarcophagi of Arles and Florence and the sarcophagus of Cardinal Albani in St. Sebastiano, see Excursus 2.

[2] H. VON CAMPENHAUSEN, *Die Passionssarkophage*, Marb. Jahrb. f. Kunstwiss. 5 (1929), pp. 29 f. GRABAR, *op. cit.*, pp. 240 ff. F. GERKE, *Die Zeitbestimmung der Passionssarkophage*, Archaeologiai Ertesitö 52 (1939), pp. 195 ff. SCHUMACHER,

The first appearance of representations of Christ in which he is unmistakably portrayed as King of the world, cannot be dated earlier than to the middle of the century. We have a group of Roman sarcophagi from the period shortly after 350, on which Christ is represented, enthroned on the personified vault of heaven, *Coelus*, and handing the law to St. Peter.¹ Two mosaics in the smaller apses of the mausoleum of Constantine's daughter Constantina—usually known as St. Costanza—would seem to be of somewhat later date. One represents Christ, clad in a purple robe, enthroned on the world-globe and giving St. Peter the keys of heaven. On the other he is shown standing between the leading Apostles on the mount of Paradise; his right hand is raised in a gesture of power, and with his left he is holding out to St. Peter a scroll bearing the inscription *Dominus pacem dat*.² In all these compositions elements have been taken over from imperial art and its representations of Caesar: holding an *adlocutio* or passing on a *mandatum*.³ It is sometimes suggested that the mosaic in the apse of the

---

"*Dominus legem dat*", pp. 15 ff. The best known representative of this group, Lat. 171 (WS I 146.3), is dated by GERKE to about A.D. 340.

¹ The best-known examples are the sarcophagus of Junius Bassus from 359 (WS I.13) and the sarcophagus hitherto called Lat. 174, but which has now been transferred to the Vatican grottos (WS I.121.4). See also WS I.28.1, 3, 29.3, WS III.284,5, 286,10. On the Bassus sarcophagus, see A. DE WAAL, *Der Sarkophag des Junius Bassus* (1900), and F. GERKE, *Der Sarkophag des Iunius Bassus* (1936). On Lat. 174 (which has not so far received any other name in literature), see H. VON SCHOENEBECK, *Die christliche Sarkophagplastik unter Konstantin*, in RM 51 (1936), pp. 326 ff., and GERKE, *Christus in der spätantiken Plastik*, 3rd ed. (1948), p. 97. GERKE dates Lat. 174 to 350–360; SCHOENEBECK considers it to be rather more recent than the Bassus sarcophagus. On the question of the imperial patterns for this representation, see above p. 12, n. 1. Cf. also p. 17, n. 1 (ROOSVAL's hypothesis).

² The most usual dating of these mosaics, which are incidentally in very bad condition, is 360–370. A quite different dating is given by G. J. HOOGEWERFF, *Il mosaico absidale di San Giovanni in Laterano ed altri mosaici romani*, AAR 27 (1953), p. 322, where he tries, somewhat surprisingly to date the mosaics to the 7th or 8th century. The two most modern works on St. Costanza, K. LEHMANN, *Sta. Costanza*, ArtB 37 (1955), pp. 194–196 and 291, and H. STERN, *Les mosaïques de l'église de Saint-Constance à Rome*, DOP 12 (1958), pp. 157–218, do not consider the apse mosaics. STERN states only (*op. cit.*, p. 160) that their dating is uncertain but that they are probably contemporary with the rest of the decoration from the middle of the 4th century.

³ SCHUMACHER, "*Dominus legem dat*", *passim*. For the question of the *traditio legis* see also the penetrating survey by G. DE FRANCOVICH, *Studi sulla scultura Ravennate* 1, FR 3.26–27 (1958), pp. 118 ff.

old Church of St. Peter, which in all probability dates from shortly after the death of Constantine,¹ represented Christ passing on the law to St. Peter. Extant copies of the mosaic destroyed in the 16th century —although it is by no means certain that this was identical with the Constantinian mosaic—show only Christ sitting between St. Peter and St. Paul,² and thus depict Christ the Philosopher rather than Christ the King.

Kollwitz has stated in a number of contexts that the turning-point, both artistic and conceptual, should be dated to the second quarter of the 4th century, i.e. after 324, when Constantine became sole ruler of the Empire, and after the Council of Nicaea, 325. It had been established at Nicaea that the Son is of one substance with the Father. All things are created through him, and he is therefore Lord of the whole world, and the object of the same honour as the Father. *Rex* and *basileus* are found among the titles appearing in *symbola* from this period.³ According to Kollwitz, there is another current of thought which contributed more than the theology of St. Athanasius and St. Hilary of Poitiers toward the transfer of the title and symbolism of Caesar to Christ: the work of the court theologians and panegyrists in general, and the later work of Eusebius in particular.

In this literature the Christian empire is represented as an image of the heavenly monarchy, and Caesar as an earthly parallel to Christ.⁴ The more this parallelism is pressed, the more epithets become transferred from Caesar to Christ.⁵ Kollwitz is of the opinion that this development may be discerned in Eusebius' Christological terminology. In the earlier writings the title *basileus* was applied to the Father, but

---

[1] E. KIRSCHBAUM, *Die Gräber der Apostelfürsten* (1957), pp. 151 ff.

[2] DE FRANCOVICH, *op. cit.*, pp. 127 ff. This fact has earlier been mentioned by L. DE BRUYNE, *La décoration des baptistères paléochrétiens*, Misc. L. C. Mohlberg, EL Bibl. 22 (1948), p. 196.

[3] KOLLWITZ, *Christus als Lehrer*, pp. 57 f. IDEM, *Das Bild*, p. 101. These creeds will be discussed below, Chap. 11.

[4] KOLLWITZ here bases his opinion primarily upon E. PETERSON, *Der Monotheismus als politisches Problem*, PThT (1951), pp. 45–147. The same problem is treated by TREITINGER, *Reichsidee*, pp. 34 ff. J. A. STRAUB, *Vom Herrscherideal in der Spätantike*, FKG 18 (1939), pp. 113 ff. (Das christliche Herrscherbild bei Eusebius von Caesarea). K. M. SETTON, *Christian Attitude towards the Emperor in the Fourth Century* (1941).

[5] See also SETTON, *op. cit.*, pp. 57 f.

this restriction disappears in later works.¹ Kollwitz' view, that the motif came into general use at about the time of the death of Constantine, is shared by other art historians—Krautheimer and Weisbach, for example.² Stange, whose position is virtually unique (see under point 3), considers that Athanasius' visit to Rome in 340 was of significance for the Roman Church's idea of Christ, and hence for Roman Church art.³

3. Stange holds the theory that Christ did not come to be regarded as King until the time at which he become the object of prayer in the liturgy, i.e. during the reign of Theodosius. It is in connexion with Jungmann's work on the history of the liturgy that Stange dates the artistic turning-point to the Theodosian period.⁴ He is therefore compelled to reject the two theories to which we have referred in points 1 and 2. Stange is also of the opinion that the basilica was intended as a throne-room—he is in fact one of the most powerful advocates of the theory—but in his view it is not Christ, but the Father, who is the ruler in the basilica.⁵ Christ is not worshipped as *rex gloriae* until liturgical prayers begin to be addressed to him—i.e. at the close of the 4th century.⁶ The rebuilt cathedral in Trier (ca. 380) is the oldest example of a church designed as the throne-room of Christ.⁷ In the

---

[1] KOLLWITZ first put forward his theory in *Das Bild*, p. 97, but here builds entirely on material he had published earlier in *Christus als Lehrer*, p. 57 f. and n. 66–68. We shall take up the question in more detail in a later chapter (Chap. 11). The difficulties of the problem are seen in the consecration speech from 314, in which, as we have seen, the Kingship of Christ is the overall theme.

[2] R. KRAUTHEIMER, *The Beginning of Christian Architecture*, RevR 3 (1938–39), p. 138: "It is during the second quarter of the fourth century, shortly before the death of Constantine, that Christ, surrounded by the Apostles, is depicted like an Emperor surrounded by his Senate; it is about this time, that he is addressed as Basileus, as King of Kings, and is represented with a halo, an imperial attribute, and in imperial dress." W. WEISBACH, *Geschichtliche Voraussetzungen einer christlichen Kunst* (1937) has not been available to the author.

[3] STANGE, *Kirchengebäude*, p. 85. This idea is, however, not carried out. It does not in fact fit into STANGE's system, because it is not until a later period that the motif—according to STANGE—breaks through.

[4] STANGE bases his hypothesis primarily on J. A. JUNGMANN, *Die Stellung Christi im liturgischen Gebet*, LF 7–8 (1925).

[5] STANGE, *op. cit.*, p. 87: "Nicht Thronsäle Christi konnten diese Basiliken sein, Thronsäle Gottes waren sie."

[6] STANGE, *op. cit.*, p. 88: "Solange Christus noch nicht als rex gloriae verehrt wurde, solange sich die liturgischen Gebete noch nicht an ihn richteten, fehlte dafür eine, die entscheidende Voraussetzung."

[7] STANGE, *op. cit.*, pp. 110 ff.

same way the mosaic in the apse of St. Pudenziana in Rome provides the first example of a pictorial representation of Christ as King.[1] Earlier representations of Christ, which we mentioned above under point 2, are explained by Stange as representing him as hero or victor, but not as King.[2] Stange's extreme position has not won very much support, but his ideas must be respected in the sense that these alterations in the form of liturgical prayer meant an important step forward in the Christological development he is discussing.[3]

As we see from this summary of some of the most generally favoured theories, the lack of unanimity in the dating of the break-through of the concept of Christ as King has to do partly with the disparate character of the material—in architecture, iconography, literature, etc.,—and partly with the many possibilities of interpretation which present themselves. Many and varied are the factors, external and internal, which are said to have contributed to this development; they range from politics and theology to Christological speculation and popular piety. Of the theological factors involved, attention is drawn to two

---

[1] STANGE, *op. cit.*, pp. 121 ff.

[2] STANGE, *op. cit.*, p. 85. On the subject of the apse mosaics in St. Costanza and the Junius Bassus sarcophagus we read: "... nun wird er als der Sieger über Tod und Sünde dargestellt, aber noch nicht als Kyrios. Und auch was nach 325 an Sarkophagen erlaubt schien, mied man in Apsiden darzustellen: wir haben keinen Anhaltspunkt, dass in irgendeiner der grossen römischen Basiliken dieser Jahrzehnte Christus als rex gloriae und Herr des Gotteshauses—was noch etwas anderes ist—sichtbar gemacht war." Quite impossible is of course STANGE's view that Christ was not believed to be *kyrios* until the Council of Nicaea, cf. below p. 28, n. 2. Further we must note that sarcophagus sculptures do not appear before 350. This type of representation of Christ is missing not only from the basilica decorations —as far as we can judge from the sparse remains—but from the catacomb paintings, which should have had the same freedom of expression as the sarcophagus sculptures. The probable explanation is that the image was first used in sculpture, and was never transferred to painting and mosaic. See DE FRANCOVICH, *op. cit.*, pp. 133 f.

[3] See the critical review by KOLLWITZ, BZ 47 (1954), p. 170 f., which also includes a resumé of KOLLWITZ' own views, of which we have given an account above. DELVOYE agrees with STANGE's dating, though not for his reasons: "Les expressions de Χριστὸς Βασιλεύς, Rex Regum, utilisées sans doute dès avant Constantin mais parmi bien d'autres prédicats du Christ, n'auraient pris une valeur prédominante que dans la deuxième moitié du IVe siècle à partir de Théodose lorsque s'est développée la théologie impériale avec la conception de l'empire chrétien image de la monarchie céleste." (*Op. cit.*, p. 220.) One wonders however whether this argument does not mean that DELVOYE agrees with KOLLWITZ' theory of the break-through of the motif during the last years of Constantine, when Eusebius set forth his imperial theology, according to which the Emperor is the image of God upon earth.

opposing systems—Athanasian orthodoxy and Arianizing court theology. If both of these theological systems in fact contributed to the concept of Christ as King, fully developed in the Theodosian period, their influence must have been quite distinct, even though both must to some extent have been determined by the political background against which the Arian struggle was fought out. However, the actualization of the idea of Christ as King belongs somewhere in this context. The development which we can trace as beginning with Eusebius' inaugural address in Tyre in 314, and which reached its full flowering during the reign of Theodosius, passed through its decisive phase some time in the middle of the century.

There is a fair consensus of opinion that the Christian Church looked upon Christ as King before the time of Constantine; it could hardly be otherwise, remembering the Messianism of the NT. But most scholars are also agreed that the motif became more prominent during the 4th century. There is however a general tendency to underestimate its significance in the pre-Constantinian period, and to overestimate its later significance,[1] evidently due to the fact that the most important work has been carried out by art historians, who have of course judged the development on a basis of their own material. But there are individual art historians who have interpreted the motif of Christ as King with the help of the pre-Constantinian doctrinal tradition and have taken into account such factors as Psalter exegesis and apocalyptic.[2]

The responsibility for the continued uncertainty as to the development of the concept must be laid primarily at the door of ecclesiastical historians and historians of doctrine, who have generally succeeded in overlooking this and many other questions of typology. For example, Harnack's *Dogmengeschichte* does not even mention the problem in its section on the Constantinian period.

The question of the development of Christological terminology between the NT and the Constantinian period has been dealt with for

[1] BAUS' essay *Das Nachwirken* provides an important corrective to this view. BAUS, as against RICHSTAETTER's one-sided stressing of the victorious Christ in the piety of the 4th century, shows the importance placed on the suffering of Christ, particularly in the preaching of St. Ambrose.

[2] S. H. GUTBERLET, *Die Himmelfahrt Christi in der bildenden Kunst* (1934), pp. 70 ff., deals with the role of Psalter exegesis in the concepts of the Ascension and parousia, but not in detail. She has no knowledge of the two most important Ascension Psalms, 23 (24) and 109 (110). F. VAN DER MEER, *op. cit.*, is the basic work on the role of Christian apocalyptic in primitive Church art.

the most part by art historians as a supplementary study. Notable contributions have been made by Kollwitz, Voelkl and others.[1] Nevertheless, their work has a number of shortcomings, due presumably to the fact that scholars have not had sufficient opportunity of carrying out adequate research in the enormous field involved. One notices in particular a difficulty in distinguishing between borrowed and newly-created terminology.[2] If reliable results are to be obtained from such terminological investigations, it is necessary to have a comprehensive overall view of the literature, of the kind which comes only from the texts themselves. There are at present no studies covering the period from the NT to the time of Constantine; Peterson's essays, though of high quality, deal only with individual points.[3]

Our theme in this dissertation will therefore be the pre-Constantinian Church's view of Christ as King, and we shall try to demonstrate what were the origins of the crisis which led eventually to the Theodosian figure of Christ the Heavenly King.

Excursus 1

Majestas Representations in pre-Constantinian Churches? L. v. Sybel has in a number of works put forward the hypothesis that the apses of several

---

[1] KOLLWITZ, *Christus als Lehrer*, *Plastik* and *Das Bild*, *passim*. VOELKL, *Kirchenbauten* (in RivAC 29), pp. 194 ff. Cf. also K. WESSEL, *Christus Rex*, AA 68 (1953), col. 118–136. (See Excursus 2 below, p. 30 f.)

[2] We have already dealt with the terminological problem p. 21, n. 4 and p. 26, n. 2. A further example of lack of clarity in the matter of the terminological development is KOLLWITZ' statement on the influence of the imperial titles on Christological expressions (*Christus als Lehrer*, p. 57): "Diese Kaisersymbolik wird nun auch auf Christus übertragen, Christus damit ebenfalls als κοσμοκράτωρ und κύριος bezeichnet." The choice of Christological titles in this case is entirely misleading. That Christ is *kyrios* has never been called in question. This word has ever since the NT been the principal title of Christ, and it is not more prominent in the 4th century than it was earlier. But on the other hand κοσμοκράτωρ was never a Christological term in the early Church, either before or after the 4th century. It is reserved in Christian language for the powers of this world, κοσμοκράτορες, whom Christ laid beneath his feet at his victory. There would have been more justification, had KOLLWITZ quoted the term παντοκράτωρ, which made its first appearance as a title for Christ during the 4th century; it had previously been reserved for the Father. But on the other hand this was no imperial title. See below, Chap. 13.

[3] PETERSON, *Christus als Imperator* and *Zeuge der Wahrheit*.

pre-Constantinian Roman churches, *tituli*, though no longer extant, were decorated with two kinds of picture of Christ. The older type portrayed Christ with a short beard, standing, his right hand raised (*aufrufend*) and an open scroll in his left hand. Another type arose later: a bearded Christ, enthroned among the Apostles (*Majestas Domini*). According to v. Sybel we have imitations of both types in the catacombs (WMKR 40.2; and 49 and 75 respectively).[1] The group of three figures, with Christ enthroned between St. Peter and St. Paul, is also believed by v. Sybel to have originated in the pre-Constantinian period.[2]

The problem of the decoration of pre-Constantinian churches in general, and Roman title-churches in particular, is met with now and again in the literature on the subject. It provides a most fascinating topic. There is however no chance of arriving at a satisfactory solution at present, since as far as we know, all the tangible evidence has disappeared (with the exception of the chapel at Dura-Europos, which incidentally provides no support for v. Sybel's thesis). There is of course no reason for supposing the liturgical room to have had the same sort of paintings as the catacombs,[3] but we have not the slightest clue as to the way in which church art and mortuary art differed, if they differed.

v. Sybel's hypothesis has been conclusively disproved—in so far as it concerns itself with matters capable of proof or disproof—by J. P. Kirsch.[4] Kirsch proves that the catacomb painting (WMKR 40.2) taken by v. Sybel to be an example of the older type, does not represent Christ at all, but a prophet or an apostle. There is in fact no evidence from this period to show that Christ was ever portrayed with a beard.

On the second type, Kirsch regards it is probable that it formed part of the decorations inside the liturgical room, and was imitated in catacomb art.[5] However, the Christ type represented here is not *Majestas Domini*, but Christ the Philosopher and his disciples. If the figure of Christ seated among the Apostles was common in the apses of pre-Constantinian churches, it is

---

[1] L. VON SYBEL, *Das Werden christlicher Kunst*, RepK 39 (1916), pp. 125 ff. IDEM, *Mosaiken römischer Apsiden*, ZKG 37 (1918), pp. 274 ff. Cf. IDEM, *Christliche Antike* 1 (1906), pp. 280 ff. and *Das Christentum der Katakomben und Basiliken*, HZ 106 (1910), pp. 23 ff. We have not had access to the two works in which VON SYBEL claims to have considered his hypothesis in most detail, i.e. *Der Herr der Seligkeit* (1913) and *Die Anfänge der Kirchenmalerei*, Christl. Kunstbl., Sept. 1915.

[2] VON SYBEL, Mosaiken, p. 278.

[3] E. MÂLE, *Rome et ses vieilles églises* (1942), pp. 52 f.

[4] J. P. KIRSCH, *Sull'origine dei motivi iconografici nella pittura cimiteriale di Roma*, RivAC 4 (1927), pp. 278 ff. and 284 ff.

[5] Cf. also KIRSCH, *op. cit.*, pp. 275 ff. and fig. 6. The apse fresco reproduced in this figure from the catacomb of Domitilla (WMKR 193) bears a striking resemblance to the mosaic of the Chapel of St. Aquilino in St. Lorenzo, Milan. N.b. *inter alia* the holder for the lecturer's scrolls. There seems to be reason for talking about an imitation of paintings in vanished churches here.

likely that this was due to a desire to represent him as the exalted Teacher
—not as King.

Excursus 2

Majestas Representations on Tetrarchic Sarcophagi? K. Wessel has said
that the origin of the *Majestas* image is to be dated to the Tetrarchic period.[1]
He maintains, as against Grabar, Kollwitz and others, that the adoption of
imperial symbolism by Christian art was not due to any sympathy felt by
the Church for Caesar; on the contrary, it is expressive of a violent polemic
against the Caesar cult of the Tetrarchic period. The theme disappeared
until a time when the political situation changed, and was later taken up
again, though in an altered form (Lat. 171).

Wessel's hypothesis is built on extremely diffuse material: on two Christian sarcophagi from the beginning of the 4th century, dated by Gerke to
the Tetrarchic period. The first is the so-called sarcophagus of Jairus, from
Arles (WS I.38.3); the second is probably somewhat more recent, and comes
from Florence (WS III.287.1). A third sarcophagus of the same type, now
in St. Sebastino, Rome, as the tomb of Cardinal Albani (WS I.40), is dated
by Gerke to the Constantinian period.

All three have the same scene: a beardless Christ, seated on a raised chair
with footstool. His right hand is raised in a rhetorical gesture; in his left
hand he holds a scroll. Christ is surrounded by six persons: two stand on
either side of the chair; two others are approaching—again, one from either
side—with hands and face concealed by a cloth; the last two lie in *proskynesis*,
their hands on the footstool.

This scene has been interpreted in various ways: as different grades of
church penance, as the prayers of the living or as Jesus' farewell discourse.
The third alternative is favoured by Wilpert, and before him by Gerke,
though with certain reservations.[2] Gerke has since stressed the undeniable
"royal" motif of the scene, pointing out that the *proskynesis*, as well as the
custom of covering hands and face, reproduce Persian court ceremonial; he
thus calls the representation "*Thronrede*".[3] Its composition evidently belongs
somewhere along the line of development from the philosophical to the royal
Christ, though the emphasis still seems to be laid on the teaching aspect.[4]

---

[1] WESSEL, *Christus Rex*, pp. 118 ff.

[2] WILPERT in WS I, pp. 49 ff. F. GERKE, *Der neugefundene altchristliche Friessarkophag im Museo Archeologico zu Florenz und das Problem der Entwicklung der ältesten christlichen Friessarkophagen*, ZKG 54 (1935), p. 19, n. 4. Cf. pp. 29 ff.

[3] GERKE, *Die christlichen Sarkophage*, p. 292, n. 1. IDEM, *Der Trierer Agricius-Sarkophag*, pp. 29 f.

[4] This is at least KOLLWITZ' view: "Mir scheint, dass auch hier ... an Gläubige zu denken ist, die nun aber nicht mehr neben Christus sitzen als seine Schüler, sondern in demütiger Haltung sich ihrem Lehrer nahen, wobei Lehrer wohl einen

The problem of iconography is a difficult one; this is no less true of the problem of dating. Although Gerke's dating of the Arles sarcophagus to 300 and the Florence sarcophagus to 310[1] has still not been challenged, Gerke himself tends to link the sarcophagi with Constantinian, rather than with Tetrarchic representations. He has characterized the scene as "*spättetrarchisch-frühkonstantinisch*",[2] and has explained that it originated from "the spirit of Lactantius and Eusebius",[3] which places the composition in the conceptual context of the beginning of the Constantinian age. A further indication that Gerke considers these sarcophagi to stand on the boundary of the Constantinian period is to be seen in the cursory treatment they receive in his comprehensive work *Die christlichen Sarkophage der vorkonstantinischen Zeit*; he evidently considers them to be outside the bounds of his period.

Furthermore, there appears to be good reason for dating all three sarcophagi to late Constantinian times.[4] Should such a dating win general recognition, those who favour the pre-Constantinian origins of the *Majestas* representation would lose their most important support.

---

sehr abgeblassten Sinn hat. Es ist einfach das Christusbild der Zeit." (*Christus als Lehrer*, pp. 51 ff., not noted by WESSEL.) KOLLWITZ further points (on p. 53) to a number of examples, showing that *proskynesis* was not unknown in the catacomb paintings and in sarcophagus art, and that in this context it had nothing to do with the *Majestas* image, but rather with the representation of Christ as miracle-worker.

[1] See above, p. 30, n. 3.
[2] *Die christlichen Sarkophage*, p. 226, n. 1.
[3] *Der Trierer Agricius-Sarkophag*, p. 30.
[4] Professor H. P. L'Orange, in conversation with the author, has said that all three sarcophagi ought to be dated later than the reliefs on the Arch of Constantine.

PART II

The Kingship of Christ in New Testament Messianism and its Development in the post-Apostolic Age

2. ROYAL TERMINOLOGY IN THE NEW TESTAMENT AND THE APOSTOLIC FATHERS

The Kingship of Christ in the New Testament is an eschatological concept, and must be seen in relation to the various Messianic concepts of Judaism. It is closely related to the NT doctrine that the Kingdom of God began to be manifested at the coming of Christ, and is soon to be consummated at the expected judgment. Christ and the Kingdom are intimately connected; as K. L. Schmidt has emphasized, Christ *is* the Kingdom: to use Origen's classical expression, he is αὐτοβασιλεία.[1] The relationship of Christ to the Kingdom has been expressed in a number of ways by different exegetes—doubtless due to the far from straightforward character of those NT texts in which the Kingdom of God is mentioned.[2] There is however a large group of NT texts in which Christ is said to be ruler in the Kingdom. God appointed Christ King over his Kingdom when he set him at his right hand at the Ascension; it is Christ, as God's representative, who will judge mankind when the Kingdom comes in its fulness.

First, then, we must be quite clear as to what is *not* meant by the Kingship of Christ in the NT. It is never a question of a this-worldly political or social entity over which Christ is in some way or other

---

[1] K. L. SCHMIDT, *Die Wortgruppe* βασιλεύς κτλ. *im N. T.*, ThWB 1 (1932–33), pp. 576–595.

[2] See the survey by J. W. DOEVE, *Jewish Hermeneutics in the Synoptic Gospels and Acts* (1953), pp. 119 ff.

ruler. That kind of Messianism was common in Judaism, and has had its day, too, in some Christian circles (e.g. that around Cerinthus). But the main stream of early Christianity looked upon Christ as the *heavenly* King, whose Kingdom is not of this world. He rules over the Church from his heavenly throne, but there is to be no overthrowing of political powers—not until the day when the present economy in its entirety ceases to exist.[1]

Nor is Christ called "King" as a way of expressing his relationship to the individual. Christ the King of the individual, controlling his desires and guiding him according to the will of God, is a motif which was soon to appear in mystical theology—from Origen onward—but of which there is no trace in the NT. When Christ is referred to as King in the NT writings, this is always understood as referring to his Kingship over the Kingdom of God, or the People of God, the new Israel, which he has purchased by his suffering. The vital aspects of the early Christian attitude to the Kingship are thus the eschatological and the collective.

These aspects are not as outstanding in the post-Apostolic age as in the NT, due mainly to the fact that the doctrine of the Church became increasingly independent of its Semitic background, once it was transferred to the Hellenistic world. The Greeks found a number of concepts used by the early Church more or less incomprehensible, the result being that the early Christian kerygma had to be reformulated in a manner which was not always adequate to express the content to be transmitted.[2] Not least the eschatological basis and the idea of the People of God were forced into the background in this situation: Christ came to be looked upon as θεός and σωτήρ.[3] The Messianic terminology of Judaism virtually disappeared, or was reinterpreted in various ways: Χριστός was understood as a personal name; ὁ υἱὸς τοῦ ἀνθρώπου as an expression of Christ's humanity; κύριος as an expression of his

---

[1] See J. Héring, *Le Royaume de Dieu et sa venue*, EHPhR 35 (1937), *passim*. J. Bonsirven, *Le Règne de Dieu*, Théologie 37 (1957), *passim*. R. Schnackenburg, *Gottes Herrschaft und Reich* (1959), *passim*. Cf. on the other hand the too-political interpretation of NT theology in A. A. T. Ehrhardt, *Politische Metaphysik von Solon bis Augustin* 2 (1959), and the critical review by P. Beskow in SEÅ 26 (1961), pp. 147–151.

[2] This problem is well presented by G. Dix, The Gospel for the Greeks, in his book *Jew and Greek* (1953), pp. 76 ff. Cf. also C. F. D. Moule, *The Influence of Circumstances on the Use of Christological Terms*, JTS 10 (1959), pp. 247–263.

[3] See below, p. 58.

Divinity. The royal aspect of Christ in particular became obscured—noticeable in the Apostolic Fathers and the Apologists (with the exception of Justin Martyr, whose writings contain a large proportion of *testimonia* material). The eschatological aspect is given little prominence in the Alexandrian authors; this leaves distinct traces in their attitude to the Kingship of Christ.

But on the other hand the Messianic categories retained their significance in certain types of conservative literature, in which the heritage of the OT and Palestinian Judaism were most clearly conserved: in apocalyptic literature, in the *testimonia* tradition and the literature of the Martyrs; this is also true, though to a lesser extent, of the liturgies. We shall find that 4th century ideas on the Kingship of Christ constantly hark back to these classes of literature.

In the following section we shall therefore consider those types of literature in which the NT ideas on the Kingship of Christ are most clearly expressed and through which they live on during the pre-Constantinian period. We have been compelled to restrict our investigation to those themes we consider vital to the pre-Constantinian development. We do not feel it necessary in this context to give a complete account of the NT doctrine of the Kingship of Christ.[1] Nor have we concerned ourselves to any great extent with Gnostic material; although the Kingship of Christ would seem to have played a certain role in Gnosticism, its meaning there was quite different. This is a by-path, and of little or no significance for our investigation of the origins and growth of the overall conception which we find fully developed during the Theodosian period.

Constant reference has been made in this debate to the royal epithets given to Christ by the early Church. However, it has not always been shown with sufficient clarity just when and in what contexts the terms in question make their appearance as Christological epithets. When there exist parallels between the terminology of the Christian Church and the Roman empire, there has often been an uncritical

---

[1] For a more complete treatment of these problems we may refer especially to the works by O. CULLMANN, *Königsherrschaft Christi und Kirche im Neuen Testament*, ThSt 10 (1941). IDEM, *Christus und die Zeit* (1948). IDEM, *Les premières confessions de foi chrétiennes*, CRHPhR 30 (1948). IDEM, *Dieu et César* (1956). IDEM, *Die Christologie des Neuen Testaments*, 2nd ed. (1958). A good survey of Prof. CULLMANN's conception of the Kingdom of Christ is given (with some critical remarks) by J. FRISQUE, *Oscar Cullmann* (1960), especially pp. 106 ff. ("La royauté du Christ et l'Église").

tendency to assume influence by the latter on the former, without stopping to examine alternative possibilities. And finally, the distinction between epithets given to Christ and those reserved for the Father has not always been clearly drawn. It is therefore necessary, if we would obtain a clear picture of the faith of the early Church in Christ the King, to examine the nature and use of this Christological terminology.

The pioneer work on the comparative terminology of Christianity and the imperial cult is Deissmann's *Licht vom Osten*.[1] Deissmann discovered a large number of cases in which the language of the earliest Christian Church corresponded with that of Hellenistic State ideology in the Greek-speaking parts of the Roman empire. He saw the main cause of this correspondence in the *Kontraststimmung* felt by the early Church over against the imperial cult.[2] The ostentatious cultic terms applied to Caesar were taken by Christians and transferred to the Son of God, whom they considered to be their rightful bearer. In this way there arose a polemic parallelism between the cult of Caesar and the cult of Christ; even when the Christological terms were originally derived from the LXX or the Gospels, they later came into conflict with similar terms from the imperial cult.

Deissmann took up most of the terms which have since come under discussion: ἄξιος, ἀρχιερεύς, ἀρχιστράτηγος, βασιλεύς, δεσπότης, εὐεργέτης, θεός, θεοῦ υἱός, ἱερὰ γράμματα, κύριος, κυριακός, σωτήρ, εὐαγγέλιον, ἐπιφάνεια, παρουσία, φιλανθρωπία.[3] He found parallels to all these in the language of the Roman imperial cult. But it must not be imagined that he was so naïve as to attempt to *derive* them all from this source. His work was however responsible for starting the debate on the relation between the terminology applied to Christ and that applied to Caesar.

Research has since shown it to be impossible to deal with all these

---

[1] G. A. DEISSMANN, *Licht vom Osten*, 1st ed. (1908); in the following pages we refer to the 4th ed. (1923). Before DEISSMANN no important work on the whole subject seems to have been published; only examinations of separate Christological terms. DEISSMANN himself refers mainly to works by classical scholars, especially to D. MAGIE, *De Romanorum iuris publici sacrique vocabulis sollemnibus in Graecum conversis* (1905).

[2] DEISSMANN, *op. cit.*, p. 287. Note, however, that Deissmann (*op. cit.*, p. 288, n. 1) criticizes the overstatements in H. WEINEL, *Die Stellung des Urchristentums zum Staat* (1908).

[3] DEISSMANN, *op. cit.*, pp. 290 ff.

terms *en bloc*. All they have in common is their parallelism with imperial terminology—a fact which tells us little or nothing about their meaning. We must therefore divide them up into a number of groups:

1. Messianic titles taken over by the NT from the LXX and from Jewish traditions. To this category belong βασιλεύς, κύριος and θεός. Another LXX word is ἀρχιερεύς: this does not however have the same explicitly royal character, since a distinction is drawn in the NT and post-canonical literature between the royal and the priestly functions of Christ.

2. Hellenistic terms which do not belong to the language of the LXX or which, when they do occur in the LXX, have no Messianic significance. Such terms are found mainly in the Pastoral Epistles: σωτήρ—σωτηρία, παρουσία, ἐπιφάνεια, φιλανθρωπία and εὐεργεσία. The terminology of Rev. may also be mentioned in this context.

3. Terms having royal character, but which in the NT are particularly linked with God, and which are first transferred to Christ at the time of the Arian conflict, viz. παντοκράτωρ and ὕψιστος.

Messianic Titles

The faith of the NT in Christ as King, ruling the world and the new People of God, drew its inspiration from the Messianic sayings of the OT. The LXX was an inexhaustible source of concepts originally connected with the sacral king, concepts which could be transferred to Christ. He is the fulfilment of all the prophecies of the OT—all the books of the OT, not least the Psalter, being regarded as prophecy. Virtually all the Christological titles in the NT are therefore royal in character: Χριστός, θεοῦ υἱός, υἱὸς τοῦ ἀνθρώπου and possibly also ἀμνός.[1] This has been clearly demonstrated by recent scholarship,

[1] On C. J. Ball's and C. F. Burney's theory, that ἀμνός as a Christological title comes from Aram. טליא, which also has the meaning of "servant" (Greek παῖς), see J. Jeremias, art. ἀμνός, ThWB 1 (1932–33), pp. 342–344. Idem, art. παῖς θεοῦ, ThWB 5 (1944–54), pp. 676–713. Idem, 'Ἀμνὸς θεοῦ—παῖς θεοῦ, ZNW 34 (1935), pp. 115–123. B. Gärtner, טליא *als Messiasbezeichnung*, SEÅ 18–19 (1953–54), pp. 98–108. C. K. Barrett, *The Lamb of God*, NTS 1 (1954–55), pp. 210–218. C. H. Dodd, who does not accept the טליא theory, nevertheless believes that ἀμνός is a Messianic title, "virtually equivalent to ὁ βασιλεὺς τοῦ Ἰσραήλ", *The Interpretation of the Fourth Gospel* (1953), p. 238. For the Messianic titles in general, see W. Staerk, *Soter* 1, BFTh 31 (1933). Idem, *Die Erlösererwartung in den östlichen Religionen*, Soter 2 (1938). V. Taylor, *The Names of Jesus* (1953).

which has shown how closely the Messianic sayings of Judaism and hence of the NT are connected with the sacral kingship of pre-exilic Israel.[1]

In the following account we must therefore limit our attention to those Messianic titles and functions which were clearly understood as being "royal" during the post-Apostolic age. The Church Fathers did not consider "the Son of Man" to be a royal title, but an expression of the humanity of Christ.[2] Not even Χριστός, which, by virtue of its being the Greek equivalent of "Messiah", ought to be the royal title *par excellence* is taken to be an expression of Christ's royal power after the NT. It becomes in general no more than a proper name for Jesus; and when its proper meaning—"anointed"—is expounded, equal emphasis is placed on its priestly or prophetic aspects and on its royal aspect.[3] The concept of the *suffering* king, so important in OT Messianism,[4] is less dominant in the early Church, where those OT sayings which have to do with the suffering of the Messiah (e.g. Isa. 53) and sayings about the Kingly power of Christ are often contrasted. There is however an expository tradition in which Ps. 95 (96).10 and Isa. 9.6 are interpreted to mean that Christ's Kingly power was purchased through suffering.[5] Those functions normally associated with the concept of "King" are those of the exalted ruler, judge and conqueror; the Kingship of Christ is therefore principally associated with the Ascension, *sessio* and parousia. We shall see that Ps. 109 (110) and Dan. 7 are central to faith in Christ as King. He is King because he has been exalted to the right hand of God; God has placed his enemies beneath his feet; and he shall come again on the clouds of heaven to judge the world.

Another complex of ideas centring on the Kingship of Christ has to

---

[1] See the literature mentioned below, p. 124.

[2] Cf. however L. BOUYER, *La notion christologique du Fils de l'homme, a-t-elle disparu dans la patristique grecque?* in Mélanges Robert, Travaux de l'Inst. Cath. de Paris 4 (1957), pp. 519–530.

[3] See below, pp. 106 ff. MOULE, *Influence*, p. 260, points out how incomprehensible the title Χριστός was to the non-Jewish Hellenistic world.

[4] I. ENGNELL, *Studies in Divine Kingship in the Ancient Near East* (1943), *passim*. IDEM, *The 'Ebed Yahweh Songs and the Suffering Messiah in "Deutero-Isaiah"*, BJRL 31 (1948), pp. 54–93. G. W. AHLSTRÖM, *Psalm 89* (1959), *passim*.

[5] See below, pp. 98 ff. It must be stressed that the motif of victory and triumph dominates over the idea of suffering in OT Messianism also; see I. ENGNELL, art. *Herrens Tjänare*, SBU 1 (1948), col. 846.

do with the authority by which he claims to be the Messiah. The main stream of Judaism required of the true Messiah that he should be a son of David; his legitimacy was confirmed by his membership of the family of David. The Kingdom he came to found should also be politically nationalist in character. There is therefore a latent revolutionary tendency in Messianism, a tendency periodically expressed in local rebellions. Jesus, by contrast, represented a form of non-political Messianism which seems to have had earlier parallels in the apocalyptic speculations of esoteric Judaism (the Enoch literature).[1] The view of the NT is that the Kingdom of God is not of this world, but otherworldly and eschatological; Christ is not an earthly ruler: he is the heavenly King. The Church did not attach a great deal of significance to the Davidic descent, and the Kingship derived therefrom. The Kingship of Christ was instead traced back to his Divine Sonship. This means that from the very first the Kingship of Christ was connected with his Divinity, and it is characteristic that the problem of his Kingship was not solved, theologically speaking, before the Council of Nicaea laid down that he is "begotten of his Father before all worlds".

βασιλεύς

The title βασιλεύς has little significance in the NT as an epithet of Christ. The Christian Church, seeking to express its faith in the royal power of Christ, normally used the title κύριος—the most common Christological term in the NT, apart from Χριστός—while βασιλεύς on the whole (the exceptions include Jn.) was used so little as to prompt Cullmann to call it "a variant of the title *kyrios*".[2]

The reason for this is not far to seek. The term βασιλεύς, which was the most usual word in Koiné Greek for "king" in a purely political sense, and which was later to become the standard designation for the Roman emperor,[3] was colourless, political and secular in character. To be sure, it had been used in the LXX and elsewhere as an equivalent to the Hebrew *mælæk* (also referring to God), and it was a common

---

[1] H. WINDISCH, *Der messianische Krieg und das Urchristentum* (1909). Cf. also literature mentioned above, p. 34, n. 1.

[2] K. L. SCHMIDT, βασιλεύς. CULLMANN, *Christologie*, p. 227.

[3] V. VON SCHOEFFER, art. βασιλεύς 1, PWK 3 (1899), col. 55-82. DEISSMANN, *Licht*, pp. 310 f. E. LOHMEYER, *Christuskult und Kaiserkult*, SGVS 90 (1919), pp. 11 ff. och *passim*. H. KLEINKNECHT, art. βασιλεύς *im Griechentum*, ThWB 1 (1932-33), pp. 562-563.

liturgical Divine title in Hellenistic Judaism,[1] but it was not so well suited as a title for the coming Messiah—though the use of *mælæk* to refer to the Messiah is not uncommon.[2]

Further evidence of the political overtones of *basileus* is to be found in the fact that most of the NT passages in which this word is applied to Jesus are found in the Gospel narratives of his trial and crucifixion. Jesus' opponents were well able to take his Messianic claims and use them as proof that he was bent on disturbing the peace; the word *basileus* fits quite naturally into this political context, as when the Roman governor was able to condemn him as a political criminal.[3] "Are you the *basileus* of the Jews?" asked Pilate (Mk. 15.2 par.). This phrase—"*basileus* of the Jews"—is used by Pilate, referring to Jesus, during the whole of the following negotiations with the Jews. "Then what shall I do with the man whom you call the *basileus* of the Jews?" (Mk. 15.12) "Do you want me to release for you the *basileus* of the Jews?" (Mk. 15.9) All four Evangelists are agreed that the superscription on Jesus' cross read ὁ βασιλεὺς τῶν Ἰουδαίων (Mk. 15.26 par.), and that one of the insults hurled at him at the crucifixion was the sarcastic title *basileus* (Mk. 15.32 par.). The crown of thorns, the purple mantle and the reed as sceptre, together with the gaudy clothes in which Herod, according to Lk. 23.11, dressed Jesus, also have to do with Jesus' claim to be a king.[4]

The title *basileus* is in this context used more frequently in the Fourth Gospel than in the Synoptics. The narrative of Jesus before Pilate in particular is filled out to the form of a conversation, in which the word *basileus* is used repeatedly; on this occasion it has theological implications which are missing from the Synoptics' passion narratives

---

[1] G. VON RAD, art. βασιλεύς *im A.T.*, ThWB 1 (1932–33), pp. 563–569. Cf. below, pp. 157 ff.

[2] P. VOLZ, *Die Eschatologie der jüdischen Gemeinde im neutestamentlichen Zeitalter* (1934), pp. 173 f.

[3] E. STAUFFER, *Jesus—Gestalt und Geschichte* (1957), pp. 97 ff. J. BLINZLER, *Der Prozess Jesu*, 3rd ed. (1960), pp. 200 ff., well points out the secular import of βασιλεύς: "Der Ausdruck 'König der Juden' ist die säkularisierte, in die Ebene des Profan-Politischen verschiedene Form für 'Messias' oder für das schon etwas stärker ins Politische überspielende Messiastitel 'König Israels'", *op. cit.*, p. 210. Cf. MOULE, *Influence*, p. 261.

[4] R. DELBRÜCK, *Antiquarisches zu den Verspottungen Jesu*, ZNW 41 (1942), pp. 124–145. T. ARVEDSON, *Jesus som narrkonung*, SEÅ 12 (1947), pp. 25–35. BLINZLER, *Prozess*, p. 210, n. 15, pp. 240 ff. (with bibliography). For Lk 23.11, see H. RIESENFELD, *Jésus Transfiguré* (1947), p. 267, n. 37.

(18.37, 19.12-15, 19.21). Further, the term *basileus* itself does not seem to have the political meaning which is so common elsewhere in the NT.[1] Asked whether he is a *basileus*, Jesus answers in the affirmative, but adds that his Kingdom is not of this world (Jn. 18.36 f.). Despite the differences in terminology, there is no doubt that the Messianism depicted in Jn. is as non-political as that of the Synoptics.

Apart from the passion narratives there are few NT passages in which Jesus is called *basileus*. It is never found in Jesus' sayings about himself (with the exception of indirect references in parables and in the saying about the judgment of the Son of Man, in Matt. 25.34-40, when Jesus speaks about the Son of Man in the third person). In the Synoptics, it is mainly in the birth narratives that Christ is described as *basileus*. In Matt. 2.2 the Magi ask, ποῦ ἐστιν ὁ τεχθεὶς βασιλεὺς τῶν Ἰουδαίων; In the course of the story of the Annunciation (Lk. 1.33) we read, καὶ βασιλεύσει ἐπὶ τὸν οἶκον Ἰακὼβ εἰς τοὺς αἰῶνας, καὶ τῆς βασιλείας αὐτοῦ οὐκ ἔσται τέλος. Neither passage can be separated from that special complex of problems connected with the Matthaean and Lucan birth narratives as a whole. Otherwise, Jesus is called *basileus* only in connexion with the triumphal entry into Jerusalem. The words ὁ βασιλεύς are incorporated by Luke into the quotation from Ps. 117 (118).26 which all four Gospels agree, was used by the crowd as a greeting for Jesus on his entry into Jerusalem (Lk. 19.38). The entry is seen by Matt. as the fulfilment of the prophecy in Zech. 9.9: "See, thy *basileus* cometh" (Matt. 21.15).

The Fourth Gospel, in its description of the entry into Jerusalem, takes up both the quotation from Zech. 9.9 (12.15) and the gloss from Ps. 117.26—the latter in the form καὶ ὁ βασιλεὺς τοῦ Ἰσραήλ (12.13).[2] Elsewhere there is little sign of the Johannine preference for *basileus* as seen in the passion narrative. "You are the *basileus* of Israel," says Nathanael to Jesus in Jn. 1.49. That the word also had distinct political associations for John is shown in Jn. 6.15, where we read that the people wished to make Jesus *basileus*.

It is hardly surprising that Jesus never called himself *basileus*. Apart from the fact that the Gospels show him to have been generally reluctant to make personal use of the commoner Messianic terms, *basileus* would seem to have been quite unsuitable for his purpose. There

---

[1] Cf. on the other hand, Jn. 6.15.

[2] See E. D. FREED, *The Entry into Jerusalem in the Gospel of John*, JBL 80 (1961), pp. 329-338.

has been a good deal of speculation as to whether Jesus' avoidance of the title of Messiah was due to its political connotations[1]—a question which lies outside the scope of this book. Be that as it may; the title of *basileus* must have been even more politically weighted. In Matt. 16.16, Jesus accepts St. Peter's confession, "You are the Messiah, the Son of the living God"; nor does he object to the people's acclamation on his entry into Jerusalem. The same applies in the Johannine version, where Jesus has no objection to Nathanael's confession of him as *basileus*. These sayings may well reflect a historical situation in which Jesus was extremely reticent about himself ("Son of Man" being the only Messianic title he uses of himself in the Gospels), while his disciples made use of a wider and more general Messianic terminology, which Jesus also accepted.

Not before the Jerusalem Passover did Jesus overcome his reluctance to make Messianic claims. When asked by the Sanhedrin whether he was the Messiah, he answered in the affirmative (Mk. 14.61 f. par.); likewise, according to the Johannine tradition Pilate's question whether he was the Jews' *basileus*. At this decisive moment the controversial terms took on a significance which they had not previously held in the Gospels.[2]

The title normally given to the Risen Jesus is Messiah, Χριστός, and *basileus* virtually disappears in Acts, the Epistles and Rev.—though it occurs in Rev. 17.14 and 19.16.[3] Again, this would seem to be largely due to its political connotations.

In Acts 17.7 we read that the rioting Jews in Thessalonica accused the Christians of being political agitators: "they are all acting against the decrees of Caesar, saying that there is another *basileus*, Jesus." But there is no concrete evidence in Acts that Jesus was in fact called *basileus* by Christians. In whatever way we judge the speeches in Acts as source-material, there can be no doubt that the situation

---

[1] Héring, *Royaume*, pp. 111 ff. W. Manson, *Jesus the Messiah* (1943), pp. 5 ff., with a criticism of Bousset's hypothesis, according to which the transcendent Messiah conception first appeared after the death of Jesus.

[2] Cf. A. H. McNeile, *The Gospel according to St. Matthew* (1915), p. 401.

[3] Some times in NT *basileus* appears as a designation for God (Matt. 5.35, 1 Tim. 1.17, 6.15, Rev. 15.5), a usage which entirely corresponds to that of OT and Judaism. See Schnackenburg, *Herrschaft, passim*. Cf. also below, p. 157. C. C. Oke's attempt to show that 1 Tim. 1.17 is said about Christ (*A Doxology not to God but to Christ*, ET 67 (1955–56), pp. 367–368), is not convincing, cf. Moule, *Influence*, p. 253.

described in Acts 17 shows just how impracticable it was for Christians to make use of the title *basileus*. Doubtless it had so many political overtones that to use it of any person other than Caesar was liable to lead to most serious consequences—even if it were used in a purely religious and non-political sense. The documents of the NT make it clear that it was precisely the "royal" character of the titles given Jesus by the early Church which laid Christians open to the charge of clandestine political activity.[1]

Thus it was that *kyrios* came to be used by the Church to denote the royal power of Christ, and *basileus* became consciously suppressed. At this time there was nothing of the later atmosphere of controversy surrounding the word *kyrios*; the turning-point was not reached until Domitian adopted *Dominus et deus* as his own private title.[2] The early Church was not interested in precipitating open political conflict with the Roman State. It is probable that a conscious effort was made to avoid political terminology, so as not to create unnecessary trouble—particularly since the early Christian Church was devoid of all form of political ambition. The political conflict came later; it is first reflected in Rev., though it may have left traces earlier, in the Pastoral Epistles.[3]

The Jewish surroundings of the early Church seem also to have contributed to the general desire to avoid a too-political terminology. It must have been difficult, in a milieu in which Messianic pretenders with political ambitions were not uncommon, to understand Jesus' statement that his Kingdom was not of this world. *Kyrios* met the needs of the early Church, with its eschatological expectations, better than did *basileus*, encumbered as it was by profane associations.

The verb βασιλεύειν, like βασιλεύς, is not often used in the NT to refer to Christ. It in fact occurs only twice: in the Annunciation narrative, καὶ βασιλεύσει ἐπὶ τὸν οἶκον Ἰακὼβ εἰς τοὺς αἰῶνας (Lk. 1.33) and

---

[1] Cf. the story told in Hegesippus' *Hypomnemata* (Eusebius, HE III. 20.1–6), according to which some relatives of Jesus were examined by the Emperor Domitian as potential rebels but were released, when they asserted that the Kingdom of Christ was not of this world. Cf. below, p. 173 f.

[2] Suetonius, Vita Caes., Domitianus 13.2. L. CERFAUX, *Le titre Kyrios et la dignité royale de Jésus*, RLC 1 (1954), pp. 3–63, especially pp. 26 ff. The common idea, that *kyrios* was a controversial title before Domitian (cf. below p. 178) is contradicted by Philo's relation of the Jewish delegation before Caligula, Legat. 356, where the Jews without any hesitation address the Emperor as *kyrios*.

[3] See below, p. 61 ff.

in connexion with a quotation from Ps. 109 (110): δεῖ γὰρ αὐτὸν βασιλεύειν ἄχρι οὗ θῇ πάντας τοὺς ἐχθροὺς ὑπὸ τοὺς πόδας αὐτοῦ (1 Cor. 15.25).[1]

It is a striking fact that in the case of βασιλεία there is no corresponding reluctance; this word is prominent, especially in the Gospels. It seems that it did not run the same risk of being interpreted politically as βασιλεύς and βασιλεύειν, particularly since in the majority of cases it is the Kingdom of *God* which is referred to. God was also commonly called *basileus* in Judaism, a practice occasionally met with in the NT,[2] and his Kingdom, מלכות שמים, is a well-known concept in Judaism.[3]

The Kingdom of the Son of Man or of Christ is only mentioned in the Gospels in material peculiar to Matt., Lk. and Jn. (Matt. 13.41, 16.28, 20.21—where the parallel in Mk. 10.37 has δόξα—Lk. 1.33, 22.29 f., 23.42, Jn. 18.36). All these passages are distinctly eschatological in character; the same applies to the other NT passages in which βασιλεία is used of the Kingdom of Christ (1 Cor. 15.24, Eph. 5.5, Col. 1.13, 2 Tim. 4.1, 18, Heb. 1.8, 2 Pet. 1.11).[4]

In the oldest post-NT literature the term *basileus* is seldom used to refer to Christ. In the Apostolic Fathers it is found as an epithet for Christ only in the *Martyrdom of Polycarp*—which belongs to the same class of literature as the Acts of the Martyrs, and which we shall therefore consider together with these,[5] and once in the *Epistle of Diognetus*.[6]

It is however possible that βασιλεύς was more common as a Christological term than the literary evidence would seem to indicate. In Justin we encounter a rich *testimonia* tradition, in which OT sayings, originally applied to the king, are transferred to Christ; βασιλεύς is one of the most common epithets here.[7] Justin is not personally responsible for this usage; it is certain that he is building on older traditions:

---

[1] βασιλεύειν is used about God in Rev. 11.15, 17 and 19.6.
[2] SCHNACKENBURG, *Herrschaft, passim*.
[3] See K. G. KUHN, מלכות שמים *in der rabbinischen Literatur*, ThWB 1 (1932–33), pp. 570–573. For βασιλεία in the NT, see SCHMIDT, βασιλεύς, pp. 580 ff.
[4] For the concept βασιλεία in the Fathers, see below, Chap. 12.
[5] See below, p. 178.
[6] Diogn. 7.4: ὡς βασιλεὺς πέμπων υἱὸν βασιλέα ἔπεμψεν. The meaning of this sentence is not quite clear. It is possible to translate it: "As a king, who sends a son, so he sent a king." A better sense is given in the translation: "As a king, who sends his son, who is also a king, so he sent (him)." This phrase therefore seems to express the conception of the pre-existent Christ as a King, a common idea in the Apostolic Fathers. Cf. below, p. 60 f.
[7] See below, p. 86.

βασιλεύς in Zech. 9.9 is already identified with Jesus in the Gospels. In later literature we find that the use of βασιλεύς, referring to Christ, is connected particularly with those OT texts which the Church has interpreted Christologically.

κύριος

The meaning of the term *kyrios* in the NT has been reckoned among the most complex of exegetical problems since 1913, when W. Bousset published his much-discussed book *Kyrios Christos*. We can undertake only a limited discussion of the exegetical question here, with reference to the meaning of the title *kyrios* in the post-Apostolic tradition.[1]

The *religionsgeschichtliche* school of the early 20th century, of which Bousset was the most prominent representative, drew upon oriental mystery and fertility cults in order to find parallels to the Christological title *kyrios*; it was thus believed that the title must have originated outside the bounds of Aramaic-speaking Jewish Christianity. Bousset believed it to have been derived from the Hellenistic syncretism of Antioch; he also believed that Paul took it over from Hellenistic Christians in that town.[2]

Bousset's thesis did not go unchallenged. A heated debate followed, in the course of which Bousset answered his critics with the book *Jesus der Herr* (1916) and published a new and revised edition of *Kyrios Christos* (1923). The further NT research progressed, the more Bousset's theories proved untenable. The real "Achilles' heel" of his hypothesis—to quote Rawlinson[3]—is that the oldest liturgical formula we know, *Maranatha*, contains the Aramaic form of the title *kyrios*.[4] Bultmann would seem to be alone among the better-known modern exegetes in accepting Bousset's findings.[5] Most are convinced that the

---

[1] Bibliographies of the extensive literature on this subject are given by W. FOERSTER, art. κύριος, ThWB 3 (1935–38), pp. 1038–1056, 1081–1098, and L. CERFAUX, art. *Kyrios*, DB Suppl. 5 (1957), pp. 200–228. Cf. also CULLMANN, *Christologie*, pp. 200–244.

[2] W. BOUSSET, *Kyrios Christos*, FRLANT N.F. 4 (1913).

[3] A. E. J. RAWLINSON, *The New Testament Doctrine of the Christ* (1929), p. 235.

[4] Cf. CERFAUX, *Le titre Kyrios*, pp. 43 f. CULLMANN, *Christologie*, pp. 214 ff.

[5] R. BULTMANN, *Theologie des Neuen Testaments* (1948–53), pp. 52 f. An original (but most unconvincing) variation of this theme is the theory of M. WERNER, *Die Entstehung des christlichen Dogmas* (1941), according to which *kyrios* is the term for an angel, secondarily applied to Christ. Cf. the criticism by W. MICHAELIS, *Zur Engelchristologie im Urchristentum* (1942), pp. 62 f.

title *kyrios* has to do with the idea of the royal power and Messiahship of Jesus.[1] L. Cerfaux in particular has produced extensive material to prove that the term *kyrios* was in common use in the Orient of NT times as a royal appellation, and that early Christianity took up the term as a synonym for the royal title.[2]

For the Semitic background of the title we are indebted principally to W. W. Graf von Baudissin, whose comprehensive work *Kyrios als Gottesname* demonstrates the importance of Near Eastern concepts of kingship for the Divine epithet;[3] this complex of ideas has also been dealt with in detail by Scandinavian scholars, such as Widengren, Engnell and Mowinckel.[4] von Baudissin has shown the extent to which the Divine and royal epithets used by all Semitic peoples are interchangeable, due to the close identification of the god and the king. Hence the Babylonians' *bēlu*, the West Semites' *baʻal*, the Hebrews' and Canaanites' *'ādōn* and the Aramaeans' *mārē* are at one and the same time titles given to a god and to the king.[5] It is in this Semitic milieu that we meet with the antecedents of the title *kyrios*, as well as of the Hellenistic imperial cult. As the God may be called king, so the king may be called god.

According to Cerfaux, whose argument is built on an extensive body of Hellenistic textual material, the title occurs as a specifically royal title in the Orient during the 1st century B.C.[6] In the following period it is associated with the Roman emperor in particular, becoming the Greek equivalent of the Latin *Dominus*, adopted by Domitian as an official imperial title. Cerfaux however urges care when attempting to link the titles *kyrios* and *dominus* with the imperial cult.[7]

---

[1] FOERSTER, κύριος, *passim*. CERFAUX, *Le titre Kyrios*, *passim*. CULLMANN, *Christologie*, pp. 222 f. Cf. also K. PRÜMM, *Herrscherkult und Neues Testament*, Biblica 9 (1928), pp. 4 ff.

[2] CERFAUX, *Le titre Kyrios*, *passim*.

[3] W. W. Graf VON BAUDISSIN, *Kyrios als Gottesname* 1-3 (1926-28).

[4] See especially ENGNELL, *Studies*, pp. 37 ff., 178 ff. Cf. S. MOWINCKEL, *Psalmenstudien* 2, Videnskapsselsk. Skrifter 2, Hist.-fil. Kl. 1921.6 (1922), p. 43. G. WIDENGREN, *Religionens värld*, 2nd ed. (1953), pp. 255 ff.

[5] VON BAUDISSIN, *Kyrios* 3, pp. 19 ff. CERFAUX, *Kyrios*, p. 202. Cf. CERFAUX's criticism of VON BAUDISSIN's theories in IDEM, *Le nom divin "Kyrios" dans la Bible grecque*, RLC 1 (1954), pp. 113-136, and IDEM, *"Adonai" et "Kyrios"*, RLC 1, pp. 137-172.

[6] CERFAUX, *Le titre Kyrios*, p. 21.

[7] CERFAUX, *Le titre Kyrios*, pp. 26-35. IDEM, *Le Christ dans la théologie de Saint Paul* (1954), pp. 20 and 350, with a criticism of the political interpretation of the

In Hellenistic Judaism the title *kyrios* is first seen in the LXX, where it is used as the Greek equivalent of Yahweh.[1] Here we may follow von Baudissin in supposing it to have been taken over from the language of Syrian and Egyptian Gentiles;[2] or Cerfaux in assuming the existence of a direct connexion with the kingship ideas of the OT (possibly as an analogy to the Palestinian Jews' practice of replacing the name Yahweh by Adonai, a practice of which there is no direct evidence in the period at which the LXX originated). In either case, *kyrios* would seem to have had a well-defined special meaning during the earliest phase of the Church, a meaning which included both "God" and "king"; it was therefore possible to use the term of Jesus in his double role of God and Messiah.[3]

Did Jesus call himself kyrios?

When we have stated that *kyrios* was a common royal title in Jesus' day, we have still not explained it fully. Nor is it enough to try and explain the title as a Greek translation of the Jewish paraphrase—Adonai—of the name Yahweh.[4] It is of course true that Jesus made Divine claims, exercised functions and adopted motives which in the OT were restricted to Yahweh (the forgiveness of sins, the 'bridegroom' motif).[5] The use of Ps. 109 (110).1 (see below) indicates that the name *kyrios* had a different meaning in the earliest Christian tradition.

---

title *kyrios*, which has been presented by LOHMEYER, *Christuskult*, and CULLMANN, *Confessions*. Cf. also W. G. KÜMMEL, *Kirchenbegriff und Geschichtsbewusstsein in der Urgemeinde und bei Jesus*, SB 1 (1943), pp. 13 ff.

[1] VON BAUDISSIN, *Kyrios*, 3, pp. 697 ff. G. QUELL, χύριος (Der at.liche Gottesname), ThWB 3 (1935–38), pp. 1056–1081. FOERSTER, χύριος, pp. 1081 ff. CERFAUX, *Le nom divin* and "*Adonai*", *passim*.

[2] VON BAUDISSIN, *Kyrios* 2, pp. 257 ff.

[3] CERFAUX, *Le nom divin*, p. 136. "*Adonai*", pp. 169 ff. VON BAUDISSIN and CERFAUX agree that the Greek translation χύριος for Yahweh is older than the Hebrew substitution Adonai for the Divine name. For other opinions on this problem, see CERFAUX, "*Adonai*", p. 172.

[4] This interpretation was common in earlier literature. In a modern version we find it in J. C. O'NEILL, *The Use of* χύριος *in the Book of Acts*, ScJTh 8 (1955), pp. 155–174. The author seems to have no knowledge of CERFAUX's works. On the title *kyrios* as an expression for the Divinity of Christ, see below, p. 55 ff.

[5] See CERFAUX, *Le titre Kyrios*, pp. 40 ff. That Jesus claimed to be Yahweh has recently been vigorously advocated by E. STAUFFER, *Jesus*, pp. 130 ff.

We are therefore compelled to ask: Did the description of Jesus as *kyrios* originate with Jesus himself?

We have said that Jesus was on the whole extremely reluctant to make personal use of any Messianic term, with the exception of "Son of Man".[1] Other terms—κύριος, βασιλεύς, Χριστός—were used of him by the early Church. The Gospels—or perhaps it would be better to say certain Gospel traditions—allow that Jesus accepted the titles Χριστός and βασιλεύς when bestowed by others.[2] The same cannot however be said of *kyrios* (ignoring the common form of polite address *kyrie* (=*mari*) used when addressing Jesus by the disciples and others). There is another sense in which *kyrios* stands in a class by itself; unlike βασιλεύς and Χριστός it was not used as a Messianic title in the Judaism of Jesus' day.[3] It is hardly likely that *kyrios* (=Aram. *marān*) as a royal title was derived from the everyday *kyrie* (=*mari*). Even though the evidence of the Gospels is not clear, we must once more ask: Was Jesus himself the originator of the title?

Kyrios, as a title given to Christ in the NT is connected from the very first with the Christological interpretation of Ps. 109 (110).1: "The Lord said unto my lord, Sit thou at my right hand, until I make thine enemies thy footstool."[4] This Psalm is among the most prominent of all OT texts in the early Christian kerygma; it is furthermore the only OT text which according to the Gospels is used by Jesus in such a way as to connect the title *kyrios* with the Son of Man. It is therefore likely

---

[1] See above, p. 41.

[2] See above, p. 41 f.

[3] BILLERBECK, *Comm.* 4, pp. 452 ff. CERFAUX, *Le titre Kyrios*, p. 38. M. PHILONENKO claims that the so-called Teacher of Righteousness is styled *kyrios* in Test. Levi 14 and Test. Benj. 9, *Les interpolations chrétiennes des Testaments des Douze Patriarches et les Manuscripts de Qoumrân* 1, RHPhR 38 (1958), pp. 324 f., 330 ff. This conclusion is however not very convincing. In the first case, God probably is meant; the second passage is still, in spite of PHILONENKO's ingenious explanations, to be regarded as a Christian interpolation. See the review by E. LARSSON in SEÅ 25 (1960), pp. 115 ff. For the expression χριστὸς κύριος in Ps. Sol. 17.32 and 18.7, see below, p. 86.

[4] On Ps. 109 (110), see L. DÜRR, *Psalm 110 im Lichte der neueren altorientalischen Forschung* (1929). H. LUDIN JANSEN, *Den 110. Psalmen*, STK 16 (1940), pp. 263–276. G. WIDENGREN, *Ps. 110 och det sakrala kungadömet i Israel*, UUÅ 1941.7.1 (1941). J. COPPENS, *La portée messianique du Psaume CX*, ALBO 3.1 (1955). IDEM, *Les apports du Psaume CX (Vulg. CIX) à l'idéologie royale israélite*, in The Sacral Kingship (1959), pp. 333–348. For further literature, see H.-J. KRAUS, *Psalmen 2* (1960), p. 752 and COPPENS, *Portée*, pp. 5 f., n. 1.

that it is this verse which is the real source of the title *kyrios* in the early Church; it also seems probable that the Christological exposition of Ps. 109.1 is derived from Jesus' own teaching.

The link between the title *kyrios* and Ps. 109.1 is thus obvious, and has often been pointed out. But the direct derivation of the title from the Psalm in question has been claimed less frequently. It usually seems to be the case that the title *kyrios* is regarded as primary, the Psalm having been chosen subsequently as a proof-text, *kyrios* being the decisive *Stichwort*.

Bousset touches upon the idea that the title may have been derived from Ps. 109.1—but only to reject it.[1] Bousset assumes the faith of the early Church in Christ to have been so *"volkstümlich"* that it could not possibly have been influenced by anything so complicated as Psalter exegesis. But recent research has shown Jesus to have been well acquainted with the ideas, expositions and methods of argument of Jewish scriptural exegesis; this means that proof-texts must be accorded much greater significance than the *religionsgeschichtliche* school imagined.[2] When Bousset talks about "misinterpreted passages in the OT" he is subjecting early Christian exegesis to a false criterion of scholarship, forgetting that such interpretations were perfectly acceptable in the early Christian milieu. A Messianic interpretation of Ps. 109.1 is not really unexpected—it is more remarkable that there is

---

[1] BOUSSET, *Kyrios Christos* (1st ed.), pp. 108 f.: "Auch wird man die Lösung des Rätsels nicht dadurch herbeiführen dürfen, dass man auf gewisse Stellen hinweist, an denen das alte Testament selbst auf Grund allerdings einer durchgehenden falschen Erklärung bereits ein überweltliches Wesen neben Jahwe oder gar mehrere Personen in der Gottheit anzunehmen und zu fordern scheint. Eine Stelle, die hier vor allen in Betracht käme, wäre etwa der Ps. 110 mit seinem: 'es sprach der Herr zu meinem Herrn.' Denn von dieser Stelle lässt sich ... nachweisen, dass sie sehr früh die Aufmerksamkeit der Christen auf sich gezogen und in ihrem Weissagungsbeweis eine Rolle gespielt habe. Schon die Theologie der Urgemeinde hat sich mit ihr beschäftigt, wie Mk 12: 35-37 beweist, und hat aus ihr die Ablehnung des messianischen Ideals des Davidssohns begründet ... Aber auch gegen diese Auskunft erheben sich die schwersten Bedenken. So geht die Entstehung eines lebendigen, volkstümlichen Glaubens niemals vor sich; ihre Christos-Kyrios-Verehrung haben die alten Christen nicht an missdeuteten Stellen des alten Testaments herausgelesen."

[2] DOEVE, *Hermeneutics*, pp. 141 ff. and *passim*. K. STENDAHL, *The School of St. Matthew* (1954), pp. 42 f. (with references to literature). B. GERHARDSSON, *The Good Samaritan—the Good Shepherd?* CN 16 (1958), pp. 22 ff. IDEM, *Memory and Manuscript*, ASNU 22 (1961), introduction, pp. 9 ff.

none to be found in the Jewish literature of the period—and we may well be justified in suspecting anti-Christian censure as the real reason behind the absence of Messianic interpretation of this passage.

The wide currency of the title *kyrios*—so wide as to compromise its use as an attribute of God—cannot be regarded as conclusive proof against the primacy of the exegesis of Ps. 109.1. The only conclusion which can be drawn from this is that the term was connected with Jesus from the very beginning; this brings us back once more to the problem of whether Jesus used it of himself in connexion with the Messianic interpretation of Ps. 109.1.

The three Synoptic Gospels all contain accounts of Jesus' use of Ps. 109.1 against Pharisees who hold that the Messiah must be the son of David (Mk. 12.35–37 par.).[1] Both Jesus and the Pharisees allow the Messianic implications of Ps. 109.1 and agree that the second *kyrios* mentioned in the verse is identical with the Messiah. The point of this story, that Jesus silences the Pharisees by quoting Ps. 109.1, in fact presupposes that the Pharisees, too, recognized the Messianic implications of the Psalm.[2] A corresponding exegesis of Ps. 109.1, this time combined with Dan. 7, is to be found in Jesus' speech before the Sanhedrin (Mk. 14.62 par.). Here there is no mention of the title *kyrios*, and Jesus refers to himself by his usual title "the Son of Man". His statement that he is to sit "at the right hand of Power" seems to go back to a combination of Dan. 7 with Ps. 109.1—the implication being that he identifies himself not only with the Son of Man in Dan. 7 but also with the *kyrios* of Ps. 109.1. Both texts seem to suggest that the title *kyrios* did not originate in the theology of the early Church, but stemmed from the teaching of Jesus.[3]

That the word does not otherwise occur as a *Selbstprädikation* in the Gospels evidently has to do with Jesus' reluctance to use Messianic titles.[4] Both Χριστός and κύριος can properly be used to refer to Christ after his victory; the royal character of both ensures that they are

---

[1] R. BULTMANN thinks that this tradition is not authentic but an expression of later *Gemeindetheologie*, *Die Geschichte der synoptischen Tradition*, 2nd ed. (1931), pp. 144 ff. Cf. on the other hand E. LOHMEYER, *Comm. ad loc.* STENDAHL, *School*, pp. 78 f. D. DAUBE has shown that this type of question has parallels in the Talmud, *Four Types of Question*, JTS N.S. 2 (1951), pp. 45–48.

[2] W. BEILNER, *Christus und die Pharisäer* (1959), pp. 197 ff.

[3] For the combination of Ps. 109 (110) and Dan. 7, see DOEVE, *Hermeneutics*, pp. 152 ff.

[4] See above, pp. 41 f.

first accurately used of the glorified Christ. God has made Jesus *kyrios* and Χριστός, proclaims St. Peter in his Pentecost address (Acts 2.36).

As Bousset pointed out, in the Gospels *kyrios* refers especially to the Risen and Glorified Lord.[1] With the exception of Lk., who uses *kyrios* of Christ on more than a dozen occasions during his earthly ministry, the term is used only in connexion with the Resurrection and Ascension narratives of the pseudo-Marcan ending and in Jn. 20–21. This is not a case of conflict between the teaching of Jesus and that of the early Church; the difference is that the Resurrection and Ascension have altered the situation entirely. Jesus is *kyrios* by virtue of his Ascension and enthronement at the right hand of the Father.

Fuller considers that the origins of the title *kyrios* are to be found in the vocative *kyrie*, but allows the full significance of Ps. 109.1, in which the word *kyrios*, from being a title of honour, became expressive of Messianic power.[2] Building largely on Jesus' use of Ps. 109.1 before the Sanhedrin, Fuller concludes that the Messianic implications of *kyrios* received the sanction of Jesus himself.[3] There would however seem to be considerable doubt as to whether the polite form of address *kyrie* was of any significance for the origin of *kyrios*. *Kyrie* was such an everyday form of address, so little befitting Jesus, that it is difficult to understand how this particular word could have developed into such a prominent Christological title. It is much more natural to see the title as being derived from Jesus' interpretation of Ps. 109.1, common among the disciples, in which the verse is regarded as a prophecy of the enthronement of the Son of Man at the right hand of God.[4] It seems likely that even during Jesus' earthly ministry, his disciples regarded him as an apocalyptic figure, revealed in the last days and destined to be enthroned in heaven as the eschatological King and judge of the world.[5] It is in this context that we must place the exegesis of Ps. 109.1 and the title *kyrios* which was linked with it.

---

[1] Bousset, *Kyrios Christos* (1st ed.), pp. 95 ff.

[2] R. H. Fuller, *The Mission and Achievement of Jesus*, StBTh 12 (1954), p. 112.

[3] Fuller, *Mission*, pp. 113 f.: "Therefore it is clear that Jesus regarded 'Adoni' as an appropriate title, not for himself in his earthly ministry, but for the Son of Man exalted at the right hand of God. That Jesus himself sanctions the process by which Maran(a) applied to him as a purely honorific title in his earthly life, becomes eventually, through the impact of subsequent events, a title applicable to him as the One exalted to the right hand of God."

[4] Cf. below, pp. 131 ff.

[5] Cerfaux has shown that Mk. does not use the term *kyrios* about Jesus even in

Kyrios in the early Christian kerygma

The title *kyrios* and enthronement of the exalted Christ at the right hand of the Father are prominent ideas in the first Christian proclamation. Both have to do with the Christological interpretation of Ps. 109 (110).1 which, as we have seen, was probably derived from Jesus' own teaching.

We also find that Ps. 109.1 was combined from the first with the title "Son of Man". The combination occurs in Jesus' address to the Sanhedrin (Mk. 14.62 par.),[1] and recurs in the story of the martyrdom of St. Stephen (Acts 7.55 f.). In the latter case, we read that Stephen saw the Son of Man *standing* at the right hand of God—an expression probably derived from early Christian apocalyptic ideas.[2] We come across the same terminology in one of the early Christian documents outside the NT, the *Hypomnemata* of Hegesippus,[3] in the passage describing the martyrdom of St. James. The Scribes and Pharisees ask which is "Jesus' door", and James answers, "Why do you ask me about the Son of Man? He is seated in heaven at the right hand of the Almighty, and he will come again on the clouds of heaven." This is obviously a further case of combination of Ps. 109.1 with Dan. 7.13 f., and may have been taken over from Jewish Messianic circles.[4]

Parallel to this we find the title *kyrios* used with particular reference to the enthronement and *sessio* of Christ. St. Peter, in his Pentecost speech—which contains a number of archaisms, and which there is good reason to believe reflected the Christology of the first Christian congregation—says that Jesus has been exalted to the right hand of God (τῇ δεξιᾷ τοῦ θεοῦ), and that he has been made both κύριος and Χριστός (Acts 2.32–36).[5] Thus not only the name κύριος but also the

---

ordinary polite forms of address. So, the word appears suddenly and mysteriously, in connexion with Jesus' entry into Jerusalem (Mk 11.3). It is the Messianic King, who will perform his earthly enthronement, which in later patristic exegesis is regarded as a type of his heavenly triumph and his parousia, *Le titre Kyrios*, pp. 40.

[1] Cf. above, p. 50.

[2] See H. Bietenhard, *Die himmlische Welt im Urchristentum und Spätjudentum*, WUNT 2 (1951), pp. 66 and 71. Schnackenburg, *Herrschaft*, p. 34. Cf. below, p. 131.

[3] Eusebius, HE II 23.12 f., GCS Eus. 2.1.168 f.

[4] C. H. Dodd, *According to the Scriptures* (1952), p. 67. Doeve, *Hermeneutics*, pp. 152 ff. J. Daniélou, *La Session à la droite du Père*, Stud. Ev., TU 73 (1959), pp. 689–698.

[5] E. Haenchen, *Die Apostelgeschichte*, 3rd ed. (1959), p. 146.

title of Χριστός were bestowed upon Jesus at his enthronement (cf. Acts 5.31, where Jesus, in connexion with his enthronement, is called ἀρχηγός and σωτήρ).[1]

The *sessio* of Christ at the right hand of God is a theme which recurs frequently in the letters of St. Paul (Rom. 8.34, Eph. 1.20, Col. 3.1, 1 Cor. 15.25, 27). The frequent allusions to Ps. 109.1 prove that St. Paul also regarded it as of vital importance as a proof-text, even though we have no passage in which he quoted it direct. It is at the same time characteristic that St. Paul uses the term *kyrios*, referring to Christ, in the context of Jesus' Messianic Kingship (Rom. 4.24, 1 Cor. 9.1, 2 Cor. 4.14).[2]

This is particularly noticeable in Phil. 2.10 f. God has exalted Jesus over all things, and has bestowed on him the name that is above every name, that at the name of Jesus every knee should bow, and every tongue confess that Jesus Christ is *kyrios*.[3] What makes this passage so interesting is that *kyrios* is here not only a royal title, but also a name—or paraphrase—of God. God has given Christ the name that is above every name, and for St. Paul this can be nothing other than the Tetragrammaton. The glorified Lord thus bears, and is entitled to bear, the name Yahweh, and he is therefore to be worshipped by the name *kyrios*, i.e. with the name used in the LXX to symbolize the Name which is too holy to be uttered.[4]

In 1 and 2 Thess. the title *kyrios* is connected in particular with the Lordship of Christ at the parousia (1 Thess. 2.19, 3.13, 4.15 f., 5.23; 2 Thess. 1.7, 2.1).[5]

The most extensive use of Ps. 109 (110) is however found in Heb.; both v. 1 and v. 4 are important, the first as proof of the Ascension and *sessio* of Christ (1.3, 13, 10.13) and the second of his office of priest after the order of Melchizedek (5.6, 7.17). It is remarkable that the introductory words of Ps. 109.1 (εἶπεν κύριος τῷ κυρίῳ μου) which elsewhere provide the normal *Stichwort* of the Psalm, are nowhere used in Heb. And this is not all. Christ is called *kyrios* on only two occasions

---

[1] Cf. below, p. 65.

[2] CERFAUX, *Le Christ*, p. 75.

[3] See E. LOHMEYER, *Kyrios Jesus*, SbHei 1927-28.4, according to which St. Paul is here quoting a primitive Christian Aramaic Psalm. Cf. CULLMANN, *Christologie*, pp. 178 ff.

[4] H. BIETENHARD, art. ὄνομα, ThWB 5 (1944-54), p. 272. CERFAUX, *Le Christ*, pp. 358 ff.

[5] See below, p. 68.

in the Epistle: in the conclusion (13.20) and in 1.10–12, with its unique use of Ps. 101 (102).26 f., referring to the work of the pre-existent Christ in creation.[1]

We also find allusions to Ps. 109 in 1 Pet. 3.22, Rev. 3.21 and 5.1, 7, none of which are linked with the title *kyrios*. The connexion between Ps. 109.1 and *kyrios* thus seems to be less marked in some NT traditions than in others.

It is a striking fact that Ps. 109.1 is neither referred to nor quoted in the Johannine literature, which at the same time makes only limited use of the title *kyrios*. It is true that in the Resurrection narrative Jesus is on several occasions called *kyrios*,[2] but the title is never used in the Johannine Epistles, and is seldom used of Christ in Rev. (The sole exceptions are 17.14 and 19.16.)

Even if we are correct in supposing *kyrios*, as a Christological title, to have been derived from a Messianic exposition of Ps. 109.1, and to have been introduced by Jesus himself—not in the form of a *Selbstprädikation* but as a title for the exalted Son of Man, it is obvious that the title *kyrios* and the kerygma of Christ's exaltation soon became separated. As far back as the NT *kyrios* began to enjoy a separate existence as a Christological term without constantly being related to Ps. 109. St. Paul often alludes to Ps. 109; his use of the *kyrios* title is even more frequent; but there is little connexion to be observed between the two, apart from the fact that both belong to the kerygma of the exaltation and glorification of Christ. In the Palestinian Church Christ seems often to have been called "Son of Man"—through the traditional combination of Ps. 109.1 and Dan. 7.13 f.—in connexion with his exaltation to the right hand of the Father. There is a very evident separation of Ps. 109.1 from the title *kyrios* in Heb. and Jn.: Heb. has a Christological exegesis of Ps. 109.1 which makes no use of *kyrios*; Jn. uses *kyrios* as a title, however infrequently, but provides no further trace of influence from Ps. 109.1.

To summarize: the evidence for the origins of the title *kyrios* in Ps. 109 (110).1 is as follows:

---

[1] See further below, p. 56.

[2] BOUSSET uses this fact to claim the secondary character of the title *kyrios*, *Kyrios Christos*, 1st ed., p. 97, an argument, which is also taken up by BULTMANN, *Theologie*, p. 383. CULLMANN's explanation seems more natural, that the title *kyrios* also for Jn. is connected with the exaltation of Jesus, *Christologie*, p. 239 and n. 2. St. Thomas' confession ὁ κύριός μου καὶ ὁ θεός μου (Jn. 20.28) is interpreted by CULLMANN as "the crowning of the Gospel".

1. The only occasion on which Jesus uses the term *kyrios* of the Messiah is in connexion with an exposition of Ps. 109.1.

2. The combination of the title *kyrios* with ideas derived from Ps. 109.1 on the enthronement of Christ at the right hand of the Father is found in St. Peter's Pentecost address, which has a number of archaisms, and which seems to reproduce some of the Christological ideas of the primitive Church.

3. Ps. 109.1 is one of the most important proof-texts in the post-Apostolic literature; from it was derived Jesus' title of *kyrios*.[1] There is no doubt that this goes back to a tradition of the Palestinian congregation, of which deposits are also to be found in the NT.

Kyrios and the Divinity of Christ

The double function of the title *kyrios*—as royal title and Divine name—complicates its interpretation. Although the title is derived from Ps. 109 (110).1, and is thus linked with the exaltation of Christ, we must ask whether there may not be some application of the term *kyrios* to Christ in the NT, an application which refers to his pre-existence, his participation in the work of creation, and his Incarnation. This use of the title is of great importance in post-Apostolic times (see below).

Cullmann has devoted one section of his book on the Christology of the NT to this question.[2] Here, as elsewhere, he distinguishes between *function* and *person*: in Cullmann's opinion, what is primary in the *kyrios* concept is faith in Jesus' Messianic function. When speculations on the nature of Jesus began to be developed—as was evidently already the case in Palestine—the title *kyrios* became filled with new content.[3]

---

[1] See below, p. 101.

[2] CULLMANN, *Christologie*, 241 ff.

[3] CULLMANN, *op. cit.*, *passim*. The distinction between "function" and "nature" is important for the whole work, and is presented in the introduction, p. 4. The same distinction is also drawn by CERFAUX, *Le titre Kyrios*, p. 62: "Le titre Kyrios a donc été imposé d'abord à Jésus à cause de sa dignité de Roi-Messie. Le developpement théologique qui s'est incorporé dans la signification de ce prédicat s'est produit par le jeu du concept de souveraineté. Le mouvement a été seulement plus intense dans le monde grec que dans le monde araméen. Les communautés judéo-chrétiennes ont pu accepter la souveraineté céleste du Christ, sans réfléchir beaucoup sur la dignité de la fonction. Les églises du monde grec, guidées par la notion

Although Cullmann thus counts sayings on the Divine nature of Christ as secondary in comparison with those which touch upon his Messianic function, he considers that there are a number of examples in the NT of *kyrios* sayings from the OT, which originally referred to Yahweh, being transferred to Christ.[1]

Only one of the examples quoted by Cullmann can be said to be unquestionably a case of transference of the OT Divine name to Jesus: Heb. 1.10 ff., with its quotation of Ps. 101 (102).26 ff.: "Thou, Lord didst found the earth in the beginning, and the heavens are the work of thy hands; they will perish, but thou remainest; they will all grow old like a garment, like a mantle thou wilt roll them up, and they will be changed. But thou art the same, and thy years will never end." This quotation provides clear proof that in the OT there has already occurred the transference to Christ of a saying about God. But this is not a rule; it is merely an isolated exception. We may also take note of the fact that Ps. 101.26 ff. is not employed as a proof-text in the post-Apostolic tradition.[2]

It is characteristic that *kyrios* in Ps. 109 (110).1 refers, not to Yahweh, but to the King: εἶπεν κύριος τῷ κυρίῳ μου. St. Justin Martyr and

---

claire de la situation unique que le Christ occupait dans la foi de l'église primitive et son culte, par l'enseignement même de Jésus, ont médité davantage sur la nature du Christ et ont professé explicitement qu'il est *Theos*. Cela s'est fait sans rupture avec les données primitives, sans poussée violente du paganisme. Les distinctions fort tranchées entre la foi primitive et la foi soidisante paulinienne ne correspondent que très imparfaitement à la réalité; s'il fallait en accepter une, nous suivrions à peu près le contre-pied de la voie tranchée par Bousset: pour nous, s'il y a un christianisme du *Kyrios*, il est caractéristique de l'église judéo-araméenne; les églises grecques sont les églises du *Christos-Theos*." Cf. on the other hand GAECHTER's review of CULLMANN' *Christologie* in ZKTh 82 (1960), p. 100; which stresses that speculations about the nature of the Messiah have existed from the beginning. Cf. also the concept "Son of God" and the Jewish ideas about the pre-existing Son of Man, which may serve as a corrective for one-sided, functional concepts of primitive Christology.

[1] CULLMANN expresses this opinion in a rather categorical form: "Überhaupt sollten wir der durchaus nicht selbstverständlichen Tatsache mehr Rechnung tragen, dass die ersten Christen nach Jesu Tode ohne weiteres auf *Jesus* übertragen haben, was das Alte Testament von *Gott* sagt", *Christologie*, p. 242.

[2] Ps. 101 (102).26 ff. is quoted by St. Irenaeus in Adv. haer. IV 3, ed. HARVEY 2.151, but is here applied to God. It is quite unknown as a proof-text for the pre-existence of Christ in the post-Apostolic literature before A.D. 200. See A. VON UNGERN-STERNBERG, *Der Alttestamentliche Schriftbeweis "De Christo" und "De Evangelio" in der Alten Kirche bis zur Zeit Eusebs von Caesarea* (1913), p. 55.

the later Fathers use this and other proof-texts to show that Christ is God and *kyrios*, without thereby identifying him absolutely with the Father. This is obviously a conscious hermeneutic principle, according to which use has been made of OT texts in which the term *kyrios* is used of someone other than Yahweh.[1]

As Cerfaux has shown, St. Paul consistently avoids taking OT *kyrios* sayings originally referring to God, and applying them to Christ.[2] Cullmann is therefore going too far when he says that after the death of Jesus the first Christians transferred to him all the OT had to say about God.[3] Had it been as simple as that, the Christological struggles of the early Church would probably never have taken place, and the Christology of the Church would have had a quite different appearance. The seed of the coming doctrine of the Trinity is to be seen here, in Christ's double character—on the one hand God and Lord; on the other separate from Yahweh.

Faith in Christ as *kyrios* and God later resulted in the transfer to Christ of such OT sayings as obviously referred to God. Heb. 1.10 ff. provides the clearest example in the NT of this process. There is a tendency in the NT, quite apart from the OT proof-texts, to use *kyrios* to refer to the pre-existence and Incarnation of Christ, though John does not use *kyrios* to refer to the Logos in his Prologue, nor does St. Paul use the term in Phil. 2.6. In each case *kyrios* is connected with Christ's exaltation. In 1 Cor. 8.6, on the other hand, it is linked with his pre-existence; the text speaks of "one *kyrios*, Jesus Christ, through whom are all things and through whom we exist". The same tendency is to be seen in 2 Cor. 8.9: "For you know the grace of our *kyrios* Jesus Christ, that though he was rich, yet for your sake he became poor, so that by his poverty you might become rich."

This tendency stands out with even greater clarity in the post-Apostolic literature. Hellenistic Christianity soon lost touch with the

---

[1] The same hermeneutic principle is followed in Heb. 1.8 f., where Ps. 44 (45).7 is used as a proof-text that Christ is θεός. Cf. CULLMANN, *op. cit.*, *ibid*. Also here a text is chosen, where God means another person than Yahweh, viz. the king: διὰ τοῦτο ἔχρισέν σε, ὁ θεός, ὁ θεός σου ἔλαιον ἀγαλλιάσεως. See further below, pp. 84 ff.

[2] L. CERFAUX, "*Kyrios*" dans les citations pauliniennes de l'Ancient Testament, RLC 1 (1954), pp. 173–188. Quite a different opinion—that St. Paul in his quotations from the LXX entirely applies the Divine name to Christ—is expressed by MICHAELIS, *Engelchristologie*, pp. 61 ff.; his conclusions, however, do not seem to be based on such a solid analysis as that of CERFAUX.

[3] See above, p. 56, n. 1.

real meaning of the Messianic titles derived from the Palestinian Church. Such terms as Son of Man, Son of David and Servant occur relatively seldom, and always in those classes of literature which were the most conservative: the *testimonia* tradition, apocalyptic literature, the liturgy. Those terms which had such wide currency in the Christian Church that they did not share the fate of the rest of the Jewish terminology (e.g. *kyrios* and *christos*), tend instead to degenerate into mere titles or to be given a meaning different from that they originally carried. Here, too, an exception is the conservative literature. The Greek-speaking world began to use other Christological terms instead, terms which must have been more readily understandable in a Hellenistic milieu. This applies particularly to θεός and σωτήρ, both of which occur only sporadically in the NT as epithets for Christ, and then mainly in the later writings.[1]

As far back as the Apostolic Fathers there is a distinct tendency to leave the kerygma of the Resurrection and Ascension of Christ, in order to concentrate instead on his pre-existence and Divine origin. The centre of gravity shifted from *kyrios* to θεός, and even when the title *kyrios* was still used, its meaning was coloured by the new emphasis on the pre-existence of Christ. This decline in the use of the title *kyrios* in post-Apostolic Christendom contradicts Bousset's theory, that *kyrios* was of Hellenistic origin and did not come into the NT until later.[2] All the evidence suggests that *kyrios*, *'ādōn* (and Aram. *marān*) was a term which could only be understood by those who spoke a Semitic language. *Kyrios* for the Greek-speaking world was only a second-class title.[3] It is most striking that in the Ignatians, *kyrios* is frequently replaced by θεός, and sometimes even by σωτήρ.[4]

In the Pauline Epistles we encounter *kyrios* in what appear to be set phrases, usually taken from the OT, but sometimes having Christological implications: the table of the Lord, the fear of the Lord, the beloved of the Lord, etc.[5] In the post-Apostolic literature such usage

---

[1] See below, p. 65.
[2] Cf. above, p. 45.
[3] See above, p. 55, n. 3.
[4] θεός appears as a Christological title in Ign. ad Eph., pref., 1.1, 7.2, 18.2, 19.3; Trall. 7.1; Rom. 3.3; Smyrn. 10.1; Polyc. 8.3. σωτήρ appears in the same sense in Ign. ad Eph. 1.1; Magn. pref.; Philad. 9.2; Smyrn. 7.1; Polyc. ad Phil. pref.; Mart. Polyc. 19.3; Diogn. 9.6; *Gospel of Peter* 4.13; 2 Clem. 20.5; Quadratus, Apol. (in Eusebius, HE IV 3.2); St. Justin, Dial. 63.5, 76.7, 128.1; St. Irenaeus, Dem. 47.
[5] CERFAUX, "*Kyrios*" *dans les citations*, pp. 185 f.

becomes more and more common, while the more pregnant *kyrios* sayings become rarer. In the *Didache* the word occurs for the most part in fixed phrases, and it is not always clear whether it is the Father or the Son who is referred to: the teaching of the Lord (title), the message of the Lord (4.13), the yoke of the Lord (6.2), the name of the Lord (9.5, 12.1), the knowledge of the Lord (11.2), the day of the Lord, κυριακή (14.1), the gospel of the Lord (15.4). The only exception to this rule is met with, characteristically, in the eschatological final chapter, 16.1, 7 f. (Quotations of Matt. 24.42 and Zech. 14.5, referring to the parousia).[1]

In the *Epistle of Clement*, *kyrios* is the standard epithet for Christ—the standard title for the Father being δεσπότης[2]—but the term is little more than a title. This is the same development as may be noted in the case of Χριστός. This is similarly true of *the Epistle of Barnabas*, though here *kyrios* normally denotes God. The only passages in which Clem. and Barn. use the title *kyrios* to refer to the glorification of Christ are quotations from the OT, and these are few in number.[3] The title has been for the most part obscured in the Ignatians and in the *Epistle of Diognetus* (occurring in the latter only twice).[4]

Kyrios, referring to Christ, is found much more frequently in the *Epistle of Polycarp* than in the Ignatians, with which Polycarp is normally reckoned for theological purposes. Polycarp draws a clear distinction in terminology between θεός=the Father and *kyrios*=the Son (1.1, 2.1, 12.2). The term also seems to be more closely linked with Christ's glorification (1.2, 2.1, 12.2) or parousia (6.2 f., 11.2) than is the case in others of the Apostolic Fathers. This is also true of the *Martyrdom of Polycarp*; the θεός-κύριος distinction is drawn (introduction), but God is called κύριε in Polycarp's prayer (14.1), in accordance with Christian prayer-tradition.[5] The use of the word *kyrios* seems to

---

[1] J.-P. AUDET, *La Didachè* (1958), pp. 468 ff. According to AUDET, *kyrios* in Did. means God, where the word stands without the definite article, *ibid.*, pp. 188 and 190, n. 1.

[2] Cf. BOUSSET, *Kyrios Christos*, 1st ed., p. 269. God is styled *kyrie* in the liturgical prayer (ch. 59–61). ὄνομα κυρίου (without any article) in 43.6 and 47.7 is also probably said about God. Further *kyrios* appears 38 times in quotations from the OT.

[3] See below, p. 101.

[4] For the title *kyrios* in Hermas, see J.-P. AUDET, *Affinités littéraires et doctrinales du Manuel de Discipline (suite)*, RB 60 (1953), pp. 45 ff.

[5] See below, p. 158.

be more controversial in character here, in conflict with the Roman State, than elsewhere in the documents of the period; one act in the imperial cult which Polycarp refused to carry out was the confession of κύριος Καῖσαρ (8.2). The *Martyrdom of Polycarp* is closely related to the later Acts of the Martyrs, and we shall consider these together.[1]

As we have seen, the language of the period is most uncertain of application. The word *kyrios* occurs with highly variable frequency in the various documents; it is sometimes a Christological epithet and sometimes a Divine name. When *kyrios* is used as a title of Christ, it is not normally connected with the idea of the glorification of Christ. Exceptions to this rule are however the expositions of proof-texts, which are for the most part conservative in character, and the *Epistle of Polycarp*. Where the word has retained its fuller implications, it is linked rather with the Divine origin of Christ than with his enthronement.

The most striking example of this is to be seen in a work of Christian apocalyptic, the *Ascension of Isaiah*, which conveys the impression of great antiquity and is closely related to Jewish apocalyptic traditions. (The document is in point of fact a long interpolation in the Jewish *Martyrdom of Isaiah*.[2]) According to this work, Isaiah is allowed to see how the Father sends the Son from the highest heaven, how he descends through the different heavens and, his work of salvation completed, reascends to the right hand of the Father. The term *kyrios* is used to refer to the Son in this pre-existent state: he is "the *kyrios* who is to be called *Christos*" (9.13) or "*kyrios Christos* who is to be called Jesus" (10.7). It is impossible to escape the idea that the motif of Christ's *descensus* has influenced the language used; just as Peter's use of *kyrios* in his speeches in Acts indicates Jesus' state after the Ascension, so it here indicates his status before the *descensus*.

The tendency, already to be seen in the NT, to use *kyrios* to express the Divine origin of Christ, is otherwise found mainly in Clem. and Barn. The name *kyrios* serves above all to express the glory of Christ in his pre-existence, the glory which he laid aside at the Incarnation: "The sceptre of the majesty of God, the *kyrios* Jesus Christ did not come with the boast of arrogance and pride, though he was able to do

---

[1] See below, p. 178.
[2] See below, p. 142.

so, but in humbleness of mind" (Clem. 16.2).[1] "If the *kyrios* endured it to suffer for our life, though he was *kyrios* of all the world, to whom God said, at the foundation of the world, 'Let us make man in our image and our likeness', then how did he endure it, to suffer at the hands of men? Learn it!" (Barn. 5.5.[2]) "So if the Son of God, though he was *kyrios*, and was to judge the living and the dead, suffered in order that his wounds might bring us life, let us believe that the Son of God could not suffer except for us" (Barn. 7.2).[3]

Thus in post-Apostolic times *kyrios* was no longer understood, as it had once been, as a typical royal title. This may serve as a partial explanation of why later periods preferred to use *basileus* to express Christ's Kingly character. But the title *kyrios* retains its character as a royal epithet, thanks to the *testimonia* tradition, which drew for its proof-texts largely upon those verses in the OT which speak of a *kyrios* distinct from God. In that class of literature, which was so much dependent upon the OT, we find throughout the early Church that the word *kyrios* has largely retained its original implications.

Hellenistic Royal Terminology in the NT

Among the NT terms taken up by Deissmann are a number of words which seem to belong to a later phase in the NT tradition, and which demonstrate striking resemblances to the Hellenistic royal terminology of the period in which the NT originated. These are: σωτήρ, παρουσία and ἐπιφάνεια, φιλανθρωπία; in Clem. εὐεργέτης also.[4] Some of these words belong to the vocabulary of the LXX; none, as far as we know, are found in the terminology of Jewish Messianism.

The unavoidable question has therefore been whether these terms were taken over from the language of the court and incorporated into the language of the Church by way of polemic against the intensifying

---

[1] τὸ σκῆπτρον τῆς μεγαλοσύνης τοῦ θεοῦ, ὁ κύριος Ἰησοῦς Χριστός, οὐκ ἦλθεν ἐν κόμπῳ ἀλαζονείας οὐδὲ ὑπερηφανίας, καίπερ δυνάμενος, ἀλλὰ ταπεινοφρονῶν.

[2] εἰ ὁ κύριος ὑπέμεινεν παθεῖν περὶ τῆς ψυχῆς ὑμῶν, ὢν παντὸς τοῦ κόσμου κύριος, ᾧ εἶπεν ὁ θεὸς ἀπὸ καταβολῆς κόσμου· ποιήσωμεν ἄνθρωπον κατ' εἰκόνα καὶ καθ' ὁμοίωσιν ἡμετέραν· πῶς οὖν ὑπέμεινεν ὑπὸ χειρὸς ἀνθρώπων παθεῖν, μάθετε.

[3] εἰ οὖν ὁ υἱὸς τοῦ θεοῦ, ὢν κύριος καὶ μέλλων κρίνειν ζῶντας καὶ νεκρούς, ἔπαθεν ἵνα ἡ πληγὴ αὐτοῦ ζωοποιήσῃ ἡμᾶς, πιστεύσωμεν ὅτι ὁ υἱὸς τοῦ θεοῦ οὐκ ἠδύνατο παθεῖν εἰ μὴ δι' ἡμᾶς.

[4] DEISSMANN, *Licht*, pp. 311 ff.

royal cult of the end of the 1st century.[1] Deissmann was most interested in demonstrating the parallelism of these expressions, with its consequent danger of conflict with the imperial powers; Lohmeyer went further, endeavouring to derive the Christological titles of the NT from this cult.[2] This attempt at a solution has been most noticeable in later exegesis of the Pastoral Epistles, though Lohmeyer's thesis has had to be modified, and has aroused violent opposition from some quarters.[3] It is beyond the scope of this book to take up this problem in detail; such would require a separate investigation. We shall therefore limit ourselves to an account of the main points in the debate, attempting to determine the extent to which the post-Apostolic age understood these terms as expressions of the rule of Christ.

Most, but not all, of those who have accepted the theory of terminological influence from the imperial cult, consider that the titles have been taken over for polemical reasons. Thus in the Pastoral Epistles Christ the King was already placed over against the Roman Emperor: a contrast clearly expressed in Rev. 17–19.[4] The eschatological ex-

---

[1] For the imperial titles in the late Roman Empire, see L. BRÉHIER, *L'Origine des titres impériaux à Byzance*, BZ 15 (1906), pp. 161–178. L. BERLINGER, *Beiträge zur inoffiziellen Titulatur der römischen Kaiser* (1935). W. SCHUBART, *Das hellenistische Königsideal nach Inschriften und Papyri*, APF 12 (1936), pp. 1–26. A. WIFSTRAND, *Autokrator, Kaisar, Basileus*, in ΔΡΑΓΜΑ, M. P. Nilsson dedicatum (1939), pp. 529–539.

[2] LOHMEYER, *Christuskult*, pp. 25 ff.

[3] So above all PRÜMM, *Herrscherkult, passim*. Cf. IDEM, *Der christliche Glaube und die altheidnische Welt* 1 (1935), pp. 161 ff.

[4] This opinion is clearly expressed by C. SPICQ, *St. Paul, Les Épîtres pastorales*, 2nd ed. (1947), pp. CLXII ff. (à propos μέγας θεός as a Christological title in Tit. 2.13): "Cette épithète comme les autres qualifications de majesté adressés à Dieu, et dont plusieurs sont nouvelles, sont choisis par saint Paul dans une intention polémique, en contraste avec le culte impérial qui prend alors une grande extension ... On adore l'Empereur et l'on décerne à son εἰκών des honneurs divins. On proclame que la divinité se manifeste en eux: ἐπιφάνεια, *praesens Deus*: qu'ils témoignent leurs faveurs (χάρις), et apportent à la ville le secours (σωτηρία), la paix (εἰρήνη), de belles espérances (ἐλπίς). Sans doute ces hommages expriment souvent une tradition conventionelle et vont de soi comme prescriptions de l'étiquette de cour, mais elles traduisent aussi une foi religieuse réelle, et sont de toutes façons sacrilèges par rapport au Dieu unique, seul Sauveur, *notre* Seigneur Jésus-Christ. Voilà pourquoi saint Paul oppose la véritable épiphanie du vrai Dieu à celle des souverains profanes, et transpose dans la foi nouvelle ces termes religieux courants en leur donnant leur sens plein et le seul vrai. Il n'y a que le Christ à être Seigneur et Sauveur du genre humain."

pectations of primitive Christianity were also contrasted with the apocalyptic speculations about a coming kingdom of peace which filled the Roman Empire, and which received their most lasting expression in Vergil's *Fourth Eclogue*.[1] The contrast between Christ and Caesar can of course be met with in other passages of the NT, and not only in the Pastorals and Rev. Lk. 2.1 ff. may well be interpreted as a conscious expression of the antithesis between Augustus' *Pax Romana* and Christ's Kingdom of Peace; similarly, the question of the paying of taxes shows how the Christ/Caesar relationship soon came to be regarded as a problem.[2] It is a very real temptation in such a context as this to fall back upon a too-speculative treatment of a material which is diffuse and often ambiguous. An investigation of the separate Hellenistic terms which may have been borrowed from the Hellenistic imperial cult reveals several possible interpretations in most cases. There are other cases in which it seems that we are dealing with a simple form of imperial terminology; here however we must get to grips with the obscure question of why and how it became integrated into the language of the Church. Did it take place in a naïve fashion, for polemical purposes, or because the imperial terminology of late Antiquity opened new possibilities for the Christian mission to the Greek-speaking peoples?

What is perhaps the most telling reason why these terms, occurring as they do largely in the Pastorals, should be reckoned as having been borrowed from imperial terminology, is that we sometimes find them in combinations of words, revealing the use of a consistent imagery. The clearest example is provided by Tit. 2.11 ff. ('Επεφάνη γὰρ ἡ χάρις τοῦ θεοῦ σωτήριος πᾶσιν ἀνθρώποις, ... ἐπιφάνειαν τῆς δόξης τοῦ μεγάλου θεοῦ καὶ σωτῆρος ἡμῶν 'Ιησοῦ Χριστοῦ) and 3.4 ff. (ὅτι δὲ ἡ χρηστότης καὶ ἡ φιλανθρωπία ἐπεφάνη τοῦ σωτῆρος ἡμῶν θεοῦ).[3] Similar combinations of terms are to be found in 1 and 2 Thess., which we consider below. In order to lay bare the meaning of these terms we must however deal with each separately—not least because their meaning appears to vary from case to case.

---

[1] So H. LIETZMANN, *Der Weltheiland* (1909). Among later literature of this kind, see especially E. STAUFFER, *Christus und die Cäsaren*, 4th ed. (1952), 84 ff. and *passim*, and IDEM, *Jerusalem und Rom* (1957), pp. 20 ff.

[2] STAUFFER, *Christus*, pp. 97 ff. (Augustus and Jesus); *ibid.* pp. 121 ff. (the tribute money).

[3] M. DIBELIUS, *Die Pastoralbriefe*, 3rd ed. (1955), pp. 108 ff.

σωτήρ

The full extent of the problem is seen in the case of the diffuse and ambiguous σωτήρ. The *religionshistorische* school—represented by Bousset and Norden—attempted to trace the word back to Hellenistic mystery religions, where it certainly played an important role.[1] But at the same time it is fully representative of the imperial cult, and ever since the turn of the century there have been attempts made to interpret its NT use in terms of a loan from imperial terminology. Even before Deissmann published his comprehensive work, Wendland and Harnack had attempted to interpret the title σωτήρ politically.[2] Later exegetical literature has followed them in allowing this explanation to lie within the realm of possibility.[3]

In the language of the Empire σωτήρ had a meaning not far removed from the sphere of eschatology; it was not uncommon for the propaganda connected with salvation from political danger to assume metaphysical dimensions. Augustus' contemporaries regarded him as a σωτήρ who had brought salvation to the Empire out of the earlier confusion, and had bestowed peace, *Pax Romana*, upon the whole of the inhabited world. Each of his successors was surrounded by similar speculations: the Emperor's accession meant the start of a new aeon; he was the object of worship, σεβαστός, and his accession could be called an ἐπιφάνεια.[4] It would, then, hardly be unreasonable to expect the Christian Church to use the title σωτήρ of Christ as the eschatological King, whose coming signalled the break-through of the new Kingdom of God. Such a usage would be all the more likely in the Hel-

---

[1] Bousset, *Kyrios Christos*, 1st ed., p. 293 ff. E. Norden, *Die Geburt des Kindes* (1924), pp. 51 ff. For the title σωτήρ in Gnostic literature, see F. J. Dölger, ΙΧΘΥΣ 1 (1910), p. 409. Most of the works here mentioned on σωτήρ also discuss the possibility of an influence from Hellenistic religions.

[2] P. Wendland, Σωτήρ, ZNW 5 (1904), pp. 335–353. A. von Harnack, *Der Heiland*, in idem, Reden und Aufsätze, 1 (1904), pp. 307 ff.

[3] For the title σωτήρ in the NT, see Lietzmann, *Weltheiland*, pp. 56 ff. Deissmann, *Licht*, pp. 311 ff. Lohmeyer, *Christuskult*, pp. 27 f. F. Dornseiff, art. Σωτήρ, PWK, Reihe 2.5 (1927), col. 1211–1221. H. Linssen, Θεὸς σωτήρ, JbL 8 (1928), pp. 1–75. Prümm, *Herrscherkult*, pp. 132 f. Idem, *Christliche Glaube*, pp. 175. Staerk, *Soter* 1, *passim*. Idem, *Erlösererwartung*, *passim*. H. Windisch, *Zur Christologie der Pastoralbriefe*, ZNW 34 (1935), pp. 227 ff. Spicq, *Épîtres pastorales*, pp. 2 f. A. D. Nock, *Soter and Euergetes*, The Joy of Study ... to Honor F. C. Grant (1951), pp. 127–148. Dibelius, *Pastoralbriefe*, pp. 74 ff. Cullmann, *Christologie*, pp. 245 ff.

[4] For the concept ἐπιφάνεια, see further below, pp. 67 ff.

lenistic world, in which the eschatological concepts of Judaism were both unknown and incomprehensible, and where there might well have been a need for a new terminology, linked with the Hellenistic royal ideology.

But it is far from certain that the NT use of the title σωτήρ really has such a direct connexion with the meaning of the word in the language of the court, even though this meaning may have had some significance when the term was taken over.

In the NT σωτήρ is used both of God and of Christ, and exclusively in those books whose language is Hellenistic; it is thus not found in Matt. and Mk., and is rare in the Corpus Paulinum, apart from the Pastoral Epistles.[1] This suggests that the word was not originally part of Christological terminology.[2] It is however found in the LXX, and it is therefore conceivable that the Church may have taken it over from that source. It is there used to refer to men who are responsible for saving acts (particularly in Judges). This is probably a case of influence from the language of Hellenism, in which such heroes could be called σωτῆρες—a parallel to the use of the word in Roman political metaphysics.[3] Of more importance is the fact that in the LXX the word is applied to God—in the set phrase θεὸς καὶ σωτήρ—particularly in the Psalter and the Prophets (Ps. 23 (24).5, 61 (62).7, Isa. 12.2, Ps. Sol. 3.6, 8.33, 16.4, 17). This would seem to be adequate evidence for the origin of the NT practice of calling God σωτήρ, and using the verb σῴζειν with God as the subject (1 Cor. 1.21, Eph. 2.5, 2 Tim. 1.9). Since the terms θεός and σωτήρ come into use at the same time as titles of Christ (see e.g. the phrase used of Christ in Tit. 2.13, 2 Pet. 1.1: θεὸς καὶ σωτήρ), we cannot dismiss the possibility that σωτήρ is here derived from the language of the LXX, and refers to Christ as God.

The word is unknown as a title for the Messiah in Judaism (with the possible exception of 1 En. 48.7); attempts have been made to trace it back to גואל, the saviour who is to crush the enemies of Israel, but

---

[1] Lk. 1.47, 2.11; Jn. 4.42; Acts 5.31, 13.23; Eph. 5.23; Phil. 3.20; 1 Tim. 1.1, 2.3, 4.10; 2 Tim. 1.10; Tit. 1.3 f., 2.10, 2.13, 3.4, 3.6; 2 Pet. 1.1, 1.11, 2.20, 3.2, 3.18; 1 Jn. 4.14; Jude 25.

[2] N.b. however that this word occurs in Acts 5.31, where Christ is called ἀρχηγὸς καὶ σωτήρ. The discourses in the Acts have certain archaic trends (cf. above, p. 52), and the occurrence of the word in this context might be evidence of an earlier integration of the word in the Christian language than is usually supposed. Cf. HAENCHEN, *Comm. ad loc.*

[3] DIBELIUS, *Pastoralbriefe*, p. 74. Cf. PRÜMM, *Christliche Glaube* 1, pp. 196 ff.

these are far from convincing.[1] It is met with in post-Apostolic literature in contexts which leave no doubt that we are dealing with influence from the logos terminology of Philo;[2] there are few traces in the NT of such an influence.

A further possibility is to interpret the word as a form of the name Jesus. This was expressed by St. Justin, who claims σωτήρ to be a translation into Greek of the name Jesus.[3] This interpretation was noted by Lietzmann,[4] but is missing from Dibelius' otherwise comprehensive study. Cullmann also considers that the name Jesus must have been of significance for the origins of the title σωτήρ.[5]

As far back as Matt. 1.21 we find a certain speculation about the name Jesus: καλέσεις τὸ ὄνομα αὐτοῦ 'Ιησοῦν· αὐτὸς γὰρ σώσει τὸν λαὸν αὐτοῦ ἀπὸ τῶν ἁμαρτιῶν αὐτῶν. The allegorical interpretation of the name which we find here seems to go back to Jewish sources: the same interpretation, this time of the name Joshua, is to be found in Sir. 46.1 (LXX): ὃς ἐγένετο κατὰ τὸ ὄνομα αὐτοῦ μέγας ἐπὶ τῇ σωτηρίᾳ ἐκλεκτῶν αὐτοῦ. In neither case is it stated explicitly that the name Joshua-Jesus means σωτήρ, but this further development would not seem to be very far removed. In Heb. 3.1 ff. we find a typological account of Joshua in which he is represented as a *typos* of Jesus; this interpretation became common in the Church Fathers.[6] There is no doubt that this typology, the main support for which was derived from the nominal resemblance, has contributed to speculation on the subject of the name Jesus. When we read, in Acts 13.23, that God κατ' ἐπαγγελίαν ἤγαγεν τῷ 'Ισραὴλ σωτῆρα 'Ιησοῦν, there appears to be an allusion to the resemblance between Joshua and Jesus, a resemblance which includes their commission to save the people.

There was no need, in countries where Semitic languages were spoken, to translate the name either of Joshua or Jesus. What appears to be a

---

[1] STAERK, *Soter* 1, p. 133. DIBELIUS, *op. cit.*, p. 75.

[2] See below, Chap. 7.

[3] Apol. 33.7: τὸ δὲ 'Ιησοῦς, ὄνομα τῇ 'Εβραΐδι φωνῇ, σωτὴρ τῇ 'Ελληνίδι διαλέκτῳ δηλοῖ.

[4] LIETZMANN, *Weltheiland*, p. 57.

[5] CULLMANN, *Christologie*, p. 249: "Daher müssen wir, zumindest überall dort, wo Kenntnis des Hebräischen vorauszusetzen ist, die Bedeutung des Eigennamens "Jesus" bei der Entstehung des Titels σωτήρ 'Ιησοῦς mit in Rechnung stellen. "Jesus" war ja für jüdische Ohren gleichbedeutend mit σωτήρ-Heiland. Dies aber wusste sicher nicht nur der Verfasser des Matthäusevangeliums."

[6] See J. DANIÉLOU, *Sacramentum futuri* (1950), pp. 203-232.

play on words in the Heb. text of Syr. 46.1 (תשועה-יהושע) takes on the character of a translation in the Greek text. It is also quite natural that Christians did not consider it necessary to translate the name of Jesus until they came into contact with such as knew neither Hebrew nor Aramaic. In such a situation the title σωτήρ might well have seemed to be the obvious translation, both as Divine epithet and as ruler's title. We note, however, that the Church Fathers' exposition of the title σωτήρ does not reckon it to be an expression for the royal power of Christ except in those cases where there has been general influence from the Philonic logos terminology. St. Justin considered it to be simply a translation of Christ's earthly name, a name which of course expressed his Messianic function, of saving (σώζειν) his people. A particularly noteworthy fact is that we have no evidence of the title σωτήρ having played a controversial role during the period of the Church's persecution.[1]

παρουσία and ἐπιφάνεια

The interpretation of these words is subject to much the same difficulties as those connected with σωτήρ; here, too, scholars have attempted to draw parallels with the imperial cult on the one hand, and with Gnostic and Hellenistic "saviour" speculations on the other.[2] Neither word is typical of the LXX, though both occur on isolated occasions, mainly in 2 and 3 Macc.,[3] and we find παρουσία in addition

---

[1] The occurrence of the word in Mart. Polyc. 19.2 does not seem to have any polemical meaning.

[2] For the word ἐπιφάνεια in the NT and the connected problems see DEISSMANN, *Licht*, pp. 318 ff. LOHMEYER, *Christuskult*, p. 31. O. CASEL, *Die Epiphanie im Lichte der Religionsgeschichte*, Bened. Monatsschr. 4 (1922), pp. 13–20. E. PFISTER, art. *Epiphanie*, PWK Suppl. 4 (1924), pp. 277–323, especially pp. 321 ff. PRÜMM, *Herrscherkult*, pp. 129 ff. IDEM, *Christliche Glaube* 1, pp. 208 ff. SPICQ, *Épîtres pastorales*, pp. 264 f. J. DUPONT, Σὺν Χριστῷ (1952), pp. 73 ff. CH. MOHRMANN, *Epiphania*, RSPhTh 37 (1953), pp. 644–670. CERFAUX, *Le Christ*, pp. 31 f. DIBELIUS, *Pastoralbriefe*, pp. 77 f. E. PAX, Ἐπιφάνεια, MThSt 10 (1955), which has a valuable survey of the present state of the discussion, pp. 3 ff.

For the word παρουσία, see DEISSMANN, *Licht*, pp. 314 ff. LOHMEYER, *Christuskult*, p. 26. M. DIBELIUS, *An die Thessalonicher I–II* (1923), p. 13 f. PRÜMM, *Herrscherkult*, pp. 131 f. A. OEPKE, art. παρουσία, ThWB 5 (1944–54), pp. 856–869. DUPONT, Σὺν Χριστῷ, pp. 49 ff. P. L. SCHOONHEIM, *Een semasiologisch onderzoek van parousia* (1953). PAX, Ἐπιφάνεια, pp. 217 ff.

[3] ἐπιφάνεια occurs in 2 Kings (Sam.) 7.23, 2 Macc. 3.24, 5.5, 12.22, 14.15; 3 Macc. 2.9, 5.8, 5.51. See DIBELIUS, *Thessalonicher*, p. 13. PAX, Ἐπιφάνεια, pp. 159

on a number of occasions in Test. XII Patr.[1] In the NT the word ἐπιφάνεια occurs only in the Corpus Paulinum, denoting either the eschatological return of Christ (2 Thess. 2.8, 1 Tim. 6.14, 2 Tim. 4.1, 8) or his birth (2 Tim. 1.10, cf. Tit. 2.11, 3.4). We encounter παρουσία largely, but not exclusively, in the Corpus Paulinum (1 Cor. 15.23, 1 Thess. 2.19, 3.13, 4.15, 5.23, 2 Thess. 2.1, 8; cf. its secular use in 2 Cor. 7.6, Phil. 1.26, 2 Cor. 10.10, 1 Cor. 16.17). In the Gospels it is found only in Matt., four times in the parousia address (24.3, 27, 37, 39). It is also found on a number of occasions in the Catholic Epistles (2 Pet. 1.16, 1 Jn. 2.28, James 5.7 f.). Unlike ἐπιφάνεια, παρουσία refers only to the coming of Christ at the judgment (with the exception of 2 Pet. 1.16, where the word refers to the Transfiguration). Not before St. Ignatius and St. Justin is the first manifestation of Jesus in the world described as parousia.[2]

Both words can, in accordance with Hellenistic practice, denote a Divine revelation. Josephus uses παρουσία in this sense to refer to the theophanies of the OT (Ant. III.5.2, 8.5, IX.4.3, XVIII.8.6). The use of ἐπιφανής and ἐπιφάνεια to refer to an invisible god who manifests himself in visible form, is disputed. It is probable that this use of the two terms was of significance when the term was adopted into the royal terminology (often in the form of the name 'Ἐπιφανής); there is however some question as to whether this title can have sacral implications at all.[3]

In the court language of the period παρουσία and ἐπιφάνεια had a definite and distinct meaning: the solemn arrival of the King or Emperor. The corresponding Latin word is *adventus*. From the time of Nero onward it was usual to stamp the inscription *Adventus Augusti* on coins minted to celebrate the coming of the Emperor to a particular province.[4] When we find the coming of Christ to the judgment described as παρουσία or ἐπιφάνεια, it is therefore only reasonable to suppose some influence from political language: Christ is compared to a ruler who visits his people. The associations with the royal cult are

---

ff. παρουσία occurs in 2 Ezra 12.6; Judith 10.18; 2 Macc. 8.12, 15.21: 3 Macc. 3.17. See SCHOONHEIM, *op. cit.*, pp. 134 ff., 270 ff.

[1] Test. Levi 8.14 f. (and a variant reading of 8.11); Test. Jud. 22.2. See SCHOONHEIM, *op. cit.*, pp. 179 ff., 277 ff.

[2] Ign. ad Philad. 9.2. On παρουσία in the writings of St. Justin, see below, p. 98.

[3] This is contested primarily by PRÜMM, *Herrscherkult*, pp. 129 ff. Cf. on the other hand PAX, 'Ἐπιφάνεια, pp. 8, 39 and 52.

[4] STAUFFER, *Christus*, pp. 36 f.

especially marked in 1 Thess. 4.15 ff., where παρουσία is linked with the concept ἀπάντησις, the term used to describe the official reception of a King on his arrival in a town.¹ The synonymous expression ὑπάντησις occurs elsewhere in the NT, always with similar associations. It is used in the parable of the ten virgins who went out to meet the bridegroom, εἰς ὑπάντησιν τοῦ νυμφίου (Matt. 25.1); the lamps they bear in procession and the cry (κραυγή) uttered when the bridegroom came are parts of the same ceremonial context.² The same characteristics are to be seen in Jn. 12.13, the account of Jesus' entry into Jerusalem: we read that the people went out εἰς ὑπάντησιν αὐτῷ, that they carried branches and cried out (ἐκραύγαζον).³

The terms παρουσία and ἐπιφάνεια seem to arouse these associations only when they are linked with the parousia. It is interesting to see that the Vulgate translates ἐπιφάνεια by *adventus* when the word means "the second coming", but with *illuminatio* when it is "the first coming" which is referred to (in 2 Thess. 2.8 τῇ ἐπιφανείᾳ τῆς παρουσίας αὐτοῦ is translated by *illustratione adventus sui*).⁴ The principle on which this translation was carried out seems to correspond to the ideas of the first centuries on the subject of the Kingship of Christ, since it was believed that his Kingship dated from the Resurrection and the Ascension. Not before the 4th century was Christ represented as King on his first coming into the world; this had consequences for the use of the term ἐπιφάνεια.⁵

What makes the analysis of the use of παρουσία in the NT so complicated is the fact that it has been incorporated into Matt., a book which otherwise bears little trace of Hellenistic influence. Schoonheim, who has discussed this problem in detail, suggests that the word may have been used with religious implications in Hellenistic Judaism (of which faint traces are to be found in Test. XII Patr.), and that the contrast between a "Hellenistic" and a "Jewish" derivation of the word is therefore only apparent.⁶ It is probable that it was already associated with the coming of the King when it was taken up by Judaism; we recall that in Test. Levi 8.15 παρουσία stands in an escha-

---

[1] E. PETERSON, *Die Einholung des Kyrios*, ZSTh 7 (1930), pp. 682–702.
[2] PETERSON, *op. cit.*, pp. 699 f.
[3] CERFAUX, *Le Christ*, pp. 36 ff.
[4] MOHRMANN, *Epiphania*, pp. 649 f.
[5] Cf. below, Chap. 12.
[6] SCHOONHEIM, *Parousia*, pp. 247, 287.

tological and royal context reminiscent of the parousia sayings of the NT.¹

There can thus be no doubt that in the NT παρουσία refers to the royal power of Christ, which is to be made manifest at the coming judgment. The same is probably true of ἐπιφάνεια as well, though this word cannot be defined so sharply. The two are often completely synonymous; Pax, who has carried out the most thorough investigation of the term ἐπιφάνεια, considers it to have been introduced by Paul as a replacement for the more colourless παρουσία.² But on the other hand he does not consider that there can have been any polemic against the Hellenistic concept of ἐπιφάνεια, since eschatology is for the most part foreign to Antiquity.³ This is of course correct; but we nevertheless wonder whether there may not have been some degree of polemic against the Hellenistic royal ideology which, as we have seen, had distinctly eschatological characteristics just at the time when the NT came into existence. The enthronement of the Emperor could be described as ἐπιφάνεια and as the coming of a new, and happier, aeon. We have however no positive evidence for such an interpretation.

φιλάνθρωπος and εὐεργέτης

It is usual in this context to name the terms φιλάνθρωπος and εὐεργέτης, though neither is really used in the NT as a Christological epithet. The adjective φιλάνθρωπος is not found at all in the NT, and the noun φιλανθρωπία only once as a theological term: in Tit. 3.4, together with a number of other terms which appear to have been derived from the language of the royal cult.⁴ It would appear to be God that is referred to here, and not Christ, but since the terms which refer to God and those referring to Christ are largely interchangeable in the Pastoral Epistles (e.g. θεός and σωτήρ are used of both), it is not impossible that φιλάνθρωπος—φιλανθρωπία was used of Christ in the milieu in which the Pastorals originated. In Diogn. 9.2 and St. Justin's Dial. 47.5 φιλάνθρωπος is linked with χρηστότης, which belongs to the same class of language, and which also occurs in Tit. 3.4.⁵ This is undoubtedly a

---

¹ *Ibid.*, pp. 184 ff., 277 f.

² PAX, 'Επιφάνεια, p. 260. According to PAX, ἐπιφάνεια is also used by St. Paul primarily about the futural parousia, *op. cit.*, p. 247.

³ PAX, *op. cit.*, p. 261.

⁴ DIBELIUS, *Pastoralbriefe*, pp. 108 ff. Cf. above, p. 63.

⁵ DIBELIUS, *op. cit.*, *ibid.* For χρηστότης, see BAG, p. 894.

case of adaptation of Hellenistic language, a tendency which became more noticeable in post-canonical literature.

εὐεργέτης is missing from the NT (except for the secular use of the word in Lk. 22.25). εὐεργεσία and εὐεργετεῖν are mentioned on several occasions as virtues: in Acts 4.9 and 10.38 (referring to Jesus), and in 1 Tim. 6.2. The fact of both roots occurring only in the Lucan literature and in the Pastoral Epistles suggests that they did not belong to the earliest phase of Christian Greek. Clem. uses the noun εὐεργέτης to describe God (19.2, 59.3).

What makes these two words so interesting in this context is that they are used in contemporary Hellenistic political literature to represent the two principal royal virtues.[1] They are standard terms, and are used by all political theorists; they are found in Isocrates and the neo-Pythagorean philosophers Ecphantus, Diotogenes and Sthenidas.[2] Philo uses the word εὐεργέτης, frequently in combination with σωτήρ, of the Emperor and of God. They do not however have a natural place in the language of the LXX, occurring only in Wisd., 2–4 Macc. and apocryphal appendices to Esther. It is of particular significance that passages in which the words are found especially frequently are the Hellenistic royal letters in Esther 8.12 (interpolated) and 3 Macc. 3. 12–30.

It therefore seems to be the case that certain parts of the NT, and the Pastoral Epistles in particular, exhibit influence from that same Hellenistic language which we encounter in political literature, where it is connected primarily with the Kingship. But it is more difficult to understand the ideological background which gave rise to their incorporation into the language of the Church. Is it a case of polemics, directed against the cult of the Emperor, exalting God or Christ as the true King in contrast to the one who has usurped the Divine titles and prerogatives? Or did the borrowing take place less dramatically,

---

[1] DEISSMANN, *Licht*, p. 311. R. KNOPF, *Die Apostolischen Väter* 1 (1920), pp. 75 f. DIBELIUS, *op. cit.*, ibid. On φιλανθρωπία, see S. LORENZ, *De progressu notionis* φιλανθρωπίας (1914). C. SPICQ, *La Philanthropie hellénistique, vertu divine et royale* (*à propos de Tit. III, 4*), STh 12 (1958), pp. 169–191. Cf. also BAG, p. 866. For εὐεργέτης, see J. OEHLER, Εὐεργέτης, PWK 6 (1907–09), pp. 978–981. DEISSMANN, *Licht*, pp. 215 f. E. SKARD, *Zwei religiös-politische Begriffe, Euergetes—Concordia*, Norske Vid.-Akad., Oslo, Avh. 2, Hist.-Fil. Kl. 1931.2. G. BERTRAM, art. εὐεργέτης, ThWB 2 (1933–35), pp. 631–653. NOCK, *Soter and Euergetes, passim*. Cf. also BAG, p. 320.

[2] On these authors, see below, pp. 188 ff.

through contact with the Hellenistic Judaism of the Diaspora, the language of which had already been subject to influence from Stoic diatribe?[1] We are inclined to favour the latter theory. Apart from Rev., there is no evidence in the NT of a clear and unambiguous attack on the Roman Empire. All attempts to demonstrate the existence of such a polemical attitude with the help of NT texts are, and must remain, hypothetical.

There are other reasons to call this theory in question. The conflict between the Church and the Empire intensified in the post-Apostolic period; the next two centuries were characterized by persecution and martyrdom, and this left clear traces in the Christian literature of the period. There grew up an extensive literature of acts and legends of the martys, in which Caesar and his minions were frequently represented as Antichrist, while the martyrs themselves were depicted as soldiers and campaigners in the cause of Christ the King.[2]

But there is little trace in this literature of the political terminology of the Pastoral Epistles. Christ is called βασιλεύς but not σωτήρ, εὐεργέτης or φιλάνθρωπος.[3] This suggests that the terminology in question was not of such controversial quality as to warrant pressing it into the service of polemics, despite the fact that the martyr literature was very definitely directed against the self-exaltation of the Roman Emperor.

On the other hand there are a number of authors, as early as the middle of the 2nd century, making Christian use of political terms taken over from Philo in particular and transferred to the realm of theology. We encounter the whole of the terminology of the Pastoral Epistles in this literature, which stemmed for the most part from Alexandria, but on this occasion without any trace of anti-imperial polemics. The authors in question have followed the example of Philo in using σωτήρ and εὐεργέτης of God and Caesar indiscriminately, without seeing anything incongruous in the practice.

We are of the opinion that we are dealing here, not with a polemical use of Caesar's titles, but with a case of borrowing connected with the Hellenization of the language of the Christian Church. The problem was to express the central Christian doctrine of the Kingship of Christ

---

[1] So according to PAX, 'Επιφάνεια, p. 246.

[2] See below, pp. 179 ff.

[3] An exception is, as previously mentioned, Mart. Polyc. 19.2, where Christ is styled σωτήρ, κυβερνήτης and ποιμήν. It is however difficult to see any anti-imperial polemic in these words. Cf. further below, Chap. 7.

for people who knew nothing of the Israelite Kingship; it seems quite natural, then, that the doctrine should have been expressed in Hellenistic terms, since these same people were well acquainted with the conduct, acclamation and titles of contemporary Hellenistic kings. It is evident that terms like ἐπιφάνεια, παρουσία and ἀπάντησις contributed to precipitate faith in the coming of Christ the King to his πόλις in order to be received by his faithful subjects.

There are however at the same time traces in the NT of the application of the terminology of political metaphysics to God and Christ. This would seem to be due to influence from Diaspora Judaism, if not from Philo himself. The development from this first beginning does not reach as far as the martyr literature and Hippolytus' criticism of the Emperor; it may be traced to the attempts made by Alexandrian theology to represent the world as a πόλις, with God as supreme ruler and the Logos as his assistant in the government of the world.

3. THE TESTIMONIA TRADITION

In the oldest Christian literature, from the NT to the 4th century, the Messianic sayings of the OT occupy a central position as proofs of the Messiahship of Jesus. The primitive Church looked upon the OT primarily as the prophetic revelation of Jesus Christ. It was not only the more obviously prophetic sayings which were applied to Christ; the whole of the OT was regarded as one great prophecy, with its personalities and events as patterns, *typoi*, of that reality which had been revealed once and for all in the coming of Christ. Typically enough, when the early Church spoke of the Scriptures, it long meant the OT. The NT revelation was of a different order from the Scriptures; it was the proclamation that the sayings of the OT were now fulfilled. That is why the first centuries saw fewer commentaries on the NT, and fewer quotations of its sayings, than of the OT. Although we possess a number of 2nd century expositions of OT texts, we have no NT commentary older than those of Origen (with the exception of the Gnostic Heracleon's commentary on Jn., of which we have a few fragments). The OT stands at the focus of interest in preaching, in catechetical teaching, in the liturgy and—not least—in discussion with the Jews; from it was drawn an inexhaustible supply of themes, images and *typoi*, which left their mark on the whole of primitive Christian soteriology.

Proof-texts are to be found liberally scattered through most Christian documents from these early centuries. It is however often possible to trace them to a definite class of literature, made up for the most part of such testimonies.[1] Most of the documents of this kind which have been preserved to our day were written with an apologetic and polemic end in view, and were usually directed against the Jews. Of the books of the NT, it is possible to reckon at least Heb. as belonging to this class; typical examples from the post-Apostolic age are the *Epistle of*

---

[1] On the use of testimonies in the ancient Church, VON UNGERN-STERNBERG, *Schriftbeweis*, is still of primary importance.

Barnabas, St. Justin's *Dialogue with Trypho* (and to some extent his first *Apology,* which is in much the same literary form as the *Dialogue,* and which also contains an anti-Jewish polemic), St. Irenaeus' *Demonstration of the Apostolic Teaching,* Tertullian's *Adversus Judaeos* (and his *Adversus Marcionem* which, though directed against Marcion, contains the same kind of argument, due to the remarkable correspondence between Jewish and Marcionite exegesis) and, finally, St. Cyprian's *Ad Quirinium,* which summarizes the earlier *testimonia* tradition.[1]

The one-sided character of these writings, as apologetics and polemics, might well give rise to the misunderstanding that the primitive Church looked upon the OT as no more than a club with which to belabour the Jews.[2] This is obviously a wrong conclusion. It is an incontestable fact that the testimonies played an extensive positive role in the inner life of the Church, in preaching, catechetical teaching and the liturgy.[3] That this application of the testimonies has tended to be obscured is due to the fact that we have so little source material illustrative of this aspect of the life of the primitive Church. OT typology is of the greatest importance in our oldest known sermons, though even these are from a later period; here we find the same proof-texts as Justin and Irenaeus use polemically, quoted for edification. There is no doubt that these sermons are based on an older homiletical tradition, but it is not easy to obtain a clear picture of its earlier stages, since it was—not unnaturally—largely oral in character and has not been

---

[1] Of the extensive literature on anti-Jewish polemic in the early Church the following works are especially worth mentioning: A. B. HULEN, *The "Dialogues with the Jews" as Sources for the Early Jewish Argument against Christianity,* JBL 51 (1932), pp. 58–70. A. LUKYN WILLIAMS, *Adversus Judaeos* (1935). B. BLUMENKRANTZ, *Die Judenpredigt Augustins,* BBG 25 (1946). SIMON, *Verus Israel.* A valuable presentation of the relation between Christian mission and Jewish proselytism (with an extensive bibliography) is given by K. THRAEDE, *Beiträge zur Datierung Commodians,* JbAC 2 (1959), pp. 90–114.

[2] Cf. the opinion expressed by M. F. WILES, *The Old Testament in Controversy with the Jews.* ScJTh 8 (1955), p. 125: "We have seen throughout this study how texts first pressed into service in the cause of anti-Jewish controversy then proceed to spill over into and to become formative of normal exegesis." This is no doubt a very one-sided view; the difference between the polemic and the homiletic use of the OT were probably not so extremely different in the beginning.

[3] GERHARDSSON, *Memory,* pp. 225 ff., 280 ff. (with references to literature). The importance of the OT in both the apologetical and catechetical context is stressed also by DANIÉLOU, *Session,* pp. 689 ff.

preserved for posterity. Thus polemics was only one of the uses to which the early Church put the testimonies, and it is therefore virtually impossible to decide whether a collection of *testimonia* like Pap. Ryl. Gk. 460 was used liturgically, homiletically or polemically.[1]

We have long known that early Christian authors used only a limited number of proof-texts, and that the same ones are as a rule used by several authors.[2] How this parallelism originated has often been discussed, but the problem has not yet been finally solved. A particularly complicated question is whether the agreement of a number of authors as to the choice of text is due to a general oral expository tradition or whether it is due to their having had access to the entire *testimonia* collection—oral or written—of Messianic texts.[3] Although we use the terms "proof-texts" and "testimonies", this does not imply that we favour the theory of *written testimonia*.

The significance of the testimonies has for the most part been estimated from the point of view of NT exegesis, though Harris' important theory is based on OT quotations in the Church Fathers. But since there are a number of modern works in which this discussion is summarized, we shall content ourselves with a very brief account.[4]

Discussion of the testimonies has long been focussed on the theory first put forward by J. Rendel Harris.[5] Harris began with the collections of OT quotations which are to be found in the work of the oldest Christian authors, showing how they took up only a limited number of texts; these are to be found in the earliest Church Fathers, in St. Justin,

---

[1] C. H. ROBERTS considered that the fragment had a liturgical use, *Two Biblical Papyri in the John Rylands Library, Manchester*, BJRL 20 (1936), pp. 219–244. L. CERFAUX in his review has presented the opposite view, that it is probably a testimony collection with an apologetical and anti-Jewish aim, RHE 33 (1937), pp. 70–72.

[2] Valuable collections of OT quotations in the early Fathers are given by VON UNGERN-STERNBERG, *Schriftbeweis*, *passim*, and J. L. KOOLE, *De overname van het Oude Testament door de christelijke Kerk* (1938), pp. 16 ff. N.b. that the collection of the latter is far from complete.

[3] For the distinction between written transmission and oral tradition with help of written notes, see below pp. 77 f.

[4] Se above all N. J. HOMMES, *Het Testimoniaboek* (1935), *passim*. DODD, *According to the Scriptures*, pp. 23 ff. K. STENDAHL, *The School of St. Matthew* (1954), pp. 207 ff. J. A. FITZMYER, "*4 Q Testimonia*" *and the New Testament*, ThSt 18 (1957), pp. 513–537.

[5] J. RENDEL HARRIS (and V. BURCH), *Testimonies* 1–2 (1916, 1920). On the earlier discussion on the testimonies, see STENDAHL, *op. cit.*, pp. 208 f.

in the *Epistle of Barnabas* and other documents from the same period. Harris' theory was that these quotations came from a lost *Book of Testimonies*, which was older than the books of the NT, and which lay behind their OT quotations.

The extreme form of Harris' theory has not won much support. His critics have tended to concentrate on two alternative possibilities. Those who have adopted a position closest to that of Harris himself have usually allowed that the early Christian authors had access to smaller collections of OT quotations, rather than the *Book of Testimonies* postulated by Harris.[1] Other scholars have rejected the idea of a written collection of testimonies, favouring instead a principle of selection without written deposit.[2] "The composition of 'testimony-books' was the result, not the presupposition, of the work of early Christian biblical scholars."[3]

The theory that there existed a definite written tradition of testimonies in early Christianity has been to some extent confirmed by the discovery of a Hebrew testimony collection in Cave 4 at Qumran.[4] The fact of the Qumran sect having made use of florilegia of Messianic texts places the existence of such texts in Christianity within the bounds of reasonable possibility, even though we have as yet no proof positive that such was the case.

The question is however whether the line of demarcation between oral and written tradition can be drawn where it has been drawn in the past. A newly published investigation of the relation between oral and written tradition in Rabbinic literature and the early Church shows how flexible the boundaries between oral tradition and private notes could in fact be. The Jewish oral midrash collections, which were either arranged on a basis of the consecutive text of Scripture, or around a certain subject, key-word or more mechanical catch-word, could also be copied down unofficially in private note-books. Such were not regarded strictly as *scripture*, but as *notes*, intended to facil-

---

[1] So WILLIAMS, *Adversus Judaeos*, pp. 3 ff. SIMON, *Verus Israel*, p. 186. P. B. W. STATHER HUNT, *Primitive Gospel Sources* (1951).

[2] T. W. MANSON, *The Argument from Prophecy*, JTS 46 (1945), p. 132. DODD, *According to the Scriptures*, pp. 23 ff. STENDAHL (*School*, p. 217), does not deny the existence of written *testimonia* collections but considers that the "composite quotations" may be explained in another way (Christian midrashes).

[3] DODD, *op. cit.*, p. 126.

[4] J. M. ALLEGRO, *Further Messianic References in Qumran Literature*, JBL 75 (1956), pp. 174 ff. FITZMYER, "*4 Q Testimonia*", 513 ff.

itate memorization.¹ A close parallel is provided by the note-books used in Hellenistic schools of rhetoric and philosophy.² It is only reasonable to suppose there to have existed a similar practice in the Church: there, too, the expository tradition was mainly oral in character, but its memorization was helped by the use of written notes.³ It seems likely that the solution of the problem of the *testimonia* lies in this direction.

When considering the post-Apostolic tradition we must not forget that they also had access to the NT; we know that its OT quotations were used by post-Apostolic authors, since a number of OT prooftexts are quoted in words which differ from every known variant of the LXX, but which agree with the NT.⁴ Further, there is no doubt that younger authors made use of testimony material from their predecessors' writings, at the same time taking over their variant readings. It is often impossible to decide to what extent a specific OT quotation is derived from one source or another, even though textual variants, composite quotations and attribution to the wrong book of the OT often give some indication of its source.

Harris considered that the agreements between Justin and Irenaeus were proof that both had made use of the same source, i.e. the hypothetical *Book of Testimonies*.⁵ It had however been suggested before Harris' theory was published that these agreements were probably due to Irenaeus having made use of Justin's writings.⁶ This view has been particularly convincingly put by Robinson, in a comparison be-

---

[1] GERHARDSSON, *Memory*, pp. 157 ff. For the disposition principles, see *ibid.*, pp. 151 ff.

[2] GERHARDSSON, *op. cit.*, pp. 159 and 162 (with references to literature).

[3] GERHARDSSON, *op. cit.*, pp. 199 ff., 333 ff.

[4] The most important survey of the problem is E. MASSAUX, *Influence de l'Évangile de saint Matthieu sur la littérature chrétienne avant saint Irénée* (1950). Of special interest among the earlier literature on this subject is W. BOUSSET, *Die Evangeliencitate Justins des Märtyrers in ihrem Wert für die Evangelienkritik* (1891), pp. 18 ff.

[5] HARRIS, *Testimonies*, 1, pp. 61 ff.

[6] A. VON HARNACK, *Die Überlieferung der griechischen Apologeten des 2. Jahrhunderts in der alten Kirche und im Mittelalter*, TU 1.1–2 (1882), p. 131. F. R. M. HITCHCOCK, *The Apostolic Preaching of Irenaeus*, JTS 9 (1907–08), pp. 284–289. L. TH. WIETEN, *Irenaeus' Geschrift "Ten bewijze der Apostolische Prediking"* (1909), mentioned by HOMMES (*Testimoniaboek*, p. 44) has not been available to the author.

tween Irenaeus' *Demonstration* and parallel passages in Justin.[1] Robinson shows that Irenaeus not only took over Justin's OT quotations (which would of course leave open the possibility of both having made use of the same *testimonia* collection), but also took over formulations from Justin's own text. These investigations show that it is highly likely that Irenaeus' *Demonstration* contains material borrowed from Justin.[2] It is consequently likely that Irenaeus' *Adversus haereses* also makes use of Justin's OT quotations, particularly since Irenaeus himself admits on a number of occasions having quoted Justin in *Adversus haereses*.[3]

Tertullian later made use, in his *Adversus Marcionem,* of both Justin and Irenaeus as sources;[4] the same material is also to be found in *Adversus Judaeos*.[5] Tertullian made use of St. Justin's writings on other occasions, too,[6] St. Cyprian later taking over material from Tertullian.[7]

Another who made extensive use of St. Justin's writings was Eusebius, in his *Ecclesiastical History*.[8] Justin appears in fact to have been read and quoted frequently throughout the Christian Church to the time of Eusebius. Only the Alexandrian literature has no clear traces of influence from Justin.[9]

---

[1] See the introduction to J. ARMITAGE ROBINSON's translation of St. Irenaeus, *The Demonstration of the Apostolic Preaching*, Transl. of Christ. Lit. Ser. IV (1920), pp. 6 ff.

[2] The generally accepted opinion, that St. Irenaeus in his *Demonstration* has used St. Justin's writing as a source, has been called in question by J. P. SMITH in the introduction to his translation of Dem., ACW 16 (1952), pp. 37 f. SMITH returns to HARRIS' hypothesis that both have used a common source, which was, however, not only a *testimonia* collection (as HARRIS believed), but also contained expositions. We know however nothing of any such source.

[3] Adv. haer. I.28.1, ed. HARVEY 1.220; IV.6.2, ed. HARVEY 2.158. Cf. Eusebius, HE IV.18.1, V.28.4. See J. ARMITAGE ROBINSON, *On a Quotation from Justin Martyr in Irenaeus*, JTS 31 (1930), pp. 374–378. Cf. HOMMES, *Testimoniaboek*, pp. 43 ff.

[4] G. QUISPEL, *De bronnen van Tertullianus' Adversus Marcionem* (1943), *passim*.

[5] QUISPEL, *op. cit.*, pp. 61 ff. N.b. that ch. 9–14 is not part of the original work, but is a clumsy interpolation made with help of an excerpt from Adv. Marc. III; the compiler has been identified by QUISPEL.

[6] VON HARNACK, *Überlieferung*, p. 132.

[7] WILLIAMS, *Adversus Judaeos*, p. 63.

[8] VON HARNACK, *op. cit.*, p. 134.

[9] *Ibid.*, p. 133. There are however certain connexions between St. Justin and the Alexandrian exegetes, which prove there to have been no watertight compartments between them, e.g. the exegesis of the ass and the colt as symbolizing the

St. Justin thus occupies a central position in the *testimonia* tradition of the early Church. Later authors used him, either directly or indirectly, as a source, but this does not of course imply that the entire tradition is collected in his writings. We do not however know what were the sources from which he derived most of his proof-texts, although a number are doubtless taken from the NT. The breadth of Justin's interpretation of Scripture compels us to assume the existence of an earlier tradition.

Of earlier or contemporary literature of the same kind we know only the *Epistle of Barnabas,* together with a number of separate testimonies in the *Epistle of St. Clement,* in the Ignatians and in *Kerygma Petri.*[1] Of these, Justin appears to have had access at least to the *Epistle of Barnabas.*[2] He may have taken some of his material from the lost writings of Aristo of Pella. The *Dialogue between Jason and Papiscus,* which is attributed to Aristo, seems to have been an earlier counterpart to Justin's *Dialogue with Trypho,* but we know virtually nothing of its contents.[3] Both Aristo and Justin were from Palestine, and it is not unlikely that their writings were responsible for propagating remnants of the tradition of the Palestinian congregation; at the same time the study of the OT was stimulated by discussion with the Jews. The whole of this literature must however be regarded in the light of what we have said above on the use of oral or written florilegia in the early Church.

Another use of proof-texts by Justin is to be seen in the context of anti-Jewish polemics. Hatch supposed that Christian testimonies were taken over from Jewish excerpt collections; against this theory Harris postulated that the *testimonia* tradition was distinctly anti-Jewish in character;[4] later scholarship has often maintained that proof-texts were used mainly in anti-Jewish polemics.[5] But the polemical situation in which the testimonies were used does not exclude the possibility of Jews and Christians having made use of a *common deposit of testimonia.* On the contrary: it is clear that the central Messianic texts of Judaism

---

Jews and the Gentiles, an exegesis which first appears in St. Justin and which later occurs in the writings of Clement and Origen. See below, Chap. 8.

[1] von Ungern-Sternberg, *Schriftbeweis,* pp. 268 ff., 273 ff.
[2] Simon, *Verus Israel,* pp. 182 ff.
[3] Williams, *Adversus Judaeos,* pp. 28 ff. Simon, *op. cit.,* p. 167, n. 3.
[4] Harris, *Testimonies,* 1, p. 2.
[5] Williams, *op. cit., passim.* Simon, *Verus Israel,* pp. 182 ff. Cf. above p. 75, n. 1.

were taken over by the Church, which believed these prophecies to have been fulfilled in Jesus Christ; as an example we may take Num. 24.17, which is to be found in the 4 Q florilegium and which was at the same time a central Christian proof-text.[1]

The testimonies are very often arranged according to a "key-word principle": this is particularly noticeable in Justin's writings. When in his *Dialogue* Justin attempts to convince the Jew Trypho that Jesus is the Messiah, he constantly refers to blocks of OT proof-texts held together by a common key-word. The key-word always provides the basis on which the OT quotations are cited and explained. It is typical that Justin often concentrates his proof-texts into separate key-words, which can later be arranged in a series. In Dial. 34.2 we read that Christ is called "King and priest and God and Lord and angel and man and captain and stone and child".[2] All these Christological titles are taken from the OT and are used by Justin as key-words for the presentation of his testimonies. Such series of key-words were obviously intended to facilitate the memorization of proof-texts to be brought out in discussion. A similar use of key-words was common in Jewish mnemonic techniques,[3] and we may therefore conclude that the *testimonia* tradition represented by Justin was closely related in its technical construction to Rabbinic expository techniques.[4] A similar form of construction, on a more or less thorough key-word principle, is also to be found in the work of later authors.[5]

---

[1] See below p. 94.

[2] The same kind of series as in *inter alia* Dial. 61.1, 86.3, 96.1, 100.4 and 126.1. St. Justin's own term for such a Christological epithet is τρόπος (86.3, 100.4). Cf. HOMMES, *Testimoniaboek*, pp. 67 f.

[3] GERHARDSSON, *Memory*, pp. 153 ff.

[4] Cf. the discussion above, p. 77 f., on the distinction between written transmission and, on the other hand, oral tradition with help of written notes.

[5] Chains of key-words appear especially in the *Dialogue between Athanasius and Zacchaeus*, ch. 46 and 49, Anecdota Oxon. 8 (1898), pp. 31 and 44. This dialogue, which is in many ways similar to St. Justin's Dial., is dated to about A.D. 325, see WILLIAMS, *Adversus Judaeos*, pp. 117 ff. Cf. also the strange chains of Christological epithets, which appear in the apocryphal Acts of the Apostles, in the *Acts of John* 98, 109, and in the *Acts of Peter* 20. The chains are here made up of epithets from the NT, and function as key-words, partly to Jesus' sayings about himself in Jn. (word, bread, door, resurrection, life, way, truth, vine), partly to the synoptic parables on the Kingdom of God (seed, salt, pearl, treasure, plough, net, mustard seed etc.). We also have other examples of Johannine titles of Christ having been collected in this way; e.g. Origen, Comm. on Jn. 1.21 ff., GCS Orig. 4.25 ff., and the

Individual proof-texts often contain more than one key-word, which means that the same proof-text can often be incorporated into more than one context. These key-words often help Justin to draw associations from one proof-text to another, and to develop his exposition with the help of new key-words—a technique with which we are well acquainted from Rabbinic exposition.

This is best illustrated by an example. In Dial. 86 Justin gathers a number of proof-texts on a basis of the key-word ῥάβδος. From the staff (ῥάβδος) with which Jacob crossed the river (Gen. 32.10) Justin proceeds to Jacob's anointing of the stone at Bethel. Further association continues along two lines: from the stone to Christ as "stone" and from the oil to Ps. 44 (45).7, in which Christ is said to be the Anointed. After this digression he returns to the consideration of another block of proof-texts based on ῥάβδος.

This technique of association seems loose, and makes the exposition appear disorganized and hard to appreciate as a whole. Justin's lack of formal literary gifts has often been remarked upon,[1] and the reader coming to Justin expecting to find a distinctive "style" is very likely to be disappointed. But this attitude to Justin as an author seems to have resulted in the underestimation of Justin's material. And a right understanding of Justin's technique of composition, though unfamiliar, can lead to a greater degree of understanding of the tradition he conveys. We must not expect to find a logically connected account in which the thought proceeds naturally from one chapter to another; if we wish to come to terms with his overall purpose, we must emulate Justin himself, starting with the key-words and comparing those proof-texts which are gathered under each such key-word. This procedure must be followed not only when reading Justin, but with all early Christian literature based on the testimonies.

---

interpolated version of Ign. ad. Philad. 9. Cf. also St. Epiphanius' statement that the Arians collected Christological epithets, taken from the creation (door, way, pillar, cloud, rock, lamb, angel, etc.) in order to prove that the Son was created. Haer. LIX.34.5 ff., GCS Epiph. 3.183 f. Cf. MICHAELIS, *Engelchristologie*, p. 178.

[1] See the critical judgment by J. GEFFCKEN, *Zwei griechische Apologeten* (1907), pp. 97 ff., and by VON UNGERN-STERNBERG, *Schriftbeweis*, p. 6: "Sowohl in der Apologie wie im Dialog finden sich häufig Wiederholungen, Abweichungen, sprunghafte Gedankenentwicklung." A more positive judgment of St. Justin's technique of composition is given by U. HÜNTEMANN, *Zur Kompositionstechnik Justins*, ThGl 25 (1933), pp. 410–428, which does not however treat St. Justin's disposition of the *testimonia*.

A key-word principle of the kind used by Justin is to be seen in the NT. One of the foundations of Harris' theory was the occurrence of "composite quotations" with λίθος as key-word in Matt. 21.42 par., 1 Pet. 2.6 ff. and Rom. 9.33.[1] Rom. 15.9–12 is a similar "composite quotation", ἔθνη being the key-word.[2] Vollmer considered this principle, as seen in the NT, to have been based on Hebrew practice.[3]

In post-canonical literature the proof from Scripture is largely dependent on earlier traditions, of which there are considerable deposits in the NT.[4] We are dealing here with sayings which were already interpreted Messianically in Judaism. It is, however, often difficult to determine the age of the traditional material, since we have so few older Jewish texts, and since Judaism exercised a certain censorship of the Messianic traditions by way of defence against Christianity.[5] One some occasions we would seem to have proof-texts which were only regarded as Messianic by the Christian Church. But these are in turn based on Messianic key-words found in the older tradition.

An eschatological interpretation of the cultic texts of the OT is to be seen within Judaism; these were considered to be no longer applicable to the cult, and were referred instead to the last days and the judgment of the world. Those sayings—and particularly those in the Psalms—which originally referred to the King were reinterpreted to point instead to a royal eschatological saviour.[6] It is probable that this tendency had a greater influence on Jewish thought than we are able to determine. The Rabbinic censorship which arose in reaction to the claims of Christianity resulted in the suppression of e.g. Messianic interpretations of Ps. 109; no such Jewish text has survived, though in Jesus' day the Psalm must have been interpreted as pointing to the Messiah.[7]

The early Christian Church took over the Messianic interpretation of the OT in its entirety and applied it to Jesus Christ. In the NT we therefore find a conscious use of the OT in which sayings about the

---

[1] Harris, *Testimonies* 1, pp. 26 ff., (Burch) 2, p. 66. Cf. Dodd, *According to the Scripture*, p. 26. Stendahl, *School*, p. 212.

[2] Fitzmyer, "*4 Q Testimonia*", p. 519.

[3] H. Vollmer, *Die alttestamentliche Citate bei Paulus* (1895), pp. 41 f. Cf. Fitzmyer, *op. cit., ibid.*

[4] von Ungern-Sternberg, *Schriftbeweis*, pp. 275 ff.

[5] Cf. below, p. 134.

[6] See below, p. 124.

[7] Billerbeck, *Comm.* 4, pp. 458 ff.

King in particular were transferred to Christ. The faith of the early Church in Christ the King is therefore coloured by the cultic texts of the OT in general and the Psalter in particular.

Christ in the NT is more than an earthly Messiah and more than an intermediate being of the sort we find in extra-canonical apocalyptic literature. He is God and Lord (cf. the confession of Thomas in Jn. 20.28). Thus even sayings which in the OT obviously have to do with God can be transferred to Christ (cf. e.g. Heb. 1.10–12 with its quotation of Ps. 101 (102).26–28).[1]

In general, however, it was another way which was followed. This had already determined the NT's choice of proof-texts and is directly named in Justin, Irenaeus and Tertullian. OT texts were chosen in which the terms κύριος and θεός occurred, but in which they referred to someone other than Yahweh. This gave the Christian expositor the opportunity to prove on a basis of the OT the existence of more than one Divine Person.[2] Such arguments were later used by the Arians to support their subordinationist Christology.[3] One of the clearest examples of the degree to which this was a conscious hermeneutical principle is to be found in St. Justin's Dial. 56.14. In this passage Justin gives a Christological interpretation of Gen. 18–19, which describes the Lord's visit to Abraham and the destruction of Sodom. It is typical of Justin that he constantly sees the Logos in the theophanies of the OT.[3] The κύριος who spoke with Abraham (Gen. 18.22 ff.) he identifies with the Logos; the κύριος who poured fire and brimstone over Sodom (Gen. 19.24) is on the other hand identified with the Father.

Justin bases his interpretation on a general rule: "It must be admitted that, apart from him who is confessed as the Creator of all things, another may be called κύριος by the Holy Spirit." As an example of this he quotes Ps. 109 (110).1 ("The Lord said unto my lord") and Ps. 44 (45).7–8 ("Therefore, o God, thy God hath anointed thee with the oil of gladness above thy fellows"). This "other", who may be called κύριος and θεός, must therefore be the Son-Logos. Justin concludes by saying (Dial. 56.15): "Do you now believe that the Holy

---

[1] See above, p. 56.
[2] VON UNGERN-STERNBERG, *Schriftbeweis*, pp. 52 ff. SIMON, *Verus Israel*, pp. 193 ff.
[3] VON UNGERN-STERNBERG, *op. cit.*, pp. 51 f. Cf. SIMON, *op. cit.*, p. 194.

Spirit can address anyone as God and Lord other than the Father of the all and his Christ?"

St. Irenaeus quotes—evidently in direct connexion with Dial. 56.14 f.—not only Ps. 109.1 and 44.7–8, but also Gen. 19.24 as proofs of the Divinity of Christ.[1] His purpose is however different from Justin's. Justin used his argument primarily in order to justify the Christological interpretation of the texts; Irenaeus as a proof of the Divinity of Christ. If he were not God, the Holy Spirit would not have called him God and Lord in the OT.

The principle was carried a step further by Tertullian and Novatian, who used a number of proof-texts in support of Trinitarian theology— here directed, not against the Jews, but against the Monarchianism of Praxeas.[2] We must however stress that Tertullian's use of the testimonies is based entirely on an older tradition, presupposing an unqualified Binitarian or Trinitarian theology. In point of fact the principle is to be found in the NT, in sayings concerning Christ as *kyrios*, where Ps. 109 (110).1 plays a decisive role. Ps. 109 (110).1 and 44 (45).7–8 occur in the list of proof-texts found in Heb. 1, and we may assume there to have been the same principle of choice here as that expounded more explicitly by Justin. Proof-texts were thus of considerable importance for the development of the doctrine of the Trinity.[3]

But there is a further principle on which proof-texts were selected— apart from the main theological principle. Since proof-texts were

---

[1] Adv. haer. III.6.1, ed. HARVEY 2.20 f.: "Neque igitur Dominus neque Spiritus Sanctus, neque Apostoli eum qui non esset Deus, definitive et absolute Deum nominassent aliquando, nisi esset vere Deus; neque Dominum appellassent aliquem ex sua persona, nisi qui dominatur omnium Deum Patrem, et Filium ejus qui dominium accepit a Patre suo omnis conditionis ..." Cf. also Dem. 44 f., which seems to depend upon St. Justin's Dial. 56 and 86; see ROBINSON's introduction to his translation of Dem., p. 12.

[2] Tertullian, Adv. Prax. 11, CCL 2.1171 f.: "Quando scripturae omnes et demonstrationem et distinctionem trinitatis ostendans a quibus et praescriptio nostra deducitur non posse unum atque eundem uideri qui loquitur et de quo loquitur et ad quem loquitur, quia neque peruersitas neque fallacia Deo congruat ut, cum ipse esset ad quem loquebatur, ad alium potius et non ad semetipsum loqueretur." The following testimonies are quoted: Isa. 42.1, 49.6, 61.1; Ps. 70 (71).18, 3.2, 109 (110).1; Isa. 45.1, 53.1 f. Cf. VON UNGERN-STERNBERG, *op. cit.*, p. 52. The same kind of argument also occurs in Novatian, De Trin. 26, ed. FAUSSET, p. 94.

[3] Cf. WILES, *The OT*, pp. 113 ff. which is however too one-sided to give a true picture of the development.

chosen and collected on the key-word principle, there was a tendency to choose texts containing one or more Christological key-words. The great majority of proof-texts for the royal character of Christ were based on the key-words κύριος, χριστός or βασιλεύς; we often come across proof-texts which contain several of these. Occasionally there was a tendency to prefer apparently dubious readings, but this was due to a wish to have further texts containing combinations of Christological key-words.[1] This process is particularly noticeable in two cases: Isa. 45.1 and Lam. 4.20.

In the case of Isa. 45.1 we find the reading εἶπεν κύριος τῷ χριστῷ μου κυρίου instead of Κύρῳ for the first time in Barn. 12.11 and then in a number of later authors.[2] This is a more or less deliberate misspelling which had been incorporated into some Christian text (possibly a testimony collection). The popularity of this testimony was not due merely to its combination of χριστός and κύριος. The verse mentions χριστὸς κύριος who is addressed by Yahweh (the first κύριος), and the proof-text therefore corresponds to the above-mentioned theological principle of selection.

A related text is Lam. 4.20, with its reading χριστὸς κύριος instead of χριστὸς κυρίου, as used by a number of early Christian authors from Justin onward.[3] In contrast to the previous example, this reading is supported by the majority of LXX manuscripts; most scholars nevertheless consider it to be a corruption of the LXX text. Apart from this passage, the expression χριστὸς κύριος occurs in the OT only in Ps. Sol. 17.32 and 18.7, but it may possibly have been a Messianic epithet in later Judaism.[4] The expression is found once in the NT, viz. in Lk. 2.2; compare however the similar expression κύριος Ἰησοῦς Χριστός in Phil. 2.11.

Lastly, the majority of proof-texts are applied with reference to their subject. Prophecies of the birth of the Messiah are interpreted as

---

[1] Cf. GERHARDSSON's account of the technique of Jewish midrash exegesis in *Memory*, pp. 33 ff. (with references to literature).

[2] St. Irenaeus, Dem. 9. Tertullian, Adv. Jud. 10.11, CCL 2.1378. St. Cyprian, Ad Quir. 1.21, CSEL 3.1.56. This testimony is however missing from the writings of St. Justin. Cf. DANIÉLOU, *Judéo-christianisme*, p. 107. The faulty reading has probably arisen in a manuscript so that ΚΥΡΩΙ has been read as ΚΥΡΙΩΙ.

[3] St. Justin, Apol. 55.5. St. Irenaeus, Dem. 71; Adv. haer. III.10.3, ed. HARVEY 2.36. See J. DANIÉLOU, *Christos Kyrios*, Mélange Lebreton 1, RSR 39 (1951), pp. 338–352. IDEM, *Judéo-christianisme*, pp. 107 f.

[4] CERFAUX, *Le titre Kyrios*, pp. 36 ff.

referring to the birth of Jesus; texts having ξύλον as key-word are interpreted as pointing to the Cross; enthronement and processional Psalms are applied to Christ's Ascension.

It may be of interest in this context to note the very minor role played in the *testimonia* tradition by Christ's title of "shepherd", which was later to become so general. This is all the more remarkable, since it is an ancient Near Eastern royal title, the implications of which are still alive in the NT tradition.[1] As the people are often called a flock, so the King of Israel is their shepherd, רעה. Gressmann has pointed out that this title has to do with the conception of the King as the one who gathers and constitutes the people; take away their King, and they are nothing but a chaotic collection of individuals.[2]

In the OT the title "shepherd" is used both of the King and of God. God is the great shepherd of Israel; the people are his flock, whom he has gathered and whom he leads to pasture.[3] "Shepherd" is already a typical Messianic title in the OT.[4] A new Messianic proof-text is Ps. 2.9 LXX (ποιμανεῖ αὐτοὺς ἐν ῥάβδῳ σιδηρᾷ),[5] a translation which also influenced Ps. Sol. 17.24,[6] and which is evidence of the use of the title "shepherd" as a Messianic epithet in Judaism. Jesus' sayings about himself as the Good Shepherd certainly go back to Jewish Messianic traditions.[7] At the same time there is a tendency in the targums to replace רעה (Aram. רעיא) as a royal epithet by other terms: פרנס (Ezek. 34.23 f.), מלכא (Zech. 13.7). The reason for this restraint is not quite clear, but it very likely has to do with Rabbinic censorship aimed at counteracting Christian use of the "shepherd" sayings of the

---

[1] For the shepherd title in the cultures of the ancient Near East, see C. J. GADD, *Ideas of Divine Rule in the Ancient East*, The Schweich Lectures 38, 1945 (1948), pp. 38 f.

[2] H. GRESSMANN, *Der Ursprung der israelitisch-jüdischen Eschatologie*, FRLANT 6 (1905), pp. 266 f.

[3] Ps. 79 (80).1, 94 (95).6 f.; Isa. 40.11; Micah 7.14. In Ezek. 34 the shepherd title is used of both God and the Messiah. See GRESSMANN, *op. cit.*, p. 267. W. JOST, ΠΟΙΜΗΝ (1939), p. 19 f. J. G. S. S. THOMSON, *The Shepherd-Ruler Concept in the Old Testament and its Application in the New Testament*, ScJTh 8 (1955), pp. 407 f.

[4] Jer. 23.4 f.; Ezek. 34.23 f., 37.24, Zech. 13.7. See THOMSON, *Concept*, pp. 411 f.

[5] JOST, ΠΟΙΜΗΝ, pp. 37 ff.

[6] *Ibid.*, pp. 39 f.

[7] On shepherd concepts in Qumran, see A. S. VAN DER WOUDE, *Die messianischen Vorstellungen der Gemeinde von Qumran* (1957), pp. 64 ff., and 85.

OT. On the other hand Rabbinic literature and especially Philo represent Moses as the shepherd *par excellence*.[1]

It is common knowledge that the title is widely used in the NT, where we also find the "shepherd" sayings of the OT used as proof of the Messiahship of Jesus. Matt. 2.6 quotes Micah 5.1 (2) in a version which says that the leader (ἡγούμενος) from Bethlehem will shepherd (ποιμανεῖ) the people of Israel. Zech. 13.7 is quoted in Matt. 26.31 and Mk. 14.27 as a prophecy of the disciples' flight on the arrest of Jesus. Ps. 2.9 is quoted in Rev. 2.26 f., 12.5 and 19.15: Christ, as King and shepherd, will shepherd all peoples with his rod of iron. Christ is clearly represented as King and shepherd in Matt. 25.31 ff.[2] The connexion between these two functions is also reflected in the fact that the titles ποιμήν and κύριος occur linked together, as in Heb. 13.20 (the only passage in Heb. where the word κύριος is used of Christ) and Rev. 19.15 f. There can be no doubt that these sayings are meant as expressions of the royal function of Christ. He is the one who carries out the task of the Messianic King, to gather all the peoples into one Kingdom.[3]

The title ποιμήν is used much less frequently in the later *testimonia* tradition of anti-Jewish polemics, compared with its use in the NT. Barn. 5.12 quotes Zech. 13.7, probably following Matt. 26.31.[4] The word is never used by St. Justin as a Christological *tropos*. He quotes a number of OT passages in which the word occurs, without however placing particular emphasis on the title "shepherd" in his exposition.[5] We find the same restraint in St. Irenaeus. Neither Dem. nor Adv. haer. contains a single "shepherd" passage.[6] ποιμήν as a Christological key-word is first found in anti-Jewish polemics, in the *Dialogue be-*

---

[1] Midrash Shemoth R. 2 (to Ex. 2.1). On Philo's use of the shepherd metaphor, see below, pp. 199.

[2] JOST, ΠΟΙΜΗΝ, pp. 45 f.

[3] GERHARDSSON, *Samaritan*, pp. 9 ff.

[4] MASSAUX, *Influence*, pp. 69 f.

[5] Isa. 40.11 in a quotation from Isa. 40.1–17 (Dial. 50.3–5); Micah 5.1 (2) according to Matt. 2.6 (Apol. 34.1 and Dial. 78.1); Zech. 13.7 (Dial. 53.6). Ps. 2 is once quoted in full (Apol. 40.11–19).

[6] Adv. haer. IV.33.11, ed. HARVEY 2.266, has a single allusion to Micah 5.1 (2) according to Matt. 2.6: "Bethlehem ... Unde et is, qui praeest et pascit populum Patris sui, venit." N.b. that the Syriac fragment, which HARVEY has published as nr. 30 (2.460 f.), and in which Christ is called shepherd, is now generally attributed to Melito of Sardis. Cf. below, p. 195.

tween *Athanasius and Zacchaeus* 79 f., which dates from the beginning of the 4th century.¹ Nor does this result in any real proof-text: Athanasius says that Christ is shepherd, to which the Jew Zacchaeus replies that in Ps. 79 (80).1 it is God who is called shepherd; Athanasius then states that this is no contradiction, since Christ is God.

It is particularly noteworthy that Ps. 22 (23).1 (κύριος ποιμαίνει με) is of no significance in the exposition of the first centuries, and is not found in anti-Jewish polemics at all. Was the introductory κύριος without article generally regarded as referring to the Father and not to Christ? The earliest commentaries on the Psalter, which must have dealt with this Psalm among others, are for the most part lost.²

The fact that the title of "shepherd" played such a little part in anti-Jewish polemics must be due to its not having been of interest to the Jews. It must be accounted likely that the choice of texts for discussion largely fell upon the most striking of the proof-texts. The "shepherd" texts evidently did not belong in this category. When we find ποιμήν used as a Christological title, it is in the context of an entirely different culture: the Hellenistic tradition of Alexandria. In Hellenistic syncretism "shepherd" is an epithet constantly used of Hermes-Logos, and Christian preachers were able to link "shepherd" and Logos as a title for Christ. We shall however return to this topic later.³ It is characteristic that one of the few allusions to Ps. 2.8 f. LXX is to be found in the Sibylline Oracles: Ῥάβδος ποιμαίνουσα σιδηρείῃ γε κρατήσει.⁴

---

¹ Anecdota Oxon. 8, pp. 44 f. For the dating, see above, p. 81 n. 5.

² A fragment of Hippolytus' Commentary on Ps. 22 (23) has been preserved in Theodoret of Cyrus (GCS Hipp. 1.2.146 f.), but is too incomplete to give a conception of Hippolytus' exegesis of this Psalm. The Commentary on Ps. 22, attributed to Eusebius (PG 23.216 f.), is of extremely dubious authenticity; the exposition however follows the Philonic concept of the relation between the functions of the shepherd and the king, which also occurs in Origen (Comm. on S. of S. 2, GCS Orig. 8.134 and Comm. on Jn. 1.28, GCS Orig. 4.35 f.): Christ is shepherd for those without reason but King for those who have been brought to reason. No traces of non-Alexandrian exegesis are to be found here. The lack of older source-material appears clearly in DANIÉLOU's treatment of the Psalm in *Bible et liturgie* (1951), pp. 240 ff.

³ See below, pp. 198 ff.

⁴ Orac. Sib. 8.248, GCS Orac. Sib. p. 157. Cf. also that the Naassenes meant that Ps. 2.9 was said about Hermes, Hippolytus, Ref. V. 7.32, GCS Hipp. 3.86.

The King of Israel

The anti-Jewish polemic of the Church Fathers stresses constantly that Jesus is the King promised in the prophecies of the OT, the King expected by the Jews. But at the same time it says that the Jews have rejected him, and that the Kingship has therefore been taken from them. The Kingship of Christ is not derived primarily from the Israelite Kingship: Christ is King because he has been anointed with the Divine nature and because after his suffering he has been enthroned at the right hand of the Father. The statements that Jesus is the Son of God, and that he is seated at the right hand of the Father have also been incorporated into the *symbola*—proof of their central position in the proclamation of the early Church. Christ's descent from the tribe of Judah and the house of David seem to have been of less importance in preaching and catechetical teaching, but came into their own in discussion with the Jews.

The question of the relationship between Jesus' Divine Sonship and his Davidic descent is already to be seen in the Synoptic tradition, in the "Son of David" passages.[1] When Jesus asks how David can address the Son of Man as Lord, if he is his son, this implies, first and foremost, that Jesus is disassociating himself from the political ideal of Messiahship linked with the concept of the Davidic descent. Though it is never explicitly mentioned, the idea of Christ as the Son of God is implied in the extension of Jesus' words.[2] It would be reading too much into his question to suggest that he *rejected* the idea that he was the Son of David.[3] Were such the case, it would be impossible to explain the importance of Son of David as a NT Christological title.[4]

---

[1] Cf. above, p. 50.

[2] Cf. CULLMANN, *Christologie*, p. 296: "Wenn er das Gespräch mit der Frage beschliesst: 'Wie ist er dann sein (sc. Davids) Sohn?', so drängt sich unwillkürlich die Frage auf, ob im Hintergrund nicht die Überzeugung steht, dass nur jene andere Sohnschaft, die Gottessohnschaft, das eigentliche Wichtige sein kann, auf das es hier ankommt. Wir können diesen Hintergrund hier nur vermuten."

[3] CULLMANN, *op. cit.*, p. 132: "Was Jesus verneint, ist nicht unbedingt seine Herkunft aus davidischem Geschlecht, sondern die von den Juden behauptete christologische Bedeutung, die dieser Abstammung im Blick auf das von ihm zu vollbringende Erlösungswerk zukommen soll." Cf. also BULTMANN, (*Geschichte*, p. 144), who thinks that this pericope expresses the Messianism of the community, rather than of Jesus himself.

[4] On the concept of Christ as the Son of David in NT theology and its background in OT, Judaism and Qumran, see E. LÖVESTAM, *Son and Saviour*, CN 18 (1961), pp. 54 ff.

Ever since NT times the main stream of Christian tradition has claimed that Christ has been King from the very first. In two respects: as the Son of God he has a share in the royal omnipotence of God; as the Son of David he can claim the Messianic Kingship promised in the OT. Though there is no developed doctrine of the double Kingship of Christ earlier than the 4th century,[1] substantially this argument was used from the time of the NT onward.

Two proof-texts in particular were of importance in shaping the doctrine of Christ as the Son of David: 2 Kings (Sam.) 7.11 ff. and Ps. 131 (132).11.[2] The two are practically identical, so much so that it is often impossible to say which of the two an author is referring to; we shall therefore consider them together, as one proof-text.

We find a number of allusions to these proof-texts in the Messianic tradition. In the Annunciation narrative Gabriel says: "He will be great, and will be called the Son of the Most High; and the Lord God will give to him the throne of his father David" (Lk. 1.32). Similarly St. Peter, in the course of his Pentecost address to the Jews, mentions the promise of God to David to "set one of his descendants upon his throne" (Acts 2.29 f.). God's promise that the Messiah is to come of the seed of David is also taken up by St. Paul in his sermon at Antioch in Pisidia (Acts 13.22 f.); that Jesus fulfilled the prophecies of a coming descendant of David was of particular significance in sermons delivered to the Jews.[3]

There are traces in the NT of other testimonies which were to become common in anti-Jewish polemic. On one occasion Paul quotes Isa. 11.1, with its promise of "a shoot out of the stock of Jesse" (Rom. 15.12). This forms part of a series of testimonies based on the keyword ἔθνη. In Rev. Christ is represented as the Lion of Judah (Gen. 49.10) and as (a shoot) out of the stock of Jesse (Isa. 11.1, 10).[4]

The question of the Davidic descent of Christ is more controversial in the post-Apostolic age than in the NT. The intense desire of the

---

[1] Cf. below, Chap. 12.

[2] 2 Kings (Sam.) 7 is known as an important Messianic text in Judaism, and also appears in the 4 Q florilegium in Qumran. See Y. YADIN, *A Midrash on 2 Sam. vii and Ps. i–ii (4 Q Florilegium)*, IEJ 9 (1959), pp. 95–98. D. FLUSSER, *Two Notes on the Midrash on 2 Sam. vii*, IEJ 9 (1959), pp. 99–109. For the relation between this text and Ps. 88 (89) and 131 (132), see AHLSTRÖM, *Psalm 89*, pp. 182 ff.

[3] LÖVESTAM, *Son and Saviour*, pp. 5 ff. and *passim*.

[4] Rev. 5.5, 22.16. Cf. BILLERBECK, *Comm.* 3, p. 801. Jesus is styled son of David also in Jn. 7.42, and 2 Tim. 2.8.

Gentile Christian Church to free itself from the Jewish tradition resulted in the idea of Jesus as the Son of David becoming obscured. The anti-Jewish author of Barn. 12.10 quotes Ps. 109 (110).1 as a contradiction of the Jews' belief that the Messiah must be the Son of David.[1] Here we note a striking intensification of Jesus' own attitude to the "Son of David" question. The anti-Jewish character of Marcionism went even further, and rejected completely the idea of the Davidic descent of Jesus.[2] At the opposite extreme, the re-Judaizing tendency of the Ebionite heresy led to the denial of Christ's Divine Sonship and the stressing of his Davidic Sonship at one and the same time.[3]

Between these two opposite poles the main stream of the Church stressed that Christ was both the Son of God and the Son of David. Paul's words to the effect that Christ was born of the seed of David as a man, but confirmed as the Son of God by the Spirit (Rom. 1.4) are also found in the Ignatians, where Christ is said to be the Son of David according to the flesh but the Son of God by the will and the power of God (Smyrn. 1.1, Eph. 18.2, 20.2; cf. Trall. 9.1, Rom. 7.3). Ignatius' emphasis on the earthly descent of Christ is here conditioned largely by his anti-Docetic purpose. He has little to say on the subject of the Kingship of Christ.

Although this attitude is typical of the post-Apostolic Church, we must note a shift of accent, due less to theological demands than to the needs of a polemical situation; it is here we encounter the doctrine of the double Kingship of Christ. It was natural in the context of a polemic directed against the Jewish Christians to stress that Christ was the Son of God; against the Marcionites, to stress that he was the Son of David. The problem is more complicated in anti-Jewish polemics. It is in the interest of the apologist to show, on the one hand, how Christ fulfilled the Messianic prophecies of the OT, and on the other to stress

---

[1] ἴδε πάλιν Ἰησοῦς, οὐχὶ υἱὸς ἀνθρώπου ἀλλὰ υἱὸς τοῦ θεοῦ, τύπῳ δὲ ἐν σαρκὶ φανερωθείς. ἐπεὶ οὖν μέλλουσιν λέγειν ὅτι Χριστὸς υἱὸς Δαυίδ ἐστιν, αὐτὸς προφητεύει ὁ Δαυίδ ... (Ps. 109.1) ... ἴδε πῶς Δαυὶδ λέγει αὐτὸν κύριον, καὶ υἱὸν οὐ λέγει.

[2] Tertullian, Adv. Marc. III.20.6 ff., CCL 1.535 f., *ibid.* IV.36.9 ff., p. 645. Cf. A. von Harnack, *Marcion*, TU 45 (1921), p. 113.

[3] Tertullian, De carne Chr. 14, CCL 2.900. Origen, Comm. on Matt. 16.12, GCS Orig. 10.513. Cf. H. J. Schoeps, *Theologie und Geschichte des Judenchristentums* (1949), pp. 71 ff. It is striking that the Pseudo-Clementines, the Ebionitic character of which is eagerly advocated by Schoeps, lay no stress upon Christ's Davidic descent. Cf. below, Chap. 10.

the way in which his coming shattered the order of the old Covenant and created something completely new.

Dom Leclercq considers that St. Justin always traced the Kingship of Christ to his Divinity; never to his Davidic descent.[1] It is however less likely that Justin differed in this respect from the rest of the anti-Jewish polemic of his time. It is true that Justin expounded Gen. 49.11 in such a way as to deny that Jesus was of human descent (Apol. 32.4, Dial. 54.2, 76.1), but this is not a polemic against his Davidic descent; it is directed against the idea of Jesus having had an earthly father. Justin claims that the Virgin Mary was descended from the family of David, and that Jesus' Davidic descent can be explained in this way (Dial. 68.5 f.).

Justin is in fact concerned to claim the Messiahship of Jesus by means of references to the OT testimonies about the coming King. In Dial. 137.2 he goes so far as to call Christ the King of Israel. Justin also has a Christological interpretation of 2 Kings (Sam.) 7.11 f.–Ps. 131.11 in which, although the only allusion to these testimonies is placed in the mouth of Trypho, the way in which Justin incorporates them into the dialogue shows that he accepted them as Christological texts (Dial. 68.5 f.).[2] 2 Kings (Sam.) 7.14 f. is quoted in Dial. 118.2, but only as a proof-text for the derivation of the Kingship of Christ from his Divine Sonship. He also stresses the fact that Jesus is the heir of the Davidic Kingship by twice quoting Micah 5.1 (2), in the version of Matt. 2.6: "And you, O Bethlehem, in the land of Judah, are by no means least among the rulers of Judah; for from you shall come a ruler (ἡγούμενος) who will govern my people Israel."[3] The fact of Christ being the Son of David and the promised King of Israel thus fills an

---

[1] J. LECLERCQ, L'Idée de la royauté du Christ dans l'œuvre de Saint Justin, AnTh 7 (1946), pp. 83–95. This essay has been reprinted as an appendix in IDEM, L'Idée de la royauté du Christ au Moyen Age (1959), pp. 215–226. (Unfortunately, the great number of misprints in the references have been reproduced in the new edition.) In the following reference is made to the pagination of the new edition. On Christ's descent from David, see ibid., pp. 222 f.

[2] For the textual form, see VON UNGERN-STERNBERG, Schriftbeweis, pp. 73 f. (the footnote).

[3] Apol. 34.1, Dial. 78.1. ἡγούμενος never occurs in the writings of St. Justin as a separate catch-word but appears in some testimonies to the Kingship of Christ, in Gen. 49.10 and Num. 24.17 (cf. below) and in Ezek. 44.3 (Dial. 118.2). For the textual form (LXX has ἄρχων where the quotation in Matt. has ἡγούμενος), see MASSAUX, Influence, pp. 496 and 524.

important function in St. Justin's debate with Trypho, though Dom Leclercq is right that the most important fact for Justin is that Christ is the Logos incarnate.

Testimonies proving Jesus to be the promised King of Israel are extremely common in the later literature.[1] Among the oldest proof-texts of this kind are Num. 24.17 and Isa. 11.1, which are often met with in combination.[2] Num. 24.17 is a well-known Messianic text in Judaism, and forms part of the florilegium of proof-texts found at Qumran.[3] St. Justin quotes this passage twice: in Dial. 106.4, where we read that a star shall come forth from Jacob and a ruler (ἡγούμενος) from Israel; and in Apol. 32.12 f., where it is combined with Isa. 11.1 to read: "A star shall come forth out of Jacob, and a flower (ἄνθος) shall spring up from the root of Jesse."[4] St. Irenaeus combines Num. 24.17 with Ps. 131 (132).11 as a proof that Christ is descended from the house of David through Mary; he is also the first to connect Num. 24.17 with the narrative of the Magi in Matt. 2.[5] Isa. 11.1 is often encountered as a proof-text; Irenaeus and Tertullian (but not Justin) make use of this passage with reference to the descent of Jesus from David.[6]

---

[1] An excellent survey is given by VON UNGERN-STERNBERG, *op. cit.*, pp. 65–80 (and *passim*; see especially the chapters on the development of the *testimonia* tradition after Tertullian). Not mentioned by VON UNGERN-STERNBERG are Orac. Sib. 6.16, GCS Orac. Sib., p. 131, 7.31 (p. 134) and 8.254 (p. 158), where Christ is represented as the son of David (with allusions to 2 Kings (Sam.) 7.11 ff. and Isa. 11.1).

[2] This combination appears very early, in Test. Jud. 24.1–6 and in Rev. 22.16, where Christ is represented as the root of David and as the clear morning-star. Cf. DANIÉLOU, *Judéo-christianisme*, pp. 241 f. HOMMES, *Testimoniaboek*, pp. 107 ff. takes up this combination, but mainly as a polemic against HARRIS.

[3] The Messianic conceptions in the Dead Sea community are also expressed in Qumran exegesis of this verse. The parallelism is interpreted as meaning the two Messiahs: the sceptre means Judah (according to Gen. 49.10), and the star therefore means the priestly Messiah. See VAN DER WOUDE, *Vorstellungen*, pp. 59 ff., 107 ff. and *passim*. FLUSSER, *Two Notes*, pp. 104 ff.

[4] The combination of these two quotations in one testimony is probably older than St. Justin's *Apology*. It is likely that Is. 11.1 had another textual form, when the combination had taken place: not ἄνθος, as in Apol. 32.12 but ῥάβδος, as in the normal text of the LXX. It was then easy to make a leap from ῥάβδος (= the sceptre in Num. 24.17) to ῥάβδος (= the scion in Isa. 11.1).

[5] Adv. haer. III.9.2, ed. HARVEY, 2.31.

[6] St. Irenaeus, Dem. 49. Tertullian, Adv. Marc. V.8.4, CCL 1.686. Cf. VON UNGERN-STERNBERG, *Schriftbeweis*, p. 75.

The entire tradition is summed up by St. Cyprian, whose *testimonia* collection contains most of these proof-texts, under the heading *Quod de semine David secundum carnem nasci haberet*.[1] Here he takes up 2 Kings (Sam.) 7.4–5, 12–14, 16; Isa. 11.1; Ps. 131 (132).11; Lk. 1.30 ff. and Rev. 5.1 ff. Num. 24.17 and Micah 5.1 (2) are contained in the previous and following chapters respectively.

We thus have a fixed tradition of proof-texts showing Jesus to be of the house of David in the anti-Jewish polemic of the first centuries; in this tradition he is represented as the promised King upon the throne of David. A number of these texts later came to occupy central positions in the Christmas and Epiphany liturgy. But when we come across them in the context of discussions with the Jews they have little of that liturgical solemnity which we find in the later ecclesiastical tradition, where the Christ-child (mainly following Matt. 2) is represented as the new-born King, worshipped by the shepherds and Magi. In this earlier context the testimonies are intended to convince the Jews that Jesus is identical with the Messiah of the house of David they have been awaiting. The Christians themselves seem to have accorded less significance to the prophecies in question. Not before Hippolytus do we find an attempt to trace in principle the Kingship of Christ to his Davidic descent—in the theory that Christ must be descended from the tribes of both Judah and Levi in order to be both King and priest.[2]

The polemical use of the Messianic texts of the OT repeatedly points out that no Israelite King fulfilled the prophecies; they have however reached their consummation in Christ. This polemic is often directed against Jewish interpretations which apply the texts in question to one or other of the Kings of Israel: that Ps. 109 (110) refers to Hezekiah,[3] or that Ps. 23 (24) or Ps. 71 (72) refers to Solomon.[4] These interpretations are unknown from Jewish literature.[5] But they seem, strangely enough, to have been incorporated into Marcionite exegesis, Judaism and anti-Judaism uniting in a common endeavour to prove

---

[1] Ad Quir. 2.11 ff., CSEL 3.1.75 ff.
[2] See below, pp. 109 f.
[3] Dial. 33.1–2, 83.1–4. Cf. LECLERCQ, *Royauté*, p. 217.
[4] Dial. 36.2–6, 34.1. LECLERCQ, *op. cit., ibid.*
[5] BILLERBECK, *Comm.* 4.1, p. 456. SIMON, *Verus Israel*, p. 192.

that Jesus had nothing to do with the OT prophecies.¹ In the anti-Jewish polemic authors return again and again to the statement that Jesus is far above the Israelite Kingship. As far back as St. Peter's address in Acts we find this characteristic, as he points out that David has not ascended into heaven (2.34). St. Justin is similarly able in an exposition of Ps. 21 (22).17 to state that no-one who has borne the name of (anointed) King has had his hands and feet pierced like Christ (Dial. 97.4). But this is a case of *reductio ad absurdum*, not unknown in the exegesis of the early Church.²

An important theme in such polemics is the idea, common as far back as the NT, that Christ became King of the Gentiles after being rejected by the Jews. The Christological interpretation of Gen. 25.23 which we find in Rom. 9.10 ff. is taken up by St. Irenaeus: the younger people received Christ when he was rejected by the elder, saying, "We have no king but Caesar" (Jn. 19.15).³ After Christ the Jews have no king at all.

The argument that the Kingship of Israel ceased with the coming of Christ is consistently referred back to Gen. 49.10, which reads in the LXX version that the sceptre shall not depart from Judah until its rightful owner comes. Justin takes up this interpretation in Apol. 32.1 ff.:

"It is yours to make accurate inquiry, and ascertain up to whose time the Jews had a lawgiver and king of their own. Up to the time of Jesus Christ, who taught us, and interpreted the prophecies which were not yet understood, (they had a lawgiver) as was foretold by the holy and divine Spirit of prophecy through Moses, 'that a ruler would not fail the Jews until he should come for whom the kingdom was reserved' (for Judah was the forefather of the Jews, from whom also they have their name of Jews): and after he (i.e. Christ) appeared, you began to rule the Jews, and gained possession of all their territory."⁴

Gen. 49.10 is one of the standard proof-texts of the later *testimonia* tradition.⁵ It is often linked with the idea that the oil with which

---

¹ Tertullian, Adv. Marc. V.9.6 ff. CCL 1.689 ff., is directed against a Marcionite exegesis, according to which Ps. 109 refers to Ezechias and Ps. 71 to Solomon. Cf. VON HARNACK, *Marcion*, p. 113.

² STENDAHL, *School*, pp. 78 f.

³ Adv. haer. IV.21.2 f., ed. HARVEY, 2.226.

⁴ Apol. 32.1 ff. Cf. Apol. 54.5, Dial. 52.2 f. (which also mentions the priesthood and the prophetic office) and Dial. 120.3.

⁵ The near-infallible VON UNGERN-STERNBERG is guilty of an error, when he states that Gen. 49.10 is not quoted by St. Irenaeus (*Schriftbeweis*, pp. 120 and 133).

kings, priests and prophets were anointed disappeared at the coming of Christ; this in its turn is often connected with an exposition of Dan. 9.24–26 LXX. The anointing, which is identified with the Spirit, passes through Christ to the Church.[1]

The most important testimony of Christ's Kingship, not only over the Jews, but also over the Gentiles, is Ps. 2.7 f.[2] Tertullian, in an anti-Jewish exposition of this text, says that David and Solomon ruled only over the Jewish people, but that Christ rules the whole world through the rays of the Gospel. Solomon was a mortal king, but Christ has an eternal throne.[3] Tertullian also has a long passage in which he says that Solomon, Pharaoh, Nebuchadnezzar and Alexander had only limited jurisdiction, and that even the Romans must defend their frontiers, but Christ's name is found everywhere; he is believed everywhere; he is honoured by all peoples; he is worshipped in all places. No king is better loved; he is King and judge of all.[4] Tertullian extends his polemic beyond the Jews, to include all earthly kingdoms. This brings us, however, to a further subject, which we shall consider in more detail later.[5]

Hippolytus' work on David and Goliath 16.5 would seem to contain a mixture of anti-Jewish and anti-imperial polemic.[6] Saul is blamed for his persecution of David, who is identified with Christ, but there can be little doubt that the text is directed equally against the Roman Emperor's persecution of the Christians. "You are king over a mere six thousand, but Christ over all creation. You are king over men in this world, but Christ over the heavens and the earth and the underworld. You are a mortal king in the fleeting ages, but Christ is an eternal ruler, perfect now and forever and throughout all eternity. Amen."

The verse is quoted in Adv. haer. IV.10.2, ed. HARVEY 2.173 f., and there is also a clear allusion to the verse in Dem. 57, which seems to be dependent on St. Justin's Apol. 32, where the verse is also quoted. Cf. ROBINSON's translation of Dem., the introduction, pp. 6 ff.

[1] This motif is dealt with in detail below, pp. 114 ff.

[2] St. Justin, Dial. 122.6. St. Irenaeus, Dem. 49.

[3] Adv. Marc. III.20.3, CCL 1.535 f. Adv. Jud. 14.12, CCL 2.1395 (which is an interpolation made with help of the preceding text).

[4] Adv. Jud. 7, CCL 2.1339.

[5] See below, pp. 173 ff.

[6] Translation from the Georgian version by G. N. BONWETSCH, TU 26.1 (1904), p. 93.

The Enthronement of the Lord

The *testimonia* tradition, as we find it in St. Justin and his successors, is always expounded in such a way as to represent the Kingship of Christ as realized in time. Although the royal power of Christ is stated to be derived from his Divinity, it is manifested in the context of the economy of salvation, and particularly in the resurrection, ascension, *sessio* and parousia of Christ. We also find that most prooftexts on the subject of the Kingship of Christ refer to his heavenly enthronement, and have *kyrios* and *basileus* as key-words. These titles therefore also refer in anti-Jewish polemic to the Risen and Glorified Lord.

The Jews were unable to reconcile the suffering and death of Christ with his Messianic claims; anti-Jewish polemics constantly return to this theme. Tryphon, in St. Justin's *Dialogue,* declares that it is unreasonable to believe that the Messiah could suffer and die like Jesus.[1] Justin replies that a distinction must be drawn between the two parousias of Christ: in his first parousia he had no visible glory, and was mortal; in the second he shall be revealed in glory on the clouds of heaven.[2] Christ had this power from the very first, though it was not manifested until the Resurrection and Ascension: he is the Logos of God, the mediator between God and the world, and his condescension at the first parousia was for our sake. His kingly nature, on the other hand, was only made manifest at the Resurrection. His passion is not regarded as royal; the Christian apologete wishes rather to stress that the suffering of Christ was his way of leaving and excelling the Jewish ideal of Kingship.[3]

Anti-Jewish polemic—as distinct from the later patristic tradition, the origins of which we can trace in Antiochene theology[4]—places little emphasis on the Kingship of Christ during his earthly ministry. St. Justin quotes the Gospel narrative of the Magi once (Dial. 78.1) and the story of Jesus' entry into Jerusalem twice (Apol. 35.11, Dial. 53.3),

---

[1] Dial. 32.1, 46.1. Cf. LECLERCQ, *Royauté,* pp. 215 ff. SIMON, *Verus Israel,* pp. 190 ff.

[2] Dial. 14.8, 52.1–4. Cf. LECLERCQ, *op. cit.,* p. 219. The term παρουσία is not used in the NT to signify the first appearance of Christ in the flesh; this use of the word is not known earlier than Ign. ad Philad. 9.2. Cf. above, pp. 67 ff.

[3] The different kinds of testimonies are conveniently arranged by VON UNGERN-STERNBERG, *Schriftbeweis, passim.*

[4] See below, pp. 231 ff.

but without stressing his Kingship other than indirectly, in the prooftexts he quotes (Micah 5.1 (2) and Zech. 9.9 respectively). These events are placed in the context of the first parousia, in which the might and glory of Christ were hidden, and Justin quotes them mainly in order to show how the prophecies were fulfilled in Jesus.[1]

The passion and death of Christ form the climax of his first parousia, and can thus be regarded as the point of departure for his coming glorification.[2] We read, in an oft-quoted reading of Ps. 95 (96).10, that "the Lord has become king from the tree" (ὁ κύριος ἐβασίλευσεν ἀπὸ τοῦ ξύλου), and this reading is often used as a proof-text showing that Christ purchased the Kingship by his suffering.[3] St. Justin—who, like his opponent Trypho, knew no Hebrew—considered his version of the LXX to be original and the normal text to be a Jewish counterfeit. There is however no doubt that this is an early Christian interpolation into the text of the LXX. It is the same reading which forms the basis of Barn. 8.5, which says that the Kingship of Jesus depends upon the tree (ἡ βασιλεία Ἰησοῦ ἐπὶ ξύλου).[4]

A similar exegesis of Isa. 9.6, "And the government shall be upon his shoulder", is made by Justin and Tertullian; the text is quoted by Justin in the form οὗ ἡ ἀρχὴ ἐπὶ τῶν ὤμων (Apol. 35.2), and is rendered by Tertullian as "cuius imperium factum est super humerum ipsius".[5] Also this text—in Tertullian combined with Ps. 95 (96).10, *regnavit de ligno*—is interpreted in the sense that Christ has purchased his King-

---

[1] LECLERCQ perhaps overemphasizes the royal import of these texts in St. Justin's writings, *op. cit.*, p. 220.

[2] Cf. St. Irenaeus, Adv. haer. III 12.9, ed. HARVEY 2.63: "The same who suffered under Pontius Pilate, is the Lord of all things, King, God and Judge."

[3] St. Justin, Apol. 41.1-4; Dial. 73.1-4, Tertullian, Adv. Marc. III.19.1, CCL 1.441. See DANIÉLOU, *Judéo-christianisme*, p. 111. LECLERCQ, *Royauté*, pp. 220 ff.

[4] This reading exists only in one Greek manuscript, the uncial 156 (in the form ἀπὸ τῷ ξύλῳ), in the Sahidic version and in one Latin manuscript (Psalterium Veronense). See WILLIAMS, *Adversus Judaeos*, p. 33. HOMMES, *Testimoniaboek*, pp. 94 ff. How this reading has arisen is a problem which has not been solved. The word ξύλα appears in verse 12, but it is not easy to understand how it may have been inserted into verse 10. A possible solution is that the faulty reading has arisen in the Hebrew text, where יהוה מלך אף תכון indistinctly written, may have been read as יהוה מלך על העץ (= ἐπὶ ξύλου).

[5] Adv. Marc. III.19.2, CCL 1.533. For the textual form, see VON UNGERN-STERNBERG, *Schriftbeweis*, pp. 76 and 95.

dom by the Cross.¹ The same exegesis of this verse also occurs in Origen, ἐβασίλευσεν γὰρ διὰ τοῦ πεπονθέναι τὸν σταυρόν.²

At an early stage we find the sufferings and death of Christ represented as a victory over death and over the demons.³ St. Justin connects the "powers of this world", over which Christ has triumphed, with the "angels of the peoples" which Jews believed to govern every nation upon earth.⁴ This meant that Christ, through his death, became King, not only of Israel, but also of the Gentiles. In the NT the same theme is linked with his glorification (Eph. 1.20 f.). It is in general typical of the attitude of the early Church that the same motif can be connected with Christ's sufferings in one context, and with his exaltation in another; the same double usage is seen in the Johannine term ὑψωθῆναι.⁵ The Resurrection, the Ascension and the Passion can be brought together in such a way as to make it almost seem that Christ was taken up into heaven direct from the Cross.⁶ Ps. 95 (96).10 is therefore not considered to contradict such testimonies as Ps. 109 (110).1 and Ps. 23 (24).7–10, which Christian interpreters regarded as proof that the enthronement of Christ took place in connexion with the Ascension.

---

[1] "Quis omnino regum insigne potestatis suae humero praefert et non aut capite diadema aut manu sceptrum aut aliquam propriae uestis notam? Sed solus potestatem et sublimitatem suam humero extulit, crucem scilicet, ut secundum superiorem prophetiam exinde dominus regnaret a ligno", Tertullian, *ibid.*

[2] Origen. Comm. on Jn. 1.38, GCS Orig. 4.49.

[3] R. LEIVESTAD, *Christ the Conqueror* (1954), pp. 62 ff., 92 ff. and *passim*. This important motif seems to be overemphasized by G. AULÉN, *Christus Victor* (1931), who has styled it "the classical doctrine of Redemption". Cf. LEIVESTAD, *op. cit.*, p. 302.

[4] Dial. 30.3, 49.8, 73.2, 83.4. Cf. Col. 2.14 f. DANIÉLOU, *Judéo-christianisme*, pp. 264 ff.

[5] Cf. G. BERTRAM, *Der religionsgeschichtliche Hintergrund der Begriff der "Erhöhung" in der Septuaginta*, ZAW 68 (1956), 60 f.

[6] BERTRAM, *Erhöhung*, p. 64: "Justin kann die Auferstehung und Himmelfahrt zusammen sehen; Christus wird unmittelbar vom Kreuz zur himmlischen Herrlichkeit erhöht. Vom Holz tritt er seine Herrschaft an, wie der christliche Zusatz zu Ps. 96.10 es ausspricht." BERTRAM earlier treated the same subject more fully in his essay *Die Himmelfahrt Jesu vom Kreuz aus und der Glaube an seine Auferstehung*, Festgabe für A. Deissmann (1927), pp. 187–217. It seems however improbable that St. Justin really meant that Christ had ascended to heaven directly from the Cross; the explanation is rather that the two motives, crucifixion and exaltation, are kept together, because they belong together theologically.

Ps. 109 (110).1

The central NT proof-texts for the exaltation of Christ retained their importance in post-Apostolic times; throughout the period of the early Church they are among the most frequently quoted passages of the OT. Unlike many other testimonies, the use of Ps. (109) 110.1 is not restricted to Christian polemic *Adversus Judaeos*, but is met with just as frequently in catechetical teaching and preaching.[1] An expression taken from this verse, that Christ is seated at the right hand of the Father, has also been incorporated into the second article of the Apostolic Creed.

This Psalm is found in the *testimonia* material used by the Apostolic Fathers (Clem. 36.5, Barn. 12.10) and is often quoted by St. Justin.[2] His purpose in quoting the verse in question is partly to demonstrate the existence of a Divine Person other than the Father.[3] The enthronement of Christ at the right hand of the Father took place at his Ascension, after the Resurrection (Apol. 45.1, Dial. 32.1-6).[4] The verse's ἕως ἄν indicates that the *sessio* of Christ will last until he has conquered the demons (at his parousia) and until the number of the good and virtuous is complete.[5] We do not have any more developed speculation on the subject of the cessation of the rule of Christ (after 1 Cor. 15.25 ff.) until Marcellus of Ancyra.[6] There is however no doubt that the way was prepared for this speculation by earlier exposition of ἕως ἄν in Ps. 109.1.

Ps. 109 (110).2

There is no Christological interpretation of Ps. 109 (110).2 ("The Lord shall send forth the rod of thy strength out of Zion") in the NT; such an interpretation is first met with in St. Justin, but is once more missing from St. Irenaeus and Tertullian. The two passages in which

---

[1] The use of Ps. 109 in the early Church is treated at length by DANIÉLOU in *Session*, pp. 689 ff. Cf. IDEM, *Bible et liturgie*, pp. 414 ff. and IDEM, *Judéo-christianisme*, pp. 282 ff.

[2] Apol. 45.2-4; Dial. 32.3-6, 33.1 f., 36.5, 56.14, 83.1, 118.1, 127.5.

[3] Dial. 56.14 f., 127.5, cf. St. Irenaeus, Adv. haer. III.6.1, ed. HARVEY 2.20 f.

[4] Cf. St. Irenaeus, Adv. haer. III.10.6, ed. HARVEY, 2.39 f.

[5] Apol. 45.1, cf. St. Irenaeus, Dem. 85, Tertullian, Adv. Marc. V.9.6, CCL 1.689 f.

[6] See below, p. 234. For the earlier exposition of this text, see DANIÉLOU, *Bible et liturgie*, pp. 417 ff., IDEM, *Judéo-christianisme*, pp. 282 f.

Justin quotes this proof-text are worded somewhat differently: the most important divergence is that in Apol. 45.5 he uses ἐξ 'Ιερουσαλήμ (as does the normal LXX text), while in Dial. 83.2 he has ἐπὶ 'Ιερουσαλήμ; in the exposition which follows, in Dial. 83.3 f., he twice uses the expression εἰς 'Ιερουσαλήμ. Despite these variants, the thought of the passages in Dial. and Apol. is identical: according to Dial. 83.2 f. "the sceptre" refers to the word of commission and conversion, offered by Jesus to the Gentiles before he reveals himself in glory at the parousia. In Apol. 45.5 "the sceptre" has to do with the word of Jesus borne out from Jerusalem by the Apostles after the Ascension. Daniélou in particular has stressed the connexion between *ascensio*, *sessio* and *missio*, as expounded here, and as earlier found in the NT (Mk. 16.19, Acts 2.33).[1] We may also note that we have here an expression of the Jewish and early Christian view of Jerusalem as the centre of the world, the place from which the word of the Lord, the Torah, proceeds.[2] The prophetic text which was responsible for establishing the classical Jewish formulation of this idea is Isa. 2.3, with the closely related Micah 4.2; this is taken up by Justin and Irenaeus as a proof-text for the Apostles' mission, bearing out the word of the Lord from Jerusalem.[3]

Ps. 109 (110).4

Verse 4 introduces a new theme into the Psalm, i.e. that the King is an eternal priest after the order of Melchizedek. We shall return to this combination of the Kingship and the priesthood in due course.[4]

---

[1] DANIÉLOU, *Session*, pp. 696 ff.

[2] GERHARDSSON, *Memory*, pp. 214 ff., 274 ff. Cf. also B. SUNDKLER, *Jésus et les païens*, AMNSU 6 (1937), pp. 21 ff.

[3] St. Justin, Apol. 39.1–3; Dial. 24.1, 109.1–3, 110.2. St. Irenaeus, Dem. 86; Adv. haer. IV.34.4, ed. HARVEY 2.271. Tertullian, Adv. Marc. III.21.3, CCL 1.537, IV.1.4 (p. 545), V.4.3 (p. 672); Adv. Jud. 3.9, CCL 2.1346. The ῥάβδος symbolism in the early Fathers is worth a separate study. Besides the exegesis of Ps. 109.2, according to which the ῥάβδος is the word of Christ, there also exists an exegesis of Isa. 11.1 in which the Messiah is called ῥάβδος, see above, p. 94. Cf. the Orac. Sib. 8.254, GCS Orac. Sib., p. 158, where Christ is styled ῥάβδος Δαυίδ, and the term σκῆπτρον for Christ in Clem. 16.2. For the Christological interpretation of Ps. 2.9 LXX, which appears as early as Rev. 2.27, 12.5, 19.15, see above, pp. 87 ff. Ps. 44.7 is interpreted in Heb. 1.8 as meaning the sceptre of Christ (cf. St. Justin, Dial. 56.17, 63.4). All these texts belong originally to the context of the sacral kingship in the Near East, see WIDENGREN, *Psalm 110*, pp. 7 f.

[4] See below, pp. 106 ff.

Ps. 23 (24).7-10

One of the most important of the early Church's testimonies to Christ's exaltation is provided by Ps. 23 (24).7-10, which is one of the most frequently quoted of proof-texts from St. Justin onward, in connexion with the Ascension.[1] No trace of this Psalm is to be found in the NT, but it is interpreted Christologically in some of the oldest of the post-canonical writings.[2]

Both the actual text and its exposition give rise to a number of complicated and as yet unsolved problems. The Greek translation (LXX) has transposed subject and object, with the result that it is not the gates which lift up their heads, but the "heads" (the heavenly guardians, *archons*) which lift up the gates ("Άρατε πύλας οἱ ἄρχοντες ὑμῶν). This translation is grammatically difficult, not least because the word ὑμῶν is virtually incomprehensible in a phrase addressed to the archons. The Vulgate text has completed the alteration by referring the possessive pronoun to the doors (*Tollite portas principes vestras*); it seems likely that the ὑμῶν of the Greek text was early understood in the same ungrammatical way.

The LXX here translates Yahweh Sebaot by κύριος τῶν δυνάμεων and not κύριος παντοκράτωρ, which is a title the early Church reserved for the Father;[3] there can be no doubt that this contributed to the Christological use of the Psalm. The two expressions κύριος τῶν δυνάμεων and βασιλεὺς τῆς δόξης emphasize that it is as King that Christ ascends to the Father, but they do not imply a use of titles still reserved for the Father.[4]

The Christological use of Ps. 23 corresponds to the *descensus-ascensio* theme, as found in extra-canonical apocalyptic literature (the *Ascension of Isaiah* and the *Epistle of the Apostles*) but not in the NT.[5] Christ,

---

[1] Dial. 29.1, 36.3 f., 85.1-4; cf. Apol. 51.7, Dial. 127.5.

[2] For the exegesis of Ps. 23 in the early Church, see J. KROLL, *Gott und Hölle*, StBW 20 (1932), pp. 46 f. and *passim*. DANIÉLOU, *Bible et liturgie*, pp. 409 ff. IDEM, *Judéo-christianisme*, pp. 284 ff.

[3] See below, Chap. 13.

[4] Both these terms are missing from the NT. MOULE (*Influence*, p. 253) indicates the similarity to the expression κύριος τῆς δόξης (1 Cor. 2.8), which does not occur in the LXX but in 1 En. and in Barn. 21.9. It is possible that κύριος τῆς δόξης is an allusion to Ps. 23, though the controversial term *basileus* has been avoided.

[5] See further below, pp. 144 f. For the similarity between Asc. Isa. and the patristic exegesis of Ps. 23, see DANIÉLOU, *Bible et liturgie*, pp. 410 f. IDEM, *Judéo-christianisme*, p. 284.

descending and ascending, had to pass through the various spheres of heaven, the gates of which were guarded by angelic powers. At his descent he hid his identity from the angels; his glory was only revealed at his Ascension.[1]

A number of very old texts connect Ps. 23 with the *descensus*, instead of the Ascension. The Greek *Physiologus* which, in its present form, dates from the end of the 4th century, but which builds on considerably older material, incorporates Ps. 23 into a description of the *descensus*; this is very reminiscent of the *Ascension of Isaiah*, and may well be based on an older, lost version of that document.[2] Other Christian apocryphal works link Ps. 23 with Christ's descent into Hell: such usage is found in the Slavonic and Latin versions of the *Gospel of Bartholomew*[3] and in the *descensus* narrative of the *Acts of Pilate*.[4] Yet another variation is seen in the *Apocalypse of Peter*, which uses the Psalm in connexion with the Transfiguration, which is here described in a way similar to the Ascension. The Lord, Moses and Elijah are taken away in a great cloud; Peter sees the heavens opened, and people who greet the three and accompany them to another heaven. "And great fear and commotion was there in heaven, and the angels pressed upon one another that the word of the scripture might be fulfilled which saith: Open the gates, ye princes."[5]

St. Justin has a fully developed version of the Ascension narrative common in later authors; here Ps. 23 is sung antiphonally between the Spirit (or the angels accompanying the Ascending Christ) and the angels (archontes) who guard the gates of heaven:

"When our Christ rose from the dead and ascended to heaven, the rulers in heaven, under appointment of God, are commanded to open the gates of

---

[1] Cf. the sayings on the angels in 1 Tim. 3.16 and 1 Pet. 1.12, and the use of Ps. 8.6 LXX in Heb. 2.7, 9.

[2] E. PETERSON, *Die Spiritualität des griechischen Physiologos* in PFJG (1959), pp. 250 f. Cf. DANIÉLOU, *Judéo-christianisme*, pp. 228 ff., 285 ff.

[3] The Slavonic version, see G. N. BONWETSCH, *Die apokryphen Fragen des Bartholomäus*, GN 1897, p. 6.

[4] *The Gospel of Nicodemus*, in C. TISCHENDORF, *Evangelia apocrypha* (1853), Greek version 5 (21), pp. 306 f.; Latin A. 5 (21), p. 377; Latin B.7 (23), p. 406. See further KROLL, *Gott und Hölle*, p. 74. DANIÉLOU, *Judéo-christianisme*, p. 232. An attempt to explain the connexion between Ps. 23 and the *descensus* motif as originating in the liturgical use of the Psalm is given by A. CABANISS, *The Harrowing of Hell, Psalm 24 and Pliny the Younger: a Note*, VC 7 (1953), pp. 63–74.

[5] ROC 5 (1910), p. 317.

heaven, that he who is King of glory may enter in, and having ascended, may sit on the right hand of the Father until he make the enemies his footstool, as has been manifest by another Psalm (109.1). For when the rulers of heaven saw him of uncomely and dishonoured appearance, and inglorious, not recognising him, they inquired: 'Who is this King of glory?' And the Holy Spirit, either from the person of his Father, or from his own Person, answers them, 'The Lord of hosts, he is the King of glory'." (Dial. 36.5 f.)

The fact that we have no earlier application of Ps. 23 to the Ascension does not of course imply that this exposition began with St. Justin. The Gnostic *Naassene sermon* uses this Psalm to describe the ascent of the individual soul through the heavenly spheres.[1] An analogous application of Ps. 117 (118).19 f. is to be seen in the description of the Ascension of Elohim in the Gnostic Justin's *Book of Baruch*.[2] The Hebrew *Book of Enoch* says that the angels opposed the ascension of Enoch; this motif would seem to be connected with Christian exposition of Ps. 23, according to which the angels refuse to open the gates to the Ascended Saviour.[3] The cosmological interpretation of the Psalm thus seems to have gained early currency.

In the description of the Ascension in the *Ascension of Isaiah*, the angels' surprise is due to the *descensus* of the Saviour having taken place in secret—a not unimportant theme in the soteriology of the post-Apostolic age.[4] In St. Justin's account, on the other hand, their inability to recognize Christ is due to his having been "of uncomely and dishonoured appearance"—the allusion being to Isa. 53.2 f.[5] It is his human nature which hides Christ's identity from the angels. It is in this respect that Justin parts company with all gnosticizing interpretations of the Ascension, and it is his interpretation which in-

---

[1] Hippolytus, Ref. V.8.18, GCS Hipp. 3.92. Cf. G. WIDENGREN, *Den himmelska intronisationen och dopet*, RoB 5 (1946), pp. 28–60.

[2] Hippolytus, Ref. V.26.15 f. GCS Hipp. 3.129. DANIÉLOU states wrongly that Ps. 23 is quoted here, *Judéo-christianisme*, pp. 284 f. Ps. 117.19 f. seems not to have been much used as a testimony in the early Church. It is quoted in Clem. 48.2 f. and in the prayer of Cyriacus, see WIDENGREN, *Den himmelska intronisationen*, p. 33, n. 1.

[3] 3 Enoch 48 (D). 6–9, ed. ODEBERG, pp. 176 ff. Cf. below, pp. 144 f.

[4] The connexion between the testimonies to *descensus* and *ascensio* appears also in St. Irenaeus, Adv. haer. IV.33.13, ed. HARVEY 2.267 f., where it is said that Christ at his Ascension returned to the place from whence he came; the Ascension is illustrated by Ps. 23, the *descensus* by Ps. 18 (19).7, which is a testimony peculiar to Irenaeus (cf. Dem. 85, where it is combined with Ps. 109.1).

[5] DANIÉLOU, *Bible et liturgie*, p. 412. IDEM, *Judéo-christianisme*, pp. 286 f.

fluences later exposition of Psalm 23. As we shall see in due course, an essential characteristic of the Nicene theology of the 4th century is that it was the human nature of Christ which was exalted at the Ascension.[1]

King, Priest, Prophet

When Christ is called King in Patristic literature, this title is often combined with two others: Priest and Prophet. The three are occasionally found together, but normally only two are used in combination, King and Priest being the most common. The combination King–Priest–Prophet, strangely enough, has been accorded most significance since the Reformation. Calvin placed the entire work of salvation in Christ under the heading *munus triplex*. Via Gerhard and Hafenreffer the concept passed into Lutheran orthodoxy, whence it was taken over in the 19th century by Catholic theology, though it has never been prominent there.[2] But it would be wrong to say that the idea of *munus*

---

[1] See below, Chap. 12.

[2] One reason why we have considered this question in such detail is that it has recently been the subject of a notable debate in Sweden. Prof. Riesenfeld's judgment on the occurrence of the threefold ministry in the NT, of which we have given an account below, has been criticized by Dr. P. E. Persson of Lund, in a book partly designed as a polemic against Uppsala exegesis, *Kyrkans ämbete som Kristusrepresentation*, StThL 20 (1961), pp. 247 ff. Prof. Riesenfeld's views are stated to be an attempt to force NT and patristic material into a mould derived from modern Protestant and Catholic theology; nothing is however said on the subject of the religio-historical background of Riesenfeld's work. Persson is not building on firsthand research. He is himself a specialist on scholastic theology, but has studied neither exegesis or patristic theology in depth. His ideas on the origins of the threefold ministry in the early Church are drawn entirely from two encyclopaedia articles, E. F. K. MÜLLER, *Jesu Christi dreifaches Amt*, in *RE 8* (1900), pp. 733–741, and M. SCHMAUS, *Ämter Christi*, in *LThK 1* (1957), pp. 457–459; all the early Church texts quoted by Persson are taken from these sources. Persson says that the idea of the threefold ministry is extremely rare in the early Church: its earliest support is in Eusebius, and after him it is not found until Peter Chrysologus, who in the course of a sermon expounds the name "Christ" in such a way as to show him to have been anointed to the three offices, Sermo 59, PL 52.363. Persson goes on to say that in St. John Chrysostom we find a saying to the effect that all Christians become prophets, priests and kings by anointing (Ep. 2 ad Cor. Hom. 3.5, PG 61.411) but dismisses it as irrelevant, since Christ is not named as being the holder of the three offices. Despite his use of these texts, he does not seem to have observed that the threefold ministry has to do with the anointing—of Christ as "the Anointed one" and the faithful as participants in his unction. Persson also considers, in line with

triplex was unknown in earlier Church tradition. Calvin derived the concept from his study of early Christian literature: so much is certain.

The trilogy of king, priest and prophet is well known from the Near Eastern cultures, in which the three offices were often united in the person of the sacral king.¹ But it is not altogether clear how this was taken over by the NT and the primitive Church. There is in fact a tendency in post-exilic Judaism to reckon with a double office—king and priest; the prophetic ministry was pushed into the background. This fits in with historical fact: the division of the sacral kingship gave rise, on the one hand to a priestly hierarchy and on the other to a political leadership. This structure is to be seen in Ezek. 44-46, with its separations of the functions of ruler and priesthood; the same is true of Zech. 4.14, where the high priest Joshua and the Davidic Zerubbabel are placed side by side as "the two anointed".²

Under the Hasmoneans, who combined priestly and royal functions, an attempt was made to retain this division of office by a formal proclamation to the effect that the Jewish people was the bearer of political power. The Hasmoneans also avoided, as far as possible, using the title *basileus*.³ Confirmation of the fact that the ancient trichotomy had not lost its actuality is provided by Josephus, who tells us that John Hyrcanus held all three offices.⁴ Later Jewish speculation on the *Urmensch* reveals considerable emphasis placed on Adam's

---

the two articles we have named, that Calvin was responsible for introducing the concept of *munus triples* into dogmatics. The only objection to this is that it is perfectly obvious that Calvin based his doctrine on a prototype found in the early Church.

¹ G. WIDENGREN has shown how the three functions are united in Moses, *The King and the Tree of Life*, UUÅ 1951.4, p. 39, cf. IDEM, *Religionens värld* (2 ed.), p. 267. On the priestly and prophetic functions of the Israelitic king, see IDEM, *Sakrales Königtum im Alten Testament und im Judentum* (1955), pp. 17 ff.

² V. APTOWITZER, *Parteipolitik der Hasmonäerzeit im rabbinischen und pseudoepigraphischen Schrifttum*, VAKMF 7 (1927), pp. 88 ff., 95 ff. R. EPPEL, *Le piétisme juif dans les Testaments des douze Patriarches* (1930), pp. 44 ff., pp. 99 ff. K. G. KUHN, *Die beiden Messias Aarons und Israels*, NTS 1 (1954-55), p. 174. VAN DER WOUDE, *Vorstellungen*, pp. 76 ff. Further references to literature in Y. YADIN, *The Dead Sea Scrolls and the Epistle to the Hebrews*, 4 (1958), p. 49, n. 33.

³ KUHN, *Messias*, pp. 175 ff.

⁴ Josephus Ant. XIII.10.7 (§ 299 f.): "He (John Hyrcanus) was by God valued worthy three of the greatest things: the lordship over the people, the office of the High Priest and the prophecy, for the Divine was with him." Cf. De bell. Iud. 2.8 (68 f.). See also LAGRANGE, *Le judaisme* (1931), pp. 122 ff.

three roles; though the Jewish Haggadah never mentions the three in combination, they are applied to him separately.[1]

An eschatological reflection of the political situation is seen in later Jewish beliefs on the subject of the two Messiahs who were to come in the last days; one was to be a priestly Messiah of the tribe of Levi: the other a king of the tribe of Judah. The priest was however the primary —an idea long known from the *Testament of the Twelve Patriarchs*.[2] Further confirmation is provided in Qumran material. In 1QSa 2.12–20 it is said that the anointed of Aaron and Israel are to take part in the eschatological banquet—a text which makes it extremely likely that the idea of the two anointed ones is present in the *Damascus Document* (Dam. 12.23, 14.19, 19.10) which, although it speaks of only *one* Messiah from Aaron and Israel, probably owes its singular form to the attentions of a Mediaeval copyist.[3] 1QS 9.11 speaks of three eschatological figures: apart from the two Messiahs, from Aaron and Israel, there is also mentioned a prophet who is to come. Here we have an eschatological projection of the old triple office.[4] In addition, Test. Levi 8 describes the coming Messiah as the bearer of three offices.[5]

---

[1] B. MURMELSTEIN, *Adam, Ein Beitrag zur Messiaslehre*, WZKM 35 (1928), p. 271. STAERK, *Erlösererwartung*, pp. 12 ff., 26 ff., 99 ff. The diffusion of this motif is seen also in an Islamic tradition, according to which Muhammed was king, priest and prophet, MURMELSTEIN, *op. cit.*, p. 271, n. 2.

[2] CHARLES' hypothesis (presented in his translation *Apocrypha and Pseudepigrapha* 2, p. 294) that the doctrine of the two Messiahs is the result of a synthesis between two originally different concepts, must be regarded as obsolete. Test. XII Patr. contains no doubt a unitary concept of two Messiahs. The relevant passages are noted by KUHN, *Messias*, p. 171. Cf. also G. R. BEASLEY-MURRAY, *The two Messiahs in the Testaments of the Twelve Patriarchs*, JTS 48 (1947), pp. 1–12. M. BURROWS, *The Messiahs of Aaron and Israel*, AThR 34 (1952), pp. 202–206. L. H. SILBERMANN, *The two Messiahs of the Manual of Discipline*, Vet. Test. 5 (1955), pp. 77–82.

[3] KUHN, *op. cit.*, pp. 173 f.

[4] *The Dead Sea Scrolls* II.2, ed. BURROWS, TREVER & BROWNLEE (1951), plate IX.11: עד בוא נביא ומשיחי אהרון וישראל. See J. T. MILIK, *Une lettre de Siméon bar Kokheba*, RB 60 (1953) pp. 276 ff., 290 f. KUHN, *op. cit.*, pp. 168 ff.

[5] Test. Levi 8.14 f.: Ὁ δὲ τρίτος ἐπικληθήσεται αὐτῷ ὄνομα καινόν, ὅτι βασιλεὺς ἐκ τοῦ Ἰούδα ἀναστήσεται καὶ ποιήσει ἱερατείαν νέαν, κατὰ τὸν τύπον τῶν ἐθνῶν εἰς πάντα τὰ ἔθνη. Ἡ δὲ παρουσία αὐτοῦ ἀγαπητή ἐστιν ὡς προφήτης ὑψίστου ἐκ σπέρματος Ἀβραὰμ τοῦ πατρὸς ἡμῶν. See MURMELSTEIN, *Adam*, p. 273. The hypothesis, presented by BOUSSET, CHARLES and BEER that it is John Hyrcanus who is meant in this text, is rejected by VOLZ, *Eschatologie*, p. 192, and MURMELSTEIN, *op. cit.*, p. 275. It is evidently a wandering motif, which cannot be tied exclusively to one historical person.

For the theology of the NT there is only one Messiah, Jesus Christ. There is occasional mention of the expected Messiah and Prophet (Mk. 8.28 par., Jn. 1.20 f., 7.40 f.), but these concepts do not belong to NT Messianism. In the NT "Messiah" means the Davidic Messiah awaited by political national eschatology. But other Messianic titles are bestowed upon him: Jesus is prophet (Lk. 7.16, Jn. 7.52, 9.17, Acts 3.22, 7.37), high priest (Heb.) and King (see previous chapter), though he is never said to represent the three eschatological saviour-figures in his person.[1]

Christ is said to be King and Priest, or King, Priest and Prophet, very early in primitive Christian literature. It would however be misleading to try and contrast the twofold and threefold Messianic office.[2] The earliest patristic exegetes were not concerned to systematize the contents of the Bible. Instead they wished to prove, with the help of the OT testimonies, that Christ had come and fulfilled the words of the prophets; they made use of the Christological titles as essential keywords. A particular combination of titles can often be explained by the fact that the words were found together in a testimony used by the author in question. This also applies to the terms we are considering here.

The two terms king and priest constantly occur together in connexion with exegesis of Ps. 109 (110); the patristic exegetes represented Christ as heavenly King, sitting at the right hand of the Father, and as everlasting High Priest after the order of Melchizedek.[3] The prophetic office is not mentioned in this context simply because it is not mentioned in the Psalm.

A more deliberate application of the twofold office is to be found in

---

[1] J. JEREMIAS, *Jesus als Weltvollender*, BFTh 33.4 (1930), pp. 7 f. STAERK, *Erlösererwartung*, pp. 26 ff. RIESENFELD, *Jésus Transfiguré*, pp. 71 f. IDEM, *Den senjudiska messianologien såsom bakgrund till kristologien*, in Bidrag till kristologien (1951), pp. 5–22. It is remarkable that PERSSON in his attack upon RIESENFELD (*Kristusrepresentation*, p. 249, n. 4) does not mention these works, where RIESENFELD gives an account of material from comparative religion but only uses the more popular essay *Ämbetet i Nya Testamentet*, in En bok om Kyrkans ämbete (1951), pp. 17–69, where RIESENFELD expounds the threefold office in brief. KUHN seems to underestimate the relation between NT Christology and Jewish Messianism, *Messias*, p. 178.

[2] This tendency appears to some extent in MÜLLER, *Dreifaches Amt*, pp. 733 f.

[3] E.g. St. Justin, Dial. 113.5, 118.1.

Hippolytus' *Commentary on the blessings of Isaac, Jacob and Moses*.[1] According to Hippolytus, Jesus is descended from both the tribe of Judah and the tribe of Levi, in order to be both King and Priest. In other words, we have a concept which is highly reminiscent of that found in Test. XII Patr. and in the Qumran texts—though the two Messiahs are here combined into one person. Hippolytus would seem to have derived his idea from some such source. Mariès has pointed out that on two occasions Hippolytus uses the verb εὑρίσκομεν twice in this context (52.8 and 72.8); this indicates that it was his own idea, and uncommon in contemporary Christian exegesis.[2] Thus when we find the same concept in St. Ambrose[3] and St. Epiphanius,[4] we may regard it as derived from Hippolytus.

A third occurrence of the twofold office is in Eusebius (HE I.3.1–5), a chapter which also contains what is perhaps the clearest reference to the threefold office in the whole of the literature of the early Church (see below). This parallel occurrence of twofold and threefold office is due neither to inconsistency nor competition. The twofold aspect is based on Eusebius' exposition of the two names Jesus and Christ, in which Jesus is said to refer back to Joshua and Christ to Aaron. Thus Moses gave the people's leader and their high priest the two names of the Saviour. Note, however, that Eusebius does not go so far as to call Joshua king, though he comes very near doing so when he says that the name of Joshua is more excellent than a royal diadem. A clearer presentation of Joshua and Aaron as the patterns of Christ's royal and priestly offices is to be found in St. Cyril of Jerusalem,[5] who develops Eusebius' theme.

As will be clear from this, the idea of the double office of Christ appears in a number of fixed combinations, dependent upon OT exegesis or (in Hippolytus' case) of later Jewish ideas. The threefold office also proves to be incorporated into similar contexts. When the early

---

[1] PO 27.1–2 (1954), pp. 52.6–9, 72.8–11, 126 f., 143–145. L. Mariès, *Le Messie issu de Lévi chez Hippolyte de Rome*, Mélange Lebreton, RSR 39 (1951), pp. 381–396. When this essay was published, the new edition had not yet appeared, and Mariès therefore refers to older editions; therefore his references are different from those given here. Cf. also idem, *Hippolyte de Rome, Sur les bénédictions d'Isaac, de Jacob et de Moïse* (1935).

[2] Idem, *Le Messie*, pp. 395 f.

[3] Exp. on Lk. 3.13, CSEL 32.4, 107 f.

[4] Haer. LXXVII 13.5, GCS Epiph. 3.464.

[5] Cat. 10.11, PG 33.676. Daniélou, *Sacramentum futuri*, pp. 215 f.

Church calls Christ King, Priest and Prophet, this is not from any desire for systematization, but an exposition of the name of Christ. The common denominator of all three categories in the thought of the Fathers is that all are anointed, χριστοί. (Cf. "the anointed of Aaron and Israel" in the Qumran texts.) When the Lord is called χριστός this implies that he has been fully anointed, receiving that which in the old Covenant was divided among the king, the priest and the prophet.[1] With the exception of the Syriac *Treasure Cave* (see below), which nevertheless retains the same background of the idea of the anointing, the threefold office is encountered in connexion with Christ, *only* in this context.

St. Justin was the first to bring together the three offices (Dial. 86–87).[2] He uses them as key-words for proof-texts demonstrating, on the one hand, Christ's perfect anointing and, on the other, the cessation of the line of Israelite office-bearers at the coming of Christ. Both purposes recur in later literature.

In Dial. 86.2–4 Justin proceeds via the key-word χρίειν from the narrative of Jacob pouring oil over the stone at Bethel to Ps. 45.7–8, "Therefore God, thy God, hath anointed thee with the oil of gladness above thy fellows." This is among the most common testimonies, since it contains the key-words χρίειν and θεός. Justin goes on to say that all anointing, whether with olive oil or with myrrh, or with a mixture of balsam, points to Christ. All kings and all anointed ones have their names from him, just as he has his names (τρόποι)—βασιλεύς, χριστός, ἱερεύς and ἄγγελος—from the Father. The leading key-word is χριστός; the other three should therefore be different categories of χριστοί. It is common knowledge that all kings and priests are anointed. But what are the implications of Christ's anointing as ἄγγελος?

The description of Christ as "angel" is one of the most discussed of the early Church's Christological titles.[3] St. Justin's use of the word

---

[1] On the anointing of Christ, see RIESENFELD, *Jésus Transfiguré*, pp. 75 f. I. DE LA POTTERIE, *L'Onction du Christ*, NRTh 90 (1958), pp. 225–252.

[2] Cf. Dial. 96.1, where Christ is called ἱερεύς, βασιλεύς and χριστός, and the *Dialogue between Athanasius and Zacchaeus*, ch. 46, Anecdota Oxon. 8, p. 31, where he is called ἄρχων, βασιλεύς, χριστός, ἱερεύς and προφήτης; *ibid.*, ch. 58 (p. 36), with the catch-words χριστός, βασιλεύς and ἱερεύς. Cf. RIESENFELD, *Ambetet*, p. 27. LECLERQ, *Royauté*, p. 224.

[3] J. MICHL, art. *Engel* (IV, christlich), RAC 5 (1960–), pp. 148 ff. (with extensive references to literature). The most important special work on this subject is J. BARBEL, *Christos Angelos* (1941). M. WERNER's theory that Christ in the primitive

is, however, fairly straightforward. He uses it to refer, not to the nature of Christ, but to one of his functions. He is called ἄγγελος because he is the messenger of God—ἄγγελος thus retaining its original meaning.

When Justin calls Christ ἄγγελος, he is referring in general to all the OT manifestations of the Logos. It was as ἄγγελος that the Logos came to visit Abraham in Mamre (Dial. 56), wrestled with Jacob (Dial. 58.10) and revealed himself to Moses in the burning bush (Dial. 60.4). For Justin the Logos is identical with the δύναμις of God, and the concepts δύναμις and ἄγγελος are coextensive. In this respect he is dependent upon Philo or views similar to those of Philo.[1]

In Apol. 63.5 the Logos is called ἄγγελος and ἀπόστολος; the two terms are synonymous expressions of the Logos' function as God's *shaliach*: his messenger who transmits the Divine revelation to men:

"He is called ἄγγελος and ἀπόστολος, for he announces (ἀπαγγέλλει) what is necessary to know, and is sent forth (ἀποστέλλεται) to announce what is revealed (ἀγγέλλεται), as also our Lord himself said: 'He who hears me hears him who sent me.'" (Lk. 10.16).[2]

ἄγγελος and ἀπόστολος are also combined in St. Justin's writings to refer to men; Joshua and the prophets are given this epithet in Dial. 75.1–3. According to Justin the Lord was referring to Joshua when he said to Moses: Ἀποστέλλω τὸν ἄγγελόν μου πρὸ προσώπου σου (Ex. 20.22, 23.20 f.). The prophets are also called ἄγγελοι and ἀπόστολοι (ὅτι δὲ καὶ ἄγγελοι καὶ ἀπόστολοι τοῦ Θεοῦ λέγοντος οἱ ἀγγέλλειν τὰ παρ' αὐτοῦ ἀποστελλόμενοι προφῆται, ἐν τῷ Ἡσαΐᾳ δεδήλωται); a further prooftext here is Isa. 6.8: Ἀπόστειλόν με. He goes on to say that it is obvious to all that Joshua became a great prophet.[3]

These texts are instructive in a number of ways. First, it is clear that Justin used the word ἄγγελος to mean, not primarily "angel" but "messenger"; similarly ἀπόστολος can have the general meaning "sent", and thus refer to the Logos (cf. Heb. 3.1). The triad of ἄγγελος–ἀπόστο-

---

Church was believed to be an angel, *Entstehung des christlichen Dogmas*, p. 307, has been convincingly refuted by MICHAELIS, *Engelchristologie*, passim.

[1] BARBEL, *Christos Angelos*, pp. 50 ff. MICHAELIS, *Engelchristologie*, pp. 146 f., 166 f. and n. 290.

[2] Cf. also Apol. 12.9, 63.14. On the concept of Christ as apostle, cf. also J. GLAZIK, *Jesus — Apostel und Hohenpriester*, ZMR 44 (1960), pp. 87–98, 175–183.

[3] Cf. Dial. 113.1, where Joshua according to Num. 13.17 is called ἀποσταλεῖς (here = "reconnoitrer"). Also Tertullian calls Joshua *angelus* and *propheta*, Adv. Marc. III.16.5, CCL 1.529, cf. Adv. Jud. 9.23, CCL 2.1371 f.

λος–προφήτης in Dial. 75 also shows that we are dealing with the prophetic functions: the proof-text Ex. 23.20 f., about Joshua as ἄγγελος and ἀπόστολος leads to the conclusion that Joshua, too, is a prophet. The office bestowed upon Christ as ἄγγελος in Dial. 86 must therefore be the prophetic office: it is clear from its combination with kings and priests that we are in fact dealing with an office.

But there is a further difficulty. Dial. 86.4 brings together ἄγγελος and χρίειν in such a way as to make it necessary to presuppose a proof-text in which Justin found the two key-words combined. No such proof-text has been preserved in any of Justin's writings. This need not imply, however, that Justin did not know of any such text.

A proof-text frequently used in the early Church, but which is seldom quoted by Justin, is Isa. 61.1–2. It is one of the earliest Christian testimonies, and according to Lk. 4.18 was used by Jesus himself in the synagogue at Nazareth: πνεῦμα κυρίου ἐπ' ἐμέ, οὗ εἵνεκεν ἔχρισέν με, εὐαγγελίσασθαι πτωχοῖς ἀπέσταλκέν με. This text is also quoted in Barn. 14.9. In Justin it is found only in the form of an allusion in Dial. 12.2, but there is no doubt that Justin, with his wide knowledge of the Christian *testimonia* tradition, was acquainted with it.

The testimony is of extreme importance in the primitive Church, since it links the Spirit with the anointing. This is the fundamental proof of Jesus' Messiahship, despite the fact that he never received any form of earthly unction.[1] The presence of the Holy Spirit, bestowed on Christ at his baptism, is sufficient of itself. Why, then, was Christ, according to Isa. 61.1, anointed with the Spirit? He was sent (ἀπέσταλκεν) in order to proclaim the Gospel (εὐαγγελίσασθαι). These two verbs contain two key-words, ἀπόστολος and ἄγγελος, which Justin was in the habit of using synonymously and in combination of Christ and the prophets. He is quite capable of taking a verb, extracting the corresponding noun, and using this as key-word; so much is clear from the above examples from Apol. 63.5 and Dial. 75.1–3.

Christ's anointing as ἄγγελος differed in character from that given a king or priest. He was anointed in order to be able to *proclaim*. The unction of the Spirit is thus connected here with the prophetic commission. This stands out with even more clarity when we turn to the following chapter (87.1–6), which has to do with the Spirit received by Christ at his baptism. This is not however directly linked with the

---

[1] M.-A. CHEVALLIER, *L'Esprit et le Messie dans le bas-judaïsme et le Nouveau Testament*, RHPhS 49 (1958), pp. 74 ff.

previous exposition of the title χριστός. Between the two is found a series of quotations having ῥάβδος as key-word; furthermore the keyword χριστός is entirely missing from Chap. 87. But the identification of the Spirit and the anointing is so common that it must be taken for granted here that it is this which is intended.[1]

In 87.1-2 Trypho asks how the doctrine of the pre-existence of Christ can be reconciled with the Messianic saying in Isa. 11.1-3, to the effect that the Messiah must be invested with the Spirit.[2] How can he have been pre-existent as God, if he stood in need of the power of the Holy Spirit? Justin answers (86.3-6) that the Spirit came upon Christ (at his baptism) not because he needed it, but in order that it should rest upon him and find its goal in him, so that there should be no more prophets in Israel.[3] He goes on to name those who were endowed with the gifts of the prophetic Spirit, as listed in Isa. 11.2: Solomon was given the Spirit of wisdom, Daniel the Spirit of understanding and counsel, Moses the Spirit of might and devotion, Elijah the Spirit of the fear of the Lord and Isaiah the Spirit of knowledge. The gifts of the Spirit, which had been divided among a number of persons, now came to rest—i.e. ceased—on the coming of the fulfiller; henceforth they are given through Christ to the faithful. After his Ascension Christ gave the Spirit to the Church, for confirmation of which Justin turns to Joel 2.28 f.: "And it shall come to pass afterward, that I will pour out my Spirit on all flesh; and your sons and your daughters shall prophesy ..."

The unction of the Spirit is here closely connected with the gift of prophecy.[4] It is thus natural that when Christ receives the fulness of the Spirit, there should arise no new prophet in Israel, but that the Spirit of prophecy should pass to the Church.

The positive aspect—that Christ received the Spirit of prophecy—

---

[1] *Ibid.*, p. 80. B. WELTE, *Die postbaptismale Salbung* (1939), p. 19.

[2] On Isa. 11.1-3 as a Messianic text in Judaism, see K. SCHLÜTZ, *Isaias 11.2*, Alttest. Abh. 11.4 (1932). CHEVALLIER, *l'Esprit*, *passim* (references to literature, p. 3). LÖVESTAM, *Son and Saviour*, pp. 59 f. and 66.

[3] The Jewish and early Christian conception that the prophetic Spirit wanders from one prophet to another, finally finding his goal in the Messiah, is clearly expressed in a fragment from the *Gospel of the Hebrews*, preserved in St. Jerome, Comm. on Isa. 11.2. See SCHLÜTZ, *op. cit.*, pp. 20 ff., 43 ff. and *passim*. STAERK, *Erlösererwartung*, pp. 105 ff. Cf. also 1 Pet. 1.10 f., St. Justin, Dial. 49.

[4] The prophetic Spirit is mentioned by St. Justin in Apol. 6. Cf. ROBINSON in his translation of St. Irenaeus' *Demonstration*, p. 24 ff.

is linked in Dial. 87 with the negative—that there is to be no new prophet in Israel. This latter aspect occurs more fully in Dial. 52, where the three offices of king, priest and prophet are directly related to one another. Justin is expounding (52.2) the blessing pronounced by Jacob over Judah (Gen. 49.10)—a common proof-text in anti-Jewish polemic—[1]and says (52.3-4):

"That in your nation there failed neither prophet (προφήτης) nor ruler (ἄρχων) from the time when it began until the time when this Jesus Christ appeared and suffered, you do not venture fearlessly to assert, nor need you prove it. For Herod, after whose reign he suffered, is called by you a high priest in spite of your saying that he was an Ashkelonite. Thus there was somebody who presented offerings according to the law of Moses and who observed the other legal ceremonies. Prophets existed in an unbroken succession until John; when your nation was carried captive to Babylon, when the land was ravaged by war and the sacred vessels carried off, there never failed to be a prophet, who was lord (κύριος) and leader (ἡγεμών) and ruler (ἄρχων) over your people. For the Spirit which was in the prophets also anointed and inaugurated kings (βασιλεῖς) for you. But since Jesus, our Anointed one (Χριστός) appeared in your nation and suffered death, there has not been and is no prophet, nay, you are no longer under your own king."

Justin is here attacking a common Jewish idea to the effect that the holy oil disappeared in Josiah's day, together with the Temple vessels and the Ark, and that the line of anointed office-bearers thus ceased long before Christ's coming.[2] Against this Justin quotes an unbroken line of office-bearers, until the day when Christ came to unite their functions in his own person. The priestly office was preserved until Herod (the Great); similarly there were prophets and kings up to the time of Christ. Then they disappeared, because the Spirit passed to Christ.[3]

---

[1] See above, p. 96 f.
[2] Horajoth 11 b ff., in *Mechilta*, ed. WINTER & WÜNSCHE (1909), p. 164. See G. A. BARTON & K. KOHLER, art. *Anointing*, JE 1 (1901), pp. 611-613. APTOWITZER, *Parteipolitik*, pp. 1 ff., 192, n. 2. Cf. Eusebius, HE I.6.7 ff., GCS Eus. 2.1.50 ff., according to which the fact that Herod was *not* a Jew and *not* a high priest is seen as the fulfilment of Gen. 49.10.
[3] Cf. also Dial. 141.3, where David is called μέγας βασιλεὺς καὶ χριστὸς καὶ προφήτης, viz. typical Christological key-words, which are evidently an allusion to Christ as the consummator of the functions. This is not contradicted by the fact that this passage deals with the sin of David: what David has prefigured in an imperfect way, appears as fulness in Christ. That David was a prophet is a fairly

A similar exposition is found in Irenaeus, who, apart from quoting Ps. 44 (45).7–8 and Isa. 11.1–3—texts taken up by Justin—also has direct quotations of Isa. 61.1. In Dem. 47 he illustrates the relationship between Father and Son from Ps. 44 (45).7–8, and then proceeds with:

"For this means that the Son, being God, receives from the Father, that is, from God, the throne of the everlasting kingdom, and the oil of anointing above his fellows. And 'oil of anointing' is the Spirit, through which he is the Anointed, and 'his fellows' are the prophets and the just and the Apostles, and all who receive fellowship of his kingdom, that is his disciples."

There follows an exposition of Ps. 109 (110).1–4 in which Christ is represented as King and Priest (Chap. 48); in Chap. 49 he takes up the question of the Kingship of Christ on the basis of the χριστός quotation in Isa. 45.1. Here, too, no cleavage is made between the offices of king, priest and prophet, though the priestly office is linked with the anointing.

The idea of Christ's anointing as Prophet is also found in Adv. haer. III.9.3:

"The Word of God, who is the Saviour of all and the ruler of heaven and earth, is Jesus ... he who took upon him flesh and was anointed by the Father with Spirit and was made Jesus Christ, as Esaias also says: ... (Isa. 11.1–4). And again Esaias, pointing out beforehand his unction and the reason why he was anointed, says: ... (Isa. 61.1). For because the Word of God was man of the root of Jesse and the Son of Abraham, the Spirit of God rested upon him, and he was anointed to preach the Gospel to the humble ... For the Spirit of God descended upon him, the Spirit of him who had promised by the prophets to anoint him."[1]

The same combination of Isa. 11 and 61 occurs in Adv. haer. III.17.1. Irenaeus, polemizing against the Gnostic doctrine that Christ descended to the man Jesus at his baptism, states that it was the Spirit, in the shape of a dove, who came upon Jesus: the same Spirit mentioned in Isa. 11.2 and 61.1 (both verses are quoted). It is the same Spirit about which is said, "it is not you who speak, but the Spirit of your Father speaking through you" (Matt. 10.20). There follows an allusion to Joel 2.29: Christ promised, through the prophets, that in the last days he would pour out his Spirit over his servants.[2]

---

common motif, connected with the prophetic character attributed to the Psalms, of which David was believed to be the author. Cf. Dial. 87.4.

[1] ed. HARVEY 2.32 f.
[2] ed. HARVEY 2.92.

This anti-Jewish polemic takes on a special form in the pseudo-Clementine *Recognitiones*, the dating of which is most uncertain. It seems likely, however, that they reproduce ideas which were current in certain circles ca. 200 A.D. or earlier.[1] In Rec. 1.45 we read that χριστός is the name given by the Jews to a king: like the Persian *Arsaces*, the Roman *Caesar* and the Egyptian *Pharaoh*. The following exposition tells how Christ was anointed with oil from the tree of life.[2]

Of particular interest to us is the continuation, in Chaps. 46 and 48, which tells how Aaron was anointed king, and how others anointed with the same oil became kings, priests and prophets. "For who is of more honour than a prophet, of more glory than a priest, more exalted than a king?" The oil disappeared on the coming of Christ, and with it the priestly, the prophetic and the kingly offices.[3]

One of the most concrete expressions of the concept of the threefold office is to be found in the Syriac *Treasure Cave*, which in its present form dates back to the 6th century, but which contains considerably older traditions. The theme which runs through the work is the tomb of Adam, situated at the centre of the world, and over which the Cross of Christ was later raised. Adam and Christ are described in the same categories; the parallelism between the two, which approaches identification, is one of the most prominent characteristics of the book.[4] The three offices are not directly linked with the anointing, but note that Christ is called Messiah (Syr. *měshīḥā*).

The document begins by describing how God, after creating Adam, instals him in his high office:

"And the angels and the powers heard the voice of God, when he said to him, 'Adam! I make thee now king, priest and prophet, as lord, head and leader for all created beings and creatures. All things shall serve thee and be thine own; I gave thee dominion over all things I have created.' When the angels heard this word, they knelt and did obeisance to him." (2.22–25.)

"Since Adam was now priest, king and prophet, God took him up to Paradise, that he might serve as priest in Eden, the holy Church." (4.1.)

---

[1] The problem of the *Pseudo-Clementines* is treated below, Chap. 10.

[2] We have here an identification of Christ with Adam, typical for PsC and stemming from certain Jewish speculations. See SCHOEPS, *Theologie*, pp. 104 ff. (from whose opinions we however differ on vital points). An analogous conception is found in the Syriac *Treasure Cave* (see below).

[3] MURMELSTEIN, *Adam*, pp. 268 ff. STAERK, *Erlösererwartung*, pp. 12 ff., 99 ff.

[4] *Die Schatzhöhle*, ed. C. BEZOLD, 1–2 (1883–88). German translation also in *Altjüdisches Schrifttum ausserhalb der Bibel*, ed. P. RIESSLER (1928), pp. 942 ff.

From Adam the threefold office passed to the Jewish people. This is in all probability an echo of the earlier idea, that the Spirit passed from Adam to the prophets, and thence to Christ. The *Treasure Cave* here links up with anti-Jewish polemic, according to which the Jews lost their offices at the coming of Christ:

"Three gifts, than which there is none costlier, were once bestowed upon the Jews: the kingship, the priesthood and the office of prophet; the office of prophet through Moses, the priesthood through Aaron and the kingship through David. These three gifts, which the families and tribes of the Israelites used for many years, were taken away from them in one day. They were deprived of these three things and were separated from them: the office of prophet by the Cross, the priesthood by the tearing of the garment and the kingship by the crown of thorns. (51.13–17.)

"On a Friday the kingship, the priesthood and the office of prophet were given to Adam, and on a Friday the kingship, the priesthood and the office of prophet were taken from the Jews." (48.29.)

Here, too, there are a number of variations in the triad. In 52.17–19 we read that before Christ, the Jews had the priesthood, the kingship and the Paschal lamb, but these three were taken from them by the crucifixion (with a reference to Dan. 9.26, which seems here to be interpreted as referring to the Messiah instead of the oil). The gifts of the Magi to Jesus are here, as in all older exegesis, interpreted symbolically (45.12–15): the gold is the mark of the king, the myrrh the healer and the incense the priest.[1] The parallel between Adam and Christ is expressed in the coming of the sons of Noah with gold, incense and myrrh to the tomb of Adam (17.6).

We thus find that in the early Church there was a tradition according to which Christ had been anointed as the perfect King, Priest and Prophet when the Spirit came upon him at his baptism. The tradition was connected with proof-texts having χριστός as key-word, particularly Ps. 44 (45).7–8, Isa. 61.1–2 and occasionally Isa. 11.1–3, which did not have the key-word χριστός but which was early associated with the baptism of Christ.[2] The coming of Christ ended the existence of the three OT offices; instead the Spirit was bestowed upon the Church, Joel 2.28–29 being the testimony by which this was confirmed. The anointing given to the faithful is here described in the categories of

---

[1] For the allegorical interpretation of the gifts, see further below, p. 220, n. 3.
[2] CHEVALLIER, *L'Esprit*, pp. 57 ff.

the prophetic unction, but the kingly and priestly aspects are not mentioned (cf. βασίλειον ἱεράτευμα in 1 Pet. 2.9).

Eusebius' description of Christ as King, Priest and Prophet in HE I.3 and Dem. ev. IV.15 is the best-known example of this in the early Church, and for this reason it is easy to imagine Eusebius to have been responsible for introducing the idea.[1] But as we shall see, Eusebius took over a largely traditional material, and followed the lines laid down *inter alia* in St. Justin's *Dialogue* and St. Irenaeus' *Demonstratio*.

The purpose of HE I.3 is to show why the Lord is called Jesus and Christ; although the name Jesus is mentioned only in 1–5, the consideration of the name Christ takes up the rest of the chapter.[2] According to Eusebius, kings, priests and prophets have one thing in common: that they have been anointed, χριστοί. That the Lord is χριστός therefore implies that he fulfils the three OT offices in his own person:

"All these (types) have reference to the true Christ, the divinely inspired and heavenly Word, who is the only high priest of all, and the only King of every creature, and the Father's only supreme prophet of prophets." (I.3.8.)

Christ had a greater power of virtue than any of the office-bearers of the OT (I.3.9), but as his dignity was derived, not from man, but from the Father (I.3.11), he had greater right than these to be called χριστός (I.3.2). At the end of the chapter there is a summing-up of the ideas expounded, in these words (I.3.19):

"It is a great and convincing proof of his incorporeal and divine unction that he alone of all those who have ever existed is even to the present day called Christ by all men throughout the world ... and even to this day is honoured as a King by his followers throughout the world, and is admired as more than a prophet, and is glorified as the true and only high priest of God."

Eusebius does not on this occasion support his exposition of the threefold office by quoting any OT texts. He refers, when dealing with χριστός as high priestly title, to the consecration by Moses of Aaron, through anointing (Ex. 29.7, 40.13, 15, 16. Cf. that the priest is called χριστός in Lev. 4.3, 5, 16 LXX). The anointing of kings and prophets

---

[1] In his article *Dreifaches Amt*, MÜLLER does not mention any existence of this idea in the early Church before Eusebius.

[2] GCS Eus. 2.1.28 ff. For the earlier exegesis of the name Jesus, see above, pp. 66 f.

is mentioned without naming any concrete case of the rite in question (3.7–8). The χριστός quotations are instead brought together in two blocks: as proof of the Jews' rejection and the call of the Gentiles (3.6) and to stress that anointing implies participation in the Divinity of the Father (3.13 f.). Further, there follows in 3.16–18 a passage in which Ps. 109 (110) is used as a testimony that Christ is King and Priest without being anointed (by the Jews).

Of the four χριστός quotations, Isa. 61.1 (3.13) and Ps. 44 (45).7–8 (3.14) are identical with those used by Justin and Irenaeus. But the two others also belong to the older tradition. Lam. 4.20 (3.6) is to be found as a proof-text as far back as Justin and Irenaeus,[1] and Ps. 2.2 had been interpreted Messianically in late Judaism, in which, incidentally, it often appears linked with Isa. 11.1–3.[2]

The same idea, though in a more developed form, is to be found in Eusebius, Dem. ev. IV.15,[3] where it is supported by quotations of Ps. 44 (45).7–8 (IV.15.15, 48, 55–64) and Ps. 109 (110) (IV.15.32–46). Eusebius stresses, in line with earlier anti-Jewish apologetics, that anointing with oil is only of secondary importance (15.21–28). Abraham, Isaac and Jacob were prophets, although they had not been anointed with oil; as proof of this Eusebius quotes Ps. 104 (105).15 and, in Abraham's case, Gen. 20.7. In the same way Isaiah calls Christ "prophet", though his anointing was not with oil, but with the Father's uncreated Divinity (15.28 f.) Isa. 61.1 is cited in support (also quoted for the same purpose in 15.43). Eusebius thus accepts the older tradition, that Isa. 61.1 deals with the anointing of a prophet.

There is a further context in which the triad of king, priest and prophet occurs in the early Church: in the prayer of consecration of oil, which appears first in Hippolytus' *Apostolic Tradition*, but which Segelberg has shown to have been used in many parts of the early Church.[4]

The passage in question reads as follows in the Latin text of the *Apostolic Tradition*:

Ut oleum hoc sanctificans das Ds sanitatem utentibus et percipien-

---

[1] DANIÉLOU, *Christos Kyrios*, pp. 338 ff.
[2] CHEVALLIER, *L'Esprit*, pp. 3 ff. and *passim*.
[3] GCS Eus. 6.173 ff.
[4] E. SEGELBERG, *Oleum sanctum*, unprinted diss., Uppsala 1952, pp. 72–107.

tibus, unde unxcisti reges sacerdotes et profetas, sic et omnibus gustantibus confortationem et sanitatem utentibus illud praebent.[1]

Segelberg has shown that the Greek prototype of this prayer is preserved in a manuscript from the Monastery of Sinai,[2] and that this was also the prototype of two Coptic prayers of consecration of oil[3] and an Armenian baptismal prayer.[4] It appears likely, on a basis of Segelberg's researches, that kings, priests and prophets were also mentioned in the prototype of a corresponding prayer in *Testamentum Domini*.[5] A prayer from the Syro-Jacobite rite,[6] and another from the Maronitic rite contain the same formula in a number of variations.

Later forms, such as the prayers for the benedictions of the chrism and of the extreme unction in the *Gelasian* and the *Gregorian Sacramentaries* (still used in the *Pontificale Romanum*) go back to the same source.[7] The same applies to the prayers for the benediction of the myron in the Byzantine[8] and Syro-Jacobite[9] rites.

Segelberg's list of office-bearers' names in the various formulae shows, apart from kings, priests and prophets, high priests (ἀρχιερεῖς) and martyrs (μάρτυρες). Both these categories are however secondary interpolations into the prayer. It is interesting to note that martyrs are called "anointed"—which evidently has to do with the growing use of *oleum martyrum*.[10] Kings are, surprisingly enough, missing from

---

[1] Ap. Trad. V.2, ed. DIX (1937), p. 10. SEGELBERG, *op. cit.*, p. 76. DIX has here two conjectures in the Latin text, which do not however seem necessary.

[2] The text is published in Π. ΤΡΕΜΠΕΛΑΣ, Μικρὸν εὐχολόγιον 1 (1950), p. 180. SEGELBERG, *op. cit.*, pp. 73 and 82.

[3] *Ibid.*, pp. 73 and 82 ff.

[4] *Ibid.*, pp. 74 and 88 f. An English translation of the text is published in *Rituale Armenorum*, ed. F. C. CONYBEARE (1905), p. 93.

[5] SEGELBERG, *op. cit.*, pp. 87 f.

[6] A Latin translation in *Ritus Orientalium*, ed. DENZINGER (1863–64), t. 2, p. 552.

[7] *Ibid.* 1, p. 341.

[8] For the Gelasian prayer, see *Liber Sacramentorum Romanae Aeclesiae ordinis anni circuli*, ed. L. C. MOHLBERG, Rer. eccl. doc. ser. maior, fontes 4 (1960), p. 61. The Gregorian prayer, see the *Gregorian Sacramentary*, ed. WILSON (1915), pp. 49 f. SEGELBERG, *op. cit.*, pp. 79 f.

[9] ΤΡΕΜΠΕΛΑΣ, Μικρὸν εὐχολόγιον 1, p. 383. SEGELBERG, *op. cit.*, pp. 93 f.

[10] The text in DENZINGER, *Ritus orientalium* 2, p. 534. SEGELBERG, *op. cit.*, p. 95.

[11] *Ibid.*, pp. 100 and 112. For the oil of the martyrs, see J. LASSUS, *Sanctuaires chrétiens de Syrie*, Inst. franc. d'arch. de Beyrouth, Bibl. arch. et hist. 42 (1944), p. 164.

an Ethiopic and a Coptic prayer, which may be due to nationalist opposition to Byzantine rule.[1]

The early occurrence and wide currency of this prayer suggests that the first prototype should be dated to the 2nd century at the very latest.[2] We therefore find that the Christian use of holy oil was from the very first linked with the concept of the use of oil in the old Covenant to anoint kings, priests and prophets.

Even though it is nowhere stated in this prayer that *Christ* is King, Priest and Prophet, it is assumed that such is the case. The Christian use of oil is based in the last resort on the fact that Jesus is Χριστός. The examples, *typoi*, of the old Covenant, whether kings, priests or prophets, reach their fulfilment in Christ; from him the *typoi* of the OT are carried on in renewed, sacramental form. The path from OT *typos* to Christian Sacrament always leads, in early Church theology, via Christ: it never goes direct.[3]

Segelberg considers the prayer to have been first used in connexion with the benediction of the chrism.[4] Since the belief of the early Church was that in the anointing of baptism the Christian came to participate in that fulness of the Spirit given to Christ at his baptism, there can be no question as to the Christological meaning of the prayer. It agrees in every way with the typological scheme we have observed in the writings of Justin, Irenaeus and Eusebius.

---

[1] SEGELBERG, *op. cit.*, p. 101.
[2] *Ibid.*, p. 102.
[3] Cf. the text by St. John Chrysostom, quoted above, p. 106, n. 2.
[4] SEGELBERG, *op. cit.*, p. 103.

4. THE APOCALYPTIC LITERATURE

The Jewish Background

We have seen in what has gone before that the NT's description of Christ as *kyrios* and *basileus* is intimately connected with those eschatological expectations which the early Church believed to have been fulfilled in him. He is called King and Lord because the Christian Church believed him to have been the eschatological King appointed by God to come on the clouds of heaven and judge mankind. His coming and his work of salvation were believed to have fulfilled the Messianic prophecies of the OT. But what the NT has to say on the subject of the Kingship of Christ is not dependent only upon the OT: the apocalyptic ideas of late Judaism, which we know from Ezek. and Dan., but which reach their climax in post-canonical Jewish apocalyptic, were also linked in their entirety with Jesus. In order to obtain a clear picture of the image of Christ the King held by the primitive Church we must therefore sketch in the background of Jewish apocalyptic literature.[1]

An important role is played in this literature by imagery drawn from the Oriental court. God is represented as a King, sitting upon his throne and surrounded by a court of angels, who are prepared to carry out his least command. The righteous, who are taken up to glory, are also given royal attributes: garments, wreaths, sceptres.[2] The saviour-figures which appear in Jewish apocalyptic literature (of whom more below) are given the same kind of attribute and are installed in their high office in forms directly reminiscent of a royal enthronement.

The reason for this is to be sought mainly in the fact that Jewish eschatology harks back to the royal ideal of the Near East, with its concentration upon the role of the king in the performance of the cult;

---

[1] On the relation between Jewish and Christian Apocalyptics, see H. H. ROWLEY, *The Relevance of Apocalyptic*, 2nd ed. (1947). Cf. IDEM, *Jewish Apocalyptics and the Dead Sea Scrolls* (1957).

[2] See below, pp. 147 ff.

in the OT this complex of ideas is seen most clearly in the Psalter.¹ During the pre-exilic period the Israelite king had a vital cultic function, primarily centred upon his enthronement at the seasonal festivals of the Israelites. The king is called "God", not least in the Psalms (Ps. 44(45). 7 f.); he is called "Son of God" (Ps. 2.7) and "Lord" (Ps. 109 (110).1) —titles taken over by the Christian Church and applied to Christ.

The Palestinian Judaism of post-exilic times experienced a thorough disintegration of the cultic scheme which had characterized Israelite religion. The cultic texts of the OT, which had earlier referred to the king, had little or no significance in the new situation of the Jewish people, and were reinterpreted eschatologically.² One result of the disintegration of the cult was that the act of salvation, previously represented in the cult of the seasonal festivals, became transferred to the eschatological level, to the coming judgment of the world; the purely cultic elements became linked with the heavenly cult before the throne of God. This in turn resulted in increased interest in cosmology and angelology.

Both in the heavenly liturgy—as depicted in the apocalyptic writings —and in the final eschatological judgment the role previously occupied by the king is transferred to a heavenly saviour-figure, who at the end of time will return mankind to its paradisal state. The "Son of Man" and Messianic ideas of late Judaism thus stand in intimate connexion with an earlier royal ideology.³ These eschatological expectations also

---

[1] The author here follows the concept of the Sacral Kingship in Israel and its relation to Jewish eschatology which has been presented especially by Scandinavian scholars. See *inter alia:* S. MOWINCKEL, *Kongesalmerne i det Gamle Testamente* (1916). IDEM, *Tronstigningssalmerne og Jahves tronstigningsfest*, NTT 18 (1917), pp. 13–29. IDEM, *Psalmenstudien* 2. H. SCHMIDT, *Die Thronfahrt Jahves am Fest der Jahreswende im alten Israel* SGVS 122 (1927). G. WIDENGREN, *Psalm 110*, IDEM, *Religionens värld*. IDEM, *Sakrales Königtum*. I. ENGNELL, *Studies*. IDEM, *Gamla Testamentet* 1 (1945) pp. 135–147. IDEM, art. *Gamla Testamentets religion*, SBU 1 col. 677 ff. IDEM, *Konung, kungadöme, ibid.* col. 1223 f. IDEM, *Messias* (GT), SBU 2, col. 245–263. IDEM, *Nyårsfester, ibid.*, col. 499. IDEM, *Psaltaren, ibid.*, col. 814 ff. RIESENFELD, *Jésus Transfiguré*, pp. 9 ff. (with extensive references to literature). H. RINGGREN, *König und Messias*, ZAW 64 (1952), pp. 120–147. AHLSTRÖM, *Psalm 89*.

[2] The transformation from a cultic to an eschatological aspect was first presented by MOWINCKEL, *Psalmenstudien* 2, pp. 89–145, 228–314. Cf. also RIESENFELD *op. cit.*, pp. 9 ff. I. ENGNELL, art. *Yttersta dagen*. (GT), SBU 2, col. 1628–1632.

[3] RIESENFELD, *op. cit.*, pp. 54 ff. 223 ff. ENGNELL, *Messias*, p. 261. IDEM, art. *Människosonen*, SBU 2, pp. 399–403.

resulted in the growth of a politically nationalist Messianism. This seems however to have been of comparatively little significance for Christianity, the basic principles of which were entirely non-political.[1]

The central action of the pre-exilic Israelite seasonal festivals, the enthronement of the king, was regarded simultaneously as being the enthronement of Yahweh. When the cultic pattern of the sacral kingship disintegrated, however, the entire action became transposed on to the level of eschatology. At the same time the conception of God became more and more transcendent; the dynamic aspect, previously so characteristic of the Israelite view of God—vitally expressed *inter alia* in the enthronement Psalms—was forced to some extent to give way to a more static conception. God was still described in royal terms, but the apocalyptic visionaries saw him as the Eternal, enthroned in the highest heaven and directing the course of the world through some intermediary.[2] Not until the last judgment will he be manifest in his full power. But even in the eschatological event the actual action is often carried out by inferior beings, of the order of the "Son of Man" of Dan. 7—the earliest example we have of such a concept.

As far back as Dan. 7 we find Yahweh described as a King, eternally enthroned high above the historical process. "The Ancient of Days", sitting on his throne, surrounded by thousands upon thousands of his servants, is an image which recurs time and time again in later Jewish apocalyptic, and which was also taken over by the Christian Church.[3] Not infrequently do we find complicated speculations as to the number of heavens, guarded by angelic powers, through which the apocalyptic visionary must pass before he can stand before the throne of the highest.[4] Descriptions of God's apparel,[5] his throne[6] and his court of angels and

---

[1] Cf. above, p. 33 f.

[2] BIETENHARD, *Himmlische Welt* pp. 53 ff. Cf. also A. WÜNSCHE, *Salomos Thron und Hippodrom*, Ex oriente lux 2.3 (1906) p. 7 (with reservation for his pan-Babylonian interpretations).

[3] 1. En. 39.12–40.10; Apoc.Abr. 17 f.; Rev. 4.1 ff. Cf. BIETENHARD, *op. cit.*, pp. 123 ff.

[4] For the number of heavens in different traditions, see BIETENHARD, *op. cit.*, pp. 3 ff.

[5] On the speculations about God's robe, see R. EISLER, *Weltenmantel und Himmelszelt* 1–2 (1910), *passim*. For the connexion between this idea and the royal and priestly robe, see RIESENFELD, *Jésus Transfiguré*, pp. 115 ff.

[6] L'ORANGE, *Studies*, pp. 48 ff. BIETENHARD, *op. cit.*, pp. 53 ff.

saints[1] are of course dependent upon the attributes of Near Eastern kings. God, like the Persian Great King, is also hidden behind curtains —a motif which recurs in Christian literature.[2]

This transcendent God, remote as he is from the daily round of the earth, is not expected to manifest his Lordship in person in the coming Kingdom of God. In Dan. 7 we see that his Kingship is exercised through the Son of Man, whose enthronement is described in 7.13 f. Although the king's enthronement was earlier taken to be a cultic representation of the enthronement of Yahweh, neither comes into the picture at this stage. The two actions have been combined into one, centred on the heavenly Son of Man, whose characteristics are both royal and divine. But he is never said to *be* God, despite the fact that the boundary between him and God remains flexible. Nor is he king, other than in a secondary sense. The supreme King on the heavenly throne is still Yahweh, and the power wielded by the Son of Man is derived from God. This posed a problem which was to cause the Christian Church many years of trouble, and which was still felt in the disputes of the Arian controversy.

The Messianic saviour had a number of features in common with the divine hypostases (Logos, Wisdom, etc.) which form a characteristic element in Jewish speculation.[3] The Son of Man and the Logos belong to two distinct theological fields: the former to apocalyptic, the latter to "Wisdom speculation". There is another profound literal sense in which they differ: the Son of Man is, by definition, human; the Logos is an aspect of God. However, in apocalyptic speculation the Son of Man is endowed with qualities which lift him above the strictly human level,

---

[1] For the idea of the heavenly council of Yahweh, see below pp. 139 and 166.

[2] 3 Enoch 45 *inter alia*. On this conception, which is common in Rabbinic Judaism, see BIETENHARD, *op. cit.*, pp. 73 f. TH. KLAUSER, *Der Vorhang vor dem Thron Gottes* JbAC 3 (1960) pp. 141–142. KLAUSER especially stresses the connexion with Persian court ceremonial; the conception of God as the Persian Great King, hidden behind the veils in his palace, will later be discussed in another context, e.g. the pseudo-Aristotelian *De mundo*, which also seems to have a Jewish origin, see below, pp. 190 f. Cf. also the name *Wilon* (= Lat. velum) for the lowest of the heavens, see WÜNSCHE, *Thron*, p. 7. BIETENHARD, *op. cit.*, pp. 8 f. and *passim*. Cf. also I. ZIEGLER, *Die Königsgleichnisse des Midrasch* (1903), pp. 277 ff. The motives are combined in Eusebius, Theoph. 1.37, GCS Eus. 3.54, where the world is represented as a πόλις, the royal palace of which is separated by a dark-blue veil, which is evidently identical with the *Wilon*.

[3] H. RINGGREN, *Word and Wisdom* (1947), *passim*.

and the distinction is thus more apparent than real. It is not by chance that the two are assimilated into the person of Jesus. Both have the character of intermediate beings; both are to some extent "royal"; and both are related to God as the supreme King. When the heavenly saviour-figure (Son of Man, Metatron, etc.) and the Logos are given royal titles, these titles do not carry the same meaning as when they are given to God; their power is derived from God.

The Heavenly Enthronement

The royal character of the heavenly saviour-figure stands out with particular clarity in those apocalyptic texts which have to do with his enthronement. We must pay particular attention to these, since it is this aspect which dominates the early Church's conception of Christ the King. This means that we cannot take up other kingly characteristics in the "Son of Man" idea: for example, the actual title "Son of Man"[1] and its relation to the concept of *Urmensch*.[2]

The Ethiopian Book of Enoch (1 En.) contains sayings on the Son of Man which would seem to be directly traceable to Dan. 7, but which contain masses of other material derived in the last resort from the royal ideology.[3] The Son of Man is here represented as having been hidden from the beginning, and revealed only in the last days (1 En. 38.2, 69.29;

---

[1] The expression בן אדם is used as a royal title in Ps. 8.5, 79.18, 145.3. AA. BENTZEN has in several works claimed its royal sense: *Det sakrale Kongedømme* (1945), pp. 49 ff. IDEM, *Kan ordet "Messiansk" anvendes om Salmernes kongeforestillinger*, SEÅ 12 (1947), pp. 36–50. IDEM, *Messias – Moses Redivivus – Menschensohn* (1948). The same conception in I. ENGNELL, art. *Adam*. IDEM, art. *Människosonen*, SBU 2, col. 400. (GT), SBU 1, col. 13–15. IDEM, review of E. SJÖBERG's *Der Menschensohn* etc. in Bibl. Or. 8 (1951), pp. 187–192. The specifically royal character of this term is denied by E. SJÖBERG, *Uttrycket "människoson" i GT*, STK 26 (1950), pp. 35–44, and IDEM, בן אדם *und* בר אנש *im Hebräischen und Aramäischen* Act. Or. 21 (1950–51), pp. 57–65, 91–107, and also by S. MOWINCKEL, *Urmensch und "Königsideologie"*, STh 2.1 (1948), pp. 71–89.

[2] On the concept of the Son of Man as *Urmensch*, see S. MOWINCKEL, *Henok og "Menneskesønnen"*, NTT 45 (1944), pp. 57–69, and IDEM, *Urmensch*. Against MOWINCKEL's conception, see I. ENGNELL, *Die Urmenschvorstellung und das Alte Testament*, SEÅ 22–23 (1957–58), pp. 265–289.

[3] For the Son of Man in the Ethiopian Book of Enoch, see E. SJÖBERG, *Der Menschensohn in äthiopischen Henochsbuch*, ASHL 41 (1946) and IDEM, *Der verborgene Menschensohn in den Evangelien*, ASHL 53 (1955). Cf. also RIESENFELD, *Jésus Transfiguré*, pp. 307 ff. S. MOWINCKEL, *He That Cometh* (1956), *passim*.

cf. 4 Ezra 7.28, 2 Bar. 29.5, 30.1, 72.2, 39.7). This parousia is in the form of an enthronement, at which the name of the Son of Man is uttered before the "Lord of Spirits" (1 En. 48.2).[1] The theme of enthronement is also clearly expressed in the idea that the Son of Man exercises his eschatological functions sitting on the throne of his glory (1 En. 45.3, 51.3, 55.4, 61.8, 62.2–5, 69.27–29). In the final eschatological event the Son of Man takes over God's function of judge.[2]

The relationship between God and the Son of Man in all these texts is flexible—typically and consistently so. The Son of Man seats himself on the throne of his glory (1 En. 69.29), but at the same time it is God who places him there (1 En. 61.8, 62.2). There has been some discussion as to whether this is God's throne or a special throne reserved for the Son of Man,[3] but such discussion seems completely pointless. The Son of Man sits on his throne, which at the same time is identical with God's throne. The shifts of meaning found in the texts[4] are obviously due to corresponding shifts in thought. We shall constantly come across similar paradoxes in the texts; as we have already pointed out, this lack of clarity was perpetuated, and was still to be seen in the problems raised by the Arian controversy.

Even more outstanding is the kingly character accorded to the Metatron, the equivalent of the Son of Man in the Hebrew Book of Enoch (3 En.). The reliability of this book as a source of information on the Jewish apocalyptic of the 1st century A.D. depends, however, upon the complex problem of its dating.[5] Most modern scholars believe it to be of considerably more recent date than Odeberg claimed, but there is a great deal of uncertainty as to the age of the various levels of tradition; it seems likely that some of them go back to the 1st century A.D.

The level of tradition which Odeberg regards as being the most ancient,[6] depicts the Metatron in distinctively royal terms. He is represented as God's highest authorized representative, through whom all communication with the world at large takes place:

---

[1] SJÖBERG, *Der Menschensohn*, pp. 61 ff. MOWINCKEL, *He That Cometh*, pp. 388 f.
[2] SJÖBERG, *op. cit.*, pp. 61 ff.
[3] SJÖBERG, *op. cit.*, pp. 63 ff. MOWINCKEL, *op. cit.*, p. 389.
[4] SJÖBERG, *op. cit.*, p. 82.
[5] H. ODEBERG, *Föreställningarna om Meṭaṭron i äldre judisk mystik (o. 50–850 e. Kr.)*, KÅ 27 (1927), pp. 1–20. IDEM, *3 Enoch* (1928). IDEM, *Fragen von Metatron, Schekina und Memra* (1942). Against ODEBERG's early dating of 3 Enoch, see G. SCHOLEM's review in OLZ 33 (1930) col. 193–197.
[6] ODEBERG, *Föreställningarna*, p. 2. IDEM, *3 Enoch*, pp. 81 f.

"This is Metatron, my servant. I have made him into a prince and a ruler over all the princes of my kingdoms and over all the children of heaven ... And every angel and every prince who has a word to speak in my presence shall go into his presence and shall speak to him ... Moreover I have set him over all the treasures of the palace of Araboth[1] and over all the stores of life that I have in the high heavens." (3 En. 10.3–6.)

Like the Son of Man, the Metatron has a throne which is an image of the throne of glory. He is the "little Yahweh"—an expression which witnesses to the extreme flexibility of the boundary between the Metatron and God himself.[2]

"I set up his throne at the door of my Hall that he may sit and judge the heavenly household on high. And I placed every prince before him, to receive authority from him, to perform his will." (3 En. 48 C. 8).

In the second level of tradition, in which Enoch is identified with the Metatron, there is a description of how the *Shekina* of God lifts Enoch up to heaven (3 En. 5.14 – 6.3).[3] It is of particular interest that this passage contains a quotation of Ps. 46(47).6—one of the most common of the Christian Church's testimonies to the Ascension of Christ. In the description of the heavenly enthronement of the Metatron we also come across the theme of the attitude of enmity shown by angelic powers in the various heavens to his exaltation. This same theme, usually connected with Ps. 23(24), is extremely common in early Christian expositions of the Ascension.[4] Since many parts of 3 En. are of relatively late date, we cannot dismiss the possibility that there may have been influence from Christian traditions here. But such need not be the case. The same theme is found in other non-Christian writings than 3 En., viz. in Justin's *Book of Baruch* (referring to the ascension of Elohim)[5] and, in a "democratized" form, in the Gnostic enthronement ritual and the concept of the ascension of the human soul through the spheres of heaven.[6]

---

[1] On Araboth as the name of the highest heaven, see WÜNSCHE, *Thron*, p. 7. BIETENHARD, *Himmlische Welt*, p. 10.

[2] ODEBERG, *Föreställningarna*, p. 3. IDEM, *3 Enoch*, p. 82. Cf. BIETENHARD, *op. cit.*, pp. 158 ff.

[3] ODEBERG, *Föreställningarna*, p. 6. IDEM, *3 Enoch*, p. 80. Cf. BIETENHARD, *op. cit.*, p. 149.

[4] See above, pp. 103 ff.

[5] Hippolytus, Ref. V. 26.15 ff., GCS Hipp. 3.129. See WIDENGREN, *Den himmelska intronisationen*, pp. 29 ff. H. LEISEGANG, *Die Gnosis*, 4th ed. (1955), pp. 156 ff.

[6] WIDENGREN, *op. cit.*, *ibid.*

What Odeberg calls the third level of tradition in 3 En. is derived from opposition to the role of Metatron, which Rabbinic Judaism considered to be an encroachment upon the sovereignty of God. But this is a later development, and of minor interest in this context.

The actual word "Metatron" would seem to have to do with this intermediate being's occupation of a throne. Odeberg quotes the opinion of Maius and others, that it was derived from a hypothetical Greek word μετάθρονος, but regards it as more likely that it came from a Greek expression ὁ μετὰ θρόνον.[1] In either case the implication would seem to be that the Metatron is God's immediate subordinate.

In post-exilic times we find a sharp distinction drawn between the priestly and royal functions, a distinction which is also projected on to the eschatology of the period. Some traditions (Qumran and Test. XII Patr.) postulate two Messiahs, one priestly and one kingly, both of whom are to be made manifest in the last days.[2] The apocalyptic literature also mentions a heavenly high priest, appointed to serve God in the celestial sanctuary. The earliest occurrence of this motif is in Zech. 3.4 ff. and 6.11–15, which describe the inauguration of Joshua as Messianic high priest. He is dressed in the sacred vestments and turban, he is crowned and set upon his throne.[3] The basis of this is the same cultic pattern as lies behind the concept of the Son of Man, though on this occasion the priestly aspect takes precedence over the royal.

A more developed form of the same scheme is found in Test. Levi 8.2–10, in the description of Levi's consecration as heavenly high priest.[4] Here, too, the description is distinctly priestly in character, corresponding to the general tendency of Test. XII Patr. Thus the majority of the insignia received by Levi are also priestly: the robe, ephod, diadem and crown (cf. the description of Aaron's consecration in Sir. 45.6–22). The last three insignia received by Levi, the purple girdle, sceptre and olive branch, do not however form part of the priestly vestment; Widengren considers them to be royal emblems. Levi is anointed with oil, washed in

---

[1] ODEBERG, *Föreställningarna*, pp. 16 ff. G. SCHOLEM is however sceptical about this etymology, see *Die jüdische Mystik in ihren Hauptströmungen* (1957) pp. 74 f.

[2] B. OTZEN, *Die neugefundenen hebräischen Sektenschriften und die Testamente der zwölf Patriarchen*, STh 1 (1953), pp. 125–157. KUHN, *Die beiden Messias, passim.* Cf. above pp. 108 ff.

[3] Cf. H. G. MAY, *A Key to the Interpretation of Zechariah's Visions*, JBL 57 (1938), pp. 173–184.

[4] See G. WIDENGREN, *Till det sakrala kungadömets historia i Israel*, Horae Soederbl. 1.3 (1947), pp. 1 ff. IDEM, *Sakrales Königtum*, pp. 49 ff.

water, receives bread and wine, and is initiated into the heavenly mysteries. Here Widengren has pointed out the resemblance to the Near Eastern enthronement ritual, as reconstructed by Hocart and later complemented by Widengren himself.[1]

There is no purely royal or purely priestly aspect in Jewish apocalyptic. Most of the Messianic figures of the apocalyptic world of ideas have both royal and priestly characteristics. The Metatron, too, can be represented as high priest, serving in the heavenly sanctuary.[2] In Christian apocalyptic we find that *standing* is linked with the priestly function, *sitting* with the royal; there is no doubt that this distinction, which is met with frequently in patristic literature, goes back to Jewish sources.[3]

NT Apocalyptic

The background of the NT faith in Christ as Son of Man and *kyrios* is to be seen not only in the Messianic sayings of the OT but also in the apocalyptic ideas current in Judaism. Passages in which it is stated that Christ is King, that he is seated upon a throne and that he will return to judge mankind are directly related to the Messianic expectations of apocalyptic groups in Jesus' day. Here, as elsewhere, the originality of Jesus lies not so much in his having broken free from the older religious tradition as in the fact that he gathered the Messianic themes of Judaism together into a new and meaningful unity.[4] The most eloquent proof of this is perhaps the term "Son of Man" used by Jesus to connect his own person with those eschatological expectations of which deposits are to be found in the Enoch literature.

On the other hand, what distinguishes the NT so sharply from contemporary Jewish literature is—with the exception of Rev.—its lack of interest in cosmology and apocalyptic. NT eschatology is as a rule free from the comprehensive mythological framework we find e.g. in Enoch or 4 Ezra. This also means that less emphasis is placed on the royal attributes given to God and the Messianic figures in the apocalyptic

---

[1] See further below, pp. 147 ff. Cf. also the royal and priestly investiture of Metatron in 3 En. 12.1-4.
[2] Num. R. 12.15. See ODEBERG, *3 Enoch*, p. 93.
[3] BIETENHARD, *Himmlische Welt*, pp. 66 and 71.
[4] RIESENFELD, *Den senjudiska messianologien*, pp. 5 ff.

literature.¹ Descriptions of the various heavens and their angelic inhabitants, common not only in apocalyptic proper but also in Rabbinic literature, are entirely missing from the NT.

When the NT represents Christ as King, it normally does so in connexion with an exposition of OT Messianic texts in which Christ is regarded as having fulfilled the prophecies. This applies in particular to two important groups of sayings: those in which, in connexion with Ps. 109(110), Christ is said to be seated at the right hand of the Father; and eschatological sayings on his parousia (following Dan. 7). Each is connected with a Christological term: Son of Man and *kyrios* respectively.²

In the Synoptic sayings of Jesus in the parousia, the royal characteristics are particularly important in the context of the representation of the glorified Son of Man. He comes in his (or his Father's) δόξα (Matt. 16.27, 24.30, 25.31, Mk. 8.38, Lk. 9.26, 21.27); this is expressive of his Divine and Kingly character, a theme taken over from Jewish Messianism.³ He is to be seated on the throne of his glory (Matt. 19.28, 25.31), which is both a seat of judgment and a royal throne, and which was already linked with the Son of Man in En. 69.29. Characteristically, Matt. 25.34–40, which deals with the subject of the judgment of the Son of Man, is one of the few passages in the NT in which Jesus is called βασιλεύς. Christ is attended by a court of angels (Matt. 16.27, 24.30 f., 25.31, Mk. 8.38, Lk. 9.26; cf. 1 Thess. 3.13, 2 Thess. 1.7, Jude 14),⁴ and his appearance is called a παρουσία—the technical expression for a king's arrival in a town.⁵ We encounter in all these sayings the same world of ideas as

---

¹ θρόνος occurs 62 times in the NT, 47 of which in Rev.; στέφανος occurs 18 times in the NT, 8 of which in Rev. The royal terminology of this kind is on the whole concentrated to Rev.

² See above pp. 50 ff.

³ See H. KITTEL, *Die Herrlichkeit Gottes*, ZNW Beih. 16 (1934), pp. 183 ff. G. KITTEL, art. δόξα in ThWB 2 (1935), pp. 236–256. RIESENFELD, *Jésus Transfiguré*, pp. 97 ff. The relation between the NT δόξα and the Jewish שכינה is stressed by DOEVE, *Hermeneutics*, pp. 151, 149 ff. DOEVE considers that the concept that the Son of Man is accompanied by his angels has developed from a midrash-like combination of Dan. 7.10, 14 with Zech. 14.5, 9. The saints have become angels through an interpretation of Isa. 6.5, where צבאות is interpreted to mean the angels. Cf. J. BONSIRVEN, *Le judaïsme palestinien au temps de Jésus-Christ*, 1 (1934), p. 224. BILLERBECK, *Comm*. 2, p. 116. Note, however, that LXX here translates צבאות with σαβαώθ, not with τῶν δυνάμεων.

⁴ Cf. 1 En. 1.9 (here about God). See MICHL, art. *Engel* pp. 76 and 147. where the most important extra-canonical material is noted.

⁵ See above, p. 68 f.

that we have met with in the apocalyptic literature. Apart from the parousia speeches, these categories occur, though more sparsely, in the Gospel narratives of the baptism and transfiguration of Jesus.[1]

The NT makes it quite clear that the eschatological authority of Christ as judge is derived from the Father. Christ has been ordained by God to be judge of the living and the dead (St. Peter's speech in Acts 10.42). God has fixed a day on which he will judge the world in righteousness by a man whom he has appointed (St. Paul's Areopagus speech, Acts 17.31). The Father has given all judgment to the Son *qua* Son of Man (Jn. 5.22, 27). All this corresponds to the picture of the Son of Man we find in Dan. 7: here the Son of Man is brought before God, who is represented as a King, enthroned and surrounded by his court of angels, and God gives him authority over all peoples. The taking over by the Son of Man of God's judicial function is a theme which recurs in Enoch.[2]

The distinction between the Son of Man and God is extremely flexible in the Gospels, as it was in the Enoch literature. The judgment of the Son of Man is identical with the judgment of God. The OT expression "the day of the Lord" is taken over by the NT, referring both to God (1 Thess. 5.2, 2 Thess. 2.2, 2 Pet. 3.10; cf. 2 Pet. 3.12) and to Christ (1 Cor. 1.8, 5.5, 2 Cor. 1.14, Phil. 1.6, 10, 2.16). The distinction between the function of Christ and the nature of Christ, which we have mentioned above, is important for the understanding of these sayings, which speak without exception of the Son of Man as exercising God's functions, but which say nothing about his nature.[3]

As the "Son of Man" sayings in the NT have to do with a Messianic interpretation of Dan. 7, so the sayings on Christ's enthronement and *sessio* have their background in the exegesis of Ps. 109(110).1. There is one striking difference between the two groups: in Ps. 109 there is no link between OT and NT, such as the "Son of Man" sayings provide in respect of Dan. 7. We know of no Jewish Messianic exegesis of Ps. 109 from pre-Christian times. It is however possible—probable, even—that

---

[1] For Jesus' baptism, see D. PLOOIJ, *The Baptism of Jesus*, in Amicitiae Corolla, presented to J. Rendel Harris (1933), where the role of the baptism as an enthronement is stressed. The same conception is found in J. KOSNETTER, *Die Taufe Jesu* Theol. Stud. d. Österr. Leogesellsch. 35 (1936) and T. ARVEDSON, *Das Mysterium Christi* (1937), pp. 123 ff. For the Transfiguration as an enthronement, see RIESENFELD, *Jésus Transfiguré, passim*.

[2] Cf. above, p. 128.

[3] Cf. above, pp. 55 f.

there was applied a Rabbinic censorship, aimed at counteracting Christian use of the Psalm.[1]

In Rabbinic literature we find conscious opposition to the idea of the Messiah *sitting* in heaven. R. Aqiba is said to have interpreted the "thrones" of Dan. 7.9 to mean that one was reserved for God and one for the Messiah; but R. Jose the Galilean rebuked him, saying that this was a profanation of the *Shekina*. Instead, he interpreted them as being the thrones of righteousness and mercy. R. Eliezer ben Azariah advised R. Aqiba not to concern himself with the haggadah, but to keep to the halakah; his own view was that the text in question referred to the throne and the footstool of God (b Sanh. 38 b). This discussion is of considerable interest, not only because it reveals the extent of Rabbinic opposition to the idea of a Messiah enthroned in heaven, but because R. Aqiba's interpretation reveals that such an idea was in fact known in early Rabbinic Judaism. It almost goes without saying that opposition to this idea and opposition to Christianity were not unconnected.

We have said that the Synoptic tradition traced the Messianic interpretation of Ps. 109(110) back to Jesus himself—to the "Son of David" question and to his interrogation before the Sanhedrin.[2] Here Jesus seemed to describe himself in apocalyptic categories: categories, moreover, which were familiar to his Jewish contemporaries. The reaction of the Jewish high priest, as recorded in the Gospels, suggests that he was perfectly well aware of the implications of Jesus' claims.

Nor is there any doubt that the early Church connected the apocalyptic view of the Ascension with faith in Christ as the *kyrios* of whom Ps. 109 spoke. The first Christians believed that he had been enthroned at the right hand of God, and that he would come again as Son of Man in the last days to execute the judgment of God upon the world. All the evidence suggests that the earlier phases in the inauguration of Christ as King—his baptism and transfiguration—were looked upon as anticipating the final enthronement, when his work of salvation would be completed.[3] It is the Ascension which occupies the central position here.

Although the NT identifies the enthronement of Christ with the Ascension—this is particularly true of Heb.—it is quite typical that

---

[1] BILLERBECK, *Comm.* 4, pp. 458 ff. Cf. above pp. 49 f., 83.

[2] See above pp. 47 ff.

[3] RIESENFELD, *Jésus Transfiguré*, p. 285: "Nous croyons pouvoir poser qu'il s'agit là d'une préfiguration partielle de l'intronisation messianique, dont la réalisation définitive suppose, selon la christologie, la mort et l'élévation qui la suit."

there is no ascension narrative of the kind seen later in e.g. the *Ascension of Isaiah*.[1] In this respect the NT is extremely reticent; little is said about the Ascension, and what is said is remarkably vague.[2] Note that not even Rev. contains any description of the Ascension.

Both Jewish and extra-canonical Christian apocalyptic writings contain descriptions of the ascension of the Saviour through the various heavenly spheres, and the same ideas seem to be hinted at here and there in the NT. Heb. 4.14 speaks of "a great high priest who has passed through the heavens". 1 Tim. 3.16 may be referring to the same theme when, in a Christological hymn, it speaks of Christ having been "seen by angels"—the reference being to the Ascension, when Christ passed the watchers, *archons*, at the gates of heaven. This idea was later to be coupled with the exegesis of Ps. 23(24). 7 ff.[3] On the whole, however, the NT is remarkably free from speculations of this kind.

Although the NT says on a number of occasions that Christ has been enthroned at the right hand of God, little interest is shown in cosmological or apocalyptic speculation in such passages. Of the books of the NT, the cosmological aspect is stressed most strongly in Heb. (Rev. being of course excepted); there Christ is represented as "a high priest ... who is seated at the right hand of the throne of the Majesty in heaven" in order to minister in the true tabernacle (8.1, 2). This description of Christ is strikingly reminiscent of that of the heavenly high priest in Test. Levi 8. Heaven is here described as a temple, rather than a throne-room; it is the tabernacle which, according to Ex. 25.40, was the heavenly prototype of the earthly (Heb. 8.5). Although more emphasis is placed on the priestly aspect, Christ in Heb. also has kingly characteristics: like Melchizedek, he is not only priest but also king (Heb. 7.1 ff.), and he is seated at the right hand of God—a clear expression of his royal dignity.

In Stephen's vision (Acts 7.55 f.) Christ is however said to be *standing* at the right hand of God. It seems likely that this difference is due to concrete apocalyptic ideas; it may be an expression of Christ's role as high priest, intercessor or witness of the martyrdom.[4]

---

[1] Cf. below, pp. 142 ff.

[2] P. Benoit, *L'Ascension*, RB 56 (1949), pp. 161-203. J. G. Davies, *He Ascended into Heaven* (1958), ch. 2 and 3.

[3] See below pp. 144 ff.

[4] Cf. above p. 131.

The Book of Revelation

In this context a special problem is posed by Rev., in which the representation of God and Christ in the royal categories of Jewish apocalyptic is more prominent than in any of the other books of the NT.[1] The main cause of this is evidently the fact that Rev. is the only book of the NT which is distinctly apocalyptic in character. Royal symbolism, which is so typical of Jewish apocalyptic literature, is taken over here, as in post-canonical Christian apocalyptic writings. God is represented as the heavenly King, and Christ as his authorized representative who carries out his works of salvation and judgment with mankind.

A theory which has often been put forward is that much of this symbolism in Rev. has been taken over from Roman imperial symbolism and applied to God and Christ as a polemic against imperial rule. According to this theory, we are dealing here with Christian polemic directed against the self-exaltation of Domitian and his persecution of the Christian Church.[2]

Erik Peterson has, in a brilliant but not altogether convincing manner, interpreted the visions of Rev. as Christian adaptation of the imperial symbolism: Christ is described in imperial categories in Rev. 1. He stands between the candle-sticks in the same way as the image of the Emperor was placed between the candelabra. His feet, shining like copper, can be traced to the *proskynesis* at the feet of Caesar. His great voice is heard above that of the earthly imperator. The seven stars in his hand are a symbol of imperial power; his face, shining like the sun, stands over against the imperial *roi soleil*. The description of the vest-

---

[1] For the relation between Rev. and the OT, see especially D. A. SCHLATTER, *Das Alte Testament in der johanneischen Apokalypse*, BFTh 16.6 (1912), *passim*. All commentaries to Rev. also mention comparative material from the OT and Jewish literature. Cf. also BIETENHARD, *Himmlische Welt*, *passim*. An extremely mythological and supra-historical interpretation of Rev. is given by E. LOHMEYER's otherwise most valuable *Die Offenbarung des Johannes*, 2nd ed., revised by G. BORNKAMM (1953). Cf. the criticism of LOHMEYER's ideas in M. RISSI, *Zeit und Geschichte in der Offenbarung des Johannes* Abh. z. Th. d. A. u. N.T. 22 (1952).

[2] This theory received its classical expression in E. PETERSON, *Christus als Imperator* and IDEM, *Von den Engeln* PThT, pp. 323–407. In the latter work the political interpretation appears mainly in the footnotes. PETERSON's interpretations of the visions in Rev. are taken over by STAUFFER, *Christus und die Cäsaren*, pp. 191 ff.

ments of the heavenly high priest is, like the imperial garment, a symbol of his power.¹

Peterson interprets Chapter 4, with its vision of the throne of God, in similar terms. The one sitting upon the throne is described periphrastically; this may be an allusion to the empty (imperial) throne. He who sits upon the throne receives the acclamation *dignus es*—a call which is also derived from the political sphere.² This is the vow of loyalty before the throne of the invisible ruler, and stands in direct contrast to the Hellenistic custom of worshipping before the monarch's empty throne. When the scroll is given to the Lamb, this is reminiscent of the way in which Caesar passed on documents to his subjects. The incense which rises from the censers of the twenty-four elders, also has to do with the imperial cult. The four riders are associated with the four parties in the circus. The connexion between the opening of the scroll and the appearance of the four riders may be that circus games provided the prelude to the taking of a new office; thus the Lordship of Christ is solemnly inaugurated with cosmic circus games.³

Rev. is evidently strongly anti-Roman and anti-imperial in style; this is clear both from the letters and the visions of the beast and the whore. The great world powers and their rulers are interpreted by Rev.—as in Dan.—as apocalyptic entities, destined to be crushed in the final eschatological conflict. But when we come to examine the description of heavenly worship before the throne of God and the visions of Christ, Jewish apocalyptic seems to be a more natural source of comparative material than the Roman imperial cult, although elements of the latter may of course have left their mark on the vision of God's supreme power.

An outstanding characteristic of Rev. is the alternation of cultic scenes and dramatic scenes. Most of the visions include descriptions of the battle between God and Satan and of God's punishment of mankind. Visions of the heavenly cult before the throne of God are inserted between these.⁴ The first and most comprehensive of these cultic descriptions consists of Chaps. 4 and 5, and further visions of the same kind follow in 7.9–17, 8.1–4, 11.15–19, 14.1–5, 15.2–8 and 19.1–10.

---

¹ *Christus als Imperator*, pp. 153 ff.

² The same interpretation of the acclamations is earlier presented in IDEM, Εἷς θεός, FRLANT N.F. 24 (1926), pp. 179 ff., 312, 418.

³ Cf. also STAUFFER, *Christus und die Cäsaren*, pp. 197 f.

⁴ This disposition of Rev. is well represented by A. FARRER in his often too-speculative book *A Rebirth of Images* (1949).

137

The introduction to the cultic vision of Chaps. 4 and 5 contains a number of characteristics which lead our thoughts to Jewish apocalyptic. John sees "an open door in heaven",¹ and a heavenly voice "like a trumpet" promises to show him what take place, without the speaker revealing himself.² At the same moment John becomes carried away "in the Spirit",³ and the vision is revealed to him.

The heaven which John sees is in the form of a throne-room or a temple: the distinction between the two being inconsiderable in Antiquity. At the centre of the sanctuary stands a throne, and on the throne one who was seated (καθήμενος), a respectful paraphrase for God himself. Around the throne there stands a circle of twenty-four thrones, on which twenty-four elders are seated, dressed in white garments, and with golden crowns on their heads; the throne is also surrounded by the four ζῷα, the throne-carrying cherubim from Ezek. 1.⁴

Most of the elements in this vision are well known from the OT and from older Jewish apocalyptic. It was an idea generally accepted in the Near East, that the earthly temple is an image of the invisible heavenly sanctuary,⁵ and vice versa, that the heavenly sanctuary is conceived of as a cosmically enlarged replica of the Temple. We have descriptions of the throne of God in Ezek. 1. 26 and 10.1, and in Rabbinic literature.⁶ It is quite certain that the twenty-four elders have to do with the concept of God's heavenly council (3 Kings 22.19, Job 1 f.), which Rabbinic Judaism considered to be the heavenly equivalent of the earthly San-

---

¹ Cf. Ezek. 1.1, Test. Levi 5.1.
² Cf. Dan. 8.16.
³ Cf. Ezek. 8.3, 11.1.
⁴ BILLERBECK, *Comm.* 3, pp. 799 f. LOHMEYER, *Comm. ad loc.* ALLO, *Comm. ad loc.* N. B. STONEHOUSE, *The Elders and the Living-Beings in the Apocalypse*, in Arcana revelata, presented to F. W. Grosheide (1951), pp. 135–148.
⁵ The heavenly temple as a pattern of the earthly one is mentioned in Ex. 25.9, 40, 26.30, 27.8, and was also a common idea in Judaism and in early Christianity; see e.g. Wisd. 9.8, Test. Levi 5.1. Acts 7.44, Heb. 8.5. According to a Jewish tradition this heavenly throne-room was created before the world as were the Torah, the penitence, Eden, the throne of the Glory and the Messiah's name. BILLERBECK, *Comm.* 1, 974. In the temple God is enthroned and there is also an altar engraved with the Messiah's name. The correspondence between the earthly and the heavenly temple is also seen in the concept that the temple of Jerusalem is situated under the heavenly temple, with the Ark of the Covenant directly under the throne of the Glory. BILLERBECK, *Comm.* 4, pp. 700 ff. Cf. also ALLO, *Comm.* pp. XLV and LVII f.
⁶ Cf. also above, pp. 125 f.

hedrin.¹ Similar speculations, connected with the ecclesiastical hierarchy, are to be found in later Christian tradition, and we cannot exclude the possibility that the representation of the heavenly worship in Rev. 4–5 also contains elements of 1st century Christian worship.² Apart from this, there is nothing in this vision which is not to be seen in any Jewish apocalypse. What makes these cultic visions so unmistakeably Christian is the figure of the Lamb, who stands before the throne, and through whom God acts in the final eschatological event. The description of Christ as a sacrificial lamb distinguished the visions of Rev. decisively from similar visions in Jewish apocalyptic. The Lamb in Rev. has however a number of striking resemblances to the intermediate beings—the Son of Man, the Metatron or Levi—with which we are acquainted from Jewish apocalyptic literature. It is not however Christ, but God, who is principally described as King in Rev. As in the Jewish apocalypses he occupies the throne in the highest heaven, and the eschatological catastrophe takes place at his command. His description in Rev. is strikingly dynamic, in contrast to the transcendence which dominates in the cultic visions. When in Rev. 4.8 he is called ὁ ἐρχόμενος this refers in all probability not only to his eternal existence in the future, but also to his coming at the judgment.³ The liturgical acclamations in 11.17 and 15.3f. tell how the Lord has manifested himself as King and revealed his judgments; the phraseology is reminiscent of the enthronement Psalms of the OT. At the same time, however, it is Christ who is represented as executing Divine judgment upon the world. The functions of God and Christ

---

[1] SCHLATTER, *Das Alte Testament*, pp. 14 ff. BIETENHARD, *Himmlische Welt*, p. 59. A. FEUILLET, *Les vingt-quatre vieillards de l'Apocalypse*, RB 65 (1958), pp. 5–32. According to FEUILLET, the presbyters are identical with the just men of the old Covenant and are therefore not directly identical with the council of angels in 3 Kings 22 and Job 1. FEUILLET compares them rather with texts such as Isa. 24.23 and Dan. 7.9. FEUILLET also points out that the presbyters are a heavenly council, *ibid.* pp. 9 f. Cf. also p. 11: "Il semble que l'Apocalypse ait voulu faire voir ainsi dans le monde céleste comme une sorte de prototype de la hiérarchie terrestre." It seems that we have here an idea corresponding to the concept of the heavenly temple; perhaps the 24 presbyters have some connexion with the 24 classes of priests in the temple of Jerusalem. On the heavenly council in the OT, see H. WHEELER ROBINSON, *The Council of Yahweh*, JTS 45 (1944), pp. 151–157.

[2] For the further development in Christian literature, see below pp. 165 ff.

[3] Cf. the expression ὁ ἐρχόμενος in Mal. 3.1 and Matt. 3.11. A dynamic interpretation of the expression is given by BIETENHARD, *op. cit.*, p. 62. For a more futural interpretation of this expression, see SCHLATTER, *Das Alte Testament*, p. 12.

combine, as we have already seen, in connexion with the "Son of Man" concept of the Enoch literature.

The Lamb, like God, has distinctly royal characteristics. In the terminology of Jewish Messianism he is called "the Lion of the tribe of Judah, the Root of David" (5.5),[1] and the same acclamation is directed to him as to God (5.12 f.).[2] But at the same time we find a similar tendency as in Jewish apocalyptic writings: the supreme King is not the Lamb, but God. It is God who is seated upon the throne, not the Lamb, who stands before the throne (5.13, 6.16, 7.9 f., 15, 17). Not until the final description of the new Jerusalem is mention made of the throne of God and the Lamb (22.1, 3).

The doctrine of the *sessio* of Christ at the right hand of the Father is hinted at on a number of occasions in Rev. Christ is seated with his Father on his throne (3.21), and the child born to the woman clothed with the sun, is caught up to God and to his throne (12.5). In the visions of the heavenly liturgy it is, however, always God who is the occupant of the throne. ὁ καθήμενος is always God and never Christ.

Christ can be given distinctly kingly characteristics outside the framework of the cultic visions. The vestments which he wears in the introductory vision (1.13 ff.) contain both priestly and kingly elements.[3] Sometimes he is represented as wearing a golden diadem (14.14, 19.12), but characteristics such as these are not found in those cultic visions in which Christ has the role of mediator and servant.

This need not be interpreted to mean that Rev. has a Christology different from that of the rest of the NT. It seems rather to be the case that these divergences are due to the difficulty of expressing NT Christology in visionary terms, particularly when the vision has to be adapted to the Jewish apocalyptic heritage. When the heavenly enthronement of Christ has to be described in the form of visions, this can only be

---

[1] See above, pp. 90 ff.

[2] For the acclamations as an expression of early liturgical usage, see below, p. 157. On the Lamb as a designation of Messiah in Rev. see W. KOESTER, *Lamm und Kirche in der Apokalypse*, in Vom Wort des Lebens, Festschrift für M. Meinertz (1951), pp. 152–164. P. A. HARLE, *L'Agneau de l'Apocalypse et le N.T.*, EtThRel 31.2 (1956), pp. 26–35. Cf. above, p. 37.

[3] ALLO, *Comm. ad loc.* G. HELLSTRÖM, *Klädnaden i Joh. Upp. 1.13*, unprinted essay (1953), has shown that the Greek word ποδήρης is probably a translation of "the ephod tunic", מעיל האפוד. See also RIESENFELD, *Jésus Transfiguré*, pp. 115 ff. Cf. above p. 130. That Christ appears in a priestly robe in Rev. 1 is noted by St. Irenaeus, Adv. haer. IV. 20.11, ed. HARVEY 2.222.

done in forms which suggest a more subordinationist Christology than that found in other books of the NT; this tendency is even more marked in post-canonical apocalyptic.

It seems, furthermore, to be the case that in Rev. the enthronement proper takes place at the parousia. Christ is not called βασιλεύς and κύριος until the decisive final conflict (17.14 and 19.16);[1] 22.1, 3 talks about the throne of the Lamb in the new Jerusalem. It is possible that the idea of a parousia enthronement was found in earlier Christian traditions as well. Clear evidence of the occurrence of this idea is not to be found before the Ethiopian *Apocalypse of Peter*.[2]

Post-canonical Apocalyptic

The first descriptions we have of Christ's descent from heaven and reascent, his work of salvation completed, to be enthroned at the Father's right hand, are to be found in the post-canonical apocalyptic literature, in works such as the *Ascension of Isaiah* and the *Epistle of the Apostles*. Although the *descensus* theme occurs on a number of occasions in the NT—particularly in Jn., where the concepts καταβαίνειν and ἀναβαίνειν are central[3]—the NT writers were reluctant to undertake the task of direct description.

---

[1] Already in Rev. 1.5 Christ is styled ὁ ἄρχων τῶν βασιλέων τῆς γῆς. For the expression βασιλεὺς βασιλέων and κύριος κυρίων (Rev. 17.14 and 19.16), see LOHMEYER, *Comm. ad loc*. It is originally a Babylonian and Iranic title for the Great King, which had already been taken over by the LXX as an attribute of God (Dan. 2.47, 2 Macc. 13.4), and also appears as an epithet for God in 1 Tim. 6.15, cf. above p. 42 n. 3. Se further: DEISSMANN, *Licht*, p. 310. LOHMEYER, *Christuskult und Kaiserkult*, p. 19. J. G. GRIFFITHS, βασιλεὺς βασιλέων, CPh 48 (1953), pp. 145–154. All these Christological titles evidently express Christ's sovereignty over all earthly rulers; this is especially manifest in Rev. with its anti-Roman attitude. Cf. also CULLMANN, *Christologie*, p. 228.

[2] ed. GRÉBAUT in ROC 5 (1910), pp. 199 and 203. Note that Christ here also receives a crown (Ethiop. *aklila*). On this text, see H. DUENSING, Ein Stücke der urchristlichen Petrusapokalypse, ZNW 14 (1913), pp. 65–78.

[3] E.g. Jn. 1.1 ff., 3.13, 6.33 f., 17.5: Phil. 2.5 ff. Heb. 1.3 ff., 2.5 (quotation of Ps. 8.5 f.). On the *descensus* motif in the NT see H. ODEBERG, *The Fourth Gospel* (1929), pp. 72–113 (on Jn. 3.13 ff.). H. SCHLIER, *Religionsgeschichtliche Untersuchungen zu den Ignatiusbriefen*, ZNW Beih. 8 (1929), ch. 1 and 2. KROLL, *Gott und Hölle, passim*. BARBEL, *Christos Angelos*, pp. 297 ff. BIETENHARD, *Himmlische Welt*, pp. 82 ff.

The *Ascension of Isaiah*, which exhibits a remarkable blend of Jewish and Christian themes, describes the topography of heaven in entire accordance with the cosmology of Jewish apocalyptic.[1] Isaiah is taken up through the heavens—seven in number[2]—and sees that each has a throne at its centre, surrounded by angels. In the seventh heaven are the thrones and the crowns prepared by God for the righteous. (Chap. 7.)

In this highest heaven there also dwell, apart from God himself, the pre-existent *kyrios* and the Spirit (or his angel) who are inferior to God in rank, and are seen to worship him (9.39).[3] The Son is called *kyrios* in his pre-existence; he is "the *kyrios* who is to be called Christ" (9.13) or "*kyrios christos*, who is to be called Jesus" (9.5, 10.7). But his real name is too holy to be uttered (8.7).

Even in his pre-existent state the *kyrios* wielded a form of royal authority: the angel who is Isaiah's guide calls him "the Lord of all these heavens and these thrones" (8.9); "Lord over all the glories which you have seen" (9.32); "Lord over the seven heavens and their angels" (10.11). Although he is seen to worship the Father and obey him (9.39, 10.16 ff.), and is thus obviously his inferior, he nevertheless occupies a position equal, or superior, to the apocalyptic figures of Judaism. He dwells in the heavens (7.37); he has an unutterable name (8.7); he is associated with the Father (7.37); and the angels praise the Father and "the Beloved" (7.17).[4]

Isaiah is then shown how the Father commands the *kyrios* to descend as far as the realm of the dead, then to return and take his place at his

---

[1] This book has been preserved in its entirety only in Ethiopian; fragments exist in Greek, Latin, Slavonic and Coptic, cf. J. FLEMMING & H. DUENSING in *Neutestamentliche Apokryphen*, ed. HENNECKE, 2nd ed. (1924), p. 303. We quote from E. TISSERANT's French translation (1909).

[2] DANIÉLOU considers that the concept of the seven heavens is a proof of the Syrian provenience of Asc. Isa., *Judéo-christianisme*, p. 23, cf. *ibid.* p. 25 (on Test. XII Patr.). It seems however that the idea of seven heavens is too common to be a sure shibboleth of the origin of Asc. Isa. M. DE JONGE, *The Testaments of the Twelve Patriarchs* (1953), to which DANIÉLOU refers, does not draw the same conclusion when he treats the motif, pp. 47 ff. That the idea of seven heavens is common in Rabbinic literature is shown by BIETENHARD, *Himmlische Welt*, pp. 8 ff., 37 ff.

[3] This type of Christology (and pneumatology) has been especially examined by G. KRETSCHMAR, *Studien zur frühchristlichen Trinitätstheologie*, BHTh 21 (1956), pp. 62 ff. Note, however, the criticism by J. BARBEL in his essay *Zur Engelchristologie im Urchristentum*, ThR 54 (1958), col. 49 ff.

[4] TISSERANT in the introduction to his translation of Asc. Isa., p. 10.

right hand (10.7–15). The Son leaves the seventh heaven (3.13, 10.17) and descends through the other six. As he passes through the different spheres he is changed, so that he comes to resemble the angels who dwell in them (10.20–27); finally he passes through the firmament (10.29) and the atmosphere (10.31). After having taken human form (3.13) he lives out his earthly life; after death he descends into Sheol.

Further, Isaiah sees how Christ rises from the kingdom of the dead and returns to the throne of the Father (3.17 f.), escorted by the righteous, whom he has liberated from Sheol. He passes through the firmament, where he is recognized and worshipped (9.17), rises from heaven to heaven (11.25–32) and finally takes his place at the right hand of the Father (11.32, cf. 10.14), where he receives from the hosts of heaven the same praise as the Father (10.15). Eventually Christ will return in his glory to judge the rulers and angels of this world (10.12). He will come with his angels and saints (4.14) to judge heaven and earth (4.18), to cast the matricide Beliar (who is decidedly reminiscent of Nero) and his hosts into Gehenna (4.14), and to consume the ungodly with the fire of his presence (4.18).

The *Epistle of the Apostles* has a very similar description of the *descensus:* here the pre-existent Christ is called "God the Son of God, who was sent of God ... Lord of lords, King of kings, Ruler of rulers, the heavenly one, that sits above the cherubim and seraphim at the right hand of the throne of the Father" (Chap. 3).[1] In Chap. 13 the Lord himself relates for the Apostles, after his resurrection, what took place when he came down to earth. As in the *Ascension of Isaiah* Christ was changed in such a way that he was able to pass unseen through the heavens; we read here that he was able to do so because the Father had given him his σοφία. The archangels have to take the place of Christ, and carry out his office before the Father (which is also mentioned in the *Ascension of Isaiah*) until his return. The *Epistle of the Apostles* bears traces of a theological development; the transformation of Christ is said to imply that he became all in all (cf. Eph. 1.10)—an interpretation of the *descensus* myth later particularly favoured by Origen.[2]

According to Chap. 14 it was Christ himself, in the form of the Arch-

---

[1] The Ethiopic text and the Coptic and Latin fragments have been edited with a German translation by C. SCHMIDT, *Gespräche Jesu mit seinen Jüngern nach der Auferstehung*, TU 43 (1919).

[2] BARBEL, *Christos Angelos*, pp. 284 ff.

angel Gabriel, who brought the message to the Virgin Mary, and who then entered into her body and became incarnate. The Ascension is of minor importance here, largely because the work claims to contain the revelation given to the Apostles by Christ *before* the Ascension. (The Ethiopian and Latin texts represent Christ as saying that he has already returned to the Father, while the Coptic text refers to the Ascension as an event still to take place.)

It is generally recognized that these two descriptions of the *descensus* are closely related. The *Epistle of the Apostles* is undoubtedly the later; its date has been variously fixed at between 130 and 180.¹ Daniélou regards the *Ascension of Isaiah* as dating from the end of the 1st century.² It goes without saying that both datings are only approximate, but it is not impossible that the former may be dependent upon the latter.

We have reason to believe that traces of this apocalyptic tradition may have been preserved elsewhere. There is a similar description of the *descensus* in the late 4th century Greek *Physiologus*. At his κατάβασις Christ became an angel with the angels, a throne with the thrones, a power with the powers and a man with men.³ When he came down in this hidden fashion he was not recognized by the heavenly watchers, and they therefore asked, "Who is this King of glory?" The Holy Spirit answered, "It is the Lord of the powers (κύριος τῶν δυνάμεων); he is the King of glory."

This text is of particular interest, since it combines the theme of the *descensus* with Ps. 23(24), which is important in the *testimonia* tradition, and which the primitive Church used both in connexion with the *descensus* and (more often) with the Ascension.⁴ The *Ascension of Isaiah* and the *Epistle of the Apostles* do not so much as hint at this Psalm;

---

¹ See the account of the different opinions as to date in QUASTEN, *Patrology* 1, pp. 150 f. DANIÉLOU dates the writing to before A.D. 180 (*Judéo-christianisme* p. 37), because the return of Christ here is expected to take place 150 years after his resurrection (ch. 17). The Coptic text seems however to reckon 120 years between the resurrection and the parousia, which may point to an even earlier date.

² DANIÉLOU, *op. cit.*, p. 23.

³ PETERSON, *Die Spiritualität des griechischen Physiologus*, pp. 250 f. DANIÉLOU, *Judéo-christianisme*, pp. 228 ff., 285 f. On the date of this writing, see PETERSON, *op. cit.*, p. 252. Cf. BARBEL, *Christos Angelos*, pp. 297 ff., with references to the older discussion on the dating.

⁴ See above, pp. 103 ff.

Peterson however considers it not improbable that the text of *Physiologus* is based on an older version of the *Ascension of Isaiah*.[1]

Be that as it may; these three *descensus* descriptions form a unity, which indicates the existence of a widespread post-Apostolic apocalyptic tradition. Another document in the same class is the *Apocalypse of Peter*, which also quotes Ps. 23(24) as a challenge to the heavenly *archons*— though here in the context of the Transfiguration, which is given the form of an ascension.[2] Daniélou, following Goppelt, considers that the *Ascension of Isaiah* and the *Apocalypse of Peter* are of Syrian origin. The Johannine characteristics of the *Epistle of the Apostles* suggest Asia Minor as its place of origin; the possibility of Syria or Egypt cannot however be excluded.[3]

Daniélou, who has attempted to classify many of the forms of early Christian literature under the somewhat inaccurate title of "Jewish Christianity", reckons all these works as belonging to Jewish Christian literature.[4] Although we cannot accept Daniélou's terminology, there is no doubt that all are closely connected with Jewish apocalyptic, and that it is here we must look for their background (The *Ascension of Isaiah* being otherwise a collection of Jewish and Christian material).

---

[1] PETERSON, *op. cit.*, pp. 250 f.

[2] ed. GRÉBAUT, in ROC 5 (1910), p. 317.

[3] DANIÉLOU, *Judéo-christianisme*, p. 37, and references to literature in QUASTEN, *Patrology* 1, pp. 150 f.

[4] At an earlier stage in the writing of this book we considered using Daniélou's term "Jewish Christianity" to cover the conservative literature, particularly that dependent upon normative Judaism; the object here was to contrast it with Hellenistic-influenced speculations, which we take up in the next section. We have not however used Daniélou's term, mainly because it is too flexible, but also because it does not altogether fit in with our arrangement of the material. Daniélou does not, for example, reckon St. Justin's scriptural exposition, which is so dependent upon Jewish midrash exegesis, as belonging to Jewish Christian literature. On the other hand he considers the Pseudo-Clementines to have a Jewish Christian character, following Schoeps and Strecker; we believe them also to contain typical examples of Hellenistic political speculation (see below, pp. 247 ff.). The problem is to escape giving the term "Jewish Christian" a random definition when trying to widen its meaning beyond that used by the Tübingen school. Christianity is built on Jewish foundations; this is none the less true of Alexandrian theology, whose indebtedness to Philo and diaspora Judaism cannot be contested. It seems therefore to be a rather hazardous undertaking to decide just how much of Jewish thought and what kind of Judaism is necessary to qualify a Christian writing for the name "Jewish Christian". For a criticism of Daniélou's terminology, see J. MUNCK, *Judekristendomen efter apostlarnas dagar*, in SEÅ 25 (1960), pp. 78–96.

This post-Apostolic apocalyptic has a number of distinguishing features, which separate it not only from Jewish apocalyptic but also the oldest Christian apocalyptic tradition as found in the NT in general, and Rev. in particular.

1) NT eschatology is centred on the parousia. Those passages in the NT in which Christ is represented in all his majesty as the apocalyptic King thus deal also with his second coming on the clouds of heaven to judge all creation. This likewise applies to Rev., in which the true royalty of Christ is only revealed at the end; although it is said that the woman "clothed in the sun" bears a child who is then caught up to God and his throne (Rev. 12.5), this is incidental to the theme. The apocalyptic which we encounter in the later writings has a different point: it is largely concerned with the description of Christ's descent to earth and his enthronement at the right hand of the Father. This is a theme which is certainly met with in the NT, but not in the terms of apocalyptic vision. That Christ has ascended to the right hand of God is central to the Christian kerygma, but there is no *description* of how this took place.[1]

2) Christ had royal characteristics in his pre-existence. He is Lord over the heavens, their thrones and their angels; his name is *kyrios*, which the earliest Christian tradition connected largely with his glorification, but which soon came to be looked upon as an expression of his Divinity.[2] But at the same time his pre-existent nature is, like that of the Spirit, inferior to the Father. Both the *kyrios* and the Spirit serve and worship God in a manner which shows that Christ's functions in his pre-existence were priestly as well as kingly.[3]

3) Christ is thus King, primarily by virtue of his (subordinate) Divine nature, in relation to which his human nature is of little significance. The involved description of the way in which Christ takes the form of the angels when descending, and reveals his true identity on his return, shows the intimate connexion between *descensio* and *ascensio*: the drama is played out on the divine, and not the human, level.

4) The enthronement of Christ implies that he was given higher status that he had before his *descensus*. In the vision descriptive of his pre-existence, the *kyrios* and the Spirit (or his angel) are seen to *stand* before

---

[1] This distinction is clearly represented by P. BENOIT, *L'Ascension*, pp. 161 ff. BIETENHARD, *Himmlische Welt*, pp. 66 ff.

[2] See above p. 55 ff.

[3] BARBEL, *Christos Angelos*, pp. 273 ff. and the parallel conception in liturgy, *ibid.*, pp. 276 f.

God in worship; when Christ is enthroned at God's right hand, the Spirit is enthroned on his left (Asc. Isa. 11.33). Both Christ and the Spirit here have clear traces of angelic beings;[1] both are inferior to God, but win equality by their deed of salvation. Speculations of this kind recur in Arianism, which believed the pre-existent Son to have attained Divine rank either at the beginning of time or after having fulfilled his work of salvation. Although the post-canonical apocalypses describe Christ in many ways as King, his Kingship is at best second-hand. His authority comes from God, the supreme and transcendent Monarch of all, whose will Christ obeys. This literature has little or no trace of the genuine NT concept, that Christ *qua* man is King of men, and particularly King over those who believe in him. Here it is cosmology which predominates; soteriology is forced into the background.

The Righteous Man as King

In the apocalypses there is a "third party" who is accorded royal attributes. Apart from God and Christ, there is the company of the saints, who are crowned by God as a reward for their righteousness. The vision described in Rev. 4 includes the twenty-four elders, who are seated on thrones. He who is faithful unto death shall obtain the crown of life (2.10, 3.11); he shall be dressed in white garments (3.4 f., 18, 6.11, 7.9, 13, 14) and be seated upon a throne (3.21, 4.4, 11.16, 20.4). The garments, the wreath or crown and the throne are attributes which recur constantly in this context.

Widengren has shown that the concept of the heavenly enthronement is closely linked with baptism.[2] The apocalyptic and Gnostic idea that the righteous are to be crowned kings corresponds to baptismal ceremonies in Mandaeism, as well as in the Syrian and Nestorian rites. In these ceremonies there was not only the white baptismal garment, known

---

[1] BARBEL, *op. cit.*, pp. 273 ff. KRETSCHMAR, *Studien*, pp. 71 ff. DANIÉLOU sums up the different associations of the Son and the Spirit with the angels, especially Michael and Gabriel, in his *Judéo-christianisme*, pp. 171 ff. It is necessary to draw a distinction between these speculations and the original "angel Christology" in the NT, which has been proposed by WERNER. See KRETSCHMAR, *op. cit.*, pp. 221 f. and BARBEL, *Zur Engelchristologie im Urchristentum*, col. 55, where also KRETSCHMAR is criticized in some respects.

[2] See WIDENGREN, *Den himmelska intronisationen*, pp. 28 ff.

all over the early Church, but also a coronation with a wreath.¹ Both the eschatological concept and the baptismal ceremony are, according to Widengren, to be traced back to the Near Eastern enthronement ritual, which Hocart's reconstruction has shown to have included a number of elements which recur here: washing, anointing, communion, the putting on of sacred garments, investiture with the attributes of power, initiation into the heavenly mysteries and enthronement (as well as the heavenly marriage, *hieros gamos*).²

The objection may be advanced that this, like all "patternism" may lead to schematization.³ But there can be no doubt that we are dealing here with a general and widely known complex of ideas; although its age and origin may be uncertain, it is to be found in Judaism, Gnosticism and Christianity during the first centuries after Christ. Hocart's and Widengren's scheme is to be seen with minor variations in Test. Levi 8, in the description of Levi's consecration to the office of heavenly high priest,⁴ in the *Naassene Sermon* (an Ophitic document preserved in Hippolytus' *Refutatio*)⁵ and in the Gnostic Justin's *Book of Baruch*.⁶

The Christian apocalypses contain most of these elements, to a greater or lesser extent. The fact of the existence of more explicit ideas on the heavenly enthronement ritual is demonstrated by a text from a 4th century Persian martyr act. A Christian woman, Martha, confesses her faith in Christ before the judge in these words:

"When he comes in glory upon the cloud-chariot, with angels and the powers of heaven and all that belongs to the wedding feast, he will purify the bodies of his brides from dust, wash them in the dew of heaven, anoint them with the oil of gladness, clothe them in the garment of righteousness, which is radiant light, give them the truth of his grace like a ring, set on their heads

---

¹ WIDENGREN, *op. cit.*, pp. 38 ff. E. SEGELBERG, *Maṣbūtā* (1958), pp. 160 ff.

² A. M. HOCART, *Kingship* (1927), pp. 70 f. On this scheme, see further WIDENGREN, *op. cit.*, pp. 28 f. IDEM, *Till det sakrala kungadömets historia*, p. 7. IDEM, *Religionens värld*, 2nd ed., pp. 179 ff. IDEM, *Sakrales Königtum*, pp. 44 ff. RIESENFELD, *Jésus Transfiguré*, pp. 223 ff.

³ A survey of this discussion is given by K.-H. BERNHARDT, *Das Problem der altorientalischen Königsideologie im Alten Testament*, Suppl. Vet. Test. 8 (1961), pp. 51 ff.

⁴ See above, pp. 130 f. WIDENGREN, *Till det sakrala kungadömets historia*, pp. 1 ff.

⁵ Hippolytus Ref. V. 8.18 ff. GCS Hipp. 3.77 ff. See WIDENGREN, *Den himmelska intronisationen*, pp. 29 ff. On the Naassene sermon, cf. further LEISEGANG, *Die Gnosis*, pp. 111 ff.

⁶ Hippolytus, Ref. V. 26.15 ff., GCS Hipp. 3.129 ff. Cf. WIDENGREN, *op. cit.*, pp. 31 ff. LEISEGANG, *op. cit.*, pp. 156 ff.

the crown of grace, which is eternal glory, place them in his glorious cloud-chariot, draw them up into the skies and take them to the heavenly bridal chamber, prepared in a house not made with hands, built in Jerusalem, the free city on high."[1]

As we see, this text contains most of the elements which Hocart and Widengren consider to be typical of the royal enthronement ritual: washing, anointing, the taking of clothes, investiture with ring and crown, enthronement (on the "cloud-chariot", which is identical with the divine throne-chariot, *Merkabah*)[2] and, finally, the heavenly marriage. What distinguishes this Christian text so sharply from Gnostic parallels is the part played by Christ and the eschatological context. The enthronement of the righteous is not, as in Gnosticism, believed to take place on a timeless, supra-historical level; it is to take place at the final judgment, when Christ comes on the clouds of heaven, surrounded by his saints. Thus the enthronement pattern, though pre-Christian in its origin, has been given an explicitly Christian interpretation.

The idea of the righteous man as king is not specifically Christian *per se*. A well-known phenomenon from pre-Christian times is the "democratization" of the kingship.[3] Logion 2 of the *Gospel of Thomas* says that he who finds "shall become king over the All", but this saying need not necessarily be derived from the NT. In the Gospels Jesus often talks about the one who seeks finding the Kingdom, but hardly says that the seeker will become King, however near such a conclusion may appear! Here we are dealing with a complex of ideas which not only has its roots in Semitic thought, but also has parallels in Greek philosophy: both Platonism and Stoicism represent the wise man as king.[4]

---

[1] *The Martyrdom of Martha, daughter of Pusai*, in Ausgewählte Akten persischer Märtyrer, German translation by O. BRAUN, BKV 22 (1915), p. 79. The text has been observed by SEGELBERG (*Maṣbūtā*, p. 160 n. 1); he states—wrongly, however —that this text belongs in a "baptismal context". There can be no doubt that the eschatological coronation of the just is meant here, not the ritual enthronement at baptism. It is especially unfortunate that SEGELBERG has omitted from his quotation of the text exactly those words, which say that Christ will come in his glory at his parousia, as well as the saying that Christ will seat his faithful on the "cloud-chariot" and carry them up into the air. We have here a good example of the confession of Christ as the eschatological King, which is typical for the martyr literature, cf. below p. 81.

[2] See below, pp. 200 ff.

[3] See ENGNELL, *Studies*, p. 215, Topical Index, *sub voce*. BENTZEN, *Det sakrale Kongedømme*, p. 52.

[4] See below, p. 214.

When the concepts of the heavenly enthronement are taken over by Christian apocalyptic, and incorporated into the Christian baptismal ritual, this takes place with constant reference to Christ as King; in this respect Christian ideas diverge from their Gnostic and Hellenistic counterparts. This is clearly seen in Rev.: "He who conquers, I will grant him to sit with me on my throne, as I myself conquered and sat down with my Father on his throne" (3.21). Through his victory Christ has won royal authority; from him the Christian receives the same authority, if he is faithful to the end.

This royal aspect of the Christian Church is usually expressed collectively by the NT: the new people of God are a royal priesthood (1 Pet. 2.5, Rev. 1.6, 5.10; cf. Ex. 19.6, Isa. 61.6, Jub. 16.18).[1] That Christians are said to be both kings and priests at one and the same time has to do with the view of the early Church that Christ was the holder of both offices, and that Christians participate in them through him; this is often linked with the anointing, which is considered to incorporate the believer into Christ's threefold function of King, Priest and Prophet.[2]

The Christians' collective kingship has a special significance in those sayings where it is said that they shall reign together with him; this theme is closely connected with that of the thousand-year kingdom in which the holy martyrs, according to Rev. 20.4, are to reign with Christ.[3] The concept, derived from Dan. 7.27, of the rule of the saints, has permeated the whole of NT eschatology. At his Ascension Christ placed all powers beneath his feet (Eph. 1.20 ff.), and the Church—which is his Body, and which shares his place in the heavenly world (Eph. 1.22 f., 2.6)—also shares his royal triumph. The Church therefore comprises a people which is exalted over all nationality (represented by the angelic powers). It is in this context we must look upon the saying in 1 Cor. 6.3, that the saints are to judge angels.

It is a common theme in the NT that Christians receive kingly and priestly authority from Christ as King and Priest. In Dan. 7.9 the prophet sees thrones placed; these recur in the Gospels as attributes of the Apostles and symbols of their role in the final judgment. "In the new world, when the Son of man shall sit on his glorious throne, you who

---

[1] L. CERFAUX, *Regale sacerdotium*, RLC 2, pp. 283–315, which also sums up the development of this idea in the post-Apostolic age. Cf. also E. G. SELWYN, *The First Epistle of St. Peter* (1952), *ad loc.*

[2] See above, pp. 106 ff.

[3] H. BIETENHARD, *Das tausendjährige Reich* (1944), *passim.*

have followed me will also sit on twelve thrones, judging the twelve tribes of Israel." (Matt. 19.28.)¹ In the Lucan version of the same text the enthronement of the Apostles is motivated from the Kingship of Christ in a manner reminiscent of Rev. 3.21: "As my Father appointed a kingdom for me, so do I appoint for you that you may ... sit on thrones judging the twelve tribes of Israel." (Lk. 22.29 f.) It is in this same context that we must see the conversation about the places of honour to Christ's right and left in his Kingdom (Matt. 20.21–23).

In the NT—apart from Rev.—the thrones are reserved largely for the Apostles. The wreath or crown, στέφανος, is however a common attribute of the saint. Sometimes it is clearly a case of wreaths of victory, awarded for victory in games (1 Cor. 9.25, 2 Tim. 2.5). Quite apart from the fact that the victor's wreath is related to the sacral use of crowns in Antiquity and therefore forms part of the same complex of ideas,² there is no doubt that the eschatological significance of the wreath in the early Church is due, at least in part, to OT sayings in which the wreath, or crown, was interpreted eschatologically.³ As Riesenfeld has pointed out, expressions such as "crown of glory" and "crown of joy" have given rise to such expressions as χαρὰ καὶ στέφανός μου (Phil. 4.1) and ἐλπὶς ἢ χαρὰ ἢ στέφανος καυχήσεως (1 Thess. 2.19).⁴ Particularly striking is the use of στέφανος in Rev.: Christ reveals himself wearing a crown (14.14);⁵ the elders in the heavenly liturgy wear crowns (4.4); he who is faithful unto death shall gain the crown of life (2.10, 3.11; cf. James 1.12).

White garments as a Christian attribute are not found in the NT outside Rev., other than in Christ's garment at the Transfiguration (Mk.

---

¹ The NT here takes over the conception that the Son of Man will come to his judgment accompanied by his angels and his saints; see above, p. 132. That the Apostles are here given a special role, is connected with the conception of the heavenly council, cf. above, p. 139, and below, p. 166. Cf. also above, p. 102 (the apostles as the sceptre of Christ).

² Baus, *Der Kranz*, pp. 143 ff.

³ So Isa. 28.5. For further examples and literature see Riesenfeld, *Jésus Transfiguré*, pp. 48 ff. N.b. the conception of the Lord as a crown, which appears in Od. Sol. 1.1–3 and in the *Acts of Thomas* 148; see the commentary in the edition of Od. Sol. by Harris & Mingana 2, pp. 207 f. On the Jewish use of wreaths see E. R. Goodenough, *The Crown of Victory in Judaism*, ArtB 28 (1946), pp. 139–159, which considers that the use is dependant on a Hellenistic influence, and against him Riesenfeld, *op. cit.*, p. 48 n. 26, who claims that there were earlier analogous uses of the wreath in Judaism.

⁴ Riesenfeld, *op. cit.*, pp. 51 f., n. 41.

⁵ Cf. Rev. 19.12 where Christ is wearing διαδήματα πολλά.

9.3 par.)[1] and as an attribute of the angels (Matt. 28.3, Lk. 24.4, Jn. 20.12, Acts 1.10, 10.30). In Rev. the white garment is worn by Christ (1.13), by the elders (4.4) and shall also be given to those who win the victory (3.4 f., 18, 6.11, 7.9, 13, 14).

The crown, the garment and the throne are also characteristics of the saints in Asc. Isa. 9.9 f. In the vision the righteous are represented dressed in white garments, but without the crown and the throne (the action being placed in the time of Isaiah). An angel explains that the two latter attributes will be given them only when the Son has come down to earth. When Christ reascends to heaven, many righteous men will ascend with him, and when Christ has returned to the seventh heaven they will be given their garments, thrones and crowns. More garments, thrones and crowns are reserved for those who are to believe in the years to come. These three attributes thus belong together, and are linked with Christ's royal authority: not until Christ has obtained the Kingship can the faithful in turn receive their authority from him. Here the enthronement of the righteous does not take place individually, as in the ascension of the Gnostic to the pleroma; it is incorporated into the scheme of salvation. The righteous who died before Christ came do not receive their thrones and crowns until the work of salvation has been fulfilled; other righteous men rise together with Christ (cf. Matt. 27.52 f.) and escort him at the Ascension. Those who in future ages are to believe will also be enthroned (9.25 f.)—at the coming judgment of the world of which 4.14 ff. speaks. Despite the striking resemblances between this and Gnostic myths of salvation, the ideas of Asc. Isa. are radically different from all forms of Gnosticism by virtue of their emphasis on the course of the history of salvation and the resurrection of the body.

The same characteristics are found in the *Apocalypse of Peter*: here the garment and the crown are distinguishing marks of Moses and Elijah at the Transfiguration[2] and of the angels.[3] At the judgment Christ himself will receive his crown at the hands of the Father[4] and will in his turn crown the righteous, making them kings.[5] The motif is less out-

---

[1] RIESENFELD, *op. cit.*, pp. 115 ff.
[2] ed. GRÉBAUT, ROC 5 (1910), p. 307. N.b. that Christ in this context is also called King.
[3] *Ibid.*, p. 311.
[4] *Ibid.*, p. 203.
[5] ed. GRÉBAUT, ROC 5 (1910), pp. 310 f.

standing in the *Epistle of the Apostles*, though it is stated that the Father (not Christ) shall crown the righteous at the judgment (Chap. 38).[1]

Christian apocalyptic has thus taken over, not merely the democratized royal enthronement as the reward of the righteous, but its close connexion with the Kingship of Christ; as Christ has been enthroned with the Father, so the Christians will be enthroned with him. The apocalyptic literature thus clearly belongs to those classes of literature which have preserved the NT idea of Christ as the eschatological King, which was later to exercise such profound influence on the royal image of Christ in art. This applies in particular to Rev., which was of decisive importance for the apocalyptic imagery of Byzantium and the Mediaeval West.[2]

Apocalyptic soon ceased to be a living class of literature, and such writings as were still in existence came to be regarded with extreme suspicion. A striking example of this is provided by the tardy recognition of Rev. as a canonical Scripture in the Church as a whole. Chiliastic speculations, which had earlier aroused the interest of such leading churchmen as Papias and St. Irenaeus, soon fell into disrepute and were forced underground. The *Ascension of Isaiah* seems to have been used mainly by heretics.

The apocalyptic themes however lived on, outside the apocalyptic literature proper. We have spoken of the baptismal ceremonies, in which special garments (and occasionally the wreath as well) were used to symbolize the kingly authority bestowed upon the righteous. The theme also spread in other forms—in Christian metaphor, as used especially by the African authors Tertullian and St. Cyprian. In their writings the wreath is taken to represent the reward given by Christ to the martyrs. There is no doubt that this has to do with the contemporary custom of crowning the victor of the games—a motif found in the NT. This image is developed by Cyprian. He speaks of the honour of competing in the presence of the Emperor and of being crowned by him, the victory won; is it not then an even greater honour to fight the good fight of faith in

---

[1] Cf. further the *Apocalypse of Paul* 24, where Christ enters the holy city with his saints as the eternal King and *ibid.* 29, where the just are seen seated on thrones; Hermas, Sim. VIII.2.1 f. and VIII.3.6; *Acts of Thomas* 158, according to which Christ has purchased a crown for the righteous by his crown of thorns.

[2] VAN DER MEER, *Maiestas Domini*, *passim*.

the presence of God and the angels, and to receive the victor's crown from Christ the Judge?[1]

Tertullian, in his *De corona*, turns to another use of the wreath: the military use. By way of introduction he reminds his readers that a soldier had just refused to take the laurel wreath he was to have worn at the reception of the *donativum:* an honour granted to the army on the occasion of the death of Septimius Severus in 211.[2] He then goes on to oppose the heathen custom of wearing the wreath.

Although it is clear that these authors are referring to the use of wreaths on various solemn occasions, it is equally clear that apocalyptic ideas play an important role in their writings on the subject. When Tertullian, in *De corona*, speaks of the wreath bestowed by Christ, contrasting it with heathen wreaths, he quotes a number of passages of Rev. in which the word *corona* is found (2.10, 6.2, 4.4, 14,14, 1.6).[3] Cyprian, who often returns to the theme of Christ's coronation of the martyrs,[4] also gives evidence of the importance with which he regards apocalyptic ideas. The most characteristic of such passages is that in *De bono patientiae* in which the suffering of Christ is related to the gifts given to the martyrs by Christ:

"He was crowned with thorns, who crowns martyrs with eternal flowers. He was smitten on the face with palms, who gives the true palms to those who overcome. He was despoiled of his earthly garment, who clothes others in the vesture of immortality. He was fed with gall, who gave heavenly food. He was given to drink of vinegar, who appointed the cup of salvation."[5]

It seems likely that this provides evidence, not only of allusions to the imagery of Rev., but of more detailed knowledge of the idea of the heavenly enthronement in the Latin West—though in this respect the

---

[1] St. Cyprian, Ep. 58.8, CSEL 3.2.663 f.: "Ad agonem saecularem exercentur homines et parantur et magnam gloriam conputant honoris sui, si illis spectante populo et imperatore praesente contigerit coronari. ecce agon sublimis et magnus et coronae caelestis praemio gloriosus, ut spectet nos certantes Deus et super eos quos filios facere dignatus est oculos suos pandens certaminis nostri spectaculo perfruatur, proeliantes nos et fidei congressione pugnantes spectat Deus, spectant angeli eius, spectat et Christus quanta est gloriae dignitas quanta felicitas praeside Deo congredi et Christo iudice coronari?" Cf. Ep. 10.4 f., CSEL 3.2.492 ff.

[2] See QUASTEN, *Patrology* 2, pp. 307 ff., with references to literature. Cf. BAUS, *Der Kranz*, pp. 162 ff.

[3] De corona 15, CCL 2.1064 f.

[4] Ep. 55.20, CSEL 3.2.638; Ep. 58.4, *ibid.* p. 659 f.; Ep. 76.1, *ibid.* p. 828 f.

[5] St. Cyprian, De bono pat. 7, CSEL 3.2.402.

passage is unique. The wreath, the palm and the garment, the food of heaven and the drink of salvation are all part of the apocalyptic scheme of things.

The African authors constantly return to the theme of the Christian, and especially the martyr, as the soldier of Christ.[1] Just as the earthly soldier is crowned by Caesar, so the martyr receives the victor's prize from Christ. The whole of this imagery links up with the concept of Christ as King and *imperator*, typical of the language of the period of the martyrs, particularly in Africa.[2] Christ himself purchased his royal authority by his suffering, and is thus not only Lord of the martyrs, but also their example in suffering and victory. Christ's Kingship from the Cross—*regnavit a ligno*—is an idea common in Tertullian.[3] When he wishes to make clear what the Christian's attitude should be to the use of the wreath, he says that Christ's wreath was the crown of thorns, and before he was greeted by the heavenly powers as *rex gloriae* (Ps. 23(24). 7 ff.) he was described, in the words of the inscription on the Cross, as *rex Iudaeorum*.[4]

The apocalyptic background is especially clear in the concept, frequently recurring in Cyprian, that the Christians shall rule together with Christ:[5] *Serui uigiles Christo dominante regnabimus*.[6] Of particular interest is the text in which Cyprian brings together this idea and the concept of Christ as αὐτοβασιλεία. Christ *is* the resurrection (Jn. 11.25), since we shall rise in him; therefore he *is* the Kingdom, since we shall reign in him.[7]

It seems that all these themes, as used by the African authors, may be derived from a study of Rev., which the West regarded as occupying an unchallenged position in the canon of the NT. We recall that the earliest commentary on Rev. is of western origin (the commentary of Victorinus of Pettau). When at a later date the imagery of Rev. was incorporated into Christian art, and when apses came to be decorated

---

[1] See further below, pp. 179 ff.
[2] See below, pp. 182 ff.
[3] See above, p. 99.
[4] Tertullian, De corona 14.3 f., CCL 2.1063. Cf. the quotation above from St. Cyprian, De bono pat. 7.
[5] See J. CAPMANY, "*Miles Christi*" *en la espiritualidad de San Cipriano*, Col. San Paciano, Ser. Theol. 1 (1956), pp. 251 ff.
[6] Cath. eccl. unit. 27, CSEL 3.1.233.
[7] De dominic. orat. 13, CSEL 3.1.275 f.

with representations of the Lamb or the throne, the elders and the martyrs with palms in their hands, wearing crowns and clad in white raiment, this development seems to have begun in the Latin West, and not least in Rome.[1]

[1] See VAN DER MEER, *Maiestas Domini, passim.* BAUS, *Der Kranz*, pp. 170 ff.

5. LITURGY AND HIERARCHY

Royal Attributes in the Liturgy

In the incipient Christian prayer tradition, as seen in the NT and other documents from the first centuries, we come across many examples of attributes having royal character. These are generally linked with the invocation of the name of God, who is called King, Lord, Almighty, etc.

Attributes of this kind are common in all Semitic religions, and are among the most usual forms of ingress to Jewish prayers, in which God is invoked as Adonai, Melek, Sebaot, etc. The use of these terms to refer to God is particularly common in the Psalter. In the deuterocanonical books of the OT (LXX) God is often addressed in prayers by the corresponding Greek terms: κύριος, βασιλεύς, παντοκράτωρ (the LXX translation of Sebaot), κοσμοκράτωρ, μεγαλοκράτωρ and ὕψιστος (the LXX translation of El Æljon).[1] The Greek magical papyri are also permeated with these and similar titles.[2]

The Christian liturgical tradition adopted most of the Divine titles used in the Jewish cult. We see this in NT prayers, in which God is invoked as κύριε (Lk. 1.68, Acts 4.29) and δέσποτα (Lk. 2.29, Acts 4.24). Royal attributes of this kind are especially common in the liturgical acclamations which have been incorporated into Rev.[3] Here God is called κύριος ὁ θεὸς ὁ παντοκράτωρ (4.8, 11.17, 15.3, 16.7, 19.6), clearly influenced by Isa. 6.3.LXX; on one occasion there is a direct quotation (4.8). Analogous attributes are ὁ κύριος καὶ ὁ θεὸς ἡμῶν (4.11) and ὁ βασιλεὺς τῶν ἐθνῶν (or αἰώνων) (15.3).

---

[1] See e.g. Esther 4.17b, 2 Macc. 1.24, 3 Macc. 6.2.

[2] Th. Schermann, *Griechische Zauberpapyri und das Gemeinde- und Dankgebet im 1. Klemensbriefe*, TU 34.2 a (1909), pp. 22 ff.

[3] For the distinction between prayer and acclamation see Peterson, Εἷς θεός, p. 313. Cf. also C. A. Piper, *The Apocalypse of John and the Liturgy of the Ancient Church*, CH 20 (1951), pp. 10–22. L. Mowry, *Revelation 4–5 and Early Christian Liturgical Usage*, JBL 71 (1952), pp. 75–84.

Distinctive of all these attributes is that they are applied not to Christ, but to the Father. This cannot be due to the fact that the early Church reserved these terms for God alone. We have already seen that in the NT κύριος was a typical Christological term,[1] and that on an occasion Christ may be called δεσπότης (Jud. 4). Although the term βασιλεύς was avoided as much as possible, it is nevertheless used of Christ here and there in the NT.[2] The only terms which can be said to have been reserved for the Father in the NT and period immediately following are παντοκράτωρ and ὕψιστος.[3]

We must seek the cause of this elsewhere: in the fact that the primitive Church seldom addressed its prayers to Christ.[4] The normal form of liturgical prayer in the pre-Constantinian Church was to pray to the Father through the Son. It was however common from the first to offer short acclamations to Christ, and in these are to be found largely the same attributes as were applied to the Father in liturgical prayer. Stephen invokes Christ as κύριε (Acts 7.59, 60).[5] Thomas confesses the Risen Lord to be ὁ κύριός μου καὶ ὁ θεός μου (Jn. 20.28). The principal oratory acclamation directed to Christ was, though, *Maranatha* (1 Cor. 16.22, Did. 10.6) together with its Greek form ἔρχου κύριε Ἰησοῦ (Rev. 22.20)—proof that acclamations of Christ originated in the Aramaic-speaking primitive Church.[6] A further acclamation, common in later Christian liturgy, κύριε ἐλέησον, cannot be demonstrated to have occurred earlier than the 4th century.[7]

All these examples are of short acclamations; not prayers in the true sense of the word. In the longer liturgical prayers in the Church Fathers, royal attributes are still connected with the Father. He is invoked as κύριε, δέσποτα and βασιλεῦ τῶν αἰώνων, and is named as

---

[1] See above, pp. 145 ff.

[2] See above, pp. 139 ff.

[3] See below, pp. 295 ff.

[4] See JUNGMANN, *Stellung Christi*, pp. 113 ff., which is of primary importance in the literature on this subject.

[5] Similar acclamations often appear in the later martyr literature, see K. BAUS, *Das Gebet der Märtyrer*, TrierThZ 62 (1953), pp. 19–32. BAUS does not however draw a clear distinction between prayer and acclamation (cf. *op. cit.*, pp. 29 f.); the long prayers to Christ which he quotes, are taken from the *Acts of Persian Martyrs*, which were written in the 4th century.

[6] See above, p. 45. Cf. also the acclamations in Rev., which are directed both to God and to the Lamb.

[7] The oldest known example is in Ap. Const. VIII; see JUNGMANN, *Stellung Christi*, p. 191.

ὕψιστος in the long prayer incorporated into Clem. 59–61; in the eucharistic prayer of the *Didache* he is addressed as δέσποτα παντοκράτωρ and κύριε (10.3 ff.),[1] and Polycarp's prayer (Mart. Polyc. 14.1) as κύριε ὁ θεὸς ὁ παντοκράτωρ.[2]

It is of particular interest to note that this terminology, limited in liturgical use to the Father, is accompanied by a different and distinctive terminology applied to Christ. The Father, the object of prayer, is invoked as κύριε; the Son, the mediator of prayer, is often given other titles befitting this function. We thus find, in Clement's prayer, Christ addressed as παῖς (59.3–4) and ἀρχιερεύς (61.3); in the eucharistic prayer of the *Didache* he is called throughout παῖς (9.3, 10.2, 3);[3] in Polycarp's prayer he is called ἀρχιερεύς and παῖς.[4] The phrase *per puerum tuum* is met with frequently in Hippolytus' *Apostolic Tradition*.[5] The object of all these titles is to express the idea of Christ as *mediator*. The royal terminology, expressive of the highest rank and the greatest power, is reserved in the liturgy for the Father. Here Christ serves as the mediator of prayer: it is worth noting the typical role played by the word διά "through thy servant", "through our high priest".[6] What we find expressed in the earliest liturgical formulae might thus be

---

[1] JUNGMANN, *op. cit.*, pp. 5 f. Cf. AUDET, *Didachè*, pp. 174 f.

[2] Polycarp's prayer has a clearly liturgical character. See H. DELEHAYE, *Les passions des martyres et les genres littéraires* (1921), pp. 33 and 63.

[3] διά 'Ιησοῦ Χριστοῦ in Did. 9.4 is considered to be a secondary interpolation; see AUDET, *op. cit.*, p. 403, and E. PETERSON, *Über einige Probleme der Didache-Überlieferung*, PFJG, pp. 146 f.

[4] A similar formula occurs in St. Peter's prayer (Acts 4.30): διὰ τοῦ ὀνόματος τοῦ ἁγίου παιδός σου 'Ιησοῦ. Cf. on the other hand Rom. 7.25: διὰ 'Ιησοῦ Χριστοῦ τοῦ κυρίου ἡμῶν and Col. 3.17: πάντα ἐν ὀνόματι κυρίου 'Ιησοῦ εὐχαριστοῦντες τῷ θεῷ πατρὶ δι' αὐτοῦ. See JUNGMANN, *Stellung Christi*, pp. 117 ff., 126 ff. CULLMANN, *Christologie*, pp. 80 f. On the title παῖς, see literature mentioned above p. 37 n. 1, and also A. VON HARNACK, *Die Bezeichnung Jesu als Knecht Gottes und ihre Geschichte in der alten Kirche*, SbB 1926, pp. 212–238, and L. CERFAUX, *La première communauté chrétienne à Jérusalem*, RLC 2, pp. 140 f. The use of the title παῖς in the NT and in the early Church has its origin in the sayings of "Deutero-Isaiah" on the Ebed Yahweh. See I. ENGNELL, *Till frågan om Ebed Jahve-sångerna och den lidande Messias hos "Deuterojesaja"*, SEÅ 10 (1945), pp. 31–65. IDEM, *The Ebed Yahweh Songs and the Suffering Messiah in "Deutero-Isaiah"*, BJRL 31 (1948), pp. 54–93. C. LINDHAGEN, *The Servant Motif in the Old Testament* (1950).

[5] Hippolytus, Ap. Trad. I. 3.6, ed. DIX, p. 6.; *ibid.* I. 4.4. (p. 7); *ibid.* I. 4.13 (p. 9) etc. See JUNGMANN, *Stellung Christi*, p. 8.

[6] On the διά formulas see JUNGMANN, *op. cit.*, pp. 117 ff. and *passim*.

characterized as a *lower* Christology than that encountered in the acclamations.

In this respect the liturgy corresponds to other classes of contemporary literature: apocalyptic writings, exemplified first by Rev. and ideally by the *Ascension of Isaiah*;[1] and representations of the hierarchy of the Church as a reflection of the heavenly hierarchy,[2] in which the Father is accorded the royal epithets and Christ is given the somewhat inferior position of a servant. Apocalyptic subordinationist theology has to do with the dependence of this literature upon its Jewish predecessors.[3] Similarly the inferior position of Christ in the liturgical prayers would seem to be largely due to their having been taken over from Jewish liturgy and supplied with διά formulae to render them suitable for Christian use.[4]

The liturgy of the *Apostolic Constitutions*, from the 4th century, still bears the same characteristics as pre-Constantinian Christian prayers. This cannot be explained away merely by reference to its undoubtedly Arian character.[5] This is a case of a general liturgical tradition, not limited to those prayers which Bousset has identified as originally Jewish; only in connexion with the Arian controversy did this tradition prove controversial. The strikingly subordinationist manner in which the liturgy expressed itself took on unexpected dogmatic significance when the Arians began to use the liturgical documents in support of their doctrine that the Son was of a different substance from the Father. On the other hand, the prayer to Christ was taken up by the orthodox theologians from the 4th century and onwards; this usage, which also implied that Christ was styled βασιλεύς and παντοκράτωρ, had a strongly anti-Arian tendency.[6]

There are however a number of examples of prayers addressed to Christ from the pre-Constantinian period, though it is true that they

---

[1] See above, pp. 136 ff.
[2] See below, pp. 165 ff.
[3] See above, pp. 123 ff.
[4] W. Bousset has proved that a certain number of the prayers in the seventh book of the Apostolic Constitutions have been taken over from Jewish sources. *Eine jüdische Gebetssammlung im siebenten Buch der Apostolischen Konstitutionen*, GN 1915 (1916), pp. 435–489. See further, E. R. Goodenough, *By Light, Light* (1935), pp. 306 ff.
[5] See B. Capelle, *Le texte du "Gloria in excelsis"*, RHE 44 (1949), pp. 439–457.
[6] See Jungmann, *Stellung Christi*, pp. 151 ff.

do not belong to the more reputable traditions. Most are to be found in the apocryphal acts of the Apostles. Here, too, Christ is given epithets otherwise reserved in prayers for the Father.

It is not surprising that in the *Acts of Thomas* the Apostle on several occasions calls out ὁ κύριός μου καὶ ὁ θεός μου:[1] this is an evident case of borrowing from Jn. 20.28. It is more remarkable that elsewhere in the Acts Thomas invokes Christ as θεὲ ἐκ θεοῦ (ὑψίστου),[2] and as κύριε and θεέ.[3] There is a long prayer in the *Acts of John* (108–115), in which Jesus is several times called θεέ and κύριε.[4] βασιλεῦ as an epithet for Christ is found in prayers in both the *Acts of John* and the *Acts of Peter*.[5]

It is usual to interpret this as an expression of an intuitive popular and perhaps Gnosticizing Christology in the Church; it is considered that the authors of the Acts failed to draw a clear distinction between the Father and the Son.[6] That there is a great deal of truth in this interpretation becomes clear when we find, in the same prayers, Christ being called πατήρ.[7]

Another aspect is however given by the fact that it seems to have been a Syrian tradition to address the eucharistic prayer not to the Father but to the Son, a tradition which may refer back to the 2nd century.[8] As Syriac is the original language of the *Acts of Thomas*, it seems reasonable that these writings have been influenced by the

---

[1] *Acts of Thomas* 10.1, AAA 114.5; *ibid.* 167 (p. 281.6); cf. *ibid.* 144.1 (p. 251.10).

[2] *Ibid.* 47 f. (p. 164.5, 16).

[3] *Ibid.* 54 (p. 171.1, 6); *ibid.* 60 f. (pp. 177.10, 21 and 178.2, 4, 7); *ibid.* 107 (p. 219.9 f.).

[4] AAA 207.1, 6, 9; 208.5; 212.1; 213.14; 215.2.

[5] *Acts of John* 22, AAA 163.15. *Vercelli Acts* 39, AAA 16.17.

[6] See F. Torm, *Valentinianismens Historie og Lære* (1901), pp. 75 ff. Jungmann, *Stellung Christi*, p. 147 and n. 87. A synod in Hippo A.D. 393 anathematized liturgical prayers to Christ as well as the abuse of confusing the titles for the Father and the Son, to mention *Patrem pro Filio* or *Filium pro Patre*, see Jungmann, *op. cit.*, p. 150.

[7] *Acts of Philip* 144 (38), AAA 84.9: κύριε Ἰησοῦ Χριστέ, ὁ πατὴρ τῶν αἰώνων, βασιλεῦ (ὅλου) τοῦ φωτός. (The text is extremely corrupt and has several variant readings.) *Acts of John* 112, AAA 212.1 f.: ὑπερουρανίων πατήρ· ὁ τῶν ἐπουρανίων δεσπότης *Gospel of Bartholomew* IV 61, ed. Bonwetsch, GN 1897, p. 26 f.: Ἀββᾶ ὁ πατήρ ... ὁ λόγος τοῦ πατρός; *ibid.* IV 64: θεέ μου καὶ πατὴρ μέγιστε καὶ βασιλεύς.

[8] G. Dix, *The Shape of the Liturgy*, 2nd ed. (1945), p. 180. Jungmann (*op. cit.*, pp. 18 ff.), mentions that the Syriac version of *Testamentum Domini* has its anaphora directed to Christ.

liturgical expressions of the Syrian Church, especially as the liturgical interest of the Acts is remarkable also in other respects. This might also explain the prayers to Christ in the other Acts, which have similar literary trends; in any case the addressing of the prayers has not been uniform in the pre-Constantinian Church.[1]

Be that as it may; the royal attributes are at all events transferred to Christ when prayers are offered to Christ. The attributes are among the fixed elements of prayer, whoever the recipient of the prayer in question may be; thus in the apocryphal acts of the Apostles Christ may be called πατήρ, a title which, it need hardly be said, is otherwise reserved exclusively for the Father.

Pliny, in his letter to the Emperor Trajan, stated that the Christians were in the habit of singing hymns to Christ as a God.[2] None of these hymns have been preserved to our day. We can however gain some impression of the hymnology of the 2nd century from the hymn-like passages in Melito's *De fide*,[3] and from the hymn which concluded the *Paedagogus* of Clement of Alexandria.[4] Among the many epithets for Christ which we find here, and which are often distinctly Hellenistic and Alexandrian in character, is βασιλεύς. Nor is it surprising to find royal attributes transferred to Christ when, as here, he is invoked in the form of a hymn.

Further evidence that there existed a certain relationship between Christology and hymnology is to be seen in the opposition of the heretics Artemon and Paul of Samosata to Christian hymn-writing. Artemon taught—according to an anonymous attack upon his heresy, some passages of which are quoted by Eusebius,[5] and which is probably identical with Hippolytus' *Little Labyrinth*[6]—that the Saviour

---

[1] In this context it may be worth mentioning the prayer, ending a Paschal homily, which seems to have been influenced by Hippolytus' *Homily on the Pasch*; see *Homélies Paschales* 1, ed. P. NAUTIN, SC 27 (1950), ch. 63, p. 27. The prayer seems to have been directed both to God and to Christ or perhaps to Christ alone: Θεὲ δέσποτα πνευματικῶς αἰώνιε (καὶ δέσποτα) βασιλεῦ Χριστέ. (The words in brackets are missing in some manuscripts.) This prayer is however probably post-Nicene and does not belong to the parts taken over from Hippolytus. Cf. QUASTEN, *Patrology* 2, pp. 178 f. Cf. further JUNGMANN, *op. cit.*, p. 199, which stresses the anti-Arian tendency in this kind of prayer formula.

[2] Pliny, Ep. 10 (ad Traj.) 96.7.
[3] See below, p. 195.
[4] See below, pp. 196 f.
[5] Eusebius, HE V. 28, GCS Eus. 2.1.500 ff.
[6] See QUASTEN, *Patrology* 2, p. 196

was a mere man; this he claimed to be the true Apostolic doctrine, preserved until the time of Victor and garbled since Zephyrinus. The anonymous author quotes Irenaeus and Melito, as proof that the Church has long taught that Christ is God; he also turns to Christian hymnody.[1] The hymns he means thus addressed Christ as θεός. We have good reason to suppose that the author of the polemic against Artemon to have mentioned these hymns just because they were rejected by Artemon and his followers.

A parallel case is to be found in the Synodal Epistle sent by the Council of Antioch to Rome and Alexandria as a result of the trial of Paul of Samosata.[2] This bishop, who had taught the monarchian heresy, and had showed indiscretion in the exercise of certain of his episcopal duties, is criticized in the Epistle *inter alia* for forbidding the singing of hymns to Christ:

"(He) stops the psalms to our Lord Jesus Christ, as being the innovations of modern men, and trains women to sing psalms to himself in the midst of the church on the great day of the Passover, which any one might shudder to hear ... He is unwilling to acknowledge that the Son of God has come down from heaven ... But those singing to him and extolling him among the people say that their impious teacher has come down as an angel from heaven."[3]

Tradition links the names of Artemon and Paul. Paul, like Artemon, is said to have taught that Christ was a mere man.[4] The Synodal Epistle says ironically that Paul is at liberty to write to Artemas (=Artemon), and that Artemas' followers are free to have communion with him.[5] It is probable that Artemas—or at least his sect—were active in Paul's day. Eusebius adds, in connexion with the condemnation of Artemon, that Paul of Samosata attempted to reintroduce Artemon's heresy;[6] a similar claim is made by Pamphilus in his *Apology for Origen*.[7] This need not imply that there was an actual link between Artemon and Paul; Bardy considers that, although there existed good communications between Rome and Antioch, the resemblances be-

---

[1] Eusebius, HE V. 28.5 (p. 500).

[2] *Ibid.* VII.30, GCS Eus. 2.2.710. Cf. further below, pp. 237 ff.

[3] *Ibid.* VII.30.10 f. (p. 710).

[4] So according to Eusebius, HE V.28.1, GCS Eus. 2.1.500; *ibid.* VII.27.2, GCS Eus. 2.2.702. See further G. BARDY, *Paul de Samosate*, SSL 4 (1923), pp. 361 ff.

[5] Eusebius, HE VII.30.17, GCS Eus. 2.2.712.

[6] *Ibid.* V.28.1, GCS Eus. 2.1.500.

[7] Pamphilus, *Apology for Origen* 5, PG 17.578 f.

tween the two were due rather to a common background than to personal contact.¹ Bardy also remarks upon the resemblance between Artemon and Paul in respect of their negative attitude to the hymns.²

We thus find no less than three resemblances between Artemon and Paul of Samosata, all of which have to do with the relation of Christology to hymnody: both taught that Christ was "mere man" (whatever this phrase may imply); both condemn the singing of hymns to Christ; and both claim to represent a more ancient form of Christianity. Artemon claims to be a representative of original Apostolic Christianity as it existed before Victor; Paul rejects hymns as a modern innovation.

The fact that Paul condemned hymns to Christ but allowed songs to be sung in his own praise cannot of course be explained away simply as an expression of his colossal egoism. It is quite obvious that Paul did not object to hearing himself praised in song—this fits in perfectly with what we know of the somewhat worldly ecclesiastical politician from Palmyra. But his refusal to countenance hymns to Christ in the context of worship was due to the fact that their contents did not agree with his own Christological ideas.

This opposition from the two heretics, Artemon in Rome and Paul in Antioch, suggests that traditional Christian hymnody represented a higher Christology than that found in the liturgical formulae, which were taken over from synagogue worship and received their Christian content at a later date. In the hymns Christ was invoked as θεός: that is why the author of the polemic against Artemon is able to cite hymnology in support of the doctrine of the Divinity of Christ, and that is why these same hymns are rejected by Artemon and Paul, since in their theology Christ was less than Divine.³ It is also understandable

---

[1] BARDY, *Paul de Samosate*, pp. 238 and 393.
[2] *Ibid.*, p. 385.
[3] It has been proposed that the acclamation ending the eucharistic prayer in Did. (10.6), ὡσαννὰ τῷ θεῷ Δαυίδ, is a confession of Christ as θεός; so J. LEBRETON, *Histoire du dogme de la Trinité* 2 5th ed. (1928), pp. 212 f. This might well be theologically and liturgically possible, because the Divine attributes are easily transferred to Christ, when he is the object of prayer. The textual witnesses, however, do not agree on this point. AUDET (*Didachè*, pp. 62 ff.) considers that the τῷ οἴκῳ Δαυίδ of the Coptic text has to be preferred according to the principle of *lectio difficilior*. AUDET also considers that not even the variant reading τῷ θεῷ Δαυίδ is to be understood as a Christological attribute, *op. cit.* p. 66: "Le modèle de l'expression n'est pas à chercher dans la foi chrétienne en la divinité de Jésus, mais avant tout dans la foi juive au 'Dieu d'Abraham, d'Isaac et de Jacob'."

that Paul rejected the hymns as modern innovations. His reasons for doing so must have been identical with Artemon's: Paul claimed to represent a more original Christology, and therefore expurgated all elements in worship which represented a higher Christology and which were at the same time of relatively recent origin.

Whether or not there was actual contact between Artemon and Paul of Samosata, we can draw the conclusion from their similar reactions that the hymns represented a higher form of Christology than the rest of the liturgy, and that they were therefore rejected by those theologians whose Christology was of a lower order. Among the attributes found in hymns to Christ were certainly, apart from θεός, a number of the other attributes used of the Father in prayers—among them some of the "royal" attributes which we have considered in this chapter.

The Hierarchy of the Church and the Hierarchy of Heaven

The image of God as King and Christ as mediator or high priest which we have seen in apocalyptic literature and in the liturgical attributes, is also reflected in a number of texts of Antiochene origin; here the hierarchy of the Church is represented as an image of the hierarchy of heaven.

The oldest example of this comparison is to be found in St. Ignatius of Antioch. In a number of his letters Ignatius compares the bishop to the Father, the deacon to Christ and the presbyters to the Apostles. In Trall. 3.1 we read:

"In the same way all must respect the deacons as Jesus Christ and the bishop as being a type (τύπος) of the Father."

He draws the same analogy in Magn. 6.1:

"I exhort you, be zealous to do everything in godly harmony, with the bishop presiding (προκαθήμενος) as the type of God, and the presbyters as the type of the council of the apostles and the deacons ... entrusted with the service of Jesus Christ."

Similarly in Smyrn. 8.1:

"You must follow the bishop, as Jesus Christ followed the Father, and you must follow the board of presbyters as the apostles, and revere the deacons as the command of God."

Conversely, God may be called the Bishop of all things (Magn. 3.1). The bishop is also occasionally compared to Christ (Trall. 2.1, Smyrn. 8.2), but is never said to be a *typos* of Christ. When the ecclesiastical hierarchy functions as a whole, each member has been given a role corresponding with the heavenly cult.

We are not mainly interested in the hierarchical organization of the cult, but rather the conception of the heavenly liturgy which it reflects. It has often been pointed out that this order corresponds closely to the description of the heavenly worship found in Rev. 4 f. On his throne at the centre of the heavenly sanctuary sits the Father, surrounded by the twenty-four elders (πρεσβύτεροι); before the throne stands the Lamb, as sacrifice and servant.[1] It would seem to be substantially the same idea of the worship of heaven which St. Ignatius sees reflected in the earthly liturgy.[2]

There is no doubt that this conception goes back to Jewish prototypes. God in the Rabbinic tradition was surrounded in heaven by a celestial court. Rabbi Meir draws a parallel between the earthly and heavenly Sanhedrin in a manner reminiscent of Ignatian typology:

"God has granted to the elders of Israel to handle the Law as the Sanhedrin sitting before God on high. 'I beheld, until thrones were set up and the Ancient of Days seated himself ... Then the court sat down and the books were opened' (Dan. 7.9 f.). In the same way God, who is called the Ancient of Days, sits and repays those who oppose him in their pride."[3]

The picture of God as King, seated among his elders, is to be seen as far back as Isa. 24.23. And Jesus' saying, that the Apostles are to sit on twelve thrones, judging the tribes of Israel (Matt. 19.28, Lk. 22.29 f.) obviously refers back to the idea of the same heavenly court. Similarly the twenty-four elders of Rev. 4 ff. are a vision of the heavenly Sanhedrin. The heavenly court and the members of the Sanhedrin share the title πρεσβύτεροι.[4]

---

[1] It would be tempting to connect the analogy between the Lamb and the deacon with the double meaning of Aram. טליא Cf. above, p. 37, n. 1.

[2] J. PASCHER, *Die Hierarchie in sakramentaler Symbolik*, in Episcopus, presented to Cardinal M. von Faulhaber (1949), p. 292. STOMMEL, *Kathedra*, p. 24.

[3] Shemoth R. 30 (to Ex. 22.1). See BIETENHARD, *Himmlische Welt*, pp. 60 and 116 ff.

[4] BIETENHARD, *op. cit.*, pp. 59 f. Cf. A. JEREMIAS, *Das Alte Testament im Lichte des Alten Orients* (1916), pp. 381 ff. On this conception, see also above, p. 139. The idea that the earthly hierarchy is an image of the heavenly council also occurs in

The typology of the Ignatian Epistles lived on in the Antiochene Church, and corresponding ideas are to be found in the Syriac *Didascalia*.[1] Here, too, the bishop is said to take the place of God: "Do thou therefore, O bishop, teach and rebuke, and loose by forgiveness. And know thy place, that it is that of God Almighty, and that thou hast received authority to forgive sins."[2] The bishop is thus compared, not only with God, but also with the king: the king's power is limited to a man's body, but the bishop exercises heavenly jurisdiction over body and soul; for that reason he is to be venerated as father, king and God.[3]

In *Didasc*. II.26 the whole hierarchical system is described: the bishop as a *typos* of God and the king, the deacon as a *typos* of Christ, the deaconess of the Holy Spirit, the presbyters of the Apostles and, finally, the widows and orphans of the altar.[4] The relationship ex-

---

Clement of Alexandria. Strom. VI.106.2 and 107.2, GCS Clem. 2.485. Cf. also *ibid*. IV.66.1 (p. 278).

[1] See R. H. Connolly's introduction to his tradition of the Syriac *Didascalia*, p. xxxviii ff.

[2] Didasc. II.18.2, ed. Connolly, p. 55. Here, as elsewhere, Funk reconstructs the Latin version from the Syriac text in his edition (p. 64). We follow the principle of quoting Funk's edition, where the text is authentic, but Connolly's translation of the Syriac text, where the original Latin text is missing. Cf. Didasc. II.11.1 f., ed. Funk, p. 46 f.: "Propterea igitur,o episcope, festina, ut mundus sis (ex) operibus, et agnosce(re) locum tuum, quoniam in omnipotentis virtute positus es observans similitudinem Dei omnipotentis. Et ita in ecclesia sede verbum faciens quasi potestatem habens iudicare pro Deo eos qui peccaverunt." Cf. Connolly's ed., pp. 40 ff.

[3] Didasc. II.34.4 f., ed. Funk, pp. 116 ff.: "Ille quidem, qui diadema portat, rex, corporis solius regnat super terram solum solvens ut ligans; episcopus autem et animae et corporis regnat ligans et solvens super terram caelesti potestate; magna enim et caelestis et deifica data est ei potestas. Episcopus ergo diligite ut patrem, timete sicut regem, honorate ut Deum." Cf. Connolly's ed., pp. 94 ff. The same concept in Didasc. II.20.1, ed. Funk, p. 70: "Diligite ergo et honorate episcopum et timete sicut patrem et dominum et secundum Deum." Cf. Connolly's ed., pp. 60 f.

[4] Didasc. II. 26.4–8, ed. Funk, pp. 104 f.: "Primus vero sacerdos vobis e(s)t levita episcopus; hic est, qui verbum vobis ministrat et mediator vester est; hic est magister et post Deum per aquam regenerans pater vester; (hic princeps et dux vester), hic est rex vester potens; hic loco Dei regnans sicuti Deus honoretur a vobis, quoniam episcopus in typum Dei praesidet vobis. Diaconus autem in typum Christi adstat; ergo diligatur a vobis. Diaconissa vero in typum sancti spiritus honoretur a vobis. Presbyteri etiam in typum apostolorum spectentur a vobis. Viduae et orphani in typum altaris putentur autem a vobis." Cf. Connolly's ed., pp. 86 ff.

isting between a deacon and a bishop can thus be compared with that between Christ and the Father: "And let the deacon make known all things to the bishop, even as Christ to his Father."[1] Contact between the congregation and the bishop takes place through the mediation of the deacons; as no one can approach God other than through Christ.[2]

The *Didascalia* also contains a description of the hierarchical order of worship, an order which doubtless corresponds to that envisaged by St. Ignatius, though his letters give us no detailed information on the subject:

"And in your congregation in the holy churches hold your assemblies with all decent order, and appoint the places for the brethren with care and gravity. And for the presbyters, let there be assigned a place in the eastern part of the house, and let the bishop's throne be set in their midst, and let the presbyters sit with him. And again, let the laymen sit in another part of the house towards the east ... But of the deacons let one always stand by the oblations of the Eucharist; and let another stand without by the door and observe them that come in; and afterwards, when you offer, let them minister together in the Church."[3]

The order here corresponds not only to the heavenly liturgy, as it is conceived of in Rev. 4 ff., but also to the placing of the Jewish Sanhedrin. According to the Mishnah Sanhedrin they sat in a semicircle, the president in the middle and the elders to right and left.[4] In Jesus' day the president was always the high priest.[5] A similar arrangement

---

[1] Didasc. II. 44.3, ed. CONNOLLY, p. 109. The Latin text is reconstructed by FUNK, p. 138.

[2] Didasc. II. 28.6, ed. CONNOLLY 90: "But let them have very free access to the deacons, and let them not be troubling the head at all times, but making known what they require through the ministers, that is the deacons. For neither can any man approach the Lord God Almighty except through Christ." The Latin text is reconstructed by FUNK, pp. 108 f. Sometimes the bishop is said to be an *imitator Christi*, but never to be a *typos* of him. Didasc. II. 20.9, ed. FUNK, p. 74: "Christi vultum portans. Per te salvator dicit his qui peccaverunt: 'Remittentur tibi peccata tua ...'" Cf. CONNOLLY's ed., pp. 64 f. Didasc. II. 24.4, ed. FUNK, p. 92: "Hunc salvatorem, regem et Deum nostrum, o episcopi, prospectorem vobis habere oportet et eius imitatores esse." Cf. CONNOLLY's ed., pp. 76 f. Cf. also Didasc. II. 25.9, ed. CONNOLLY, p. 81: "For thou art an imitator of Christ."

[3] Didasc. II. 57.2 ff., ed. CONNOLLY, p. 119. Reconstruction of the Latin text by FUNK, pp. 158 ff.

[4] C. Sanh. 4.3. See S. B. HOENIG, *The Great Sanhedrin* (1953), p. 56.

[5] E. SCHÜRER, *Geschichte des jüdischen Volkes im Zeitalter Jesu Christi* 2, 4th ed. (1907), pp. 248 ff.

was observed by the Qumran sect.[1] There is thus no doubt that the Church's order was derived from that of the Jewish Sanhedrin; hence, too, was derived the typological conception of the hierarchy as a reflection of God's court. That is why the bishop, as president (προκαθήμενος)—cf. Ign. ad Magn. 6.1—was understood to be the *typos*, not of Christ, but of the Father. It is the deacon instead who is considered to fulfil Christ's functions. Christ stands before the Father's throne and carries out his commandments, just as the deacon is always prepared to serve the bishop. The character of "king" is linked to the bishop and God; that of "servant" to the deacon and Christ. The whole of this ministerial typology corresponds to the apocalyptic vision of heaven, as seen in Rev. and—even more intensively—in the *Ascension of Isaiah*; the liturgical structure of the Antiochene tradition thus corresponds to a distinctly subordinationist Christology.

It is in this context that we must place the origin of the bishop's throne.[2] They were in use in pre-Constantinian times, and as far back as ca. 200 A.D. the "cathedra" had become a metaphor denoting "the office of bishop".[3] In all probability there are references to the bishop's throne and the presbyters' bench in Hermas.[4] Here, too, the Christian tradition harks back to Jewish prototypes: Stommel has written on the subject of "Moses' chair", the ideas connected with it and the metaphorical use of the term.[5] It is not entirely unthinkable that this corresponds to a cult object which actually existed in Jewish synagogues.[6] Stommel also has a hypothesis, which is interesting but requires more detailed investigation and proof, that the bishop's throne in early churches corresponds to the Torah niche in the synagogue and, further, that this arrangement corresponded to the idea of the bishop as a sort

---

[1] C. RABIN, *Qumran Studies*, in Scripta judaica 2 (1957), pp. 103 ff.

[2] STOMMEL, *Kathedra*, passim. IDEM, *Bischofsstuhl*, passim.

[3] *Canon Muratori*, ed. G. RAUSCHEN in *Monumenta minora saeculi secundi*, FP 3 (1905), p. 34. Tertullian, De praescr. haer. 36.1, CCL 1.216; IDEM, Adv. Valentinianos 11.2, CCL 2.762. See STOMMEL, *Kathedra*, p. 17 and n. 3.

[4] Hermas, Vis. III. 1.4–8. See STOMMEL, *Kathedra*, pp. 20 ff.

[5] STOMMEL, *Kathedra*, p. 18.

[6] M. GINSBURGEN (*La chaire de Moïse*, REJ 90 (1931), pp. 161–165), rejects the idea that "Moses' chair" was a real piece of furniture in the synagogue. Later discoveries, especially of the synagogue in Doura Europos, seem however to favour the theory of the chair as a liturgical object. See C. ROTH, *The 'Chair of Moses' and its Survivals*, PEQ 81 (1949), pp. 100–111. E. STAUFFER, *Der Stand der Neutestamentlichen Forschung*, in Theologie und Liturgie (1952), pp. 66 f. A cautious judgment is given by I. RENOW, *The Seat of Moses*, IEJ 5 (1954), pp. 262–267.

of νόμος ἔμψυχος, a personification in the cult of Divine revelation.¹ It is worth noting in our context that in pre-Constantinian times the bishop's throne is never associated with the throne of Christ.² On the other hand, however, the bishop, carrying out God's function of judge in the centre of the liturgical room, is soon regarded as a king, the king himself being also looked upon as the representative of Divinity, if not Divine in his own person.³ This made it possible, as in *Didascalia*, to give the bishop the title of king. It is also likely that the pre-Constantinian liturgical room, centred as it was on the cathedra instead of the altar, was highly suggestive of an imperial or royal basilica.

It is thus entirely consistent that the *Pseudo-Clementines* (which are also of Antiochene origin) defend the monarchical episcopate on a basis of political arguments. St. Peter, in his speech made on the occasion of Zacchaeus' consecration as bishop, says that it is necessary, for the sake of peace and harmony, to have a leader to follow. That is why God has appointed Christ King over the age to come, and that is why the faithful must follow the bishop, honouring him as the image (εἰκών) of God.⁴ Here the bishop is not regarded as the representative of Christ. In the *Pseudo-Clementines* the king is the image of God; this applied to Noah in the past, to Christ in the age to come and to the bishop in the age of the Church.⁵

The tendency to link the bishop with the Father and the deacon with Christ continued, and even became intensified, in the *Apostolic Con-*

---

¹ STOMMEL, *Kathedra*, pp. 29 ff. We hope to be able to investigate this hypothesis in another context. The throne as the place of revelation has been pointed out especially by G. WIDENGREN, *The Ascension of the Apostle and the Heavenly Book*, UUÅ 1950.7, *passim*. IDEM, *Religionens värld*, 2nd ed., pp. 469 ff. IDEM, *Muhammad the Apostle of God and his Ascension*, UUÅ 1955. 1, *passim*. IDEM, *Uppenbarelsebringaren på tronen*, in IDEM, *Kungar, profeter och harlekiner* (1961), pp. 112–117. Cf. also F. BOLL, *Aus der Offenbarung Johannis*, ΣΤΟΙΧΕΙΑ 1 (1914), pp. 136 ff. (excursus "Könige als Offenbarungsträger"). It seems that the practice of placing the Gospels on a throne during certain councils in the early Church (see above, p. 15) belongs in the same context.

² An exception is perhaps the pseudo-Clementine Hom. 3.70. GCS PsC. Hom., p. 82; it is said here that it is necessary to honour the bishop, because those things which are carried to him, are carried on to Christ, and from him to God. It is therefore fitting to honour the throne of Christ, even as we are commanded to honour Moses' chair, though it is possessed by sinners.

³ STOMMEL, *Kathedra*, pp. 24 ff.

⁴ See further below, p. 246.

⁵ Cf. below, p. 253.

stitutions.¹ In Ap. Const. II.26.5 we read, in an appendix to the text of the *Didascalia*, that the deacon must be prepared to serve the bishop as Christ serves the Father: to serve him irreproachably, just as Christ does nothing on his own initiative but always carries out the will of the Father.² This is entirely in line with the subordinationist Christology of the *Apostolic Constitutions*.

The functions of the bishop are however linked with those of Christ in the interpolated version of the Epistles of Ignatius, which is contemporary with the *Apostolic Constitutions* and shares the same tendencies. Here it is made perfectly clear that it is in his priestly, and not his kingly functions that the bishop is the image of Christ. When we read in (Ps.-) Ign. ad Eph. 6 that the bishop is to be regarded as the Lord himself, standing before the Lord (the Father), ὡς αὐτὸν τὸν κύριον δεῖ προσβλέπειν, τῷ κυρίῳ παρεστῶτα,³ it is Christ the High Priest who is meant: this is clear from the reference to Christ standing—a general expression for his priestly function.⁴ The situation is even more clearly reflected in Smyrn. 9, which says that the bishop is the bearer of the εἰκών of God, i.e. the image of God as a ruler, and the

---

¹ Pascher (*Hierarchie*, p. 294) and, following him, Stommel (*Kathedra*, p. 27 n. 80) states without verification, and wrongly, that the *Apostolic Constitutions* see the bishop as a type of Christ and not as a type of the Father.

² ὁ δὲ διάκονος τούτῳ παριστάσθω ὡς ὁ Χριστὸς τῷ πατρί, καὶ λειτουργείτω αὐτῷ ἐν πᾶσιν ἀμέμπτως, ὡς ὁ Χριστός, ἀφ' ἑαυτοῦ ποιῶν οὐδέν, τὰ ἀρεστὰ ποιεῖ τῷ πατρὶ πάντοτε. Cf. the addition to II.44.3, ed. Funk, p. 139, where it is said about the deacon: λαβὼν παρὰ τοῦ ἐπισκόπου τὴν ἐξουσίαν, ὡς ὁ Χριστὸς παρὰ τοῦ πατρὸς τὸ προνοεῖν.

³ ed. Lightfoot, p. 838.

⁴ The same situation is to be seen in Ap. Const. VI.30.9, Funk p. 385, in an expanded version of Didasc. VI. 23.8, ed. Funk p. 382 f.: "sedentis ad dexteram sedis omnipotentis Dei super Cherubin" (cf. Connolly's ed., p. 258). Ap. Const. cites Ps. 109 (110).1 b, but goes on to quote the vision of Stephen, according to which the Son of Man *stands* at the right hand of Power, ὡς ἀρχιερέα πάντων τῶν λογικῶν ταγμάτων, which is clearly the most important factor for Ap. Const. The very fact of Christ here being represented as standing meant that this narrative played a not unimportant role as an Arian argument. St. Ambrose also takes up this question in his anti-Arian polemic, and represents Christ in both his functions: "He sits as Judge of the quick and the dead; he stands as his people's Advocate. He stood, then, as a Priest, whilst he was offering to his Father the sacrifice of a good martyr." (De fide 3.17 (137), PL 16.616 f.). Cf. G. H. Williams, *Christology and Church-State Relations in the Fourth Century*, CH 20. 4 (Dec. 1951), pp. 17 f. On the question of Christ standing and sitting, see also Bietenhard, *Himmlische Welt*, pp. 66, 71.

image of Christ as a priest.[1] Anyone opposing the bishop is thus guilty of disrespect to God and Christ Jesus, the first-born and the Father's only high priest by nature.[2] We find the same expression in Magn. 4, where Christ is called the first bishop and the only high priest by nature.[3] Elsewhere Christ is called in interpolations by strikingly subordinationist terms.[4] When a list of the heavenly powers mentions Christ's βασιλεία (Trall. 5), it is immediately followed by the statement that the power of God is incomparably greater.[5] Hierarchical speculation, according to which the king is subordinate to the bishop, the bishop to Christ and Christ to God, (Philad. 4 and Smyrn. 9) is dealt with in a later passage.[6] Since the bishop is the image of Christ as priest, the function of the deacon differs from that in the early tradition; according to Trall. 7 he represents the angelic powers.

---

[1] ed. LIGHTFOOT, p. 808: (τίμα) ἐπίσκοπον δὲ, ὡς ἀρχιερέα θεοῦ εἰκόνα φοροῦντα· κατὰ
[2] τὸ ἄρχειν, θεοῦ, κατὰ δὲ τὸ ἱερατεύειν, Χριστοῦ.
μὲν Ibid., p. 809: ... οὐκ ἄνθρωπον ἀτιμάζει, ἀλλὰ θεὸν, καὶ Χριστὸν Ἰησοῦν, τὸν πρωτότοκον, καὶ μόνον τῇ φύσει τοῦ πατρὸς ἀρχιερέα.
[3] Ibid., p. 752: ὁ ἀληθινὸς καὶ πρῶτος ἐπίσκοπος, καὶ μόνος φύσει ἀρχιερεύς.
[4] On Christ as ἀρχιστράτηγος in Smyrn. 8, see below, p. 267.
[5] Ibid., p. 737: ... τοῦ τε πνεύματος τὴν ὑψηλότητα, καὶ τοῦ κυρίου τὴν βασιλείαν, καὶ ἐπὶ πᾶσι τὸ τοῦ παντοκράτορος θεοῦ ἀπαράθετον.
[6] See below, p. 322.

6. CHRIST THE KING AND THE PAGAN EMPEROR

The attitude of the Christian Church to the Roman state is one of the most widely discussed aspects of the history of the first centuries A.D.[1] There are two main schools of thought on this question: those who, basing their views on Rom. 13, consider the Christian Church to have been entirely loyal to the Roman government, and those who consider early Christianity to have been a revolutionary movement directed against the Empire.[2] Neither view, when expressed in its extreme form, is accurate. The main interest of the Christian Church was eschatological, not political, and when the Church confessed Christ as King it did so, convinced that the present age and all its temporary political organization would soon disappear, to be replaced by the other-worldly Kingdom of Christ. The Christian view of the politics of the time was thus usually that they were no more than provisional arrangements; they were regarded as being of merely relative worth. Typically enough, the NT and later traditions claimed political power to have been derived from the angels: ordained by God but not of Divine nature. This power, too, was broken by Christ's work

---

[1] The literature on the relation between the early Christian Church and the Roman state is extremely comprehensive. The following works are worthy of special mention: LOHMEYER, *Christuskult*. H. WINDISCH, *Imperium und Evangelium* (1931). F. J. DÖLGER, *Zur antiken und frühchristlichen Auffassung der Herrschergewalt von Gottes Gnaden*, AC 3 (1932), pp. 117–127. K. L. SCHMIDT, *Das Gegenüber von Kaiser und Staat in der Gemeinde des Neuen Testaments*, ThBl 16 (1937), col. 1–16 (with further bibliography). G. KITTEL, *Christus und Imperator* (1939). O. ECK, *Urgemeinde und Imperium*, BFTh 42.3 (1940), pp. 301–434. M. DIBELIUS, *Rom und die Christen im ersten Jahrhundert*, SbHei 1941–42.2. W. DURANT, *Caesar und Christus* (1949). STAUFFER, *Christus und die Cäsaren*. CULLMANN, *Dieu et César*. H. RAHNER, *Kirche und Staat im frühen Christentum* (1961), pp. 21–71.

[2] An extreme example of the interpretation of early Christianity as a revolutionary movement is given by EHRHARDT, *Politische Metaphysik* 2. Cf. above, p. 34.

of salvation, when at his Ascension he laid all angelic powers beneath his feet (Eph. 1.20 ff.).[1]

In the NT we find the Christian Church already claiming to be the new people of God, separated from the rest of mankind through the saving work of Christ, just as the old Israel was constituted as a people by the Exodus from Egypt and the Sinai Covenant.[2] The pre-Constantinian Church often claimed to be a *tertium genus*: a separate race alongside the Jews and the Gentiles.[3] This race-consciousness was of course non-political in conception. Jesus had said that his Kingdom was not of this world (Jn. 18.36); the Church in turn emphasized that the Kingdom to which it owed its allegiance was not earthly but heavenly.[4] The Christian's citizenship was double: of earth and of heaven—an idea which received one of its clearest expressions in Diogn. 5–6.

But the Church's claim to constitute a separate people proved extremely dangerous from the political point of view. The Roman authorities came to look upon Christians as a threat to the unity of the Empire, a state within the state, a group whose loyalty was in doubt. It is in this context that compulsory participation in the imperial cult and the persecutions must be seen.

The Christians' attitude to Caesar stood in close relation to their outward circumstances. Christian documents from the first centuries— e.g. the works of the Apologetes and the Alexandrian theologians— were often strikingly positive in their estimation of the imperial authorities.[5] Time and again Jesus' saying on the imperial tax was taken as a *modus vivendi*; "Pay Caesar what is due to Caesar, and pay

---

[1] See SCHMIDT, *Gegenüber*, col. 14 f. CULLMANN, *Dieu et César*, pp. 55 ff.

[2] See N. A. DAHL, *Das Volk Gottes*, Skrifter utg. av Det Norske Vid.-Akad. 2, Hist.-filos. Kl. 1941.2.

[3] VON HARNACK has a chapter on this theme in his *Mission* 1, pp. 206–234.

[4] Cf. Justin, Apol. 11.1–2. We have already mentioned the notice in Hegesippus' *Hypomnemata* (Eusebius, HE III 20.1–6), according to which some of Jesus' relatives were examined by the Emperor Domitian but were released, when they declared that the Kingdom of Christ was not earthly but heavenly and eschatological.

[5] See E. PETERSON, *Kaiser Augustus im Urteil des antiken Christentums*, Hochland 30.2 (1933), pp. 289–299. IDEM, *Monotheismus, passim*. A well-balanced representation of positive and negative elements (with stress on the positive trends) is given by RAHNER, *Kirche*, pp. 21 ff.

God what is due to God" was a common definition of Church–Caesar relations in the pre-Constantinian Church.[1]

A striking fact is that the martyr literature contains occasional examples of a positive attitude to the Emperor. This is expressed most clearly in the *Acts of Apollonius*, which is probably based on an authentic report of the trial of the Christian philosopher, martyred under the Emperor Commodus.[2] On being exhorted to sacrifice to the image of Caesar, Apollonius answered that all Christians offer an unbloody and pure sacrifice to God, who is παντοκράτωρ, but that they pray to those images which Divine Providence has established to rule on earth.[3] He went on to say that Christians pray for Commodus daily, since they recognized that his power was derived from the One God.[4]

It is clear that Apollonius' views go back to Hellenistic ideas on the role of the Emperor, similar to those expressed by Philo and other early authors, ideas which we shall later consider in more detail.[5] Typical of this school of thought is the characterization of the Emperor as the image of God, but this is the first occasion on which we find it in Christian literature. Thus during the latter half of the 2nd century it was natural for a Christian theologian familiar with Hellenistic philosophy to look upon the Emperor as God's instrument for the government of the world.

When the Emperor began to interfere with God's proper sphere of activity, either by forbidding Christian worship or by claiming the right to be worshipped as divine, there arose open conflict. Caesar came to be regarded differently—as Antichrist, to whom God has granted power for a time in order to test the Christians' faith, but who is destined soon to be overthrown when Christ the King comes in glory.

This political interpretation of the final eschatological conflict is

---

[1] First in St. Justin, Apol. 17. Cf. St. Irenaeus, Adv. haer. III 8.1, ed. HARVEY 2.27. Tertullian, De corona 12.4, CCL 2.1059, Scorp. 14.2, CCL 2.1096, De idol. 15.3, CCL 2.1115 f., De fuga 12.9 f., CCL 2.1152 f.

[2] *Ausgewählte Märtyrerakten*, ed. KNOPF & KRÜGER (1929), pp. 30 ff. Cf. QUASTEN, *Patrology* 1, pp. 183 f. (with references to literature).

[3] *Acts of Apollonius* 8 (p. 31): τὴν δι' εὐχῶν μάλιστα ⟨ὑπὲρ νοητικῶν⟩ καὶ λογικῶν εἰκόνων τῶν τεταγμένων ὑπὸ τῆς προνοίας τοῦ θεοῦ βασιλεύειν ἐπὶ τῆς γῆς.

[4] *Ibid.* 9 (p. 31): εὐχόμεθα ... ὑπὲρ τοῦ βασιλεύοντος ἐν τῷδε τῷ κόσμῳ Κομόδου, εἰδότες ἀκριβῶς ὅτι οὐκ ὑπὸ ἄλλου τινός, ἀλλὰ ὑπὸ μόνης τῆς τοῦ ἀνικήτου θεοῦ βουλῆς, τοῦ τὰ πάντα ἐμπεριέχοντος, ὡς προεῖπον, βασιλεύει ἐπὶ τῆς γῆς. On the prayer for the Emperor, see DIBELIUS, *Pastoralbriefe*, pp. 30 f. DÖLGER, *Herrschergewalt*, pp. 118 ff.

[5] See below, pp. 253 f.

found in several of the earliest Christian apocalypses. Best-known among these is the description of the "beast" in Rev. 13.1 ff., which there is no doubt refers to the Roman Emperor. The beast is the last of the kings who are to come (Rev. 7.11). He is given power over all tribes and peoples and tongues and nations (13.7). He mocks God, persecutes the saints and claims the right to be worshipped (13.5 ff.). But the beast and the other kings are destined to be overcome by the Lamb and his servants, since the Lamb is Lord of lords and King of kings. Christ is thus described as King over against the earthly political authorities, i.e. in their pseudo-religion and godlessness.[1]

The *Ascension of Isaiah* has the same characteristics. Beliar, this book's version of Antichrist, has committed matricide (4.2), thus recalling the Emperor Nero.[2] Like the beast of Rev., Beliar is to be a king with power over the whole world, and is to persecute the Christian Church. One of the Twelve is to be left at his mercy; this is probably a reference to Peter's martyrdom under Nero. Beliar is to make himself a god, and his statue is to be worshipped by the people (4.2–13). His kingdom, like that of Antichrist, will be overthrown in the last days: *Kyrios* will come with his angels and saints and cast Beliar into Gehenna (4.14).

Among the Church Fathers Hippolytus is the one who most clearly maintained an attitude of enmity to the Roman Empire. The Empire he considered to be the fourth kingdom of the world (Dan. 2.40 ff.) which was to be replaced by the eternal Kingdom.[3] It is typical that Hippolytus, the author of the first Christian commentary on Daniel, was dominated by the same kind of eschatological speculation as that which we find in the Christian apocalypses, including their political interpretation of the role of Antichrist. Here, too, we find early attempts at a Christian philosophy of history—on this occasion distinctly dualistic. The fact that Christ was born during the reign of the Emperor Augustus—later used by Eusebius as proof of Augustus' divine commission—is taken by Hippolytus instead to be a sign of how Antichrist gathered his forces in face of the coming trial of strength with the heavenly King.[4]

---

[1] See CULLMANN, *Dieu et César*, pp. 77 ff.

[2] It is however a matter of doubt, if the writing may be dated on this ground to the time of Nero, as is proposed by DANIÉLOU, *Judéo-christianisme*, pp. 22 f.

[3] Hippolytus, De Antichr. 25, GCS Hipp. 1.2.17.

[4] Hippolytus, Comm. on Dan. 4.9, GCS Hipp. 1.1.206 ff.

According to Hippolytus, one of the signs of Antichrist is his faithful imitation of Christ in all things. The kingdom of Antichrist is thus a shameless copy of the Kingdom of Christ. It was prophesied that Christ would resemble a lion in his royal dignity and his glory (Gen. 49.10); in the same way the Scriptures call Antichrist a lion in his tyranny and violence (1 Pet. 5.8). There can be little doubt that the godless kingdom of Antichrist is here meant to represent the Roman Empire.[1]

This anti-Roman attitude is however most strongly expressed in the martyr literature. Christian opposition to Caesar drew freely for its imagery upon the OT, and upon Dan. in particular, in which Nebuchadnezzar, Belshazzar and Darius are represented as typical godless rulers, claiming divine rights of worship and other insults to the holiness of God, only to be overthrown at the last.[2]

Against such rulers Daniel stands up as the mouthpiece of God, proclaiming that it is God who possesses true power. Interpreting Nebuchadnezzar's dream of the colossus with feet of clay, he says that Nebuchadnezzar's power comes from God (2.37). But in time God will make an end of all kingdoms, and found a kingdom which can never be destroyed (2.44; cf. 4.3, 4.34, 6.27). From Dan. 7.14 we see that this kingdom is identical with that of the Son of Man. Thus at this early stage we have the double aspect: that the earthly king derives his might from God, but that like all earthly power, it is destined to perish in the last days, when the eschatological king appointed by God assumes all power. A contrast may be drawn between the earthly king and the heavenly, as when Nebuchadnezzar is punished with the loss of reason and then on his recovery gives thanks to the King of heaven (Dan. 4.34 f., 37).[3]

A more direct predecessor of the Christian martyr tradition, with which we shall deal in the following pages, is to be seen in the Jewish martyrdoms.[4] In one of the classical Jewish martyr texts, 2 Macc. 7.9,

---

[1] Hippolytus, De Antichr. 6, GCS Hipp. 1.2.7 f.

[2] Claims of Emperor cult are made both by Nebuchadnezzar (ch. 3) and by Darius (ch. 6). Belshazzar made a banquet with the vessels carried away from the temple of Jerusalem (ch. 5).

[3] On this motif and connected problems, see B. RIGAUX, *L'Antéchrist et l'opposition au royaume messianique dans l'Ancient et le Nouveau Testament* (1932), *passim*.

[4] The connexion between Jewish and Christian martyr literature is pointed out

one of the seven brothers cruelly executed by Antiochus Epiphanes says to the king, "You outlaw, although you may remove us from this life, the King of the whole world will raise us up, who have died in defence of his law, to new life, an eternal life." This text was well known among early Christians, and is also given a Christian interpretation, according to which "the King of the whole world" is Christ.[1]

One of the chief characteristics of the martyr literature is therefore that the martyr in question, when examined before Caesar or his representative, confesses Christ as the true King. There is no doubt that such actually took place, strengthening the case against Christians as enemies of the state.[2] The oldest example of this we have is the *Martyrdom of Polycarp*, in which Polycarp is commanded to sacrifice to the Emperor and say "Kyrios Kaisar" (8.2)[3] but instead confesses Christ as his King (9.3).[4] The practice of addressing the Emperor as *kyrios* was not otherwise considered to be apostasy either by Jews or Christians. We have earlier pointed out how according to Philo, Jews used the title *kyrios* before Caligula,[5] and in the *Martyrdom of Paul*, the martyr Patroclus uses the same title before the Emperor Nero.[6] But the title took on a quite different controversial tone when, in connexion with the Caesar cult, it was made a confession of the divinity of the Emperor—a development which began when Domitian adopted the title *Dominus et Deus*, thus coming into conflict with the language of the Christian Church.[7] We see, in this situation, how the confession

---

especially by H. W. Surkau, *Martyrien in jüdischer und frühchristlicher Zeit* (1938). H. von Campenhausen has tried to minimize the Jewish influence on Christian Acts of Martyrs, *Die Idee des Martyriums in der alten Kirche* (1936), but this attempt has not been accepted in the later discussion.

[1] St. Cyprian, Ad Quir. 3.17, CSEL 3.1.132, Ad Fortunatum 11, *ibid.*, p. 339. St. Hilary, Contra Constantium 6, PL 10.582.

[2] von Harnack, who seems to underestimate the role of the persecutions, considers that "some hotspurs" confessed that God or Christ was their only King or Emperor, and so incurred a just punishment, but that such cases were very rare, *Mission* 1, p. 221 n. 2.

[3] Cf. above p. 60.

[4] πῶς δύναμαι βλασφημῆσαι τὸν βασιλέα μου, τὸν σώσαντά με;

[5] See above, p. 43 n. 2.

[6] See below, p. 180.

[7] The controversial theme in Mart. Polyc. seems to be less the title *kyrios* than the other cultic acts which Polycarp was commanded to perform: to swear by the genius of the Emperor and to curse the godless (= the Christians). Cerfaux is certainly right when he says that "la formule *kyrios Caesar* regarde plus l'aspect politique des persecutions que leur aspect religieux", *Le titre Kyrios*,

of Christ as *basileus* became more important as a protest against the imperial cult. When the Emperor claimed to be divine, the Christian instead affirmed that Christ was King (cf. Mart. Polyc. 17.3).[1] The two aspects of this attitude to the title *kyrios* are clearly shown in a statement of Tertullian:

"Augustus, the founder of the empire, would not even have the title Lord; for that, too, is a name of Deity. For my part, I am willing to give the emperor this designation, but in the common acceptance of the word, and when I am not forced to call him Lord as in God's place."[2]

It is thus not correct to say—as has often been said—that the use of the title *kyrios* by the Emperor was condemned out of hand. But when linked with the imperial cult it could be highly controversial, and *kyrios Christos* could be set up in opposition to *kyrios Kaisar*. It was more usual, however, to use the title *basileus* or the Latin *imperator* as titles of Christ in contexts in which a distinction was to be drawn between the eternal King and the temporal Emperor.

A common element in the acts of the martyrs is that the Christian confesses himself to be a soldier of Christ.[3] This theme—the Christian as a soldier of Christ—goes back to the language of the NT;[4] a factor which contributes to its occurrence in the acts of the martyrs is of course the element of heroics, together with the idea of martyrdom as a victorious struggle against the powers of darkness. But over and above this, a good number of martyrs seem actually to have been soldiers.[5] The refusal to fight in war was, alongside the refusal to

---

[1] On the title βασιλεύς for Christ, see above, pp. 39 ff. The title βασιλεύς for God may also appear in Christian Acts of Martyrs in its controversial sense. See e.g. the relation of the martyrdom of Lucius in St. Justin's App. (2 Apol.).2: "He professed his thanks, knowing that he was delivered from such wicked rulers, and was going to the Father and King of the heavens."

[2] Apolog. 33.3–34.2, CCL 1.143 f.

[3] The best survey of this motif is still that given by von HARNACK, *Militia Christi*. For the occurrence of the motif in St. Cyprian, see CAPMANY, "*Miles Christi*", passim.

[4] von HARNACK, *Militia Christi*, pp. 8 ff. LEIVESTAD, *Christ the Conqueror*, pp. 138 ff.

[5] von HARNACK, *Mission* 2, pp. 48 f. On the other hand, H. DELEHAYE points out that there is a tendency in the Martyr legends to make soldiers out of such saints, who seem to have had no military profession, *Les légendes grecques des saints militaires* (1909), pp. 112 f. He doubts, however, that the reason for this development is the idea of the Christian as a soldier of Christ: "Le symbolisme est une

sacrifice to Caesar, probably the most common cause of death sentences passed on Christians.

One of the best examples of this confession—of Christ as King and the Christian as his soldier—is found, not in any of the authentic acts of the martyrs, but in the apocryphal *Martyrdom of Paul*.[1] The theme runs through the whole work, but is especially prominent in Chaps. 2 f. The context is this: that Nero's cup-bearer Patroclus has fallen out of a window and been killed, but has been brought back to life by Paul (cf. Acts 20.9–12). The continuation is so characteristic that we shall quote it in extenso:[2]

"And Caesar, when he heard that Patroclus was alive, became afraid and would not go in. But when he went in, and saw Patroclus, he was shocked and said, 'Patroclus, are you alive?' And he said, 'Yes, Caesar, I am alive.' And he said, 'Who brought you back to life?' And the boy, filled with faith, said, 'Jesus Christ, the King of the ages (ὁ βασιλεὺς τῶν αἰώνων).' And Caesar was troubled and said, 'Shall he, then, be the King of the ages and overthrow all kingdoms?' Patroclus answered him, 'Yes, he overthrows all kingdoms (πάσας τὰς βασιλείας τὰς ὑπ' οὐρανόν), and he alone shall exist eternally, and no kingdom shall escape him.' And he struck him in the face, saying, 'Patroclus, are you also a soldier of that King?' (καὶ σὺ στρατεύῃ τῷ βασιλεῖ ἐκείνῳ;) And he said, 'I am, Lord Caesar (κύριε Καῖσαρ), for he brought me back to life when I was dead.' And Barsabas Justus of the broad feet, and Urion the Cappadocian, and Festus the Galatian, Caesar's chief men, said, 'We are also soldiers of the King of the ages.' And when he had tortured them, he threw them into prison, though he loved them; and he commanded the soldiers of the Great King (τοὺς τοῦ μεγάλου βασιλέως στρατιώτας) to be sought out, and published a decree to the effect that all who were found to be Christians and soldiers of Christ should be killed.

And Paul was brought in together with many others, in bonds, and all his fellow-prisoners paid attention to him. Caesar recognized that

---

explication commode et peut suffire dans certains cas, à calmer l'imagination. Malheureusement, elle est bien superficielle, et le plus souvent, ne répond nullement à la réalité. A moins d'en saisir l'application dans un cas concret, l'hypothèse mérite toutes les défiances," *ibid.*, p. 118.

[1] On this writing, see QUASTEN, *Patrology* 1, p. 132.

[2] AAA pp. 108 f. Cf. SCHUBART's & SCHMIDT's edition of the papyrus fragments, (1936), p. 60.

he was the leader of the camp (ὅτι ἐκεῖνος ἐπὶ τῶν στρατοπέδων ἐστίν) and said to him, 'You may be the servant of the Great King, but you are my prisoner. How did you think you could infiltrate into Roman territory and recruit soldiers (στρατολογεῖν) from my province?' But Paul, filled with the Holy Spirit, said in the presence of all, 'O Caesar, it is not only from your province that we recruit soldiers, but from the whole world. For we have been commanded that no man should miss the opportunity of serving my King (στρατευθῆναι τῷ ἐμῷ βασιλεῖ).' "[1]

This account is of course pure legend. Its historical value lies in the fact of its being such an outstanding expression of the faith of the martyr Church in Christ the King. His Kingdom is other-wordly and eschatological in character; he is the King of the ages, who is to come and overthrow all the kingdoms of the earth. His Kingdom is supranational; his soldiers are drawn from the four corners of the earth. The trial which his soldiers must undergo is to bear witness to their Lord; this has the quality of high drama when it has to be done before an earthly king (cf. Ps. 118 (119).46, Matt. 10.18 f.). Indeed, the very word "martyr" would seem to mean "one who bears witness".[2]

Typical of the acts of the martyrs is that the usual system of dating —giving the year of the Emperor's reign, the Consuls' office, etc.—is found prefacing passages in which Christ is called the true King. An example is in the secondary conclusion of the *Martyrdom of Polycarp* (Chap. 21), where the dating has been supplemented by βασιλεύοντος δὲ εἰς τοὺς αἰῶνας Ἰησοῦ Χριστοῦ.[3] A more common formula is however κατὰ δὲ βασιλεύοντος τοῦ κυρίου ἡμῶν Ἰησοῦ Χριστοῦ, which occurs in a

---

[1] Other typical examples of the contrast between God or Christ and the earthly rulers occur in the *Acts of Persian Martyrs*, German transl. by O. Braun in BKV²: The *Martyrdom of Mar Simon and Companions* 15 (p. 23), 16 (p. 25), 22 (p. 31), 38 (p. 46). The *Martyrdom of Martha* contains a confession of Christ as the eschatological King, which has already been quoted above, p. 149. The same tendency appears also in the *Passion of St. Felix of Thibiuca* 19, AB 39 (1921), p. 254: "quia bonum est oboedire Deo perpetuo regi et inmortali quam imperatori huius saeculi iniqui iubenti."

[2] We have not had access to the latest work on this problem, N. Brox, *Zeuge und Märtyrer*, Stud. z. N. u. A.T. 5 (1961).

[3] The same formula also in the *Martyrdom of Agape, Eirene, Chione and Companions* 7, ed. Knopf & Krüger, p. 100. A variant formula is ἐν οὐρανοῖς βασιλεύοντος τοῦ κυρίου ἡμῶν Ἰησοῦ Χριστοῦ, *The Acts of Dasius* 12, ed. Knopf & Krüger, pp. 94 f.

number of the acts.¹ The Latin acts have the corresponding formula "regnante (uero) domino nostro Iesu Christo".² We shall not attempt to discuss which of these versions, the Latin or the Greek, is the older. Their style as standard expressions, and their constant position in the dating of the acts has enabled them to be incorporated secondarily on a number of occasions. Conceptually they belong in the context of the acts of the martyrs, and it is certain that they derive their origin from the time of the persecutions.

One of the best known examples of a martyr's confession of Jesus as King is found in the *Passion of the Martyrs of Scilli*. St. Speratus is commanded to swear by the genius of the Emperor, but answers, "I do not know the empire of this age, but rather serve God, whom no man has seen or can see with his eyes ... for I know my Lord, the King of kings and the Emperor (*imperator*) of (the kings of) the nations."[3]

Of particular interest here is the fact that Christ is called not only *rex* but also *imperator*. The use of the word *imperator* as a title of Christ has been dealt with in detail by Peterson,[4] who shows that the term is by no means unusual, and that it is directed against the Roman imperial authority. Certain of his statements are, however, capable of modification.

---

[1] The *Acts of Pionius* 23, ed. KNOPF & KRÜGER, p. 57. The *Martyrdom of St. Apollonius* 47 b, *ibid.*, p. 35. The secondary epilogue to the *Acts of the Martyrs of Scilli* 17, ed. GEBHARDT, p. 27. The *Martyrdom of St. Theodor* 9, according to Codex Parisinus 1470 and 520. On the last mentioned martyrdom, see DELEHAYE, *Légendes grecques*, p. 135.

[2] The *Acts of St. Cyprian* 6, ed. KNOPF & KRÜGER, p. 64. The *Acts of St. Maximus* 3, *ibid.* p. 61. The *Acts of Carpus, Papylus and Agathonice* 7, *ibid.*, p. 66. The *Acts of Marcellus* (manuscript group N) 5, *ibid.*, p. 89. The *Passion of Irenaeus, bishop of Sirmium*, 6, *ibid.*, p. 105.

[3] The *Acts of the Martyrs of Scilli* 5 f. in *Acta Martyrum Selecta*, ed. GEBHARDT (1902), p. 23, ed. KNOPF & KRÜGER, p. 29. The textual conditions are not quite clear here. GEBHARDT's text has the form "dominum meum et imperatorem regum omnium gentium". KNOPF's & KRÜGER's edition has "domnum meum, regem regum et imperatorem omnium gentium". A Greek translation has τὸν κύριον ἡμῶν καὶ βασιλέα τῶν βασιλέων καὶ δεσπότην πάντων τῶν ἐθνῶν. It seems probable that the Greek text is a translation from the original Latin text, which is then identical with the text in KNOPF & KRÜGER. It is however possible that the end of the sentence ought to have the form "imperatorem regum omnium gentium" according to Rev. 1.5.

[4] PETERSON, *Christus als Imperator*, *passim*. Cf. DÖLGER, *Herrschergewalt*, pp. 122 ff.

Peterson limits his inquiry, quite naturally, to the Latin language, since *imperator* is a Latin word. But it is of no small interest to compare the term with its Greek equivalents.

The normal Greek equivalent of *imperator* as a title of Caesar was αὐτοκράτωρ.[1] As far as we know the word never occurs in the language of the Church as a predication either for God or for Christ: nor does the Greek loan-word ἰμπεράτωρ. If the title is in fact intended as anti-imperial polemic, this probably originated in the Latin-speaking world. However, it seems unlikely that the demands of a polemical situation were in themselves sufficient to create new epithets for Christ, without other influences playing their part. We may therefore expect the title *imperator* to have occurred in the older tradition in some way. The fact that the Greek-speaking Church confessed Christ as *kyrios* and *basileus* but not αὐτοκράτωρ and ἰμπεράτωρ is of course due to the occurrence of the former in the LXX and the NT, and hence in the Church's own language, and the profane political overtones of the latter.

A further Greek equivalent advanced by Peterson is the title ἄρχων in Rev. 1.5; this he considers to be an allusion to the Emperor[2]—a suggestion which is far from being intrinsically improbable. As Peterson points out, the Vulgate translation of this word is not *imperator*, but *princeps*. But the Church's Latin translation of Greek terms was extremely flexible during the early centuries, and in fact one Itala manuscript (cod. h) has the translation *imperator*.[3] As we mentioned above, it seems possible that St. Speratus' confession referred to Rev. 1.5, and that his use of *imperator* was as a translation of ἄρχων. The verse seems however not to have been very well-known in the early Church and is hardly ever quoted in the pre-Constantinian Latin literature.

But *imperator* was originally a military, and not a political, title, even though it soon came to be understood as a technical term for the Emperor—and not only in his capacity as commander-in-chief of the army.[4] In some of the texts quoted by Peterson *imperator* has an ex-

---

[1] A. ROSENBERG, art. *Imperator*, PWK 9 (1914–16), pp. 1139 f.

[2] PETERSON, *Christus als Imperator*, pp. 153 f.

[3] *Thesaurus* 7.1, col. 560.

[4] D. MCFAYDEN, *The History of the Title Imperator under the Roman Empire* (1920), pp. 66 f.: "As a matter of fact, the use of *imperator* as a full synonym of *princeps* became not uncommon under the Flavians and their successors. It tended to lose its military reference and to be employed in the sense of "autocrat", a sense which corresponded with its derivation (*imperator* = *qui imperat*) and with the provincial understanding of its Greek equivalent. It was thus, as we have seen,

press military significance, connected with the above-mentioned conception of the Christian as a soldier of Christ; this is true of the quotations from Tertullian and Cyprian in particular.[1] It is therefore impossible in this context to consider the word primarily as an imperial title; it must be seen against the background of the general introduction of military terminology into the language of Latin Africa, its meaning being "general".[2] Peterson points out that *imperator* and *rex* are often found together, and that care must be exercised when translating them as military terms.[3] As we have seen, there is a constant tendency to shift between the representation of Christ as King and as General, when the Christian is called his soldier. Of course the Church came into conflict with the language of politics over this point; ample witness to this is borne by the death sentences passed on innumerable Christians as enemies of the state. But the epithets we are discussing do not appear to have originated in this conflict situation; on the contrary: the conflict arose from the collision of the language of the Church and the language of the Roman state.

A somewhat different problem is posed by the use of the word *imperium* to refer to the reign of God and Christ, a term which Peterson takes up in connexion with the title *imperator*.[4] The two words *imperator* and *imperium* cannot be connected exactly as Mommsen and many later scholars would have them connected, to make *imperator* the one who exercises that power which is called *imperium*; or vice versa, to explain *imperium* as the authority wielded by an *imperator*. Valuable light is shed on this subject by the use of the word *imperium* in the

---

that Dio interpreted the title in the third century. The word *princeps*, however, still remained the commonest word for "emperor"; Latin-speaking peoples never quite forgot that *imperator* was originally a military term. The reaction against the "*tumultuarii imperatores*" of the third century led to the former term being preferred in the succeeding period."

[1] Tertullian, De exhort. cast. 12, CCL 2.1031, De fuga 10.1, CCL 2.1147. St. Cyprian, Epist. 15.1, CSEL 3.2.513. The letter of the confessors in Cyprian's collection (Epist. 31.5), CSEL 3.2.561. Quite incomprehensible is EHRHARDT's criticism of PETERSON (*Politische Metaphysik* 2, p. 178 n. 2), who is wrongly said not to have mentioned Cyprian.

[2] Cf. στρατηγός in Clement of Alexandria, below, pp. 209 f. *Imperator* occurs as a title for God also in Cicero, De rep. 3.33 and De senectute (Cato maior), 73, both in military context.

[3] PETERSON, *Christus als Imperator*, p. 152.

[4] *Op. cit., ibid.*

Latin translation of the NT: it reproduces the strikingly non-political κράτος.

It is common knowledge that the NT uses a large number of words to denote power or might: ἀρχή, δύναμις, ἐνέργεια, ἐξουσία, ἰσχύς, κράτος. In the Vulgate (as in the Old Latin translations) these are translated by various Latin terms: ἀρχή is translated by *principatus* (or *principium initium* or *principes*), δύναμις by *virtus* (sometimes by *fortitudo* or *potestas*), ἐνέργεια by *operatio*, ἐξουσία by *potestas*, ἰσχύς by *virtus* (sometimes by *vires* or *fortitudo*), κράτος by *imperium* (sometimes by *potentia*, and once—in Rev. 5.13—by *potestas*). *Imperium* also reproduces two other words: ἐπιταγή and ἡγεμονία—the latter occurring only once (Lk. 3.1), where it has a purely political meaning (the reign of Tiberius Caesar).¹

A number of these words can serve as equivalents of *imperium* in its political meaning. Apart from ἡγεμονία, ἀρχή and ἐξουσία can refer to the Roman imperial power.² κράτος, on the other hand, has no particular connexion with the Empire.³ In the NT the word is found mainly in doxologies directed to God or Christ (1 Tim. 6.16, 1 Pet. 4.11, 5.11, Jude 25, Rev. 1.6. On one occasion (in Heb. 2.14) κράτος is used to denote the power of the devil. It implies sovereign and irresistible power, and it seems to be this meaning which the Latin-speaking Church wished to stress by its use of *imperium*.⁴

This use of this word *imperium* may be compared with that found in the Itala OT, which sometimes translates βασιλεία with *imperium* (Ps. 21 (22). 29, 144 (145).13, Sir. 46.13, 47.21),⁵ and in the Latin translation of Irenaeus, where *imperium* consistently reproduces ἀρχή, even in its political meaning.⁶ Once the Latin text speaks about the *imperium* of the angels; here, too, it probably translates ἀρχή.⁷ Of greatest in-

---

[1] The different senses of the NT words for "power" and "force" are well represented by H. SCHLIER, *Der Brief an die Epheser* (1957), pp. 85 f.

[2] A. ROSENBERG, art. *Imperium*, PWK 9 (1914–16), col. 1201.

[3] W. MICHAELIS, art. κράτος. ThWB 3 (1935–38), pp. 905–910.

[4] Cf. H. WAGENVOORT, *Roman Dynamism* (1947), pp. 66 ff. (with reservation for his interpretation of *imperium* as a "mana" concept).

[5] *Thesaurus* 7.1, col. 576. Cf. Tertullian's translation of ἀρχή in Isa. 9.6 with *imperium* (above, p. 99).

[6] Irenaeus, Adv. haer. III. 21.3, ed. HARVEY 2.115, *ibid.* V. 30.3, p. 410.

[7] *Ibid.*, I. 23.3, ed. HARVEY 1.194.

terest is the text in which divine omnipotence is compared to the Roman Empire.[1]

Had the Latin translation of the NT reproduced βασιλεία, ἀρχή or ἐξουσία—meaning the power of God or Christ—in this way by the word *imperium*, we should have been more justified in talking about a conscious adaptation of Roman political terminology. As things are, the problem is far from having been solved.

---

[1] *Ibid.*, II. 6.2, ed. HARVEY 1.264.

PART III

The Kingship of Christ in pre-Constantinian Speculative Systems

7. THE LOGOS AS KING

The 2nd century saw the development within the Church of the logos theology, which to determine the entire course of subsequent Christological discussion. It is to be found in Justin Martyr and Irenaeus, and in a more definite form in Clement of Alexandria. In each case it is recognized that the ideological background of the doctrine is to be seen in the Hellenistic Judaism of Alexandria in general, and of Philo in particular.

Christ the Logos and Christ the King have often been placed in sharp contrast; the Logos has been considered to have had connexions with the concept of Christ as Philosopher and Revealer, rather than Christ as Cosmic Ruler. Art historians in particular have stressed the distinction between these two conceptions in their attempts to sketch in the background to the new, royal characteristics which appear in the 4th century representations of Christ.[1]

The distinction is not unjustified. If we compare Alexandrian theology with the NT, and with authors such as Justin and Irenaeus, it soon becomes evident that the typological interpretation of Scripture and the basic eschatological presuppositions of the Alexandrians are forced into the background by the Hellenistic allegorical tradition stemming from Philo. The Judaism with which the Alexandrian theologians were confronted, and which came to exercise a considerable influence on the Alexandrians' exegesis, had a character which seems to have differed considerably from that of normative Palestinian

---

[1] KOLLWITZ, *Christus als Lehrer*, pp. 48 ff. GERKE, *Sarkophage*, pp. 226 ff., L'ORANGE, *Studies*, pp. 139 ff.

Judaism, especially in its lack of eschatological Messianism. The heritage of Palestinian Jewish Messianism, preserved within the Church more especially in the *testimonia* tradition, is therefore largely missing from the Christian theology of Alexandria. In the writings of Clement of Alexandria and of Origen, Christ seldom appears as the eschatological King; instead, he appears primarily as the eternal Logos of God; the power by which God directs and reveals his law to the world, and in which all things cohere.

But we must not therefore conclude that Christ is never represented as King in Alexandrian theology. Both the eternal Logos and the earthly Christ are often depicted in royal categories, the distinction being that the metaphors are drawn, not from the OT but from the concept of the ideal king, as found in contemporary Hellenism. It becomes possible, through the identification of the Son with the Logos of Hellenistic philosophy, to apply the ideas of political metaphysics to Christ. That is why the logos concept plays such a significant role in the development of "kingship" theology. It is in point of fact one of the main elements in the complex of problems surrounding the Caesar *versus* Church conflicts of the Constantinian period.

During the first centuries A.D. metaphysical speculations on the Kingship were extremely prominent in Hellenistic philosophy; this is seen particularly in those speeches and documents which bear the name of Περὶ βασιλείας. A political philosophy of this kind is found in Philo and in the anonymous author of *De mundo*, in the Neo-Pythagorean philosophers Ecphantus, Sthenidas and Diotogenes, and in the work of Trajan's political adviser Dio Chrysostom—to mention only the most important of its exponents. All these authors take it for granted that the king does not merely occupy the highest position in the human hierarchy; his rule also reflects God's government of the world, and it is therefore a constantly recurring demand that the king shall strive to imitate God.[1] Philo connects this view in a special way with the doctrine of the Logos of God's governing and organizing power; his royal ideal, which he sees realized in Moses, is that of the wise man, who is able to govern the people because he himself is governed by the Logos.

---

[1] For this literature, see E. R. GOODENOUGH, *The Political Philosophy of Hellenistic Kingship*, YCS 1 (1928), pp. 55-102. IDEM, *The Politics of Philo Judaeus* (1938). L. DELATTE, *Les Traités de la Royauté d'Ecphante, Diotogène et Sthénidas*, BFPhL 97 (1942).

These ideas did not originate in Hellenistic times; they have a long history, reaching back to the political writings of Plato and Aristotle, to Stoic and Pythagorean philosophy and even to those religious ideas connected with the sphere of the sacral kingship. Nor were these speculations worked out in a vacuum; they are closely linked with the political aspirations of their day, not least with the growing imperial cult.

The central figure in this picture is Philo, who is also one of the most influential of the Hellenistic political philosophers on Christian theology. As we shall see, Alexandrian theology took over a number of important elements from Philo's political writings and applied them to Christ as King. If we ask whence Philo himself derived these ideas, it is all the more difficult to give a definite answer: here we encounter the same near-insoluble problem as that posed by all eclectic Hellenistic philosophy.

Bréhier and Goodenough, followed by Tarn, believe Philo's speculations on the Kingship to be derived first and foremost from the Neo-Pythagorean philosophers Ecphantus, Sthenidas and Diotogenes, with whom Philo shows extensive agreement, and whose writings are normally dated to early Hellenistic times.[1] This has however been sharply criticized by Delatte, who dates the Neo-Pythagorean fragments on philological grounds to the 1st or 2nd centuries A.D. Delatte considers the relationship between these authors and Philo to be the exact opposite of that postulated by earlier scholars: it is the Neo-Pythagoreans who have made use of Philo's metaphysics to refer to the Kingship.[2]

Delatte's conclusions are based on thorough philological investigations, and his dating of the writings in question has been generally accepted.[3] But the relationship between these and Philo is probably more complex than Delatte imagines: it is less likely that Philo has influenced the Neo-Pythagoreans, than that both have made use of common sources.[4]

---

[1] E. Bréhier, *Les idées philosophiques et religieuses de Philon d'Alexandrie* (1908), pp. 17 ff. Goodenough, *Philosophy*, *passim*. W. W. Tarn, *Alexander and the Unity of Mankind*, PBA (1933), pp. 123–166.

[2] Delatte, *Traités*, pp. 284 ff. and *passim*.

[3] See the review by M. P. Charlesworth in CR 63 (1949), pp. 22 f. and by J. S. Morrison in JHS 69 (1949), pp. 91 f.

[4] According to A. D. Nock it is improbable that Philo influenced any pagan writers at all. See Charlesworth, *op. cit.*, p. 23.

Philo's representation of the monarchy has a number of Stoic characteristics, suggesting that at least some elements of his system have been derived from Stoic authors.[1] We know that in Hellenistic times there was a whole Stoic literature dealing with the kingship (Zeno, Cleanthes, Sphairos, Perseus, Dionysius).[2] All have now been lost, but we have some idea of the ideas to which they gave expression. The dominant view of Stoicism was cosmopolitanism: the view of the world as a *polis*. The analogies between the state and the world which are of such importance in Philo and the Neo-Pythagoreans may therefore be of Stoic origin. That scholars have not normally accepted the Stoic background to later Hellenistic kingship writings has to do with the fact of the Stoics' sharp criticism of the kingship; in the opinion of the Stoics the wise king is independent of his position in society. But they also favour the idea of the wise man as the ideal head of state, an idea which recurs in Philo's political writings.[3]

We can also trace Pythagorean elements in Philo's writings, elements which Philo shares with the Neo-Pythagorean philosophers. The analogies between the various governing functions, which we consider in more detail below, are found as far back as Archytas. It is hardly likely that the Neo-Pythagorean philosophers took over this older tradition via Philo; both seem instead to be indebted to older Pythagorean sources, as was the author of *De mundo*.[4]

During the first centuries A.D. there thus existed a literature in which the kingship was treated metaphysically. It is probable that this literature was centred upon Alexandria, and that Philo was one of its leading figures. We find it however impossible to accept the idea that Philo's attitude was entirely non-political and that the responsibility for transplanting the Philonic terms from the level of general metaphysics to that of politics must be laid at the door of the Neo-Pythagoreans, and Ecphantus in particular.[5] Philo was distinctly interested in

---

[1] "La conception de la royauté que l'on trouve dans les oeuvres de Philon d'Alexandrie apparait comme profondement influencée par la doctrine stoïcienne," DELATTE, *op. cit.*, p. 150.

[2] DELATTE, *op. cit.*, p. 140.

[3] DELATTE, *op. cit.*, pp. 140 f.

[4] GOODENOUGH considers that these analogies, as seen in Philo, exhibit clear traces of influence from Pythagoreanism, *Politics*, pp. 96 f. DELATTE, too, allows that it is "not forbidden" to reckon with a direct connexion between the Neo-Pythagoreans and the old Pythagorean school, *op. cit.*, p. 87.

[5] DELATTE sometimes tends in the same direction, *op. cit.*, p. 288.

politics, and what he has to say about the kingship parallels sayings from earlier authors than the Neo-Pythagoreans.¹ Later authors, such as Dio Chrysostom and Aelius Aristides also show important agreements, without there being any influence, direct or indirect, from Philo.²

Political metaphysics, as seen in the Roman Empire, probably had its roots in Alexandria. A special line of development is followed by Philo, a line in which the ideas of the Greek philosophers were linked with Jewish monotheism, and in which the earthly monarchical kingship is personified in the figure of Moses. We therefore regard it as natural to suppose that Philo drew his ideas from contemporary Hellenistic political philosophy. The question of which author or authors Philo used is another matter, which we cannot go into here. In the following pages we may take the Neo-Pythagorean writings, and Dio, as examples of the nature of those contemporary political theories which we include under the term "Hellenistic political metaphysics".

Political metaphor plays an important part in Hellenistic philosophy. The pseudo-Aristotelian *De mundo* describes God in terms of a Persian Great King, enthroned in the innermost state apartment of his palace and hidden behind veils. He governs the world indirectly, through his *dynamis*, which sets the sun and moon in motion, which directs the paths of the heavens and sustains the whole world.³ According to this image it is God who is King: his *dynamis* fulfils the functions of a subsidiary co-regent or satrap. The contrast becomes even more distinct when this conception becomes dualistic, and the good God is confronted by the demiurge, who is evil, or whose good is a limited good.⁴ Numenios draws a radical distinction between God's functions as βασιλεύς and πατήρ on the one hand, and the functions of the demiurge on the other.⁵

The hypostasizing process is even more concrete in Plotinus. God is

---

¹ DELATTE, *op. cit.*, pp. 149 ff., quotes Seneca, Musonius and Plutarch as examples of authors of the imperial period who, together with Philo, demonstrate parallelism with the Neo-Pythagorean fragments.

² GOODENOUGH, *Politics*, p. 46.

³ De mundo, 398a, ed. LORIMER, pp. 82 ff. On the world-view of De mundo, see A.-J. FESTUGIÈRE, *La révélation d'Hermès Trismégiste II, Le Dieu Cosmique* (1949), pp. 460–518.

⁴ The standard works on God as Great King and the Logos as his vicegerent are PETERSON, *Monotheismus*, and STRAUB, *Herrscherideal*, pp. 113 ff.

⁵ H.-CH. PUECH, *Numénius d'Apamée et les théologies orientales au second siècle* (Mélange Bidez 2), AIPh 2 (1934), pp. 745–778.

represented as the King of kings; he has delegated his powers as ruler to Zeus, who is his son and εἰκών, and who is now the real governor of the cosmos. Around and below him are the ranks of the lower hierarchy: the nearer they approach the King, the more royal they become.[1] It is thus possible, as in this case, for the Logos to be accorded royal character; it is nevertheless always assumed that his powers are derived from the supreme King, who is God.

This entire complex of ideas was taken over by the Church, largely via Philo. We find that Philo himself was deeply interested in politics, and particularly in the monarchy.[2] Thus his view of the world and his anthropology are characterized by his use of political metaphor. It is in fact one of Philo's most outstanding characteristics that he uses the same metaphors to describe God in his relation to the world and the individual's logos or νοῦς in relation to man. This form of analogy—or macrocosm–microcosm imagery—constantly gives rise to abrupt shifts in thought, which make it much more difficult to grasp Philo's meaning. But since we are concerned in this chapter with the logos theology, we shall pause to consider Philo's use of metaphor in connexion with the Logos. We cannot however isolate this usage entirely from those contexts in which the metaphors are applied to God, to the wise man or to man in general.

"As the King is to the State, so is God to the world."[3] Such a use of analogy, normal in Hellenistic philosophy, is in Philo combined with the Stoic concept of the world as a πόλις and of God as its King.[4] In Agr. 50 f. we encounter the same world of ideas as in *De mundo*, with God as the Great King and the Logos as his satrap. To be a shepherd (τὸ ποιμαίνειν) is so excellent that it is attributed not only to kings and wise men, but also, with perfect justification, to God, the director of all things (πανηγεμόνι). Every God-fearing man and the world-all should therefore join in singing Ps. 22(23).1, "The Lord is my shepherd": "for like a shepherd, God the Shepherd and King directs earth

---

[1] Plotinus Enn. V. 5.3. E. Benz, *Marius Victorinus und die Entwicklung der abendländischen Willensmetaphysik*, FKG 1 (1932), pp. 234 ff.

[2] Peterson, *op. cit.*, pp. 54 ff., I. Heinemann, *Philons griechische und jüdische Bildung* (1932), pp. 182–202, Goodenough, *Politics*, pp. 86–120.

[3] Philo Prov. fragm. 2 (in Eusebius Praep. ev. VIII. 14). Diotogenes ap. Stob. IV. 7.61, ed. Delatte, p. 38.

[4] The world as a *polis* in Philo, see Spec. leg. III. 189, Opif. 143, QE II. 42. Goodenough, *By Light, Light*, pp. 51 ff., K. L. Schmidt, *Die Polis in Kirche und Welt*, Rektoratsprogramm der Univ. Basel 1939.

and water and air and fire and all the plants and animals in them, things mortal and divine; and in addition he directs the nature of heaven, the revolutions of the sun and moon, and the variations and harmonious dances of the other stars; he directs them according to δίκη and νόμος, for he has appointed τὸν ὀρθὸν αὐτοῦ λόγον καὶ πρωτόγονον υἱόν, who receives the guardianship of this sacred flock like a viceroy (ὕπαρχος) of the Great King."[1]

Philo adopts analogies from Hellenistic philosophy between various kinds of directive function. What the ruler is to the State, so is the head man in the village, the husband in the house, the doctor among the sick, the general in the camp, the admiral among the crew and complement, the ship-owner for merchant-ships and trading vessels, and the pilot for the sailors.[2] There are a number of terms which Philo uses as expressions of the guiding activity of the Logos: the Logos is leader (ἡγεμών), shepherd (ποιμήν), pilot (κυβερνήτης), charioteer (ἡνίοχος); a term less frequently used is βασιλεύς, since this title is given to those who fulfil the highest of all functions, and the Logos occupies only the second place in the hierarchy.[3]

These terms are used with a clearly political meaning in Hellenistic philosophy. Diotogenes states that the king must save (σώζειν) his people as the pilot saves the ship, the charioteer the chariot and the doctor the sick.[4] Similarly we read in *De mundo* that as the pilot is on board ship, as the charioteer in his chariot, the coryphaeus in a chorus,

---

[1] Agr. 50 f., cf. Post. 68. English translation by GOODENOUGH, *By Light, Light*, pp. 57 f. On the expression ὀρθὸς λόγος, see GOODENOUGH, *Politics*, pp. 93 f.

[2] Spec. leg. IV.186: ὅπερ γὰρ πόλεως βασιλεύς, τοῦτο καὶ κώμης ὁ πρῶτος καὶ οἰκίας δεσπότης καὶ νοσούντων ἰατρός, καὶ στρατοπέδου μὲν στρατηγός, ναύαρχος δ' ἐμβατικοῦ καὶ πληρωμάτων, καὶ πάλιν φορτίδων μὲν καὶ ὁλκάδων ναύκληρος, κυβερνήτης δὲ πλωτήρων.

[3] The Logos is called βασιλεύς in Mut. 116. When Philo on one occasion calls Melchizedek king, priest and Logos (Leg. alleg. III. 81 f.) it is the priestly, rather than the kingly function he stresses. See H. LEWY, *Sobria ebrietas*, ZNW Beih. 9 (1929), pp. 21 f., GOODENOUGH, *Politics*, p. 99. That the Logos is called ἀρχιερεύς by Philo is a common expression of the function of the Logos as mediator (Gig. 52, Migr. 102, Fuga 108).

[4] Diotogenes ap. Stob. IV.7.61, ed. DELATTE, p. 38: κυβερνάτα μὲν γὰρ ἔργον ἐντὶ τὰν ναῦν σώζεν, ἀνιόχω τὸ ἅρμα, ἰατρῶ δὲ τὼς νοσίοντας, βασιλέως δε καὶ στραταγῶ τὼς ἐν πολέμῳ κινδυνεύοντας. Cf. DELATTE, *op. cit.*, pp. 249 f., 252 f. The analogy is to be found already in Archytas, ap. Stob. III.1.112: στρατεύματος μὲν γὰρ ἀγεῖται στραταγός, πλωτήρων δὲ κυβερνάτας, τῶ δὲ κόσμω θεός.

the lawgiver in a town and the commander (ἡγεμῶν) in a military camp, so is God in the world.¹

This system of analogies is early taken over by Christian theology, mainly in Alexandria but also in other traditions (Melito of Sardis, the *Martyrdom of Polycarp*, Hippolytus). Christ (especially in his Logos aspect) is called not only King, but also shepherd, charioteer, pilot and general—the titles obviously being taken from the political terminology used by Philo to describe the governing function of the Logos.

Since these terms enumerated here may vary considerably in meaning and application, we have chosen to deal with each separately as it occurs in the writings of the earliest Fathers of the Church. We do not consider that a summary account of Philo's terminology would be justified in this context.²

St. Justin Martyr and St. Irenaeus seldom refer to the Logos in royal terms. In both authors the royal titles are linked with the proofs of the Messiahship of the incarnate Christ, as found in the *testimonia* tradition.³ Nor does either author make use of the Philonic terminology of the Logos as world-governor. Not even ποιμήν is used to refer to the Logos.⁴

---

¹ De mundo 400 b. 6 ff., ed. LORIMER, p. 94: ὅπερ ἐν νηῒ μὲν κυβερνήτης, ἐν ἅρματι δὲ ἡνίοχος, ἐν χορῷ δὲ κορυφαῖος, ἐν πόλει δὲ νομο<θέτη>ς, ἐν στρατοπέδῳ δὲ ἡγεμών, τοῦτο θεὸς ἐν κόσμῳ. The same analogies are also found in Dio Chrysostom, Or. 4.24 f., Teubn. Dio Chrys. 1.76: ὁ γὰρ βασιλεὺς ἀνθρώπων ἄριστός ἐστιν, ἀνδρειότατος ὢν καὶ δικαιότατος καὶ φιλανθρωπότατος καὶ ἀνίκητος ὑπὸ παντὸς πόνου καὶ πάσης ἐπιθυμίας. ἢ σὺ οἴει τὸν ἀδύνατον ἡνιοχεῖν ἡνίοχον εἶναι τοῦτον; ἢ τὸν ἄπειρον τοῦ κυβερνᾶν κυβερνήτην, ἢ τὸν οὐκ ἐπιστάμενον ἰᾶσθαι ἰατρόν; οὐκ ἔστιν. For the terminology in Philo and Hellenistic political philosophy, see G. RUDBERG, *Forschungen zu Poseidonios*, HVSS 20: 3 (1918), pp. 194 ff.

² A good account of Philo's terminology is given in RUDBERG, *loc. cit.* The reader is further referred to the books by BRÉHIER and GOODENOUGH.

³ When E. J. GOODSPEED claims that Justin calls the Logos βασιλεύς and ἱερεύς, *The Theology of Justin Martyr* (1923), p. 172, this is evidently due to the fact that he has failed to observe the distinction between the language used by Justin of the pre-existent Logos and of the incarnate Saviour. A possible exception may be Apol. 12.7: ὁ λόγος ... οὗ βασιλικώτατον καὶ δικαιότατον ἄρχοντα μετὰ τὸν γεννήσαντα θεὸν οὐδένα οἴδαμεν ὄντα.

⁴ EHRHARDT's assumption that *princeps* in Adv. haer. III. 16.6, ed. HARVEY 2.88, is a translation of ἡγεμών is baseless, *Politische Metaphysik* 2, p. 109, n. 2. In the Latin translation of Irenaeus *princeps* translates ἄρχων or ἀρχηγός throughout (once *principes* translates μεγιστᾶνες in a quotation from Prov. 8.15); see REYNDERS, *Index* II, p. 253. Had Irenaeus used the term ἡγεμών of the Logos, it is probable that this would have been translated by *dux*; the word is used to reproduce ὁδηγός,

An important exception is however provided by the famous passage in Irenaeus, the first in Christian literature to make use of the four cherubim of Ezek. 1 as prefiguring the four Gospels.[1] Here the Logos is represented as enthroned upon the cherubim, reference being made to Ps. 79(80).1: "Thou that sittest on the cherubim, shine forth." The text is of outstanding interest, since a clear identification is made of the Logos with Yahweh, the Logos being called "charioteer" (on this latter topic, see below).[2]

Otherwise, it would seem that by the middle of the 2nd century the political logos terminology had become common currency in much of the Church. It is to be found *inter alia* in three ancient texts: in the fragment *De fide*, in the *Martyrdom of Polycarp* and in the hymn which concludes the *Paedagogus* of Clement of Alexandria, but which is probably based on older sources. We shall therefore begin by examining these three texts, in which we find typical examples of the Philonic system of analogies.

The fragment *De fide* was at first attributed to Irenaeus, but is now generally considered to be the work of Melito of Sardis.[3] The concluding passage of the fragment reads as follows, in the Latin translation:[4]

    pastor eorum qui salvi sunt[5]
    sponsus ecclesiae,

ἀρχηγός, ἡγούμενος (in a quotation of Num. 24.17, cf. Justin Dial. 106.4, and of Gen. 49.10); on one occasion *duces* translates ἡγεμόνας (in quotation of Matt. 10.18, meaning "local governor"), REYNDERS, *Index* II, p. 101. EHRHARDT's assumption must be seen in connexion with his general tendency to read political terminology and ideology into entirely non-political contexts.

[1] Adv. Haer. III. 11.8, ed. HARVEY 2.47; cf. IV. 33 13, ed. HARVEY 2.268, where St. Irenaeus quotes Ps. 98 (99).1.

[2] See below, pp. 200 ff.

[3] Fragm. XV in Corpus Apolog. Christ. IX, ed. OTTO (1872), fragm. 68 in Florilegium Edessenum, ed. I. RUCKER, BAS 1933: 5, pp. 55 ff. On textual traditions and editions, see P. NAUTIN, *Le dossier d'Hippolyte et de Méliton* (1933), pp. 43–46, 64 f. HARNACK and JORDAN favour the theory of St. Irenaeus as author; KRÜGER favours Melito. Among modern scholars who have accepted Melito as author are C. BONNER, *The Homily of the Passion by Melito Bishop of Sardis and some Fragments of the Apocryphal Ezekiel*, SD 12 (1940). pp. 48–50, and O. PERLER, *Ein Hymnus zur Ostervigil von Meliton?* (Papyrus Bodmer XII), Par 15 (1960), p. 24 f. NAUTIN alone seems to accept the view that the fragment is the work of neither Irenaeus nor Melito, op. cit., pp. 64–72.

[4] *Op. cit.*, p. 66.

[5] Only in the so-called Irenaeus version.

>   Cherubim ἡνίοχος
>   princeps exercitus angelorum,
>   Deus a Deo, Filius ex Patre,
>   Iesus Christus, rex in saecula, Amen.

Here we find a number of epithets for Christ, expressing his divine and royal character; they have so much in common that, with the exception of *rex* (=βασιλεύς), they do not occur in contemporary anti-Jewish polemic, but are well known from the writings of Philo. Christ is ποιμήν and ἡνίοχος (*princeps* is probably a translation of ἀρχιστράτηγος).[1] Earlier in the fragment Christ is called "*in legibus lex*" (=νόμος) "*in regibus dux*" (prob. =ἡγεμών) and κυβερνήτης (of Noah).

We encounter the same combination of titles in the *Martyrdom of Polycarp* 19.2.[2] As in *De fide*, the enumeration of epithets is carried out in a rhetorical hymn-style:

> δοξάζει τὸν θεὸν καὶ πατέρα παντοκράτορα
> καὶ εὐλογεῖ τὸν κύριον ἡμῶν Ἰησοῦν Χριστόν,
> τὸν σωτῆρα τῶν ψυχῶν ἡμῶν
> καὶ κυβερνήτην τῶν σωμάτων ἡμῶν
> καὶ ποιμένα τῆς κατὰ τὴν οἰκουμένην καθολικῆς ἐκκλησίας.

The terms used here are not only κυβερνήτης and ποιμήν, but σωτήρ as well—the latter being a title characteristic of Hellenistic Christianity, with more or less explicit political connotations.[3]

The third text is provided by the closing hymn in Clement of Alexandria's *Paedagogus*.[4] In what has gone before Clement has summarized the character of the Logos as paedagogue, using analogies of the same order as those we meet in Philo: the horse is controlled by the bit (χαλινῷ) and the bull by the yoke (ζυγῷ), but man is formed by the Logos.[5] In this context the Logos is called the charioteer of Israel (ἡνίοχε Ἰσραήλ). This calls to mind the exposition of Jesus' entry into

---

[1] BARBEL, *Christos Angelos*, p. 234.

[2] It is not possible in this context to go into the question of the genuineness of the verse in question. H. VON CAMPENHAUSEN's theory that it comes from the so-called Euangelion editor and is contemporary with Eusebius' text of the martyrdom, lacks adequate evidence; see H. VON CAMPENHAUSEN, *Bearbeitung und Interpolationen des Polycarpmartyriums*, SbHei 1957: 3, pp. 13 f., 37 f.

[3] Cf. above, pp. 64 ff.

[4] Paed. III. 101.3, GCS Clem. 1. 211 f.

[5] *Ibid.* 99.1, p. 290.

Jerusalem, which we discuss elsewhere, and according to which the ass and the foal symbolize the Jews and the Gentiles, yoked together by Christ and driven into the heavenly city.[1]

The closing hymn summarizes a great deal of the frequently obscure imagery of Hellenistic Christology: here Christ the Logos is not called ἡνίοχος, but a bridle for unbroken foals (στόμιον πώλων ἀδαῶν); not κυβερνήτης, but instead a reliable rudder for ships (οἴαξ νηῶν ἀτρεκής). Both the expressions have to do with the concept of God as the supreme pilot and the Logos as his instrument upholding the world. Christ is the shepherd of royal lambs (ποιμὴν ἀρνῶν βασιλικῶν). The same imagery recurs time and time again in connexion with the Logos: Christ is ποιμήν, βασιλεύς, οἴαξ, στόμιον. The analogy drawn between the various "directive" functions is perfectly clear: Christ, as shepherd, shall lead the rational sheep; as King, he shall lead the untouched children (ἡγοῦ προβάτων / λογικῶν ποιμὴν ἄγι', ἡγοῦ / βασιλεῦ παίδων ἀνεπάφων).[2]

In the writings of Clement of Alexandria in general, we find that he has taken over the Philonic terminology in its entirety. As in Philo, and as in *De mundo*, the Logos is represented as being an activity (ἐνέργεια) of God, and as God's power (δύναμις) through which he directs the world.[3] The political metaphors recur in Clement, expressing the directive and governing activity of the Logos: he is ποιμήν, στρατηγός and κυβερνήτης,[4] ἡγεμών, βασιλεύς, νόμος, θεσμός, σωτήρ, μονογενής.[5]

It is of particular interest to note how in these texts the metaphors occur in various combinations, but never in isolation. The only reasonable explanation is that the authors were well aware of the doctrine of analogy which formed the basis of Philo's use of metaphor. Since Christ is the Logos of God, his activity can be expressed by means of images drawn from various walks of life. His relation to the world corresponds to that of the King to the State, the shepherd to the flock, the pilot to the ship, etc. When we meet with sayings in later texts where Christ is stated to be, for example, a pilot or charioteer, we must

---

[1] See below, pp. 222 f.

[2] The distinction here is dependent upon Philo's concept of the relationship between the functions of shepherd and king. See below, p. 199.

[3] Strom. VII. 7.7, 9.1, GCS Clem. 3.7 f.; cf. Exc. ex Theod, 4.2, GCS Clem. 3.106.

[4] Paed. I. 54.3, GCS Clem. 1.122; see H. Rahner, *Antenna Crucis II, Das Meer der Welt*, ZKTh 66 (1942), p. 117. Cf. Paed. I. 65.3, p. 128.

[5] Strom. VII. 16.5, GCS Clem. 3.12.

keep in mind the context in which these metaphors belonged when they were taken over by Christian theology. They were part of the terminology of political speculation, expressing in a number of ways that it is the Logos who is King—who has been entrusted by God with the task of directing and governing the world. The Logos is thus also the bearer of political authority. When Clement, following Philo, portrays Moses as an ideal king on the Hellenistic pattern,[1] he describes him as "animated law", νόμος ἔμψυχος, because he was guided by the Logos (τῷ χρηστῷ λόγῳ κυβερνώμενος).[2] As far as Christology is concerned, the real problem is that the Logos was in point of fact not regarded as King, but as God's viceroy in the world; further, that the human nature of Christ was pushed into the background. The earthly Christ is King because he is guided by the Logos. As we have earlier had occasion to point out, the idea that the sovereignty of Christ is primarily dependent upon his Divine nature (and not, for example, upon his descent from David) formed part of the deposit of tradition which we find in anti-Jewish polemic and elsewhere. When Clement describes Christ in the same categories as those used by Philo to describe Moses, the sovereignty of Christ is limited thereby. He becomes the ideal king, humanly speaking, but seen *sub specie aeternitatis* he seems to be little more than the earthly manifestation of God's Logos, to whom God, the Great King, has delegated governmental powers. He is not a king in his own right; he is a king at three removes.

As far back as in Philo we encounter political terminology linked with the corresponding terms in the OT. The fact that the Logos is described as ἡνίοχος and ποιμήν is explained on a basis of allegorical OT exegesis; other terms, such as ἡγεμών and κυβερνήτης, are not derived from the Holy Scriptures. Since the various terms suggest different associations, they are incorporated by the Church Fathers into different allegorical contexts. But as we have already pointed out, it is noteworthy that they occur in the oldest texts as expressions of the Philonic doctrine of analogy.

ποιμήν

The word ποιμήν, shepherd, appears in each of the three texts we have quoted. This may seem unremarkable, remembering the popula-

---
[1] See below, p. 214.
[2] Strom. I. 167.3, GCS Clem. 2.104.

rity of the "shepherd" image in early Christian art and literature.¹ But as we mentioned earlier,² the title of "shepherd" plays very little part in the *testimonia* tradition. That this imagery became so common in the early Church was evidently due to influence from Hellenistic thought, and from Philo in particular, though it goes without saying that Jesus' sayings in Jn. 10 about his own person are mainly responsible for the ease with which Hellenistic "shepherd" imagery became assimilated to the Christian tradition.

Philo treats the concepts "shepherd" and "King" as synonymous,³ and uses them over and over again in combination to refer to the Logos.⁴ Since God is King, he is also shepherd,⁵ and the work of the Logos is expressed partly in that he keeps the world-all together like a shepherd, and partly that he curbs the desires of the individual, and shapes him according to reason.⁶

At this point Philo is building upon political metaphors drawn from Greek literature. The Homeric king was described as "shepherd of the people", and the "shepherd" imagery recurs frequently in the work of the political theorists.⁷ Plato uses it in several contexts,⁸ and among the pagan authors it is found *inter alia* in Ecphantus and Dio Chrysostom; the latter author in particular produces the shepherd image, with variations, on a number of occasions in his four speeches Περὶ βασιλείας.⁹ But although Philo was influenced by Hellenistic

---

¹ On the question of the image of the shepherd in the early Church, see J. QUASTEN, *Der Gute Hirte in hellenistischer und frühchristlicher Logostheologie*, in Heilige Überlieferung, Festgabe ... I. Herwegen (1938), pp. 51–58. JOST, ΠΟΙΜΗΝ, *passim*. T. K. KEMPF, *Christus der Hirt* (1942), particularly pp. 97–149, which gives a review of Hellenistic, Gnostic and Christian material on the application of the "shepherd" motif to the Logos. The most recent work on the iconographical question is TH. KLAUSER, *Studien zur Entstehungsgeschichte der christlichen Kunst* I and III, JbAC 1 (1958), pp. 20–51 and 3 (1960), pp. 112–133.

² See above, pp. 87 ff.
³ See below, p. 199.
⁴ Mut. 116, Post. 67–69.
⁵ Agr. 50 f.
⁶ Sacr. Abel et Cain, 104 f. On the "shepherd" metaphor in Philo, see QUASTEN, *op. cit.*, pp. 51 ff., JOST, *op. cit.*, pp. 21 f., KEMPF, *op. cit.*, pp. 107 ff. All seem to underestimate the political implications of the metaphor.
⁷ Cf. DELATTE, *Traités*, p. 227.
⁸ Rep. 416a, 440d, Polit. 275a f.
⁹ Ecphantus ap. Stob. IV. 7.64, ed. DELATTE, p. 32: ὅλαν δὲ τὰν εὔνοιαν χρὴ παρασκευάζεσθαι πρῶτα μὲν παρὰ τῶ βασιλέως ἐς τὼς βασιλευομένως, δεύτερον δὲ παρὰ

political thought, he was also very much dependent upon the OT: this is evident from those passages in which he describes Moses as a shepherd.¹ In this respect he was preparing the way for the Christian theologians, who linked the shepherd sayings of the OT and NT with the political use of the title of shepherd, as it appeared in Hellenistic philosophy. The actual connexion is in fact far from being a superficial one; both the OT and the Hellenists, in their identification of the functions of shepherd and king, refer back to ancient Near Eastern concepts of kingship.²

ἡνίοχος

Although the Christological epithet of shepherd has been the subject of a great many studies, there is as far as we are aware no study dealing with Christ, the Logos, as charioteer, ἡνίοχος, in Christian theology. We must therefore pay rather more attention to this metaphor than to the others with which we are concerned in this chapter.³

ἡνίοχος has also been taken over from the terminology of Philo, who uses it in both the macrocosmic and microcosmic meaning: God and the Logos are called ἡνίοχος,⁴ but so is man, as the highest created being,⁵ and reason in the individual man.⁶

It would take far too long to trace the image of God as charioteer back to its origin, and we cannot undertake to do so here. We may however mention that it goes back to the general Indo-European conception of the charioteer-god, which in Greek thought came to

---

τῶνδε ἐς τὸν βασιλέα, ὁποία γεννάτορος πότι υἱέα καὶ ποτὶ ποίμναν νομέως καὶ νόμῳ ποτὶ χρωμένως αὐτῷ. Cf. DELATTE, *op. cit.*, p. 227. Dio Chrys. Or. 1.11 ff., 2.71, 3.41–50, 4.62. See L. FRANÇOIS, *Julien et Dion Chrysostome, Les* Περὶ βασιλείας *et le second panegyrique de Constance*, REG 28 (1915), p. 427, V. VALDENBERG, *La théorie monarchique de Dion Chrysostome*, REG 40 (1927), p. 145.

¹ Cf. below, p. 218.
² GOODENOUGH, *Kingship in Early Israel*, JBL 48 (1929) pp. 169–205.
³ We have discovered, since the preparation of this section, that the same material has been dealt with, on rather different principles, by J. DANIÉLOU, *Les symboles chrétiens primitifs* (1961), pp. 77–93.
⁴ For the concept of God as ἡνίοχος and κυβερνήτης, see Opif. 46, Cherub. 24, Heres. 99, Decal. 53, 60, Spec. leg. I. 14. For the Logos as ἡνίοχος, see Leg. alleg. III. 118, 134, 224, Fuga 101, Heres. 301.
⁵ Opif. 88, where man is also called, ὕπαρχος τοῦ πρώτου καὶ μεγάλου βασιλέως with the same terminology as that used by Philo in Agr. 51 to refer to the Logos.
⁶ Cf. below, n. 44.

be connected with Helios in particular.¹ In his *Phaedrus*, Plato speaks of the winged chariot which Zeus drives across the heavens, together with the chariots of the gods; their microcosmic equivalents are the souls of men, which are pulled by two horses, one good and one evil, and which must be governed by reason if the entire team is not to come to grief.²

In political philosophy ἡνίοχος is generally used, often in connexion with κυβερνήτης, as one of the analogies expressing the directive function of the king. The term is to be found in the passages from Diotogenes, *De mundo* and Dio Chrysostom which we quoted above.³ Philo has also taken the metaphor into his logos concept, as well as its analogical use: "The Logos rules over the world-all like a charioteer or a pilot, for he guides the ship of the world, in which all things are transported, and he steers the winged chariot, the entire heaven, by virtue of his independent and unlimited governing power."⁴

However, Philo also links ἡνίοχος with an allegorical exposition of the cherubim upon the mercy-seat. According to Philo, the cherubim represent God's creative and sovereign power. The invisible Logos, which stands over them, thus functions as ἡνίοχος. Philo refers to Ex. 25.22: "I will commune with thee from above the mercy-seat, from between the two cherubim." God rides upon the cherub-throne, which is also a chariot, and gives the Logos the necessary directions, so that he steers the chariot aright.⁵

It has often been supposed that in this text Philo is dependent upon Jewish *Merkabah* speculation,⁶ But whether or not such a developed

---

¹ J. Bidez & F. Cumont, *Les mages hellénisés* 2 (1938), p. 142 n. 4. L'Orange, *Studies*, pp. 37 ff.

² Phaedr. 246 A ff. The image is also taken over by Philo to refer to the individual's reason, Leg. alleg. II. 99, 102, Agr. 82 ff., Somn. II. 269 f., usually connected with an allegorical exposition of Ex. 15.1. Cf. Clem. Alex. Strom. V. 52.5, GCS Clem. 3. 362.

³ See above, p. 194; Rudberg, *Forschungen*, pp. 197 f.

⁴ Heres. 301: ... ἐποχούμενον τοῖς ὅλοις ἡνιόχου τρόπον ἢ κυβερνήτου. πηδαλιουχεῖ γὰρ τὸ κοινὸν τοῦ κόσμου σκάφος, ᾧ τὰ πάντα ἐμπλεῖ, καὶ τὸ πτηνὸν ἅρμα, τὸν σύμπαντα οὐρανόν, ἡνιοχεῖ χρώμενον αὐτεξουσίῳ καὶ αὐτοκράτορι βασιλείᾳ.

⁵ Fuga 100 f. Cf. H. A. Wolfson, *Philo* 1-2, 2nd ed. (1948), pp. 136 f., 345: "The Term Logos expresses the totality of power." Cf. Goodenough, *By Light, Light*, pp. 28 ff.

⁶ Thus K. Kohler, art. *Merkabah*, JE 8.498 ff.; W. Neuss, *Das Buch Ezechiel in Theologie und Kunst bis zum Endes des XII. Jahrhunderts* 1-2 (1912), pp. 30 f. van der Meer, *Maiestas Domini*, pp. 224 f.

speculation existed as early as in Philo's day and in Alexandria is, and must remain, uncertain. Jewish tradition traces the *Merkabah* speculation no farther back than to Rabban Jochanan ben Zakkai, i.e. to about the time of the Fall of Jerusalem.[1]

Anyone who, like Philo, was widely read in both the OT and Hellenistic literature, would have found it easy to associate the cherub-throne with Helios' chariot. For the cherub-throne is God's chariot, in which he rides when he "rides upon a cherub" (Ezek. 1, Ps. 17(18).11). Both Helios' chariot and Yahweh's throne would seem to have a common origin in Near Eastern gods' thrones, which were often chariot-formed.[2] That the two were identified in Hellenistic syncretism is clear from two Jewish charms quoted by Goodenough, which call upon "Helios on the Cherubim".[3]

Goodenough has brought together Philo's use of the term ἡνίοχος with pictures in Jewish synagogues representing Helios as a charioteer surrounded by the signs of the zodiac.[4] Goodenough draws the conclusion from a number of passages in Philo that Helios here represents God himself. But is it not also possible that Helios may represent the Logos who, according to Philo, is both sun and charioteer?[5] Is it not much more likely that the artist intended to portray the Logos, rather than paint an image of God? If the Logos is represented in Jewish art as Helios on his chariot, this would be a conceivable prototype of the newly-discovered Christ-Helios mosaic in the Julian tomb beneath St. Peter's in Rome.[6]

One of the titles bestowed upon Christ in Melito's fragment *De fide* is "the ἡνίοχος of the cherubim".[7] Here we have an example of the way in which the Philonic conception of the Logos as the charioteer on the cherub-throne has been transferred to Christ. We have also found the idea of the Logos enthroned upon the cherubim in Irenaeus,[8] although

---

[1] The latest work on the *Merkabah* speculations is SCHOLEM, *Jüdische Mystik* (1957): see Chap. 2, pp. 43 ff.

[2] L'ORANGE, *Studies, passim*.

[3] GOODENOUGH, *Jewish Symbols* 8, p. 172.

[4] *Ibid.*, pp. 214 f.

[5] On the Logos as sun in Philo, see F. J. DÖLGER, *Die Sonne der Gerechtigkeit und der Schwarze*, LF 2 (1918), pp. 100 f.

[6] On this topic see below, p. 205.

[7] See above, p. 196.

[8] See above, p. 195. On this passage in Irenaeus, see NEUSS, *op. cit.*, pp. 26 ff., VAN DER MEER, *op. cit.*, pp. 223 ff.

he does not use the term ἡνίοχος. As God and Logos, Christ has his place upon the throne of God. When at a later date this is connected with the idea of the Logos as the world's supreme governing power, we get the strange combination of Helios' *quadriga* and Yahwe's throne-chariot, borne by four cherubim, with the Logos as charioteer. But at the same time we cannot exclude the possibility, in these later texts, of influence from Jewish *Merkabah* speculation.

The earliest allegory of Christ as charioteer would seem to be that which we find in Melito's fragment on the washing of Baptism (Περὶ λουτροῦ).[1] Here Christ is compared to the sun who, after having completed his daily journey with his chariot (ἱππεύμασι can hardly refer other than to Helios' team of four horses),[2] disappears into the ocean, only to rise again on the following day, purified in the bath. If the sun and stars and the moon bathe in the ocean, why should not Christ be baptized in the Jordan? "The King of heaven, the commander (ἡγεμών) of creation, the rising sun, who was also revealed unto the dead in Hades and mortals on earth. Like the one true sun he arose from heaven."[3]

The image of Christ as the sun was, as Dölger has pointed out, extremely common in the earliest period of the Church. Helios was also king, and the Roman emperors were quite willing that their portraits should appear on his *quadriga*.[4] Thus when Melito represents Christ as Helios, he does so in order to stress that he is βασιλεύς, ἡγεμών and ἡνίοχος at one and the same time.

Hippolytus, who, more than any other writer of the period, developed motives into complicated allegories, also represents the Church as a chariot, with Christ as the charioteer.[5] The Apostles are the horses,

---

[1] Text in *Die ältesten Apologeten*, ed. GOODSPEED, p. 310 f. See further F. J. DÖLGER, *Sol Salutis, Gebet und Gesang im christlichen Altertum*, LF 4–5 (1920), pp. 264 ff. The text's Hellenistic character is pointed out by R. M. GRANT, *Melito of Sardis on Baptism*, VC 4 (1950), pp. 33–36.

[2] DÖLGER, *Sol Salutis*, p. 265 n. 2.

[3] βασιλεὺς οὐρανῶν καὶ κτίσεως ἡγεμών, ἥλιος ἀνατολῆς, ὃς καὶ τοῖς ἐν ᾅδου νεκροῖς ἐφάνη καὶ τοῖς ἐν κόσμῳ βροτοῖς, καὶ μόνος ἥλιος οὗτος ἀνέτειλεν ἀπ' οὐρανοῦ.

[4] This became very common as a result of the introduction of the cult of Sol Invictus into Rome. See L'ORANGE, *Sol Invictus*, pp. 86–114. On the concept of βασιλεὺς Ἥλιος see F. CUMONT, *La théologie solaire du paganisme romain*, Mém. par div. sav. Acad. Inscr. Paris 12: 2 (1913), pp. 452 f.

[5] Comm. on S. of S. 8.2 ff. transl. BONWETSCH, TU 23: 2c (1902), pp. 39 ff. The complete document is found only in Georgian translation, though there exist a number of Old Slavonic and Armenian fragments.

yoked together in the harness of faith; the chariot is the ἐκκλησία of the Gentiles; the Evangelists are the wheels, and the Logos is the charioteer. The chariot is fourfold, being made up of the four creatures, and thus identical with the cherub-throne. We know from another source that Hippolytus identified the Evangelists and the cherubim.[1] This allegory is a rather curious mixture of OT and Greek elements: the Apostles as horses do not appear to fit in particularly well with the OT cherub-throne; the prototype is however Helios' *quadriga*, though the number of horses has been increased to twelve.[2]

The motif becomes even more complicated when Christian allegory takes over the Iranian myth according to which the horses drawing God's chariot are the four elements personified—a concept introduced into Hellenism by Dio.[3] Methodius identifies the cherub-throne with Dio's chariot, and is thus able to connect the four creatures with the elements: Man—air; lion—fire; ox—earth; eagle—water. "Now God who, as the old word says, has the beginning and end and middle of all that exists, who holds together and maintains air and earth, water and fire, the greatest animals by his own will; he guides the all ineffably as though eternally driving a four-yoked chariot."[4]

---

[1] Fragm. 1 in Ezek., GCS Hipp. 1.2.183.

[2] It may be worth noting in this context that in another passage of the same book, Comm. on S. of S. 22, it is said that Christ arises like a great star and is revealed like the eye of the sun of righteousness, to be praised together with the Father. This is probably a case of the same kind of imagery as that noted in connexion with Melito's work on the washing of baptism. Cf. DÖLGER, *Die Sonne der Gerechtigkeit*, p. 108. The word meaning "eye", which is found in the Georgian text, but not in the Slavonic, has been ingeniously interpreted as being a mistranslation, due to the misunderstanding of the Armenian translation which formed the basis of the Georgian translation: see intro. to BONWETSCH'S trans., p. 16. But it is likely that the word occurred in the original text, since it was extremely common for the "sun of righteousness" to be compared with an eye. See DÖLGER, *op. cit.*, pp. 97 ff.

[3] BIDEZ & CUMONT, *Les mages hellénisés* 1, pp. 91 ff., Dio Chrys. Or. 36.39, Teubn. Dio Chrys. 2.14 f., fragm. 0.8 in BIDEZ & CUMONT, *op. cit.* 2, pp. 142 ff. According to Dio the hymn forms part of the mysteries (ἀπόρρητοι τελεταί), probably the mysteries of Mithra. The comparison of the elements with the horses before a quadriga are derived, according to BIDEZ & CUMONT, from the Zervanite theology (*op. cit.* 1 p. 92, cf. p. 66). The hymn of Dio is in later Hellenistic literature applied to Helios, the horses being the elements (ex. in BIDEZ & CUMONT, *op. cit.* 2, p. 147 n. 2).

[4] Methodius, De resurr. II.10.4–6, GCS Meth. p. 351 f.: ὁ τοίνυν θεός, ὥσπερ ὁ παλαιός φησιν λόγος, ἀρχὴν καὶ τελευτὴν καὶ μέσα τῶν ὄντων ἁπάντων ἔχων, ἀέρα καὶ γῆν, ὕδωρ τε αὖ καὶ πῦρ, τὰ μέγιστα ζῷα τῇ βουλῇ συνέχων τῇ ἑαυτοῦ καὶ διακρατῶν καθάπερ ὄχημα τέτρωρον πρὸς διαμονὴν εὐθύνων ἀρρήτως ἡνιοχεῖ τὸ πᾶν. The text in

Recent excavations beneath St. Peter's in Rome have revealed, among other things, a mausoleum containing a number of mosaics; surprisingly, these included for the first time a representation of Christ as Helios.[1] The walls are covered with a net of vine-ornaments, and we also find pictures of a fisherman with his line, of Jonah being cast into the sea, and of the good shepherd. The most important picture is however to be found on the arch. It is of Helios standing on his chariot, which is drawn by white horses; his head is surrounded by a halo of light, which may possibly be intended to represent a cross; in his left hand he holds the world-globe, while his right hand has probably been raised in the gesture of power of Sol Invictus.[2]

Since the murals are undoubtedly Christian, the Helios mosaic must also be regarded as being Christian, although we have no earlier example of Helios in Christian art.[3]

Reference has been made—and rightly so—to the researches of Dölger, who has clearly demonstrated the importance of Christian sun-symbolism in the earliest Church.[4] However, the fact that Christ the Logos was there called ἡνίοχος—a title linked with Helios in particular—provides us with an important complement. Christ is βασιλεύς Ἥλιος, the cosmic charioteer, who holds the world in his hand. The astral symbolism adopted by the Roman emperors was also, though on a more limited scale, taken up by Christian mortuary art. Thus before ever the *Majestas* picture was drawn, Christ was represented in iconography as King, but in the categories of Hellenistic political philosophy. Representations of Christ on the cherub-throne date from a much later period.[5]

---

question has aroused little attention. It is not taken up by NEUSS, who says that St. Jerome was the first to connect the four creatures with the elements, *op. cit.*, p. 66. The evangelists' symbols and the elements are dealt with from the point of view of iconography by D. TSELOS, *Unique Portraits of the Evangelists*, ArtB 34 (1952), pp. 257–277, who however follows NEUSS in respect of the Church Fathers.

[1] KIRSCHBAUM, *Die Gräber*, pp. 29 ff. We have not had access to IDEM, *Ein christliches Mausoleum unter der Peterskirche*. Das Münster 1948–49, pp. 400–406 or O. PERLER, *Die Mosaiken der Juliergruft im Vatikan* (1953).

[2] Cf. L'ORANGE, *Studies*, pp. 139 ff., DÖLGER, *Sol Salutis*, pp. 289 ff.

[3] Cf. DÖLGER, *Sol Salutis*, p. 288 n. 5.

[4] KIRSCHBAUM, *Die Gräber*, pp. 35 f. On Christian "sun" symbolism see particularly DÖLGER, *op. cit.*, pp. 282 ff.

[5] On the representation of Christ enthroned between the Cherubim, see VAN DER MEER, *op. cit.*, pp. 255 ff.

This interpretation of the mosaic is further confirmed by the pictures with which it is surrounded. Kirschbaum points out that "fisherman" and "shepherd" are among the titles bestowed upon Christ in the concluding hymn of Clement's *Paedagogus*.[1] As we have already seen, ἡνίοχος belongs among the enumerated epithets of Christ, not actually in the hymn itself but in the song of praise immediately preceding it.[2] It is not necessary for that reason to assume direct influence from Clement. As we have pointed out, Clement's hymn has traditional characteristics, which are also to be found in more ancient writings, in the Melito fragment and in the *Martyrdom of Polycarp*. It would therefore seem to be a justifiable conclusion that the representation of Christ as fisherman, shepherd and charioteer go back to an early Christian tradition of hymn-writing, a tradition which is also reflected in Clement.

κυβερνήτης

The Logos is described not only as charioteer, but also as pilot, κυβερνήτης. The two metaphors are often used synonymously in Hellenistic political philosophy.[3] The use of ἡνίοχος links up with the common idea that the divine king rides in a chariot; the use of κυβερνήτης to the idea of the world as a ship.[4] The image of the State as a ship, with the King as its pilot, has been well-known in classical Greek literature ever since the time of Plato,[5] who also applied the image microcosmically, so that the soul became the κυβερνήτης of the body.[6] From Greek political philosophy the metaphor passed on to Philo,

---

[1] KIRSCHBAUM, *op. cit.*, p. 35.

[2] Cf. above, p. 196. In the hymn itself Christ is called στόμιον πώλων ἀδαῶν: an analogous but even more subordinationist use of imagery.

[3] RUDBERG, *op. cit.*, pp. 197 f. We find κυβερνήτης, used by Archytas in analogies, ap. Stob. III. 1.112, and by Diotogenes, ap. Stob. IV. 7.61, ed. DELATTE p. 38; cf. IDEM, *op. cit.*, pp. 249 f., in Dio Chrys. Or. 12.34, 36.50, Teubner Dio Chrys. 1, p. 208, 2, p. 18, and in De mundo 400b.6 f. Cf. above, p. 193.

[4] RAHNER, *Antenna Crucis* III (1942), pp. 196–227, has a full account of the occurrence of nautical imagery in Classical and Hellenistic literature, pp. 210 ff. Cf. DELATTE, *op. cit.*, pp. 249 f. K. GOLDAMMER, *Das Schiff der Kirche*, ThZ 6 (1950), pp. 232–237, lays particular emphasis upon the political character of the symbol of the ship, but refers mainly to Latin literature.

[5] Pol. 302A, Gorgias 67 (511d), Rep. VI. 488 a–e. In the last passage in particular Plato makes use of the metaphor of the ship to express his political principle that the rule of the state should be committed to one man.

[6] Leges 12.10 (961).

who uses it to refer to God, to the Logos, to man as the crown of creation and to reason as the governing power in man.[1] The word is later found in the *Martyrdom of Polycarp* and in Clement of Alexandria, following Philo.[2]

The term κυβερνήτης is particularly used in the nautical allegories which we find in various branches of early Christian literature.[3] In his work *De Antichristo* Hippolytus describes the Church as a ship sailing on the ocean of the world, with Christ as its skilled pilot.[4] Incidentally, we have here a parallel to that exposition of Jesus' entry into Jerusalem according to which Christ, as ἡνίοχος, steers the Jews and the Gentiles; according to Hippolytus the two (as a rule) rudders symbolize the two Covenants (οἴακες δύο αἱ δύο διαθῆκαι).[5]

A similar allegory is to be found in the so-called *Epistle of Clement to the Apostle James*, which stands as an introduction to the pseudo-Clementine homilies.[6] Here, as in Hippolytus, the Church is compared to a ship. The ship is owned by God and the (head) pilot is Christ:

> For the whole business of the Church is like unto a great ship, bearing through a violent storm men who are of many places, and who desire to inhabit the city of the good kingdom. Let therefore God be your shipowner, and let the pilot be likened to Christ.[7]

---

[1] Cherub. 36, Migr. 67, Sacr. Abel et Cain 51, Leg. alleg. III. 118, 224, Heres. 301—the latter quoted above, p. 201. For man as κυβερνήτης, see above, p. 200, quotation of Opif. 88.

[2] See above, p. 197. Clement used the word in a nautical allegory, as in the famous passage in which the Christian is compared with Ulysses, bound to the mast as he passes the Sirens, Protr. 118.4, GCS Clem. 1.83, Rahner, *Antenna Crucis* I, pp. 136 ff. Cf. Protr. 100.4, GCS Clem. 1.72: the Logos is the helmsman, and the wind of the Holy Spirit will waft the boat into the safe harbour of heaven. The common form of analogy is found in Paed. I. 54.2, GCS Clem. 1.122: the Logos is στρατηγός and κυβερνήτης.

[3] Rahner, *Antenna Crucis* III, pp. 196 ff.

[4] De Antichr. 59, GCS Hipp. 1.2.39: θάλασσα δέ ἐστιν ὁ κόσμος, ἐν ᾧ ἡ ἐκκλησία ὡς ναῦς ἐν πελάγει χειμάζεται μὲν ἀλλ' οὐκ ἀπόλλυται. ἔχει γὰρ μεθ' ἑαυτῆς τὸν ἔμπειρον κυβερνήτην Χριστόν. The text is dealt with by Dölger, *Sol Salutis*, pp. 210 ff., and more briefly by Rahner, *op. cit.*, p. 199 n. 13.

[5] Rahner, *op. cit.*, p. 199 n. 13 (οἴαξ) and PWK Suppl. 5, pp. 941 f.

[6] Epist. Clem. ad Jac. 14.1-2, GCS PsC 1.16.

[7] Ἔοικεν γὰρ ὅλον τὸ πρᾶγμα τῆς ἐκκλησίας νηὶ μεγάλῃ διὰ σφοδροῦ χειμῶνος ἄνδρας φερούσῃ ἐκ πολλῶν τόπων ὄντας καὶ μίαν τινὰ ἀγαθῆς βασιλείας πόλιν οἰκεῖν θέλοντας. ἔστω μὲν οὖν ὑμῖν ὁ ταύτης δεσπότης θεὸς καὶ παρεικάσθω ὁ μὲν κυβερνήτης Χριστῷ ... Dölger, *Sol Salutis*, pp. 215 f., Rudberg, *op. cit.*, pp. 200 f.

We catch an unusually clear glimpse of Hellenistic logos theology here in the dichotomy of God and Christ. God owns the ship, but Christ the Logos directs it. God does not concern himself with the course of events in the world; instead he guides the world through the mediation of his Logos. "Le roi règne, mais il ne gouverne pas." Thus when Christ is described as κυβερνήτης, the metaphor is not chosen at random. It still conveys much of the same meaning as it did in Hellenistic political philosophy and in Philo.[1]

ἡγεμών

The title ἡγεμών, which is found in the same literature as the other Logos titles we have discussed, does not have so many associations. It belongs among the analogies which we have encountered in Hellenistic political philosophy,[2] from whence it was adopted by Philo.[3] On those occasions on which the word occurs as an epithet for Christ we may assume influence from this direction. The word is not used to refer to Christ in the NT or in the earliest subsequent literature. Christ may be called ἄρχων or ἀρχηγός;[4] in expositions or quotations of Gen. 49.10, Num. 24.17 and Micah 5.1(2) he is sometimes called ἡγούμενος,[5]

---

[1] On the further development of the theme in patristic literature, see RAHNER, *op. cit.*, pp. 201 ff. There are a few examples of Christ having been represented as κυβερνήτης in early Christian art: see DÖLGER, *op. cit.*, pp. 212 ff., 216. Of particular interest is the lamp in the form of a ship, mentioned by DÖLGER, in which Christ stands in the bows, his hand raised in the gesture of power, and Peter sits in the stern as oarsman. The lamp bears the inscription "Dominus legem dat". Illustration in W. F. VOLBACH and M. HIRMER, *Frühchristliche Kunst, Die Kunst der Spätantike in West- und Ostrom* (1958), plate 12b. On the "ship" motif in early Christian art, see G. STUHLFAUTH, *Das Schiff als Symbol der altchristlichen Kunst*, RivAC 19 (1942), pp. 111–141.

[2] Dio Chrys. 12.27, 36.31 f., Teubn. Dio Chrys. 1, p. 206, 2, pp. 12 f. De mundo 400b, 6 f., RUDBERG, *op. cit.*, pp. 196 f.

[3] Plant. 60, Migr. 174, Leg. alleg. III. 150, Vita M. I. 26, Spec. leg. IV. 92.

[4] ἄρχων: Rev. 1.5, Justin, Apol. 12.7, Dial. 14.4. The word is otherwise not common as a predicate of Christ, being used more frequently to refer to the Devil as "prince of this world", Ign. ad Eph. 17.1, 19.1; Mag. 1.3, Trall. 4.2, Rom. 7.1, Philad. 6.2, Barn. 4.13, 18.2. Cf. the title ἄρχοντες for the powers of this world: see M. DIBELIUS, art. *Archonten*, RAC 1 (1941–50), ed. 631–633. ἀρχηγός: Acts 3.15, Heb. 12.2, 2 Clem. 20.5; *princeps* = ἄρχων or ἀρχηγός used of Christ in Irenaeus, Adv. haer. II. 22.4, III. 12.5, 16.6, IV. 24.1, 25.1. On ἄρχων as a term for the Devil, cf. also F. X. GOKEY, *The Terminology for the Devil and Evil Spirits in the Apostolic Fathers* (1961), pp. 50, 74 f.

[5] See above, p. 93.

but ἡγεμών evidently had no place in the earliest Christian terminology.[1] The word occurs in Melito's document on the washing of Baptism, and probably also in the original text of *De fide*;[2] it is also to be found several times in Clement of Alexandria.[3] Its occurrence is of particular interest, in that it is considerably more political in meaning than is ἄρχων, and bears witness of influence from the political thought of the Hellenistic world.[4]

στρατηγός

The word στρατηγός is closely related to ἡγεμών in meaning; it is found as a political metaphor in Archytas and Diotogenes,[5] and is taken up, together with the other metaphors, by Philo to express the activity of the Logos.

It is common knowledge that military allegories play a prominent role in the earliest Church. Christ is represented as commander and the individual Christian as his soldier.[6] Military terms occur particularly often in the work of the African Latin authors. However, the NT and the earlier Greek authors contain passages in which the Christian's life is compared with that of the soldier.[7]

The term στρατηγός, referring to Christ, is found neither in the NT nor in the earliest post-NT Christian literature. Not before Clement of Alexandria does the word occur in this meaning; there the context is such that it is perfectly evident that it has been taken over from Philo. On a number of occasions we find στρατηγός combined with κυβερνήτης,[8] and it also occurs together with βασιλεύς and νομοθέτης.[9] The most

---

[1] EHRHARDT assumes wrongly that Irenaeus uses ἡγεμών as a title of Christ. See above, p. 194 n. 4.

[2] See above, pp. 196 and 203.

[3] See above, p. 197.

[4] RUDBERG (*op. cit.*, p. 196) points out that ἄρχων has a less pregnant meaning than ἡγεμών.

[5] Archytas, ap. Stob. III. 1.112. Diotogenes, ap. Stob. IV. 7.61, ed. DELATTE, p. 38. Both reproduced above, p. 193 n. 4. See further DELATTE, *op. cit.*, pp. 249 f.

[6] See above, p. 179. HARNACK, *Militia Christi, passim*. PETERSON, *Christus als Imperator*, pp. 149–154.

[7] A review of the most important text is to be found in HARNACK, *Militia Christi*, pp. 93 ff.

[8] Protr. 100.4, GCS Clem. 1.72, Paed. I. 54.2, *ibid.* p. 122.

[9] Strom. I. 168.4, GCS Clem. 2.105, here referring not to the Logos but to the wise man, who has all the attributes of the Logos, since he is governed by the Logos. See below, p. 214.

detailed text is that in which military punishments are used to illustrate the disciplinary activity of the Logos. Here the Logos is compared to a commander, who can punish miscreants by imposing fines, corporal punishment, imprisonment, or even the death penalty, but in all this he has the good of the wrongdoer at heart.[1]

What is characteristic of all these passages is that it is not the incarnate Christ, but the Logos of God, who is the general. This, too, is proof that the term στρατηγός is not derived primarily from the military terminology of the NT but from the political metaphysics of Philo.[2]

The word ἀρχιστράτηγος is different in meaning; it belongs to the *testimonia* tradition, and means, with reference to Joshua 5.14, "captain of the heavenly host".[3] It is found, in contrast to στρατηγός, in Justin Martyr and Irenaeus, but not in Clement of Alexandria. It is striking, the way in which these two terms, so closely related to each other, are used quite separately, and seldom appear together in the same class of literature.[4] The word does not otherwise occur in Hellenistic political philosophy; nor is it to be found in Philo.

σωτήρ

We have earlier mentioned that σωτήρ belongs among the Hellenistic royal titles, and that there has been some discussion, whether or not its occurrence in the NT has to do with this usage.[5] On that occasion we also pointed out that we are far from certain as to the origin of the word as a Christological title. But in the post-Apostolic literature the word σωτήρ is used in contexts which lead us to assume the influence of political terminology.

Most Hellenistic political theorists stressed that it was the duty of the head of state to save, σώζειν, his people.[6] This is found *inter alia* in

---

[1] Paed. I.65.2 f., GCS Clem. 1.128: ... ὡσαύτως καὶ ὁ μέγας ἡμῶν ἐκεῖνος στρατηγός, ὁ τῶν ὅλων ἡγεμὼν λόγος ... Military allegories are also found in Protr. 100.4, GCS Clem. 1.72 and Strom. VII. 100.1, GCS Clem. 3.70. See further HARNACK, *op. cit.*, pp. 96 ff.

[2] HARNACK, *op. cit.*, pp. 23 ff., includes no special investigation of the term στρατηγός in his discussion of Clement.

[3] See below, pp. 265 f.

[4] An exception is Methodius, who uses both ἀρχιστράτηγος and στρατηγός to refer to the Logos as the leader of the heavenly powers (both connected with ποιμήν in the same sense), Symp. III. 6.63 f., GCS Meth. pp. 32 f., IV. 6.107, p. 52. Eusebius uses both terms, but in different contexts. Cf. below, pp. 264 ff.

[5] See above, pp. 64 ff.

[6] DELATTE, *Traités*, p. 249.

Diotogenes; the king should save his subjects as the steersman saves the ship, etc.¹ But the word σωτήρ is not used by Philo in his account of the kingship. Nevertheless, we have reason to suppose that he was well acquainted with the idea.² Philo seems to have used the title to refer to the Emperor, and sometimes to refer to God. In both cases he uses the fixed expression σωτήρ καὶ εὐεργέτης, which is thus—typically enough—both metaphysical and political in meaning.

We may assume Christian literature to have been influenced by this terminology when we find the word in connexion with other Philonic terms: a case in point is the connexion of σωτήρ with εὐεργέτης. In the *Martyrdom of Polycarp* 19.2 we find σωτήρ together with κυβερνήτης and ποιμήν; this, as we have said, is a typical combination of political metaphors. The word σωτήρ is found in combinations of this kind mainly in Eusebius.³

When faced with metaphors such as these it may be justifiable to ask to what extent they have retained their political meaning in Christian theology. They were used by Philo (and by other Hellenistic authors as well) to refer not only to the king but also to God, and to the individual man according to the macrocosmos–microcosmos speculation, which was so common in eclectic Hellenistic philosophy. The focus of interest for Alexandrian theology was often the individual's νοῦς, rather than the government of the world. In Origen we see the regression of political philosophy.

We shall see that the political implications of these terms were still consciously applied, particularly in the writings of Eusebius, in which the Logos is described as the ruler of the world and is referred to by those metaphors we have been considering.

The Emperor may be described in the same kind of metaphor, since he is governed by the Logos, and is the image of God and his instrument for the realization of the world order. This Philonic tradition was thus of great importance for the 4th century attitude to the Kingship of Christ, and also left its mark upon the Mediaeval conception of the ideal relations between God and the king. The cosmic aspect of the Kingship of Christ is the contribution of Alexandrian theology to the growth of the doctrine, and stands in sharp contrast to the economic and eschatological Christology of the Antiochene school.

---

[1] See above, p. 193 n. 4.
[2] GOODENOUGH, *Politics*, p. 97.
[3] See below, p. 264.

8. THE INCARNATE CHRIST AS KING IN ALEXANDRIAN THEOLOGY

It has often been pointed out that the royal aspect of Christ is not expressed so clearly in Clement and Origen as in the NT and the oldest Church tradition. Theologians in the highly Hellenized milieu of Alexandria did not think in terms of eschatology. Philo had interpreted the OT in such a way as to minimize the importance of a historical process; he was not the first Jewish theologian in Alexandria to do so. The Biblical figures are made to function as symbols of a super-earthly and super-historical reality. Even Moses, who receives a central position in Philo's thought, is really no more than an expression in time of the eternal Law.

Clement, following in Philo's footsteps, wished to present Christianity as the perfect philosophy and as a saving gnosis; for him, Christ was mainly the Revealer, the Philosopher and the Teacher. (That Christ is the Revealer of Divine truth is of course an important aspect of NT Christology but is given a Hellenistic accent in Alexandrian theology.) The NT doctrine of Christ as the eschatological King and Judge of the world, on the other hand, has little significance in Clement's work.

It is only natural, therefore, that the Alexandrian Christ has often been set up in contrast to the 4th century theology of Christ as King.[1] A number of art historians have pointed out that Alexandrian theology is also clearly reflected in the art of the period: the sarcophagi and catacomb paintings of the 3rd century show Christ sitting, in the manner of the ancient philosophers, with a scroll in his hand, discussing with his disciples. Not until the beginning of the 4th century, when other motives began to dominate, did the majestic characteristics of the image of Christ become more apparent.[2]

---

[1] KOLLWITZ, *Christus als Lehrer*, pp. 48 ff., IDEM, *Das Bild*, p. 96, L'ORANGE, *Studies*, pp. 188 ff.

[2] Cf. above, pp. 11 ff.

The distinction between Christ the Teacher and Christ the King should not however lead us to a one-sided estimation of the Alexandrian theologians' image of Christ. Clement and Origen also played a considerable part in spreading the concept of the Kingship of Christ, as it began to make its mark on the young Byzantine Empire. It is true that Clement (and to some extent Origen also) makes no use of those forms of literature with which the royal ideology seems to have been particularly connected during the sub-Apostolic age. We have few examples of exegesis of OT texts, such as we find in the anti-Jewish polemic of Justin Martyr and Irenaeus. Apocalyptic descriptions are entirely absent; little interest is shown in matters of liturgy. We do however find elements in the Alexandrian theologians which seem to be missing from the older tradition. We find a Hellenistic ideal of Kingship, taken over from Philo, and an incipient Hellenistic-inspired political metaphysic. While expositions of the NT are extremely rare in the early post-Apostolic age, we find a rich deposit of NT exegesis in Origen; this includes expositions in which Jesus appears as King.

Clement of Alexandria

Despite having little interest in politics as such, Clement's views on Kingship show that he was very much dependent upon Philo's political writings, even if he has also studied other political authors. Clement himself refers to Plato and the Stoics when he wishes to enlist Greek philosophy in support of his views. It is common knowledge that he believed Plato to have derived his ideas from Moses.[1]

"The King is to the state as God is to the world."[2] Clement, in common with Philo and the Pythagorean philosophers, makes the category of Kingship refer to various stages of rule. God and the Logos rule over the world-all, the lawgiver-king rules over the people, and the wise man rules himself. These various forms of rule are interdependent, in a ladder of hierarchy: the wise man gains his knowledge from the wiser lawgiver, who in turn represents the Logos of God. Consequently, when Christ is represented as King in Clement's works, he is described in terms of the lawgiver.

---

[1] Strom. I. 165.1, GCS Clem. 2.103; II. 20.1, GCS Clem. 2.123. Cf. E. MOLLAND, *The Conception of the Gospel in the Alexandrinian Theology* (1938), pp. 52 ff.

[2] Philo Prov. fragm. 2 (in Eusebius Praep. ev. VIII. 14). Diotogenes, ap. Stob. IV. 7.61. Cf. GOODENOUGH, *Hellenistic Kingship*, pp. 66–68.

The concept of "the universal Kingship" is developed in a number of passages of the *Stromateis*. According to the philosophers, it is only the wise king, lawgiver or general who is righteous, holy and God-fearing.[1] The wise man *par excellence* is Moses, not only for Philo but also for Clement; he is prophet, lawgiver, tactician, general (στρατηγός), statesman and philosopher.[2] These functions are hierarchically interrelated; the task of the tactician is a part of the general, which is part of that of the King. It is not only legislation and justice, but also divinity, which is summed up in the principle of Kingship. The Kingship thus stands at the head of the hierarchy of values, and includes in itself all other functions.[3] According to this passage, the King is the one who determines the laws, and has the power of reason, enabling him to rule voluntary servants,[4] just like the Lord, who rules over those who believe in him and in Christ, and under whose feet God has placed all things.

The common Hellenistic concept of the wise man as King recurs in a number of passages of Philo's works, and it is certain that Clement has taken over the idea from him, though he refers to Plato and other Greek philosophers as well.[5]

Philo is however, unlike Clement, very much interested in politics, and the "democratization" of the Kingship is therefore linked in his

---

[1] Strom. I. 168.4, GCS Clem. 2.105. Cf. Strom. II. 19.4, GCS Clem. 2.123. The wise man is called νόμος ἔμψυχος in Strom. II. 18.4, GCS Clem. 2.122.

[2] Strom. I. 158.1, GCS Clem. 2.99.

[3] Strom. I. 158–159, GCS Clem. 2.99 ff.

[4] It is a general principle in Hellenistic political philosophy that one of the characteristics of the true kingship is to rule, unlike the tyrant, over voluntary subjects. Cf. Philo, Leg. alleg. III. 79 f.

[5] In Strom. II. 18.1–19.4, GCS Clem. 2.121 f., Clement refers to Plato's Euthydemos and the Statesman, in which the wise man is called royal, even when a private citizen, and to Pindar, Speusippus and Chrysippus. In Philo the idea is found particularly in Mut. 151 f., Post. 127–129, Sobr. 56 f. and Somn. II. 243 f. Cf. StVF ed. von Arnim, 617, 618 and 622. Cf. also R.-A. Gauthier, *Magnanimité, L'idéal de la grandeur dans la philosophie païenne et dans la théologie chrétienne*, Bibl. thomiste 28 (1951). The fact of the wise man as king has to do with the image of wisdom as a "royal road", see J. Pascher, Η ΒΑΣΙΛΙΚΗ ΟΔΟΣ, StGKA 17. 3–4 (1941), F. Tailliez, ΒΑΣΙΛΙΚΗ ΟΔΟΣ, OCP 13 (1947), pp. 299–354, J. Leclercq, *La voie royale*, Suppl. de a Vie Spirituelle (1948), pp. 338–352. On the same idea in the work of the later Fathers, see Y. M.-J. Congar, *Jalons pour une théologie du laïcat* (1954), pp. 314 ff. Cf. also Schmidt art. βασιλεία.

work with a distinct emphasis upon the monarchy.¹ The King, for Philo, is of extreme importance, particularly as lawgiver; he is in fact animated law, νόμος ἔμψυχος.² Moses, as mediator of the consummate Law, is also the ideal King.

We have said that Philo was dependent upon that form of Hellenistic political philosophy which also appears in the Pythagoreans, and that there are large areas of terminological and material agreement between him and Diotogenes, Sthenidas and Ecphantus.³ It has been claimed by historians of religion that Philo's views were derived from Hellenistic syncretism; but this is an unwarranted conclusion, and recent years have seen greater emphasis placed on his Jewish and OT background. Thus Goodenough has shown that when Philo speaks of the King as νόμος ἔμψυχος, although his terminology is taken from Hellenistic philosophy, the concept refers back to the Kingship patterns of the Near East. Although the term is not used, the concept is found in both Babylonia and Israel.⁴ The character of the Israelite King as righteousness incarnate has been stressed by other modern scholars.⁵ This idea of the King as νόμος ἔμψυχος is thus an excellent example of the way in which OT-Jewish and Greek material is interwoven in Philo; so much so, that it is a hazardous undertaking to attempt to distinguish its various original components.⁶

It is characteristic of Philo that his supra-historical *Weltanschauung* leaves no room for the Messianic idea.⁷ Moses, who is depicted as the

---

[1] On the subject of Philo's view of the kingship, see principally I. HEINEMANN, *Philons Bildung*, pp. 182-202 and GOODENOUGH, *Politics*, pp. 86-120. See also WOLFSON, *Philo* II, pp. 325 ff.

[2] On this idea, see H. E. STIER, ΝΟΜΟΣ ΒΑΣΙΛΕΥΣ (1927) and A. STEINWENTER, ΝΟΜΟΣ ΕΜΨΥΧΟΣ, Anzeiger der Akad. d. Wiss. in Wien, Phil.-hist. Kl. 83 (1946), pp. 250-268.

[3] BRÉHIER, *Idées de Philon*, pp. 18 ff., DELATTE, *Traités*, pp. 245 ff.

[4] GOODENOUGH, *Kingship in Early Israel*, pp. 169-205.

[5] J. PEDERSEN, *Israel* III-IV (1940), p. 93 f. G. ÖSTBORN, *Tōrā in the Old Testament* (1945), pp. 77 ff.

[6] HEINEMANN, *Philons Bildung*, pp. 182-202; cf. criticism by GOODENOUGH, *Politics*, p. 86 n. 1. According to GOODENOUGH, HEINEMANN, despite his efforts to do justice to the influence from the two traditions, placed too much emphasis on the Greek tradition.

[7] F. GRÉGOIRE, *Le Messie chez Philon d'Alexandrie*, ETL 12 (1935), pp. 28-50, J. DE SAVIGNAC, *Le messianisme de Philon d'Alexandrie*, Nov. Test. 4 (1960), pp. 319-324. Both stress that there is no real messianism here. DE SAVIGNAC does not consider the relationship between Moses and Messiah.

ideal King, and given all the epithets usually reserved for the Messiah, stands instead at the focus of Philo's system.[1] Moses is thus called King and priest[2] and above all lawgiver.[3] Apart from this particular function, he is regarded as having the three classical functions of King, priest and prophet.[4] He must be King in order to fulfil the function of lawgiver, priest in order to have insight into the cult, and prophet in order to be the recipient of divine inspiration.[5] An interesting observation made by Philo is that the kings (even the kings of Israel) were originally priests as well.[6] Moses, by virtue of his Kingship, is also priest, lawgiver and judge.[7] This combination of attributes is commonly combined with Diotogenes' statement that the Kingship includes the offices of general, judge and priest.[8] It is only reasonable to suppose that the triad of King, priest and prophet goes back to more ancient Jewish traditions.[9]

We have already seen how the image of Christ in the early Church was coloured by the Messianic expectations of Palestinian Judaism. Both the apocalyptic world of concepts and the Messianic interpretation of the OT were taken over by Jesus and, after him, by the Church, in the conviction that the prophecies had been fulfilled and that the eschatological King had come. But Alexandrian theology was connected with an entirely different Jewish tradition. It was presumably not only Philo who substituted Moses for the Messiah at the heart of his theology; we may suppose it to have been a general tendency in Alexandrian Judaism. Consequently the Christian Church in Alexandria came to represent Christ as the new and consummate Moses. This tendency can be discerned as early as in the Epistle to the Hebrews, which appears to have originated in Alexandria.[10]

---

[1] GRÉGOIRE, *op. cit.*, pp. 37 ff.

[2] Virt. 54.

[3] BRÉHIER, *op. cit.*, pp. 18 ff. GOODENOUGH, *By Light, Light*, pp. 188 ff.

[4] Vita M. II. 3.

[5] Vita M. II. 1–8, Praem. 54–56.

[6] QE II. 105, cf. Vita M. II. 31.

[7] Vita M. 148–163, II. 4, 292.

[8] Diotogenes, ap. Stob. IV. 7.61. See BRÉHIER, *op. cit.*, pp. 19 ff., GOODENOUGH, *By Light, Light*, p. 190, DELATTE, *op. cit.*, pp. 249 ff.

[9] Cf. above, pp. 106 ff.

[10] C. SPICQ, *L'Épître aux Hébreux* 1 (1952), pp. 64 ff. In SPICQ's view Heb. is directly dependent upon Philo, *op. cit.*, pp. 39–91. Although R. P. C. HANSON accepts the Alexandrian origin of the Epistle, he criticizes this theory sharply:

The parallelism between Moses and Christ is presented all the more clearly in the work of Clement, who describes both in the same terms and connects the same idea with both. It one extended passage he describes Moses as a Hellenistic ideal king, and supplies Moses with all the epithets normally reserved for such a King.[1] He is not only a wise king and lawgiver; he is even called νόμος ἔμψυχος.[2]

According to Clement, Christ has the same qualities, though they are even more pronounced than in Moses' case: Christ is the true King, high priest and lawgiver. Christ has proved himself to be King, since he was addressed as such by the unbelieving Jews, by little children and by the prophets; his Kingdom is so great that he was able to refuse the offer of the world and all its gold when it was made by the adversary. He is the one and only High Priest, since he alone knows the nature of true worship; he is the King of peace Melchizedek, who is best fitted to lead the human race. He is lawgiver, since it was he who proclaimed the Law through the mouths of the prophets, and he who taught, in the clearest possible terms, what we ought to do and what we ought not to do.[3]

Moses was the mouthpiece of the Logos for men. Christ is himself the Logos incarnate. In this Clement goes far beyond Philo. But when he describes Christ's royal qualities, he is so close to Philo's description of Moses that it is virtually impossible to distinguish the two. It is significant that in the passage we have just summarized, Clement appears to refer to the three-fold ministry of King, priest and prophet. Although he does not mention the prophet, his description of the lawgiver fits in with the character of the prophet.

Similarly, both Moses and Christ are called "shepherd": a title which in Alexandrian theology is particularly important as referring to the Logos.[4] As we have already pointed out,[5] the titles of shepherd and King are synonymous in the Near East and in the OT. Philo, too, uses

---

Heb. he considers to be influenced not by Philo, but by another Jewish theology in Alexandria, related to that of Philo, *Allegory and Event* (1959), pp. 83 ff.

[1] Strom. I. 158–168, GCS Clem. 2.99–105; cf. above, p. 214. Strom. II. 21.1, GCS Clem. 2.123.

[2] Strom. I. 167.3, GCS Clem. 2.104.

[3] Strom. II. 21.1–5, GCS Clem. 2.123 f.

[4] Protr. 116.1, GCS Clem. 1.81. Paed. I. 52.2–3, *ibid.*, pp. 121 f.; 84.1–85.2, pp. 139 f. Cf. above, pp. 198 ff.

[5] See above, p. 87.

the two synonymously.¹ The title of shepherd is given not only to Kings and wise men (Kings of course being wise men as well), but also to God, the King of the world-all.²

On the human level, the shepherd *par excellence* is naturally Moses.³ His care for Jethro's sheep (Ex. 3.1) is seen by Philo as being a preparation for his coming Kingship. Since Kings are called "shepherds of the people", Philo considers that a King's education ought to include a measure of practical experience in caring for sheep.⁴ Moses demonstrates himself to be the good shepherd primarily in his function of lawgiver, because he leads the senses to observe the universal Law.⁵

When Clement describes Christ as the good shepherd, he does so on the pattern of Moses as King and lawgiver. The above-mentioned passage in which he characterizes Moses as a Hellenistic ideal king,⁶ is followed by a description of Christ as the true shepherd and lawgiver:

"As then we say that it is the shepherd's office to care for the sheep, for "the good shepherd gives his life for the sheep"; so we also say that the office of the lawgiver is to establish the virtue of men, by kindling as far as possible what is good in man, because it is his office to guard and to care for the flock of men. And if the flock, which the Lord speaks about in a parable, is nothing but a flock of men, then he himself will be the shepherd and the good lawgiver of one single flock of sheep who hear him."⁷

The concept of shepherd here corresponds to the Hellenistic ideal of Kingship, which we have also seen in Philo. The shepherd-king is the one who gives mankind the divine law and leads men along the path of the royal wisdom. The concepts God, king and shepherd, each in its own area of experience, are analogous: as the shepherd is to the flock and the king for the people, so is God for the world.⁸

The hymn which concludes Clement's *Paedagogus* is a particularly

---

[1] Agr. 66, Jos. 2, Prob. lib. 30–31, Legat. 44.
[2] Agr. 50 f., cf. *ibid.*, 41.
[3] Virt. 58.
[4] Vita M. I. 60–62, cf. Jos. 2 f.; GOODENOUGH, *By Light, Light*, p. 184. Clement takes up Philo's exposition in Strom I. 156.3, GCS Clem. 2.98.
[5] Agr. 43–49; GOODENOUGH, *op. cit.*, p. 229.
[6] See above, p. 217.
[7] Strom. I. 169.1–2, GCS Clem. 2.105.
[8] Strom. VII. 42.7, GCS Clem. 3.32. Cf. Protr. 116.1–4, in which Christ is compared with a shepherd for the flock and a king for the army, GCS Clem. 1.81 f. N.b. the military terminology.

expressive description of Christ as Shepherd and King; here he enumerates the titles of Christ, and returns time and time again to the words "Shepherd" and "King".[1] It is probable that there are connexions between this and an older tradition of hymn-writing, and that the epithets given to Christ by Clement refer back to an early liturgical usage.[2]

Origen

There are certain standard difficulties encountered in each and every attempt to describe Origen's theology; this is no less true of the attempt to give an overall picture of Origen's doctrine of the Kingship of Christ. His general presentation varies, between a more or less traditional Biblical theology and Platonic speculation, depending upon the part of his work to which we turn.[3] There is little about Christ as King in either *Contra Celsum* or *De principiis*; the commentaries and homilies, on the other hand, contain a number of sayings on the Kingship of Christ. There would seem to be little reason, after the discovery of the Toura texts, to call in question the authenticity of the works of Biblical theology; it is clear that the fact that we have here a more traditional type of theology than in *Contra Celsum* and *De principiis* is due to the different character of the works in question.[4] It is however possible, even within the framework of the Biblical theology, to come across different estimations of the Kingship of Christ. The more traditional eschatological concepts are to be found mainly in the *Commentaries on Matthew and John,* while the OT homilies and the *Commentary on the Song of Songs* contain a theology strikingly spiritual in character. It has been said that the more orthodox character of the commentaries is due to the fact that they were intended for an inner circle of Christians, the homilies being designed to be read by a wider public; this view, first put forward by Pamphilus in his *Apology for Origen,* is however most improbable.[5] Modern scholarship has demonstrated how difficult

---

[1] Paed. III.101.3, GCS Clem. 1.291 f.

[2] See above, pp. 196 f.

[3] On Origen as exegete, see J. DANIÉLOU, *Origène* (1948), H. DE LUBAC, *Histoire et Esprit* (1950), HANSON, *Allegory and Event.*

[4] On the Toura texts, see e.g. L. DOUTRELEAU, *Que savons-nous aujourd'hui des papyrus de Toura?* RSR 43 (1955), pp. 162-193.

[5] Pamphilus, Apol. 1 (82), PG 17.557.

it is to draw a line of demarcation between Origen's two types of exposition.[1] He is nevertheless more "spiritual" in character when expounding the OT than when commenting on the NT. In his *Commentary on the Song of Songs* he links the royal theme with the theme of the bridegroom, symbolizing the relationship between Christ and the individual believer.[2]

The oldest preserved commentaries on the text of the NT are to be found in Origen; these are of particular interest for us, since they provide the earliest examples of an exposition of the actions and words with which Jesus manifests himself as the Messiah. Apart from unimportant passages in Justin and Irenaeus,[3] the only pre-Origen commentary on the NT which we possess is a highly fragmentary commentary on John by the Valentinian theologian Heracleon.[4] It is probable that Origen was inspired to undertake his commentaries by

---

[1] E. KLOSTERMANN, *Formen der exegetischen Arbeiten des Origenes*, ThLZ 72 (1947), pp. 203-208.
[2] W. VÖLKER, *Das Vollkommenheitsideal des Origenes* (1931), pp. 100 ff. Cf. below, pp. 228 ff.
[3] In this context we may mention the exposition of the Matthaean account of the gifts of the Magi; we first find it in St. Irenaeus, according to whom the gold refers to the king, the incense to God and the myrrh to the coming burial, Adv. haer. III.9.2, ed. HARVEY 2.32: "Myrrham quidem, quod ipse erat, qui pro mortali humano genere moreretur et sepeliretur: Aurum vero, quoniam Rex, cujus Regni finis non est; Thus vero, quoniam Deus, qui et notus in Judaea factus est, et manifestus eis qui non quaerebant eum." The same interpretation is found in Origen, Cat. fragm. 29, GCS Orig. 12.27: χρυσὸς ὃν προσφέρει τὰ ἔθνη πλουτοῦντα ἔργοις ἀγαθοῖς, λίβανος ἡ εἰς θεὸν ὁμολογία, σμύρνα γνῶσις τοῦ ὑπὲρ ἀνθρώπων ἀποθανεῖν Χριστὸν τῇ ἁμαρτίᾳ καὶ ταφῆναι κατὰ τὰς γραφάς, and Cat. fragm. 30 (p. 28): Δῶρα μὲν προσήνεγκαν αὐτῷ χρυσὸν καὶ λίβανον καὶ σμύρναν ὑπὸ θεοῦ ὁδηγούμενοι, ἵνα δείξωσιν αὐτὸν πᾶσι καὶ βασιλέα καὶ θεὸν τέλειον, καὶ ὡς μέλλοντα θνῄσκειν ὑπὲρ ὑμῶν. The occurrence of this interpretation in both Origen and Irenaeus suggests that it was widespread in the Church. In later tradition it became common property, being used by both orthodox and Arians; it was taken up by St. Ambrose in De fide 1.4 (31), PL 16.535 and Exp. in Luc. 2.44, CSEL 32.4.66, but also in the Arian *Contra Judaeos*, PL 57.801 (On this writing, see below, p. 270). In all these texts the gold indicates the Kingship and the incense God (even in the Arian writings); only in respect of the myrrh is there a conflicting interpretation, according to which it means not only the suffering, death and burial, but the human nature as a whole. See J. LEMARIÉ, *La manifestation du Seigneur*, Lex Orandi 23 (1957), pp. 241 f., 254.
[4] The Heracleon fragments preserved in Origen's commentary are gathered in A. E. BROOKS' edition, TS 1: 4 (1891); cf. also W. FOERSTER, *Von Valentine zu Heracleon*, ZNW Beih. 7 (1928).

Heracleon, and he has also taken over a proportion of Heracleon's exegesis, in a more or less modified form.¹

The traditional Christian idea that the Kingship of Christ was made manifest above all at the Ascension is also to be found in Origen, largely in his exposition of the descriptions in Matt. and Jn. of Jesus' entry into Jerusalem.² The entry is, according to Origen, an anticipation of the Ascension of Christ, his entry into the heavenly city. The Zion which rejoiced and the Jerusalem which proclaimed the good tidings (Zech. 9.9) cannot in Origen's view be identical with the earthly Jerusalem, over which Jesus wept—the town which murdered the prophets and crucified Christ. The prophecy refers instead to the heavenly Zion (Heb. 12.22) and the Jerusalem above, which is free (Gal. 4.26).³ The ass and the foal symbolize the Jews and the Gentiles, who are freed by Christ from their bonds and led into the heavenly city.⁴

Origen has taken over these allegorical interpretations from earlier traditions, of which no more than a few traces remain. In the *testimonia* tradition the entry into Jerusalem is seen only as the fulfilment of Zech. 9.9 and Gen. 49.11.⁵ Irenaeus on one occasion represents the entry into Jerusalem as the coming of the expected King, but says nothing about it being an anticipation of the Ascension.⁶ The background of Origen's exegesis must be sought instead in Alexandrian theology. Clement has a passage in which he represents the entry into Jerusalem as anticipating the Ascension.⁷ A similar interpretation of

---

¹ HANSON, *Allegory*, pp. 144, 161. The degree to which Clement and Origen are dependent upon Gnostic exegesis is strongly emphasized by J. DANIÉLOU, *The Fathers and the Scriptures*, ECQ 10 (1954), pp. 265-273. Similarly VÖLKER, *Vollkommenheitsideal*, pp. 128 f., 143. Cf. HANSON's criticism in *op. cit.*, pp. 148 f.

² Comm. on Matt. 16.14-19, GCS Orig. 10.518 ff. Comm. on Jn. 10.28-32 (18), GCS Orig. 4.201 ff.

³ Comm. on Matt. 16.15, p. 522 f.

⁴ Comm. on Matt. 16.15, p. 523 f. Comm. on Jn. 10.29 (18), p. 202, cf. *ibid.* 13.13, p. 238. The same theme is dealt with in a more summary fashion in Comm. on Matt. 16.3, GCS Orig. 10.468 f. When the true Jerusalem received Jesus, when he ascended on the ὑποζύγιον which was his body, the earthly Jerusalem—which was a shadow of the heavenly—and its Temple, were destroyed. We find the same contrast in Comm. on Matt. 12.20, p. 115: Jesus was killed in the Jerusalem here below, but after his resurrection reigns on mount Zion and in the Jerusalem which is the city of the living God (here the Latin version has a quotation from Ps. 2.6).

⁵ Justin Apol. 32.2, 35.11.

⁶ Adv. haer. IV. 11.3, ed. HARVEY 2.175 f.

⁷ Protr. 121.1, GCS Clem. 1.85.

the same event is to be found in Heracleon; the resemblance between this interpretation and those of Clement and Origen is striking, though the former is dominated by Heracleon's Valentinian theology. The entry symbolizes the ascension of the Saviour from the hylic to the psychic sphere, the pneumatic sphere being represented by the holy of holies in the Temple: the place where, according to Heracleon, the cleansing of the Temple took place.[1]

Although we know that Clement and Origen were not entirely uninfluenced by Gnostic exegesis,[2] it would nevertheless be quite wrong to regard this interpretation as originally Gnostic. It is entirely in accord with the parallelism between the heavenly and the earthly Jerusalem, which is already to be seen in Judaism, and which is reflected in the NT, and particularly in those passages quoted by Origen: Gal. 4.26 and Heb. 12.22, as well as Rev. 21–22.[3] The heavenly city is regarded both as the pattern of the earthly Jerusalem and as an eschatological reality, which will be revealed in the last days.[4] We have already pointed out that in *testimonia* there is a tendency to interpret the processional Psalms as referring to the Ascension.[5] The King, entering the Temple in procession, is taken to be a *typos* of Christ enthroned in the heavenly sanctuary. It is fully in agreement with this interpretation when Origen interprets the entry into Jerusalem as prefiguring the coming Ascension. The Valentinian and Naassene doctrine that Jerusalem is an image of the pleroma is derived from an older Jewish tradition,[6] and it is probable that both Clement and Origen derived their doctrine of the entry as a pattern of the Ascension from an earlier Alexandrian Christian theology. We must remember that Heb., with its doctrine of Christ's entry into the heavenly sanctuary, is probably of Alexandrian origin.[7]

Origen, as he himself admits, took over the typological interpretation

---

[1] Origen Comm. on Jn. 10.33 (19), p. 206. Taken up as fragm. 13 in BROOKS' edition (pp. 68 f., cf. 46) and as fragm. 11 in FOERSTER, *op. cit.*, pp. 9 ff.

[2] Cf. above and n. 49.

[3] SCHLIER, *Comm. ad loc.*, SPICQ, *Comm. ad loc.*

[4] SCHMIDT, *Polis*, pp. 67 ff. Cf. IDEM, *Jerusalem als Urbild und Abbild*, Eranos-Jahrbuch 18 (1950), pp. 207–248, BIETENHARD, *Himmlische Welt*, pp. 192 ff.

[5] PEDERSEN, *Israel* II, p. 437, KROLL, *Gott und Hölle*, p. 254 and *passim*, DANIÉLOU, *Bible et Liturgie*, p. 426; cf. above, pp. 101 ff.

[6] Hippolytus, Ref. VI. 34.3 ff., GCS Hipp. 3.162 f.; cf. SCHMIDT, *Jerusalem*, p. 248.

[7] Cf. above, p. 216.

of the ass and the foal as the Jews and the Gentiles from an earlier exposition.¹ Clement was evidently also familiar with this exegesis,² and it is explicitly mentioned in Justin.³ The problem of how Jesus was able to ride on both the ass and the foal, which caused difficulties for all the early Church's exegetes, is dealt with by both Clement and Origen in such a way as to make it appear that Jesus yoked the two to a cart.⁴ It goes without saying that neither Clement nor Origen believed Jesus to have entered Jerusalem in this way. Nevertheless, the fact of there being two animals was used by the allegorizers in order to represent Christ as ἡνίοχος: He is the Logos, who yokes the two races of man and leads them into the holy city.⁵

The parallelism between Jesus' entry into Jerusalem and the Ascension is to be found in another passage, in which Origen places the people's question "Who is this person?" (Matt. 21.10) over against the angels' inquiry at the Ascension.⁶ Here we are dealing with the same motif as we have already encountered in Apocalyptic and in the *testimonia* tradition. Apart from Ps. 23 (24).7 ff., a proof-text frequently associated with this tradition, we find Origen also using Isa. 63.1: "Who is this that comes from Edom, in crimsoned garments from Bozrah?" The angels' wonderment is increased by the fact that at the time of his Ascension, Christ still bears the marks of his Passion.⁷

The prophecy of the coming prince of peace, who is to cast chariots and horses out of Jerusalem and destroy the bows of war (Zech. 9.10) is taken by Origen and given a special interpretation agreeing with

---

¹ Comm. on Jn. 10.29 (18), p. 202.
² Protr. 121.1, GCS Clem. 1.85.
³ Dial. 53.2.
⁴ Clemens, Protr. 121.1, Origen, Comm. on Jn. 10.29 (18), p. 202. One reason for this interpretation is that Hellenistic kings normally rode in chariots, cf. ALFÖLDI, *Ausgestaltung*, pp. 106 ff. But they did not know that the ass was the common form of transport in the Orient—even for kings. See also St. John Chrysostom, Hom. 67 in Matt., PG 58, 628: Christ did not ride in a chariot like other kings, οὐχὶ ἅρματα ἐλαύνων, ὡς οἱ λοιποὶ βασιλεῖς.
⁵ Cf. Clem. Paed. III. 101.1, GCS Clem. 1.290 f., in which the Christ-Logos is called ἡνίοχε 'Ισραήλ and *ibid.*, 101.3 (p. 291), in which he is called στόμιον πώλων ἀδαῶν. Cf. above, pp. 196 f.
⁶ Comm. on Matt. 16.19, pp. 539 f.
⁷ The same combination of Ps. 23 and Isa. 63 recurs in Comm. on Jn. 6.56, pp. 164 f., and is later taken over by Ambrose, De myst. 36 CSEL 73.103 f. Cf. DANIÉLOU, *Bible et Liturgie*, pp. 412 ff., IDEM, *Judéo-christianisme*, pp. 286 f.

his exposition of Jesus' entry into Jerusalem. Before the coming of Christ, the heavenly Jerusalem was ruled by the spiritual powers of darkness in the heavenly places (Eph. 6.12), but these were cast out when he entered, just as he cast out the merchants from the Temple after his entry into Jerusalem (Matt. 21.12 par.).[1] The NT sayings about the fall of Satan (Lk. 10.18, Jn. 12.31, Rev. 12.7–9) are connected by Origen with the Ascension; despite their somewhat unusual form, these are older ideas which have been taken over from the NT (cf. Rev. 12.5 ff.).[2] One element in the enthronement of Christ is that his enemies are laid beneath his feet. "He has disarmed the principalities and powers of the spiritual world." Nor is the connexion with the cleansing of the Temple the original work of Origen; we have already seen how Heracleon, in a Gnostic exposition, connected the entry and the purification of the Temple.

As the entry of Jesus into Jerusalem prefigures the coming Ascension, so the episode in which Jesus is mocked is taken to prefigure the coming Kingship.[3] The crown of thorns and the mantle do not however give rise to any presentation of the Kingship. The reed which Jesus held in his hand is reminiscent of the broken reed upon which we supported ourselves before we believed (Isa. 36.6). Jesus took the reed, and gave us in its place the sceptre of the Kingdom of Heaven, of which it is written: "The sceptre of thy kingdom is the sceptre of righteousness" (Ps. 44 (45).7). There follow two quotations in which the word ῥάβδος is the key-word: 1 Cor. 4.21 and Ex. 12.11; the technique used is reminiscent of Justin's, with one difference—that Origen also makes use of NT quotations among his proof-texts.

Origen saw the Kingship of Christ as manifested in his Ascension, which at the same time was his enthronement. This view is particularly prominent in his commentary on Matt. 20.20 ff.,[4] the pericope in which the mother of the sons of Zebedee comes to Jesus with the request that her sons may be allowed to sit, one on the right hand and one on the left hand of Jesus in his Kingdom. Origen points out that her request is typical of the Kingdoms of the world, in which it is accounted an

---

[1] Comm. on Jn. 10.29, pp. 202 f.
[2] BIETENHARD, *Himmlische Welt*, pp. 209 ff., "Der Satan als himmlisches Wesen."
[3] Comm. on Matt., Comm. ser. 125, GCS Orig. 11.262.
[4] Comm. on Matt. 16.4, GCS Orig. 10.471 ff.

honour to sit together with the king, dressed in his finery and bearing his regalia.[1]

In this context Origen produces a large number of proof-texts from the OT and the NT, showing what is meant by the *sessio* of Christ. He begins with a series of OT texts in which God is represented as seated upon his throne: 3 Kings 22.19, 2 Chron. 18.18, Isa. 6.1, Dan. 7.9, Ezek. 1.25 f., Ps. 109 (110).1, Ps. 79 (80).1 and Ps. 46 (47).9. There follow quotations from the Gospels, in which Jesus speaks of the revelation of the Son of Man upon his throne: Matt. 19.28, 25.31, 26.64, Mk. 14.62 and Lk. 22.69.[2] Origen goes on to say that the throne of God is spiritual, and so is the throne of Christ. The fact that Christ is seated at the right hand of Power must also be understood spiritually.[3] To imagine that it would be possible to sit at the right and left hand of the throne of Christ is therefore both worldly and absurd. That Christ has been installed in his Kingship and has received power must be understood as meaning that he has destroyed sin, which ruled in our mortal bodies (cf. Rom. 6.12) and ruled over every evil ἀρχή and ἐξουσία and δύναμις; this is the meaning of Christ's enthronement on the throne of his glory.[4]

Origen often criticizes the naïve literalism which evidently flourished in contemporary, less well-educated expositors.[5] His criticism of a too-naïve view of Heaven must be seen against this background. When he rejected the "local" Heaven of the apocalyptic literature he opened the way for a new understanding of the Ascension of Christ. Instead of the descriptive, we have the conceptual understanding, on a basis of which the theology of the Ascension was to develop.[6]

It is mainly in the homilies and the commentaries on the books of

---

[1] συγκαθεζόμενοι τῷ βασιλεῖ ἐν τῇ βασιλικῇ ἐσθῆτι καθεζομένῳ καὶ ὁτιποτοῦν τῶν τῆς βασιλικῆς πραγμάτων διέποντι (*ibid.* p. 473).

[2] *Ibid*, pp. 474 ff.

[3] *Ibid*, p. 477.

[4] *Ibid*, p. 478; cf. Comm. on Matt., Comm. ser. 111, GCS Orig. 11.231 (to Matt. 26.64).

[5] Hanson, *Allegory*, pp. 148 ff.

[6] Criticism of a too-naïve attitude to the heavenly world is to be seen as early as Irenaeus, Adv. haer. IV. 3, ed. Harvey 2.150 f. This was later taken up in particular by St. John Chrysostom, who says in his commentary on Isaiah that the prophet cannot have seen God, that God has no throne, the seraphim no wings and there is no altar in heaven, Comm. on Isa. 6, PG 46.68–70. Cf. J. Lécuyer, *Le sacerdoce céleste du Christ selon Chrysostome*, NRTh 82/72 (1950), pp. 561–579, which gives a clear picture of the way in which the rich visual imagery of Chrysostom by no means excludes a spiritual understanding of things heavenly.

the OT that Origen places sayings having to do with the Kingship of Christ in the context of Philonic allegory. It is characteristic that he says in his commentary on the Gospel of John that the Jerusalem entered by Christ is the heavenly city, but at the same time gives the microcosmical interpretation, that Jerusalem is the soul and the ass the OT released by the disciples, i.e. when they draw out its spiritual meaning.[1] This is an exposition in the manner of Philo, in which the Biblical statements are interpreted, not as prophecies of the eschatological events, but as symbols of psychological or moral truths.[2]

In these allegorical expositions Origen often returns to the theme of "royalty"; it is seldom that he is referring to the Kingship of Christ when he does so. He took over instead the idea of the wise man as king, which we have previously encountered in Philo and Clement. For Origen it is the word of Scripture which is the source of wisdom: the true king is he who penetrates the word and appropriates the wisdom hidden therein.[3] On a number of occasions he returns to an allegorical interpretation of Num. 21.18, which speaks of the well which the princes dug and the nobles of the people delved;[4] that Origen is here dependent upon Jewish exegesis has been shown by the discovery of the Damascus Document, in which the passage is explained in such a way that the well refers to the law and "the nobles of the people" the penitents of Israel.[5] In Origen's version, too, the well stands for the word. The parallelism between the "princes" and the "nobles" he interprets as referring to two kinds of people; the princes dug and the kings delved: the kings are thus those who delve the deepest and penetrate the secrets of God. In connexion with this Origen sets out what royalty implies: Christians are called "a royal people" (cf. 1 Pet. 2.9). The Apostles and those who rule the churches are even more entitled to be called kings, and the Lord is thus called "the King of

---

[1] Comm. on Jn. 10.28 (18), p. 201. Cf. HANSON, *Allegory*, pp. 267 f. An interpretation of Jerusalem as the individual into which Christ makes his entry is found as far back as Orac. Sib. 8.324 ff., GCS, Orac. Sib. p. 163. Cf. Od. Sol. 7.16–17. A third interpretation, according to which Jerusalem is the Church, is given by Origen in Comm. on Jn. 6.42, p. 151.

[2] HANSON, *Allegory*, p. 48 and *passim*.

[3] Apart from this Origen also has a representation of the wise man as priest; VÖLKER, *Vollkommenheitsideal*, pp. 187 ff.

[4] Hom. on Num. 12.2, GCS Orig. 7.99 ff., Comm. on S. of S. Prol., GCS Orig. 8.81.

[5] Dam. 8.5 ff., HANSON, *Allegory*, p. 21.

kings", since he rules over kings. Origen also mentions the fact that Paul calls the Christians in Corinth kings, though ironically, in 1 Cor. 4.8. His exposition closes with a summary. True kings and rulers are necessary to take away the earth from the well, i.e. take away the superficial meaning of the letter of Scripture and penetrate to the inner rock, which is Christ, and bring out the spiritual meaning like living water. Kings are thus those who have driven out the rule (*regnum*) of sin from their bodies and have accepted the reign of righteousness in their limbs. To be great in the Kingdom (Matt. 5.19) means to be a king.

A similar exposition is given by Origen of Judg. 5.3, "Hear, ye kings, and listen, ye rulers". Here he says that kings are those who are called to observe the word of God, i.e. the people of God. On this occasion, too, he refers to 1 Pet. 2.9.[1] Since Christians are kings, Christ is called King of kings and Lord of lords.

"It makes you a king over all things if Christ rules in you, for a king (*rex*) comes to rule (*regendo*). Thus if the spirit (*animus*) rules in you and your body obeys, if you place the lusts of the flesh beneath the yoke of rule, if you govern your sins even harder with the reins of your temperance, you shall have the right to be called king, since you are able to rule yourself aright. When you have been made thus, you shall worthily have been called as king to hear the divine words."[2]

This text has mainly to do with Christ as the Logos, and should perhaps have been more at home in the previous section. But what is stressed here is that in these contexts the Kingship of Christ is introduced only secondarily. Origen wishes to represent the wise man, i.e. the Christian, as king. Since Christ rules over all Christians, he is the King of kings: this spiritualized interpretation becomes common in later allegorical Scripture exposition, influenced as it was by Origen.[3] We see at the same time that the Apostles, who were not only able to control themselves, but also were commissioned to govern others, may be called kings in a special sense. The "democratization" of the royal ideal which is found in these texts thus does not exclude the

---

[1] The Latin text has a somewhat different wording here than previously.
[2] Hom. on Judg. 6.3, GCS Orig. 7.501.
[3] The idea of Christ as *rex regum* is often found in Origen, with this interpretation; see Hom. on Num. 1.4, GCS Orig. 7.84 f., *ibid.*, 12.2 (p. 100), *ibid.*, 28.4 (p. 285). Hom. on Judg. 6.3, GCS Orig. 7.501.

principle of hierarchy. The idea that the king, and above all the lawgiver, is the wise man *par excellence* has been seen in Philo and to some extent in Clement, though his political interest was slight. In Origen we find the political argument in the passage in question being transferred to the ecclesiastical level. The Church's office-bearers are possessors of the kingship in a special sense: it is this same thought which is to be found in the Pseudo-Clementines and the Syriac *Didascalia*.[1]

The allegorical interpretation of the Kingship of Christ is especially noticeable in Origen's commentaries on the Song of Songs. His contemporaries believed the book to have been written by Solomon, who is thus identical with the king and the bridegroom in the song.[2] Certain trends in Rabbinic exegesis had already interpreted the poem as referring to the love between God and Israel,[3] and early Christian interpretation (first in Hippolytus and Origen) was able to link up with Jewish exegesis.[4]

The writings of Hippolytus and Origen on the Song of Songs are practically contemporaneous. It is uncertain whether there has been any influence exercised in one or other direction, though it seems that Hippolytus is more likely to have influenced Origen than vice versa.[5]

In his commentary Hippolytus has a Christological interpretation of the poem according to which the bridegroom is Christ and the bridalchamber is the Church. The King in S. of S. 1.4 and 1.12 is thus obviously Christ.[6] But at the same time we find that there has been some influence from Philo, in Hippolytus' psychological interpretation of the text of Scripture.[7]

This tendency is even more marked in Origen, according to whom Solomon is a pattern of Christ, partly as King of peace, partly because the Queen of the East came to hear his wisdom. "In plurimus Solo-

---

[1] See above, p. 167 and below, p. 246.
[2] Origen. Comm. on S. of S. Prol., GCS Orig. 8.83 f.
[3] See BONSIRVEN, *Exegèse*, pp. 214 ff. J. E. KELLER, *Der Bräutigam im Gleichnis der zehn Jungfrauen* (1940). A. NEHER, *Le symbolisme conjugal : expression de l'histoire dans l'A.T.*, RHPhR 34 (1954), pp. 30–49. J. GUILKA, "*Bräutigam*" — *spätjüdisches Messiasprädikat?* TrierThZ 69 (1960), pp. 298–301.
[4] HANSON, *Allegory*, pp. 33 f.
[5] *Ibid.*, pp. 115 f.
[6] Hippolytus, Comm. on S. of S. 3.1, ed. BONWETSCH, TU 23:c (1902), p. 34 (translation from the Georgian text).
[7] HANSON, *op. cit.*, p. 117.

monem typum Christi ferre vel secundum hoc quod pacificus dicitur vel secundum, quod regina austri venit a finitibus terrae audire sapientiam Solomonis, non puto dubitandum."[1] The idea of Christ as King of peace also occurs on a number of occasions in the commentary to S. of S. 1.4.[2]

Here the commentator varies between an ecclesiological and an individual interpretation: the expression *introduxit me rex in cubiculum suum* (S. of S. 1.4) refers on the one hand to Christ and the Church, and on the other to the Logos and the soul.[3] The bridal-chamber is sometimes the Church: "Cubiculum regis; discit in hac domo, quae est ecclesia Dei vivi"; but it can also denote the perfection of the soul.[4]

S. of S. 1.12, where the (variant) Latin translation harks back to the LXX, "Ἕως οὗ ὁ βασιλεὺς ἐν ἀνακλίσει αὐτοῦ is also interpreted in a number of ways: in the homilies this verse is combined with Num. 24.9, and that the King rests like a lion is said to refer to his suffering.[5] In the commentary this passage is said to refer to the dwelling of the Logos in the soul: "Igitur haec fieri convenit, usque quo rex sit in recubito suo, id est usque quo in id proficiat huiusmodi anima, ut capiat regem recumbentem in semet ipsa. Sic enim dicit hic rex quia: 'habitabo in iis et inambulabo in iis' ... Habet ergo rex iste qui est sermo Dei, in ea anima, quae iam ad perfectum venerit, recubitum suum."[6]

Christ is thus described here more as bridegroom than as King. There is little trace of either OT or Hellenistic ideas on the kingship. That Christ is King is drawn directly from the text, without being placed in closer relation to the wider circle of royal ideas and themes.

A link with the *testimonia* tradition's representation of Christ as King is found in the use of the exposition of Ps. 44 (45) in connexion with the exegesis of S. of S.; there is no doubt that Ps. 44 was of great importance for the interpretation of the Kingship of Christ and the

---

[1] Origen, Comm. on S. of S. Prol., p. 84.
[2] *Ibid.*, pp. 119 f.
[3] *Ibid.*, p. 108.
[4] *Ibid.*, p. 109. Hom. on S. of S. 1.5, GCS Orig. 8.70.
[5] Hom. on S. of S. 1.10 (pp. 41 f.) and 2.2 (p. 43), cf. 2.9 (p. 55). On the lion as a Christological symbol, cf. A. GRILLMEIER, *Der Logos am Kreuz* (1956), pp. 81 ff.
[6] Comm. on S. of S. 2, pp. 164 f.

Church as his bride, and for the growing Marian typology.[1] However, the description of Christ as King in the context of a bride–bridegroom mysticism lies outside the development which we are describing here.

[1] Hom. on S. of S. 1.2 (pp. 63 f.), 2.3 (p. 83). Cf. St. Justin, Dial. 63, St. Irenaeus, Adv. haer. IV.39.2, ed. HARVEY 2.298 f.

9. THE ANTIOCHENE TRADITION

We are by no means so well informed about the Antiochene school in pre-Constantinian times as we are about the Alexandrian school. We have virtually no material on the doctrine of the Kingship of Christ, and the little we have is a most unsatisfactory foundation on which to base any definite conclusions.

F. Loofs has in a number of works made an attempt, which is both learned and deserving of respect, to sketch the outlines of an Antiochene theological tradition, from Theophilus of Antioch via Paul of Samosata to Eustathius and Marcellus of Ancyra.[1] The results of his work are nevertheless most unconvincing. This is because the keystone of his argument, the hypothesis that Theophilus' work *Contra Marcionem* can be reconstructed from Irenaeus' *Adversus haereses*, is now rejected by most scholars. This means that the source-material on which our knowledge of pre-4th century Antiochene theology is based is reduced to Theophilus' *Ad Autolycum*, a few fragments of St. Lucian's writings and some acts from the legal proceedings against Paul of Samosata. If we want more detailed information about the Antiochene theologian's views on the Kingship of Christ, we must turn to 4th century authors; a suitable starting-point is provided by Marcellus of Ancyra.

Marcellus of Ancyra

It is generally accepted that Marcellus belongs in the stream of Antiochene tradition.[2] His opponents pointed out the resemblances

---

[1] F. Loofs, *Theophilus von Antiocha adversus Marcionem und die anderen theologischen Quellen bei Irenäus*, TU 46: 2, 1930. See also earlier works by the same author: *Leitfaden zum Studium der Dogmengeschichte*, 4th ed. (1906), and *Paulus von Samosata*, TU 44: 5 (1924), together with the works quoted below on Marcellus of Ancyra.

[2] F. Loofs, *Die Trinitätslehre Marcells von Ancyra und ihr Verhältnis zur älteren Tradition*, SBA 1902; *Marcellus von Ancyra*, RE (3rd ed.) 12 (1903), pp. 259–265,

between his theology and that of Paul of Samosata. Later research has confirmed this judgment, and has shown that there are definite resemblances.[1] We shall see that this also applies to their respective views on the Kingship of Christ.

Marcellus of Ancyra has a place in the history of doctrine primarily as an advocate of a distinctly economical doctrine of the Trinity, which his opponents held to be a new variant of Sabellianism, or of the monarchianism of Paul of Samosata. Whether such was in fact the case has often been discussed —without,however, any definite result being reached.[2] The Synod of Rome, 340, and the Council of Serdica, 343–344, acquitted him of the charge of heresy, but he was condemned as a heretic by the Council of Constantinople, 381. That it is so difficult adequately to estimate his position has to do with apparent contradictions in his own writings. It is probable that his visit to Rome, with Athanasius, to have his case tried, modified his opinions somewhat.[3]

We see from the preserved fragments of Marcellus' theology that he held the Logos to be *homoousios* with the Father.[4] But unlike Athanasius, and like Paul of Samosata, he draws a distinction between the Logos and the Son.[5] Prior to the Incarnation we can speak only of the Logos; other titles, such as υἱός, πρωτότοκος and βασιλεύς, can be applied

---

cf. 24 (1913), p. 64. The only comprehensive recent work on Marcellus, W. GERICKE, *Marcell von Ancyra*, ThA 10 (1940), gives a valuable survey of research on Marcellus and the main problems connected with his theology, but is in many respects unsatisfactory. GERICKE is very much dependent upon LOOFS, not least in respect of his Theophilus hypothesis, and is too preoccupied with matters of confessional Protestantism to be fully scientific. Further, his account is largely based on his own translation of the Marcellus fragments, a translation which is in many cases quite unreliable. On the latter point, see F. SCHEIDWEILER, *Marcell von Ancyra*, ZNW 46 (1955), pp. 202–214.

[1] So H. LIETZMANN, *Geschichte der alten Kirche* III³ (1953), p. 185; LOOFS, *Paulus von Samosata*, p. 294; IDEM, *Theophilus von Antiochia*, p. 445. We shall not comment upon LOOFS' claim to be able to trace the theological tradition back to the times before the apologetes, a claim which we are unable to accept.

[2] See the review of research on Marcellus in GERICKE, *Marcell*, pp. 28–70, which mentions the most important Marcellus literature up to World War II.

[3] GERICKE, *Marcell*, pp. 14 ff.

[4] The Marcellus fragments are published in KLOSTERMANN's edition of Eusebius' anti-Marcelline writings, GCS Eus. 4. We follow KLOSTERMANN's numbering here, and consider it unnecessary to quote RETTBERG's as well.

[5] GERICKE, *Marcell*, pp. 132 ff. T. E. POLLARD, *The Origins of Arianism*, JTS NS 9 (1958), pp. 103–111, gives an excellent account of the relation between the concepts "Logos" and "Son" in the theology of Paul of Samosata and Marcellus.

only to the Incarnate Christ.¹ The Kingship of the Logos, which plays such an important role in Alexandrian theology, has no place in Marcellus' system, since he regards the Logos as not having the hypostatic independence postulated by Origen. The divine Monas of which the Logos forms a part, Marcellus calls παντοκράτωρ,² and he is able to say that the Logos reigns together with God and the Father.³ But he restricts the title βασιλεύς to the Incarnate Christ, and it is evident from the fragments that the concepts βασιλεύς and βασιλεία are purely economic in character.

Thus according to Marcellus the Kingship of Christ is connected with a definite time in the history of salvation. He stresses on a number of occasions that the Kingship of Christ was originally the Kingship of man—the man who was expelled from Heaven. "At all events, he who came down and took flesh through the Virgin has been set as King over the Church, doubtless in order that man, who was once expelled from Heaven, might attain the Kingship through the Logos."⁴ "... And man, who was once led astray, will be made King through the Logos, and he shall destroy the power and strength and might of the devil."⁵ "For the Logos did not inaugurate his Kingdom in himself; man, who was led astray by the devil, became King through the power of the Logos, in order that he, once he had become King, might conquer the devil, who once led (him) astray."⁶ Marcellus therefore

---

[1] It is clear from Eusebius' polemic that for Marcellus the Logos is not βασιλεύς; Eusebius states, as against Marcellus, that the Logos is not only πρωτότοκος and υἱός but also βασιλεύς, Contra Marcellum I. 1.22, GCS Eus. 4.6; II. 1.3 (p. 32); II. 3.39 (p. 52); II. 4.22 (p. 56).

[2] See below, p. 307.

[3] Fragm. 117: συμβασιλεύει γὰρ τῷ θεῷ καὶ πατρί, οὗ ὁ λόγος ἦν τε καὶ ἐστίν.

[4] Fragm. 111: ὁ γοῦν καταβὰς καὶ τὴν σάρκα διὰ τῆς παρθένου προσλαβὼν κατεστάθη βασιλεὺς ἐπὶ τὴν ἐκκλησίαν, δηλονότι ἵνα διὰ τοῦ λόγου ὁ τῆς βασιλείας τῶν οὐρανῶν πρότερον ἐκπεπτωκὼς ἄνθρωπος βασιλείας τυχεῖν δυνηθῇ. τοῦτον οὖν τὸν ἄνθρωπον τὸν πρότερον διὰ τὴν παρακοὴν τῆς βασιλείας ἐκπεπτωκότα κύριον καὶ θεὸν γενέσθαι βουλόμενος ὁ θεὸς ταύτην τὴν οἰκονομίαν εἰργάσατο. ὁ οὖν ἁγιώτατος προφήτης Δαυὶδ προφητικῶς λέγει· ὁ κύριος ἐβασίλευσεν, ἀγαλλιάσθω ἡ γῆ.

[5] Fragm. 113: διὰ τοῦτο γὰρ καὶ βασιλεύει ἐν τῇ ἀνθρωπίνῃ σαρκὶ γενόμενος, βασιλεύς τε καταστὰς διὰ τοῦ λόγου ὁ ἀπατηθεὶς πρότερον ἄνθρωπος πᾶσαν ἀρχὴν τοῦ διαβόλου καὶ δύναμιν καὶ ἐξουσίαν καταργήσει ...

[6] Fragm. 117: οὐ δὲ γὰρ αὐτὸς καθ'ἑαυτὸν ὁ λόγος ἀρχὴν βασιλείας εἴληφεν, ἀλλ'ὁ ἀπατηθεὶς ὑπὸ τοῦ διαβόλου ἄνθρωπος διὰ τῆς τοῦ λόγου δυνάμεως βασιλεὺς γέγονεν, ἵνα βασιλεὺς γενόμενος τὸν πρότερον ἀπατήσαντα νικήσῃ διάβολον.

emphasizes that the Kingship of man, through the Logos, was inaugurated less than 400 years earlier.[1]

Just as the Kingship of Christ had a beginning in time, so it will also have an end in time, when "all things have been placed beneath his feet". Here Marcellus is particularly dependent on 1 Cor. 15.24 ff.,[2] which he subjects to a double exegesis: on the one hand, at the end of time the Kingship of Christ will cease, as regards his human nature; but on the other, the Logos will also cease to exist as an independent person, and will be taken up into the divine Monas. Thus not only the human, but also the divine economy, is destined to come to an end after the judgment.[3]

The doctrine that the Kingship of Christ has a beginning in time is built by Marcellus on OT proof-texts: Ps. 2.6; 96 (97).1; 98 (99).1[4]—proof-texts with which we are familiar from the early *testimonia* tradition, and which were extensively used by Marcellus.[5] When the text says that the Lord has become King, this for Marcellus is proof that he was not always King. Marcellus is here standing in an line of ancient tradition, a line which we have already discussed. Justin and Irenaeus both saw the Kingship of Christ as manifested in time. We have earlier had occasion to point out that the sayings in the OT proof-texts to the effect that Christ has become King were connected in the oldest *testimonia* tradition with his exaltation after suffering—a trend which is to be found in the NT, where Jesus said to have become κύριος as a result of his victory.[6] At the same time those sayings which are applied to the Lord as χριστός were connected with Jesus' baptism, which is

---

[1] Fragm. 115: καὶ ὅλως μυρίων ῥητῶν πρὸς μαρτυρίαν ἔστιν εὐπορήσαντα δεῖξαι, ὅτι ἀρχὴν βασιλείας εἴληφεν ὁ ἄνθρωπος διὰ τοῦ λόγου. εἰ οὖν εἴληφεν ἀρχὴν βασιλείας πρὸ ἐτῶν ὅλων οὐ πλειόνων ἢ τετρακοσίων ... Cf. fragm. 116.

[2] Fragm. 113, 114, 117; see GERICKE, *Marcell*, pp. 142 ff.

[3] GERICKE, *Marcell*, p. 144.

[4] Fragm. 111, 112, 115. Cf. G. W. H. LAMPE, *The Exegesis of some Biblical Texts by Marcellus of Ancyra and Pseudo-Chrysostom's Homily on Ps. XCVI.1*, JTS 49 (1948), pp. 169–175.

[5] Marcellus' standing as a Biblical theologian was stressed by TH. ZAHN, *Marcellus von Ancyra* (1867). Unfortunately GERICKE, *op. cit.*, makes no attempt to relate Marcellus to his historical background on the matter of exegesis, but instead indulges in fruitless speculations as to whether Marcellus is to be regarded as a "biblicist", since he regards "dogma" as "the work of men" over against the Biblical revelation—an idea found in fragm. 86 and taken over by GERICKE: see pp. 181 ff.

[6] See above, pp. 52 f.

interpreted as being a form of Messianic inauguration.[1] But in Marcellus the beginning of the Kingship of Christ is in point of fact simply the Incarnation, seen as man's *recapitulatio* through his union with the Logos. That the Kingship of Christ is destinated to cease at the end of time also implies, therefore, that the connexion between the divine and the human is to cease, and that the Logos is once more to be taken up into the Monas.

Marcellus' doctrine of the Kingship of Christ is very much reminiscent of Irenaeus' doctrine of recapitulation, and it is certain that it is in the last resort based upon that doctrine. The difference is that Irenaeus is so dependent upon Justin in his exposition of the OT that it does not occur to him to connect the doctrine of recapitulation with the Kingship. Christ, through the Incarnation, has summed up and renewed the whole of mankind. But he did not become King until the moment of his installation at the right hand of the Father. It is therefore characteristic that Ps. 98 (99).1, which Marcellus interprets as referring to the Incarnation, is instead linked by Irenaeus with the Ascension.[2]

There is no trace in Marcellus of the *descensus-ascensio* theme, which is principally manifested in Irenaeus' exposition of Ps. 23 (24). His emphasis on the unity of the Godhead and the economic character of the Logos leaves no room for the twin concepts of the descent and exaltation of the Logos. What is changed by the Incarnation is not primarily the Logos, but human nature. The purpose of the economy of salvation is not the Kingship of the Logos, but of man. The focus of the history of salvation is therefore not the exaltation which took place at the Ascension, but the union of man with the Logos, of which the exaltation to the right hand of the Father is a fruit. Since the basis of the Kingship of man is his union with the Logos, Marcellus is perfectly logical when he dates the beginning of that Kingship to the Incarnation.

It is entirely understandable that the baptism of Jesus is of no significance for Marcellus. The idea that Christ was made King through his baptism had been spoiled by Gnostic and Adoptionist speculations, according to which the "Incarnation" began only at the moment of Jesus' baptism, when the Logos became united with the man Jesus.

Marcellus interprets Ps. 109 (110) in traditional terms, as referring

---

[1] See above, p. 114.
[2] Adv. haer. IV. 33.13, ed. HARVEY 2, 268.

to the Ascension. Here, too, the human nature of Christ is more evident than in the earlier *testimonia* tradition. According to Marcellus, "the Logos of God made it possible, through the resurrection, for human flesh to become immortal, and to sit on the right hand of God, crowned with the victor's wreath".[1] He is particularly interested, when expounding Ps. 109 (110).1, in its ἕως ἄν, "until I make thine enemies thy footstool"—a primary proof for him that the Kingship of Christ will come to an end.[2] The subject of the Lordship of Christ over the Church during the period between the Ascension and the parousia is scarcely mentioned in the preserved fragments; this need not of course mean that he never dealt with the subject in his writings. It is more likely that this particular aspect of Marcellus' theology, not being controversial, was not taken up by Eusebius, and has thus not been preserved for posterity. As it is, the *sessio* of Christ is mentioned only in a quotation of Acts 3.21, which is also included as a support for the doctrine that the Kingship of Christ will come to an end.[3]

Compared with the school of Origen, Marcellus' theology is strikingly traditional, in both its terminology and its contents. That goes a long way toward explaining why Marcellus has been regarded as representing a more "unphilosophical", "unhellenistic" and original Christology.[4] But when we compare him with earlier representatives of the *testimonia* tradition and exegesis, Justin Martyr and Irenaeus, we find that there is a distinctly speculative element in Marcellus—which hardly suggests an "unphilosophical" theologian. To be sure, his philosophical background is not that of the Philonic tradition; he must be placed, both theologically and philosophically, in an Antiochene tradition, on whose earlier stages we are regrettably little informed.[5]

---

[1] Fragm. 127: (ἔφη) τὸν τοῦ θεοῦ λόγον τὴν ἀνθρωπίνην σάρκα διὰ τῆς ἀναστάσεως ἀθάνατον γενέσθαι παρασκευακέναι καὶ ὥσπερ τινὰ νίκης στέφανον ἀναδησάμενον ἐν δεξιᾷ τοῦ πατρὸς καθέζεσθαι.

[2] Fragm. 117.

[3] *Ibid.*

[4] See e.g. Gericke, *op. cit.*, pp. 130 f.

[5] We cannot in this context go into the complicated question of the extent to which the Christology of the Antiochene theologians may have been influenced by Aristotelian philosophy. The discussion of this topic has, remarkably enough, stagnated since the end of the 19th century. See the account given by H. S. Nash, *The Exegesis of the School of Antioch, A Criticism of the Hypothesis that Aristotelianism was a Main Cause in its Genesis*, JBL 11 (1892), pp. 22–37. R. V. Sellers, *Two Ancient Christologies* (1954), pp. 106, 109, takes an Aristotelian influence for granted.

Paul of Samosata

The Alexandrian theologians linked the concept of Kingship primarily with the Logos as the governing power in the world; we have evidence that Antiochene theology, on the other hand, connected the idea of Kingship mainly with the Incarnate Christ. These contrasting views are reflected in an *argumentum* to Ps. 109 (110), written by an anonymous, though obviously well-informed, 6th or 7th century author. According to this writer, the followers of Arius and Eunomius interpreted the Psalm as referring to the Logos of God before, as well as after, the Incarnation, while the disciples of Paul of Samosata, Photinus and Sabellius allowed that it referred to man alone (εἰς ψιλὸν ἄνθρωπον).[1] If this be correct, it is of the utmost importance for our problem. Ps. 109 is the central proof-text for the royal character of Christ. According to this author, though he is of a later period, we have here two entirely different interpretations of the Psalm: the Arians considered it to refer to the divine nature of Christ; the Antiochenes (and Sabellians) to human nature.

We shall deal with the question of the Arians' attitude to the Kingship of Christ in a subsequent chapter. We can however make the preliminary observation that this fits in well with what we already know of the Alexandrian tradition, which connects the royal qualities with the Logos first and foremost. Although the Arians cannot be regarded simply as the extreme left wing of the school of Origen, but must be regarded as a having a number of Antiochene characteristics,[2] what is essential in this content is that they laid greater emphasis on the preexistence of the Son than did the Antiochenes—a circumstance which is evidently due to influence from Origen.

Paul of Samosata and Marcellus' disciple Photinus,[3] in common with Sabellius, are said to have interpreted Ps. 109 εἰς ψιλὸν ἄνθρωπον. It goes without saying that this statement cannot be accepted just as it stands. It is based on an accusation of "psilanthropism", directed against a number of heretics in the early Church. According to Eusebius, Theo-

---

[1] *Expositio patrum graecorum in psalmos*, ed. B. CORDERIUS, III (1643), p. 238. Quoted after LOOFS, *Paulus von Samosata*, p. 143: οἱ μὲν περὶ Ἄρειον καὶ Εὐνόμιον εἰς τὸν θεὸν λόγον εἰρῆσθαι λέγουσι τὸν ψαλμὸν καὶ πρὶν σαρκωθῆναι, οἱ δὲ περὶ Παῦλον τὸν Σαμοσατέα καὶ Φωτεινὸν καὶ Σαβέλλιον εἰς ψιλὸν ἄνθρωπον.

[2] See T. E. POLLARD, *Logos and Son in Origen, Arius and Athanasius*, SP 2 (1957), pp. 282–287; IDEM, *The Origins of Arianism*, pp. 103–111.

[3] GERICKE, *Marcellus*, pp. 19 ff.

dotus the Tanner was the first to teach that Christ was ψιλὸς ἄνθρωπος,[1] and the same doctrine is attributed by him to Artemon, Paul of Samosata and Marcellus.[2] The same accusation was later levelled against other theologians having Antiochene sympathies.[3]

This information, as far as Sabellius is concerned, it entirely worthless. Even the early Church was extremely vague as to the teachings of this particular heretic and his disciples. Both Paul of Samosata and Marcellus of Ancyra had been accused by their opponents of attempting to renew Sabellian modalism,[4] and it is therefore only natural that the name of Sabellius should be connected with theirs. Incidentally, this combination is an extremely common one in the register of heretics.

The subject of the Kingship of Christ is dealt with in a summary of Paul's theology preserved in one of the pseudo-Athanasian writings, *Contra Apollinarem*.[5] Bardy and (with reservations) Loofs are willing to accept this document as a source for Paul's theology.[6] Its genuineness has however since been challenged by Riedmatten; what he finds in the text is Apollinarian theology disguised as the heresy of Paul.[7] The sayings on the Kingship of Christ in particular have no parallel in what we know of Apollinarius' own writings, and since the text as a whole contains a mixture of expressions taken from Paul of Samosata and Apollinarius it seems probable that the sayings on the Kingship of Christ can also be taken to be genuine.

The fragment begins with these words:

Τὸν θεὸν ἐκ τῆς παρθένου, θεὸν ἐκ Ναζαρὲτ ὀφθέντα, καὶ
ἐντεῦθεν τῆς ὑπάρξεως τὴν ἀρχὴν ἐσχηκότα καὶ ἀρχὴν
βασιλείας παρειληφότα ...

---

[1] Eusebius HE V. 28.6, GCS Eus. 2.1.500 f.: πρῶτον εἰπόντα ψιλὸν ἄνθρωπον τὸν Χριστόν. Elsewhere he ascribes the same doctrine to the Ebionites, III. 27.1 f., GCS Eus. 2.1.254 f., VI. 17, GCS Eus. 2.1.554 f.

[2] Eusebius HE V. 28.1, GCS Eus. 2.1.500 (on Artemon and Paul): ψιλὸν ἄνθρωπον γενέσθαι τὸν σωτῆρα. Cf. VII. 27.2, GCS Eus. 2.2.702. The same accusation is levelled against Marcellus in Eccl. theol. I. 20.(91).43.

[3] See LOOFS, *Paulus von Samosata*, pp. 60 f., n. 3.

[4] BARDY, *Paul de Samosate*, p. 29 n. 5. GERICKE, *Marcell*, p. 12.

[5] 2 Contra Apollinarem 3, PG 26.1136 f.

[6] BARDY, *Paul de Samosate*, fragm. 17 (p. 339); cf. LOOFS, *Paulus von Samosata*, pp. 138 ff. Loofs' procedure seems to be quite arbitrary when attempting to reconstruct an original text from this fragment and a similar one preserved in 1 Contra Apollinarem 20, PG 26.1128.

[7] H. DE RIEDMATTEN, *Les Actes du procès de Paul de Samosate*, Par. 6 (1952), pp. 100 ff.

The expression that Christ received the beginning of his Kingship, ἀρχὴν βασιλείας παρειληφότα, is reminiscent of sayings we have previously encountered in Marcellus of Ancyra: ὥσπερ ἀρχὴν βασιλείας ... λαβόντος (fragm. 112); ἀρχὴν ἐσχηκένα βασιλείας ... ἀρχὴν βασιλείας εἴληφεν ὁ ἄνθρωπος (fragm. 115). For this reason we cannot entirely dismiss the idea that the author of *Contra Apollinarem* may be reproducing, not the theology of Paul, but that of Marcellus.

In those fragments of Paul which are generally accepted as authentic, we encounter a number of other sayings, sayings which confirm that Paul and Marcellus were substantially in agreement on this point. Paul, over-emphasizing the human nature of Christ as he did, probably linked the Kingship of Christ, as did Marcellus, to his humanity. The clearest evidence of this is to be found in a fragment preserved in Leontius of Byzantium:

"Ἄνθρωπος χρίεται, ὁ λόγος οὐ χρίεται. ὁ ναζωραῖος χρίεται, ὁ κύριος ἡμῶν, καὶ γὰρ ὁ λόγος μείζων ἦν τοῦ Χριστοῦ ... Λόγος μὲν γὰρ ἄνωθεν, Ἰησοῦς δὲ Χριστὸς ἄνθρωπος ἐντεῦθεν.[1]

The title Χριστός has been bestowed on the Lord as the Anointed One. According to Paul, the name can therefore be applied only to the human nature anointed by its connexion with the Logos at the Incarnation.

We are therefore compelled to conclude that Paul of Samosata and Marcellus of Ancyra demonstrate a large measure of agreement on the subject of the Kingship of Christ. Both regard its function as centring exclusively on the economy of salvation, and as having its beginning in time. Both regard the Kingship as having begun with the Incarnation. Although it would be wrong to say that they look upon the Kingship of Christ as having to do with "man alone", it is obvious that it can be relevant only for man when united with the Logos.

Is it possible from this to draw the conclusion that Marcellus is dependent upon Paul of Samosata? The idea is tempting, particularly when we remember that certain of Marcellus' contemporaries accused him of trying to renew the heresy of Paul. But the matter is not as straightforward as all that. We come across similar characteristics in

---

[1] Bardy, *Paul de Samosate*, fragm. 2a (p. 309), Loofs, *Paulus von Samosata*, fragm. 13 (p. 77), Riedmatten, *Actes*, fragm. S. 26 (p. 153). On this fragment, see further Bardy, *op. cit.*, pp. 310 ff., Loofs, *op. cit.*, pp. 118 ff., Riedmatten, *op. cit.*, pp. 30 ff.

the work of Antiochene authors of a later date than Marcellus,[1] and we are therefore compelled to ask whether this might not be evidence for the existence of a general Antiochene tradition, of which Paul of Samosata and Marcellus of Ancyra are extreme representatives.

St. Lucian of Antioch

We must however observe the greatest caution here. From Antioch originated, not only Marcellus' economic Christology, but also Arianism. The Antiochene theology of the 3rd century is represented not only by Paul but also by St. Lucian, who also founded a school; heretics like Arius, Eusebius of Nicomedia and Asterius called themselves "collucianists", although whether or not Lucian would have accepted them as disciples is of course a different matter.

St. Alexander of Alexandria, in a letter, describes Lucian as a follower of Ebion, Artemas and Paul of Samosata,[2] thus placing him in the heretical theological tradition we have called typically Antiochene. But it is scarcely possible to accept the statement, although it is not easy to say why Alexander should have defined Lucian's position in this way. It has often been discussed whether he misunderstood Lucian's theology, deliberately misrepresented him, or was perhaps attacking another Antiochene theologian of the same name; such questions however lie outside the bounds of this study.[3]

As far as we can see from the preserved fragments of St. Lucian's writings, his theology can be described as being the direct opposite of Paul's. Paul taught a distinct monarchianism, denying the independence of the divine hypostases; Lucian taught a subordinationist trinitarianism, closely related to that of Origen, which anticipated Arianism.[4] Like the Alexandrian theologians, Lucian places particular emphasis upon the divine nature of Christ: this is clear from the Lucian formula adopted by the Arianizing Synod of Antioch, 341.[5] In this formula the pre-existent Son is also called βασιλεὺς ἐκ βασιλέως, thus

---

[1] See LAMPE, *Exegesis, passim.*
[2] Theodoretus, HE I.4.46, PG 82.900.
[3] See G. BARDY, *Recherches sur saint Lucien d'Antioche et son école* (1936), pp. 47 ff. BARDY himself believes that the person mentioned in St. Alexander's letter is not St. Lucian, *op. cit.*, pp. 58 f.
[4] BARDY, *op. cit.*, p. 56.
[5] See below, p. 273.

using a terminology later to be taken over by the Arians. Lucian thus regarded Christ as being King by virtue of his Divine nature, but at one remove, as the εἰκών of the Father. We are thus dealing with a point of view which, on a basis of the definitions we have been using, can be called Alexandrian rather than Antiochene.

But it seems likely that we can explain this paradox perfectly satisfactorily. The trial of Paul and his deposition in 268 probably led to a theological change of atmosphere in Antioch. The bishops, in opposition to Pauline Sabellianism, instead swung round to a left-wing Origenist position, represented by Lucian, who was appointed Paul's successor.[1] Lucian then went on to found a school, which proved in its later Arian form to have taken up both Alexandrian and Antiochene elements.[2]

But at the same time the economic doctrine of the Trinity and the emphasis placed upon Christ's humanity lived on in the Antiochene Church, and found a new champion in Marcellus of Ancyra. When at the end of the 4th century the stronghold of Arianism in Syria was overcome, the economic Christology recurred in the Antiochene authors, Theodoret of Cyrus and Theodore of Mopsuestia, and was later to give rise to a new heresy, Nestorianism. As we shall see, it was especially the Antiochene theologians who were to connect the Kingship of Christ with the Incarnation during the 4th and 5th centuries.

---

[1] See BARDY, *op. cit.*, p. 46.
[2] See below, p. 269.

10. THE POLITICAL THOUGHT OF THE PSEUDO-CLEMENTINES

The most thoroughgoing pre-Constantinian application of the political thought of Hellenism to Christ as King is without any shadow of a doubt to be found in the pseudo-Clementine writings. This has however been generally overlooked in the more notable works on this literature; this gives us all the more reason for considering the political thought of the *Pseudo-Clementines* (PsC) in some detail here. It is true that the writings are considerably removed from the main stream of the Church's development; it is nevertheless of interest to observe the way in which political concepts stood in the forefront of the particular tradition represented by PsC. They probably also reflected speculations which were current in the main stream of the Church's tradition. It is also possible that the investigation of this complex of ideas will throw fresh light on the theological position of PsC.

When we investigate the political thought of PsC, we are led to a result which is not particularly favourable to those who have postulated that the writings can be divided up into a number of different sources.[1] As we shall see, the political thought of PsC is strikingly consistent, and cuts across many of the divisions by which scholars have sought to separate the various source-documents.

Schoeps and, following him, Strecker, see in the political thought of PsC no more than a general attitude of enmity toward the Kingship as such.[2] This very much over-simplified view is based on the two authors' hypothesis of the "Ebionite" origin of PsC, and leads to a serious underestimation of the Hellenistic elements in the writings. Schoeps had a general tendency to interpret each and every text in

---

[1] In this chapter Hom. is quoted after GCS PsC, Rec. after PG 1. On the hypothesis of source division, see G. STRECKER, *Das Judenchristentum in den Pseudoklementinen*, TU 70 (1958), intro.

[2] SCHOEPS, *Theologie*, pp. 242 f.; STRECKER, *op. cit.*, pp. 184 f.

"Ebionite" terms, and he has unfortunately been followed in this by Strecker, who has accepted his views without question.

Schoeps claims that there is in PsC an attitude of enmity to the Kingship in principle; this is directed against the Kings of Israel in particular.[1] Strecker accepts and develops this view, claiming at the same time that it is possible to distinguish between different traditions. The hypothetical source-book, *Kerygma Petri*, thus criticizes the Kingship in Israel, while other traditions are concerned with the Kings of the Gentiles in their polemic. But even Strecker cannot accept his own conclusions, and he is therefore compelled to assume the existence of *Sonderquellen*, in which the material does not agree with the tendency he has postulated in the respective traditions.[2] In a situation like this, it is far better to ignore the "source" hypothesis altogether, and treat the material as a unity—though recognizing at the same time that many different traditions have been combined to form PsC.

Schoeps'—and to some extent Strecker's—theory that the polemic of PsC is directed against the Kingship in Israel, is not supported by the material. Schoeps claims that Hom. 3.52 says that the Israelite Kingship disappeared because it was not divine πρόσταγμα;[3] but in point of fact the text speaks only of βασιλεῖαι in general, without closer definition. Strecker accepts Schoeps' view here, saying that the context (sacrifices and prophecies by "those that are born of women") shows that it is the Israelite Kingship which is being referred to.[4] Although

---

[1] SCHOEPS quotes a passage in Epiphanius (Haer. XXX. 18.4) in support of his thesis, stating that according to this text the Ebionites were anti-royalist, *op. cit.*, p. 243. What Epiphanius actually said was that the Ebionites recognized Abraham, Isaac and Jacob, Moses and Joshua, but not David, Solomon and the prophets. It is thus not the kingship that is rejected by the Ebionites, but the whole of the Israelite tradition after the migration into Canaan.

[2] On this basis the source division is unfortunate, not least because the only passage in PsC in which the Israelite kingship is expressly criticized is in Rec. (1.38), which according to STRECKER, is *not* a polemic against the Israelite kingship, *op. cit.*, p. 185. STRECKER's argument on Rec. 1.69 seems particularly unnecessary; in this passage the Apostle James states when and how the Books of Kings are to be read. But the reader is nowhere told what the Apostle said; the text informs us only that he spoke on the subject. STRECKER however assumes this passage to be anti-royalist. But since he does not permit Rec. to contain attacks on the kings of Israel, he is given an excuse to bring in yet another "Sonderquelle", *op. cit.*, p. 185.

[3] *Op. cit.*, p. 243.

[4] *Op. cit.*, p. 184 n. 1.

the Kings of Israel may well be included in this saying, the plural βασιλεῖαι suggests that here, as in other passages of PsC, we are dealing with a general criticism of Kingship as such.

There is a tendency in PsC which may perhaps be called anti-royalist, but it is directed only in part against the Israelite Kingship. The judgments passed are for the most part in general terms, and can of course apply to Israelite Kings, as well as to any others. The only passage in which there is an unmistakable reference to the Kings of Israel is that in Rec. 1.38, where they are accused of having built the Temple; this is clearly a polemic against the cult, rather than against the Kingship.

We read in Rec. 1.48 that the oil used to anoint priests, prophets and kings has disappeared, since the true prophet has come. Here, again, we are not dealing with an attitude of direct enmity to the Israelite Kingship, or to the priesthood or the prophets. This is an example of a thought which is common in anti-Jewish polemics (in connexion with Gen. 49.10 and Dan. 9.24–26), that the ministry and cult of the old Covenant disappeared at the coming of the Messiah.[1]

But even this general "anti-royalism" is more than an generally negative attitude to the institution of Kingship. In PsC, the word βασιλεύς is strikingly ambivalent in meaning. It is typical that it is used of both Christ and Satan (Hom. 3.19, 8.21–22, Rec. 2.32). Noah is called "king" (Hom. 9.3) in a context which makes it clear that the title is a positive one. What Schoeps and Strecker call "anti-royalism" is in point of fact only one aspect of a remarkably consistent political theology—a theology related to that which we encounter in the work of other Christian authors during the first centuries A.D.

The clearest expression of the basic political attitude of PsC is to be found in Hom. 9.2:

"You are wicked against the God of all, worshipping lifeless images instead of him or along with him, and attributing his divine name to every kind of senseless matter. In the first place, therefore, you are unfortunate in not knowing the difference between *monarchy* and *polyarchy* (μοναρχίας καὶ πολυαρχίας)—that *monarchy*, on the one hand, is productive of *concord* (ὁμόνοια), but polyarchy is effective of wars (πόλεμοι). For oneness (τὸ ἕν) does not fight with itself, but multitude (τὰ πολλά) has occasion of undertaking battle one against another."

---

[1] See above, pp. 96 f.

Immediately following this passage, in Hom. 9.3, we find a description of man's progressive degradation from the beginning. Noah is described as a king of a golden age. He lived for 350 years *in concord* (ἐν ὁμονοίᾳ) with those peoples who were his descendents, and he was a king *after the image of the one God* (τοῦ μόνου θεοῦ κατ' εἰκόνα). But after his death his descendents began to wage war upon one another, because each wanted to be king. This was the start of polyarchy, which replaced the original state of happiness and harmony. When at a later date, kings began to allow themselves to be worshipped as gods, the result was polytheism (Hom. 9.5). Just as monotheism is connected with the monarchy (for Noah was king after the image of the one God), so polytheism and polyarchy are inseparably linked together.[1]

This complex is incorporated into the dualistic world-view which dominated PsC. This present age is entirely under the sway of Satan, who is called ὁ πρόσκαιρος βασιλεύς or ὁ τῶν παρόντων βασιλεύς (Hom. 8.21). This age is represented by the female (evil) prophecy: when she becomes pregnant and bears temporary kings (πρόσκαιροι βασιλεῖς), she causes war and bloodshed (Hom. 3.24). Over against the present evil age with its polyarchy, polytheism, dissention and war is placed, on the one hand, the original state of man (Noah) and, on the other, the age to come, in which Christ is King, ὁ μέλλοντος αἰῶνος βασιλεύς (Hom. 3.19) or ὁ μελλόντων βασιλεύς (Hom. 8.21). Both these harmonious ages are characterized by their monarchy, which guarantees unity and peace.

The relation between the Kingdom of Christ and that of Satan is clearly described in St. Peter's speech in Hom. 20.2:

> Listen, therefore, to the truth of the harmony (ἁρμονίας τὴν ἀλήθειαν) in regard to the evil one (Satan). God appointed *two kingdoms*, and established two ages, determining that the present world should be given to the evil one, because it is small and passes quickly away; but he promised to preserve for the good one (Christ) the age to come, as it will be great and eternal. He therefore created man with free-will, and possessing the capability of inclining to whatever actions he wishes.

Peter goes on to say that man consists of three evil, feminine elements and three good, masculine elements.

---

[1] Cf. also Rec. 1.21: the eighteen generations of men who represent one of the lowest levels of dissolution also imply that it was then that rulers began to allow themselves to be worshipped as gods. Both passages go back to Jewish traditions. Cf. Jub. 11.2, 4.

Wherefore also two ways have been laid before him[1]—those of obedience and disobedience to law; and *two kingdoms* have been established—the one called the kingdom of heaven, and the other the kingdom of those who are now kings upon earth. Also *two kings* have been appointed, of whom one is selected to rule by law over the present and transitory world, his nature being such that he rejoices in the destruction of the wicked. But the other, the good King, the King of the age to come, loves the whole nature of man; but not being able to have boldness in the present world, he counsels what is advantageous, like one who tries to conceal his real identity.[2]

What we have here in Peter's speech is an explicit theocratic principle. Those who are kings now belong to the present evil age: in the world to come there shall be only one ruler: Christ. We pointed out earlier that in Hom. 9.2–3 there is a politically coloured argument in favour of monarchy rather than polyarchy. Monarchy is said to be the ideal form of government, a form which was characteristic of the original golden age, and which will once more be seen in the age to come; polyarchy and disunity belong to the present evil age.

We come across the same ideas in Hom. 3.61–62: St. Peter's speech on the occasion of Zacchaeus' consecration as bishop. Peter says that the faithful should be obedient to someone, so that they can live in *concord* (ὁμόνοια). The *monarchy* guarantees *peace* (εἰρήνη) because of the *order* (εὐταξία) it brings with it, but if everyone is determined to rule (φιλαρχοῦντες) and no one is willing to obey a single ruler, the result is *disunity* (διαίρεσις). Similarly, there is constant war (πόλεμοι) because there are many *kings* on earth, and each one makes the other's power into an excuse for waging war. But if there were but one leader (ἡγεμών), there would be no reason to wage war, and all would be able to live together in peace. That is why God, in the age to come, has appointed one *king* over the all (βασιλεὺς τοῦ παντός): so that *monarchy* might establish *peace*. It is therefore necessary to follow one leader (ὁδηγός) and venerate him as *the image of God* (ὡς εἰκόνα θεοῦ); the leader in turn must be familiar with the way that leads to the heavenly city. This argument leads to the conclusion that the monarchical bishop is a necessity for the unity of the Church.

Not only the position of the bishop as leader of the Christian con-

---

[1] For the doctrine of the two ways see G. Klein, *Der älteste christliche Katechismus und die jüdische Propagandaliteratur* (1909), pp. 157 ff. Dölger, *Sonne der Gerechtigkeit*, pp. 124 ff. Audet, *Didachè*, pp. 254 ff.

[2] The two kingships, between which man must choose by his own free will, are also mentioned in Rec. 3.52; see also Dölger, *op. cit.*, pp. 126 f.

gregation, but also the Kingship of Christ, can be motivated in political terms. We read in Hom. 3.19 that Christ (who is on this occasion also called *father*) shall be *king* over his own children, in order that there might be eternal *peace*, ensured by his fatherly love and the reverence of his children. "For when the man who speaks well (ὁ εὔλογος) reigns, there is true joy among his subjects on account of him who reigns."[1]

In PsC we thus encounter a combination of two thought-patterns: a dualistic world-view and a form of monism according to which the one God in Heaven has his counterpart in one King on earth: Christ. The bridge between the two patterns, which appear to be of divergent origin, is the doctrine of the two ages. The present aeon, which is under Satan's rule, is characterized by its wars and disunity; the age to come, over which Christ is King, will be an age of peace and harmony. The monarchichal government of the Church, though motivated on a basis of the need for peace and order, also serves to reflect conditions in the age to come.

A point on which neither Schoeps nor Strecker has anything to say is that these sections of PsC make use of a terminology with which we are already familiar from contemporary Hellenistic political literature: μοναρχία, πολυαρχία, εἰρήνη, εὐταξία, etc. There is no doubt that these terms have been taken over from political metaphysics, and applied to the Christian history of salvation, as understood by the author of this part of PsC.

Monarchy and Polyarchy

The twin concepts monarchy and polyarchy are well known in Greek literature. The Greek philosophers often stress that monarchy is to be preferred over all other forms of government: Plato, Aristotle and the earlier Stoics all make mention of this.[2] In Hellenism there is a special

---

[1] εὔλογος evidently refers to the previous sentence in chap. 3.19, which tells how Christ blessed those who abused him (εὐλόγει τοὺς λοιδοροῦντας). The word is seldom used of persons, in the meaning of "rational".

[2] On the position of the monarchy in Greek philosophy, see E. GOODENOUGH, *Hellenistic Kingship*, pp. 55–102, TARN, *Alexander and the Unity of Mankind*. M. H. FISCH, *Alexander and the Stoics*, Am. Jour. of Philol. 58 (1937), pp. 59–82, 129–151 (with criticism of the two previous works). GOODENOUGH complements his account in *Politics*, p. 44 n. 7. L. DELATTE, *Traités* contains a detailed account of the development of theories of the monarchy in Greek political thought, pp. 123–162.

class of literature devoted to the praise of monarchy which seems also to have influenced Philo.¹ οὐκ ἀγαθὸν πολυκοιρανίη, εἷς κοίρανος ἔσθω, reads a familiar verse in the Iliad,² a verse which is often quoted in the literature of Antiquity; it is, then, of considerable importance that when we meet with it at the end of Book XII of Aristotles' *Metaphysics*, it has been transposed from the political to the metaphysical sphere.³

Peterson has shown how the concept of "monarchy" in Philo (particularly Spec. leg. 1.12) and in later Christian literature is used as a collective term, denoting both the Lordship of God and political power.⁴ From the superiority of monarchy as a political system is drawn the metaphysical conclusion that monotheism is a superior religion.⁵ And vice versa: the monarchy of God is bearer of political *auctoritas*; the one God in Heaven has his counterpart in the one King on earth. The Roman Empire is motivated in these terms—a metaphysical argument which we later find in Eusebius of Caesarea and others.⁶

The use of the terms monarchy and polyarchy in PsC must be seen against this background, and we must remember that at the same time they have the meaning of monotheism and polytheism. A political *apologia* for monotheism is to be found in Hom. 9.2;⁷ the same political arguments are advanced in favour of the Lordship of Christ in Hom. 3.61 f.⁸ A typical argument in political terms, both for and against polytheism,⁹ may be seen in Hom. 10.12,15 and Rec. 5.19, 22.

The pseudo-Clementine literature was able to link up with the political metaphysics of Philo and other Jewish authors; it also had connexions with earlier political speculation in the Church, though of this latter, few traces now remain. Both Justin Martyr and Irenaeus

---

¹ See above, p. 192.
² II 204.
³ Peterson, *Monotheismus*, pp. 49 ff.
⁴ Peterson, *op. cit.* Comprehensive documentation is also to be found in L. Verhoeven, *Studien over Tertullianus' Adversus Praxean* (1948), pp. 71 ff. Cf. Idem, *Monarchia dans Tertullien, Adversus Praxean*, VC 5 (1951), pp. 43–48. Verhoeven seems however not to be acquainted with Peterson's pioneer work.
⁵ Cf. Philo, Agr. 49: the monarchy of God is motivated by saying that the heaviest burden of all is to be compelled to obey many masters.
⁶ See below, p. 318.
⁷ See above, p. 244.
⁸ See above, p. 246.
⁹ Peterson, *Monotheismus*, pp. 71 ff.

wrote on the subject of monarchy, but their writings have been lost, and we do not know what they may have contained.¹

The earliest example of Christian criticism of polyarchy would seem to be a short sentence in Tatian, saying that the Greeks are better informed on the subject of multiple government (πολυκοιρανίη) than on monarchy.² The archaism obviously refers to the famous verse in the Iliad; the Acts of the Martyrs often use the same verse against the Emperor.³ The quotation is also used in the pseudo-Justinian *Cohortatio ad Graecos* in a way which is reminiscent of PsC: "That the rule of many is not good (οὐκ ἀγαθὸν πολυκοιρανίη) but, on the contrary, evil has been shown in his work (by Homer), when he tells of the wars which arose as a result of multiplicity (πλῆθος) and battles and revolutions and civil disturbances. For it is a characteristic of monarchy to be peaceful (ἄμαχος)."⁴

The course traced by Peterson from Aristotle and *De mundo* via Philo and the Church Fathers to Eusebius, is not entirely relevant when it comes to determining the background of the political thought of PsC with more precision. The material he uses is largely concerned with God as the supreme governor of the world (and in Eusebius, with Augustus and Constantine as God's instruments for the realization of the kingdom of peace on earth). There is on the other other hand little about Christ as King of peace. This is to some extent due to the special complex of problems aroused by the term "monarchy" in 3rd century theological discussion. The concept has become almost a motto for that heresy usually called monarchianism, which endeavoured to save the unity of the Godhead and the divinity of the Son by identifying the Father and the Son.⁵ Tertullian, answering Praxeas, made a curious attempt to defend the position of the Son as an independent Person in the Godhead by drawing an analogy with the double principate of the

---

¹ Eusebius, HE IV. 18.4, GCS Eus. 2.1.364; V. 20.1 (p. 480); cf. PETERSON, *Monotheismus*, pp. 62 f., 67 f. There is some doubt as to whether St. Irenaeus, as PETERSON believes, is here dependent upon Theophilus of Antioch. PETERSON builds unfortunately on F. LOOFS' dubious work *Theophilus von Antiochia*.

² Or. ad Gr. 14.1; cf. PETERSON, *Monotheismus*, pp. 64 f.

³ Eusebius, Mart. Pal., GCS Eus. 2.2.907 f. The *Martyrdom of St. Coratus*, AB 1 (1882), p. 451. Cf. L. CERFAUX, *Le titre Kyrios*, p. 57.

⁴ Ps.-Just., Cohort. ad Gr. 17, PG 6.273.

⁵ G. BARDY, Art. *Monarchianisme*, DThC 10.2 (1928–30), col. 2193 ff. VERHOEVEN, *op. cit.*, pp. 30 ff.

Roman Empire.¹ The discussion between Dionysius of Alexandria and Dionysius of Rome shows how difficult it was to combine Christological speculation with the concept of monarchy.² The author(s) of PsC seem to be unfamiliar with this argument; this may be evidence for the antiquity of PsC, or at least, for the fact that we have in PsC a tradition little influenced by other theological developments.

Another of the elements which has been incorporated into the political metaphysics of PsC is the Jewish speculation on Israel and the Gentiles or—on the theological level—the God of Israel and the "angels of the peoples".³ This "angel" concept, which plays an important part in Hen., occurs in PsC in Hom. 18.4 and Rec. 2.42. In the Jewish tradition God was believed to have set an angel over each of the Gentile races (an exposition of Deut. 32.8 f.); the people of Israel were under Michael or under God himself. These angels were considered to be closely linked with the Gentile kings,⁴ and they therefore came to be a kind of divine guarantee for nationalism and even for polytheism.⁵

But in some traditions the angels play a negative role, and were believed to cause disorder and discord in the world: this idea is found in Hen., Jub. and elsewhere. There was also an idea in Jewish eschatology that the day of judgment will see the punishment of the angels first, and the Gentiles afterward.⁶ As the Gentiles make war on earth,

---

¹ Tert. Adv. Prax. 3, CCL 2.1161 f. Cf. PETERSON, *Monotheismus*, pp. 69 f., VERHOEVEN, *op. cit.*, p. 64.

² PETERSON, *Monotheismus*, pp. 76 ff.

³ B. REICKE, *The Disobedient Spirits and Christian Baptism* (1946), pp. 85 ff., E. PETERSON, *Das Problem des Nationalismus im alten Christentum*, in PFJG, pp. 51–63. Cf. also above, p. 100.

⁴ As REICKE points out (*op. cit.*, pp. 85 f.) there is in the "parables" of 1 Enoch a definite connexion between the angels and "the Kings and the Mighty and those who reside on earth" (1 En. 55.4; 62.1, 3, 6, 9; 63.1, 12; 67.8, 12). The passage 1 En. 67.4–69.1 deals with the judgment of the Kings and the Mighty, and the angels are constantly coming into the picture. Similarly in 1 En. 90.22–25 there is a constant tendency to shift between the kings and the astral powers. The role of the angels is strikingly negative, hence REICKE's characterization of them as "the fallen angels".

⁵ Behind this is the OT idea of the heathen gods as "the sons of God"; on the textual tradition of Deut. 32.8 f., see literature quoted in PETERSON, *Nationalismus*, pp. 51 f. The LXX text is supported by a Qumran fragment; see P. W. SKEHAN, *A Fragment from the "Song of Moses" (Deut. 32) from Qumran*, BASOR 136/1954, p. 12.

⁶ God never punishes a people without first having punished its angelic ruler in heaven, Billerbeck, *Comm.* 3, p. 50, PETERSON, *Nationalismus*, p. 53.

so the angels make war in heaven: a common idea.[1] This is particularly true of gnosticizing theology, according to which the powers which rule the world were believed to be evil, and the plurality in the government of the world sufficient proof that the government must be a bad one. According to Simon Magus the goverment of angels is bad, because each one is striving after power.[2]

The attitude of PsC on this point is ambivalent. Peter states in Rec. 2.42 against Simon Magus (representing polytheism) that the angels can be called gods, because they are sent by God; "for the honour of the sender, that his authority may be full, he that is sent is called by the name of him who sends".[3] God has divided the peoples of the world into 72 sections, and has appointed an angel as lord over each. Thus not only the angels, but also the rulers of the world, can be regarded as gods. (Moses and the Judges are quoted as examples, though already mentioned in 2.41.) Peter goes on to quote Ex. 22.28: "Thou shalt not curse the gods, and thou shalt not curse the prince of thy people." The true God is however neither angel nor man, but Christ, the judge of all.[4] Thus we read in 2.44 that the cult of these lower gods is forbidden, and that only the highest God may be worshipped, "Therefore Moses, when he saw that the people were advancing, by degrees initiated them in the understanding of the *monarchy* and the faith of the one God (*paulatim eos as intelligentiam monarchiae et fidem Dei unius initiavit*), as he says in the following words: 'Thou shalt not make mention of the names of other gods' (Josh. 23.7 LXX)."

Since Christ became King by his victory and Ascension, the angels, according to the belief of the early Church, have been deprived of their power. Christ, when he was enthroned, placed all the powers of the earth under his feet. Both Jews and Gentiles are called to membership in the Kingdom of Christ: in political terms, polyarchy has been replaced by the monarchy of Christ. To this extent PsC is in full agreement with the Church's tradition. What is peculiar to PsC is however

---

[1] PETERSON, *op. cit.*, p. 54, particularly n. 6 with its bibliography.

[2] Irenaeus, Adv. haer. I. 23.3, ed. HARVEY 1.193, Hippolytus Ref. VI. 19.6, GCS Hipp. 3.147: κακῶς γὰρ διοικούντων τῶν ἀγγέλων τὸν κόσμον διὰ τὸ φιλαρχεῖν αὐτούς ... Cf. φιλαρχεῖν as the cardinal sin, connected with polyarchy, in Hom. 3.61.

[3] PG 1.1268: "ob honorem mittentis, ut plena sit ejus auctoritas, hoc dicitur iste qui missus est quod est ille qui misit."

[4] PG 1.1269: "Principes ergo singularum gentium dii appellantur. Principum Deus Christus est, qui est omnium judex. Vere ergo neque angeli, neque homines, neque ulla creatura dii esse possunt."

the identification of unity and the good with the masculine principle and disunity and the evil with the feminine—Gnostic speculations probably derived from Hellenistic philosophy, either Pythagorean or (possibly) Platonic.[1]

Eirene and Homonoia

Linked with the concept of monarchy in PsC are the two virtues εἰρήνη and ὁμόνοια—a combination which bears the unmistakable marks of Hellenistic political philosophy. The twin concepts—*pax* and *concordia* in Latin—were political catch-words in the Hellenistic world, denoting the ideal conditions which the monarchy—and later the Roman principate—was considered to bring.[2] The virtue of ὁμόνοια is stressed by the Stoics in particular; we find the word only once, however, in the neo-Pythagorean fragments on the kingship.[3]

But it is far from being the case that εἰρήνη and ὁμόνοια were used exclusively in a political sense in Hellenistic literature. Philo often uses the word without any political connotation whatever. ὁμόνοια is not found in the NT, but occurs fairly frequently in the Apostolic Fathers: in the Ignatians and the *Shepherd of Hermas*, but in Clement most of all. It has been said, apparently with a good deal of justification, that the latter bears traces of Stoic influence; there is, though, no evidence that the word has political overtones in Clement.[4]

In PsC, both εἰρήνη and ὁμόνοια are used in a distinctly political sense, both being connected with the monarchy as the ideal form of government. The monarchy creates ὁμόνοια (Hom. 9.2). Noah's ancient monarchy was characterized by its ὁμόνοια (Hom. 9.3). Since the monarchy brings εἰρήνη, the faithful ought to live together with the

---

[1] The speaker here is not Moses but Joshua. Cf. also the briefer Hom. 16.14.

[2] E. Zeller, *Die Philosophie der Griechen* III.2 (1903), pp. 129, 139 f. On the occurrence of the speculation in the primitive Church, see Dölger, *Sonne*, pp. 90ff.

[3] On ὁμόνοια as a political concept, see G. Kramer, *Quid valeat ὁμόνοια in litteris Graecis* (1915). H. Zwicker, art. *Homonoia*, PWK 8 (1912–13), col. 2265–2268. H. Fuchs, *Augustin und der antike Friedensgedanke*, Neue Philol. Forsch. 3 (1926), pp. 109 ff. Tarn, *Alexander*, p. 128. W. W. Tarn & G. T. Griffith, *Hellenistic Civilization* 3 (1952), pp. 90 f. On εἰρήνη, see Fuchs, *op. cit.*, pp. 166 ff. C. Koch, art. *Pax*, PWK 18.2 (1949), ed. 2430–2436.

[4] Ecphantus ap. Stob. IV. 7.64, ed. Delatte, p. 32. See Goodenough, *Hellenistic Kingship*, pp. 83 f., Tarn, *Alexander*, p. 128. On the Stoic conception of Kingship, see Fisch, *Alexander and the Stoics*, pp. 69 ff.

bishop in ὁμόνοια (Hom. 3.61). *Pax* and *concordia* are the signs of the monarchy, and they are therefore an integral part of the order of the Church. Similarly, the monarchical rule of Christ in the coming age will be characterized by εἰρήνη (Hom. 3.62, 3.19).

In the Constantinian period ὁμόνοια became a characteristic motto of imperial union policy.[1] Eusebius was also responsible for supplying Constantine with the metaphysical foundation on which to build up the doctrine that the new Roman Empire was the Kingdom of peace, promised by God.[2] The same terminology is used in the relevant sections of PsC, which most scholars consider to be pre-Constantinian; it is applied in this case to eschatology and to the ministry of the Church.[3]

The King as Imago Dei

Noah, according to Hom. 9.3, was king after the image of the one God (τοῦ μόνου θεοῦ κατ' εἰκόνα). In the same way the faithful, according to Peter's "consecration" speech (Hom. 3.62), honour the bishop as the image of God (ὡς εἰκόνα θεοῦ). Here the office of bishop is described in monarchical categories,[4] as we have seen; the expression "the image of God", as used here, is typical of the monarchy.

For Byzantine and Mediaeval speculation over the nature of the Kingship, the concept of the King as the image of God is quite usual.[5] It is normally derived from Ecphantus on the Kingship.[6] Other neo-

[1] On the occurrence of εἰρήνη and ὁμόνοια Clem., see L. SANDERS, *L'hellénisme de Saint Clément de Rome et le paulinisme*, Stud. hell. 2 (1943), pp. 124 ff. and *passim*.

[2] H. DOERRIES, *Das Selbstzeugnis Kaiser Konstantins*, GAb 3 Folge 34 (1954), pp. 317 ff.

[3] See below, p. 256.

[4] On the bishop as a τύπος of God, see above, pp. 165 ff.

[5] E. H. KANTOROWICZ, *Kaiser Friedrich II.*, p. 173 and n. 29 f. Cf. IDEM, *Deus per naturam, Deus per gratiam*, HThR 45 (1952), pp. 253–277.

[6] DELATTE, *op. cit.*, pp. 177 ff., KANTOROWICZ, *Friedrich II.*, p. 173. The passage in question in Ecphantus (ap. Stob. IV. 7.64, ed. DELATTE, p. 32) has been discussed particularly, since the same passage is found in Clement of Alexandria, Strom. V. 5.29, as a quotation from Eurysos and referring to mankind in general as the image of God. According to DELATTE, whose views are shared by KANTOROWICZ, Ecphantus borrowed from Eurysos and transferred the "image" idea from mankind to the king. Here the image of God is called ἀρχέτυπον; the concept of the king as God's εἰκών is met with in Plutarch, Ad princ. iner. 780 f. and in later literature. See DELATTE, *op. cit.*, p. 180, TARN, *Alexander*, p. 143 and n. 127.

Pythagorean "kingship" fragments, and other categories of Hellenistic political literature, contain the idea that the king is to imitate God.[1] The idea of the King as *imago Dei* and *imitator Dei* is so natural that it seems superfluous to try and derive the idea of the King as the image of God from this one passage in Ecphantus—quite apart from the fact that the idea may well have been expressed in other lost political documents.

The idea that the king is the image of God is in point of fact extremely ancient in Near Eastern culture. "The shadow of God is Man/ and men are the shadow of Man / Man that is the King / (who is) like the image of God", reads a Sumerian proverb quoted by Engnell.[2] In Jewish traditions these speculations are connected particularly with the concept of Adam as the image of God and the King of creation.[3] The pseudo-Clementine writings estimate Adam very highly indeed; he is said to have been anointed as the first prophet (Rec. 1.47). Over and over again it is stressed that he was the image of God.[4] The extensive deposit of Hellenistic political philosophy in those texts in which the King is said to be the image of God suggests, however, that we must look to Hellenistic works on the Kingship for the source of this idea, too.

As we mentioned earlier, the Acts of Apollonius contain an example of the way in which the 2nd century Christian Church had already come to look upon the king as the image of God, appointed by God to carry out his function of government on earth.[5] Apollonius, who was trained in Greek philosophy, is certainly dependent here upon that kind of political metaphysic found in Ecphantus. PsC would seem to have derived the idea of the king as the image of God from this source, though the entire complex has been influenced by Jewish ideas of Adam as *Urmensch* and king.

---

[1] Philo, Spec. leg. IV. 187 f. Diotogenes ap. Stob. IV. 7.62 (conclusion), Sthenidas ap. Stob. IV. 7.63 (conclusion). Dio Chrys. Or. 37.42-46. On the latter, see VALDENBERG, *La théorie monarchique*, pp. 148 f.

[2] *Divine Kingship*, motto. IDEM, *Urmenschvorstellung*, p. 271 n. 9.

[3] MURMELSTEIN, *Adam*, p. 271.

[4] Hom. 2.16, 8.10, 10.3. Cf. KANTOROWICZ, *Friedrich II.*, n. 29.

[5] See above, p. 175.

The King as Father

Christ is called "father" in Hom. 3.19; he shall be king over his own children, and his fatherly love for them and their love and reference for him will bring about eternal peace.[1]

It is unusual for Christ to be called πατήρ in writings from this period. Not unnaturally, the title is reserved for God. Nor does the Messianic title "eternal father" in Isa. 9.6 have any significance as a proof-text. There are isolated examples of Christ being called πατήρ in prayers.[2] It therefore seems most likely that we must seek elsewhere for the origin of the title—again, in political philosophy.

The King is often referred to as a father in Hellenistic political literature.[3] The neo-Pythagorean Kingship fragments stress that the King is to imitate God, even in respect of his fatherhood.[4] This mutual relationship is emphasized by Ecphantus in particular,[5] and is also taken up by Philo.[6] It is common knowledge that the Roman emperor was called *pater patriae* and *pater orbis*, a terminology having its roots in earlier political philosophy.[7]

In Hom. 3.19, when Christ is called King and Father, and when his relationship to his people is said to resemble the mutual love of a father and his children, we may be quite sure that we are dealing with influence from Hellenistic political ideology.

The result of this examination of a number of concepts in PsC—which could of course be extended to include other terms—is that we

---

[1] τοῦτο πατήρ, τοῦτο προφήτης, τοῦτο εὔλογον τὸ αὐτὸν ἰδίων τέκνων βασιλεῦσαι, ἵνα τῇ ἐκ πατρὸς πρὸς τέκνα στοργῇ καὶ τῶν τέκνων πρὸς τὸν πατέρα ἐνδιαθέτῳ τιμῇ αἰώνιος εἰρήνη γενέσθαι δυνηθῇ.

[2] See above, p. 161.

[3] The parable seems to have been of Stoic origin; see L. BERLINGER, *Beiträge*, p. 78. GOODENOUGH, *Politics*, pp. 95 ff. DELATTE, *Traités*, p. 227.

[4] Diotogenes, ap. Stob. IV. 7.62, ed. DELATTE, p. 45; Sthenidas ap. Stob. IV. 7.63, ed. DELATTE, p. 46; Ecphantus, ap. Stob. IV. 7.64, ed. DELATTE, p. 32.

[5] Ecphantus, *ibid.*: ὅλαν δὲ τὰν εὔνοιαν χρὴ παρασκευάζεσθαι πρῶτα μὲν παρὰ τῷ βασιλέως ἐς τὼς βασιλευομένως, δεύτερον δὲ παρὰ τῶνδε ἐς τὸν βασιλέα, ὁποία γεννάτορος ποτὶ υἱέα ...

[6] Philo Spec. leg. IV. 184: τὸν γὰρ ἄρχοντα οὕτως χρὴ προεστάναι τῶν ὑπηκόων ὡς πατέρα παίδων, ἵνα καὶ αὐτὸς ὡς ὑπὸ γνησίων υἱῶν ἀντιτιμᾶται. Prov. fragm. 2 (in Eusebius Praep. ev. VIII. 14): βασιλεῖ δὲ οὐκ ἔστι πρόσρησις οἰκειοτέρα πατρός. ὁ γὰρ ἐν ταῖς συγγενείαις πρὸς τέκνα γονεῖς, τοῦτο βασιλεὺς μὲν πρὸς πόλιν, πρὸς δὲ κόσμον ὁ θεός. GOODENOUGH, *Politics*, pp. 95 ff. Cf. Dio Chrys. Or. 1.22.

[7] ALFÖLDI, *Insignien*, p. 88. BERLINGER, *Beiträge*, pp. 77 ff., DELATTE, *Traités*, p. 146.

have found evidence of a considerable deposit of Hellenistic political speculation, reminiscent of that found in Philo and in the neo-Pythagorean Kingship fragments. The passages in question are drawn largely from the Homilies; we have no certain evidence for the politics of Rec. It is easy, on a basis of this fact, to conclude that the ideas in question were not present in that document which formed the common foundation for Hom. and Rec. Such a conclusion however contradicts the hypothesis of divided sources, which claims that the texts with which we have been dealing are derived from a hypothetical *Kerygma Petri*.[1] We have not the slightest desire to increase the goodly measure of confusion which already exists on the subject of PsC, by introducing a new basis for source division. It is sufficient for our purposes to point out that in one section of PsC there is a deposit of Greek speculation, which has nothing whatever to do with more or less hypothetical "Ebionite" concepts.

The derivation of these ideas cannot be determined with any degree of exactness. The closest parallels are found in Eusebius and in the *Apostolic Constitutions*;[2] both would appear to be of later date, however, and in them the peace-bringing monarchy is identified with the Roman Empire, and not with the eschatological Kingdom of Christ. Of political writings from the period before Constantine, Philo provides a number of parallels, but does not use εἰρήνη and ὁμόνοια politically, in connexion with the monarchy.

It seems likely that PsC, Eusebius and the *Apostolic Constitutions* refer back to a common tradition. The concept of the end of polyarchy and the restoration of peace through the eschatological monarchy (of Christ or of Constantine) is so characteristic that there can be little question of chance resemblances due to the similar political atmosphere of the milieus in which the respective traditions were formed. It is more difficult to determine whether this earlier tradition was Gentile, Jewish or Christian, though the identification of the monarchy with monotheism seems to rule out its having been a Gentile tradition. This identification is first found in Philo, and it is possible that the theological concept of monarchy was first formed in Alexandrian Judaism.[3] If the pattern was originally Jewish, that would help to explain the ease with which Eusebius was able to apply the eschatological sayings

---

[1] SCHOEPS, *Theologie*, passim, STRECKER, *Judenchristentum*, passim.
[2] See below, pp. 318, 321.
[3] Thus VERHOEVEN, *Studien*, p. 78; IDEM, *Monarchie*, p. 45.

to Constantine. Had he been building upon Christian eschatology, and then transferred the concepts from Christ to the Emperor, it would have been more of a stumbling-block. It is, however, unlikely that the first application of this political ideology to Christ took place in such an obscure and carelessly compiled document as PsC. There were in all probability Christian traditions before PsC, in which it was claimed that the Hellenistic world's hopes of unity, harmony and peace had been fulfilled in Christ. But we cannot be certain. What we can be certain about is that in the 4th century conflicts between Caesar and Church, the Church possessed a powerful political consciousness, connected with faith in the Church as the new people, *tertium genus*, whose King was Christ.

PART IV

The Kingship of Christ in the Arian Conflict

Introduction

We have seen that the position occupied by the idea of the Kingship of Christ in the early 4th century theological tradition was far from insignificant. The *testimonia* tradition was still alive, conveying the Christian interpretation of the Messianic sayings of the OT. Traditional proof-texts are to be found at this time not only in anti-Jewish literature, but in every kind of Christian writing, whatever theological tendency they represent. The same proof-texts can be found in the Arians and Athanasius, in Eusebius and Marcellus of Ancyra; that authorities disagree as to their interpretation is another matter. The choice of proof-texts was invested with such intrinsic authority that no one challenged its validity. When the point at issue was the Kingship of Christ, the same texts were used again and again—Ps. 2, 44 (45) and 109 (110) being the most important of these.

Before ever the Arian conflict broke out we note that there were distinct divergences of opinion on the matter of the Kingship of Christ between the two main theological schools of the time, the Alexandrian and the Antiochene. The left wing of theological opinion, represented by Eusebius, connected the Kingship of Christ for the most part to the Logos as the vicegerent of God in the world. Among the Antiochenes, whose outstanding representative was Marcellus of Ancyra, the Kingship of Christ was connected with his humanity or, to be more precise, with his human nature from the moment when that nature became united with the Logos. Of the two tendencies it is the Antiochene which is related most closely to the *testimonia* tradition and hence to the Messianism of Palestinian Judaism; the Alexandrians on the other hand were indebted to the Hellenistic Judaism of Alexandria in general, and to Philo in particular.

From the time of the Arian controversy there appeared two other schools which both, despite their differences, may be said to unite Alexandrian and Antiochene: Arianism and Nicene orthodoxy. In their doctrines of the Kingship of Christ both have combinations of ideas which we have already seen in the earlier schools. Thus by the middle of the 4th century we have no less than four main schools of thought on the Kingship of Christ: the Alexandrian, in which the Philonic tradition lived on, the Antiochene, the Arian and the Nicene. We have already given account of the two former; we shall now proceed to a consideration of the Arian and Nicene traditions.

11. EUSEBIUS AND THE ARIANS

Eusebius and the Kingship of Christ

Our investigation so far has shown that the idea of the Kingship of Christ was by no means forgotten during the years between the NT and the Constantinian period. On the contrary: it dominates much of the Christian literature of the time. It is true that the Messianism of the NT is pushed into the background in Christian theology, influenced as it was by Alexandrian Judaism, but instead the Hellenistic ideal of kingship, though political, was transferred to both the heavenly Logos and the earthly Christ. The political speculations of the Pseudo-Clementines show that in the pre-Constantinian period there were already attempts being made to centre a scheme of political metaphysics on the figure of Christ the King. But at the same time the Messianism of the NT lived on in the more conservative classes of literature, particularly in anti-Jewish polemics and probably in sermons as well—though little of this latter class has come down to posterity.

It is nevertheless undeniable that the theme is much more prominent in the Christian literature and art of the Constantinian period. Although the difference between the pre-Constantinian and the Constantinian images of Christ is by no means as great as has sometimes been supposed, there is clear evidence that the "royal" theme comes more and more into the foreground during the 4th century.

Kollwitz considers that these new tendencies are to be observed principally in Eusebius. What he means is that the subject of the Kingship of Christ is more prominent in Eusebius' later writings than in his earlier work. Further, he claims that in these writings Eusebius transfers to Christ epithets previously reserved for the Father; a case in point is βασιλεύς.¹ It has often been said that Eusebius was of considerable importance in laying the metaphysical foundations of Constantine's Emperorship, and that he regarded the new order as the fulfilment of the OT prophecies of peace.² We are not however aware that his views on the Kingship of Christ have ever been subjected to closer scrutiny.

Eusebius is far from being an original theologian. His gifts were largely apologetical,³ and his theological writings are very largely dependent upon earlier theology. It is thus unlikely that such an unoriginal and dependent author could have been the originator, or even the leading representative, of that new tendency in Christology with which we are dealing.

Detailed study shows that in his presentation of the Kingship of Christ Eusebius is dependent upon both the *testimonia* tradition and the Alexandrian tradition. Deposits of the former are to be found mainly in HE and Dem ev., and in his letter to Constantine's sister Constantia, in which he uses the traditional exposition of Ps. 23.7–9 as Scriptural proof of the *ascensio* and *sessio* of Christ.⁴ Apart from the

---

[1] KOLLWITZ, *Das Bild*, p. 97: "Hob sich in den ersten drei Jahrhunderten die Vorstellung von Christus als einem himmlischen König keineswegs besonders aus dem Kreis der übrigen Vorstellungen heraus, so tritt darin seit der Friedenszeit ein Wandel ein. Der Umschwung ist deutlich in den Schriften Eusebius zu spüren. Beschränkt er in seinen frühen Werken den Basileus-Titel noch vorwiegend auf den Vater, so fällt diese Beschränkung in seinen späteren Schriften ganz fort. Christus ist gleich dem Vater μέγας βασιλεύς, παμβασιλεύς, τοῦ σύμπαντος ἡγεμών κόσμου." KOLLWITZ here (*op. cit.*, p. 18) supports his view with quotations from Laus C. and Theoph., earlier published in his *Christus als Lehrer*, p. 58 and n. 66–68. In this earlier work he does not however draw the same conclusions, but considers that these expressions are borrowed from the imperial ceremonial of the Constantinian court: "Diese Parallellität zwischen Christus und dem Kaiser wird dann im folgenden eingehend entwickelt. Je eingehender das geschieht, desto mehr Prädikate wandern auch vom Kaiser auf Christus", *Christus als Lehrer*, pp. 57 f. Cf. IDEM art. *Christus Basileus* in RAC, col. 1259 f.

[2] PETERSON, *Monotheismus*, pp. 89 ff. H. BERKHOF, *Die Theologie des Eusebius von Caesarea* (1939), pp. 54 ff.

[3] BERKHOF, *op. cit., passim*.

[4] The letter has been edited in PG 20.1545 ff. It is treated in the following works, which however mainly discuss its iconoclastic tendencies: H. KOCH, *Die altchristliche Bilderfrage nach den literarischen Quellen*, FRLANT 10 (1917). W. ELLIGER, *Die Stellung der alten Christen zu den Bildern in den ersten vier Jahrhunderten*. StChD (1930), pp. 47 ff. G. FLOROVSKY, *Origen, Eusebius and the Iconoclastic Controversy*, CH 19 (1950), pp. 84 ff. M. V. ANARTOS, *The Argument for Iconoclasm*

letter to Constantia, which is difficult to date, we find that Eusebius' use of proof-texts to determine the Kingship of Christ is limited to works written before the Council of Nicaea.[1] Kollwitz is thus mistaken when he says that the Kingship of Christ is of no significance in Eusebius' early work. This is contradicted principally by Eusebius' speech at the consecration of the basilica at Tyre, 314, which is one of the Constantinian period's clearest expressions of faith in Christ's Kingship.[2]

The Alexandrian tradition is dominant in the view of the Kingship expressed in Eusebius' writings from the 330's: the Syriac *Theophany*, *Laus Constantini* and *De ecclesiastica theologia*.[3] These are filled with "royal" terminology, and it is this which has led Kollwitz to believe that these express Eusebius' faith in the Kingship of Christ more clearly than his earlier works. As in Clement, the role accorded to the incarnate Christ in these later works is comparatively insignificant.

Here we find the Alexandrian theologians' image of God as the Persian Great King, hidden in his state apartments behind veils, who communicates only through his servants.[4] The visible power at work in the world is his Logos, the mediator between the invisible God and the world; this is the organizing power and constitutive force of the universe. All these are characteristics we have previously seen in Philo and the Christian theology of Alexandria.[5]

The Logos is therefore frequently described in terms indicative of

---

as presented by the Iconoclastic Council of 754, in Late Class. and Mediev. Stud. in honor of A. M. Friend, Jr. (1955), pp. 183 f.

[1] For the dating of Eusebius' works, see E. SCHWARTZ, *Eusebius von Caesarea*, PWK 6 (1909), col. 1370–1439.

[2] See above, pp. 19 ff.

[3] The *Laus Constantini*, which has been composed in two different parts, the so-called Tricennalia oration and an apology, stands in a complex relationship to the Syriac *Theophany*. It is believed that Eusebius used Theoph. when writing Laus C., especially in its later part (from ch. 11). See I. A. HEIKEL, *Kritische Beiträge zu den Constantin-Schriften des Eusebius*, TU 36.4 (1911), pp. 82 ff.

[4] Theoph. 1.22, GCS Eus. 4.45 ff. Laus C. 12.1 ff. GCS Eus. 1.229 f. On the concept of God as the Great King, see BERKHOF, *Eusebius*, p. 97. STRAUB, *Herrscherideal*, pp. 113 ff.

[5] GRESSMANN points out in his edition of Theoph., pp. XXIV ff., that this writing is dependent on Philo's Prov., also used by Eusebius in Praep. ev. VI.6. Cf. P. WENDLAND, *Philos Schrift über die Vorsehung*, (1892). On Eusebius' logos theology, see BERKHOF, *op. cit.*, pp. 67 ff. The most important texts are Theoph. 1.23 (pp. 45 f.), 1.38 (p. 56), 1.41 (p. 58), 1.43 (p. 60), 1.45 (p. 62).

his subordination: he is the Great King's ὕπαρχος, ἀρχιστράτηγος, ἀρχιερεύς, etc.¹ But since God has given him royal ἐξουσία,² he can also be called βασιλεύς or even παμβασιλεύς.³ This has nothing to do with Nicene tendencies. Eusebius is perfectly faithful to the Alexandrian tradition which, following Philo, uses the same terminology somewhat vaguely to refer to God and the Logos, to the king and the wise man.⁴

The Alexandrian element in these texts is to be seen not least in the application of the entire Hellenistic political terminology to the Logos. The Logos is thus ποιμήν,⁵ κυβερνήτης,⁶ ἡγεμών,⁷ and στρατηγός;⁸ but seldom, if ever, ἡνίοχος.⁹ These terms are also found in typical combinations of analogies,¹⁰ and σωτήρ in typical expressions derived from the Philonic logos theology.¹¹

The situation is thus practically the opposite of that postulated by Kollwitz. Eusebius' earlier writings are dominated by faith in the incarnate Christ as the one appointed by God to be the ruler of the world. This concept is later obscured by the idea of God's Logos as the power by which he governs the world, a power which takes visible form

---

[1] Laus C. 3.6 (p. 202).
[2] Theoph. 1.23 (p. 46).
[3] Laus C. 6.4 (p. 206), 12.16 (p. 234), Theoph. 1.3 (p. 41), 1.34 = Laus C. 12.16 (p. 52), 2.13 (p. 84), 2.97 (p. 125), 3.1 (p. 126), 3.38 (p. 140), 3.61 (pp. 157 f.). The Greek fragment to the last mentioned of the texts (p. 13) has παμβασιλεύς, and so has also Laus C. 12.16 = Theoph. 1.34.
[4] See above, p. 192. Cf. BERKHOF, Eusebius, p. 95.
[5] Laus C. 7.9 (p. 214) = Theoph. 2.83 (p. 119), Eccl. theol. I.13 (74).2, GCS Eus. 4.73. On the Logos as shepherd in Eusebius, see QUASTEN, Der Gute Hirte, pp. 57 f.
[6] Dem. ev. IV.2.1, GCS Eus. 6.152, Laus C. 7.9 (p. 214) = Theoph. 2.83 (p. 119), Eccl. theol. I.13 (74).2 (p. 73).
[7] Dem. ev. IV.1.4 (p. 151) and IV.7.2 (p. 161): both these texts have ἡγεμὼν καὶ βασιλεὺς τῶν ὅλων; probably ἡγεμών also occurred in the original text to Theoph. 1.4 (p. 42), "Führer und Lenker" in GRESSMANN's translation.
[8] Laus C. 7.9 (p. 214) = Theoph. 2.83 (p. 119).
[9] The verb ἡνιοχεῖν occurs, referring to the Logos, in Laus C. 6.4 (p. 206), 11.2 (p. 227) = Theoph. 1.5 (p. 42) and 12.16 (p. 234) = Theoph. 1.34 (p. 52).
[10] Laus C. 7.9 (p. 214) = Theoph. 2.83 (p. 119): τί ἐχρῆν τὸν τῶν καταπονουμένων βασιλέα (θεόν) διαπράξασθαι; ... ἀλλ' οὔτε κυβερνήτης οὕτω ποτ' ἂν λεχθείη σοφός, ... οὔτε στρατηγὸς οὕτω ποτ' ἂν γένοιτο ἀφειδής, ... ἀλλ' οὐδὲ ποιμὴν ἀγαθὸς τῆς αὐτοῦ ποίμνης τὸ πεπλανημένον ἀπαθῶς παρίδου ἂν θρέμμα, ... So also Eccl. theol. I.13 (74).2 (p. 73): πάντων γὰρ ἀθρόως τῶν τε κατ' οὐρανὸν καὶ τῶν ἐπὶ γῆς ποιμένα καὶ σωτῆρα κηδεμόνα τε καὶ φύλακα καὶ ἰατρὸν καὶ κυβερνήτην μόνον αὐτὸν ὁ γεννήσας ἀνέδειξεν πατήρ, ...
[11] Eccl. theol. III.15.5 (p. 172) σωτῆρι καὶ βασιλεῖ τῶν ὅλων.

in the person of the Emperor Constantine. Hellenistic political terminology is used so consistently, not in order to glorify Christ, but the Roman Emperor. Characteristically, Eusebius never uses the epithet βασιλεύς in these writings to refer to the incarnate Christ.¹

The political terminology used by Eusebius of the Logos has been taken over from Alexandrian theology, and in the last resort from Philo. We cannot trace any more direct influence from political thought on the logos terminology in his writings. There are no grounds for the assertion that the new positive attitude to the Empire influenced his Christological terminology.

A special case is provided by the term ἀρχιστράτηγος, which is fairly common in Eusebius,² and which Kollwitz reckons as one of the terms indicating influence from the imperial cult.³ In point of fact ἀρχιστράτηγος, unlike στρατηγός, which Eusebius took over from Alexandrian theology,⁴ is derived from the *testimonia* tradition. It has nothing whatever to do with the language of the imperial court or Caesar's titles.

In the LXX ἀρχιστράτηγος is used to describe the captain of the hosts of the Lord who, according to Josh. 5.13 f., revealed himself to Joshua. It is thus used to refer to an archangel,⁵ but came to be used at an early stage of the pre-existent Christ.⁶

The word is found in a number of passages in Justin's Dialogue as a Christological key-word (34.2 and 61.1); there is no doubt that this refers to Josh. 5.14, which is also quoted in 62.5. In the chains of key-words the word is brought in together with ἄγγελος and ἄνθρωπος, the latter also occurring in Josh. 5.13.

Ἀρχιστράτηγος δυνάμεως κυρίου, as the captain of the host is called in Josh. 5.14, is used by a number of pre-Constantinian authors as a Christological title. Strangely enough, it is found mainly in Latin authors and in Latin translations of Greek Fathers: *princeps exercitus angelorum* in Melito,⁷ *princeps angelorum* in Irenaeus,⁸ *princeps militiae*

---

¹ BERKHOF, *Eusebius*, p. 120. Cf. *ibid.*, p. 124.
² HE I.2.3, GCS Eus. 2.1.10, I.2.11 (p. 16), X.4.15 (p. 867), Dem. ev. V.19.3 (p. 249), Praep. ev. VII.15.2, GCS Eus. 8.1.391, Laus C. 3.6 (p. 202).
³ *Christus als Lehrer*, pp. 58 f., n. 75.
⁴ See above, p. 209.
⁵ DEISSMANN, *Licht*, pp. 368 ff.
⁶ BARBEL, *Christos Angelos*, pp. 234 f.
⁷ Melito, De fide, cf. above, p. 196.
⁸ Syriac fragment in H. JORDAN, *Armenische Irenäusfragmente*, TU 36.3 (1913), fragm. 57 A 11.

celestis in Origen,[1] *angelorum omnium princeps* in Novatian[2] and *dux magnus caelitus* or *dux sanctae militiae* in Lactantius.[3]

The expression is connected with the pre-existent Logos as far back as Justin, who considered the OT theophanies to have been revelations of the Logos. The Logos is the δύναμις of God, a concept which for Justin is the equivalent of ἄγγελος.[4] In Josh. 5.13 f. Christ appeared as the highest δύναμις, as the leader of the divine powers. It is thus understandable that the term ἀρχιστράτηγος is connected with the Logos, and that it often occurs in combination with another Christological title taken from the OT, viz. μεγάλης βουλῆς ἄγγελος (from Isa. 9.6 LXX). The latter title is used twice by Justin as a Christological epithet (in Dial. 76.3, 126.1), the second occasion being in a chain of key-words.[5] From here the term has passed into the work of Irenaeus and Novatian.[6]

Eusebius uses both terms—ἀρχιστράτηγος and μεγάλης βουλῆς ἄγγελος —of Christ, frequently in combination.[7] We also find in HE I.2.11 that he has derived the term from Josh. 5.14. Further, it is typical that the word occurs on several occasions in HE, but only once in Laus C.; it belongs to the *testimonia* tradition and is therefore taken up by Eusebius in those writings in which he is most dependent upon that tradition.

In Laus C. 3.6 ἀρχιστράτηγος is used together with other titles clearly intended to stress the inferior position of the Son. The titles in question are μεγάλου βασιλέως ὕπαρχος, ἀρχιερεύς, προφήτης and μεγάλης βουλῆς ἄγγελος. This is in no way intended to express Christ's absolute equality with the Father and his kingly power; on the contrary, it shows with unusual clarity how he was considered to be no more than

---

[1] Hom. on Ezek. 1.7, GCS Orig. 8.331.

[2] Novatian, De Trin. 11, ed. FAUSSET, p. 36. On the occurrence of the term in Novatian, see J. BARBEL, *Zur "Engelchristologie" bei Novatian*, Trier ThZ 67 (1958), pp. 96–105.

[3] Lactantius, Div. inst. 4.25, CSEL 19.272, *ibid.*, 7.19.5 (p. 645).

[4] BARBEL, *Christos Angelos*, p. 60.

[5] BARBEL, *op. cit.*, p. 60 n. 68.

[6] St. Irenaeus, Adv. haer. III.16.3, ed. HARVEY 2.84, Dem. 56. Novatian, De Trin. 18, ed. FAUSSET, p. 16. See further BARBEL, *Christos Angelos* and "*Engelchristologie*", *passim*.

[7] HE I.2.3 (p. 10), X.4.15 (p. 867), Praep. ev. VII.15.2 (p. 391), Dem. ev. V.19.3 (p. 249), Laus C. 3.6 (p. 202).

the Father's vicegerent. The same is true of Praep. ev. VII.15.2,¹ which has the combination εἰκὼν θεοῦ, θεοῦ δύναμις, θεοῦ σοφία, θεοῦ λόγος, ἀρχιστράτηγος δυνάμεως κυρίου and μεγάλης βουλῆς ἄγγελος. It is not then surprising that the title was adopted by the Arians; the Arian interpolation in Ign. ad Smyrn. 8.2 describes Christ as ἀρχιστράτηγος τῆς δυνάμεως κυρίου.²

Eusebius' views on the Kingship of Christ are most clearly expressed in his anti-Marcelline writings. It is typical that his defence of the Kingship of Christ takes place in this context: it is the royal character of the Logos which, according to his Alexandrian principles, he is desirous of defending.

In his writings Marcellus had attacked the Arian party, and particularly Asterius the Sophist and Eusebius of Nicomedia. After Marcellus had been deposed by the Arian Synod of Constantinople, 336, Eusebius wrote *Contra Marcellum* and his *Ecclesiastical Theology*, in which he defended the Arian position and attacked Marcellus, whom he considered to be an advocate of the heresies of Sabellius and Paul of Samosata.

We have said that Marcellus of Ancyra refused to call the pre-existent Logos anything but just plain Logos.³ Eusebius objected, saying that the pre-existent Logos can very well be called βασιλεύς, εἰκών, πρωτότοκος πάσης κτίσεως, ἀγαπητός, υἱός, Ἰησοῦς and Χριστός.⁴ At the same time he attacked Marcellus' doctrine that the Kingship of Christ will come to an end, referring to Lk. 1.33, which the later tradition also adopted as its most important proof-text confuting Marcellus' heresy. Eusebius was one of the first to advance the classical solution of the problem of how Lk. 1.33, which says that the Kingdom of Christ shall have no end, is to be reconciled with 1 Cor. 15.28, according to which at the end of time Christ is to render the Kingdom to his Father. He pointed out that βασιλεία can mean both Kingship and Kingdom: Christ will not cease from being King, but he will render to the Father "the Kingdom", i.e. those who are ruled by him.⁵

---

¹ P. 391.
² Ed. LIGHTFOOT, p. 808. For the Arian tendency of this version, see below, p. 305 n. 2.
³ See above, pp. 232 f.
⁴ Contra Marc. I.1.22, GCS Eus. 4.6, II.1.3 (p. 32), 3.39 (p. 52), 4.22 (p. 56).
⁵ Eccl. theol. III.16.3 (p. 175). Cf. below, pp. 286 f.

The essential point here is that Christ's Kingship has existed from the beginning, since Christ is the Logos, and that this power has no end. The Kingship of the incarnate Christ, on the other hand, is not equally important to Eusebius. It is impossible to find a more thoroughgoing opposition between Alexandrian and Antiochene than that revealed in the controversy between Marcellus and Eusebius: the one regarded the Kingship of Christ as being bound to the human nature, determined by the economy of salvation and limited to a definite period of time; the other connected the Kingship to the eternal Logos, a cosmic power which, though revealed in time, belongs to eternity and to the supra-historical sphere.

Eusebius, too, recognized the difficulty of reconciling the doctrine of the Logos with the concept of the monarchy: one of the most stubborn of the 3rd century theological problems, and one which was actualized by the Monarchianist heresy.[1] Peterson considers that the term μοναρχία was of no particular significance in Alexandria; he reports that the word is not found in the writings of Clement, Origen or Athanasius.[2] But Eusebius uses the term μοναρχία in his polemic against Marcellus: belief in two hypostases leads to loss of the monarchical Godhead. Since there is only one God, who is without beginning, and since the Son is born of him, there can only be *one* monarchy and *one* kingship.[3]

The relationship between God and Christ can therefore also be compared to that existing between the Emperor and his image. The person who honours the image, honours Caesar; in the same way the person who honours Christ, the εἰκών of God, honours God at the same time.[4] This analogy was later adopted by St. Basil, and thus won the approval of Cappadocian theology.[5] But as used by Eusebius it was distinctly subordinationist, and must therefore have been unacceptable to Nicene orthodoxy. Despite the fact that he is called βασιλεύς, the Logos is really not a king, but an image of the one who is the real King.

---

[1] Peterson, *Monotheismus*, pp. 76 ff.

[2] *Op. cit.*, p. 78.

[3] Eccl. theol. II.7.1 (p. 104): ἀλλὰ φοβῇ, ὦ ἄνθρωπε, μὴ δύο ὑποστάσεις ὁμολογήσας δύο ἀρχὰς εἰσαγάγοις καὶ τῆς μοναρχικῆς θεότητος ἐκπέσοις; μάνθανε τοίνυν ὡς, ἑνὸς ὄντος ἀνάρχου καὶ ἀγεννήτου θεοῦ τοῦ δὲ υἱοῦ ἐξ αὐτοῦ γεγεννημένου μία ἔσται ἀρχὴ μοναρχία τε καὶ βασιλεία μία ...

[4] Ibid. II.7.16 (p. 106), cf. II.23.3 (pp. 133 f.).

[5] De Spir. Sancto 18.45, PG 32.149. Cf. below, p. 329.

The Arians and the Kingship of Christ

Our main difficulty, when trying to determine the Arians' attitude to the Kingship of Christ, is the lack of source material. It is common knowledge that the greater part of the Arians' literature has been lost, and we must therefore be content with relatively late material, often of uncertain date. A review of the existent source material shows, however, that the concept of the Kingship of Christ was important in Arianism, and that the Arians supported this doctrine with the traditional proof-texts, though these were interpreted in their own peculiar fashion.

Arianism was highly eclectic. It embraced elements from the school of Origen and from Antiochene theology, and cannot be described as a branch of any one theological movement of the earlier period.[1] This is particularly true of the logos theology, the kernel of Arianism. Arius was dependent upon the subordinationist logos theology of the Philonic tradition, but at the same time he drew upon the Antiochenes for their distinction between the Logos and the Son, a distinction which he reshaped in his own way. Paul of Samosata, followed by Marcellus of Ancyra, distinguished between the Logos and the Son in such a way as to understand "the Son" as referring only to the incarnate Logos. On a basis of this definition it is possible to claim that the Logos has existed from all eternity, while the Son had a beginning in time. Arius adopted this terminology, but moved the existence of the Son back in time to his pre-existent state. When Arius went on to say that the Logos is eternal but the Son has an origin in time, he meant that God created the Son after his own Logos, which thus corresponds closely to ὁ πατρικὸς λόγος of Clement of Alexandria.[2]

Turning to the idea of the Kingship of Christ, this strange eclecticism led to the conclusion that the Kingship was something which belonged to the Son in his pre-existence (thus far in agreement with the Alexandrians) but which has been granted him in time (the view of the Antiochenes). This is seen most clearly in the matter of the Arians' interpretation of the Scriptures.

The traditional proof-texts of the Lord's Kingship are considered in the NT and later tradition to refer to his glorification after suf-

---

[1] See POLLARD, *Logos and Son*, pp. 282 ff., and IDEM, *Origins*, pp. 103 ff.

[2] POLLARD, *Origins*, ibid. Cf. R. P. CASEY, *Clement and the two Divine Logoi*, JTS 25 (1924), pp. 43–56.

fering. But in the Antiochene tradition there is a tendency to link them instead with the Incarnation. The Arians favoured a third interpretation: the words refer to events which took place at the beginning of time, when God appointed the Son he had created as vicegerent over the world. The fact that Arius and Eunomius are said to have taught that Ps. 109 (110) refers to the Son before the Incarnation[1] agrees completely with what we know from such of the Arians' expositions as have been preserved.

It is characteristic that the Arian *Contra Judaeos* (attributed to the Arian bishop Maximinus),[2] although it uses proof-texts common in anti-Jewish polemics, applies them in an altogether new way. It aims at giving a chronological presentation of the history of salvation, and therefore begins with the birth of the Son, quoting as proof-texts Ps. 2.7, 44 (45).7 and 109 (110).1. Traditionally the two latter are interpreted as pointing to the Incarnate Christ; in the exegesis of the school of Origen and the African Fathers Ps. 2.7 was taken to refer to the eternal generation of the Son.[3] An even better example of Arian exegesis is provided in a tractate on the Gospel of Luke,[4] in which the author expounds the doctrine of the Kingship of Christ with a starting point in Lk. 1.32.[5]

The words *filius altissimi vocavitur* are expounded, in line with older tradition, to mean that Christ is not the son of Joseph, nor of David, nor of Abraham, but the Son of the Most High. But at the same time the author attacks the Nicenes' view of the Son as ὕψιστος (*non altissimus, sed altissimi*).[6] Does he, then, have the same throne and the same

---

[1] See above, p. 237.

[2] Ed. by C. H. TURNER, JTS 20 (1919), pp. 293–310. (Earlier printed in PL 57.793 ff.) See further B. CAPELLE, *Un homiliaire de l'évêque arien Maximin*, RevBén 34 (1922), pp. 81–108.

[3] See below, p. 289. A corresponding exposition of Ps. 109.1 and Ps. 44.7 occurs in an Arian fragment from Maius' collection, where it is also evident that it is the pre-existent Son who is meant: "Hic Spiritus non est Deus nec Dominus, quoniam nec creator ... quoniam non est Deus sed minister Christi Filii Dei sui ... Hic a se non loquitur, sed quaecumque audierit, loquetur, et docet, et futura annuntiat credentibus. Hic Christus Dominum et Deum suum profitetur esse dicens: Dixit Dominus Domino meo ... Et iterum ad Christum Deum suum dicit idem Spiritus: Sedes tua Deus in saeculum saeculi ...", fragm. 3, PL 13.601 f. On this text, see further CPL 705 and PL Suppl. 1.326.

[4] Tract. in Luc., PL Suppl. 1.327 ff.

[5] *Ibid.*, col. 331 ff.

[6] Cf. below, p. 311.

glory as the Father? No, replies the Arian author, with a characteristic reinterpretation of the rest of the verse. He quotes it as *Et davit illi Deus sedem patris sui*, thus leaving out the words about "the father" being David. The saying is then interpreted as referring to the enthronement of the Son at the beginning of time, as postulated by the Arians. In the beginning God gave a throne to the Son, but this is inferior to his own (*sicut ante saecula sedem dedit; non sibi comparem, sed subiectam; rex regalem constituens; pater filio affectualem non aequalem*). Prov. 16.12 and Ps. 44 (45).7 follow as proof-texts (n.b. particularly the latter). Christ thus rules *non in tempore sed in aeternum*. The Kingship of the Son has a beginning, but no end (*habet principium, nescit finem; quia te perfectus pater perfectum filium genuit; ut in genitura praestaret initium, et in regno nulla invidia successionem perficeret*). There follow a number of passages of Scripture as proof of the beginning in time of the Kingship of the Son (Jn. 1.1, 8.25, Ps. 109 (110).3, Prov. 8.22 f., Rev. 1.8). The key-word of each is *principium*, which the author interprets to mean "beginning in time". The passage ends with a series of traditional proof-texts of the Kingship of the Lord (Ps. 144 (145).13, 46 (47).9, 94 (95).3, 46 (47).8, Isa. 33.17, Ps. 92 (93).1, 96 (97).1).

Lk. 4.18 (*Spiritus Domini super me*) is interpreted in a similar way.[1] Christ has been anointed twice: in the beginning God anointed the Son as God (*Deus ante saecula uncxit me Deum*), in proof of which is quoted Ps. 44 (45).8. In time he became anointed with Holy Spirit and power (Acts 10.38). It is of course not possible to give the phrase *ante saecula* a Nicene interpretation.

It is thus clear that the Arians were by no means strangers to the idea of calling Christ βασιλεύς; nor were they unacquainted with the traditional proof-texts of his Kingship. Nor is it possible to regard the actual use of the word βασιλεύς as due to the influence of Nicene theology (as Kollwitz tends to suppose). This is shown principally by the fact that the two *symbola* from the 4th century in which the Son is described as βασιλεύς both come from the Arianizing consecration Synod of Antioch, 341. In the first creed the Son is called διαμένοντα βασιλέα καὶ θεόν;[2] in the second βασιλέα ἐκ βασιλέως.[3] Kollwitz' as-

---

[1] *Ibid.*, col. 336.

[2] C. J. Hefele, *Conciliengeschichte* 1 (1855), pp. 503 f. The sources are Athanasius, De synodis 22, ed. Opitz, p. 249, and Socrates, HE 2.10, PG 67.201. The text is published in Mansi 2, col. 1339 f.

[3] Hefele, *op. cit.* 1, pp. 504 f. The sources are Athanasius, De synodis 23, ed.

sumption that this is proof of the continuance of Nicene theology falls down completely when we recall the Arian tendency of the Synod as a whole.¹

The problem is further complicated by the fact that neither of the creeds seems actually to have been compiled at the Council; it is certain that both were taken over from older traditions. What were these traditions, and to what extent were the creeds revised by the Council?

The first clause διαμένοντα βασιλέα καὶ θεὸν εἰς τοὺς αἰῶνας is to all intents and purposes a variant of concluding clauses to the second article, as found in a number of early *symbola*. The best known of these, οὗ τῆς βασιλείας οὐκ ἔσται τέλος (Lk. 1.33), is to be found in the Jerusalemite creed,² in Epiphanius³ and in the Apostolic Constitutions;⁴ it also concludes the second article in the Nicene-Constantinopolitan creed. Another variant is οὗ ἡ βασιλεία ἀκατάλυτος (or ἀκατάπαυστος) in the so-called fourth Antiochene creed.⁵

There is no doubt that the formula, as used in the first Antiochene creed, was directed against Marcellus of Ancyra and his doctrine that the Kingdom of Christ was to cease at the judgment.⁶ Marcellus' doctrine is based on the connexion he established between the Kingship of Christ and his human nature and hence the economy of salvation. It is certain that the Synod, dominated as it was by representatives of the school of Origen and Arians, linked the Kingship with the pre-existent Son as the vicegerent of God. The Arians also believed that his Kingdom would have no end (cf. the exposition of Lk. 1.32 mentioned above). Even such an outstanding Arian as Eunomius adopted the formula in one of his creeds.⁷

OPITZ, p. 249, Hilary, De synodis 29, PL 10.502, cf. *ibid.* 33 (col. 505 f.), Socrates, HE 2.10 (col. 201). The text is published in MANSI 2, col. 1341.

[1] KOLLWITZ, *Christus als Lehrer*, p. 57: "Es ist von Interesse, wie gerade diese Konsequenz des nicaenischen Dogmas in den Symbolen, die aus dem Kreis der Synode von Antiochien (341) stammen, ausgebaut wird." KOLLWITZ here quotes the first Antiochene creed in Socrates' version and the second creed according to St. Hilary. Cf. IDEM, *Das Bild*, p. 101.

[2] St. Cyril of Jerusalem, Cath. 15.2, PG 33.871-872.

[3] Epiphanius, Ancor. 118: 10, GCS Epiph. 1.147.

[4] Ap. Const. VII.41.6, ed. FUNK, p. 446.

[5] St. Athanasius, De synodis 25, ed. OPITZ, p. 251. Socrates, HE 2.18, col. 221 f.

[6] See above, p. 234.

[7] Eunomius, Apol. 27, PG 30.865. On this creed, which is closely related to the creed in Ap. Const. VII.41, see M. ALBERTZ, *Untersuchungen über die Schriften des*

The second creed was, according to Sozomenos, compiled by St. Lucian of Antioch.¹ Kattenbusch considers that Sozomenos is wrong, and that it is the fourth creed which is Lucian's work.² The second creed should be attributed instead to Asterius the Sophist, in whose work we find similar turns of phrase.³ The Lucian authorship of the second creed has been defended by Loofs, whose argument seems entirely convincing.⁴ He shows that there is a late tradition according to which Lucian was present at the Council of Antioch, and he considers it likely that both Asterius and the second Antiochene creed are dependent upon the same prototype, which was probably derived from Lucian. In favour of this is, apart from Sozomenos' account, the fact that Asterius was a disciple of Lucian. It may even have been he who put forward the Lucian creed at the Council. This means that the creed must be dated back to the second half of the 3rd century. Further, the formula βασιλεὺς ἐκ βασιλέως, which we also find in Asterius, must also be accounted part of the original text. It was thus probably Lucian's formula which was adopted by the Council of Antioch.

The phrase βασιλεὺς ἐκ βασιλέως is *per se* far from unambiguous. It can be given a Nicene interpretation (like the Nicene creed's *Deum de Deo*);⁵ it can be interpreted in accordance with the school of Origen (the Logos is God's authorized regent over the world) and even in line with pure Arianism (the Son has received royal power from God). It is interesting in this connexion to compare the above-mentioned text from Asterius with a similar passage in the Arian *Contra Judaeos*.

Eunomius (1908), pp. 37 ff. In the following Eunomius also uses 1 Cor. 15.28 as a proof that the Son is subordinate to the Father, but without the conclusion drawn by Marcellus, that the Kingdom of the Son will come to an end. G. H. WILLIAMS seems to make a mistake in considering that the Kingdom of Christ will come to an end according to the Arians, *Christology* 2, p. 17. Cf. below, p. 287 n. 4.

[1] Sozomenus, HE III.5.9, GCS Soz., pp. 106 f.
[2] P. KATTENBUSCH, *Das apostolische Symbol* 1 (1894), pp. 255 ff.
[3] On Asterius, see BARDY, *Saint Lucien*, pp. 316 ff.
[4] F. LOOFS, *Das Bekenntnis Lucians, der Märtyrers*, SbB 1915, pp. 576–603. BARDY, *Saint Lucien*, pp. 85 ff., 91 ff., 96 n. 41. Cf. above, p. 240.
[5] The formula is interpreted in this way by St. Hilary, De synodis 29 ff.

Asterius[1]	Contra Judaeos[2]
Deum de Deo, totum ex toto, unum ex uno, perfectum de perfecto, regem de rege, Dominum de Domino.	unus unum genuit, solus solum, Deus Deum, rex regem, ingenitus ingenitum, Pater Filium, auctor Verbum, creator creatorem, aeternus aeternum, spiritus spiritum, lux lucem, splendor splendorem, pius pium, bonus bonum, misericors misericordem, perfectus perfectum.

Christ can also be described as βασιλεύς in more or less typical Arian formulae. A number of liturgical formulae in the Apostolic Constitutions, among them the close of the Gloria, call Christ βασιλεύς (or κύριος or θεός) πάσης αἰσθητῆς καὶ νοητῆς φύσεως.[3] Capelle has shown how this formula occurs in other documents having Arian tendencies. The interpolated version of Ign. ad Smyrn. 8.2 (the interpolations of which show a moderate Arianism) does not, it is true, call Christ βασιλεύς, but instead ἀρχιστράτηγος,[4] and it is similarly said about him διανομεῖ πάσης νοητῆς φύσεως. Similar expressions referring to the Kingship of the Son are to be found in Maius' Arian fragments, in which the Son is described as the King of creation, but the vicegerent of God: *natum subditum Deo non nato: dominum totius creaturae natum, ministrum verum Domini non nati: regere totius creaturae natum sub potestate regis non nati.*[5] *Filius autem Patri non est Deus, sed omni creaturae Dominus et Deus et Filius.*[6] *Regimur a Patre per Filium, quia Pater jussit Filio, et Filius regit nos.*[7]

The tendency of these texts is perfectly evident. The Son can be called βασιλεύς, but in that case what is meant is that he functions as

---

[1] Asterius' formulas are included in the Marcellus fragments preserved in Eusebius' Contra Marc. and Eccl. theol. The text is included in Contra Marc. 1.4, GCS Eus. 4.25, also printed as fragm. 96 (p. 205) in the same volume. We here quote the Latin text of St. Hilary.

[2] *Contra Judaeos*, PL 57.795.

[3] Ap. Const. VII.42.3, ed. FUNK, p. 448, 47.3 (p. 456), VIII.12.7 (p. 498), 12.49 (p. 514), cf. VIII.15.9 (p. 520). For this formula, see CAPELLE, *Le texte du "Gloria in excelsis"*, pp. 450 f.

[4] On this epithet, see above, pp. 265 ff.

[5] Fragm. 1, PL 13.598.

[6] Fragm. 4 (col. 605).

[7] Fragm. 8 (col. 612).

God's vicegerent over creation. He is not βασιλεύς in any absolute sense, but always with the qualification πάσης ... φύσεως: only in relation to the created universe, just as he is God only over the universe. The human nature of Christ is never mentioned in these texts; it is always the pre-existent Son who is referred to. The Arians' interest in the incarnate Christ and his Kingship was slight. Arianism denied the divinity of the Son, and had little interest in the human nature of Christ. In this respect Arianism is Alexandrian, rather than Antiochene. It was the Nicene theology, and not Arianism, which was to take up and develop the doctrine of the Kingship of the incarnate Christ.

12. THE NICENE THEOLOGIANS AND THE KINGSHIP OF CHRIST

It was not only the Arians whose doctrine of the Kingship of Christ combined Alexandrian and Antiochene elements: the same is true of the Nicene theologians. But here the resemblance ends. The Arians were mainly interested in metaphysics; St. Athanasius and the other Nicenes in soteriology. The Philonic doctrine of the Logos as governor of the world is seldom seen in Nicene theology, though it was of course not unknown, nor was it rejected by the Nicenes. In his *Contra Gentes*, probably published before the outbreak of the Arian controversy,[1] St. Athanasius was able to compare the Logos to a King, giving many kinds of order during the building of a city; further, he could describe how the Logos rules the cosmos with a gesture, and ensures that each and every creature carries out its proper functions.[2] The concept of the Logos as the power which binds the universe together was also to become common in Nicene orthodoxy.[3]

The most important tasks facing the Nicene theologians in their conflict with Arianism were, on the one hand, to show how the Son is of the same nature as the Father and, on the other, to stress that he was also true man. St. Athanasius and the other Nicene theologians wished to contradict the harmonizing theology of e.g. Eusebius, which made Christ into an intermediate being between God and man, by stressing the tension between the divine and the human, paradoxically expressed in the Incarnation.[4] Athanasius therefore made conscious

---

[1] On the dating, see QUASTEN, *Patrology* 3, p. 25.

[2] Orat. c. Gent. 43, PG 25.85: ἔοικεν οἰκοδομηθείσῃ μάλιστα μεγάλῃ πόλει, καὶ οἰκονομουμένῃ ἐπὶ παρουσίᾳ τοῦ καὶ ταύτην οἰκοδομήσαντος ἄρχοντος καὶ βασιλέως. *Ibid.*, col. 88: ὑπὸ γὰρ μιᾶς ῥιπῆς νεύματός τινος τοῦ θεοῦ λόγου ὁμοῦ τὰ πάντα διακοσμεῖται, καὶ τὰ οἰκεῖα παρ' ἑκάστου γίγνεται ...

[3] On this conception, see E. STOMMEL, Σημεῖον ἐκπετάσεως, RQ 48 (1953), pp. 21–42.

[4] Cf. OPITZ' judgment below, p. 316 n. 4.

use of terms previously reserved for the Father, transferring them to Christ: the Son is not only the Logos and the Son but also παντοκράτωρ and ὕψιστος. The terminological boldness of this step must have been unwelcome, not only to Arians and Alexandrians, but to all who were used to the earlier language.[1] Both words are titles of God as the Almighty and the Highest, and they are used by Athanasius to refer to the *homoousia* of the Son—to express that the Son is God in the highest meaning, and that he is possessed of all the divine attributes except that of being the Father. Like the whole of the left wing—but unlike Marcellus of Ancyra—Athanasius taught that the Son possessed the quality of Kingship in his pre-existence.[2] But he has not been appointed in time (as the Arians maintained), nor is he God's vicegerent (as according to the Arians and the school of Origen); He is God, and hence the supreme monarch, the eternal *pantocrator*.

But at the same time Athanasius stressed, more strongly than the Arians, the human nature of Christ. With regard to his Kingship, Athanasius shared the views of the Antiochenes, that the incarnate Christ obtained a Kingdom for our sakes. He thus regarded Christ as having a *double Kingship*: as God he is King by nature; as man he has become King through his work of salvation. This was also to provide a solution of the problem which occupied the minds of subsequent orthodox Nicene theologians.

Although Athanasius, unlike Marcellus, taught that Christ is King *qua* God, he emphasized that those passages of Scripture which the early Church interpreted as having to do with the *inauguration* of Christ into his royal office, refer to his human nature. This must be so, since the Logos participates in divine omnipotence from the beginning, and cannot have been given further divine attributes in the course of time. The saying in Ps. 2.6 to the effect that Christ has been inaugurated as King (κατεστάθην) also refers, according to Athanasius, to his human nature—as do those sayings in which he is said to have been created.[3] Here St. Athanasius often crosses swords with Arian exegetes, who claim that the pre-existent Son has been exalted, or that the incarnate Logos obtained, through his work of salvation, divine at-

---

[1] See below, pp. 295 ff.
[2] That according to St. Athanasius, the title βασιλεύς belongs to Christ also by virtue of his Divine nature is clear from Orat. 2 c. Arian. 17, PG 26.181, and De synod. 49.5, ed. OPITZ, p. 274. See further examples in the following pages.
[3] Orat. 2 c. Arian. 11, PG 26.169.

tributes which he lacked prior to the Incarnation. This kind of polemic is particularly common in the two first discourses against the Arians.

In his first discourse St. Athanasius states that ὑπερύψωσεν in Phil. 2.9 refers to the human nature of Christ. "That he was 'highly exalted' does not signify that the essence of the Word was exalted, for he was ever and is 'equal to God', but the exaltation is of the manhood."[1] It is against this background that we must set Athanasius' anxiety to stress that the Son is ὕψιστος. Since he is ὕψιστος by nature, the term ὑπερύψωσεν cannot refer to him, but must have to do with his human nature.

Athanasius is dependent here upon more than the Antiochene tradition of exposition. The same idea is to be found in Origen's commentary on John. On Jn. 13.31 Origen says that Christ's exaltation has nothing to do with his divine aspect, since the Word was in the beginning with God, and hence cannot be exalted (ὑπερυψωθῆναι)—a term taken direct from Phil. 2.9. The exaltation instead applies to the Son of Man (here the equivalent of the human nature), descended from the seed of David, which has glorified God through his death.[2] Origen does not say that Christ is ὕψιστος as God, but this is mainly a matter of terminology. Athanasius means that the Son is ὕψιστος, and this is identical with what Origen has already said. The most important difference is that since the question has now become controversial, Athanasius is compelled to express his views more emphatically than Origen.

In the earlier exegetical tradition Ps. 23 (24) was used as a proof-text not only for Christ's Ascension but also for his *descensus*. The angelic powers fail to recognize him at his Ascension because his descent took place in secret.[3] From the beginning, therefore, the exposition of Ps. 23 was intimately connected with that view of the Incarnation according to which Christ to some extent laid aside his divine nature at his descent: "Thou didst make him for a little while lower than the angels" (Ps. 8.6, Heb. 2.7). But for Athanasius it was inconceivable that the divinity of the Son was lessened by the Incarnation. If he is God, he has always been God. What is described in

---

[1] Orat. 1 c. Arian. 41, PG 26.96.

[2] Origen, Comm. on Jn. 32.25, GCS Orig. 4.470: ὁ γὰρ λόγος ἐν ἀρχῇ πρὸς τὸν θεόν, ὁ θεὸς λόγος, οὐκ ἐπεδέχετο τὸ ὑπερυψωθῆναι. ἡ δὲ ὑπερύψωσις τοῦ υἱοῦ τοῦ ἀνθρώπου (= the human nature).

[3] See above, pp. 103 f.

Ps. 23 is the ascent of the human nature to the throne of God, the work of salvation completed.

"... we must take the present phrase, 'he highly exalted him' (Phil. 2.9), not that he himself should be exalted, for he is the highest (ὕψιστος γάρ ἐστιν), but that he may become righteousness for us, and we may be exalted in him, and that we may enter the gates of heaven, which he has also opened for us, the forerunners saying, 'Lift up your gates, O ye rulers, and be ye lift up, ye everlasting doors, and the King of Glory shall come in' (Ps. 23.7). For here also not on him were shut the gates, as being Lord and Maker of all, but because of us is this too written, to whom the door of paradise was shut. And therefore in a human relation, because of the flesh which he bore, it is said of him, 'Lift up your gates' and 'shall come in', as if a man were entering; but in a divine relation on the other hand it is said of him, since 'the Word was God', that he is the 'Lord' and the 'King of Glory' ... (Quote Ps. 88 (89).17). And if the Son be righteousness, then he is not exalted as being himself in need, but it is we who are exalted in that Righteousness, which is he."[1]

In this exposition of Ps. 23 Athanasius reverts to a theme found in earlier exegesis of the Psalm. We have already pointed out that Justin said that the reason why the angels failed to recognize Christ at the Ascension was his "uncomely and dishonoured appearance" due to his human nature; this element recurs in all later expositions of the Psalm.[2] What Athanasius does is to isolate this characteristic by excluding every suspicion of a lessening of the divine nature; he thereby makes the Ascension into an enthronement of the human nature of Christ.

As we have seen,[3] the Arians interpreted Ps. 44 (45).7 f. as referring to the pre-existent Son, anointed by God in order that he might be appointed King over the cosmos. This Psalm is also interpreted by Athanasius as a reference to the human nature of Christ—an interpretation fully in line with earlier expository tradition:

"He is here anointed, not that he may become God, for he was so even before; not that he may become King, for he had the Kingdom eternally,

---

[1] Orat. 1 c. Arian. 41, PG 26.97. The same exegesis of the Psalm occurs in the short recension of De incarnatione 25, ed. ROBERTSON, reprinted and supplied with a critical apparatus by R. P. CASEY, StD 14.2 (1946), p. 38. It is however missing in the longer and original recension.

[2] See above, p. 105. This motif appears clearly in a fragment of Hippolytus' Psalm commentary preserved in Theodoret of Cyrus, GCS Hipp. 1.2.147: πρῶτον νῦν φαίνεται ταῖς δυνάμεσι ταῖς οὐρανίαις σὰρξ ἀναβαίνουσα.

[3] See above, pp. 270 f.

existing as God's image, as the sacred oracle shows; but in our behalf is this written, as before. For the Israelitish kings, upon their being anointed, then became kings, not being so before, as David, as Hezekiah, as Josiah, and the rest; but the Saviour on the contrary, being God, and ever ruling in the Father's Kingdom, and being himself he that supplies the Holy Ghost, nevertheless is here said to be anointed, that, as before, being said as man to be anointed, with the Spirit, he might provide for us men, not only exaltation and resurrection, but the indwelling and the intimacy of the Spirit."[1]

Athanasius further attacks the kind of exposition of St. Peter's speech in Acts 2.36 which makes it appear that the Logos only became κύριος and Χριστός after the completion of his earthly work of salvation, declaring that this is a new version of the heresy of Paul of Samosata. The Logos is Lord and King from all eternity. Here Athanasius advances the well-known proof-texts from the earliest *testimonia* tradition, Gen. 19.24, Ps. 109 (110).1, Ps. 44 (45).6 and Dan. 7.14.

"It is plain that even before he became man, he was King and Lord everlasting, being image and Word of the Father. And the Word being everlasting Lord and King, it is very plain again that Peter said that the essence of the Son was made, but spoke of his Lordship over us, which 'became', when he became man, and redeeming all by the cross, became Lord of all and King."[2]

It is clear from this text that the Incarnation did not mean that the royal power possessed by the divine nature of Christ from the beginning, in any way lessened:

"For though the Word existing in the form of God took a servant's form, yet the assumption of the flesh did not make a servant of the Word, who was by nature Lord; but rather, not only was it that emancipation of all humanity which takes place by the Word, but that very Word who was by nature Lord, and then was made man, hath by means of a servant's form been made Lord of all and Christ, that is, in order to hallow all by the Spirit."[3]

In the following Athanasius argues that the text "I shall be their God" (Lev. 26.12) cannot reasonably be interpreted to mean that God has not always been God; nor can the saying that Christ has become Lord and eternal King mean that his Kingship has thereby increased. This Kingship is that which he has been given according to the flesh. (Ps. 109 (110).1 is given as proof-text.)[4]

Athanasius' views are here expressed with great clarity. Christ has

---
[1] Orat. 1 c. Arian. 46, PG 26.105 f.
[2] Orat. 2 c. Arian. 13 PG 26.173.
[3] *Ibid.*, 14, col. 176.
[4] *Ibid.*, col. 176 f.

a double Kingship: as the Logos he participates in the Kingship of God, and is *pantocrator*; as man he has been granted a Kingship in time, for our sakes. We have already noted that Alexandrian theology laid particular emphasis on the Logos as King (though he was not always considered to be King in the absolute sense favoured by Athanasius, and at least the left wing of the school of Origen thought of him as "the vicegerent of God"). Antiochene theology, as seen in its extreme representative Marcellus of Ancyra, connected the Kingship instead with his human nature (a view which has to do with an undue emphasis on the human nature, characterized by its opponents as "psilanthropism"). When we find Athanasius saying that both the Logos and the human nature are bearers of Kingship, each in its own way, this should not however be regarded as a compromise between the two views, though it may seem so at first sight. What is vital for Athanasius is the *homoousia* of the Son; his participation in the divine omnipotence is only a consequence of this. He rejects everything which might indicate that the Son is inferior in any way to the Father; for example, that he laid aside certain of his divine attributes at the Incarnation. Athanasius refuses to have anything to do with any form of *kenosis* theology. It is therefore necessary that what took place at his exaltation must have reference to his human nature, which is granted royal dignity. Athanasius' doctrine of the double Kingship is thus fully in agreement with his basic theology, and must be estimated against this background.

There is one striking difference between the views of the temporal Kingship of the Son favoured by Athanasius and Marcellus: the former did not regard the Incarnation as the sole point of departure in the same way as the latter. In his interpretation of the proof-texts Athanasius is much more nearly in line with traditional exegesis, according to which Christ was installed in his Kingship at his glorification, which followed his suffering (see e.g. Athanasius' interpretation of Ps. 23 and Acts 2.36).

There are however a number of passages in Athanasius which link the Kingship of Christ with the Incarnation. This is true of the infrequent passages dealing with Ps. 2.6 which, as we have seen, are of primary importance for Marcellus as Scriptural proofs of the temporal beginning of the Kingship of Christ—i.e. at the Incarnation.[1] It is im-

---

[1] See above, p. 234. In the *testimonia* tradition Ps. 2.6 plays an unimportant role. Ps. 2 is quoted in its entirety by St. Justin in Apol. 40.11–19. Otherwise it occurs

possible, in Athanasius' view, for the statement that Christ has been enthroned (καθεστάθην) as King on Zion to refer to his divine nature, which has possessed the Kingship from the beginning. It must mean that he has become man.¹ That he has become King on Zion means that he allowed his divine power to shine forth from Zion in human form, in order to save men and bring them to his Father's Kingdom.² "Zion" is interpreted literally as referring to the Jewish people.

Athanasius seems to be dependent here upon the Antiochene exegetical tradition. The Alexandrians interpreted the verse as referring to the Resurrection and Ascension—in line with the general allegorical principle according to which sayings on Jerusalem were interpreted as meaning the heavenly city.³ Such an interpretation is to be found in Origen⁴ and in St. Hilary of Poitiers.⁵

Ps. 44 (45).7 is also used by Athanasius as a proof-text for the Incarnation.⁶ In the earlier *testimonia* tradition this Psalm was linked with the baptism of Jesus, when he was anointed with the Spirit.⁷ But as we have seen, the Arians considered that this Psalm referred to the Son's anointing as God by the Father at the beginning of time.⁸ The important point for Athanasius is that it is the human nature of Christ which was made King by the divine unction; there can be no change in the divine nature. It may be that Athanasius is dependent here upon Antiochene tradition. Gnosticizing groups maintained that at his baptism the man Jesus was united with the heavenly Christ; it is likely, against this view, that the Psalm was early used to refer to the Incarnation, at which the Spirit became identified with the Logos. This development is to be seen in the passage from Paul of Samosata which

---

only in St. Cyprian, Ad Quir. 2.29, CSEL 3.1.97, as a testimony to Christ's eternal Kingship.

¹ Orat. 2 c. Arian. 11, PG 26.169.

² *Ibid.* 52, col. 257. Another exegesis, according to which Zion is the Church, appears in a catena fragment to Ps. 2.6, Op. Ath, ed. Maurina 1.2 (1777), pp. 805 f. It is probable that this text is authentic: see R. DEVREESSE in DB Suppl. 1, col. 1125.

³ Cf. above, pp. 221 ff.

⁴ Comm. on Jn. 13.58 (57), GCS Orig. 4.288 f. Comm. on Matt. 12.20 (the Latin version), GCS Orig. 10.115. Cf. Comm. on Jn. 6.39 (p. 147) and Comm. on Matt. Comm. ser. 130, GCS 11.267.

⁵ Tract. in Ps. 2, ch. 26, CSEL 22.56 f.

⁶ Epist. ad Marc. 6, PG 27.16. Cf. above, p. 279.

⁷ See above, p. 116.

⁸ See above, pp. 270 f.

we have quoted above,¹ and this may be taken to represent the wider Antiochene tradition.

As a final example of Athanasius' tendency to connect the Kingship with the Incarnation we may cite an exegesis of Ps. 109 (110), the authenticity of which is not satisfactorily established. In this exegesis v. 1 carries the double meaning of the human birth of Christ and his Ascension; ἡμέρα τῆς δυνάμεώς σου in v. 3 refers to his birth and ἐν ταῖς λαμπρότησι τῶν ἁγίων to the angels in the birth narrative.² But Athanasius' normal interpretation of this Psalm is the traditional one, according to which it refers to the Ascension of Christ.

It is not surprising to find such a tendency in Athanasius, even though it is far from prominent. If it is in fact true that the Kingship was granted to Christ's human nature through its connexion with the Logos, it follows that the Kingship began to exist as from the instant when the human nature and the Logos combined—at the Incarnation. Marcellus had already drawn this conclusion, and the close connexion between the two can scarcely have failed to influence the latter—quite apart from the fact that Marcellus seems on this point to favour a form of Antiochene exegesis which may have reached Athanasius along other paths.

The tendency, however, becomes much more marked in the later tradition, and particularly among exegetes with an Antiochene tendency. As far back as the 4th century the Kingship of Christ had begun to be shifted back from his glorification to his birth. This is typical of Byzantine theology, and is expressed most clearly in the growing observance of Christmas and in the development of Epiphany as the festival of the Kingship of Christ. Later development leads in the same direction: when the Council of Ephesus, 431, laid down that the Virgin Mary is *Theotokos*, this led to her being represented as a queen, seated upon a throne with the Christ Child upon her knee (see e.g. the mosaic on the triumphal arch of St. Maria Maggiore in Rome); the magi become kings, worshipping the true King, the infant Jesus.³

This shift in emphasis is especially noticeable in the interpretation

---

[1] See above, p. 239.

[2] Op. Ath, ed. Maurina 1.2.950.

[3] See H. BARRÉ, *La Royauté de Marie pendant les neuf premiers siècles*, RSR 29 (1939), pp. 129–162. The iconographical problem has recently been thoroughly investigated by G. A. WELLEN, *Theotokos* (1960), *passim* (with comprehensive references to literature). Cf. also GRABAR, *L'Empereur*, p. 198.

of the traditional testimonies of the Kingship of Christ, which come more and more to be referred to the Incarnation instead of the Ascension. The change became permanent in the Church's Scriptural exegesis, and the new emphasis is normative even today. It is of considerable interest to observe the central role played by the royal Psalms in the Christmas liturgy of the present-day Roman and Byzantine rites.[1]

We consider it highly likely that this change of emphasis is to be traced back to a pre-Constantinian tradition of exposition, found in its extreme form in Marcellus of Ancyra and applied in a more moderate form by Athanasius. Subsequent development took place largely in accordance with the views of Athanasius: Marcellus' denial that the Logos is King and his idea that the Kingdom of Christ will cease to exist at the end of time were never adopted, and the latter was condemned as heresy by the Council of Constantinople in 381.

Lampe has examined a number of expositions of the doctrine of Christ's temporal Kingship, and considers that we are here dealing with a group of ideas influenced by Marcellus, despite his reputation as a heretic.[2] Although extremely well documented, Lampe's monograph lacks precision. He fails to draw a clear distinction between those authors who favour the general idea of an "economic" Kingship, and those who emulate Marcellus in linking the Kingship with the Incarnation. Nor does he allow there to have been an Antiochene tradition existing alongside Marcellus, which resembled Marcellus' views without being identical. Further, the name of St. Athanasius is conspicuous by its absence from Lampe's essay.

Lampe points out that the interpretation of Ps. 2.6 and 96.1 to refer to the Incarnation is typical of Marcellus' theology, and considers that this characteristic is to be found in the work of a number of later authors. But a number of the expositions quoted by Lampe do not actually connect these verses with the Incarnation; they say only that the statement that Christ has become King must apply to his human nature, since he possesses the Kingship from the beginning, being God.

---

[1] A good survey of these motives in the liturgy of the Christmas cycle is given by LEMARIÉ, *La manifestation du Seigneur*, pp. 93 ff. and *passim*. Cf. also A. MANSER, *Christkönigszüge im römischen und benediktinischen Adventsgottesdienst*, in Heilige Überlieferung, Festgabe ... I. Herwegen (1938), pp. 124–135.

[2] LAMPE, *Exegesis*, pp. 169 ff. Cf. also IDEM, *Some Notes on the significance of* ΒΑΣΙΛΕΙΑ ΤΟΥ ΘΕΟΥ, ΒΑΣΙΛΕΙΑ ΧΡΙΣΤΟΥ, *in the Greek Fathers*, JTS 49 (1948), pp. 58–73, where the same texts are discussed from somewhat different aspects.

This exegesis, as found in the two Antiochene theologians Theodoret of Cyrus[1] and Theodore of Mopsuestia,[2] corresponds to the general post-Athanasian doctrine of the Nicenes. It is likely that these authors, particularly remembering their Antiochene background, really considered that according to Ps. 2.6, the human nature became King by being united with the Logos at the Incarnation. But since neither said anything about which element in the economy of salvation was intended, it is conceivable—at least in theory— that one or both, in common with the Alexandrian exegetes, believed the verse in question to refer to the enthronement of the human nature in the heavenly city at the Ascension.

There are two other texts quoted by Lampe: one is a fragment of a catena attributed to Cyril of Alexandria, but of dubious authenticity.[3] The other is a homily on Ps. 96 (97).1 among the *spuria* of St. John Chrysostom, and which in all probability dates from the 4th century.[4] Neither of these authors has any hesitation in connecting the Kingship with the Incarnation, and it seems likely that both are of Antiochene origin. But we have no reason to suppose there to have been any influence from Marcellus. We might equally well speak of influence from Athanasius, who used the same exegesis, but it may well be a case of influence from that tradition upon which both Marcellus and Athanasius drew for their link between the Kingship and the Incarnation. The hypothesis of influence from Marcellus is also contradicted by the fact that Pseudo-Chrysostom's homily includes a polemic directed expressly against Marcellus and his doctrine that the Kingdom of Christ is destined to cease in time.[5]

---

[1] In Ps. 2.6, ed. SCHULZE 1.2 (1769), p. 620. Note however that the authenticity of Theodoretus' Psalm commentary, preserved only in the form of catena fragments, has not yet been sufficiently demonstrated. SCHULZE's edition (also reprinted in PG 80), builds mainly on two manuscripts, *Monac.* 478 and 527, which do not seem quite reliable. A. RAHLFS has made a list of older manuscripts of Theodoret's Psalm commentary in his *Verzeichnis der griechischen Handschriften des Alten Testaments für das Septuaginta-Unternehmen aufgestellt*, GN 1914, Beiheft, pp. 405 ff. DEVREESSE also mentions among his *desiderata* a critical edition founded on these manuscripts, (DB Suppl. 1, col. 1134), but such an edition has not yet been published.

[2] In Ps. 2.6, ed. DEVREESSE, p. 11.

[3] In Ps. 2.6, PG 69.720 f. The authenticity of Cyril's Psalm commentary, consisting of catena fragments, is so dubious that it is impossible to use it in its present state for scientific work.

[4] In Ps. 96.1, PG 55.604 f.

[5] This is also pointed out by LAMPE, *Exegesis*, p. 173.

Lampe is much too one-sided in his derivation of the doctrine of the Kingship κατὰ σάρκα from Marcellus; he is also far too prone to find reminiscences of Marcellus' interpretation of 1 Cor. 15.28 in the work of later authors. One of these is St. Gregory of Nazianzus, who is deserving of mention not only on this account, but also because he has an excellent summary of the doctrine of the double Kingship of Christ, as earlier seen in St. Athanasius:

"He is said to be King, in one sense because he is *Pantocrator* and King over those who desire it or not, and in another sense ... because he has placed under his sway ourselves who voluntarily accept his government. Of his Kingdom conceived in the former sense there is no end; of his second Kingdom what shall be the end? The reception of us, saved, under his hand."[1]

It is quite out of the question that St. Gregory would have expressed his approval of a doctrine which his contemporaries had generally condemned as heretical. It is only reasonable to suppose that his interpretation of 1 Cor. 15.28 was different from that of Marcellus. Lampe himself seems to have provided us with the solution. Referring to his quotation of Pseudo-Chrysostom's homily he draws our attention to the efforts of 4th-century theologians to resolve the tension between Lk. 1.33 and 1 Cor. 15.28—how the βασιλεία of Christ can be eternal and at the same time be subjected to the Father at the end of time. As Lampe points out, we find in Eusebius and later in Gregory of Nyssa and the homily Lampe himself quotes a solution of the problem according to which βασιλεία is taken to mean both Kingship and Kingdom. The Kingship of Christ—his kingly and sovereign power—is eternal; the Kingdom which he renders to the Father consists of those who are ruled by him (τοὺς ὑπ' αὐτοῦ βασιλευομένους).[2] The same view is reflected in the text from St. Gregory of Nazianzus which we quoted above.

But the validity of this explanation is even more extensive than it would appear from Lampe's account. St. Athanasius uses precisely the same argument, saying that the Kingdom which is rendered to the Father is identical with the faithful.[3] The same statement is found in

---

[1] St. Gregory of Nazianzus, Orat. 30.4, PG 36.108.
[2] Eusebius, Eccl. theol. III.16.3, GCS Eus. 4.175.
[3] De incarn. et c. Arian. 20, PG 26.1020 f.: Ἡμεῖς γάρ ἐσμεν οἱ ἐν αὐτῷ ὑποτασσόμενοι τῷ πατρί ...

both St. Hilary[1] and St. Ambrose;[2] they are agreed that Christ does not lose the Kingdom by rendering it to the Father.[3]

Thus during the 4th century there was a widespread exegetical tradition of exposition of 1 Cor. 15.28, according to which Christ is to render his Kingdom (the Church) to the Father, but continue to reign over it for all eternity. An exception to this rule is Marcellus, whose ideas on the subject are to be traced not only to his distinctive doctrine of the Incarnation (which anticipated Nestorianism), but also to his economical doctrine of the Trinity, according to which the Logos will be incorporated into the Monas at the end of time. The mere fact of an author talking about the end of the Kingdom of Christ, and basing his conclusions on 1 Cor. 15.28, need not imply influence from Marcellus; other agreements are necessary before the case for influence can be considered proven. The parallels which Lampe has shown to have existed between Marcellus and later authors are due rather to their having had a common background—remembering that their two main points, that Christ's βασιλεία κατὰ σάρκα had a beginning in time (Ps. 2.6) and will have an end in the last days (1 Cor. 15.28), are both to be found in Athanasius.[4]

---

[1] St. Hilary, De Trin. 11.39, PL 10.424: "Non enim ait: 'Tradet suum regnum'; sed 'Tradet regnum' ... Nos itaque tradet in regnum."

[2] St. Ambrose, De fide 5.12 (146), PL 16.677 f.: "Venit in hunc mundum, ut regnum sibi pareret ex nobis." Ibid. 5.12 (147): "Venit ergo Jesus in hanc terram regnum accipere de nobis, quibus ait: 'Regnum Dei intra vos est' (Lk 17.21). Hoc est regnum quod Christus accepit, hoc est quod Patri tradidit. Nam quomodo regnum accepit, qui erat rex sempiternus." Ibid. 5.12 (150), col. 678: "Tradet igitur Patri regnum suum Filius? Non deperit Christo regnum quod tradit, sed perficit. Nos sumus regnum, quia nobis dictum est: 'Regnum intra vos est' (Lk 17.21)."

[3] St. Hilary, De Trin. 11.29, PL 10.418 f.: "... videamus an traditio regni defectio sit intelligenda regnandi; ut quod tradit Filius Patri, tradendo non teneat. Quod si quis stultae impietatis furore contendet; fateatur necesse est Patrem, cum tradidit omnia Filio, amisisse tradendo si tradidisse traditis egere significat. Ait enim Dominus: 'Omnia mihi tradita sunt e patre meo' (Lk 10.22) et rursum: 'Data est mihi omnis potestas in caelo et in terra' (Matt. 28.18). Si igitur tradidisse caruisse est; Patre quoque his quae dedet caruit. Quod si Pater tradendo non caruit; ne Filius quidem intelligi potest his egere quae tradit."

[4] 1 Cor. 15.28 is also quoted by Eunomius, Apol. 27, PG 30.865; from this quotation G. H. WILLIAMS (*Christology* 2, p. 17) has drawn the rash conclusion that according to the Arians the Kingdom of Christ would come to an end. This is however not the Arian conception; see above, p. 272. That an author quotes 1 Cor. 15.28 is of course no proof of his theological position. 1 Cor. belonged to the canonical writings in the early Church!

The Nicene theologians exhibit a general tendency to interpret the Kingship of Christ economically; so much can be said without needing to bring in the subject of the influence of Marcellus. The Kingship which he possesses by nature *qua* God has been passed on to man in his work of salvation, and man has been granted royal dignity thereby. The background of this tendency is to be seen rather in St. Athanasius' doctrine of the double Kingship than in Marcellus' one-sided linking of the Kingship with Christ's human nature alone.

The change of emphasis from the divine to the human nature of Christ is clearly seen in the Nicene exposition of Ps. 2.7, "Thou art my son, this day I have begotten thee"—a verse which the post-Nicene exegetical tradition has generally supposed to refer to the birth of Christ, but which at an earlier period was interpreted in a different way. It is one of the most outstanding of the Messianic texts quoted in the NT,[1] but its application varies considerably: it is connected with Jesus' baptism (Mk. 1.11 par.),[2] transfiguration[3] and resurrection (Acts 13.33). The text has little significance in the oldest *testimonia* tradition: the latter part of the verse is used in anti-Jewish polemics to show that Christ is King, not only of the Jews, but of the Gentiles as well.[4]

St. Justin quotes the verse once in connexion with the baptism of Jesus,[5] and Tertullian once, though in connexion with the transfiguration.[6] There are also slight indications from the earliest period

---

[1] PLOOIJ, *Baptism*, pp. 246 f. KOSNETTER, *Taufe, passim*. ARVEDSON, *Mysterium Christi*, pp. 123 ff. CHEVALLIER, *L'Esprit*, pp. 3 ff. LÖVESTAM, *Son and Saviour*, *passim*.

[2] It has been claimed that Mk 1.11 is founded only on Isa. 42.1, which has no doubt influenced the later part of the proclamation, and υἱός is thus a translation of עבד in Isa. 42.1. So J. JEREMIAS, *The Servant of God*, SBT 20 (1957), pp. 80 ff., and CULLMANN, *Christologie*, p. 65 (who considers that Ps. 2.7 may also have influenced the text). LÖVESTAM's investigation shows however that it is hardly possible to eliminate Ps. 2.7 from the proclamation at Jesus' baptism, *op. cit.*, pp. 94 ff. Cf. also CHEVALLIER, *op. cit.*, pp. 62 ff.

[3] RIESENFELD, *Jésus Transfiguré*, pp. 250 ff., especially points out how the proclamation of Jesus as the Son of God in the Transfiguration narrative implies his enthronement as King. On Ps. 2.7 as a royal enthronement hymn, see *ibid.*, p. 68.

[4] St. Justin, Dial. 122.5. St. Irenaeus, Dem. 49. Tertullian, Adv. Marc. III.20.3, CCL 1.535, Adv. Jud. 12.1, CCL 2.1384.

[5] Dial. 88.8.

[6] Adv. Marc. IV.22.8, CCL 1.602.

that it was referred to Jesus' birth: in the *Dialogue between Timothy and Aquila*, which has been dated to ca. 200.[1]

Ps. 2.7 was put to new use in anti-Modalist polemics as a proof-text for the Son's eternal birth from the Father. The verse is used in this way by Tertullian[2] and, following him, by Novatian.[3] The same interpretation is to be found in Alexandrian exegesis, in Origen[4] and Eusebius;[5] it is likely that the Arians derived this use of the verse from Alexandrian tradition, together with their general tendency to refer testimonies to the Kingship of Christ back to his pre-existence.[6]

It is not quite clear what was St. Athanasius' attitude to the interpretation of Ps. 2.7, but it seems likely that in accordance with his general principles he considered it to refer to the temporal birth of Christ.[7] At all events, this interpretation is to be found in later An-

---

[1] Anecdota Oxon. 8, p. 70. On the dating, see A. L. WILLIAMS, *Adversus Judaeos*, pp. 67 ff.

[2] Adv. Prax. 7.2 and 11.3, CCL 2.1165, 1171.

[3] De Trin. 26, ed. FAUSSET, p. 94.

[4] Comm. on Jn. I. 29 (31) GCS Orig. 4.37. According to a catena fragment in Codex *Vindob.* 8, attributed to Origen, Ps. 2.7 referred to the birth of Christ in the flesh, see *Commentaires inédits des Psaumes*, ed. R. CADIOU (1936), p. 72. CADIOU considers that this exegesis is an archaïc feature, expressing Origen's opinion during his earlier years (*op. cit.*, p. 42). The attribution is however uncertain, as in most catena fragments. Nor does the exegesis seem to be very ancient; as we have seen, no ancient expositions of Ps. 2.7 in which the verse is said to be a prophecy of the Incarnation are known.

[5] In Ps. 71 (72).1, PG 23.792 f. According to this catena fragment the human nature in Christ is another King than the King speaking in Ps. 2.6 f.: thus this Psalm refers to the Divine nature, according to Eusebius. The text comes from *Coislin* 44, and is certainly authentic, see DEVREESSE in DB Suppl. 1, col. 1122 f. Another fragment of a commentary in Ps. 2.7, attributed to Eusebius (PG 23.88), in which the verse is said to refer to the birth according to the flesh, comes from a manuscript which DEVREESSE characterizes as "totalement négligeable", *op. cit.*, col. 1123.

[6] Cf. above, pp. 270 f.

[7] According to a catena fragment on Ps. 2.7, attributed to St. Athanasius (PG 27.68), the words "Thou art my Son" are said about the eternal existence; "to-day I have begotten thee" about the birth κατὰ σάρκα. Its authenticity is however most uncertain. This text is not taken from the Maurine edition (as are most Athanasian chains quoted here) but belongs to a part of MIGNE's edition, which is reprint from MONTFAUCON's *Collectio nova Patrum* 2. The text is taken from a rather late manuscript, *Ambros.* B. 134 sup., which is a compilation from different chains in Escorial. See DEVREESSE in DB Suppl. 1, col. 1125. Also the pseudo-Athanasian Orat. 4 c. Arian. 11, PG 26.169 and *ibid.* 52, col. 257, claims that Ps. 2.7 is said about Christ's

tiochene-influenced exegetes—in Theodoret of Cyrus[1] and Theodore of Mopsuestia,[2] both of whom reckon the verse as referring to the birth of Christ κατὰ σάρκα. A western Nicene theologian, St. Hilary of Poitiers, gives a totally different interpretation: that the verse, in connexion with Acts 13.33, refers to the Resurrection.[3] The Alexandrians', and Tertullian's, earlier opinion that it had to do with the eternal generation of the Son, has evidently been pushed into the background as suspected Arianism. The main cause of this was that the word σήμερον (today) could all too easily suggest the Arians' doctrine that the Son was born of the Father in time, although Origen had already tried to evade such an interpretation by declaring the expression to be allegorical.[4] It is however of interest to note that the Nicene theologians' interpretations vary, and that the Antiochene theologians' opinion, that it had to do with the birth of Jesus, is in line with their general tendency to stress the significance of the Incarnation.

We have a similar situation in connexion with Ps. 71 (72).1: again a verse which is of little significance in the *testimonia* tradition,[5] but which is taken up and given an allegorical interpretation in Alexandrian exegesis. The parallelism of the verse (Give the king thy judgements, O God, and thy righteousness unto the king's son.) is used by Origen as a basis upon which to expound his doctrine of the double Kingship of Christ—which in this respect anticipates Athanasius. "The king"

---

birth in time. On this writing, see QUASTEN, *Patrology* 3, pp. 27 f. (with references to literature).

[1] In Ps. 2.7, ed. SCHULZE 1.2.621. On the matter of authenticity, see above, p. 285 n. 1.

[2] In Ps. 2.7, ed. DEVREESSE, p. 13. The catena fragment on Ps. 2.7, which (probably wrongly) is attributed to Cyril of Alexandria (PG 69.721) may possibly be of Antiochene origin. On the chains of St. Cyril, see above, p. 285 n. 3. Here, too, Ps. 2.7 is said to be a prophecy of Christ's birth κατὰ σάρκα. The text is a natural sequel to the (ps.-)Cyrillic exegesis of Ps. 2.6, mentioned above.

[3] Tract. in Ps. 2, ch. 30, CSEL 22.59.

[4] According to Comm. on Jn. 1.29, it is said "today", because it is always "today" with God.

[5] The verse is quoted, in St. Justin, Dial. 34.2 and 64.6, but Justin's main interest is to claim that the Psalm does not refer to Solomon. The same polemic also occurs in Tertullian, Adv. Marc. V.9.6 ff., CCL 1.689 f. On the relation between Jewish and Marcionite exegesis, see above, pp. 95 f. St. Cyprian takes up the verse as a testimony that Christ is Judge and King, Ad Quir. 2.30, CSEL 3.1.99.

refers to the divine nature: "the king's son" to the human nature;[1] this interpretation was later taken over by Eusebius.[2]

This exegesis, assuming as it did that the human nature of Christ was really not accorded royal character, was forced to give way for other interpretations advanced by the orthodox theologians. One exegesis of the Psalm, ascribed to St. Athanasius and probably authentic, says, referring to this verse, that both "the king" and "the king's son" refer to the human nature. Further, that it is because of the human nature that the King may be said to receive righteousness, although he is himself the righteousness of the Father (in his divine nature).[3] This interpretation is completely in line with Athanasius' anti-Arian exposition of Scripture: since there can be no change in the pre-existent Son, the text cannot mean that the Father gives the Son a righteousness that he did not possess by nature; it must therefore be the human nature that is referred to. The ascription of this exegesis of the Psalm to St. Athanasius thus seems to be justified, not only textually, but also with respect to its contents.

The parallelism, which plays no real part in St. Athanasius' exegesis, recurs in a catena fragment attributed to Theodoret of Cyrus.[4] Here Christ is not only King but also the King's Son, both as God and as man: as God he is Son of the All-King (παμβασιλεύς); as man he is Son of David, and he has received righteousness as a man. This exegesis has to do with the fully developed doctrine of the double Kingship of Christ, as we have earlier observed it in the post-Nicene tradition.

Finally, the same tendency is to be seen in the development of exegesis of two other verses from the Psalter: Ps. 96 (97).1 and 98 (99).1, both of which were used by Marcellus as proof-texts of the temporal Kingship of the Son, beginning at the Incarnation. The former is of no importance in the *testimonia* tradition;[5] Ps. 98.1, however, is found on a number of occasions in St. Justin as a testimony to the Kingship of Christ, without going into details,[6] and St. Irenaeus

---

[1] Comm. on Jn. 1.28, GCS Orig. 4.35 f.: ἡγοῦμαι οὖν βασιλέα μὲν λέγεσθαι τὴν προηγουμένην τοῦ πρωτοτόκου πάσης κτίσεως φύσιν, ἣ δίδοται διὰ τὸ ὑπερέχειν τὸ κρίνειν· τὸν δὲ ἄνθρωπον, ὃν ἀνείληφεν ὑπ' ἐκείνης μορφούμενον κατὰ δικαιοσύνην ⟨καὶ⟩ ἐκτυπούμενον, υἱὸς τοῦ βασιλέως.

[2] In Ps. 71.1, PG 23.792 f. The text is certainly authentic, see above, p. 289 n. 5.

[3] Op. Ath., ed. Maurina, 1.2.897.

[4] In Ps. 71.1, ed. Schulze 1.2.1102. On its authenticity, see above, p. 285 n. 1.

[5] Only St. Cyprian, Ad Quir. 2.29, CSEL 3.1.98.

[6] Dial. 37.2–4 and 64.4.

interprets it as referring to the Ascension.¹ There is no example earlier than Marcellus of either of these Psalms being referred to the Incarnation; still St. Jerome referred both to Christ's glorification, thus reproducing in all likelihood an older Christological interpretation.² On the other hand we have in the catenas attributed to Theodoret of Cyrus as exposition according to which both verses refer not only to the human nature of Christ, but also to his epiphany.³ Pseudo-Chrysostom's homily on Ps. 96.1 contains a similar exposition.⁴ The author, partly for anti-Arian reasons, states that the Kingship which is referred to is the Kingship of Christ κατὰ σάρκα. He also dates the inauguration of the Kingship to the Incarnation. The Kingship adopted by Christ is that previously possessed by David, but usurped by daemons; he supports this view with a quotation from Lk. 1.32 (Ps. 131.11) "And the Lord God will give to him the throne of his father David". The interpretation of the name Jesus—"for he will save his people from their sins" (Matt. 1.21)—the author considers to prove that Christ had "a people" which he could call his own even before his Passion.⁵ The one who is to receive the throne from God is he who has been born in the human economy: the throne which God gives him is not the heavenly throne, of which Christ was already the possessor, but the throne of David.⁶ The homily concludes with a polemic aimed

¹ Adv. haer. IV.33.13, ed. Harvey 2.268.

² Tract. in Ps. 96.1, CCL 78.157 f., says that the Psalm is speaking about the exultation of the saved people. The interpretation of the Psalm is more clearly seen in Tract. in Ps. 98.1, CCL 78.167 ff. St. Jerome here treats the Psalms which begin with the words *Dominus regnavit*: according to him Ps. 96 ought to come after Ps. 98, which, according to St. Jerome, refers to the passion and glorification of Christ. Thus Ps. 96 according to St. Jerome has to do with the Kingship that Christ received after his suffering.

³ In Ps. 96.1, ed. Schulze 1.2.1296: βασιλεῦσαι δὲ τὸν κύριον ἔφη, οὐχ ὡς τὸ τηνικαῦτα τὴν βασιλείαν δεξάμενον, ἀλλ' ὡς τότε τοῖς ἀνθρώποις τὴν οἰκείαν δείξαντα βασιλείαν. In Ps. 98.1, p. 1306: προαγορεύει δὲ καὶ σωτῆρος ἡμῶν τὴν ἐπιφάνειαν, καὶ τῶν Ἰουδαίων τὴν ἀπιστίαν. For its authenticity, see above, p. 285 n. 1. The conception that Ps. 96.1 refers to the epiphany of Christ also appears in the (ps.-) Cyrillic fragment on Ps. 96.1, PG 69.1248. For this use of the term ἐπιφάνεια, which is different from that discussed above, pp. 67 ff., see Mohrmann, *Epiphania*, p. 657.

⁴ Ps.-Chrysostom, In Ps. 96.1, PG 55.604 f. See Lampe, *Exegesis*, pp. 171 ff., which also has an account of the contents of the homily.

⁵ *Ibid.*, col. 604: λέγει τὸν λαὸν αὐτοῦ, ἵνα μάθης, ὅτι οὐ μετὰ τὸ πάθος λαὸς ὁ λαός · ἵνα μάθης, ὅτι οὐ μετὰ τὸ πάθος ἐκληρονόμησε λαόν, ἀλλ' εἶχε μὲν τὸν λαὸν, ὡς δεσπότης τοῦ λαοῦ, καὶ πρὸ τοῦ πάθους, ἀνεκτήσατο δὲ τῷ πάθει τὴν οἰκουμενικὴν ἐκκλησίαν.

⁶ *Ibid.*, καὶ δώσει αὐτοῦ κύριος. Τίνι; τῷ ὑπὸ σοῦ τικτομένῳ τῇ ἐνσάρκῳ οἰκονομίᾳ.

at Marcellus' doctrine of the temporal limitation of the Kingdom of the Son.

Without claiming to be an authority in the history of art, we should like to record our opinion here that the ideological background of the origin of the *Majestas* image is not to be sought for in the political metaphysics of Eusebius, but in Nicene theology. Stange is quite right when he points out, without however drawing the natural consequences of his argument, that the *Majestas* image became popular in the West after St. Athanasius came to Rome in 340 and won over the Roman Church for his cause.[1] Not until the end of the century did the first *Majestas* images appear in the hitherto Arian-dominated East.[2]

The idea of the Kingship of Christ is, as we have seen, by no means foreign either to the Arians or to Eusebius, but his Kingship is traditionally linked with his role as God's vicegerent over the world. A symbolic representation of this tradition, influenced as it was by Philonic ideas, has long existed in art, where Christ is represented as shepherd, as steersman or as charioteer in accordance with the political metaphors which were transferred to the Logos. Although there were no *Majestas* images in the pre-Constantinian period, there were representations of Christ as King in the terms of early Logos theology.[3]

What distinguishes the 4th century *Majestas* image from these representations is that Christ is depicted as a King also in respect of his human nature. He is depicted as enthroned upon the vault of heaven, i.e. as the incarnate and ascended Lord. He is depicted in royal garments, giving the law to St. Peter—this too being a sign of the royal authority granted to the glorified Lord. The apocalyptic ideas of Rev. are of importance in this iconographical context.[4]

In the continuing struggle against Arianism it was not only art, but also the liturgy, which came to be used as a weapon. Prayers to Christ and doxologies are of importance, as are the royal epithets con-

---

[1] STANGE, *Kirchengebäude*, p. 85.

[2] VAN DER MEER, *Maiestas Domini*, pp. 255 ff.

[3] Cf. J. FINK, *Die Anfänge der Christusdarstellung*, ThR 51 (1955), pp. 241–252, who considers that the representation of Christ in iconography was influenced by imperial art as far back as the 3rd century. That the Arians were not opposed to imperial symbolism is clear from the decorations in the Arian baptistery in Ravenna, where the *etimasia* has a central position: see NORDSTRÖM, *Ravennastudien*, pp. 34 ff.

[4] VAN DER MEER, *op. cit., passim.*

nected with the invocations in the prayers.[1] This complex of ideas however lies outside the bounds of this study.

---

[1] J. A. JUNGMANN, *Stellung Christi*, pp. 151 ff. IDEM, *Die Abwehr des germanischen Arianismus und der Umbruch der religiösen Kultur im frühen Mittelalter*, ZKT 69 (1947), pp. 36–99. Cf. above, p. 160.

13. PANTOCRATOR AND HYPSISTOS

Christus Pantocrator

In the history of art the word *Pantocrator* is used to describe a particular form of the *Majestas* image; it is often used more generally of representations of Christ as King.[1] We cannot go into the question of why just *Pantocrator* has been used in this way. But the term is well chosen, since παντοκράτωρ came into use as a Christological title at about the same time as the first *Majestas* representations originated, i.e. at the beginning of the 4th century. The word παντοκράτωρ is used in the NT and the post-Apostolic age before ca. 300 A.D. only of the Father; not until Athanasius' anti-Arian polemic was its meaning widened to include the Son. As far as we are aware there is no study in existence of the use of the term in the early Church, and we shall therefore attempt to remedy the omission by giving a short account of its development.

The word παντοκράτωρ (from πᾶν, *all*, and κρατεῖν, *to rule*), came relatively late to Greek, being of Hellenistic origin. The older and more common word is παγκρατής, often used as an attribute of Zeus, and it is probable that παντοκράτωρ has developed from it, in connexion with such word-forms as κοσμοκράτωρ, αὐτοκράτωρ, etc.[2] We have evidence that the word was also used as an attribute of Hermes, Attis, Mandulis and other gods (παντοκράτειρα occurs as a title of Isis). But there is little or no evidence that the word was ever used as a royal title or elsewhere in political or legal contexts.[3]

---

[1] So L'ORANGE, *Studies*, pp. 165 ff.

[2] W. MICHAELIS, art. παντοκράτωρ, ThWB 3 (1935–38), pp. 913–914, gr. KRUSE, art. *Pantokrator*, PWK 18.2 (1949), col. 829–830. BAG, pp. 613 f.

[3] Cf. KATTENBUSCH, *Das apostolische Symbol* 2, p. 526. According to KATTENBUSCH παντοκράτωρ is a political term which has secondarily been transferred to God, but he gives no evidence for this view. It is often said that παντοκράτωρ has a political sense (so of course also by EHRHARDT, *Politische Metaphysik* 2, p. 27), but we still have seen no reason for this presumption.

It is characteristic of the Greek style of hymnody that the gods are given epithets combined with πᾶν.[1] The god nourishes and supports all, sees all, hears all, knows all and is ruler over the all. Later we shall consider two adjectives combined with πᾶν: παντοδύναμος and παμβασιλεύς.

In Hellenistic Judaism παντοκράτωρ was adopted as an attribute of Yahweh; this usage occurs in two inscriptions from Gorgippia and extremely often in the magical papyri.[2] But most significant is the fact that it was introduced into the LXX in the phrase κύριος παντοκράτωρ, the word being the equivalent of צבאות or שדי.[3] The expression יהוה צבאות is however sometimes translated by κύριος σαβαώθ or κύριος τῶν δυνάμεων. Ps. 23 (24).10, which the early Church interpreted as referring to Christ, uses the latter translation. The word was later taken over by the Christian Church, either from the LXX or from the language of the synagogue.

In the NT παντοκράτωρ is found once only outside Rev.: in 2 Cor. 6.18, which is a reminiscence from the LXX.[4] In Rev., on the other hand, the word occurs nine times (1.8, 4.8, 11.17, 15.3, 16.7, 14, 19.6, 15, 21.22). Rev. 4.8 is a quotation from Isa. 6.3 LXX; in most of the other passages the word occurs in set phrases, having the character of formal acclamations, and highly liturgical in their nature.[5] Their background is to be sought in the LXX and the synagogue liturgy.

One particular use is together with expressions of God's existence in the beginning, now and to eternity: Ἐγώ εἰμι τὸ ἄλφα καὶ τὸ ὦ, λέγει κύριος ὁ θεός, ὁ ὢν καὶ ὁ ἦν καὶ ὁ ἐρχόμενος, ὁ παντοκράτωρ (1.8); ἅγιος ἅγιος ἅγιος κύριος ὁ θεὸς ὁ παντοκράτωρ, ὁ ἦν καὶ ὁ ὢν καὶ ὁ ἐρχόμενος (4.8); εὐχαριστοῦμέν σοι, κύριε ὁ θεὸς ὁ παντοκράτωρ, ὁ ὢν καὶ ὁ ἦν (11.17). The author of Rev. is evidently very fond of connecting the word

---

[1] See K. Keysner, *Gottesvorstellung und Lebensauffassung im griechischen Hymnus*, WStA 2 (1932), pp. 28 ff., 45.

[2] G. F. Moore, *Judaism in the first Centuries of the Christian Era* 1 (1927), pp. 374 ff. C. H. Dodd, *The Bible and the Greeks* (1934), p. 19. Michaelis, pp. 913 f. According to St. Gregorius of Nazianzus (Orat. 18.5, PG 35.990 f.), the Jewish syncretistic movement, called *Hypsistarians* (see below, pp. 307 f.), only prayed to the παντοκράτωρ.

[3] Schermann, *Zauberpapyri*, p. 23. Kruse, *Pantokrator*, col. 829 f.

[4] Windisch, *Comm. ad loc.*

[5] Peterson, Εἷς θεός, pp. 313 ff.

παντοκράτωρ with these phrases, particularly as an expression of God's Lordship, not only over the cosmos, but also over time.¹

In all these passages παντοκράτωρ refers to God, and the author has obviously avoided using it of Christ, despite the fact that many other attributes are predicated in Rev. of the Father and the Son indiscriminately.² Nor is the typical expression ὁ ὢν καὶ ὁ ἦν etc. (1.4, 8, 4.8, 11.17) used of Christ, who is instead called ὁ πρῶτος καὶ ὁ ἔσχατος (1.17, 22.13) or ἡ ἀρχὴ καὶ τὸ τέλος (21.6, 22.13). In 1.14 a clear distinction is drawn between ὁ ὢν καὶ ὁ ἦν καὶ ὁ ἐρχόμενος and Christ, who is called ὁ μάρτυς ὁ πιστός. The author seems to be following certain definite principles for drawing a terminological distinction between the Father and the Son; it is, however, difficult to determine the nature of the principles in question. So much is clear: that παντοκράτωρ is one of the terms used only of the Father. We can discern the influence of the LXX and its use of the title παντοκράτωρ to render Yahweh Sebaot.

This rule, that παντοκράτωρ is reserved for the Father, continues to apply in the post-canonical literature up to the 4th century. There is no evidence from this period that the title παντοκράτωρ was ever used to refer to Christ.³ The word is most familiar as an attribute of the Father in the most ancient Christian *symbola*.⁴ This seems to indicate that the term παντοκράτωρ was understood as being restricted to the

---

¹ The use of παντοκράτωρ as a noun is dependent on the Jewish conception of Sabaoth as a special name of God. See A. MARMORSTEIN, *Zur Erklärung der Gottesnamen bei Irenäus*, ZNW 25 (1926), pp. 255 f. SCHLATTER, *Das Alte Testament*, pp. 12 f. and ALLO, *L'Apocalypse*, p. 7, point out that ὁ ὤν etc. is a paraphrase of the name Yahweh Sabaoth. Cf. also 1 Tim. 1.17 where God is styled βασιλεὺς τῶν αἰώνων.

² Cf. LOHMEYER, *Comm. ad loc.*

³ A Coptic magical text in which Christ is invoked with the formula ιαω ιαω πεχ̅ρ̅ παητοκρατωρ, cannot be reckoned as belonging to Christian literature, *Ausgewählte koptische Zaubertexte*, ed. A. M. KROPP (1930–31): the text is edited in tome 1, pp. 22 ff. (see especially lines 4, 39, 63, 82), a translation follows in tome 2, pp. 149 ff. and a commentary in tome 3, § 49 (pp. 32 f.). The text has a strongly syncretistic tendency, and the epithets for Christ are taken from the most diverse religious traditions. Cf. V. STEGEMANN, *Die Gestalt Christi in den koptischen Zaubertexten*, QSGKAM 1 (1934), pp. 19 ff. For the identification of Christ with Iao, see DÖLGER, ΙΧΘΥΣ 1, pp. 268 ff.

⁴ Comprehensive, though far from complete, surveys of the use of παντοκράτωρ in the early Church are given by KATTENBUSCH, *Das apostolische Symbol* 2, pp. 520 ff., 537 ff. and *passim*, and by H. HOMMEL, *Pantokrator*, ThV 5 (1953–54), pp. 348 ff.

Father, in more or less the same way as ἅγιος was restricted to the Spirit.

Such exceptions as we encounter only serve to prove the rule. In the *Epistle of St. Clement* and in the *Shepherd of Hermas* παντοκράτωρ serves as an adjectival qualification of ὄνομα. Note, however, that in Jewish practice *the Name* referred to God himself.[1] Clement of Alexandria twice uses παντοκράτωρ as an adjectival qualification of ὁ πατρικὸς λόγος.[2] This is due to Clement's distinctive Logos theology, and does not imply that the Son was given the epithet in question.[3]

So late as in a 4th century author like Eusebius, παντοκράτωρ was still being used to refer only to the Father. In *Praeparatio evangelica* and *De ecclesiastica theologia* he uses the word παντοκράτωρ seven times in all, always in connexion with θεός and πατήρ.[4] A more common term in Eusebius is παμβασιλεύς, which is not confined to the Father, but can equally well refer to the Logos.[5]

We first meet the word παντοκράτωρ referring to Christ in the work of St. Athanasius, and there can be little doubt that it was he who introduced the term in this meaning, or at least, that it was he who ensured that it became known and used in the Church.[6]

When we examine Athanasius' use of the title παντοκράτωρ, we

---

[1] Clem. 60.4, Hermas, Vis. III.3.5. See BIETENHARD, art. ὄνομα p. 276 n. 225, where it is pointed out that ὄνομα has become a hypostasis in Hermas. DANIÉLOU's opinion that ὄνομα in Hermas means the Son (*Judéo-christianisme*, pp. 203 ff.) is not quite convincing. N.b. that παντοκράτωρ or παντοκρατορικός stands as an epithet for God's βούλημα in Clem. 8.5.

[2] Paed. I.9.84, GCS Clem. 1.139. *Ibid.*, III.7.39, p. 259.

[3] In none of those texts the Logos-Son (ὁ υἱὸς λόγος) is meant, but both have reference to the νοῦς of the Father. This is clear from the first mentioned text, where the expression ὁ πατρικὸς λόγος is used, a term, typical of Clement and used to distinguish the Logos of the Father from the Logos-Son. In the second text λόγος stands as an attribute to θεός. It is thus God, who is at the same time παντοκράτωρ and λόγος. On these distinctions, see CASEY, *Clement and the two Divine Logoi*, pp. 43 ff. The word παντοκράτωρ occurs in Paed. only in these two passages. It is entirely missing from Protr., but in Strom. it occurs no less than 52 times, all about God or the Father (with one exception, Strom. V.4.4, GCS Clem. 2.328, where the word is used about the Marcionite demiurge). In Eclog. proph. the word occurs twice, both about God.

[4] See Indices in GCS Eus. 4 and 8.2, *sub voce*.

[5] On the term παμβασιλεύς for Logos, see above, p. 264. For παμβασιλεύς as a liturgical formula, see LINSSEN, Θεὸς σωτήρ, pp. 28 and n. 122, 48 f., 67 ff.

[6] On St. Athanasius' use of the word παντοκράτωρ, see G. MÜLLER, *Lexicon Athanasianum* (1944–52), col. 1079 f.

notice at once that there is a great difference between those passages referring to the Father and those about the Son. When παντοκράτωρ is applied to the Father, it takes place without comment, and we are aware that this is common linguistic practice. When the word is used of the Son, it is always motivated, and we are equally aware that this is a controversial issue. Athanasius is consciously making use of attributes previously limited to the Father, but which he transfers to the Son in order to stress the *homoousios* of the two Divine Persons. Since the Son is of one substance with the Father, he shares his attributes, with one exception: the attribute of Fatherhood.[1] Thus he is God, since the Word was God (Jn. 1.1) and he is παντοκράτωρ, i.e. ὁ ἦν καὶ ὁ ὢν καὶ ὁ ἐρχόμενος, ὁ παντοκράτωρ.[2] Athanasius is well aware of the connexion between the title παντοκράτωρ and the expression ὁ ἦν etc.[3] He is also conscious that παντοκράτωρ is an equivalent expression for Sebaot, saying perfectly consistently that it is the Son who is praised in the Psalter under the name of the Lord of Hosts.[4]

St. Athanasius motivates his application of παντοκράτωρ to the Son by referring to the words of Jesus in Jn. 16.15, "All that the Father has is mine,"[5] and in Jn. 17.10, "All that is mine is thine, and what is thine is mine."[6] This argument is not limited to the title of παντοκράτωρ, but is also used of other attributes, such as θεός, ἄτρεπτος, etc., which he uses of Christ.[7] The solution of the problem thus appears to be extremely simple. Athanasius, in the course of his struggle with Arianism,

---

[1] Orat. 3 c. Arian. 4, PG 26.329.

[2] *Ibid.*: "οἷον τὸ θεός· καὶ θεὸς ἦν ὁ λόγος· τὸ παντοκράτωρ· τάδε λέγει ὁ ἦν, καὶ ὁ ὤν, καὶ ὁ ἐρχόμενος, ὁ παντοκράτωρ."

[3] Cf. also Epist. 2 ad Serap. 2, PG 26.609: "παντοκράτωρ ἐστὶν ὁ πατήρ. παντοκράτωρ ἐστὶ καὶ ὁ υἱός, λέγοντος τοῦ Ἰωάννου· 'ὁ ὤν, ὁ ἦν, ὁ ἐρχόμενος, ὁ παντοκράτωρ'."

[4] Orat. 2 c. Arian. 23, PG 26.197: "'Ἔστι γὰρ αὐτός, ὥς οἵ τε ἄλλοι προφῆται λέγουσι, καὶ Δαβὶδ ψάλλει κύριος τῶν δυνάμεων. κύριος Σαβαώθ, ὃ ἑρμηνεύεται, κύριος τῶν στρατιῶν, καὶ θεός ἀληθινὸς καὶ παντοκράτωρ, κἂν οἱ Ἀρειανοὶ ἐν τούτῳ διαρρηγνύωσιν ἑαυτούς."

[5] Epist. ad Afros episc. 8, PG 26.1041: "πάλιν δὲ εἰπάτωσαν, εἰ δύναται τὰ γενητὰ εἰπεῖν· πάντα, ὅσα ἔχει ὁ πατὴρ ἐμά ἐστιν; Ἔχει δὲ τὸ κτίζειν, τὸ δημιουργεῖν τὸ ἀΐδιον, τὸ εἶναι παντοκράτωρ, τὸ ἄτρεπτον ..."

[6] De synod. 49, Opitz, p. 273: αὐτὸς γὰρ εἶπεν ὁ υἱός. 'πάντα ὅσα ἔχει ὁ πατὴρ ἐμά ἐστι', τῷ τε πατρὶ ἔλεγε· 'πάντα τὰ ἐμὰ σά ἐστι καὶ τὰ σὰ ἐμά', οἷον τὸ θεός. 'θεὸς' γὰρ 'ἦν ὁ λόγος' τὸ 'παντοκράτωρ' τάδε λέγει 'ὁ ὤν καὶ ὁ ἦν καὶ ὁ ἐρχόμενος ὁ παντοκράτωρ'.

[7] Cf. further Athanasius, Exp. Fidei 1, PG 25.201 (where the Son is styled παντοκράτωρ ἐκ παντοκράτορος), De decr. Nic. syn. 30.3, ed. Opitz, p. 26, Epist. 2 ad Serap. 3, PG 26.612.

was the first to transfer the term to Christ, his object being to express that the Son is *homoousios* with the Father; from this beginning the concept *Christus Pantocrator* gradually became established in the Christian vocabulary. But we must pause to inquire: What meaning was attached to the word παντοκράτωρ? May it not be the case that Athanasius is breaking, not only linguistically but also theologically, from the tradition of the Church? Once more we must examine the question from the beginning.

It is not easy to determine the exact meaning of the word παντοκράτωρ. We have seen that it was originally used in a number of set phrases: in Hellenistic Greek as an attribute of the gods, in the LXX as an equivalent of a Hebrew Divine name. This conventional usage means that we must be rather careful when trying to fix its meaning.

H. Hommel has put forward a hypothesis to the effect that παντοκράτωρ was of Stoic origin, and meant *omnitenens*; this is entirely out of the question.[1] Of more interest is the earlier discussion as to whether

---

[1] H. HOMMEL, *Pantokrator*, ThV 5 (1953/54), pp. 322–378. HOMMEL bases his argument on the fact that κρατεῖν with the genitive has the usual meaning "rule", while with the accusative it means "keep". It is this latter meaning which HOMMEL considers to lie behind the term παντοκράτωρ, the translation of which should therefore be "omnitenens", not "omnipotens"; the word he regards as being of Stoic origin. Although the translation "omnitenens" is not unknown in the early Church, it first appears at a relatively late date (the oldest recorded uses are in Augustine, Confessions XI.13.15 and De Gen. ad litt. IV.2); the reason for the occurrence of the word in this debate seems to be its supposed use by Tertullian. The first to suggest its use there was J. PEARSON, *Expositio symboli apostolici* (1691), p. 74 n. 2, from which source the idea was taken over by C. CASPARI, *Ungedruckte, unbeachtete und wenig beachtete Quellen zur Geschichte des Taufsymbols und der Glaubensregel* 3 (1875), p. 211 n. 362 and by KATTENBUSCH, *Die apostolische Symbol*, p. 534 n. 90. Both CASPARI and KATTENBUSCH sought in vain for the word in Tertullian. HOMMEL however found the passage mentioned by PEARSON: in point of fact the word is found once in the pseudo-Tertullian *Carmen adversus Marcionitas* V. 202,CCL 2.1453. It would be as well to delete it from further discussion of the symbola, not least because it is bad Latin.

HOMMEL's attempt to derive the word παντοκράτωρ from Stoicism seems to have failed; the word is never used by the Stoics. He is therefore compelled to postulate secondary derivations, e.g. that the word occurs (in the conventional meaning) in a passage of the Letter of Aristeas (185) which "shows Stoic influence", or that παντοκράτωρ in Rev. is used together with the A Ω formula, which HOMMEL considers to have originated in Stoic ἀρχή and τέλος speculations. This statement he derives from the formula SATOR-AREPO, which he also considers to be Stoic, and on which he has written a separate essay (ThV 1952), explaining an obscure situation in even

the word was active in meaning, "ruler of all", or passive, "almighty". The problem is further complicated by the fact that it often occurs together with a similar, but not altogether synonymous, word: παντοδύναμος.

Kattenbusch has summarized previous interpretations of the two words in question, in which a number of scholars in succession appear to have taken over substantially the same material.[1] Pearson noted the distinction between παντοκράτωρ and παντοδύναμος, interpreting παντοκράτωρ as "ruler of all", and παντοδύναμος as "almighty"—the obvious interpretation, remembering the root meaning of the Greek words.[2] This view was developed by Westcott: παντοκράτωρ implies a "moral conception of universal dominion" while παντοδύναμος implies "the metaphysical conception of omnipotence".[3] Caspari draws a similar conclusion: that God is παντοδύναμος provides the condition on which he can be παντοκράτωρ.[4] Kattenbusch himself adopts these interpretations: παντοκράτωρ has an active meaning of "ruling"; παντοδύναμος a passive meaning of "almighty".[5] Dodd is also in agreement with this view.[6] Michaelis, on the other hand, gives παντοκράτωρ another meaning, considering it to be "conceived of more statically than dynamically".[7] We cannot however come to a definite decision without first examining the meaning of the word παντοδύναμος.

---

greater obscurity. See C. SCHNEIDER's critical review of HOMMEL's essays in ZRG 10 (1958), pp. 179–181.

There is little of positive value to be derived from HOMMEL's investigations, other than the fact that God's sustaining power was regarded as being of great importance, not least by the apologetes. Here it is sometimes possible to interpret παντοκράτωρ philosophically: thus Theoph. ad Autolyc. 1.6: παντοκράτωρ δὲ (λέγεται) ὅτι αὐτὸς τὰ πάντα κρατεῖ καὶ ἐμπεριέχει. But is clear that this is a secondary use of the word. HOMMEL, too, has observed that the title παντοκράτωρ is later transferred to Christ, but he does not connect this with the Arian conflict; instead he regards the word as having paled and lost its original meaning of "maintainer". Christ is κύριος βασιλεὺς πάντων κρατῶν, not πατὴρ πάντα κρατῶν. HOMMEL regards the word as meaning nothing but "omnitenens"; his whole hypothesis falls down at this point.

[1] KATTENBUSCH, *Das apostolische Symbol* 2, p. 533.
[2] PEARSON, *Expositio* (unavailable to the author).
[3] B. F. WESTCOTT, *The Historic Faith* (1885), p. 218.
[4] CASPARI, *Quellen* 3, n. 362.
[5] KATTENBUSCH, *Das apostolische Symbol* 2, p. 533.
[6] DODD, *The Bible and the Greeks*, p. 19.
[7] MICHAELIS, art. παντοκράτωρ, p. 914.

παντοδύναμος.

Kattenbusch and all the scholars he quotes have one thing in common, that all are authorities on the Creeds; the exegetical basis of their argument, on the other hand, is relatively weak. None of these authors has attempted to examine the OT texts, which it is only reasonable to assume to have contributed to the Christian use of the word παντοκράτωρ.[1]

In the LXX, though the word is uncommon, it nowhere occurs in the meaning of abstract, passive omnipotence. Its use is limited to three passages in Wisd., where it is used to refer to the Divine hypostases, πνεῦμα, λόγος and χείρ. In Wisd. 7.23 we read, referring to σοφία: Ἔστι γὰρ ἐν αὐτῇ πνεῦμα παντοδύναμον. In Wisd. 18.15 it is instead the λόγος which is said to be παντοδύναμος: ὁ παντοδύναμός σου λόγος ἀπ᾽ οὐρανῶν ἤλατο. There is also a reference to the hand of God, hypostasized and given the attribute παντοδύναμος (Wisd. 11.17): οὐ γὰρ ἠπόρει ἡ παντοδύναμός σου χείρ.

This is exactly the opposite of what might have been expected. In the Hellenistic Judaism represented by Wisd., God himself has rather a passive function, and works in the world through his hypostases.[2] God might therefore have been expected to have been called by the passive term παντοδύναμος, the active hypostases being given the epithet παντοκράτωρ. But as we see, exactly the opposite has taken place. This must mean that the words in the LXX have a meaning other than Kattenbusch and his predecessors supposed.

The solution would appear to lie in the fact that in Hellenistic Greek, the meaning of παντοδύναμος was much more concrete and active than the above-mentioned scholars thought. The word expresses as a rule, not some abstract concept of power, but the concrete power, δύναμις, of God, at work through his Divine hypostases.

We have earlier had occasion to point out that God is described in the pseudo-Aristotelian *De mundo* and in other Hellenistic literature as a Persian Great King, living the hidden life of a recluse in his palace, or as a puppet-master, at work behind the scenes.[3] Nothing is visible in

---

[1] KATTENBUSCH states (*op. cit.*, p. 533) that Caspari has investigated the sense of παντοδύναμος and of παντοκράτωρ in Jewish sources. We have not however found any such investigation in the mentioned work of CASPARI (*Quellen* 3).

[2] RINGGREN, *Word and Wisdom*, p. 157 and *passim*.

[3] See above, p. 191. See further E. FASCHER, art. *Dynamis*, in RAC 4 (1959), col. 415–458 and K. PRÜMM, *Dynamis in griechisch-hellenistischer Religion*, ZKTh 83 (1961), pp. 393–430.

the world but his δύναμις, which permeates the whole cosmos and sets in motion the sun and the moon. This δύναμις is contrasted with the ἀρχή, the reigning power, of God. God is μόναρχος—a political metaphor found in Plato and in Christian authors after about the middle of the 2nd century.[1] His δύναμις is the hypostasis through which he rules the world: God reigns, but his δύναμις rules.

Philo understands δύναμις as a real hypostasis of God.[2] There is however a corresponding tendency in the Lucan tradition, in which the words πνεῦμα and δύναμις are used synonymously (Lk. 1.17, 35, Acts 1.8, 10.38); the fact that the angel of the Annunciation is called Gabriel (גבריאל) would seem to have to do with the δύναμις (גבורה) overshadowing Mary, (Lk. 1.35).[3] The Gnostic version of δύναμις as a divine hypostasis is found in Acts; where Simon Magus is called ἡ δύναμις τοῦ θεοῦ ἡ καλουμένη μεγάλη (Acts 8.10).[4] In Justin Martyr the word δύναμις is used of the Logos.[5]

It therefore seems likely that the decisive clue to the meaning of παντοδύναμος is to be found in its use in the LXX. Since God rules the world through his δύναμις, the word παντοδύναμος, "the power which is capable of all things", can be applied both to this attribute and to God himself. The word is otherwise uncommon: it occurs neither in NT nor in Philo, but in the pre-Nicene fathers is sometimes used synonymously with παντοκράτωρ. It is used in a special sense in connexion with the lists of qualities and attributes which are so typical of Greek religious texts, and in which divine πᾶν-epithets play a leading role.[6] When the two Greek manuscripts *Cod. Sangall.* and *Cod. Cantabrig.* use the word παντοδύναμος in the second article of the Apostolic Creed (καθεζόμενον ἐν δεξιᾷ θεοῦ πατρὸς παντοδυνάμου), this is because it is a translation from Latin *omnipotens*.[7] A reminiscence of the LXX

---

[1] See above, pp. 247 ff.
[2] W. Grundmann, art. δύναμαι etc., ThWB 2 (1933–35), p. 299.
[3] R. Laurentin, *Traces d'allusions étymologiques en Luc. 1–2* (I), Biblica 37 (1956), pp. 447 ff.
[4] See Fascher, *op. cit.* col. 448 f.
[5] Cf. above, p. 112.
[6] So Clement of Alexandria, Eclog. proph. 26.2, GCS Clem. 3.144: ὁ θεὸς παντοδύναμος καὶ παντοκράτωρ. *The Liturgy of St. James:* ἅγιος εἶ παντοκράτωρ, παντοδύναμε, φοβερέ, ἀγαθέ etc. The text in *The Greek Liturgies,* ed. Swainson (1884), pp. 270 f.
[7] Caspari, *Quellen* 3, pp. 208 f.

use of the word is to be found in Methodius: Ἔστι δὲ ὁ υἱός, ἡ παντοδύναμος καὶ κραταιὰ χεὶρ τοῦ πατρός.[1]

The term παντοδύναμος is thus connected mainly with the divine hypostases in Hellenistic Judaism, but these have little significance in the earliest Christian literature. There is, then, little point in weighing the word against the much commoner παντοκράτωρ. We may note that παντοδύναμος is never used as a Christological title, even by those authors whose Christology is distinctly subordinationist. It is probable that the word had too many associations to be used in this way.

Most explanations of the title παντοκράτωρ suffer from one basic error, that they approach the word from a philosophic angle. This criticism applies to Hommel's hypothesis in particular, but is also relevant in the case of the credal scholars and their discussions of the active *versus* the passive meaning of παντοκράτωρ. We must remember that παντοκράτωρ is primarily a LXX word, the equivalent of *Sebaot*, and that it belongs in the religious sphere of Judaism. The Heb. Sebaot has also been the object of energetic discussion, but there is no doubt that it denotes Yahweh in his aspect of ruler, "Yahweh, enthroned on Zion, from whence he rules; the maintainer of the Covenant; the shield and protector of the chosen people against every enemy and every unfriendly power; the all-conquering and omnipotent national god".[2] It was this royal aspect which gave rise to the title Sebaot, and which led to the choice of the Greek παντοκράτωρ as its equivalent. Its *Sitz im Leben* is not philosophical, but liturgical; that is why we find it in the liturgical texts of Rev., where God is described in terms which we recognize from Dan. 7, enthroned as the cosmic ruler and surrounded by his court of angels and saints. That is also why the word παντοκράτωρ is adopted as a title for God in the introductory phrases of Christian prayers.[3] It is often used by the Fathers, but almost invariably as a title of honour for God. It should be remembered that for the Christians of the first centuries, the LXX was living literature, and that they were thus well acquainted with the vocabulary of the OT, both in meaning

---

[1] De creatis 9, GCS Meth. p. 498. The Spirit is styled παντοδύναμον and πανεπίσκοπον by St. Ambrose (in connexion with Wisd. 7.22), De Spir. Sancto 3.22 (169), PL 16.815.

[2] I. Engnell, art. *Sebaot*, SBU 2, col. 1072 f.

[3] See above, p. 157.

and overtones. It is sometimes explained that παντοκράτωρ is a translation of Sebaot.[1]

St. Athanasius, introducing the concept Χριστὸς παντοκράτωρ, was concerned to emphasize the cosmic supremacy of Christ as a corrective to the Arians' doctrine of his inferiority. We therefore find the Arians opposing the use of the title of παντοκράτωρ for Christ; the pseudo-Ignatians and the *Apostolic Constitutions* contain repudiations of the doctrine of Christ as παντοκράτωρ, interpreted as ὁ ἐπὶ πάντων θεός.[2]

St. Ambrose has a passage in which he describes the last days, when the Gentiles, the Jews and the Manichaeans are forced to bow before the power of Christ; the Arians, too, will have to confess the Almighty, whom they have denied. For St. Ambrose, then, denial of the omnipotence of Christ was typical of the Arians.[3]

The Nicene theologians, on the other hand, shared the Athanasian doctrine of the Son as παντοκράτωρ. St. Ambrose and Didymus draw upon their philological knowledge to motivate this doctrine, in an exposition of Ps. 23 (24), a Psalm which had long been used as a proof-text for the royal power and the Ascension of Christ. Here Christ is called κύριος τῶν δυνάμεων; we have already pointed out that the fact that this expression, and not κύριος παντοκράτωρ, is used to translate Yahweh Sebaot was an important cause of the Psalm's being adopted as a proof-text in the Christian tradition.[4] In their expositions Ambrose and Didymus bring together the Hebrew name and its two translations: if Christ is κύριος τῶν δυνάμεων, then he must also be Yahweh Sebaot, of which κύριος τῶν δυνάμεων is a translation; and since he is Yahweh Sebaot, he must be κύριος παντοκράτωρ, which is another translation.

---

[1] Origen, C. Cels. 5.45, GCS Orig. 2.50. Athanasius, Orat. 2 c. Arian. 23, see above, p. 299.

[2] Ps.-Ign. ad Philipp. 7.1, ed. LIGHTFOOT, p. 778: πῶς δὲ πάλιν οὐκέτι σοι δοκεῖ ὁ Χριστὸς εἶναι ἐκ τῆς παρθένου, ἀλλ' ὁ ἐπὶ πάντων θεός, ὁ ὤν, ὁ παντοκράτωρ; cf. Ps.-Ign. ad Tars., 2.1, 5.1, ed. LIGHTFOOT, pp. 765 and 767. Ap. Const. VI.26.2, ed. FUNK, pp. 367 f.: ἕτερον ἐξ αὐτῶν αὐτὸν εἶναι τὸν Ἰησοῦν τὸν ἐπὶ πάντων θεὸν ὑποπτεύουσιν etc. Cf. VI.18.4, ed. FUNK, p. 343. CAPELLE, *Le texte du "Gloria in excelsis"*, pp. 444 ff., demonstrates the Arian tendency in these texts. On the relation between the long recension of the Ignatian Epistles and the Ap. Const., see F. E. BRIGHTMAN, *Liturgies Eastern and Western* 1 (1896), pp. xxvii f. and xxxiv–xlii.

[3] St. Ambrose, De fide 5.14 (182), PL 16.685: "... cum Gentilis crediderit, cum Judaeus agnoverit, quem crucifixit; cum Manichaeus adoraverit, quem in carne venisse non credidit; cum Arianus omnipotentem confessus fuerit, quem negavit ..."

[4] Cf. above, p. 103.

Ergo, the Son is almighty.¹ It is characteristic that this exposition is to be found in the work of Origen's two most outstanding exegetical disciples. There can be no doubt that the philological argument is derived from the school of textual criticism in Alexandria, the principal monument of which was the *Hexapla.* It is not inconceivable that Athanasius was inspired to call the Son παντοκράτωρ from this source; he does not however motivate his action from Ps. 23. There may have been earlier philological expositions of Ps. 23, but none now survive.

In the context in which St. Gregory of Nazianzus expounds his doctrine of the double Kingship,² παντοκράτωρ is brought together with the Kingship Christ possesses as God. "He is said to be King, in one sense because he is *Pantocrator* and King over those who desire it

---

¹ St. Ambrose, De fide 4.1 (14), PL 16.619 f.: "Dominus virtutum, ipse est rex gloriae. Ergo Dominus virtutum ipse est Filius. Et quomodo infirmum Ariani dicunt, quem Dominum virtutum sicut et Patrem credimus? Quomodo Ariani discretiones faciunt potestatis, cum Dominum sabaoth Patrem, Dominum sabaoth Filium legerimus? Nam et hic sic positum plerique codices habent, quod Dominus sabaoth ipse sit rex gloriae; sabaoth autem interpretes alicubi Dominus virtutum (=Aquila), alicubi regem, alicubi omnipotentem interpretati sunt. Ergo quoniam qui ascendit Filius est: qui ascendit autem, Dominus est sabaoth; omnipotens utique Dei Filius est." Didymus, In Ps. 23 (24).10, PG 39.1297 f.: "'κύριος τῶν δυνάμεων', εἰποῦσαι, 'αὐτός ἐστιν ὁ βασιλεὺς τῆς δόξης'. Δυνάμεων δὲ κύριον αὐτὸν εἶπον, ὡς ἄρχοντα στρατοπέδων. Σημειωτέον δὲ ὅτι οἱ τὰ Ἑβραίων ἠκριβωκότες φασίν, τὴν 'Σαβαὼθ' φωνήν, ἐν τῷ Ἑβραϊκῷ κειμένην, εἰς Ἑλλάδα φωνὴν οἱ Ἑβδομήκοντα μεταλαμβάνοντες, ὅτε μὲν τὸ 'κύριος τῶν δυνάμεων', ὅτε δὲ 'κύριος στρατιῶν', ὅτε δὲ τὸ 'παντοκράτωρ' ἔταξαν. Λέγουσι γοῦν καὶ ἐν τῷ τόπῳ τούτῳ κειμένου τοῦ 'Σαβαώθ', μετάληψις εἰς τὸ 'κύριος τῶν δυνάμεων', γέγονεν. εἰ δὲ τὸ 'Σαβαὼθ' ἐπὶ τοῦ σωτῆρος εἴρηται, ἑρμηνεύεται δὲ καὶ εἰς τὸ 'παντοκράτωρ', εἰκότως ἡ 'παντοκράτωρ' φωνή, τοῦ σωτῆρος κατηγορηθείη. Εἰ γὰρ πάντα δι' αὐτοῦ γέγονεν, καὶ αὐτός ἐστιν πρὸ πάντων, καὶ τὰ πάντα ἐν αὐτῷ συνέστηκεν, κρατεῖ δὲ προνοητικῶς τῶν δι' αὐτοῦ πάντων γεγενημένων, καὶ πρὸ πάντων ἐστὶν τῶν ἐν αὐτῷ συστάντων, ἀκολούθως παντοκράτωρ λέγεται ... (Zech. 2: 8 f.) παντοκράτωρ γὰρ ὑπὸ παντοκράτορος ἀποστελλόμενος, ὁ υἱός ἐστιν ὑπὸ τοῦ πατρὸς πεμπόμενος. The authenticity of this text seems to be well proved. MIGNE's text is a reprint of A. MAIUS, *Nova bibliotheca patrum* 7.1 (1854), p. 201, which here is supported by both of the manuscripts used, Vat. gr. 1789 (A) and 1682–83 (B). On the textual problem, see DEVREESSE in DB Suppl. 1, col. 1125 f. A shorter version of this text (with some variant readings) is taken up as belonging to Origen's Psalm commentary in PG 12.1269, an attribution which does not deserve confidence, cf. DEVREESSE, *op. cit.*, col. 1120 f. A better knowledge of Didymus' exegesis of the Psalms will probably be won when the Psalm commentary in the Toura texts is published. See A. GESCHÉ, *Un document nouveau sur la christologie du IVᵉ s.*, SP 3 (1961), pp. 205–213.

² Cf. above, p. 286.

or not, and in another sense ... because he has placed under his sway ourselves who voluntarily accept his government."[1]

The use Marcellus of Ancyra makes of the title παντοκράτωρ is worth noting here: in the first article of his Creed the word πατέρα is missing, which has brought παντοκράτορα into apposition with θεόν.[2] Caspari and—to some extent—Kattenbusch regard this variant as a copyist's error; Zahn, followed by Gericke, consider that πατέρα has been omitted for theological reasons.[3] Gericke points out that in the preserved fragments Marcellus never uses παντοκράτωρ in apposition to πατήρ, but always to θεός.[4] It therefore seems only reasonable to adopt Gericke's view, that Marcellus uses παντοκράτωρ as a title, not only for God, but for the whole of the Divine Monas. This would then be a link—one among many—between Marcellus and Athanasius in this field.

Hypsistos as a Christological title

The development of the title παντοκράτωρ becomes clearer if we compare it with the closely similar development of the term ὕψιστος as an attribute of God. Here, too, we are dealing with a word used in the LXX as the equivalent of a Divine name in Hebrew, a word which the early Church applied only to the Father, but which Athanasius later used also of the Son. It may therefore be of interest to give some account of its development, though the word does not have the same "royal" character as παντοκράτωρ, and though no one has claimed ὕψιστος to be an expression used in civil law.

Unlike παντοκράτωρ, ὕψιστος is used in classical Greek (by Pindar and Aeschylus), being commonly applied to Zeus as the highest of the Olympian gods. Its real popularity was however derived from Hellenism, particularly in its use as an expression for the monotheistic tendency in Jewish-Hellenistic religious syncretism. The intermingling

---

[1] Gregory of Nazianus, Orat. 30.4, PG 36.108: Βασιλεύειν γὰρ λέγεται, καθ' ἓν μέν, ὡς παντοκράτωρ, καὶ θελόντων καὶ μή, βασιλεύς· καθ' ἕτερον δὲ, ὡς ἐνεργῶν τὴν ὑποταγὴν, καὶ ὑπὸ τὴν ἑαυτοῦ βασιλείαν τιθεὶς ἡμᾶς· ἑκόντας δεχομένους τὸ βασιλεύεσθαι.

[2] Epiphanius, Haer. LXXII.3.1, GCS Epiph. 3.258. HAHN § 17.

[3] CASPARI, Quellen 3, pp. 99 ff. KATTENBUSCH, Das apostolische Symbol 2, pp. 71 ff. ZAHN, Marcellus von Ancyra, p. 15 n. 1. GERICKE, Marcell von Ancyra, pp. 14 ff. (n. 38) and 116 ff. (and n. 20).

[4] Fragm. 19, 31, 60, 117.

of the Jews of the diaspora with Hellenistic Greeks gave rise to a syncretistic movement, which in turn led to the formation of a particular sect, called *Hypsistarians* (σεβόμενοι θεὸν ὕψιστον).[1] The word was not unknown in Christianity, but was limited largely to popular literature having few theological pretensions: it is found in certain set phrases in the letter papyri[2] and in Christian apocryphal writings.[3]

R. H. Charles[4] has shown statistically that the word was extremely common in Jewish literature during the 2nd century B.C. (Sir. and Dan., LXX, Jub.) There followed a period when the word was little used, but it once more came into use during the 1st century A.D. (NT, Apoc. Baruch, 4 Ezra, Test. 12 Patr.).[5] It was used by Philo and Josephus, and also occurs in the Sibylline oracles.[6]

In the LXX ὕψιστος normally translates two Hebrew Divine names: עליון and עלי. This usage is most frequent in Dan., Sir. and Wisd.

The NT has ὕψιστος as a name for God only nine times in all. Of these, only one is to be found in the Epistles (Heb. 7.1, which is a quotation from the LXX). The others are divided between one passage in Mk. (5.7) and seven in the Lucan literature (5 in Lk., 2 in Acts); this is not really surprising, in view of the fact that the word is good Greek, and was mainly used beyond the boundaries of Palestinian Judaism. It is perhaps not pure chance that the word is used by the Hellenist Stephen in his speech (Acts 7.48) and by the Greek slave-girl in Thyatira (Acts 16.17).

Particularly striking is the use of ὕψιστος in Lk. 1: υἱὸς τοῦ ὑψίστου (1.32), δύναμις ὑψίστου (1.35), προφήτης ὑψίστου (1.76).[7] It is the rule in the NT that ὕψιστος refers to the Father: never to Christ, who is instead called υἱὸς τοῦ ὑψίστου (Mk. 5.7, Lk. 1.32, 8.28).

The use of the word in the post-Apostolic Church is of little interest. It occurs for the most part in quotations from the LXX (Gen. 14,

---

[1] F. Cumont, art ″Υψιστος, PWK 9 (1914–16), col. 444–450. BAG, pp. 857 f.

[2] G. Ghedini, *Lettere cristiane dei papiri greci del III e IV secolo* (1923), p. 38. Ex. nr. 30–32, pp. 211 ff.

[3] Cf. below, p. 309 n. 6.

[4] *The Book of Jubilees*, ed. R. H. Charles (1902), p. 213 n. 16.

[5] On the occurrence of ὕψιστος in Test. XII Patr., see R. Eppel, *Le piétisme juif dans les Testaments des douze Patriarches* (1920), p. 53. See further *The Greek Version of the Testaments of the Twelve Patriarchs*, ed. R. H. Charles (1908), index *sub voce*.

[6] BAG, p. 858.

[7] On ὕψιστος in Lk 1.32 and 1.35, see Laurentin, *Traces* (II), Biblica 38 (1957), pp. 10 f.

Dan. 7, etc.) and from Lk. 1.32 and 1.35.¹ On those occasions when the word is used more independently, it is always connected with God the Father: God is called πατὴρ ὕψιστος in St. Ignatius' *Epistle to the Romans* (ingress); in one passage Aristides calls Christ ὁ υἱὸς τοῦ θεοῦ τοῦ ὑψίστου (Apol. 15.1). The Latin translation of Irenaeus often uses *altissimus* to translate ὕψιστος: St. Irenaeus, expounding the Hebrew Divine name, says that God is called *deus omnipotens* (=παντοκράτωρ) *et altissimus*, thus reproducing the Heb. Sebaot and El Æljon.² Here also ὕψιστος is used exclusively of the Father; this is clear from such expressions as *sedentem ad dextram patris altissimi* and *ab altissimo patre genituram*³—both of which are reminiscent of the corresponding use of the title παντοκράτωρ. Such independent use of the word is however exceptional.

In Marcionism and other branches of Gnosticism ὕψιστος was used to denote the Supreme God, as distinct from the Demiurge. The term is used by Irenaeus in this meaning to refer to Marcion's Supreme God.⁴ Similarly we learn from Hippolytus that the *Elkhasaites* prescribed a second baptism in the name of the Supreme God and his Son, the Great King.⁵ This Gnostic use of the word corresponds closely with what we know from other sources of its popularity in syncretistic circles.

The term ὕψιστος is not used to refer to Christ, even in the apocryphal Acts of the Apostles, in which Christ is often given epithets not used elsewhere in the Christian literature of the period. Though ὕψιστος is common in this type of writing, it is reserved (as is παντοκράτωρ) for God.⁶ A special problem is posed by a passage in Test. XII (Test. Levi

---

¹ Ὕψιστος occurs 5 times in Clem., all in quotations from LXX. In St. Justin's Apol. the word occurs only once (33.5), in a quotation from Lk 1.32. In Dial. God is 14 times styled ὕψιστος, always in quotations (Gen. 14.18, Ps. 49 (50).14, Ps. 81 (82).6, Dan. 7.22–27, Lk 1.35). St. Irenaeus seems to have used the word about 20 times in Adv. haer., mainly in quotations (Gen. 14.22, Deut. 32.8, Ps. 49 (50).14, Ps. 81 (82).6, Dan. 7.22–27, Lk 1.32, 35). See REYNDERS' Irenaeus Index 2, p. 26.

² MARMORSTEIN, *Erklärung*, pp. 253 ff.

³ Adv. haer. III.16.2, ed. HARVEY 2.85, III.19.2, *ibid.*, p. 104.

⁴ Adv. haer. II.6.2, ed. HARVEY 1.264.

⁵ Hippolytus, Ref. IX.15, GCS Hipp. 3.253 f.: βαπτισάσθω ἐκ δευτέρου ἐν ὀνόματι τοῦ μεγάλου καὶ ὑψίστου θεοῦ καὶ ἐν ὀνόματι υἱοῦ αὐτοῦ ‹τοῦ› μεγάλου βασιλέως.

⁶ Ὕψιστος is a rather common word in the Acts of Thomas: Thomas is styled ἀπόστολος τοῦ ὑψίστου in ch. 39, 45 (42), 49 (46), 150, AAA pp. 156, 162, 165, 260. The Greek text has ἀπόστολος (τοῦ) Χριστοῦ τοῦ ὑψίστου in 78 and 125 app., AAA

4.1), which speaks of τῷ πάθει τοῦ ὑψίστου; De Jonge has interpreted this as referring to the sufferings of Christ.¹ Any estimation of this passage obviously depends upon which of the theories about the origin of Test. XII is favoured: whether it is regarded as being from Qumran, or Christian, or Jewish with Christian interpolations.² De Jonge, who considers Test. XII to be Christian, though based to some extent on Jewish material, maintains that this unusual phrase is due to the fact that the author had no satisfactory formula to express the relationship between Christ and God. ὕψιστος occurs on one other occasion in Test. Levi 4; there is no doubt that here it means "God". In whatever way this text may be interpreted, it is unreasonable to draw from it the conclusion that ὕψιστος is a typical Christological title.³ This is contradicted by all the rest of the tradition.

Here, as in the case of παντοκράτωρ, it is St. Athanasius who transfers the title from the Father, and uses it equally of the Son. This is naturally motivated by the *homoousios* of the Son, though we do not meet with the same detailed argument as that for παντοκράτωρ. In particular he opposes the Arian argument that Christ cannot be ὕψιστος by his nature, since it would in that case be pointless to talk about his having been exalted; he further argues that the exaltation of Christ affected, not his Divine nature, which is ὕψιστος, but his human nature.⁴ Athanasius also applies the name κύριος σαβαώθ to Christ, quoting two passages from the Psalms (Ps. 86.5 and 96.9) as proof that Christ is ὕψιστος.⁵

---

pp. 193, 234. The Syriac version, which is considered to be more original, has here also "the Apostle of the Most High", ed. WRIGHT (1871), 2, pp. 214 and 262. In 48 (45) Christ is styled 'Ιησοῦ ὕψιστε, φωνή, but from the Syriac text it is evident that ὕψιστος here is an attribute to the voice and not to Jesus, ed. WRIGHT, 2, p. 187. It seems thus that Christ has not been styled ὕψιστος even in these acts.

¹ DE JONGE, *Testaments*, p. 126.
² On this discussion, see OTZEN, *Sektenschriften*, pp. 125 ff.
³ This premature conclusion is drawn by DANIÉLOU, *Judéo-christianisme*, p. 264.
⁴ Orat. 1 c. Arian. 38, PG 26.92: οὐκοῦν εἰ καὶ πρὸ τοῦ τὸν κοσμὸν γενέσθαι τὴν δόξαν εἶχεν ὁ υἱὸς καὶ κύριος τῆς δόξης ὕψιστός τε ἦν καὶ ἐξ οὐρανοῦ κατέβη ... Ibid. 40, col. 93 f.: Εἰ γὰρ θεὸς ὢν γέγονεν ἄνθρωπος, καὶ ἐξ ὕψους καταβὰς λέγεται ὑψοῦσθαι, ποῦ ὑψοῦται θεὸς ὤν; Δηλοῦ ὄντος πάλιν τούτου, ὅτι, τοῦ θεοῦ ὑψίστου ὄντος, ἐξ ἀνάγκης εἶναι δεῖ καὶ τὸν τούτου λόγον ὕψιστον ... Cf. ibid. 41 (col. 97), 43 f. (col. 101), De incarn. et c. Arian. 3, PG 26.989: οὐ γὰρ ὁ ὕψιστος ὑψοῦται, ἀλλ' ἡ σὰρξ τοῦ ὑψίστου ὑψοῦται. Cf. DAVIES, *He Ascended*, pp. 97 ff.
⁵ De incarn. et c. Arian. 22 (col. 1027): Ὁ δὲ Δαβὶδ λέγει· Μήτηρ Σιὼν ἐρεῖ· "Ἄνθρωπος καὶ ἄνθρωπος ἐγεννήθη ἐν αὐτῇ, καὶ αὐτὸς ἐθεμελίωσεν αὐτὴν ὁ ὕψιστος. Οὗτος γὰρ ὁ

The concept of Christ as ὕψιστος provided one of the main points of controversy in the Arian struggle. The Arian tractate on Luke, which we have earlier had occasion to mention, says, referring to Lk. 1.32, that Christ is the Son of the Most High, but that he is not himself the Most High.[1]

Nicene theology, on the other hand, like Athanasius, claimed Christ to be ὕψιστος. A particularly important proof-text is Ps. 86 (87).5, already used by Athanasius, a text which not only serves to confirm the doctrine of Christ as ὕψιστος, but which is also interpreted as referring to the Incarnation. Further proof-texts are Ps. 17 (18).14, 82 (83).19 and Lk. 1.76, all of which are quoted by St. Ambrose in his anti-Arian polemic.[2] In Ambrose's view Arius was guilty of the sin of Lucifer in Isa. 14.14—"I will make myself like the Most High"—not by exalting himself to the dignity of the Godhead but pulling Christ down to his own human level.[3] Theodoretus of Cyrus further emphasizes what Athanasius has already said, that Christ is ὕψιστος by virtue of his Divine nature, and that his exaltation therefore refers only to his

---

ἄνθρωπος ὁ γεννηθεὶς ἐν αὐτῇ, αὐτός ἐστιν ὁ ὕψιστος, καθὼς ἐν ἄλλῳ ψαλμῷ λέγει. καὶ γνώτωσαν, ὅτι ὄνομά σου κύριος — σὺ μόνος ὕψιστος ἐπὶ πᾶσαν τὴν γῆν.

[1] Tract. in Luc., PL Suppl. 1.331: "non altissimus sed altissimi." Cf. Contra Varimadum 1.53, CCL 90. 64 f. On this writing, which is an anti-Arian treatise from the 5th century, see B. Schwank, *Zur Neuausgabe von "Contra Varimadum"*, SE 12 (1961), pp. 112-196, where textual tradition, provenience and theological tendency are discussed.

[2] St. Ambrose, De fide 5.2 (7 ff.), PL 16.591: "Mater Sion dicet: Homo, et homo factus est in ea, et ipse fundavit eam Altissimus (Ps. 86 (87).5 ... Qui autem altissimus, idem homo, nisi Mediator Dei, et hominum, homo Christus Jesus, qui dedit semetipsum redemptionem pro nobis (1 Tim. 2.5 f.)? ... Quis autem neget Christum esse altissimum significatum? Nam qui aliter sentit, Deo Patri sacramentum incarnationis ascribit. Sed hinc dubitari non potest quod altissimus Christus sit; cum etiam alibi dixerit de mysterio passionis: Dedit vocem suam Altissimus, et mota est terra (Ps. 17.14). Et in Evangelio habes: Et tu puer, propheta Altissimi vocaberis; praeibis enim ante faciem Domini parare vias ejus (Lk 1.76). Qui altissimus? Dei Filius. Ergo qui altissimus Deus, Christus est. Et solus utique cum dicitur Deus, non separatur etiam Dei Filius. Qui enim altissimus, solus, sicut scriptum est: Et cognoscant quoniam nomen tibi Dominus, tu solus altissimus super omnem terram (Ps. 82 (83).19)."

[3] *Ibid.* 5.19 (238), PL 16.698: "Sed non Arius raptus in caelum, quamvis eum secutus sit, qui jactatione damnabili divina praesumeret, dicens: Ponam thronum meum super nubes, et ero similis Altissimo (Isa. 14.14); sicut enim ille dixit: Ero similis Altissimo: sic et Arius altissimum Dei Filium sui similem vult videri: quem non in divinitatis aeternae majestate veneratur, sed ex carnis infinitate metitur."

human nature. He possesses the Kingship as God, but receives it as man.¹ Here we have the doctrine of the double Kingship of Christ fully developed, though there can be no doubt that Athanasius was responsible for the first steps.

According to Didymus the Blind, the title ὕψιστος is appropriate not only to the Father and the Son, but to all three Persons in the Godhead; this applies equally to κύριος, βασιλεύς and other titles.² Didymus also interprets Ps. 82 (83).19 (Σὺ εἶ μόνος ὕψιστος ἐπὶ πᾶσαν τὴν γῆν) as referring to Christ.³ When this saying was incorporated into the *Gloria* of the Mass (*Tu solus Altissimus*), it would thus seem to have been for anti-Arian reasons; the formula however seems to have been accepted only gradually, and to have won an assured position only in the 9th century.⁴ It is difficult to determine the exact age of this liturgical phrase. It is missing from the oldest versions of the *Gloria*, and that it is also missing from the *Apostolic Constitutions* is not unnatural, remembering the Arian tendency of the document in question.⁵

---

¹ Theodoretus, In Ps. 2.6, ed. SCHULZE 1.2.620: ... ἀλλ' ὅμως καὶ ἔχει τὴν βασιλείαν ὡς θεός, καὶ λαμβάνει ὡς ἄνθρωπος. Οὕτως ὕψιστος ὀνομαζόμενος ὡς θεός, ὑψώθη ὡς ἄνθρωπος. In Ps. 109.1 (p. 1392): Οὐ γὰρ ταπεινὸς ὢν ὑψώθη, ἀλλ' ὕψιστος ὢν καὶ ἐν μορφῇ θεοῦ ὑπάρχων, ἐταπείνωσεν ἑαυτὸν μορφὴν δούλου λαβών. Cf. also St. Ambrose, De excess. fratr. Satyr. 1.12, PL 16.1294, where Christ according to Ps. 86 (87).5 is called "Homo utique corpore, altissimus potestate".

² De Trin. 3.23, PG 39.926: "Η συνθῶνται, ὡς τὸ 'ὁ θεός' καὶ 'κύριος' ἐπίκοινόν ἐστιν ὄνομα τῶν τριῶν ὑποστάσεων, ὡς καὶ βασιλεύς, καὶ ὕψιστος, καὶ ἄχραντος, καὶ ἀκατάλυτος, καὶ ἅγιος, καὶ ὅσα πρέπει λέγειν περὶ θεοῦ.

³ *Ibid.*, col. 925 f. Cf. U. HOLZMEISTER, *Unbeachtete patristische Agrapha*, ZKTh 38 (1914), p. 128.

⁴ See C. BLUME, *Der Engelhymnus Gloria in excelsis Deo*, StML 73 (1907), pp. 60 f. BLUME has however not seen the connexion between this formula and the Arian controversy: "Ursprünglich und fürs gewöhnliche ist dasselbe mehr ein Attribut *Gottes überhaupt*, besagt nicht etwas dem *Sohne Gottes* Eigentümliches, und so lässt sich mit Recht fragen, wie und wann gerade dieses eingefügt werde ... Erst seit dem 9. Jahrhundert lautet es ständig: *tu solus altissimus.*" As we have seen, ὕψιστος was in pre-Constantinian times not used for all the three Divine Persons but exclusively for the Father, and it is the doctrine of the *homoousios* which transfers the title to the Son. The apparently illogical expression that the Son *only* is ὕψιστος comes from Ps. 82 (83).19, and is commented already in the Didymus text, mentioned above. Cf. also JUNGMANN, *Missarum Sollemnia* 1, p. 440.

⁵ CAPELLE, *Le texte du "Gloria in excelsis"*, pp. 444 ff.

14. CHRIST THE KING AND THE CHRISTIAN EMPEROR

The question of the relationship of Caesar and Church during the 4th century has been discussed by many scholars, and we have no reason in work of this nature to consider the problem in detail. There is, however, one special reason why we should look more closely at the ecclesiastical situation when seeking to clarify the Church's attitude to the Kingship of Christ at this time.

There is no doubt that the Constantinian Empire and the breakthrough of the idea of Christ as King are in some way related. In the introductory chapter of this study we gave a brief account of Kollwitz' theory that this break-through was due to the new and positive attitude to the Roman Emperor. On the other hand it has been stressed that the idea of Christ as King was used, especially by the orthodox opponents of the Emperor Constantius, to counteract the idea of imperial supremacy over the Church and in support of the Church's demand for independence. Here we shall take up the matter of Church–State relations, in the period in question, only in so far as they have to do with the concept of Christ as the supreme King.

The Arians (to which party Eusebius has often been regarded, quite wrongly, as belonging) have long served as a paradigm of a conciliatory attitude, concerned only with the maintenance of their own position with the help of the state. The reason for the popularity of this interpretation is to be seen in the unnecessarily biased polemics of St. Athanasius, St. Ambrose and Lucifer of Calaris, together with the fact that we have so little first-hand Arian material. It is also typical that a number of works on the subject have been published in critical ecclesiastical situations. J. H. Newman's presentation of the Arians' attitude to the state would seem to have been conditioned largely by his own attitude to English Erastianism.[1] Peterson's works on political metaphysics

---

[1] J. H. NEWMAN, *The Arians of the Fourth Century* (1833).

and its problems were published in the days of Hitler's *Machtübernahme*,[1] and the most important of these, *Der Monotheismus als politisches Problem*, took the form of an answer to Carl Schmitt's "political theology".[2] Similarly H. Berkhof, in his book *Kerk en Kaiser*, wrote that he was compelled to hide from the German forces of occupation for many months.[3] Those who fought for the freedom of the Church from the interference of the state or opposed the reshaping of the Church by Nazi collaborators, found much material in the Arian controversy, as it is related in the preserved documents. But although ecclesiastical history has been peculiarly enriched by modern ecclesiastical conflict situations, it is not unthinkable that these very situations have given rise to a highly biassed estimation of the ancient documents. In the following pages we shall attempt to see whether such is in fact the case.

At the end of his book *Der Monotheismus als politisches Problem* Peterson shows how impossible it is to base a "political theology", of the kind expounded by Eusebius of Caesarea, on the Christian doctrine of the Trinity. If we claim the existence of a triune God, this rules out the idea of a unified theological and political monarchy, with the one God in heaven corresponding to the one Caesar on earth.[4] In his review of Peterson's essay Dölger called this conclusion in question,[5] pointing out that we have an example from the end of the 7th century of the doctrine of the Trinity giving rise to a demand for a

---

[1] E. PETERSON, *Göttliche Monarchie*, ThQ 112 (1931), pp. 537–564. IDEM, *Kaiser Augustus* (Hochland 1933) and *Monotheismus* (first published 1935).

[2] Cf. C. SCHMITT, *Politische Theologie*, (1922). SCHMITT's and PETERSON's views are critically discussed by A. MARXEN, *Das Problem der Analogie zwischen den Seinsstrukturen der grossen Gemeinschaften* (1937).

[3] H. BERKHOF, *Kirche und Kaiser* (German translation 1947), p. 5.

[4] PETERSON, *Monotheismus*, pp. 104 f.: "Doch die Lehre von der göttlichen Monarchie musste an der christlichen Eschatologie scheitern. Damit ist nicht nur theologisch der Monotheismus als politisches Problem erledigt und der christliche Glaube aus der Verkettung mit dem Imperium Romanum befreit worden, sondern auch grundsätzlich der Bruch mit jeder 'politischen Theologie' vollzogen, die die christliche Verkündigung zur Rechtfertigung einer politischen Situation missbraucht. Nur auf dem Boden des Judentums oder Heidentums kann es so etwas wie eine 'politische Theologie' geben. Doch die christliche Verkündigung von dem drei-einigen Gotte steht jenseits von Judentum und Heidentum, gibt es doch das Geheimnis der Dreieinigkeit nur in der Gottheit selber aber nicht in der Kreatur."

[5] Review in BZ 36 (1936), pp. 225 f.

triumvirate at the head of the Empire. Treitinger, on the other hand, has accepted Peterson's result, considering that the reason why the Emperor embraced the Arians' cause was that the doctrine of the Trinity was regarded as being a threat to the divine monarchy which formed the foundation of the Roman Empire.[1]

We cannot escape the fact that the ecclesiastical and secular politics of the 4th century recognized a link between the divine monarchy and monarchical rule on earth. This attitude was not limited to the Arians or to the imperial court theologians. An important memento is provided by Theodoret's account of the Papal schism in Rome in the 350's. While Pope Liberius was on a visit to Milan in 357 the Emperor Constantius appointed a deacon, Felix, as Bishop of Rome. When Liberius later returned to Rome, and claimed his position, Constantius decided that he was only to be allowed to share it with Felix. When this extraordinary decision was made public in the circus, the people began to propose in jest that each bishop should have his own party in the circus, and then shouted in chorus, "One God, one Christ, one bishop."[2] Those who protested in this way against the Emperor's interference in a matter which concerned only the Church may well be said to have claimed the independence of the Church.[3] It is however characteristic that this protest against imperial supremacy was itself just as monarchical in character as the Constantinian court theology ever was. Just as the monarchy of God demands imperial monarchy, according to Eusebius, so, according to the defenders of the freedom of the Church, there must be a unified Church government. In this case the doctrine of the Trinity did not tend to undermine the monarchy (supposing that the Roman Christians in the 350's were in fact Trinitarians), and it is common knowledge that later trinitarian theology did not weaken the Papacy. Remembering all this, we must ask whether Peterson's theory, despite its superficial elegance, is in fact anything more than a construction without historical foundation.

The American mediaeval historian G. H. Williams has gone further than either of these, claiming in a long essay that there existed a close relationship between Christology and ecclesiastical politics during the

---

[1] TREITINGER, *Reichsidee*, pp. 45 f.
[2] Theodoretus, HE 2.17, GCS Theod. p. 137.
[3] So RAHNER, *Kirche*, pp. 91 f.

4th century.¹ In Williams' view Arianism (under which term he also includes Eusebius) could not avoid taking up a positive attitude to the Emperor: this on account of its cosmological understanding of the Logos-Son. The basic soteriology of the Nicene orthodox emphasis upon the Incarnation led, equally unavoidably, to independentism. We must pause to examine Williams' theory in more detail, since he regards the doctrine of the Kingship of Christ as having been of decisive importance in the ecclesiastical situation.

Williams' objective is to demonstrate the importance of the Biblical —and in particular the OT—background for the decision of the Council of Nicaea and for the struggle of the Nicene theologians against the Arianizing Caesars, particularly Constantius. He therefore sets out the two contrasting views of Christ, the Catholic and the Arian, schematically: these correspond to the two views of the relation of the Empire to the Church. The Arians considered Caesar to be the bishops' bishop; the Catholics included him within the Church.² These two viewpoints may be increased to four, if we include the Donatists, who rejected all contact between Caesar and Church, and the incipient doctrine of the two swords, according to which Caesar and Church each have the right to rule their respective areas of authority.³

According to Williams there were three levels of disagreement between Catholics and Arians: (i) The Arians regarded the Logos-Son primarily as a mediator in a cosmological sense; the Catholics regarded him as a mediator between a righteous God and sinful man in the context of historical redemption. While the orthodox preserved the tension between reason and revelation, the Arians harmonized the two.⁴ (ii) The Arians stressed the subordination of the Son in order to have a mediator between God and the world; the Catholics were

---

¹ G. H. WILLIAMS, *Christology and Church-State Relations in the Fourth Century*, CH 20 (1951), nr. 3, pp. 3–33 and nr. 4, pp. 3–26. The two parts of WILLIAMS' essay are hereinafter called WILLIAMS 1 and 2.

² WILLIAMS, *op. cit.* 1, p. 9.

³ *Ibid.*, n. 32.

⁴ WILLIAMS here founds his concept on H. G. OPITZ, *Eusebius von Caesarea als Theologe*, ZNW 34 (1935), p. 19; this author however is not talking about the Arians but about Eusebius: "Für Euseb gibt es keine Spannung zwischen Vernunft und Offenbarung, weil der offenbare Sohn Gottes selbst die Vernunft ist, die sich im Weltgeschehen manifestiert ... Bei Athanasius und in Rom liesst man die Parodoxie von Vernunft und Offenbarung bestehen, behauptete geradezu, dass in dieser Paradoxie das göttliche Geheimnis am deutlichsten fassbar wird."

mainly interested in defending the divinity of the Logos. (iii) The Catholics regarded Christ as Lord over Rome; the Arians subjected the historical Christ to the living law (νόμος ἔμψυχος) in the person of the Emperor, whose position is established by the Logos.[1]

These disagreements became critical on four points: (a) the authority of Caesar in matters of faith and ecclesiastical law; (b) the Eucharist; (c) the prophetic office of the bishop; and (d) the Kingship of Christ.[2] The second of these points is of minor interest for our investigations, though it contains much illustrative material. Williams takes up the question of the role played by the Kingship of Christ and the Logos in 4th century ecclesiastical politics in connexion with the other points.

There are a number of virtues in Williams' account, not least in that he has demonstrated the significance of the doctrine of the Kingship of Christ in the debates of the period. His book is a welcome corrective to those exaggerated accounts of the harmonious relations subsisting between Church and Caesar given by Kollwitz in particular.[3] But on the other hand, its schematization tends to lead to undue generalizations on the subject of the relation of Christology to ecclesiastical politics.

Williams' account of the imperial ideology of the Arians is based largely on Eusebius and Themistius.[4] This choice of source-material to some extent shows up the weakness in his argument, since neither was an Arian. Eusebius was a left-wing representative of the school of Origen;[5] Themistius was not a Christian at all.[6] It is not an easy matter to find out what the Arians really thought on these questions, since most of their literature has vanished irretrievably.[7]

---

[1] WILLIAMS, *op. cit.*, 1, pp. 11 ff.
[2] *Ibid.*, p. 14.
[3] Cf. above, p. 24.
[4] WILLIAMS, *op. cit.*, 1, pp. 14 ff.
[5] This is admitted also by WILLIAMS, *ibid.*, p. 15.
[6] *Ibid.*, p. 21.
[7] Such examples as we are able to quote of the Arians' ideas are almost without exception drawn from Athanasius' *Historia Arianorum*, the polemical character of which means that we must observe caution when accepting what it says, SETTON, *Attitude*, pp. 78 ff. Athanasius here attacks the Arians for not having any king but Caesar (Hist. Arian. 32.4, ed. OPITZ, p. 201), which is obviously a reference to Jn. 19.15, intended to represent the Arians as the enemies of Christ: WILLIAMS, *Christology* 1, p. 25 n. 128, SETTON, *op. cit.*, p. 82. In another context he similarly accuses the two Arian court bishops Ursacius and Valens of denying the eternity of the Son and calling the Emperor "eternal" at the same time, αἰώνιον δὲ αὐτὸν βασιλέα

Eusebius' political metaphysic has often been the object of historical research.[1] But a just estimation—which has not always been made hitherto—must take into account not only its relation to the Logos theology of Origen but also to the background of Philonic political speculation.[2] Eusebius' imperial ideal and Philo's conception of the monarchy coincide entirely: Constantine is an image of the monarchical power of God in heaven;[3] he is the epitome of the wise man, and an incarnation of the law.[4] Such sayings as these should not of course be understood as a near-blasphemous transfer by Eusebius of the attributes of Christ to Constantine. He has the political speculations of the Pythagoreans and Philo to fall back upon—the same speculation as that which contributed to the Alexandrian theologians' view of Christ as the ideal King. But Eusebius has also a definite opinion on the relationship existing between Christ and Caesar: he equates the Logos of the political philosophers with Christ, whose Kingship he connects, as did the Alexandrians, with his divine nature. The great difference between Eusebius and Philo is that Eusebius has a historical perspec-

---

εἰρήκασιν, De synod. 3.2, ed. OPITZ, p. 232, SETTON, *op. cit.*, p. 82. On "eternal" as a title of the Emperor, see H. V. INSTINSKY, *Kaiser und Ewigkeit*, Hermes 77 (1942), pp. 313–355. The ironical characterization of the court theologians is certainly accurate: both certainly combined Arian theology with unwavering support of Caesar. But it is a long step from this situation to an ideological or metaphysical connexion between the two. Even less of theological lesson is taught in the anecdote from Eusebius Vita Const. 4.48 quoted by Williams (*op. cit.*, n. 53); according to this a priest stood up at the Arianizing Council of Jerusalem and said that in the age to come Constantine would share the rule with Christ; he was rebuked by Constantine himself. This grotesque flattery cannot of course be accepted as genuine Arianism. How could it be reconciled with Williams' (faulty) statement, that the Arians, in common with Marcellus of Ancyra, taught that the Kingship of Christ was to cease in the age to come? (Cf. WILLIAMS, *op. cit.* 2, p. 17.)

[1] PETERSON, *Monotheismus*, pp. 86 ff. N. BAYNES, *Eusebius and the Christian Empire*, Mélange Bidez 2, Univ. libre de Bruxelles, Ann. de l'Inst. de philol. et d'hist. orient. 2 (1934), pp. 13–18. STRAUB, *Herrscherideal*, pp. 113 ff. BERKHOF, *Eusebius*, pp. 53 ff. and *passim*. IDEM, *Kirche*, pp. 100 ff. SETTON, *Attitude*, pp. 40 ff. and *passim*. On the concept of the Christian Empire as the Kingdom of God, see the valuable account by G. B. LADNER, *The Idea of Reform* (1959), pp. 118 ff.

[2] Cf. above, pp. 189 f. The relation between Eusebius' theory of the Empire and earlier political speculation is stressed especially by BAYNES, *op. cit.*

[3] Eusebius, Laus. C. 5, GCS Eus. 7.204: Constantine's empire is τὸ μίμημα τῆς μοναρχικῆς ἐξουσίας. *Ibid.* 7, p. 215: The Emperor is ὁ δ' ἐξ ἑνὸς εἷς βασιλεύς, εἰκὼν ἑνὸς τοῦ παμβασιλέως.

[4] *Ibid.* 11, p. 223: Constantine is ὁ ἐκ θεοῦ σεσοφισμένος.

tive which Philo lacks: he sees the unification of the Roman Empire under a single ruler and the unexpected rise to power of the Christian Church as an eschatological manifestation of the work of the Logos. The kingdom of peace, of which the Scripture of the OT spoke so often, has now come.[1] His weak doctrine of the Incarnation facilitates an interpretation of the victory of Constantine in terms of the history of salvation. Just as, three centuries earlier, the earthly Christ became the instrument of the Logos, the Logos has now taken Constantine into his service in order to realize his scheme of salvation. That Eusebius is capable of pressing his speculations to this extreme point is due not least to the fact that he invests the Logos with cosmological, ordering significance; the Emperor thus corresponded to what he considered to be the Logos' primary function.[2]

If we compare what Eusebius has to say about the role of Caesar with the account given by Themistius in his panegyrics, we find undeniable parallels, striking in their extent.[3] Here, too, we must seek the cause of these in common dependence upon earlier political speculation, though in Themistius' case without any particularly Christian significance.

Have we, then, any reason for saying that Eusebius' political metaphysic was also adopted by the Arians? It is an unchallengeable fact that the Arians sought the support of the Emperor, and that the Emperor Constantius gave the Arians extensive support, resulting in opposition from the Nicene theologians as defenders of the independence of the Church. But it is a long step from this position to Williams' assertion that Arianism as such was state-church minded and that the Nicene theology *per se* led to a demand for the independence of the Church.

There is no doubt that political considerations were often of greater significance than the basic theological attitude in these matters. It is an established fact that the struggle against Caesaropapism was waged

---

[1] See especially PETERSON, *Monotheismus*, pp. 86 ff.

[2] WILLIAMS, *Christology* 1, p. 18. On the other hand, WILLIAMS seems to overstate Eusebius' view, when saying (*ibid.*, p. 17): "In thus enthusiastically comparing Caesar and Christ it was indeed hard for Eusebius not to leave the impression that the work of a Christian Caesar was of more importance than the work of Christ." It is perhaps possible to get this impression when studying only Laus C. and Theoph., but this judgment must be notably modified, when Eusebius' other writings are taken into consideration: e.g. Dem. ev. and Praep. ev.

[3] Cf. WILLIAMS, *op. cit.* 1, pp. 21 ff.

not only in the Arian camp but also among the orthodox, at least when the orthodox were in fact able to reckon with the support of the Emperor. Incidentally, it was in Byzantium, with its Nicene orthodoxy, that the Emperor's power within the Church was felt most keenly during subsequent years. From Constantine onwards it was recognized by all parties except the Donatists that the Emperor had his power from God, and this concept created new problems in the field of Church-state relations.

This situation is reflected in a number of 4th century documents. The orthodox St. Optatus of Mileve stressed against the Donatists, who had opposed all connexion between Caesar and Church (*quid est imperatori cum ecclesia?*), that the Church is in the state—the same expression as that used by Williams to denote the attitude of the Arians.[1] The same accusations as those directed by St. Athanasius and St. Ambrose against the Arians[2] were turned by the Luciferians against Pope Damasus and the orthodox, once the wind had changed and the orthodox had been assured of the support of the Emperor. Those who were now bishops were accused of having previously feared Caesar more than the true God and the eternal Emperor, Christ; Damasus was also accused of maintaining his power with the support of the Emperor.[3]

There is some evidence that certain Arians demanded that Caesar should be subordinate to the Church—a claim which Williams considers to have been made only by the Nicene orthodox. This trend is found in the *Apostolic Constitutions*, the Arian tendency of which is no

---

[1] Optatus Milev., De schism. Donat. 3.3. CSEL 26.73 f.: "… enim respublica est in ecclesia, sed ecclesia in republica, id est in imperio Romano, quod Libanum appellat Christus in canticis canticorum, cum dicit: ueni, sponsa mea inuenta, ueni de Libano (S. of S. 4.8), id est de imperio Romano, ubi et sacerdotia sancta sunt et pudicitia et uirginitas, quae in barbaris gentibus non sunt et, si essent, tuta esse non possent, merito Paulus docet orandum esse pro regibus et potestatibus, etiamsi talis imperator sunt, qui gentiliter uiueret; quanto magis quod christianus, quanto quod deum timens, quanto quod religiosus, quanto quod misericors, ut ipsa res probat!" (*Ibid.*, p. 74.)

[2] Cf. above, p. 317 n. 7.

[3] The letter of the Luciferians to the Emperor Theodosius, CSEL 35.1.11: "… episcopi plus iram regis terreni timuerunt quam Christum, uerum deum et sempiternum regem." *Ibid.*, p. 30: Pope Damasus reigns "accepta auctoritate regali". Cf. RAHNER, *Kirche*, p. 102.

longer questioned,¹ and in the related interpolations in the letters of St. Ignatius.² Williams mentions Ap. Const., saying however that it represents—in common with Arianism in general—the political theories of Eusebius;³ this is hardly accurate.

The observation that the attitude of Ap. Const. to the Caesar and the Roman Empire is a positive one, is *per se* correct. We read on a number of occasions that Christians must fear the king, since he has been appointed by God.⁴ Its positive evaluation of the Roman Empire is even more striking. Christ, in fulfilment of Dan. 2.34, has destroyed polyarchy and polytheism, and has established the Roman monarchy.⁵ The passage in criticism of the kingship in 1 Kings (Sam.) 8.10–17, quoted in Didasc. II.34,⁶ is removed by Ap. Const.

None of these passages in Ap. Const. has however anything to say about the relations between Caesar and Church. It is hardly surprising that the end of the 4th century saw a more positive attitude to the Emperor, compared with the time of the persecutions. The idea of the divine appointment of the Emperor would seem to have been accepted by most camps, with the exception of the Donatists. The statement that monarchy has destroyed polytheism provides, it is true, an interesting parallel to Eusebius' political metaphysic, but as Peterson has pointed out, this idea is by no means foreign to the pre-Constantinian Church.⁷ The political speculations of PsC in particular indicate that it goes back to an ancient Antiochene tradition taken up by Ap. Const.⁸

Williams' interpretation is rendered impossible by Ap. Const. VI.1–3, which he quotes but misinterprets. The Didascalia, in a parallel passage, has a warning against schism, and refers to Korah's revolt against Moses. Ap. Const. builds out this passage, referring to 2

---

¹ C. H. TURNER, *Notes on the Apostolic Constitutions* 1, JTS 16 (1914–15), pp. 54–61. Cf. CAPELLE, *Le texte du "Gloria in excelsis"*, pp. 439 ff.

² The best representation of the relation between Ap. Const. and the interpolated version of the Ignatians is still BRIGHTMAN, *Liturgies Eastern and Western* 1, pp. xxvii f. and xxxiv ff.

³ WILLIAMS, *Christology* 1, pp. 20 f.

⁴ Ap. Const. IV.13, ed. FUNK, pp. 233 f. *Ibid.* VII.16, p. 402.

⁵ Ap. Const. V.20.11, ed. FUNK, p. 207. Cf. PETERSON, *Monotheismus*, p. 101 and n. 161.

⁶ Ed. CONNOLLY, p. 94; Lat. fragm., *ibid.*, p. 95.

⁷ *Monotheismus*, pp. 64 ff.

⁸ Cf. above, p. 256.

Chron. 26.16–21, which deals with the way king Uzziah usurped the priestly office, and was punished with leprosy.[1] Williams takes note of this passage, which is hardly positively inclined to the kingship, but states that in the following passage Moses is called both high priest and king. But this is wrong: what is said is that certain men have set themselves up against David in respect of the kingship, but that others challenged Moses for the leadership (περὶ πρωτείων).[2]

That this text has nothing whatever to do with the power of Caesar over the Church becomes perfectly clear when we compare it with the parallel passage in the interpolated version of Ign. ad Smyrn. 9—a text of which Williams makes no mention. We shall set out the texts in parallel columns in order to demonstrate their areas of agreement:

Ap. Const. VI.2.1	Interpol. Smyrn. 9
εἰ γὰρ ὁ βασιλεῦσιν ἐπεγειρόμενος κολάσεως ἄξιος ... πόσῳ μᾶλλον ὁ ἱερεῦσιν ἐπανιστάμενος ὅσῳ γὰρ ἱεροσύνη βασιλείας ἀμείνων ...	εἰ γὰρ ὁ βασιλεῦσιν ἐπεγειρόμενος κολάσεως ἄξιος δίκαιος γενήσεται ... πόσῳ δοκεῖτε χείρονος ἀξιωθήσεται τιμωρίας ὁ ἄνευ ἐπισκόπου τι ποιεῖν προαιρούμενος ...

Both these texts deal with the importance of obeying the king, but only with the object of presenting the priestly office as even more sacrosanct: the bishop is even more worthy of obedience, since he occupies an even higher office. It need scarcely be said that both texts place the priesthood over the Empire in order of merit.

Here the interpolated version of Ign. ad Smyrn. goes on to describe the ecclesiastical hierarchy: the layman should obey the deacons, who obey the presbyters, who obey the bishop, who obeys Christ, who obeys God.[3] The place of the Emperor in the hierarchical ladder is clearly seen from the interpolated Ign. ad Philad. 4: the governors (ἄρχοντες) should obey the Emperor (Καῖσαρ), and the soldiers should obey the governors. In the same way the deacons should obey the presbyters, who are here also called ἀρχιερεῖς. But all these, presbyters, deacons and the rest of the clergy, the people, the soldiers, the governors and

---

[1] Ap. Const. VI.1.3, ed. Funk, p. 303.

[2] Ap. Const. VI.2.2, ed. Funk, p. 305: οἱ μὲν γὰρ τῷ Δαυὶδ περὶ βασιλείας, οἱ δὲ τῷ Μωϋσεῖ περὶ πρωτείων ἐπανέστησαν ἁμιλλώμενοι.

[3] Οἱ λαϊκοὶ τοῖς διακόνοις ὑποτασσέσθωσαν, οἱ διάκονοι τοῖς πρεσβυτέροις· οἱ πρεσβύτεροι τῷ ἐπισκόπῳ. ὁ ἐπίσκοπος τῷ Χριστῷ, ὡς αὐτὸς τῷ πατρί.

the Emperor, should obey the bishop; the bishop in turn should obey Christ as Christ obeys the Father.[1] In this case the subordinationist Christology involved does not lead to the conclusion that the Emperor has a right to rule over the Church. On the contrary: the emphasis laid upon Christ as ἀρχιερεύς leads to a more positive evaluation of the priesthood.

How does Ap. Const. fit into this picture? Here we have no statements of such clarity as those we have quoted. Its repeated reference to king Uzziah seems however to point to the idea that the king should avoid interfering with the work of the priesthood.[2] VI.1-2 in particular comprise an outright criticism of Caesar's claim to supremacy over the Church. Other 4th century authors made use of the Uzziah narrative in the context of anti-imperial polemic,[3] and it is begging the question to interpret these texts, as Williams has done, as a polemic against a lower grade of the priesthood which has usurped the functions of the higher priesthood.[4]

It is by no means surprising to find the Arians claiming the independence of the Church over against the command of the Emperor. Ap. Const. and the interpolations in the Ignatian epistles date back to ca. 380, i.e. the period of Theodosius' decree against non-Christian religions, with which he grouped all manner of heresy.[5] This placed the Arians in the conflict situation previously occupied by the orthodox, and they were undoubtedly forced to stress their Church's independence from imperial pressure.

Williams characterizes the Nicenes' attitude as being that the Emperor is obedient to Christ, not only to the eternal Logos (Eusebius' view) but to the historical, incarnate Christ, whose authority has passed on to the Church.[6] This is largely correct. The Nicene theologians evaluated the

---

[1] Οἱ ἄρχοντες πειθαρχείτωσαν τῷ Καίσαρι· οἱ στρατιῶται τοῖς ἄρχουσιν· οἱ διάκονοι τοῖς πρεσβυτέροις ἀρχιερεῦσιν· οἱ πρεσβύτεροι καὶ οἱ διάκονοι καὶ ὁ λοιπὸς κλῆρος, ἅμα παντὶ τῷ λαῷ καὶ τοῖς στρατιώταις καὶ τοῖς ἄρχουσι καὶ τῷ Καίσαρι, τῷ ἐπισκόπῳ· ὁ ἐπίσκοπος τῷ Χριστῷ, ὡς ὁ Χριστὸς τῷ πατρί.

[2] Allusions to the Uzziah narrative occur in II.27.4, ed. FUNK, p. 107, III.10.3 (p. 201), VIII.46.8 (p. 560).

[3] Lucifer of Calaris, De non parc. 8, CSEL 14.220 f. Cf. BERKHOF, Kirche, p. 158. St. John Chrysostom, In illud, Vidi dominum hom. 5.2, PG 56.132, Ecloga 21: De imperio, PG 63.697. Cf. SETTON, Attitude, p. 190.

[4] This use of the text occurs only in VIII.46.8, ed. FUNK, p. 560.

[5] W. ENSSLIN, Die Religionspolitik des Kaisers Theodosius des Grossen, BAS 1953.2, pp. 15 ff.

[6] WILLIAMS, Christology, 2, pp. 15 ff.

imperial authority in a positive way (though this often came in sharp contrast to personal attacks on the Emperor), but they stressed continually that the Emperor's power is derived from Christ. That the one who bestows this power is the incarnate Christ and not, as in Eusebius, the eternal Logos, leads to a more critical attitude to the Emperor. He is understood not primarily as being a manifestation of God's monarchy or as νόμος ἔμψυχος, whose will is law, both for the Empire and the Church; instead his position is regarded as being assured by Christ, to whom he is responsible for his actions.

It is to this end that Athanasius stresses on a number of occasion in his Apology to Constantius that the Emperor's authority is derived from Christ the King;[1] it is probably the same idea which recurs in the Catholic bishops' letter to Constantius from the Synod of Ariminium.[2]

This attitude was of course liable to be intensified into a conflict between the earthly Caesar and Christ the King, a conflict which was still remembered as having existed during the period of the persecutions. An excellent example of this is the story of how St. Antony received a letter from Constantine and his sons Constans, to which the Emperor demanded an answer. Antony regarded the Emperor's attentions as unwelcome, and at first refused to answer. But he eventually answered, at his monks' request, "commending them for worshipping Christ, and giving them salutary advice not to think highly of the things of this world, but rather to bear in mind the judgment to come; and to know that Christ alone is the true and eternal King."[3]

---

[1] Apol. ad Const. 10, SC 56, p. 98: ... ὁ κύριος, ὁ ἐπακούσας καὶ χαρισάμενος ὁλόκληρόν σοι τὴν ἐκ προγόνων βασιλείαν. Ibid. 12 (p. 100); Δέσποτα παντοκράτορ, βασιλεῦ τῶν αἰώνων, ὁ πατὴρ τοῦ κυρίου ἡμῶν Ἰησοῦ Χριστοῦ, σὺ διὰ τοῦ σοῦ λόγου τὴν βασιλείαν ταύτην τῷ σῷ θεράποντι Κωνσταντίῳ δέδωκας ... Ibid. 35 (pp. 131 f.): Ἀλλὰ χάρις τῷ κυρίῳ τῷ τὴν βασιλείαν σοι δεδωκότι ... (Constantius is exhorted to restore the orthodox bishops) ... σὺ δὲ καὶ νῦν καὶ ἐν ἡμέρᾳ κρίσεως ἔχῃς παρρησίαν εἰπεῖν τῷ κυρίῳ καὶ σωτῆρι ἡμῶν καὶ παμβασιλεῖ Ἰησοῦ Χριστῷ. Οὐδένα τῶν σῶν ἀπώλεσα. Cf. K. F. HAGEL, *Kirche und Kaisertum in Lehre und Leben des Athanasius* (1933), pp. 53 f.

[2] The letter of the Ariminium synod to Constantius, CSEL 65.79: "... per ipsum deum et dominum nostrum Iesum Christum, saluatorem imperii tui et largitorem salutis tuae ..." Cf. the Greek text in Athanasius, De synod. 10, ed. OPITZ, p. 237: ... διὰ τοῦ κυρίου ἡμῶν Ἰησοῦ Χριστοῦ ἐκήρυξαν, τοῦ καὶ τῆς σῆς βασιλείας φρουροῦ καὶ τῆς σῆς ῥώσεως προστάτου ... Cf. also the synod in Milan 355, where the bishops referred to the belief that the Emperor is established by God, Athanasius, Hist. Arian. 34.1, ed. OPITZ, p. 202. See RAHNER, *Kirche*, p. 89.

[3] Athanasius, Vita Antonii 81, PG 26.956 f. In this context it is worth mentioning that the catena fragment on Ps. 2.7, attributed to St. Athanasius (see above,

It is seldom that we meet with such an explicit eschatology in 4th century authors. There is no doubt however that expectations of the parousia had their place in the Nicene camp; the Arians and the leftwing representatives of the school of Origen were far too dependent upon the supra-historical view derived from Alexandria to have much time left for eschatology. It is here, and not in the matter of their attitude to the Emperor, that we must look for the deepest level of opposition between the views of the Arians and the orthodox on the Kingship of Christ.

Berkhof has attempted to trace their mutual differences to an Eastern versus a Western mentality.[1] It is true that the Arians' stronghold was in the East, while Athanasius was supported largely by the West. This explanation enables Berkhof to draw a natural line of development between the 4th century and the Middle Ages, with a Caesaropapistic Byzantium in the East and the battle for the Church's liberty being fought out in the West.[2] The vulnerable point in his argument is the term "mentality": it is never safe to build an argument on such a vague idea. Berkhof's speculations are as a result sometimes too bold, as when he brings together the Greeks and the Javanese as peoples with "Eastern" characteristics.[3]

---

p. 289 n. 7), also mentions that some authorities consider that it is the Roman Empire that is governed by Christ with the rod (= the cross). This interpretation is not common in earlier exegesis of the Psalm. We find it however in Rabbinic exegesis, in Gen. R. 97, see LÖVESTAM, *Son and Saviour*, p. 22 n. 2. According to this interpretation the Messiah will chastise the State, probably the Roman Empire. It seems probable that the exegesis mentioned in the Athanasius fragment has the same negative import, even if the Psalm is here quoted in its ordinary LXX form with ποιμανεῖ (= "shepherd").

[1] BERKHOF, *Kirche und Kaiser*, pp. 191 ff.

[2] *Ibid.*, p. 198: "Wir erkennen nunmehr auch, dass dieser Mentalitätsunterschied zwischen Osten und Westen für unsern Gegenstand nicht nur indirekt, als Hintergrund der verschiedenartigen Reaktion auf das arianische Problem, von Bedeutung ist, sondern auch direkt zur Erklärung des Byzantinismus einerseits und des theokratischen Bewusstseins andrerseits beiträgt. Das Schwergewicht des Byzantinismus liegt in seiner Passivität dem Kaiser gegenüber, während das theokratische Bewusstsein sich in einer aktiven prophetisch-kritischen Haltung gegenüber dem Kaiser verwirklicht. Jene Passivität gehört zum Osten, wie diese Aktivität eine Eigenart des Westens ist."

[3] *Ibid.*, p. 196. K. ALAND has also noted a weak point in BERKHOF's theory, that St. Athanasius is reckoned by BERKHOF among the Western theologians, *Kaiser und Kirche von Konstantin bis Byzans*, in IDEM, Kirchengeschichtliche Entwürfe (1960), p. 263.

Without attempting to refute hypotheses of this nature, which are by nature incapable of proof or disproof, we can go so far as to say that one clear distinction between the Latin and Greek forms of Christianity in the middle of the 4th century was that the greater part of the Eastern half of the Empire was characterized by its Origenism (with certain variations in Antioch), while in the West was to be found an eschatological emphasis without its like in the East. Clear proof of this is provided by the West's positive attitude to Rev.: the oldest commentary we have on this book was written by the Latin Victorinus of Pettau.[1] This meant that the West was in a better position than the East to accept the Nicene theologians' emphasis on Christ as incarnate and as the eschatological King.

In his work on the *Majestas* image, van der Meer has stressed the importance of Rev. for the earliest pictorial representations of Christ as King.[2] It is not Christ the Logos who is represented here; it is the eschatological ruler and judge.[3] Typically, the most ancient pictures of this kind are found in the West. Kollwitz seems to have been guilty of a grave error in seeing in the earliest *Majestas* images an expression for the new appreciation of the Emperor, which he traces to Eusebius.[4] The Christ represented on Roman sarcophagi from ca. 350, enthroned on the vault of heaven and passing on his law to Peter,[5] is definitely not the Logos of Origenist speculation, but the cosmic judge who is to awaken the dead. It may be well to recall here that as far back as 340 Pope Julius adopted the views of Athanasius, after which the West became distinctly Nicene.[6]

The eschatological conception of Christ as King was thus strongest in the West; the Nicene theologians of the East connected the royal theme mainly to the cult. This characteristic is seen most of all in a number of theologians having Antiochene tendencies: John Chrysostom, Theodore of Mopsuestia and Narses.[7] Here, too, Kollwitz seems to be mistaken in discerning the influence of Eusebian theology from the

---

[1] On the canonicity of Rev. in the early Church, see A. WIKENHAUSER, *Einleitung in das Neue Testament* (1953), pp. 404 ff.

[2] VAN DER MEER, *Maiestas Domini*, pp. 21 ff. and *passim*.

[3] On this point we cannot quite agree with VAN DER MEER, who tends to describe the beardless *Majestas* image as a picture of the Logos.

[4] Cf. above, p. 24.

[5] Cf. above, p. 293.

[6] E. SCHWARTZ, *Zur Geschichte des Athanasius*, new ed. (1959) pp. 291 ff.

[7] Cf. above, pp. 15 f.

imperial court.¹ It is not Christ the Logos who is mentioned here as being King, but the incarnate and ascended Lord, who is seated at the right hand of the Father and present in the form of bread and wine whenever the holy mysteries are celebrated.

In St. John Chrysostom we find the kingly characteristics of Christ dominating the priestly entirely. According to Chrysostom, the priesthood of Christ belongs to his human nature; but at his enthronement he is seated as a King, and does not stand in the manner of priests. Chrysostom explains all expressions which appear to contradict this as a συγκατάβασις for our sakes.² This royal power of Christ is manifested especially in the Eucharist, which Chrysostom does not, remarkably enough, interpret as an image of the cult of heaven; on the contrary, the worship of heaven, as described in Isa. 6, is the pattern of the Eucharist. The Eucharist *is* the heavenly cult, properly so-called. Chrysostom can even go so far that he claims everything in the celebration to be invisible in principle.³ From this point it is a logical consequence that the liturgy is shaped as the court ceremonial of the heavenly King, and that the ceremonies of the imperial court should be taken over by the Church. On the other hand, but parallel with this development, we find Theodore of Mopsuestia laying great emphasis on the priesthood of Christ.⁴

The emphasis laid upon the Kingship of Christ by these authors had entirely different implications from the point of view of ecclesiastical politics than those seen in the West. When the Kingship of Christ is considered to be realized above all in the cult, the areas of conflict diminish accordingly. We also find that later Byzantinism could be combined perfectly well with a high view of the Kingship of Christ.

In its trial of strength with Caesar, the Church tended to fall back rather upon the priesthood than the Kingship of Christ. As far back as ca. 200 A.D. it was common to speak of priests in general, and bishops in particular, as ἱερεῖς,⁵ and it became usual in the 4th century political

---

¹ *Plastik*, pp. 145 ff. *Das Bild*, pp. 109 ff.
² See LÉCUYER, *Le sacerdoce céleste*, pp. 564 f.
³ St. John Chrysostom, In illud: Vidi Dominum, hom. 6, PG 46.138 f.; hom. 19, PG 63.139. Cf. LÉCUYER, *op. cit.*, p. 571.
⁴ See J. LÉCUYER, *Le sacerdoce chrétien et le sacrifice eucharistique selon Théodore de Mopsueste*, RSR 36 (1949), pp. 481–516.
⁵ See P.-M. GUY, *Remarques sur le vocabulaire antique du sacerdoce chrétien*, in Études sur le Sacrement de l'Ordre. Lex Orandi 22 (1957), pp. 141 f.

conflicts of the Church to make use of sayings referring to the priesthood of the OT, as applying to the priests of the new Covenant.

St. Ambrose opposed Caesar Valentinianus II, who wished to give up the basilica in Milan to the Arians, with a sharp demand for the independence of the Church;[1] it was in this context that he made his famous statement that the Emperor is in the Church and not over the Church (*imperator enim intra ecclesiam, non supra ecclesiam*).[2] It is a striking fact that we have here no reference to the Kingship of Christ. But he made use in the course of the same dispute that it was the priests in the old Covenant who ruled the empire. They had not usurped it. On the contrary: the kings (*imperatores*) had endeavoured to gain the priesthood, rather than vice versa. The priests had never been tyrants; but they had often suffered under tyrants.[3]

It is natural, when comparing the priesthood of the old and new Covenants in this way, to draw upon the OT for concrete examples to serve as a warning to Caesar. We have already mentioned the story of king Uzziah, who was stricken with leprosy because he usurped the functions of the priesthood.[4] St. Ambrose makes special mention of Nathan before King David and Elijah before Ahab as examples of the way in which kings have been rebuked by prophets and priests when they have committed some crime.[5]

From this position is but a short step to the exaltation of the priesthood over the kingship. We can find this tendency as early as in Lucifer of Calaris, who claimed that it is the duty of the Emperor to obey the priests of the Lord.[6] Chrysostom states that the bishop is himself a ruler (ἄρχων) and is of higher rank than the Emperor; "the sacred laws take and place under his hand even the royal head, and when

---

[1] SETTON, *Attitude*, pp. 109 ff.

[2] St. Ambrose, Sermo c. Auxent. 36, PL 16.1061. Cf. SETTON, *op. cit.*, p. 148. RAHNER, *Kirche*, p. 101.

[3] Epist. 20.23, PL 16.1013: "Si haec tyrannidis videntur, habeo arma, sed in Christi nomine: habeo offerendi mei corporis potestatem. Quid moraretur ferire, si tyrannum putaret? Veteri iure sacerdotibus donata imperia, non usurpata, et vulgo dici quod imperatores sacerdotium magis optaverunt quam imperium sacerdotes ... Habemus tyrannidem nostram. Tyrannis sacerdotis infirmitas est ... addidi quia numquam sacerdotes tyranni fuerunt, sed saepe sunt passi." Cf. SETTON, *Attitude*, pp. 149 f.

[4] Cf. above, pp. 321 f.

[5] See SETTON, *Attitude*, p. 141. BERKHOF, *Kirche*, pp. 183 f. WILLIAMS, *Christology* 2, p. 9 and n. 44.

[6] See STRAUB, *Herrscherideal*, pp. 136 ff.

there is need of any good thing from above, the Emperor is wont to resort to the priest, but not the priest to the Emperor."¹ The priest is therefore just as much more worthy of honour and reverence than the ruler, as his priesthood is higher than the kingship.² Kings and priests have their separate areas of influence.³ The task of the king is to rule over temporal matters; the authority of the priest is derived from heaven, and what the priest does on earth is confirmed by God in heaven. The king is obeyed by bodies; the priest by souls. The king uses material weapons; the priest spiritual weapons. The priest's power (ἀρχή) is therefore superior to that of the king, and the head of the king is therefore set under the hand of the priest.⁴

The Church thus did not lay particular emphasis upon the Kingship of Christ in its struggle with Caesar; such would have led to revolution and the demand for theocracy. The stress was instead placed upon the priesthood, which was accorded higher rank than the kingship. The same characteristics are to be seen in the writings of St. Basil⁵ and, more surprisingly, in Ap. Const. and the interpolated version of the Ignatian epistles.⁶ But it was quite natural for an Arianizing theology

---

[1] St. John Chrysostom, Hom de stat. 3.2, PG 49.50. Cf. SETTON, *op. cit.*, p. 189.

[2] Hom. de Anna 2.4, PG 54.648. Cf. SETTON, *op. cit.*, p. 189.

[3] In Ps. 121 Expos. 2, PG 55.349 f. Cf. SETTON, *op. cit.*, p. 191.

[4] In illud: Vidi dominum, hom. 4.4 f., PG 56.126; Ecloga 21, de imperio, PG 63.697. Cf. SETTON, *op. cit.*, p. 192. Of less interest in our context is S. VEROSTA, *Johannes Chrysostomus, Staatsphilosoph und Geschichtstheologe* (1960); cf. however pp. 318 ff.

[5] G. F. REILLY, *Imperium and Sacerdotium according to St. Basil the Great* (1945), *passim*. In this context it is worth mentioning a mistake made by WILLIAMS (*Christology* 2, p. 17). According to WILLIAMS St. Basil has argued "that the emperor can at best claim to be an image of the heavenly King by grace, whereas Christ is the image of God by identity of nature." WILLIAMS here gives no reference, but certainly means De Spir. Sancto 18.45, PG 32.149, treated by SETTON, *op. cit.*, p. 199, and by KANTOROWICZ, *Deus per naturam*, pp. 266 f. where also other examples of this imagery are given. What St. Basil says here is however quite different from what WILLIAMS states. He takes up the same parable of the emperor and his image, which Eusebius also uses in defence of the Divine monarchy (see above, p. 268). The image of the Emperor is often called "the Emperor", but this does not imply that there are two emperors. In the same way the monarchy of God is not divided, because Christ is the image of God, and he who venerates the Son, venerates also the Father, whose image the Son is. Here St. Basil adds the modification, that the Emperor's image is a case of pictorial likeness (μιμητικῶς), but the Son is an image by nature (φυσικῶς). Thus the text does not contain anything about the concept of the Emperor as the image of God.

[6] Cf. above, pp. 321 ff.

to emphasize the priesthood as a reflection of the heavenly priesthood of Christ.

In the period which followed, the subject of the Kingship of Christ was thus no longer the same source of conflict. Both the *imperium* and the priesthood were traced back to Christ, but the one was administered by the Emperor and the other by the Church. When the Church came to oppose the Emperor, it did so on a basis of the superiority of the priesthood to the *imperium*. The royal ideology of the Hellenistic world lived on, down to the Middle Ages and beyond.[1] The Kingship of Christ was thus in all probability of less importance as an argument in the struggle for the Church's freedom than one might suppose, from its undoubted popularity as a motif for ecclesiastical art and its occurrence in the cult. As Dom Leclercq has well shown, the eschatological Kingship of Christ plays a central role in the homiletic tradition of the Middle Ages.[2] It thus seems that it is the inner life of the Church and not ecclesiastical politics that has gained the greatest profit from faith in Christ's eternal Kingship.

---

[1] We here primarily refer to KANTOROWICZ' pioneer works. See especially *Dante's "Two Suns"*, in Univ. of California. Publ. in Sem. Philol. 11 (1951), pp 217–231. IDEM, *Kaiser Friedrich II*. IDEM, *Deus per naturam*. IDEM, *The King's Two Bodies* (1957).

[2] *Royauté, passim*.

BIBLIOGRAPHY

A. *Texts and translations*

Biblia Hebraica ..., ed. R. KITTEL, 8th ed. by P. KAHLE, A. ALT & O. EISSFELDT. Stuttgart 1952.
Die Weisheit des Jesus Sirach, hebräisch und deutsch, herausg. von R. SMEND. Berlin 1906.
Septuaginta ... ed. A. RAHLFS. 1-2. Stuttgart 1943.
Origenis Hexaplorum quae supersunt ... concinnavit, emendavit et multis partibus auxit F. FIELD. 1-2. Oxonii 1875.
Biblia Sacra iuxta Vulgatam versionem cura et studio monach. abbat. pont. S. Hieronymi in urbe OSB ed. 10 (Liber Psalmorum). Romae 1953.
Novum Testamentum Graece ... ed. E. NESTLE & K. ALAND. 23rd ed. Stuttgart 1957.
Nouum Testamentum D. Nostri Iesu Christi Latine, ... rec. I. WORDSWORTH. 1-3. Oxonii 1889-1954.
Apocrypha and Pseudepigraphs of the Old Testament in English ..., ed. R. H. CHARLES. 1-2. Oxford 1913.
Ascension d'Isaïe, éd. E. TISSERANT. (= Documents pour l'étude de la Bible.) Paris 1909.
3 Enoch or The Hebrew Book of Enoch, ed. ... by H. ODEBERG. Cambridge 1928.
The Book of Jubilees, ed. by R. H. CHARLES. London 1902.
The Odes and Psalms of Solomon, re-ed. ... by R. HARRIS & A. MINGANA. 1-2. Manchester 1916-20.
The Greek Versions of the Testaments of the Twelve Patriarchs, ed. ... by R. H. CHARLES. Oxford 1908.
Neutestamentliche Apokryphen in deutscher Übersetzung, ed. E. HENNECKE. 2nd ed. Tübingen 1924.
Neutestamentliche Apokryphen in deutscher Übersetzung, ed. E. HENNECKE & W. SCHNEEMELCHER. 1, 3rd ed., Tübingen 1959.
Acta Apostolorum Apocrypha, herausg. von R. A. LIPSIUS und M. BONNET. 1-2. Leipzig 1891-1903.
ΠΡΑΞΕΙΣ ΠΑΥΛΟΥ, *Acta Pauli.* Nach dem Papyrus der Hamburger Staats- und Univ.-Bibl. unter Mitarbeit v. W. SCHUBART herausg. v. C. SCHMIDT. Veröffentl. aus der Hamburger Staats- und Univ.-Bibl. 1. Hamburg 1928.
Apocrypha Anecdota ... ed. by M. R. JAMES. TSt 2.3. Cambridge 1893.
Les Apocryphes coptes, publiés et traduits par E. REVILLONT. 1. PO 2. Paris 1907.

Gespräche Jesu mit seinen Jüngern nach der Auferstehung, Ein katholisch-apostolisches Sendschreiben des 2. Jahrhunderts nach einem koptischen Papyrus herausgegeben, übersetzt und untersucht v. C. Schmidt. Übersetzung des äthiopischen Textes v. I. Waijnberg. TU 43. Leipzig 1919.

Littérature éthiopienne pseudo-clémentine, ed. S. Grébaut. ROC 5 (1910), pp. 198-214, 307-323, 425-439.

Altjüdisches Schrifttum ausserhalb der Bibel, übersetzt und erläutert v. P. Riessler. Augsburg 1928.

The Dead Sea Scrolls of St. Mark's Monastery II.2: Plates and Transcriptions of the Manual of Discipline, ed. M. Burrows, J. C. Trever & W. H. Brownlee. New Haven 1951.

The Zadokite Documents, ed. C. Rabin. 1: The Admonition, 2: The Laws. 2nd ed. Oxford 1958.

The Babylonian Talmud translated into English, ed. I. Epstein. 5-6. (Sanhedrin 1-2.) London 1935-48.

Midrash Rabbah translated into English ..., ed. H. Freedman & M. Simon. 3, 6. London 1939.

Mechilta, Ein tannaitischer Midrasch zu Exodus, ed. J. Winter & A. Wünsche. Leipzig 1909.

Flavii Iosephi opera omnia, ed. S. A. Naber. 1-4. Leipzig 1888-1896.

Philonis Alexandrini opera quae supersunt, ed. L. Cohn & P. Wendland. 1-7. Berlin 1896-1930.

Philo with an English Translation by F. H. Colson (& G. H. Whitaker). 1-9. (LCL.) London 1929-1949.

Philo, Suppl. 1-2, transl. by R. Marcus. (LCL.) London 1953.

Die apostolischen Väter. Neubearbeitung der Funkschen Ausgabe 1, ed. K. Bihlmeyer, W. Schneemelcher. (= SQ II.1.1.) 2nd ed. Tübingen 1956.

The Apostolic Fathers, ed. J. B. Lightfoot, Part II, S. Ignatius, S. Polycarp, vol. II.2. London 1885.

Die ältesten Apologeten ... herausg. von E. J. Goodspeed. Göttingen 1914.

Corpus Apologetarum Christianorum saeculi secundi, ed. J. C. Th. Otto. 9. Jenae 1872.

Sancti Ambrosii Mediolanensis Episcopi opera omnia ... t. 2. PL 16. Parisiis 1845.

Sancti Ambrosii opera, pars septima ... rec. O. Faller. CSEL 73. Vindobonae 1955.

Arnobii Adversus Nationes libri VII, rec. C. Marchesi. 2nd ed. (= Corp. Script. Lat. Parav. 62), Aug. Taurinorum 1953.

Athanasii Alexandrini opera omnia quae exstant vel quae ejus nomine circumferuntur ... opera & studio monachorum Ordinis S. Benedicti et Congregatione S. Mauri. 1.2. Patavii 1777.

S.P.N. Athanasii ... opera omnia quae exstant, ... t. 1-3. PG 25-27. Paris 1857.

Athanasius Werke, herausg. v. H. Opitz. 2.1. Berlin & Leipzig 1935.

The De Incarnatione of Athanasius. Part 1, The long recension manuscripts by G. J. Ryan. Part 2, The short recension by R. P. Casey. StD 14.1-2. London 1945-46.

Athanase d'Alexandrie, Apologie à l'Empereur Constance. Apologie pour sa fuite ... ed. J.-M. SZYMUSIAK. SC 56. Paris 1958.
Sancti Aureli Augustini De Genesi ad litteram libri duodecim ..., rec. ... I. ZYCHA. CSEL 28. Pragae, Vindobonae & Lipsiae 1895.
Sancti Augustini Confessionum libri tredecim, rec. ... P. KNÖLL. CSEL 32. Pragae, Vindobonae & Lipsiae 1896.
S.P.N. Basilii ... opera omnia quae exstant, ... t. 2. (contains also Eunomii impii apologia). PG 30, 32. Paris 1857.
S. Clementis I, ... opera omnia 1. PG 1 (1857).
Clemens Alexandrinus. Protrepticus and Paedagogus, Herausgegeben ... von O. STÄHLIN. GCS Clem. 1. Leipzig 1905.
Clemens Alexandrinus. Stromata, Buch I-VI. Herausg. von O. STÄHLIN, in dritter Auflage neu herausg. v. L. FRÜCHTEL. GCS Clem. 2. Leipzig 1960.
Clemens Alexandrinus, Stromata, Buch VII und VIII — Excerpta ex Theodoto — Eclogae Propheticae — Quis dives salvetur — Fragmente. Herausg. v. O. STÄHLIN. GCS Clem. 3. Leipzig 1909.
Clemens Alexandrinus. Register von O. Stählin. GCS Clem. 4. Leipzig 1934-36.
S. Thasci Caecili Cypriani opera omnia, rec. G. HARTEL. CSEL 3.1-2. Vindobonae 1868-71.
S.P.N. Cyrilli Archiepiscopi Hierosolymitani opera quae exstant omnia. PG 33. Paris 1857.
S.P.N. Cyrilli Alexandriae Archiepiscopi opera quae reperiri potuerunt omnia ... t. 2. PG 69. Paris 1859.
Didymi Alexandrini opera omnia ... PG 39. Paris 1858.
Epiphanius, Ancoratus und Panarion haer. De fide. Herausg. von K. HOLL. GCS Epiph. 1-3. Leipzig 1915-33.
Eusebii Pamphili ... opera omnia quae exstant ... t. 5. PG 23. Paris 1857.
Eusebius. Über das Leben Constantins. Constantins Rede an die heilige Versammlung. Tricennatsrede an Constantin. Herausg. von I. A. HEIKEL. GCS Eus. 1. Leipzig 1902.
Eusebius. Die Kirchengeschichte. Die lateinische Übersetzung des Rufinus. Über die Märtyrer in Palästina. Einleitungen. Übersichten und Register. Herausg. v. E. VON SCHWARTZ und T. MOMMSEN. GCS Eus. 2.1-3. Leipzig 1903-09.
Eusebius. Das Onomastikon der biblischen Ortsnamen. Die Theophanie. Die griechischen Bruchstücke und Übersetzung der syrischen Überlieferungen. Herausg. v. E. KLOSTERMANN (Onomastikon) und v. H. GRESSMANN (Theophanie). GCS Eus. 3. Leipzig 1904.
Eusebius. Gegen Marcell. Über die kirchliche Theologie. Die Fragmente Marcells. Herausg. v. E. KLOSTERMANN. GCS Eus. 4. Leipzig 1906.
Eusebius. Die Demonstratio Evangelica. Herausg. v. I. A. HEIKEL. GCS Eus. 6. Leipzig 1913.
Eusebius. Die Praeparatio Evangelica 1-2. Herausg. v. K. MRAS. GCS Eus. 8.1-2. Berlin 1956.
S.P.N. Gregorii Theologi vulgo Nazianzeni, ... opera quae exstant omnia, ... t. 2. PG 36. Paris 1858.

The Fragments of Heracleon, ed. by A. E. BROOKE. TSt 1.4. Cambridge 1891.
S. Hieronymi Presbyteri Opera, Pars 2, Opera homiletica. CCL 78. Turnholti 1958.
Sancti Hilarii Pictaviensis Episcopi opera omnia ... t. 2. PL 10.2. Parisiis 1845.
S. Hilarii Episcopi Pictaviensis Tractatus super Psalmos, rec. A. ZINGERLE. CSEL 22. Pragae, Vindobonae & Lipsiae 1891.
S. Hilarii Episcopi Pictaviensis opera, pars quarta, rec. ... A. FEDER. CSEL 65. Vindobonae & Lipsiae 1916.
Hippolytus. Exegetische und homiletische Schriften. Die Kommentare zu Daniel und zum Hohenliede. Kleinere exegetische und homiletische Schriften. Herausg. v. G. N. BONWETSCH und H. ACHELIS. GCS Hipp. 1. Leipzig 1897.
Hippolytus. Refutatio omnium haeresium. Herausg. v. P. WENDLAND. GCS Hipp. 3. Leipzig 1916.
Hippolyts Kommentar zum Hohenlied auf Grund von N. Marrs Ausgabe des grusinischen Textes herausg. von G. N. BONWETSCH. TU 23.2c. Leipzig 1902.
Die georgisch erhaltene Schriften von Hippolytus, herausg. v. G. N. BONWETSCH. Der Segen Jakobs, Der Segen Moses, Die Erzählung von David und Goliath. TU 26.1a. Leipzig 1904.
Hippolyte de Rome sur les bénédictions d'Isaac, de Jacob et de Moïse ... ed. M. BRIÈRE, L. MARIÈS & B.-CH. MERCIER. PO 27.1-2. Paris 1954.
Sancti Irenaei ... Libros quinque Adversus haereses ... ed. W. W. HARVEY, 1-2. Cantabrigiae 1857.
Armenische Irenaeusfragmente mit deutscher Übersetzung nach W. Lüdtke ... herausg. v. H. JORDAN. TU 36.3. Leipzig 1913.
St. Irenaeus. The Demonstration of the Apostolic Preaching, Translated from the Armenian with introduction and notes by J. ARMITAGE ROBINSON. London 1920.
St. Irenaeus, Proof of the Apostolic Preaching, transl. and ann. by J. P. SMITH. ACW 16. Westminster, Md. & London 1952.
S.P.N. Joannis Chrysostomi ... opera omnia quae exstant ... t. 2, 4-6, 8, 12. PG 49, 54-56, 58, 63. Paris 1859-60.
S.P.N. Justini Philosophi et Martyris opera quae exstant omnia ... PG 6. Paris 1857.
Luciferi Calaritani opuscula, rec. G. HARTEL. CSEL 14. Vindobonae 1886.
Sancti Maximi Episcopi Taurinensis opera omnia ... PL 57. Parisiis 1847.
Methodius. Herausg. von G. N. BONWETSCH. (GCS.) Leipzig 1917.
Novatiani Romanae urbis Presbyteri De Trinitate Liber — Novatian's Treatise on the Trinity, ed. W. Y. FAUSSET. Cambridge 1909.
S. Optati Milevitani Libri VII, rec. C. ZIWSA. CSEL 26 Pragae, Vindobonae & Lipsiae 1893.
Origenis opera omnia ... t. 7. PG 17. Paris 1857.
Origenes. Die Schrift vom Martyrium. Gegen Celsus. Die Schrift vom Gebet. Herausg. v. P. KOETSCHAU. GCS Orig. 1-2. Leipzig 1899.
Origenes. Jeremiahomilien. Klageliederkommentar. Erklärung der Samuel-

und Königsbücher. Herausg. v. E. KLOSTERMANN. GCS Orig. 3. Leipzig 1901.

Origenes. Der Johanneskommentar. Herausg. v. E. PREUSCHEN. GCS Orig. 4. Leipzig 1913.

Origenes. De Principiis. (ΠΕΡΙ ΑΡΧΩΝ), herausg. v. P. KOETSCHAU. GCS Orig. 5. Leipzig 1913.

Origenes. Homilien zum Hexateuch in Rufins Übersetzung. 1–2. Die Homilien zu Numeri, Josua und Judices. Herausg. v. W. A. BAEHRENS. GCS Orig. 6–7. Leipzig 1920–21.

Origenes. Homilien zu Samuel I, zum Hohelied und zu den Propheten. Kommentar zum Hohelied. In Rufins und Hieronymus' Übersetzung. Herausg. v. W. A. BAEHRENS. GCS Orig. 8. Leipzig 1925.

Origenes. Die Homilien zu Lukas in der Übersetzung des Hieronymus und die griechischen Reste der Homilien und des Lukas-Kommentars. 2. Aufl. Herausg. v. M. RAUER. GCS Orig. 9. Berlin 1959.

Origenes. Origenes Matthäusererklärung I–III. (Die griechisch erhaltene Tomoi, die lateinische Übersetzung der Commentariorum Series, Fragmente und Indices.) I–III.1 herausg. unter Mitw. v. E. BENZ u. E. KLOSTERMANN. III.2 herausg. v. E. KLOSTERMANN u. L. FRÜCHTEL. GCS Orig. 10–12. Leipzig 1933–41.

Socratis Scholastici, Hermiae Sozomeni Historia ecclesiastica. PG 67. Paris 1859.

Sozomenus. Kirchengeschichte. Herausg. von J. BIDEZ (†). Eingel. zum Druck besorgt und mit Register versehen von G. CH. HANSEN. (GCS.) Berlin 1960.

Quinti Septimi Florentis Tertulliani Opera 1–2. CCL 1–2. Turnholti 1954.

B. Theodoreti Opera omnia ex rec. I. SIRMONDI denuo edidit ... I. L. SCHULZE. 1.2. Halae 1769.

Theodoreti, Cyrensis Episcopi ... opera omnia ... t. 1. PG 80. Paris 1860.

Le Commentaire de Théodore de Mopsueste sur les Psaumes (I–LXXX), ed. R. DEVREESSE. ST 93. Città del Vaticano 1939.

ΑΠΟΣΤΟΛΙΚΗ ΠΑΡΑΔΟΣΙΣ. The Treatise on the Apostolic Tradition of St Hippolytus of Rome, ed. G. DIX. London 1937.

Ausgewählte Akten persischer Märtyrer. German transl. by O. BRAUN. BKV 22 (1915).

Bibliothek der Symbole und Glaubensregeln der alten Kirche, herausg. v. A. HAHN, dritte vielfach veränderte und vermehrte Auflage v. G. L. HAHN. Mit einem Anhang v. A. HARNACK. Breslau 1897.

Sacrorum Conciliorum nova et amplissima collectio ... (ed.) J. D. MANSI. 2. Florentinae 1759. New ed. Paris & Leipzig 1901–1927.

Contra Varimadum. CCL 90. Turnholti 1961.

The Dialogues of Athanasius and Zacchaeus and of Timothy and Aquila, ed. ... by F. C. CONYBEARE. Anecdota Oxon. Class. Ser. 8. Oxford 1898.

Didascalia et Constitutiones Apostolorum, ed. F. X. FUNK. 1–2. Paderbornae 1905.

Didascalia Apostolorum, ed. R. H. CONNOLLY. Oxford 1929.

Epistulae Imperatorum Pontificum aliorum ... Avellana quae dicitur collectio, rec. O. GUENTHER. 1-2. CSEL 35.1-2. Pragae, Vindobonae & Lipsiae 1895-98.

Μικρὸν εὐχολόγιον, ed. Π. Ν. ΤΡΕΜΠΕΛΑΣ 1. 'Αθῆναι 1950.

Expositio Patrum Graecorum in Psalmos, ed. B. CORDERIUS. Roma 1642.

Florilegium Edessenum anonymum ⟨syriace ante 562⟩. Herausg. v. I. RUCKER. BAS 1933.5. München 1933.

Homélies Paschales 1. Une homélie inspirée du traité sur la Pâque d'Hippolyte, ed. ... par P. NAUTIN. SC 27. Paris 1950.

Liber Pontificalis, ed. L. DUCHESNE. 1. Paris 1884-86.

Liber Sacramentorum Romanae Aeclesiae ordinis anni circuli, ed. L. C. MOHLBERG. Rerum eccl. documenta, ser. maior, fontes 4. Roma 1960.

Greek Liturgies, chiefly from Original Authorities, ed. C. A. SWAINSON. Cambridge 1884.

The Gregorian Sacramentary under Charles the Great, ed. ... by H. A. WILSON. Henry Bradshaw Soc. 49. London 1915.

Ausgewählte Märtyrerakten und andere Urkunden aus der Verfolgungszeit der christlichen Kirche, herausg. v. O. VON GEBHARDT (= Acta Martyrum Selecta). Berlin 1902.

Ausgewählte Märtyrerakten, ed. R. KNOPF & G. KRÜGER. (3rd ed.) SQ 3. Tübingen 1929.

Monumenta minora saeculi secundi, ed. G. RAUSCHEN. FP 3. Bonn 1905.

Patrologiae cursus completus a J. P. Migne editus ... Series Latina. Supplementum accurante A. Hamman ... vol. 1. Paris 1958-59.

Die Pseudoklementinen. 1. Homilien, herausg. ... v. B. REHM. (GCS.) Berlin 1953.

Sanctorum Damasi Papae et Paciani necnon Luciferi Episcopi Calaritani opera omnia ... (contains also Monumenta vetera ad Arianorum doctrinam pertinentia, col. 557-672). PL 13. Parisiis 1845.

Die Schatzhöhle, ed. C. BEZOLD. 1-2. Leipzig 1883-88.

Die Oracula Sibyllina. Bearbeitet von J. GEFFCKEN. (GCS.) Leipzig 1902.

La Passion de S. Félix de Thibiuca, ed. H. DELEHAYE. AB 39 (1921), pp. 241-276.

Rituale Armenorum, ed. F. C. CONYBEARE. Oxford 1905.

Ritus Orientalium in administrandis sacramentis, ed. H. DENZINGER. 1-2. Wirceburgi 1863-64.

Ausgewählte koptische Zaubertexte, herausg. v. A. M. KROPP. 1-3. Bruxelles 1930-31.

Aelius Aristides Smyrnaei quae supersunt omnia, ed. B. KEIL. II. Berlin 1898.

Aristotelis ... De Mundo, ed. W. L. LORIMER ... acc. capitum V, VI, VII interpretatio Syriaca ab E. KÖNIG. Paris 1933.

Cicero. Scripta, rec. C. F. W. MUELLER. 4.2-3. Lipsiae 1898.

Dionis Chrysostomi Orationes ... ed. G. DE BUDÉ. 1-2. (Bibl. Teubn.) Lipsiae 1916-19.

Platonis Opera, rec. ... I. BURNET. 1-5. (Script. Class. Bibl. Oxon.) Oxonii 1900-07 (new impression 1946-1950).

Plotin, Ennéades V. Texte établi et traduit par E. Bréhier. (Coll. Budé.) Paris 1931.
Plutarchi Chaeronensis Moralia, rec. G. N. Bernardakis. 5. (Bibl. Teubn.) Lipsiae 1893.
Ioannis Stobaei Anthologii Libri duo posteriores, rec. O. Hense. 1–2. (= Ioannis Stobaei Anthologium, rec. C. Wachsmuth et O. Hense. 3.) Berolini 1894–1909.
Stoicorum Veterum Fragmenta, collegit I. ab Arnim. 1–3. Lipsiae 1903–05.

B. *Literature*

Ahlström, G. W., *Psalm 89*. Eine Liturgie aus dem Ritual des leidenden Königs. Diss. Uppsala. Lund 1959.
Aland, K., *Kaiser und Kirche von Konstantin bis Byzanz*. Idem, Kirchengeschichtliche Entwürfe, Gütersloh 1960, pp. 257–279.
Albertz, M. *Untersuchungen über die Schriften des Eunomius*. Diss. Halle–Wittenberg. Wittenberg 1908.
Alföldi, A., *Die Ausgestaltung des monarchischen Zeremoniells am römischen Kaiserhofe*. RM 49 (1934), pp. 1–118.
— *Insignien und Tracht der römischen Kaiser*. RM 50 (1935), pp. 1–171.
Allegro, J. M., *Further Messianic References in Qumran Literature*. JBL 75 (1956), pp. 174–187.
Allo, P. E.-B., *Saint Jean, L'Apocalypse*. (Études Bibliques.) Paris 1933.
Anartos, M. V., *The Argument for Iconoclasm as presented by the Iconoclastic Council of 754*. Late Classical and Medieval Studies in honor of A. M. Friend, Jr. Princeton, N.J. 1955, pp. 177–188.
Anrich, G., *Das antike Mysterienwesen in seinem Einfluss auf das Christentum*. Göttingen 1894.
Aptowitzer, V., *Parteipolitik der Hasmonäerzeit im rabbinischen und pseudoepigraphischen Schrifttum*. VAKMF 5, Wien 1927.
Arvedson, T., *Das Mysterium Christi*, Eine Studie zu Mt 11.25–30. Diss. Uppsala. Uppsala 1937.
— *Jesus som narrkonung*. SEÅ 12 (1947), pp. 25–35.
Audet, J.-P., *Affinités littéraires et doctrinales du Manuel de Discipline* (suite). RB 60 (1953), pp. 41–82.
— *La Didachè*. Instruction des Apôtres. Paris 1958.
Aufhauser, J. B., *Die sakrale Kaiseridee in Byzanz*. Sacral Kingship, pp. 531–542.
Aulén, G., *Christus Victor*. London 1931.
Bandmann, G., *Mittelalterlicher Architektur als Bedeutungsträger*. Berlin 1951.
Barbel, J., *Christos Angelos*. Bonn 1941.
— *Zur "Engelchristologie" bei Novatian*. TrierThZ 67 (1958), pp. 96–105.
— *Zur Engelchristologie im Urchristentum*. ThR 54 (1958), col. 49–58, 103–112.
Bardy, G., *Paul de Samosate*. SSL 4, Louvain 1923.
— art. *Monarchianisme*. DThC 10 (1927–30), col. 2193–2209.

— *Recherches sur saint Lucien d'Antioche et son école*. Paris 1936.
BARRÉ, H., *La Royauté de Marie pendant les neuf premiers siècles*. RSR 29 (1939), pp. 129–162.
BARRETT, C. K., *The Lamb of God*. NTS 1 (1954/55), pp. 210–218.
BARTON, G. A. & K. KOHLER, art. *Anointing*. JE 1 (1901), pp. 611–613.
BAUDISSIN, W. W. Graf VON, *Kyrios als Gottesname*. 1–3. Giessen 1926–28.
BAUER, W., W. F. ARNDT & F. W. GINGRICH, *A Greek-English Lexicon of the New Testament and other Early Christian Literature*. A translation of W. BAUER's Griechisch-Deutsches Wörterbuch zu den Schriften des Neuen Testaments und der übrigen urchristlichen Literatur. 4th ed. 1952, by W. F. ARNDT and F. W. GINGRICH. Cambridge & Chicago 1957.
BAUS, K., *Der Kranz in Antike und Christentum*. Theophaneia 2. Bonn 1940.
— *Das Gebet der Märtyrer*. TrierThZ 62 (1953), pp. 19–32.
— *Das Nachwirken des Origenes in der Christusfrömmigkeit des heiligen Ambrosius*. RQ 49 (1954), pp. 21–55.
BAYNES, N. H., *Eusebius and the Christian Empire*. Mélange Bidez 2, Univ. libre de Bruxelles. Ann. de l'Institut de philol. et d'hist. orient. 2 (1934), pp. 13–18.
BEASLEY-MURRAY, G. R., *The two Messiahs in the Testaments of the Twelve Patriarchs*. JTS 48 (1947), pp. 1–12.
BEILNER, W., *Christus und die Pharisäer*. Wien 1959.
BENOIT, P., *L'Ascension*. RB 50 (1949), pp. 161–203.
BENTZEN, AA., *Det sakrale Kongedømme*. Festskrift udg. af Københavns Univers. Nov. 1945. København 1945.
— *Kan ordet "Messiansk" anvendes om Salmernes Kongeforestillinger?* SEÅ 12 (1947), pp. 36–50.
— *Messias, Moses Redivivus, Menschensohn*. Abh. z. Theol. d. A. u. NT 17, Zürich 1948.
BENZ, E., *Marius Victorinus und die Entwicklung der abendländischen Willensmetaphysik*. FKG (1932).
BERKHOF, H., *Die Theologie des Eusebius von Caesarea*. Diss. Leiden. Amsterdam 1939.
— *Kirche und Kaiser*. Zollikon–Zürich 1947.
BERLINGER, L., *Beiträge zur inoffiziellen Titulatur der römischen Kaiser. Eine Untersuchung ihres ideengeschichtlichen Gehaltes und ihrer Entwicklung*. Diss. Breslau. Breslau 1935.
BERNHARDT, K.-H., *Das Problem der altorientalischen Königsideologie im Alten Testament*. Suppl. Vet. Test. 8. Leiden 1961.
BERTRAM, G., *Die Himmelfahrt Jesu vom Kreuz aus und der Glaube an seine Auferstehung*. Festgabe für Adolf Deissmann, Tübingen 1927, pp. 187–217.
— *Der religionsgeschichtliche Hintergrund des Begriffs der "Erhöhung" in der Septuaginta*. ZAW 68 (1956), pp. 57–71.
BIDEZ, J. & F. CUMONT. *Les mages hellénisés. Zoroastre, Ostanès et Hystaspe d'après la tradition grecque*, 1–2. Paris 1938.
BIETENHARD, H., *Das tausendjährige Reich*. Bern 1944.
— art. ὄνομα. ThWB 5 (1944–54), pp. 242–283.

— *Die himmlische Welt im Urchristentum und Spätjudentum.* Tübingen 1951. WUNT 2.

BILLERBECK, P., see STRACK, H. L. & P. BILLERBECK.

BLINZLER, J., *Der Prozess Jesu.* 3rd ed., Regensburg 1960.

BLUME, C., *Der Engelhymnus Gloria in excelsis Deo.* Sein Ursprung und seine Entwicklung. StML 73 (1907), pp. 43–62.

BLUMENKRANTZ, B., *Die Judenpredigt Augustins.* Ein Beitrag zur Geschichte der jüdisch-christlichen Beziehungen in den ersten Jahrhunderten. BBG 25 (1946).

BOLL, F., *Aus der Offenbarung Johannis.* ΣΤΟΙΧΕΙΑ 1. Leipzig & Berlin 1914.

BONNER, C., *The Homily on the Passion by Melito Bishop of Sardis and some Fragments of the Apocryphal Ezekiel.* StD 12, London 1940.

BONSIRVEN, J., *Le judaïsme palestinien au temps de Jésus-Christ.* 1–2. 2nd ed., Paris 1934–35.

— *Le Règne de Dieu.* Théologie (Études publiées sous la direction de la faculté de Théologie S. J. de Lyon-Fourvière) 37. Paris 1957.

BOUSSET, W., *Die Evangeliencitate Justins des Märtyrers in ihrem Wert für die Evangelienkritik.* Göttingen 1891.

— *Kyrios Christos.* Göttingen 1913 (2nd ed. 1921).

— *Jesus der Herr.* Nachträge und Auseinandersetzungen zu Kyrios Christos. Göttingen 1916.

— *Eine jüdische Gebetssammlung im siebenten Buch der Apostolischen Konstitutionen.* GN 1915 (1916), pp. 435–489.

BOUYER, L., *La notion christologique du Fils de l'homme, a-t-elle disparu dans la patristique grecque?* Mélanges Bibliques rédigés en l'honneur de A. Robert, (Travaux de l'Inst. Cath. de Paris 4), Paris 1957, pp. 519–530.

BRANDON, S. G. F., *The Effect of the Destruction of Jerusalem in A.D. 70 on Primitive Christian Soteriology.* Sacral Kingship, pp. 471–477.

BRÉHIER, L., *L'Origine des titres impériaux à Byzance.* BZ 15 (1906), pp. 161–178.

BRÉHIER, E., *Les idées philosophiques et religieuses de Philon d'Alexandrie.* Paris 1908.

BRIGHTMAN, F. E., *Liturgies Eastern and Western.* 1. Oxford 1896.

BROWNLEE, W. H., *Messianic Motifs of Qumran and the New Testament.* NTS 3 (1956–57), pp. 12–30, 195–210.

DE BRUYNE, L., *La décoration des baptistères paléochrétiens.* Misc. L. C. Mohlberg I, EL (Bibl.) 22 (1948), pp. 189–220.

BULTMANN, R., *Die Geschichte der synoptischen Tradition.* 2 ed., Göttingen 1931.

— *Theologie des Neuen Testaments.* Tübingen 1948–53.

BURROWS, M., *The Messiahs of Aaron and Israel.* AThR 34 (1952), pp. 202–206.

CABANISS, A., *The Harrowing of Hell, Psalm 24, and Pliny the Younger: a Note.* VC 7 (1953), pp. 65–74.

CADIOU, R., *Commentaires inédits des Psaumes.* Étude sur les textes d'Origène contenus dans le manuscript *Vindobonensis 8,* Paris 1936.

CAMPENHAUSEN, H., Frhr VON, *Die Passionssarkophage.* Marburger Jahrbuch für Kunstwissenschaft 5 (1929), pp. 15–47.
— *Die Idee des Martyriums in der alten Kirche.* Göttingen 1936.
— *Bearbeitung und Interpolationen des Polycarpmartyriums.* SbHei 1957: 3.
CAPELLE, B., *Un homiliaire de l'évêque arien Maximin.* RevBén 34 (1922), pp. 81–108.
— *Le texte du "Gloria in excelsis".* RHE 44 (1949), pp. 439–457.
CAPMANY, J., *"Miles Christi" en la espiritualidad de San Cipriano.* Colectanea San Paciano, Ser. Theol. 1, Barcelona 1956.
CASEL, O., *Die Epiphanie im Lichte der Religionsgeschichte.* Bened. Monatsschr. 4 (1922), pp. 13–20.
CASEY, R. P., *Clement and the two Divine Logoi.* JTS 25 (1924), pp. 43–56.
CASPARI, C., *Ungedruckte, unbeachtete und wenig beachtete Quellen zur Geschichte des Taufsymbols und der Glaubensregel.* 3. Kristiania 1875.
CECCHELLI, C., *Il trionfo della croce. La croce e i santi segni prima e dopo Costantino.* Roma 1954.
CERFAUX, L., *Le titre "Kyrios" et la dignité royale de Jesus.* RLC 1, pp. 3–64.
— *Le nom divin "Kyrios".* RLC 1, pp. 113–136.
— *"Adonai" et "Kyrios".* RLC 1, pp. 137–172.
— *"Kyrios" dans les citations pauliniennes de l'Ancien Testament.* RLC 1, pp. 173–188.
— *La première communauté chrétienne à Jérusalem.* RLC 2, pp. 125–156.
— *Regale sacerdotium.* RLC 2, pp. 283–315.
— *Le Christ dans la théologie de Saint Paul.* Paris 1954.
— *Kyrios.* DB Suppl. 5 (1957), col. 200–227.
— *Le conflit entre Dieu et le Souverain divinisé dans l'Apocalypse de Jean.* Sacral Kingship, pp. 459–470.
CERFAUX, L. & J. TONDRIAU. *Un concurrent du christianisme. Le culte des souverains dans la civilisation gréco-romaine.* (Bibliothèque de théologie, série III, vol. 5) Tournai 1957.
CHEVALLIER, M.-A., *L'Esprit et le Messie dans le bas-judaïsme et le Nouveau Testament.* EHPhS 49, Paris 1958.
CONGAR, Y. M.-J., *Jalons pour une théologie du laïcat.* Paris 1954.
COPPENS, J., *La portée messianique du Psaume CX.* Analecta Lov. Bibl. et Orient. 3. 1, Louvain & Gembloux 1955.
— *Les apports du Psaume CX (Vulg. CIX) à l'idéologie royale israélite.* Sacral Kingship, pp. 333–348.
CULLMANN, O., *Königsherrschaft Christi und Kirche im Neuen Testament.* ThSt 10. Zürich 1941.
— *Christus und die Zeit.* Zürich 1948.
— *Les premières confessions de foi chrétiennes.* CRHPhR 30. Paris 1948.
— *Dieu et César. Le procès de Jésus. St. Paul et l'Autorité. L'Apocalypse et l'État totalitaire.* Neuchâtel–Paris 1956.
— *Die Christologie des Neuen Testaments.* 2nd ed., Tübingen 1958.
CUMONT, F., *La théologie solaire du paganisme romain.* Mém. par div. sav., Acad. Inscr. Paris 12. 2 (1913), pp. 447–479.
— art. Ὕψιστος. PWK 9 (1914–16), col. 444–450.

DAHL, N. A., *Das Volk Gottes.* Eine Untersuchung zum Kirchenbewusstsein des Urchristentums. Skrifter utg. av Det Norske Vid. Akad. 2, Hist.-fil. Kl. 1941.2, Diss. Oslo. Oslo 1941.

DANIÉLOU, J., *Origène.* Paris 1948.

— *Sacramentum futuri.* Études sur les origines de la typologie biblique. Paris 1950.

— *Bible et liturgie.* Lex Orandi 11. Paris 1951.

— *Christos Kyrios.* Une citation des Lamentations de Jérémie dans les Testimonia. Mélanges Lebreton 1, RSR 39 (1951), pp. 338–352.

— *The Fathers and the Scriptures.* ECQ 10 (1954), pp. 265–273.

— *Théologie du Judéo-Christianisme.* 1. Tournai 1958.

— *La session à la droite du Père.* Stud. Ev., TU 73 (1959), pp. 689–698.

— *Les symboles chrétiens primitifs.* Paris 1961.

DAUBE, D., *Four Types of Question.* JTS N.S. 2 (1951), pp. 45–48.

DAVIES, J. G., *He Ascended into Heaven.* London 1958.

DEISSMANN, G. A., *Licht vom Osten.* (1st ed. Tübingen 1908.) 4th ed. Tübingen 1923.

(DEKKERS, E. & AE. GAAR.) *Clavis Patrum Latinorum* qua in novum Corpus Christianorum edendum optimas quasque scriptorum recensiones a Tertulliano ad Bedam commode recludit E. DEKKERS opera usus qua rem praeparavit et iuvit AE. GAAR Vindobonensis. SE 3. Bruges 1951.

DELATTE, L., *Les Traités de la Royauté d'Ecphante, Diotogène et Sthénidas.* BFPhL 97, Liège & Paris 1942.

DELBRÜCK, R., *Die Consulardiptychen.* SSK 2 (1929).

— *Das spätantike Kaiserornat.* Die Antike 8 (1932), pp. 1–21.

— *Spätantike Kaiserportraits.* SSK 8 (1933).

— *Antiquarisches zu den Verspottungen Jesu.* ZNW 41 (1942), pp. 124–145.

DELEHAYE, H., *Les légendes grecques des saints militaires.* Paris 1909.

— *Les passions des martyres et les genres littéraires.* Bruxelles 1921.

DELVOYE, C., *Recherches récentes sur les origines de la basilique paléochrétienne.* AJPh 14 (1954–57), pp. 205–228.

DESCAMPS, A., *Le messianisme royal dans le NT.* (J. C. L. Coppens:) L'Attente du Messie, Paris 1954, pp. 57–84.

DEVREESSE, R., art. *Chaînes exégétiques grecques.* DB Suppl. 1 (1928), col. 1084–1233.

DIBELIUS, M., *An die Thessaloniker I–II.* Handbuch z. NT, herausg. v. H. Lietzmann, 11. Tübingen 1923.

— *Rom und die Christen im ersten Jahrhundert.* SbHei 1941–1942. 2.

DIBELIUS, M. & H. CONZELMANN. *Die Pastoralbriefe.* 3rd ed. Handbuch z. NT, herausg. v. H. Lietzmann, 13. Tübingen 1955.

DIX, G., *The Shape of the Liturgy.* 2nd ed. London 1945.

— *Jew and Greek.* London 1953.

VON DOBSCHÜTZ, E., ΚΥΡΙΟΣ ΙΗΣΟΥΣ. ZNW 30 (1931), pp. 97–123.

DODD, C. H., *The Bible and the Greeks.* London 1934.

— *According to the Scriptures.* London 1952.

— *The Interpretation of the Fourth Gospel.* Cambridge 1953.

DOERRIES, H., *Das Selbstzeugnis Kaiser Konstantins*. GAb 3 F., 34. Göttingen 1954.
— *Konstantin der Grosse*. Stuttgart 1958.
DOEVE, J. W., *Jewish Hermeneutics in the Synoptic Gospels and Acts*. Diss. Leiden. Assen 1953.
DÖLGER, F. J., ΙΧΘΥΣ. 1. Rom 1910.
— *Die Sonne der Gerechtigkeit und der Schwarze*. LF 2, Münster i. W. 1918.
— *Sol Salutis*. Gebet und Gesang im christlichen Altertum. LF 4–5. Münster i. Westf. 1920.
— *Zur antiken und frühchristlichen Auffassung der Herrschergewalt von Gottes Gnaden*. AC 3 (1932), pp. 117–131.
DORNSEIFF, F., art. Σωτήρ. PWK 2 Reihe 5 (1927), col. 1211–1221.
DOUTRELEAU, L., *Que savons-nous aujourd'hui des papyrus de Toura?* RSR 43 (1955), pp. 162–193.
DUENSING, H., *Ein Stück der urchristlichen Petrusapokalypse enthaltender Traktat der äthiopischen pseudo-klementinischen Literatur*. ZNW 14 (1913), pp. 65–78.
DUPONT, O. J., *Filius meus es tu*. L'interprétation de Ps. II, 7 dans le Nouveau Testament. RSR 35 (1948), pp. 522–543.
— Σὺν Χριστῷ. L'Union avec le Christ suivant St. Paul. Bruges, Louvain & Paris 1952.
DURANT, W. *Cäsar und Christus*. Bern 1949.
DÜRR, L., *Psalm 110 im Lichte der neueren altorientalischen Forschung*. Univ. Progr. Braunschw. Akad. Kirchhain N.-L. 1929.
DYGGVE, E., *Fra evangeliekirke til magtkirke*. Studier til sanctuariets udviklingshistorie. KÅ 58 (1958), pp. 11–52.
DÜRIG, W., *Pietas liturgica*. Regensburg 1958.
ECK, O., *Urgemeinde und Imperium*. Ein Beitrag zur Frage nach der Stellung des Urchristentums zum Staat. BFTh 42.3 (1940), pp. 301–434.
EGGER, G., *Römischer Kaiserkult und konstantinischer Kirchenbau*. JAIW 43 (1958), pp. 120–132.
EHRHARDT, A., *Christian Baptism and Roman Law*. Festschrift Guido Kisch, Stuttgart 1955, pp. 147–166.
— *Politische Metaphysik von Solon bis Augustin*. 2. Tübingen 1959.
EISLER, R., *Weltenmantel und Himmelszelt*. I–II. München 1910.
ELLIGER, W., *Die Stellung der alten Christen zu den Bildern in den ersten vier Jahrhunderten*. StChD 20, Leipzig 1930.
ENGNELL, I., *Studies in Divine Kingship in the Ancient Near East*. Diss. Uppsala. Uppsala 1943.
— *Gamla Testamentet 1*. Uppsala 1945.
— *Till frågan om Ebed Jahve-sångerna och den lidande Messias hos "Deuterojesaja"*. SEÅ 10 (1945), pp. 31–65.
— *The 'Ebed Yahweh Songs and the Suffering Messiah in "Deutero-Isaiah"*. BJRL 31 (1948), pp. 54–93.
— Articles in SBU: *Adam*, SBU 1, col. 13–15. *Gamla Testamentets religion*, col. 673–685. *Herrens Tjänare*, col. 844–846. *Konung, Kungadöme*, col. 1221–1226. *Messias* (GT), SBU 2, col. 245–263. *Människosonen*, col.

399-403. *Nyårsfester*, col. 497-503. *Psaltaren*, col. 787-832. *Sebaot*, col. 1072-1073. *Yttersta dagen*, col. 1628-1632.
— Rev. of E. Sjöberg, *"Der Menschensohn"*. BO 8 (1951), pp. 187-192.
— *Die Urmenschvorstellung und das Alte Testament*. SEÅ 22-23 (1957-58), pp. 265-289.
ENSSLIN, W., *Gottkaiser und Kaiser von Gottes Gnaden*. BAS 1943. 6. München 1943.
— *Die Religionspolitik des Kaisers Theodosius d. Gr.* BAS, 1953. 2.
EPPEL, R., *Le piétisme juif dans les Testaments des douze Patriarches*. Strasbourg 1930.
FARRER, A., *A Rebirth of Images*. London 1949.
FASCHER, E., *Gottes Königtum im Urchristentum*. Numen 4 (1957), pp. 85-113.
— *Dynamis*. RAC 4 (1959), col. 415-458.
FESTUGIÈRE, A. J., *La révélation d'Hermès Trismégiste*. II. Le dieu cosmique. Paris 1949.
FEUILLET, A., *Les vingt-quatre vieillards de l'Apocalypse*. RB 65 (1958), pp. 5-32.
FINK, J., *Die Anfänge der Christusdarstellung*. ThR 51 (1955), pp. 241-252.
FISCH, M. H., *Alexander and the Stoics*. AJPh 58 (1937), pp. 59-82, 129-151.
FITZMYER, J. A., *"4 Q Testimonia" and the New Testament*. TS 18 (1957), pp. 513-537.
FLOROVSKY, G., *Origen, Eusebius and the Iconoclastic Controversy*. CH 19 (1950), pp. 77-96.
FLUSSER, D., *Two Notes on the Midrash on 2 Sam. vii*. IEJ 9 (1959), pp. 99-109.
FOERSTER, W., *Von Valentin zu Heracleon*. Untersuchungen über die Quellen und die Entwicklung der valentinianischen Gnosis. ZNW Beih. 7 (1928).
— Κύριος. ThWB 3 (1935-38), col. 1038-1056, 1081-1098.
FRANÇOIS, L., *Julien et Dion Chrysostome*. Les Περὶ βασιλείας et le second panégyrique de Constance. REG 28 (1915), pp. 417-439.
DE FRANCOVICH, G., *Studi sulla scultura Ravennate. 1 — I sarcofaghi*. FR 3.26-27 (1958), pp. 5-172; 3.28 (1959), pp. 5-175.
FREED, E. D., *The Entry into Jerusalem in the Gospel of John*. JBL 80 (1961), pp. 329-338.
FRISQUE, J., *Oscar Cullmann*. Une théologie de l'histoire du salut. Cahiers de l'actualité religieuse 11. Paris 1960.
FUCHS, H., *Augustin und der antike Friedensgedanke*. NPhU 3. Berlin 1926.
FULLER, R. H., *The Mission and Achievement of Jesus*. StBTh 12. London 1954.
GADD, C. J., *Ideas of Divine Rule in the Ancient East*. The Schweich Lectures of the British Academy (38) 1945. London 1948.
GAGÉ, J., Σταυρὸς νικοποιός. *La victoire impériale dans l'empire chrétien*. RHPhR 13 (1933).
GÄRTNER, B., טליא *als Messiasbezeichnung*. SEÅ 18-19 (1953-54), pp. 98-108.
GAUTHIER, R.-A., *Magnanimité*. L'idéal de la grandeur dans la philosophie païenne et dans la théologie chrétienne. Bibl. thomiste 28. Paris 1951.

GEFFCKEN, J., *Zwei griechische Apologeten*. Leipzig & Berlin 1907.
GERHARDSSON, B., *The Good Samaritan—the Good Shepherd?* CN 16. Lund & Copenhagen 1958.
— *Memory and Manuscript*. Oral Tradition and Written Transmission in Rabbinic Judaism and Early Christianity. ASNU 22. Diss. Uppsala. Uppsala, Lund & Copenhagen 1961.
GERICKE, W., *Marcell von Ancyra*. Der Logos-Christologe und Biblizist. Sein Verhältnis zur antiochenischen Theologie und zum Neuen Testament. ThA 10, Halle 1940.
VON GERKAN, A., *Die profane und die christliche Basilika*. RQ 48 (1953), pp. 128–146.
GERKE, F., *Ist der Sarkophag des Junius Bassus umzudatieren?* RivAC 10 (1933), pp. 105–118.
— *Der neugefundene altchristliche Friessarkophag im Museo Archeologico zu Florenz und das Problem der Entwicklung der ältesten christlichen Friessarkophage*. ZKG 54 (1935), pp. 18–39.
— *Der Sarkophag des Iunius Bassus*. Berlin 1936.
— *Die Zeitbestimmung der Passionssarkophage*. Archaeologiai Ertesitö 52 (1939), pp. 191–251.
— *Die christlichen Sarkophage der vorkonstantinischen Zeit*. SSK 11 (1940).
— *Ideengeschichte der ältesten christlichen Kunst*. ZKG 59 (1940), pp. 1–102.
— *Christus in der spätantiken Plastik*. 3rd ed. Mainz 1948.
— *Der Trierer Agricius-Sarkophag*. Ein Beitrag zur Geschichte der altchristlichen Kunst in den Rheinlanden. Trier 1949.
GESCHÉ, A., *Un document nouveau sur la christologie du IVe s.*: le Commentaire sur les Psaumes decouvert à Toura. SP 3 (1961), pp. 205–213.
GHEDINI, G., *Lettere cristiane dei papiri greci del III e IV secolo*. Milano 1923.
DE GHELLINCK, J., *Pour l'histoire du mot "sacramentum"*. SSL, Études et docum. 3 (1924).
GINSBURGEN, M., *La chaire de Moïse*. REJ 90 (1931), pp. 161–165.
GLAZIK, J., *Jesus — Apostel und Hohenpriester*. Skizze einer biblischen Missionslehre. ZMR 44 (1960), pp. 87–98, 175–183.
GOKEY, F. X., *The Terminology for the Devil and Evil Spirits in the Apostolic Fathers*. The Cath. Univ. of America, Patristic Studies. 93. (Diss.) Washington 1961.
GOLDAMMER, K., *Das Schiff der Kirche*. Ein antiker Symbolbegriff aus der politischen Metaphorik in eschatologischer und ekklesiologischer Umdeutung. ThZ 6 (1950), pp. 232–237.
GOODENOUGH, E. R., *The Political Philosophy of Hellenistic Kingship*. YCS 1 (1928), pp. 55–102.
— *Kingship in Early Israel*. JBL 48 (1929), pp. 169–205.
— *By Light, Light*. The Mystic Gospel of Hellenistic Judaism. New Haven 1935.
— *The Politics of Philo Judaeus*. New Haven 1938.
— *The Crown of Victory in Judaism*. ArtB 28 (1946), pp. 139–159.

— *Jewish Symbols in the Greco-Roman Period.* 8. Bollingen Series 37. New York 1958.

GOODSPEED, E., *The Theology of Justin Martyr.* Jena 1923.

GOPPELT, L., *Typos.* Die typologische Deutung des Alten Testaments im Neuen. BFTh R. 2, 43 (1939).

GRABAR, A., *L'Empereur dans l'art byzantin.* PFLS 75. Paris 1936.

GRANT, F. C., *The Idea of the Kingdom of God in the New Testament.* Sacral Kingship, pp. 437–446.

GRÉGOIRE, F., *Le Messie chez Philon d'Alexandrie.* ETL 12 (1935), pp. 28–50.

GRESSMANN, H., *Der Ursprung der israelitisch-jüdischen Eschatologie.* FRLANT 6. Göttingen 1905.

GRIFFITHS, J. G., Βασιλεὺς βασιλέων. Remarks on the History of a Title. CPh 48 (1953), pp. 145–154.

GRUNDMANN, W., art. δύναμαι etc. ThWB 2 (1933–35), pp. 286–318.

GUILKA, J., *"Bräutigam" — spätjüdisches Messiasprädikat?* TrierThZ 69 (1960), pp. 298–301.

GUTBERLET, S. H., *Die Himmelfahrt Christi in der bildenden Kunst, von den Anfängen bis ins hohe Mittelalter.* Samml. Heitz, Akad. Abh. z. Kulturgesch., R. 3, 1. Strassburg 1934.

GUY, P.-M., *Remarques sur le vocabulaire antique du sacerdoce chrétien.* Études sur le Sacrement de l'Ordre, Lex Orandi 22. Paris 1957, pp. 125–145.

HAENCHEN, E., *Die Apostelgeschichte.* (Krit.-exeg. Komm. über d. NT. Begr. v. H. A. W. Meyer.) 3rd ed. Göttingen 1959.

HAGEL, K. F., *Kirche und Kaisertum in Lehre und Leben des Athanasius.* Diss. Tübingen. Leipzig 1933.

HANSON, R. P. C., *Allegory and Event.* London & Richmond, Virginia 1959.

HARLE, P. A., *L'Agneau de l'Apocalypse et le N. T.* EtThRel 31.2 (1956), pp. 26–35.

VON HARNACK, A., *Die Überlieferung der griechischen Apologeten des 2. Jahrhunderts in der alten Kirche und im Mittelalter.* TU 1.1–2 (1882).

— *Militia Christi.* Tübingen 1905.

— *Der Heiland.* IDEM, Reden und Aufsätze 1. 2nd ed. Giessen 1906, pp. 307–311.

— *Mission und Ausbreitung des Christentums in den ersten drei Jahrhunderten.* 1–2. Leipzig 1906.

— *Marcion.* Das Evangelium vom fremden Gott. TU 45 (1921).

— *Die Bezeichnung Jesu als Knecht Gottes und ihre Geschichte in der alten Kirche.* SbB 1926, pp. 212–238.

HARRIS, J. RENDEL (and V. BURCH). *Testimonies.* I–II. Cambridge 1916, 1920.

HEFELE, C. J., *Conciliengeschichte.* 1. Freiburg i. Br. 1855.

HEIKEL, I. A., *Kritische Beiträge zu den Constantin-Schriften des Eusebius.* TU 36.4 (1911).

HEINEMANN, I., *Philons griechische und jüdische Bildung.* Kulturvergleichende Untersuchungen zu Philons Darstellung der jüdischen Gesetze. Breslau 1932.

HELLSTRÖM, G., *Klädnaden i Joh. Upp. 1.13*. En lexikografisk undersökning av det grekiska ordet ποδήρης betydelse. Unprinted essay. Uppsala 1953.
HÉRING, J., *Le Royaume de Dieu et sa venue*. EHPhR 35. Paris 1937.
HITCHCOCK, F. R. M., *The Apostolic Preaching of Irenaeus*. JTS 9 (1907–08), pp. 284–289.
HOCART, A. M., *Kingship*. London 1927.
HOENIG, S. B., *The Great Sanhedrin*. Philadelphia & New York 1953.
HOLZMEISTER, U., *Unbeachtete patristische Agrapha*. ZKTh 38 (1914), pp. 113–143.
HOMMEL, H., *Pantokrator*. ThV 5 (1953–54), pp. 322–378.
HOMMES, N. J., *Het Testimoniaboek*. Studiën over O.T. citaten in het N.T. en bij de patres, met critische beschouwingen over de theorieën van J. Rendel Harris en D. Plooy. Diss. Amsterdam, Amsterdam 1935.
HOOGEWERFF, G. J., *Il mosaico absidale di San Giovanni in Laterano ed altri mosaici romani*. AAR 27 (1953), pp. 297–326.
HULEN, A. B., *The "Dialogues with the Jews" as Sources for the Early Jewish Argument against Christianity*. JBL 51 (1932), pp. 58–70.
HUNT, P. B. W. STATHER. *Primitive Gospel Sources*. London 1951.
HÜNTEMANN, U., *Zur Kompositionstechnik Justins*. Analyse seiner ersten Apologie. ThGl 25 (1933), pp. 410–428.
IHM, C., *Die Programme der christlichen Apsismalerei vom vierten Jahrhundert bis zur Mitte des achten Jahrhunderts*. FKCA 4. Wiesbaden 1960.
INSTINSKY, H. U., *Kaiser und Ewigkeit*. Hermes 77 (1942), pp. 313–355.
— *Bischofsstuhl und Kaiserthron*. München 1955.
JEREMIAS, A., *Das Alte Testament im Lichte des Alten Orients*. Leipzig 1916.
JEREMIAS, J., *Jesus als Weltvollender*. BFTh 33.4 (1930).
— art. ἀμνός. ThWB 1 (1932–33), pp. 342–344.
— ’Αμνὸς θεοῦ — παῖς θεοῦ. ZNW 34 (1935), pp. 115–123.
— art. παῖς θεοῦ. ThWB 5 (1944–54), pp. 676–713.
JEREMIAS, J. & W. ZIMMERLI, *The Servant of God*. Transl. by H. Knight. StBTh 20. London 1957.
DE JONGE, M., *The Testaments of the Twelve Patriarchs*. Assen 1953.
JOST, W., ΠΟΙΜΗΝ. Das Bild vom Hirten in der biblischen Überlieferung und seine christologische Bedeutung. Diss. Giessen. Giessen 1939.
JUNGMANN, J. A., *Die Stellung Christi im liturgischen Gebet*. LF 7–8. Münster 1925.
— *Die Abwehr des germanischen Arianismus und der Umbruch der religiösen Kultur im frühen Mittelalter*. ZKTh 69 (1947), pp. 36–99.
— *Missarum Sollemnia*. 1–2. Wien 1948.
KANTOROWICZ, E. H., *Dante's "Two Suns"*. Semitic and Oriental Studies presented to W. Popper. University of California Publications in Semitic Philology 11 (1951), pp. 217–231.
— *Kaiser Friedrich II und das Königsbild des Hellenismus*. Varia Variorum, Festgabe für Karl Reinhardt. Münster & Köln 1952, pp. 169–193.
— *Deus per naturam, Deus per gratiam*. A Note on Medieval Political Theology. HThR 45 (1952), pp. 253–277.

— *The King's Two Bodies*. A Study in Medieval Political Theology. Princeton, N. J. 1957.

KATTENBUSCH, F., *Das apostolische Symbol*. I–II. Leipzig 1894–1900.

KELLER, J. E., *Der Bräutigam im Gleichnis der zehn Jungfrauen*. Gehlberg 1940.

KEMPF, T. K., *Christus der Hirt*. Ursprung und Deutung einer altchristlichen Symbolgestalt. Rom 1942.

KEYSNER, K., *Gottesvorstellung und Lebensauffassung im griechischen Hymnus*. WStA 2. Würzburg 1932.

KIRSCH, G. P., *Sull'origine dei motivi iconografici nella pittura cimiteriale di Roma*. RivAC 4 (1927), pp. 259–287.

KIRSCHBAUM, E., *Die Gräber der Apostelfürsten*. Frankfurt a. M. 1957.

KITTEL, G., art. δόξα. ThWB 2 (1935), pp. 236–256.

KITTEL, H., *Die Herrlichkeit Gottes*. Studien zu Geschichte und Wesen eines Neutestamentlichen Begriffs. ZNW Beih. 16 (1934).

KLAUSER, TH., *Aurum coronarium*. RM 59 (1944), pp. 129–153.

— *Der Ursprung der bischöflichen Insignien und Ehrenrechte*. Bonner Rektoratsrede 11.12.1948. Krefeld 1949.

— art. *Ciborium*. RAC 3 (1955–57), col. 68–86.

— *Studien zur Entstehungsgeschichte der christlichen Kunst*. 1 and 3. JbAC 1 (1958), pp. 20–51, and 3 (1960), pp. 112–133.

— *Der Vorhang vor dem Thron Gottes*. JbAC 3 (1960), pp. 141–142.

KLEIN, G., *Der älteste christliche Katechismus und die jüdische Propaganda-Literatur*. Berlin 1909.

KLEINKNECHT, H., art. βασιλεύς *im Griechentum*. ThWB 1 (1932–33), pp. 562–563.

KLOSTERMANN, E., *Formen der exegetischen Arbeiten des Origenes*. ThLZ 72 (1947), col. 203–208.

KNOPF, R., *Die Apostolischen Väter*. 1. Handbuch z. N. T., herausg. v. H. Lietzmann, Erg.-bd. Tübingen 1920.

KOCH, C., art. *Pax*. PWK 18.2 (1949), col. 2430–2436.

KOCH, H., *Die altchristliche Bilderfrage nach den literarischen Quellen*. FRLANT 10. Göttingen 1917.

KOESTER, W., *Lamm und Kirche in der Apokalypse*. Vom Wort des Lebens, Festschrift für M. Meinertz (= Neutest. Abh. Erg. Bd. 1). Münster i. W. 1951, pp. 152–164.

KOHLER, K., art. *Merkabah*. JE 8 (1904), pp. 498–500.

KOLLWITZ, J., *Christus als Lehrer und die Gesetzesübergabe an Petrus*. RQ 44 (1936), pp. 45–66.

— *Oströmische Plastik der theodosianischen Zeit*. SSK 12 (1941).

— *Rev. of L. Kitschelt, Die frühchristliche Basilika als Darstellung des himmlischen Jerusalems*. BZ 42 (1942), pp. 273–276.

— *Das Bild von Christus dem König in Kunst und Liturgie der christlichen Frühzeit*. ThGl 1 (1947), pp. 95–117.

— art. *Christus Basileus*. RAC 2 (1951–54), col. 1257–1262.

KOOLE, J. L., *De overname van het Oude Testament door de christelijke Kerk*. Hilversum 1938.

KOSNETTER, J., *Die Taufe Jesu.* Theol. Stud. d. Österr. Leogesellsch. 35 (1936).
KRAMER, H., art. *Homonoia.* PWK 8 (1912–13), col. 2265–2268.
— *Quid valeat* ὁμόνοια *in litteris Graecis.* Diss. Göttingen. Göttingen 1915.
KRAUS, H.-J., *Psalmen.* 1–2. Neukirchen 1960.
KRAUTHEIMER, R., *The Beginnings of Christian Architecture.* RevR 3 (1938–39), pp. 127–148.
KRETSCHMAR, G., *Studien zur frühchristlichen Trinitätstheologie.* BHTh 21. Tübingen 1956.
KROLL, J., *Gott und Hölle. Der Mythus vom Descensuskampfe.* StBW 20. Berlin 1932.
KRUSE, gr., art. *Pantokrator.* PWK 18.2 (1949), col. 829–830.
KUHN, K. G., *Die beiden Messias Aarons und Israels.* NTS 1 (1954–55), pp. 168–179.
— מלכות שמים *in der rabbinischen Literatur.* ThWB 1 (1932–33), pp. 570–573.
KÜMMEL, W. G., *Kirchenbegriff und Geschichtsbewusstsein in der Urgemeinde und bei Jesus.* SB 1. Uppsala 1943.
LADNER, G. B., *The Idea of Reform.* Its Impact on Christian Thought and Action in the Age of the Fathers. Cambridge, Mass. 1959.
LAGRANGE, M.-J., *Le judaïsme avant Jésus-Christ.* Paris 1931.
LAMPE, G. W. H., *Some notes on the Significance of* ΒΑΣΙΛΕΙΑ ΤΟΥ ΘΕΟΥ, ΒΑΣΙΛΕΙΑ ΧΡΙΣΤΟΥ *in the Greek Fathers.* JTS 49 (1948), pp. 58–73.
— *The Exegesis of some Biblical Texts by Marcellus of Ancyra and Pseudo-Chrysostom's Homily on Ps. XCVI.1.* JTS 49 (1948), pp. 169–175.
LANG, S., *A few suggestions toward a new solution of the Origin of the Early Christian Basilica.* RivAC 30 (1954), pp. 189–208.
LANGLOTZ, E., *Der architektonische Ursprung der christlichen Basilika.* Festschr. f. H. Jantzen, Berlin 1951, 30–36.
LANGLOTZ, E. & F. W. DEICHMANN, art. *Basilika.* RAC 1 (1941–50), pp. 1225–1249 (Langlotz), pp. 1249–1259 (Deichmann).
LASSUS, J., *Sanctuaires chrétiens de Syrie.* Inst. fr. d'arch. de Beyrouth, Bibl. arch. et hist. 42. Paris 1944.
LAURENTIN, R., *Traces d'allusions étymologiques en Luc. 1–2.* (I–II.) Biblica 37 (1956), pp. 435–456; 38 (1957), pp. 1–23.
LEBRETON, J., *Histoire du dogme de la Trinité des origines au concile de Nicée.* 1–2. 5th ed. Paris 1919–1928.
LECLERCQ, J., *L'Idée de la royauté du Christ au Moyen Age.* Paris 1959.
LÉCUYER, J., *Le sacerdoce chrétien et le sacrifice eucharistique selon Théodore de Mopsueste.* RSR 36 (1949), pp. 481–516.
— *Le sacerdoce céleste du Christ selon Chrysostome.* NRTh 82 (1950), pp. 561–579.
LEISEGANG, H., *Die Gnosis.* 4th ed., Stuttgart 1955.
LEHMANN, K., *Sta. Costanza.* ArtB 37 (1955), pp. 193–196 and p. 291.
LEIVESTAD, R., *Christ the Conqueror.* Ideas of Conflict and Victory in the New Testament. Diss. Oslo. London 1954.
LEMARIÉ, J., *La manifestation du Seigneur.* La Liturgie de Noël et de l'Épiphanie. Lex Orandi 23. Paris 1957.

LEWY, H., *Sobria ebrietas*. Untersuchungen zur Geschichte der antiken Mystik. ZNW Beih. 9 (1929).
LIETZMANN, H., *Geschichte der alten Kirche*. 3. 2 uppl. Berlin 1953.
— *Der Weltheiland*. Bonn 1909.
LINDHAGEN, C., *The Servant Motif in the Old Testament*. A Preliminary Study to the 'Ebed-Yahweh Problem' in Deutero-Isaiah. Diss. Uppsala. Uppsala 1950.
LINSSEN, H., Θεὸς σωτήρ. Entwickelung und Verbreitung einer liturgischen Formelgruppe. JL 8 (1928), pp. 1–75.
LOHMEYER, E., *Christuskult und Kaiserkult*. SGVS 90. Tübingen 1919.
— *Kyrios Jesus*. Eine Untersuchung zu Phil. 2: 5–11. SbHei 1927–28 Abh. 4.
LOHMEYER, E. & G. BORNKAMM, *Die Offenbarung des Johannes*. 2nd ed. Handbuch z. NT, herausg. v. H. Lietzmann, 16. Tübingen 1953.
LOOFS, F., *Die Trinitätslehre Marcells von Ancyra und ihr Verhältnis zur älteren Tradition*. SbB 1902.
— *Leitfaden zum Studium der Dogmengeschichte*. 4th ed. Halle 1906.
— *Das Bekenntnis Lucians, des Märtyrers*. SbB 1915, pp. 576–603.
— *Paulus von Samosata*. TU 44.5 (1924).
— *Theophilus von Antiochia adversus Marcionem und die anderen theologischen Quellen bei Irenäus*. TU 46.2 (1930).
L'ORANGE, H. P., *Sol invictus imperator*. SO 14 (1935), pp. 86–114.
— *Kejseren på himmeltronen*. Oslo 1949.
— *Studies on the Iconography of Cosmic Kingship in the Ancient World*. Inst. f. sammenl. kulturforskn. A. 23. Oslo 1953.
— *Expressions of Cosmic Kingship in the Ancient World*. Sacral Kingship, pp. 481–492.
LORENZ, S., *De progressu notionis* φιλανθρωπίας. Diss. Leipzig. Leipzig 1914.
LÖVESTAM, E., *Son and Saviour*. A Study of Acts 13, 32–37. With an Appendix: 'Son of God' in the Synoptic Gospels. CN 18. Lund & Copenhagen 1961.
DE LUBAC, H., *Histoire et esprit*. Paris 1950.
LUDIN JANSEN, H., *Den 110. Psalmen*. STK 16 (1940), pp. 263–276.
— *The Consecration in the eighth Chapter of Testamentum Levi*. Sacral Kingship, pp. 356–366.
MCFAYDEN, D., *The History of the Title Imperator under the Roman Empire*. Diss. Chicago. Chicago 1920.
MCNEILE, A. H., *The Gospel according to St. Matthew*. The Greek Text with Introduction, Notes and Indices. London 1915.
MAGIE, D., *De Romanorum iuris publici sacrique vocabulis sollemnibus in Graecum sermonem conversis*. Leipzig 1905.
MÂLE, E., *Rome et ses vieilles églises*. Paris 1942.
MANSER, A., *Christkönigszüge im römischen und benediktinischen Adventsgottesdienst*. Heilige Überlieferung, Festgabe ... I Herwegen, Münster 1938, pp. 124–135.
MANSON, T. W., *The Argument from Prophecy*. JTS 46 (1945), pp. 129–136.
MANSON, W., *Jesus the Messiah*. London 1943.

MARIÈS, L., *Hippolyte de Rome. Sur les bénédictions d'Isaac, de Jacob et de Moïse*. Paris 1935.
— *Le Messie issu de Lévi chez Hippolyte de Rome*. Mélange Lebreton 1, RSR 39 (1951), pp. 381–396.
MARMORSTEIN, A., *Zur Erklärung der Gottesnamen bei Irenäus*. ZNW 25 (1926), pp. 253–258.
MARROU, H. I., *L'idée de Dieu et la divinité du Roi*. Sacral Kingship, pp. 478–480.
MARXEN, A., *Das Problem der Analogie zwischen den Seinsstrukturen der grossen Gemeinschaften* (dargestellt in engeren Anschluss an die Schriften von Carl Schmitt und Erick Peterson). Diss. Bonn. Würzburg 1937.
MASSAUX, E., *Influence de l'Évangile de saint Matthieu sur la littérature chrétienne avant saint Irenée*. Univ. Cath. Lov. Diss. Theol. II: 42. Louvain & Gembloux 1950.
MAY, H. G., *A Key to the Interpretation of Zechariah's Visions*. JBL 57 (1938), pp. 173–184.
VAN DER MEER, F., *Maiestas Domini. Théophanies de l'Apocalypse dans l'art chrétien*. StAC 13. Rom & Paris 1938.
MICHAELIS, W., art. κράτος. ThWB 3 (1935–38), pp. 905–910.
— art. παντοκράτωρ. ThWB 3 (1935–38), pp. 913–914.
— *Zur Engelchristologie im Urchristentum*. Basel 1942.
MICHL, J., art. *Engel*. RAC 5 (1960–), pp. 109–200.
MILIK, J. T., *Une lettre de Siméon bar Kokheba*. RB 60 (1953), pp. 276–294.
MOHRMANN, CH., *Epiphania*. RSPhTh 37 (1953), pp. 644–670.
MOLLAND, E., *The Conception of the Gospel in the Alexandrinian Theology*. Diss. Oslo. Oslo 1938.
MOORE, G. F., *Judaism in the first Centuries of the Christian Era*. 1. Cambridge, Mass. 1927.
MOULE, C. F. D., *The Influence of Circumstances on the Use of Christological Terms*. JTS 10 (1959), pp. 247–263.
MOWINCKEL, S., *Kongesalmerne i det Gamle Testamente*. Kristiania 1916.
— *Tronstigningssalmerne og Jahves tronstigningsfest*. NTT 18 (1917), pp. 13–79.
— *Psalmenstudien* II. Das Thronbesteigungsfest Jahwäs und der Ursprung der Eschatologie. Videnskapsselsk. Skrifter II, Hist.-filos. Kl. 1921 n° 6. Kristiania 1922.
— *Henok og "Menneskesønnen"*. NTT 45 (1944), pp. 57–69.
— *Urmensch und "Königsideologie"*. STh 2.1 (1948), pp. 71–89.
— *He That Cometh*. Oxford & Bristol 1956.
MOWRY, L., *Revelation 4–5 and Early Christian Liturgical Usage*. JBL 71 (1952), pp. 75–84.
MUILENBURG, J., *The Son of Man in Daniel and the Ethiopic Apocalypse of Enoch*. JBL 79 (1960), pp. 197–209.
MÜLLER, E. F. K., *Jesu Christi dreifaches Amt*. RE 8 (1900), pp. 733–741.
MÜLLER, G., *Lexicon Athanasianum*. Berlin 1952.
MUNCK, J., *Judekristendomen efter apostlarnas dagar*. SEÅ 25 (1960) pp. 78–96.

MURMELSTEIN, B., *Adam. Ein Beitrag zur Messiaslehre.* WZKM 35 (1928), pp. 242–275.
NASH, H. S., *The Exegesis of the School of Antioch. A Criticism of the Hypothesis that Aristotelianism was a Main Cause in its Genesis.* JBL 11 (1892), pp. 22–37.
NAUTIN, P., *Le dossier d'Hippolyte et de Méliton.* Paris 1953.
NEHER, A., *Le symbolisme conjugal: expression de l'histoire dans l'A.T.* RHPhR 34 (1954), pp. 30–49.
NEUSS, W., *Das Buch Ezechiel in Theologie und Kunst bis zum Ende des XII Jahrhunderts.* BGAM 1–2. Münster i. Westf. 1912.
NEWMAN, J. H., *The Arians of the Fourth Century.* (Cardinal Newman's Works.) London 1908.
NOCK, A. D., *Soter and Euergetes.* The Joy of Study, Papers on New Testament and Related Subjects Presented to Honor F. C. Grant, ed. by S. E. Johnson, New York 1951, pp. 127–148.
NORDEN, E., *Die Geburt des Kindes.* Geschichte einer religiösen Idee. Berlin 1924.
NORDSTRÖM, C.-O., *Ravennastudien.* Figura 4. Stockholm 1953.
ODEBERG, H., *Föreställningarna om Meṭaṭron i äldre judisk mystik.* (o. 50–850 e. Kr.) KÅ 27 (1927), pp. 1–20.
— *The Fourth Gospel. Interpreted in its Relation to Contemporaneous Religious Currents in Palestine and the Hellenistic Oriental World.* Uppsala & Stockholm 1929.
— *Fragen von Metatron, Schekina und Memra.* Lund 1942.
OEHLER, J., Εὐεργέτης. PWK 6 (1907–09), pp 978–981.
OEPKE, A., art. παρουσία. ThWB 5 (1944–54), pp 856–869
OKE, C. C., *A Doxology not to God but to Christ.* ET 67 (1955–56), pp. 367–368.
O'NEILL, J. C., *The Use of κύριος in the Book of Acts.* ScJTh 8 (1955), pp. 155–174.
OPITZ, H.-G., *Euseb von Caesarea als Theologe.* ZNW 34 (1935), pp. 1–19.
ÖSTBORN, G., *Tōrā in the Old Testament. A Semantic Study.* Diss. Uppsala. Lund 1945.
OTZEN, B., *Die neugefundenen hebräischen Sektenschriften und die Testamente der zwölf Patriarchen.* STh 7 (1953), pp. 125–157.
PASCHER, J., ΒΑΣΙΛΙΚΗ ΟΔΟΣ. *Der Königsweg zu Wiedergeburt und Vergöttung bei Philo von Alexandrien.* Paderborn 1941.
— *Die Hierarchie in sakramentaler Symbolik.* Episcopus, Festschr. f. Kard. M. Faulhaber. Regensburg 1949, pp. 278–295.
PAX, E., Ἐπιφάνεια. *Ein religionsgeschichtlicher Beitrag zur biblischen Theologie.* MThSt 1.10 (1955).
PEDERSEN, J., *Israel. Its Life and Culture.* I–IV. London & Copenhagen 1926–1940.
PERLER, O., *Ein Hymnus zur Ostervigil von Meliton?* (Papyrus Bodmer XII.) Par. 15 (1960).
PERSSON, P. E., *Kyrkans ämbete som Kristusrepresentation. En kritisk analys av nyare ämbetsteologi.* StThL 20. Lund 1961.
PETERSON, E., Εἷς θεός. FRLANT N.F. 24. Göttingen 1926.

— *Die Einholung des Kyrios.* ZSTh 7 (1930), pp. 682–702.
— *Göttliche Monarchie.* ThQ 112 (1931), pp. 537–564.
— *Kaiser Augustus im Urteil des antiken Christentums.* Hochland 30.2 (1933), pp. 289–299.
— *Der Monotheismus als politisches Problem.* IDEM, Theologische Traktate, München 1951, pp. 45–147.
— *Christus als Imperator.* Ibid., pp. 149–164.
— *Zeuge der Wahrheit.* Ibid., pp. 165–224.
— *Von den Engeln.* Ibid., pp. 323–407.
— *Das Problem des Nationalismus im alten Christum.* IDEM, Frühkirche, Judentum und Gnosis, Rom, Freiburg & Wien 1959, pp. 51–63.
— *Über einige Probleme der Didache-Überlieferung.* Ibid., pp. 146–182.
— *Die Spiritualität des griechischen Physiologos.* Ibid., pp. 236–253.
PFISTER, E., art. *Epiphanie.* PWK Suppl. 4 (1924), pp. 277–323.
PHILONENKO, MARC, *Les interpolations chrétiennes des Testaments des douze Patriarches et les manuscrits de Qoumrân.* RHPhR 58.4 (1958).
PIPER, O. A., *The Apocalypse of John and the Liturgy of the Ancient Church.* CH 20 (1951), pp. 10–22.
PLOOIJ, D., *The Baptism of Jesus.* Amicitiae Corolla, presented to J. Rendel Harris, London 1933, pp. 239–252.
POLLARD, T. E., *Logos and Son in Origen, Arius and Athanasius.* SP 2 (1957), pp. 282–287.
— *The Origins of Arianism.* JTS N.S. 9 (1958), pp. 103–111.
DE LA POTTERIE, I., *L'Onction du Christ.* Étude de théologie biblique. NRTh 90 (1958), pp. 225–252.
PRÜMM, K., *Herrscherkult und Neues Testament.* Biblica 9 (1928), pp. 1–25, 129–142, 289–301.
— *Der christliche Glaube und die altheidnische Welt.* 1–2. Leipzig 1935.
— *Dynamis in griechisch-hellenistischer Religion und Philosophie als Vergleichsbild zu göttlichen Dynamis im Offenbarungsraum.* ZKTh 83 (1961), pp. 393–430.
PUECH, H.-CH., *Numénius d'Apamée et les théologies orientales au second siècle.* Mélange Bidez 2, AIPh 2 (1934), pp. 745–778.
QUASTEN, J., *Der Gute Hirte in hellenistischer und frühchristlicher Logostheologie.* Heilige Überlieferung, Festgabe … I. Herwegen. Münster 1938, pp. 51–58.
— *Patrology.* 1–3. Utrecht & Brussels 1949–1960.
— *Mysterium tremendum.* Eucharistische Frömmigkeitsauffassungen des vierten Jahrhunderts. In Vom christlichen Mysterium, Gesamm. Arb. z. Gedächtnis v. O. Casel, Düsseldorf 1951, pp. 66–75.
QUELL, G., κύριος. (Der at.liche Gottesname). ThWB. 3 (1935–38), pp. 1056–1081.
QUISPEL, G., *De bronnen van Tertullianus' Adversus Marcionem.* Diss. Utrecht. Leiden 1943.
RABIN, C., *Qumran Studies.* Scripta judaica 2. Oxford 1957.
VON RAD, G., art. βασιλεύς *im AT.* ThWB 1 (1932–33), pp. 563–569.

Rahlfs, A., *Verzeichnis der griechischen Handschriften des Alten Testaments für das Septuaginta-Unternehmen aufgestellt.* GN 1914, Beiheft.

Rahner, H., *Antenna Crucis.* I. Odysseus am Mastbaum. ZKTh 65 (1941), pp. 123–152. II. Das Meer der Welt, ZKTh 66 (1942), pp. 89–118. III. Das Schiff aus Holz, ZKTh 66 (1942), pp. 196–227.

— *Kirche und Staat im frühen Christentum.* München 1961. (Rev. ed. of Idem, *Abendländische Kirchenfreiheit,* 1943.)

Rawlinson, A. E., *The New Testament Doctrine of the Christ.* The Bampton Lectures for 1926. London, New York & Toronto 1929.

Reicke, B., *The Disobedient Spirits and Christian Baptism.* Diss. Uppsala. København 1946.

Reynders, B., *Lexique comparé du texte grec et des versions latine, arménienne et syriaque de l'« Adversus haereses » de saint Irénée.* 1–2. CSCO Subs. 5–6. Louvain 1954.

Richstaetter, C., *Christusfrömmigkeit in ihrer historischen Entfaltung.* Köln 1949.

de Riedmatten, H., *Les Actes du procès de Paul de Samosate.* Étude sur la christologie du IIIe au IVe siècle. Par. 6. Freiburg i. Br. 1952.

Riesenfeld, H., *Jésus Transfiguré.* København 1947.

— *Ämbetet i Nya Testamentet.* En bok om Kyrkans ämbete, Uppsala 1951, pp. 17–69.

— *Den senjudiska messianologien såsom bakgrund till kristologien.* Bidrag till kristologien, Bringstrup 1951, pp. 5–22.

Rigaux, B., *L'Antéchrist et l'opposition au royaume messianique dans l'Ancien et le Nouveau Testament.* Diss. Louvain. Gembloux & Paris 1932.

Ringgren, H., *Word and Wisdom.* Diss. Uppsala. Lund 1947.

— *König und Messias.* ZAW 64 (1952), pp. 120–147.

Rissi, M., *Zeit und Geschichte in der Offenbarung des Johannes.* Abh. z. Theol. d. A. u. N.T. 22. Zürich 1952.

Roberts, C. H., *Two Biblical Papyri in the John Rylands Library, Manchester.* BJRL 20 (1936), pp. 219–244.

Robinson, J. A., *On a Quotation from Justin Martyr in Irenaeus.* JTS 31 (1930), pp. 374–378.

Roosval, J., *Petrus- och Moses-gruppen bland Roms sarkofager.* Konsthist. Tidskr. 1 (1932), pp. 77–88.

— *Junius Bassus' sarkofag och dess datering.* Arkeologiska studier tillägnade HKH Kronprins Gustaf Adolf, Stockholm 1932, pp. 273–287.

Roth, C., *The 'Chair of Moses' and its Survivals.* PEQ 81 (1949), pp. 100–111.

Rowley, H. H., *The Relevance of Apocalyptic.* A Study of Jewish and Christian Apocalyptics from Daniel to the Revelation. 2nd ed. London & Redhill 1947.

— *Jewish Apocalyptics and the Dead Sea Scrolls.* London 1957.

Rudberg, G., *Forschungen zu Poseidonios.* HVSS 20: 3 (1918).

Sanders, L., *L'hellénisme de Saint Clément de Rome et le paulinisme.* Stud. hell. 2. Louvain 1943.

Sas-Zaloziecky, W., *Westrom oder Ostrom.* JÖBG 2 (1952), pp. 150–152.

DE SAVIGNAC, J., *Le messianisme de Philon d'Alexandrie.* Nov. Test. 4 (1960), pp. 319–324.
SCHEIDWEILER, F., *Marcell von Ancyra.* ZNW 46 (1955), pp. 202–214.
SCHERMANN, TH., *Griechische Zauberpapyri und das Gemeinde- und Dankgebet im 1. Klemensbriefe.* TU 34. 2a (1909).
SCHLATTER, D. A., *Das Alte Testament in der johanneischen Apokalypse.* BFTh 16.6 (1912).
SCHLIER, H., *Religionsgeschichtliche Untersuchungen zu den Ignatiusbriefen.* ZNW Beiheft 8. Giessen 1929.
— *Der Brief an die Epheser.* Ein Kommentar. Düsseldorf 1957.
SCHLÜTZ, K., *Isaias 11.2.* (Die sieben Gaben des Hl. Geistes in den ersten vier christlichen Jahrhunderten.) Alttest. Abh. 11.4. Münster i. W. 1932.
SCHMAUS, M., *Ämter Christi.* LThK (2nd ed.) 1 (1957), pp. 457–459.
SCHMIDT, H., *Die Thronfahrt Jahves am Fest der Jahreswende im alten Israel.* SGVS 122. Tübingen 1927.
SCHMIDT, K. L., art. *Die Wortgruppe βασιλεύς κτλ. im NT.* ThWB 1 (1932–33), pp. 576–595.
— *Das Gegenüber von Kaiser und Staat in der Gemeinde des Neuen Testaments.* ThBl 16 (1937), Col. 1–16.
— *Die Polis in Kirche und Welt.* Eine lexikographische und exegetische Studie. Rektoratsprogramm der Univ. Basel 1939.
— *Jerusalem als Urbild und Abbild.* Eranos-Jahrbuch 18 (1950), pp. 207–248.
SCHMITT, C., *Politische Theologie.* München 1922.
SCHNACKENBURG, R., *Gottes Herrschaft und Reich.* Freiburg i. Br. 1959.
SCHNEIDER, A. M., *Die altchristlichen Bischofs- und Gemeindekirchen und ihre Benennung.* GN 1952. 7, pp. 153–161.
SCHNEIDER, C., *Studien zum Ursprung liturgischer Einzelheiten östlicher Liturgien.* 1. καταπέτασμα. Kyrios 1 (1936), pp. 57–73. 2. θυμιάματα. Kyrios 3 (1938), pp. 149–190.
— *Geistesgeschichte des antiken Christentums.* 1–2. München 1954.
VON SCHOEFFER, V., art. βασιλεύς 1. PWK 3 (1899), col. 55–82.
VON SCHOENEBECK, H., *Die christliche Sarkophagplastik unter Konstantin.* RM 51 (1936), pp. 238–336.
SCHOEPS, H. J., *Theologie und Geschichte des Judenchristentums.* Tübingen 1949.
SCHOLEM, G., *Die jüdische Mystik in ihren Hauptströmungen.* Zürich 1957.
SCHOONHEIM, P. L., *Een semasiologisch onderzoek van parousia.* Met betrekking tot het gebruik in Mattheüs 24. Diss. Utrecht. Aalten 1953.
SCHUBART, W., *Das hellenistische Königsideal nach Inschriften und Papyri.* APF 12 (1936), pp. 1–26.
SCHUMACHER, W. N., *"Dominus legem dat."* RQ 54 (1959), pp. 1–39.
SCHÜRER, E., *Geschichte des jüdischen Volkes im Zeitalter Jesu Christi.* 1–3. 3rd and 4th ed. Leipzig 1901–1909.
SCHWANK, B., *Zur Neuausgabe von "Contra Varimadum" nach dem Codex Paris B. N. Lat. 122 17 im Corpus Christianorum Series Latina XC.* SE 12 (1961), pp. 112–196.

Schwartz, E., *Eusebios von Caesarea*. PWK 6 (1909), col. 1370–1439.
— *Zur Geschichte des Athanasius.* (= Gesammelte Schriften 3.) Berlin 1959.
Segelberg, E., *Oleum sanctum.* Unprinted diss. Uppsala 1952.
— *Maṣbūtā, Studies in the Ritual of the Mandaean Baptism.* Diss. Uppsala. Uppsala 1958.
Sellers, R. V., *Two Ancient Christologies. A Study in the Christological Thought of the Schools of Alexandria and Antioch in the Early History of Christian Doctrine.* London 1954.
Selwyn, E. G., *The First Epistle of St. Peter.* London 1952.
Seston, W., *Le culte impérial et les origines de la basilique chrétienne.* Bull. de la Soc. Nat. des Antiquaires de France. 1948–49, pp. 200–201.
— *Le culte impérial, le culte des morts et les origines de la basilique latine chrétienne.* REL 27 (1949), pp. 82–83.
Setton, K. M., *Christian Attitude towards the Emperor in the Fourth Century.* New York 1941.
Silbermann, L. H., *The two Messiahs of the Manual of Discipline.* VT 5 (1955), pp. 77–82.
Simon, M. *Verus Israel.* Étude sur la relation entre chrétiens et juifs dans l'empire romain. Bibl. d'écoles franç. d'Athènes et de Rome, Fasc. 166. Paris 1948.
Sjöberg, E., Der Menschensohn im äthiopischen Henochsbuch. ASHL 41. Lund 1946.
— *Uttrycket "människoson" i GT.* STK 26 (1950), pp. 35–44.
— בן אדם und בר אנש im Hebräischen und Aramäischen. AO 21 (1950–51), pp. 57–65, 91–107.
Skard, E., *Zwei religiös-politische Begriffe.* Euergetes-Concordia. Norske Videnskaps-Akad. Oslo, Avh. II, Hist.-Filos. Kl. 1931: 2.
Skehan, W., *A Fragment from the "Song of Moses" (Deut. 32) from Qumran.* BASOR 136/1954, pp. 12–15.
Spicq, C., *La philanthropie hellénistique, vertu divine et royale* (à propos de Tit. III, 4). STh 12 (1958), pp. 169–191.
— *Les Épîtres pastorales.* 2nd ed. Paris 1947.
— *L'Épître aux Hébreux.* 1. Paris 1952.
Staerk, W., *Soter.* 1. BFTh 31. Gütersloh 1933.
— *Die Erlösererwartung in den östlichen Religionen.* Untersuchungen zu den Ausdrucksformen der biblischen Christologie (Soter II). Stuttgart & Berlin 1938.
Stange, A., *Das frühchristliche Kirchengebäude als Bild des Himmels.* Köln 1950.
Stauffer, E., *Das theologische Weltbild der Apokalyptik.* ZSTh 8 (1930–31), pp. 203–215.
— *Der Stand der Neutestamentlichen Forschung.* Theologie und Liturgie, Kassel 1952, pp. 35–105.
— *Christus und die Cäsaren.* 4th ed. Hamburg 1952.
— *Messias oder Menschensohn?* Nov. Test. 1 (1956), pp. 81–102.
— *Jerusalem und Rom.* Bern 1957.
— *Jesus.* Gestalt und Geschichte. Bern 1957.

STEGEMANN, V., *Die Gestalt Christi in den koptischen Zaubertexten.* QSGKAM 1. Heidelberg 1934.
STEINWENTER, A., ΝΟΜΟΣ ΕΜΨΥΧΟΣ. Zur Geschichte einer politischen Theorie. Anzeiger der Akad. d. Wiss. in Wien, Philos.-hist. Kl. 83 (1946), pp. 250-268.
STENDAHL, K., *The School of St. Matthew.* Diss. Uppsala. Uppsala 1954.
STERN, H., *Les mosaïques de l'église de Sainte-Constance à Rome.* DOP 12 (1958), pp. 157-218.
STIER, H. E., ΝΟΜΟΣ ΒΑΣΙΛΕΥΣ. Studien zur Geschichte der ΝΟΜΟΣ-Idee vornehmlich im V und IV Jahrhundert v. Chr. Diss. Berlin 1927.
STOMMEL, E., *Die bischöfliche Kathedra im christlichen Altertum.* MThZ 3 (1952), pp. 17-32.
— *Bischofsstuhl und Hoher Thron.* JbAC 1 (1958), pp. 52-78.
STONEHOUSE, N. B., *The Elders and the Living-Beings in the Apocalypse.* Arcana revelata, aangeboden aan F. W. Grosheide, Kampen 1951, pp. 135-148.
STRACK, H. L. & P. BILLERBECK, *Kommentar zum Neuen Testament aus Talmud und Midrasch.* 1-4. München 1922-28.
STRAUB, J. A., *Vom Herrscherideal in der Spätantike.* FKG 18 (1939).
STRECKER, G., *Das Judenchristentum in den Pseudoklementinen.* TU 70 (1958).
STUHLFAUTH, G., *Das Schiff als Symbol der altchristlichen Kunst.* RivAC 19 (1942), pp. 111-141.
SUNDKLER, B., *Jésus et les païens.* AMNSU 6 (1937), pp. 1-38.
SURKAU, H. W., *Martyrien in jüdischer und frühchristlicher Zeit.* Göttingen 1938.
VON SYBEL, L., *Das Werden christlicher Kunst.* RepK 39 (1916), pp. 118-129.
— *Christliche Antike.* Einführung in die altchristliche Kunst, I. Marburg 1906.
— *Das Christentum der Katakomben und Basiliken.* HZ 106 (1910), pp. 1-38.
— *Mosaiken römischer Apsiden.* ZKG 37 (1918), pp. 273-318.
TAEGER, F., *Charisma.* Studien zur Geschichte des antiken Herrscherkultus. 1-2. Stuttgart 1957-1960.
TAILLIEZ, F., ΒΑΣΙΛΙΚΗ ΟΔΟΣ. Les valeurs d'un terme mystique et le prix de son histoire littérale. OCP 13 (1947), pp. 299-354.
TARN, W. W., *Alexander and the Unity of Mankind.* PBA 1933, pp. 123-166.
TARN, W. W. & G. T. GRIFFITH, *Hellenistic Civilisation.* 3rd ed. London 1952.
TAYLOR, V., *The Names of Jesus.* London 1953.
TEEUWEN, S. W. J., *Sprachlicher Bedeutungswandel bei Tertullian.* Ein Beitrag zum Studium der christlichen Sondersprache. StGKA 14.1. Paderborn 1926.
THOMSON, J. G. S. S., *The Shepherd-Ruler Concept in the Old Testament and its Application in the New Testament.* ScJTH 8 (1955), pp. 406-418.
THRAEDE, K., *Beiträge zur Datierung Commodians.* JbAC 2 (1959), pp. 90-114.
TORM, F., *Valentinianismens Historie og Lære.* København 1901.

TREITINGER, O., *Die oströmische Kaiser- und Reichsidee nach ihrer Gestaltung im höfischen Zeremoniell.* Jena 1938.

TSELOS, D., *Unique Portraits of the Evangelists.* ArtB 34 (1932), pp. 257–277.

TURNER, C. H., *Notes on the Apostolic Constitutions.* 1. JTS 16 (1914–15), pp. 54–61.

VON UNGERN-STERNBERG, A., *Der Alttestamentliche Schriftbeweis "De Christo" und "De Evangelio" in der Alten Kirche bis zur Zeit Eusebs von Caesarea.* Halle 1913.

VALDENBERG, V., *La théorie monarchique de Dion Chrysostome.* REG 40 (1927), pp. 142–182.

VERHOEVEN, L., *Studien over Tertullianus' Adversus Praxean.* Diss. Utrecht. Amsterdam 1948.

— *Monarchia dans Tertullien.* VC 5 (1951), pp. 43–48.

VEROSTA, S., *Johannes Chrysostomus, Staatsphilosoph und Geschichtstheologe.* Graz, Wien & Köln 1960.

VISSER, W. J. A., *Die Entwicklung des Christusbildes in Literatur und Kunst in der frühchristlichen und frühbyzantinischen Zeit.* Diss. Utrecht. Bonn 1934.

VOELKL, L., *Die konstantinischen Kirchenbauten nach Eusebius.* RivAC 29 (1953), pp. 49–66, 187–206.

— *Die konstantinischen Kirchenbauten nach den literarischen Quellen des Okzidents.* RivAC 30 (1954), pp. 99–136.

VOGT, J., *Berichte über Kreuzeserscheinungen aus dem 4. Jahrh. nach Chr.* Mélange Grégoire 1, AIPH 9 (1949), pp. 593–606.

VOLBACH, W. F. & M. HIRMER, *Frühchristliche Kunst. Die Kunst der Spätantike in West- und Ostrom.* München 1958.

VÖLKER, W., *Das Vollkommenheitsideal des Origenes.* Tübingen 1931.

VOLLMER, H., *Die alttestamentlichen Citate bei Paulus, textkritisch und biblisch-theologisch gewürdigt nebst einem Anhang über das Verhältnis des Apostels zu Philo.* Freiburg & Leipzig 1895.

VOLZ, P., *Die Eschatologie der jüdischen Gemeinde im neutestamentlichen Zeitalter.* Tübingen 1934.

DE WAAL, A., *Der Sarkophag des Junius Bassus.* Rom 1900.

WAGENVOORT, H., *Roman Dynamism. Studies in ancient Roman thought, language and custom.* Oxford 1947.

WARD PERKINS, J. B., *Constantine and the Origins of the Christian Basilica.* PBSR 22 (1954), pp. 69–90.

WEINEL, H., *Die Stellung des Urchristentums zum Staat.* Tübingen 1908.

WELLEN, G. A., *Theotokos. Eine ikonographische Abhandlung über das Gottesmutterbild in frühchristlicher Zeit.* Diss. Nijmegen. Utrecht & Antwerpen 1960.

WELTE, B., *Die postbaptismale Salbung. Ihr symbolischer Gehalt und ihre sakramentale Zugehörigkeit nach den Zeugnissen der alten Kirche.* Diss. Freiburg i. Br. Freiburg i. Br. 1939.

WENDLAND, P., *Philos Schrift über die Vorsehung.* Berlin 1892.

— Σωτήρ. ZNW 5 (1904), pp. 335–353.

WERNER, M., *Die Entstehung des christlichen Dogmas.* Basel 1941.

WESSEL, K., *Kranzgold und Lebenskronen.* AA 65–66 (1950–51), Col. 103–114.
— *Christus Rex.* Kaiserkult und Christusbild. AA 68 (1953), Col. 118–136.
WESTCOTT, B. F., *The Historic Faith.* London & Cambridge 1885.
WHEELER ROBINSON, H., *The Council of Yahweh.* JTS 45 (1944), pp. 151–157.
WIDENGREN, G., *Psalm 110 och det sakrala kungadömet i Israel.* UUÅ 1941. 7.1.
— *Den himmelska intronisationen och dopet.* RoB 5 (1946), pp. 28–60.
— *Till det sakrala kungadömets historia i Israel.* Horae Soederbl. 1. Stockholm 1947.
— *The Ascension of the Apostle and the Heavenly Book.* UUÅ 1950.7.
— *The King and the Tree of Life.* UUÅ 1951: 4.
— *Religionens värld.* 2nd ed. Uppsala 1953.
— *Sakrales Königtum im Alten Testament und im Judentum.* Franz Delitzsch-Vorlesungen 1952. Stuttgart 1955.
— *Muhammed, the Apostle of God and his Ascension.* (King and Saviour V.) UUÅ 1955.1.
— *Uppenbarelsebringaren på tronen.* IDEM, Kungar, profeter och harlekiner, Stockholm 1961, pp. 112–117.
WIFSTRAND, A., *Autokrator, Kaiser, Basileus.* Bemerkungen zu den griechischen Benennungen der römischen Kaiser. ΔΡΑΓΜΑ. Martino P. Nilsson A.D. IV ID. IUL. anno MCMXXXIX dedicatum, Lund 1939, pp. 529–539.
WIKENHAUSER, A., *Einleitung in das Neue Testament.* Freiburg i. Br. 1953.
WILES, M. F., *The Old Testament in Controversy with the Jews.* ScJTh 8 (1955), pp. 113–126.
WILLIAMS, A. L., *Adversus Judaeos.* A Bird's-eye View of Christian Apologiae until the Renaissance. Cambridge 1935.
WILLIAMS, G. H., *Christology and Church–State Relations in the Fourth Century.* CH 20 (1951), nr. 3, pp. 1–33 and nr. 4, pp. 1–26.
WILPERT, J., *Die Malereien der Katakomben Roms.* Freiburg i. Br. 1903.
— *Die römischen Mosaiken und Malereien der kirchlichen Bauten vom IV. bis zum XIII Jahrhundert.* I–IV. Freiburg i. Br. 1916.
— *I sarcofaghi cristiani antichi.* Testo, tavole. I–III. Mon. dell'ant. crist. Roma 1929–36.
WINDISCH, H., *Der messianische Krieg und das Urchristentum.* Tübingen 1909.
— *Der zweite Korintherbrief.* (Krit.-exeg. Komm. über d. NT. Begr. v. H. A. W. Meyer.) Göttingen 1924.
— *Imperium und Evangelium.* Kiel 1931.
— *Zur Christologie der Pastoralbriefe.* ZNW 34 (1935), pp. 213–238.
WOLFSON, H. A., *Philo.* Foundations of Religious Philosophy in Judaism, Christianity, and Islam. 1–2. 2nd ed. Cambridge, Mass. 1948.
VAN DER WOUDE, A. S., *Die messianischen Vorstellungen der Gemeinde von Qumran.* Van Gorcum & Assen 1957.
WÜNSCHE, A., *Salomos Thron und Hippodrom.* Abbilder des babylonischen Himmelsbildes. Ex oriente lux II: 3. Leipzig 1906.

YADIN, Y., *The Dead Sea Scrolls and the Epistle to the Hebrews.* SH 4 (1958), pp. 36–55.
— *A Midrash on 2 Sam. vii and Ps. i–ii (4 Q Florilegium).* IEJ 9 (1959), pp. 95–98.
ZAHN, TH., *Marcellus von Ancyra.* Gotha 1867.
ZELLER, E., *Die Philosophie der Griechen.* III. 2nd ed. Leipzig 1903.
ZIEGLER, I., *Die Königsgleichnisse des Midrasch beleuchtet durch die römische Kaiserzeit.* Breslau 1903.

C. Abbreviations

AA Archäologischer Anzeiger. Beiblatt zum Jahrbuch des Deutschen Archäologischen Instituts. Berlin.
AAA Acta Apostolorum Apocrypha, ed. R. A. Lipsius & M. Bonnet.
AAR Atti della Pontificia Accademia Romana di Archeologia, Rendiconti, Roma.
AB Analecta Bollandiana. Brussels.
AC Antike und Christentum, ed. F. J. Dölger, Münster i W. 1929–1950.
ACW Ancient Christian Writers, ed. by J. Quasten och J. C. Plumpe. Westminster, Md. och London.
AIPh Université libre de Bruxelles, Annuaire de l'Institut de philologie et d'histoire orientales et slaves. Paris & Bruxelles.
AJPh American Journal of Philology. Baltimore.
AnTh L'Année théologique. Paris.
AMNSU Arbeiten und Mitteilungen aus dem neutestamentlichen Seminar zu Uppsala. Uppsala.
AO Acta Orientalia. Leiden.
APF Archiv für Papyrusforschung. Leipzig & Berlin.
ArtB Art Bulletin. New York.
ASHL Acta Regiae Societatis Humaniorum Litterarum Lundensis. Lund.
ASNU Acta Seminarii Neotestamentici Upsaliensis edenda curavit A. Fridrichsen. Uppsala.
AThR Anglican Theological Review. New York.
BAS Sitzungsberichte der Bayerischen Akademie der Wissenschaften, Philos.-philol.-hist. Klasse, München.
BASOR Bulletin of the American Schools of Oriental Research. Jerusalem.
BBG Basler Beiträge zur Geisteswissenschaft. Basel.
BFPhL Bibliothèque de la Faculté de Philosophie et Lettres de l'Université de Liège. Liège & Paris.
BFTh Beiträge zur Förderung christlicher Theologie. Gütersloh.
BGAM Beiträge zur Geschichte des alten Mönchtums. Münster in Westf.
BHTh Beiträge zur historischen Theologie. Tübingen.
BJRL Bulletin of John Rylands Library. Manchester.
BKV Bibliothek der Kirchenväter. 2nd ed. Kempten & München 1911 ff.
BO Bibliotheca Orientalis. Leiden.
BZ Byzantinische Zeitschrift. Leipzig.
CCL Corpus Christianorum, Series Latina. Turnhout & Paris.

CH Church History. Chicago, Ill.
CN Coniectanea Neotestamentica. Lund & Copenhagen.
CPh Classical Philology. Chicago.
CRHPhR Cahiers de la Revue d'histoire et de philosophie religieuses. Strasbourg.
CSCO Corpus Scriptorum Christianorum Orientalium. Louvain.
CSEL Corpus Scriptorum Ecclesiasticorum Latinorum. Wien.
DB Dictionnaire de la Bible, ed. F. Vigoreux. Paris 1895–1912. Suppl. 1926 ff.
DOP Dumbarton Oaks Papers. Cambridge, Mass.
DThC Dictionnaire de théologie catholique, ed. A. Vacant, E. Mangenot och E. Amann. Paris 1903–1950.
ECQ Eastern Churches Quarterly. Ramsgate.
EHPhR Études d'Histoire et de Philosophie Religieuse. Paris.
EHPhS Études d'histoire et de philosophie de la faculté de théologie protestante de l'Université de Strasbourg. Paris.
EL (Bibl.) Ephemerides Liturgicae (Bibliotheca). Roma.
ET The Expository Times. Edinburgh.
EtThRel Études théologiques et religieuses. Montpellier.
ETL (Bibl.) Ephemerides Theologicae Lovanienses (Bibliotheca). Louvain (Gembloux).
FKCA Forschungen zur Kunstgeschichte und christlichen Archäologie. Wiesbaden.
FKG Forschungen zur Kirchen- und Geistesgeschichte. Stuttgart.
FP Florilegium Patristicum. Bonn.
FR Felix Ravenna. Ravenna.
FRLANT Forschungen zur Religion und Literatur des Alten und Neuen Testaments. Göttingen.
GAb Abhandlungen der Gesellschaft der Wissenschaften zu Göttingen. Phil.-hist. Klasse. Göttingen.
GCS Die griechischen christlichen Schriftsteller der ersten drei Jahrhunderte, herausg. v. der Kirchenväter-Kommission der Preussischen Akademie. Leipzig, Berlin.
GGA Göttingsche Gelehre Anzeigen. Göttingen.
GN Nachrichten von der Gesellschaft der Wissenschaften zu Göttingen, Phil.-hist. Klasse. Göttingen.
HThR Harvard Theological Review. Cambridge, Mass.
HVSS Skrifter utgivna av Humanistiska Vetenskapssamfundet i Lund. Lund.
HZ Historische Zeitschrift. München & Berlin.
IEJ Israel Exploration Journal. Jerusalem.
JAIW Jahreshefte des Österreichischen Archäologischen Institutes. Wien.
JbAC Jahrbuch für Antike und Christentum. Münster.
JBL Journal of Biblical Literature. New Haven & Boston.
JE The Jewish Encyclopedia. New York & London 1891–1906.
JL Jahrbuch für Liturgiewissenschaft. Münster.
JTS Journal of Theological Studies. London & Oxford.

JÖBG Jahrbuch der Österreichisch-byzantinischen Gesellschaft. Wien.
KÅ Kyrkohistorisk Årsskrift. Stockholm, Göteborg & Uppsala.
Lat Lateran Museum, Rome.
LCL Loeb Classical Library. London.
LF Liturgiegeschichtliche Forschungen. Münster.
LThK Lexikon für Theologie und Kirche, 2nd ed., Freiburg i. Br. 1957 ff.
MANSI Sacrorum Conciliorum Nova et Amplissima Collectio, ed. J. D. Mansi.
MThSt Münchener Theologische Studien, Hist. Abt. München.
MThZ Münchener Theologische Zeitschrift. München.
N.F. Neue Folge.
NPhU Neue Philologische Untersuchungen. Berlin.
NRTh Nouvelle revue théologique. Tournai.
N.S. New Series.
NTS New Testament Studies. London & New York.
NTT Norsk teologisk tidsskrift. Oslo.
OCP Orientalia christiana periodica. Roma.
OLZ Orientalistische Literaturzeitung. Leipzig.
Par Paradosis. Freiburg i. Br.
PBA Proceedings of the British Academy. London.
PBSR Papers of the British School at Rome. Rome.
PEQ Palestine Exploration Quarterly. London.
PFJG E. Peterson, Frühkirche, Judentum und Gnosis.
PFLS Publications de la Faculté des lettres de l'Université de Strasbourg. Paris.
PG Patrologiae cursus completus, Series Graeca, ed. J. P. Migne.
PL Patrologiae cursus completus, Series Latina, ed. J. P. Migne.
PO Patrologia Orientalis, ed. R. Graffin och F. Nau, Paris.
PThT Erik Peterson, Theologische Traktate.
PWK Realencyklopädie der klassischen Altertumswissenschaft, ed. Pauly–Wissowa–Kroll–Ziegler. Stuttgart 1893 ff.
QSGKAM Quellen und Studien zur Geschichte und Kultur des Altertums und des Mittelalters. Heidelberg.
RAC Reallexikon für Antike und Christentum, ed. Th. Klauser. Leipzig & Stuttgart.
RB Revue Biblique. Paris.
RE Realencyklopädie für protestantische Theologie und Kirche, ed. A. Hauck. Leipzig.
REG Revue des études grecques. Paris.
REJ Revue des études juives. Paris.
REL Revue des études latines. Paris.
RepK Repertorium für Kunstwissenschaft. Berlin & Stuttgart.
RevBén Revue Bénédictine. Maredsous.
RevR The Review of Religion. New York.
RHE Revue d'histoire ecclésiastique. Louvain.
RHPhR Revue d'Histoire de la Philosophie religieuses. Strasbourg.
RivAC Rivista di Archeologia Cristiana. Rom.
RLC Recueil Lucien Cerfaux. 1–2 ETL Bibl. 6–7. Gembloux 1954.

RM Mitteilungen des Deutschen Archäologischen Instituts. München, Röm. Abt.
RoB Religion och Bibel. Uppsala.
ROC Revue de l'Orient chrétien. Paris.
RQ Römische Quartalschrift. Freiburg i. Br.
RSPhTh Revue des sciences philosophiques et théologiques. Paris.
RSR Recherches de science religieuse. Paris.
Sacral Kingship The Sacral Kingship. Contributions to the Central Theme of the VIIIth International Congress for the History of Religions. (Rome, April 1955.) Leiden 1959.
SB Symbolae Biblicae Upsalienses. Uppsala.
SbB Sitzungsberichte der Preussischen Akademie der Wissenschaften, Phil.-hist. Klasse. Berlin.
SbHei Sitzungsberichte der Heidelberger Akademie der Wissenschaften, Phil.-hist. Klasse. Heidelberg.
SBT Studies in Biblical Theology. London.
SBU Svenskt Bibliskt Uppslagsverk, utg. av I. Engnell och A. Fridrichsen, 1st ed. Gävle 1948.
SC Sources chrétiennes, ed. H. de Lubac & J. Daniélou. Paris.
ScJTh Scottish Journal of Theology. Edinburgh & London.
SE Sacris Eruditi, Jaarboek voor godsdienstwetenschappen. Bruges.
SEÅ Svensk exegetisk årsbok. Uppsala.
SGVS Sammlung gemeinverst. Vorträge und Schriften aus dem Gebiet der Theologie- und Religionsgeschichte. Tübingen.
SH Scripta Hierosolymitana. Jerusalem.
SO Symbolae Osloenses. Oslo.
SP Studia Patristica. 1–6. Papers Presented to the International Conferences on Patristic Studies held at Christ Church Oxford 1955 and 1959. TU 63–64 (1957) and 78–81 (1961).
SQ Sammlung ausgewählter Quellenschriften zur Kirchen- und Dogmengeschichte. Tübingen.
SSK Studien zur Spätantiken Kunstgeschichte. Berlin.
SSL Spicilegium Sacrum Lovaniense. Louvain.
SSO Studier fra sprog- og oltidsforskning. København.
ST Studi e Testi, Publicazioni della Biblioteca Vaticana. Roma.
StAC Studi di antichità cristiana. Roma & Paris.
StBTh Studies in Biblical Theology. London.
StBW Studien der Bibliothek Warburg. Berlin.
StChD Studien über christliche Denkmäler. Leipzig.
StD Studies and Documents, ed. K. Lake & S. Lake. London & Philadelphia.
StGKA Studien zur Geschichte und Kultur des Altertums. Paderborn.
STh Studia Theologica. Lund.
StH Studia Hellenistica. Louvain.
StThL Studia Theologica Lundensia. Lund.
STK Svensk teologisk kvartalsskrift. Lund.
StML Stimmen aus Maria Laach. Freiburg i. Br.

ThA Theologische Arbeiten zur Bibel-, Kirchen- und Geistesgeschichte. Halle.
ThBl Theologische Blätter. Leipzig.
ThGl Theologie und Glaube. Paderborn.
ThLZ Theologische Literaturzeitung. Leipzig.
ThQ Theologische Quartalschrift. Tübingen & Stuttgart.
ThR Theologische Revue. Münster.
ThSt Theologische Studien. Zürich.
ThV Theologia Viatorum. Berlin.
ThWB Theologisches Wörterbuch, ed. G. Kittel. Stuttgart 1932 ff.
ThZ Theologische Zeitschrift. Basel.
TrierThZ Trierer Theologische Zeitschrift. Trier.
TS Theological Studies. Woodstock, Md.
TSt Texts and Studies, ed. by J. A. Robinson. Cambridge.
TU Texte und Untersuchungen, ed. Gebhardt, Harnack & Schmidt. Leipzig.
UUÅ Uppsala Universitets Årsskrift. Uppsala.
VAKMF Veröffentlichungen der Alexander Kohut Memorial Foundation. Wien.
VC Vigiliae Christianae. Amsterdam.
VT Vetus Testamentum. Leiden.
WMKR J. Wilpert, Die Malereien der Katakomben Roms.
WMM J. Wilpert, Die römischen Mosaiken und Malereien.
WS J. Wilpert, I sarcofaghi cristiani antichi.
WStA Würzburger Studien zur Altertumswissenschaft. Würzburg.
WUNT Wissenschaftliche Untersuchungen zum Neuen Testament. Tübingen.
WZKM Wiener Zeitschrift für die Kunde des Morgenlandes. Wien.
YCS Yale Classical Studies. New Haven.
ZAW Zeitschrift für die alttestamentliche Wissenschaft. Giessen & Berlin.
ZKG Zeitschrift für Kirchengeschichte. Stuttgart.
ZKTh Zeitschrift für katholische Theologie. Innsbruck.
ZMR Zeitschrift für Missionswissenschaft und Religionswissenschaft. Münster.
ZNW Zeitschrift für die neutestamentliche Wissenschaft und die Kunde der ältesten Kirche. Giessen.
ZRG Zeitschrift für Religions- und Geistesgeschichte. Marburg.
ZSTh Zeitschrift für Systematische Theologie. Gütersloh.

INDEX OF AUTHORS

Ahlström 38, 91, 124
Aland 325
Albertz 272 f.
Alföldi 11, 13 f., 223, 255
Allegro 77
Allo 138, 140, 297
Anartos 262 f.
Anrich 16
Aptowitzer 107, 115
Arvedson 40, 133, 288
Audet 59, 159, 164, 246
Aulén 100

Ball 37
Bandmann 14
Barbel 111 f., 141 ff., 146 f., 196, 265 f.
Bardy 163 f., 238 ff., 249, 273
Barré 283
Barrett 37
Barton 115
von Baudissin 46 f.
Baus 17 f., 27, 151, 154, 158
Baynes 318
Beasley-Murray 108
Beer 108
Beilner 50
Benoit 135, 146
Bentzen 127, 149
Benz 192
Berkhof 262 ff., 314, 318, 323, 325, 328
Berlinger 62, 255
Bernhardt 148
Bertram 71, 100
Bidez 201, 204
Bietenhard 52 f., 125 f., 129, 131, 136, 139, 141 f., 146, 150, 166, 171, 222, 224, 298

Billerbeck 48, 83, 91, 95, 132, 134, 138
Blinzler 40
Blume 312
Blumenkrantz 75
Boll 170
Bonner 195
Bonsirven 34, 132, 228
Bousset 45, 49, 51, 54, 56, 59, 64, 78, 108, 160
Bouyer 38
Bréhier, E. 189, 194, 215 f.
Bréhier, L. 62
Brightman 305, 321
Brox 181
de Bruyne 24
Bultmann 45, 50, 54, 90
Burney 37
Burrows 108

Cabaniss 104
Cadiou 289
von Campenhausen 22, 178, 196
Capelle 160, 270, 274, 305, 312, 321
Capmany 155, 179
Casel 67
Casey 269, 279, 298
Caspari 300 ff., 307
Cecchelli 17
Cerfaux 11, 43, 45 ff., 51, 53, 55, 57 f., 67, 69, 76, 86, 150, 159, 178, 249
Charles 108
Charlesworth 189
Chevallier 113 f., 118, 120, 288
Congar 214
Connolly 167
Coppens 48

Cullmann 35, 45 ff., 53 ff., 64, 66, 90, 141, 159, 173 f., 176, 288
Cumont 201, 203 f., 308

Dahl 174
Daniélou 52, 66, 75, 86, 89, 94, 99 ff., 102, 110, 120, 142, 144 f., 147, 176, 200, 219, 221 ff., 298, 310
Daube 50
Davies 135, 310
Deissmann 16, 36, 39, 61, 64, 67, 71, 141, 265
Delatte 188 ff., 193, 199 f., 206, 209 f., 215 f., 247, 253, 255
Delbrück 11, 40
Delehaye 159, 179, 182
Delvoye 13 f., 26
Devreesse 282, 285, 289, 306
Dibelius 63, 65 ff., 70 f., 173, 175, 208
Dix 34, 161
Dodd 37, 52, 76 f., 83, 296, 301
Doerries 253
Doeve 33, 49 f., 52, 132
Dölger 64, 173, 175, 182, 202 ff., 207 f., 246, 252, 297
Dornseiff 64
Doutreleau 219
Duensing 141 f.
Dupont 67
Durant 173
Dürig 16
Dürr 48
Dyggve 13

Eck 173
Egger 13 f.
Ehrhardt 16, 34, 173, 184, 194 f., 209, 295
Eisler 125
Elliger 262
Engnell 38, 46, 124, 127, 149, 159, 304
Ensslin 323
Eppel 107, 308

Farrer 137
Fascher 302 f.
Festugière 191
Feuillet 139
Fink 293
Fisch 247, 252
Fitzmyer 76 f., 83
Flemming 141
Florovsky 262
Flusser 91, 94
Foerster 45 ff., 220, 222
François 200
de Francovich 23 f., 26
Freed 41
Frisque 35
Fuchs 252
Fuller 51

Gadd 87
Gagé 16
Gärtner 37
Gauthier 214
Geffcken 82
Gerhardsson 49, 75, 78, 81, 86, 88, 102
Gericke 232, 234, 236 ff., 307
von Gerkan 14 f.
Gerke 13, 17 f., 22 f., 30 f., 187
Gesché 306
Ghedini 308
de Ghellinck 16
Ginsburgen 169
Glazik 112
Gokey 208

Goldammer 206
Goodenough 151, 160, 188 ff., 200 ff., 211, 213, 215 f., 218, 247, 252, 255
Goodspeed 194
Grabar 11 f., 15 ff., 22, 30, 283
Grant 203
Grégoire 215 f.
Gressmann 87, 263
Griffiths 141, 252
Grillmeier 229
Grundmann 303
Guilka 228
Gutberlet 27
Guy 327

Haenchen 52, 65
Hagel 324
Hanson 216 f., 219, 221, 225 f., 228
Harle 140
von Harnack 16, 20 f., 27, 64, 78 f., 92, 96, 159, 174, 178 f., 195, 209 f.
Harris 76, 78, 80, 83, 94
Hefele 271
Heikel 263
Heinemann 192, 215
Hellström 140
Héring 34, 42
Hitchcock 78
Hocart 131, 148
Hoenig 168
Holzmeister 312
Hommel 297, 300 f.
Hommes 76, 78 f., 81, 94, 99
Hoogewerff 23
Hulen 75
Hunt 77
Hüntemann 82

Ihm 12
Instinsky 15, 318

Jeremias, A. 166
Jeremias, J. 37, 109, 288

De Jonge 142, 310
Jost 87 f., 199
Jungmann 15 f., 25, 158 ff., 294, 312

Kantorowicz 17, 253 f., 329 f.
Kattenbusch 273, 295, 297, 300 ff., 307
Keller 228
Kempf 199
Keysner 296
Kirsch 29
Kirschbaum 24, 205 f.
Kitschelt 14
Kittel, G. 132, 173
Kittel, H. 132
Klauser 15, 17, 126, 199
Klein 246
Kleinknecht 39
Klostermann 220
Knopf 71
Koch, C. 252
Koch, H. 262
Koester 140
Kohler 115, 201
Kollwitz 11 ff., 22, 24 ff., 28, 30 f., 187, 212, 262, 265, 272
Koole 76
Kosnetter 133, 288
Kramer 252
Kraus 48
Krautheimer 25
Kretschmar 142, 147
Kroll 103 f., 141, 222
Kruse 295
Kuhn 44, 107 ff., 130
Kümmel 47

Ladner 318
Lagrange 107
Lampe 234, 240, 284 ff., 292
Lang 14, 19
Langlotz 13
Lassus 121

Laurentin 303, 308
Lebreton 164
Leclercq 93, 95, 98 f., 111, 214, 330
Lécuyer 225, 327
Leisegang 129, 148
Lehmann 23
Leivestad 100, 179
Lemarié 220, 284
Lewy 193
Lietzmann 63 f., 66, 232
Lindhagen 159
Linssen 64, 298
Lohmeyer 39, 50, 53, 62, 64, 136, 141, 173, 297
Loofs 231 f., 237 ff., 249, 273
L'Orange 12 f., 31, 125, 187, 201 ff., 205, 212, 295
Lorenz 71
Lövestam 90 f., 114, 288, 325
de Lubac 219
Ludin Jansen 48

McFayden 183
McNeile 42
Magie 36
Mâle 29
Manser 284
Manson, T. W. 77
Manson, W. 42
Mariès 110
Marmorstein 297, 309
Marxen 314
Massaux 78, 88, 93
May 130
van der Meer 12, 27, 153, 156, 201 f., 205, 293, 326
Michaelis 45, 57, 82, 112, 185, 295 f., 301
Michl 111, 132
Milik 108
Mohrmann 67, 69, 292
Molland 213
Moore 296

Morrison 189
Moule 34, 38, 40, 42, 103
Mowinckel 46, 124, 127
Mowry 157
Müller, E. F. K. 106, 119
Müller, G. 298
Munck 145
Murmelstein 108, 117, 254

Nash 236
Nautin 195
Neher 228
Neuss 201 f., 205
Newman 313
Nock 64, 71, 189
Norden 64
Nordström 13, 293

Odeberg 128 ff., 141
Oehler 71
Oepke 67
Oke 42
O'Neill 47
Opitz 276, 316
Östborn 215
Otzen 130, 310

Pascher 166, 171, 214
Pax 67 f., 70, 72
Pearson 300 f.
Pedersen 215, 222
Perler 195, 205
Persson 106 f.
Peterson 16, 24, 28, 69, 104, 136 f., 144 f., 157, 159, 174, 182 ff., 191 f., 248 ff., 262, 268, 296, 314 f., 318 f., 321
Pfister 67
Philonenko 48
Piper 157
Plooij 133, 288
Pollard 232, 237, 269
de la Potterie 111
Prümm 46, 62, 64 f., 67 f., 302
Puech 191

Quasten 16, 144 f., 154, 162, 175, 180, 199, 264, 276, 290
Quell 47
Quispel 79

Rabin 169
von Rad 40
Rahlfs 285
Rahner 173 f., 197, 206 ff., 315, 320, 324, 328
Rawlinson 45
Reicke 250
Reilly 329
Renow 169
Richstaetter 18, 27
Riedmatten 238 f.
Riesenfeld 40, 106, 109, 111, 124 f., 127, 131 ff., 140, 148, 151 f., 288
Rigaux 177
Ringgren 124, 126, 302
Rissi 136
Roberts 76
Robinson 79, 85, 97, 114
Roosval 17, 23
Rosenberg 183, 185
Roth 169
Rowley 123
Rudberg 194, 201, 206 ff.

Sanders 253
Sas-Zaloziecky 14
de Savignac 215
Scheidweiler 232
Schermann 157, 296
Schlatter 136, 139, 297
Schlier 141, 185, 222
Schlütz 114
Schmaus 106
Schmidt, H. 124
Schmidt, K. L. 33, 39, 44, 173 f., 192, 214, 222
Schmitt 314
Schnackenburg 34, 42, 44, 52
Schneider, A. M., 14 f., 22

Schneider, C. 13, 15, 19, 301
von Schoeffer 39
von Schoenebeck 23
Schoeps 92, 117, 242 f., 256
Scholem 128, 130, 202
Schoonheim 67 ff.
Schubart 62
Schumacher 12, 22 f.
Schürer 168
Schwank 311
Schwartz 263, 323
Segelberg 120 ff., 148 f.
Sellers 236
Selwyn 150
Seston 13 f.
Setton 24, 317 f., 323, 328 f.
Silbermann 108
Simon 20, 75, 77, 80, 84, 95, 98
Sjöberg 127 f.
Skard 71
Skehan 250
Smith 79
Spicq 62, 64, 67, 71, 216
Staerk 37, 64, 66, 108 f., 114, 117
Stange 14, 19, 25 f., 293
Stauffer 40, 47, 63, 68, 136 f., 169, 173
Stegemann 297
Steinwenter 215
Stendahl 49 f., 76 f., 83, 96
Stern 23
Stier 215
Stommel 15, 19, 166, 169 ff., 276
Stonehouse 138

Strack, see Billerbeck
Straub 24, 191, 263, 318, 328
Strecker 242 f., 256
Stuhlfauth 208
Sundkler 102
Surkau 178
von Sybel 28 ff.

Taeger 11
Tailliez 214
Tarn 189, 247, 252 f.
Taylor 37
Teeuwen 16
Thomson 87
Thraede 75
Tisserant 142
Tondriau 11
Torm 161
Treitinger 11, 13, 24, 315
Tselos 205
Turner 321
von Ungern-Sternberg 56, 74, 76, 80, 82 ff., 93 f., 96, 98 f.

Valdenberg 200, 254
Verhoeven 248 ff., 256
Verosta 329
Visser 11
Voelkl 14, 19, 21, 28
Vogt 16 f.
Volbach 208
Völker 220 f., 226
Vollmer 83
Volz 40, 108

de Waal 23
Wagenvoort 185
Ward Perkins 14
Weinel 36
Weisbach 25
Wellen 283
Welte 114
Wendland 64, 263
Werner 45, 111 f., 147
Wessel 17, 28, 30 f.
Westcott 301
Wheeler Robinson 139
Widengren 16, 46, 48, 102, 105, 107, 124, 129 f., 147 f., 170
Wieten 78
Wifstrand 62
Wikenhauser 326
Wiles 75, 85
Williams, A. L. 75, 77, 79 ff., 99, 289
Williams, G. H. 171, 273, 287, 316 ff., 328 f.
Wilpert 30
Windisch 39, 64, 173, 296
Wolfson 201, 215
van der Woude 87, 94, 107
Wünsche 125 f., 129

Yadin 91, 107

Zahn 234
Zeller 252
Ziegler 126
Zwicker 252

INDEX OF PASSAGES

Old Testament

GENESIS
14.18: 309
14.22: 309
18 f.: 84
18.22 ff.: 84
19.24: 84 f., 280
20.7: 120
25.23: 96
32.10: 82
49.10: 91, 93 f., 96, 115, 177, 195, 208, 244
49.11: 93, 221

EXODUS
2.1: 88
3.1: 218
12.11: 224
15.1: 201
19.6: 150
20.22: 112
22.28: 251
23.20 f.: 112 f.
25.9: 138
25.22: 201
25.40: 135, 138
26.30: 138
27.8: 138
29.7: 119
40.13: 119
40.15 f.: 119

LEVITICUS
4.3: 119
4.5: 119
4.16: 119
26.12: 260

NUMBERS
13.17: 112
21.18: 226
24.9: 229
24.17: 81, 93 ff., 195, 208

DEUTERONOMY
32.: 309
32.8 f.: 250

JOSHUA
5.13 f.: 265 f.
5.14: 210, 265 f.
23.7: 251

JUDGES
5.3: 227

1 KINGS (SAMUEL)
8.10–17: 321

2 KINGS (SAMUEL)
7: 91
7.4 f.: 95
7.11 f.: 93
7.11 ff.: 91, 94
7.12–14: 95
7.14 f.: 93
7.16: 95
7.23: 67

3 (1) KINGS
22.19: 138 f., 225

2 CHRONICLES (PARALIPOMENA)
18.18: 225
26.16–21: 321 f.

2 EZRA (NEHEMIAH)
12.6: 68 (=Neh. 2.6)

JUDITH
10.18: 68

ESTHER
4.17 (interpol.): 157
8.12: 71

JOB
1 f.: 138 f.

PSALMS
2: 88, 281
2.2: 120
2.6: 221, 234, 277, 281, 284 f., 287
2.6 f.: 289
2.7: 124, 270, 288 ff.
2.7 f.: 97
2.8 f.: 89
2.9: 87 ff., 102
3.2: 85
8.5: 127
8.6: 104, 278
17 (18).11: 202
17 (18).14: 311
18 (19).7: 105
21 (22).17: 96
21 (22).29: 185
22 (23).1: 89
23 (24): 27, 95, 103 ff., 129, 144 f., 223, 235, 278 f., 281, 305 f.
23 (24).5: 65
23 (24).7: 279
23 (24).7 ff.: 135, 155, 223
23 (24).7–9: 262
23 (24).7–10: 100, 103
23 (24).10: 296
44 (45): 229
44 (45).6: 280
44 (45).7: 57, 82, 102, 224, 270 f., 282
44 (45).7 f.: 84 f., 111, 116, 118, 120, 124, 279

44 (45).8: 271
46 (47).6: 129
46 (47).8: 271
46 (47).9: 225, 271
49 (50).14: 309
61 (62).7: 65
70 (71).18: 85
71 (72): 95 f.
71 (72).1: 290 f.
79 (80).1: 87, 89, 195, 225
79 (80).18: 127
81 (82).6: 309
82 (83).19: 311 f.
86 (87).5: 310 ff.
88 (89): 91
88 (89).17: 279
91 (92).1: 271
94 (95).3: 271
94 (95).6 f.: 87
95 (96).1: 271
95 (96).10: 38, 99 f.
96 (97): 292
96 (97).1: 234, 284 f. 291 f.
96 (97).9: 310
98 (99): 292
98 (99).1: 195, 234 f., 291
101 (102).26 f.: 54
101 (102).26 ff.: 56
101 (102).26–28: 84
104 (105).15: 120
109 (110): 27, 38, 44, 48, 53 f., 83, 95 f., 101, 109, 120, 132 ff., 235, 237, 270, 283
109 (110).1: 47–56, 84 f., 92, 100 f., 105, 124, 133, 171, 225, 236, 270, 280
109 (110).1–4: 116
109 (110).2: 101 f.
109 (110).3: 271, 283
109 (110).4: 53
117 (118).19 f.: 105
117 (118).26: 41
118 (119).46: 181
131 (132): 91
131 (132).11: 91, 93 ff., 292

144 (145).13: 271
145 (146).3: 127

PROVERBS
8.15: 194
8.22 f.: 271
16.12: 271

SONG OF SONGS
1.4: 228 f.
1.12: 228 f.
4.8: 320

WISDOM
7.22: 304
7.23: 302
9.8: 138
11.17: 302
18.15: 302

SIRACH
45.6–22: 130
46.1: 66 f.
46.13: 185
47.21: 185

ISAIAH
2.3: 102
6: 327
6.1: 225
6.3: 157, 296
6.5: 132
6.8: 112
9.6: 38, 99, 185, 255, 266
11: 116
11.1: 91, 94 f., 102
11.1–3: 114, 116, 118, 120
11.2: 114, 116
11.10: 91
12.2: 65
14.14: 311
24.23: 139, 166
28.5: 151
33.17: 271
36.6: 224
40.1–17: 88
40.11: 87 f.

42.1: 85, 288
45.1: 85 f., 116
49.6: 85
53: 38
53.1 f.: 85
53.2 f.: 105
61: 116
61.1: 85, 113, 116, 120
61.1 f.: 113, 118
61.6: 150
63.1: 223

JEREMIAH
23.4 f.: 87

LAMENTATIONS
4.20: 86, 120

EZEKIEL
1: 138, 195, 202
1.1: 138
1.25 f.: 225
1.26: 138
8.3: 138
10.1: 138
11.1: 138
34: 87
34.23 f.: 87
37.24: 87
44.3: 93
44–46: 107

DANIEL
2.34: 321
2.37: 177
2.40 ff.: 176
2.44: 177
2.47: 141
4.3 (3.33): 177
4.34 f. (4.31 f.): 177
4.37 (4.34): 177
5: 177
6: 177
6.27 (26): 177
7: 38, 50, 125 ff., 132 f.
7.9: 134, 139, 150, 225
7.9 f.: 166

7.10: 132
7.13 f.: 52, 54, 126
7.14: 132, 280
7.22–27: 309
7.27: 150
8.16: 138
9.24–26: 97, 244
9.26: 118

Joel
2.28 f.: 114, 118
2.29: 116

Micah
4.2: 102
5.1 (2): 88, 93, 95, 99, 208
7.14: 87

Zechariah
3.4 ff. 130
4.14: 107
6.11–15: 130
9.9: 41, 45, 99, 221
9.10: 223
13.7: 87 f.
14.5: 59, 132
14.9: 132

Malachi
3.1: 139

2 Maccabees
1.24: 157
3.24: 67
5.5: 67
7.9: 177
8.12: 68
12.22: 67
13.4: 141
14.15: 67
15.21: 68

New Testament

St. Matthew
1.21: 66, 292
2: 94 f.
2.2: 41
2.6: 88, 93
3.11: 139
5.19: 227
5.35: 42
10.18: 195
10.18 f.: 181
10.20: 116
13.41: 44
16.16: 42
16.27: 132
16.28: 44
19.28: 132, 151, 166, 225
20.20 ff.: 224
20.21: 44
20.21–23: 151
21.10: 223
21.12: 224
21.15: 41
21.42: 83
24.3: 68
24.27: 68
24.30 f.: 132
24.37: 68
24.39: 68
24.42: 59
25.1: 69
25.31: 132, 225
25.31 ff.: 88
25.34–40: 132
26.31: 88
26.64: 225
27.52 f.: 152
28.3: 152
28.18: 287

St. Mark
1.11: 288
5.7: 308
8.28: 109
8.38: 132
9.3: 151 f.
10.37: 44
11.3: 52
12.35–37: 49, 50
14.27: 88
14.61 f.: 42
14.62: 50, 52, 225
15.2: 40
15.9: 40
15.12: 40
15.26: 40
15.32: 40
16.19: 102

St. Luke
1.17: 303
1.30 ff.: 95
1.32: 91, 270, 272, 292, 308 f., 311
1.33: 41, 43 f., 267, 272, 286
1.35: 303, 308 f.
1.47: 65
1.68: 157
1.76: 308, 311
2.1 ff.: 63
2.2: 86
2.11: 65
2.29: 157
3.1: 185
4.18: 113, 271
7.16: 109
8.28: 308
9.26: 132
10.16: 112
10.18: 224
10.22: 287
17.21: 287
19.38: 41
21.27: 132
22.25: 71
22.29 f.: 44, 151, 166
22.69: 225
23.11: 40
23.42: 44
24.4: 152

St. John
1.1: 271, 299
1.1 ff.: 141
1.20 f.: 109
1.49: 41

3.13: 141
4.42: 65
5.22: 133
5.27: 133
6.15: 41
6.33 f.: 141
7.40 f.: 109
7.42: 91
7.52: 109
8.25: 271
9.17: 109
11.25: 155
12.13: 41, 69
12.15: 41
12.31: 224
13.31: 278
16.15: 299
17.5: 141
17.10: 299
18.36: 44, 174
18.36 f.: 41
19.12–15: 41
19.15: 96, 317
19.21: 41
20–21: 51
20.12: 152
20.28: 54, 84, 158, 161

Acts

1.8: 303
1.10: 152
2.29 f.: 91
2.32–36: 52
2.33: 102
2.34: 96
2.36: 51, 281
3.15: 208
3.22: 109
4.9: 71
4.24: 157
4.29: 157
4.30: 159
5.31: 53, 65
7.37: 109
7.44: 138
7.48: 308

7.55 f.: 135
7.59 f.: 158
8.10: 303
10.30: 152
10.38: 71, 271, 303
10.42: 133
13.22 f.: 91
13.23: 65 f.
13.33: 288
16.17: 308
17.7: 42
17.31: 133

Romans

1.4: 92
4.24: 53
6.12: 225
7.25: 159
8.34: 53
9.10 ff.: 96
9.33: 83
15.9–12: 83
15.12: 91

1 Corinthians

1.8: 133
1.21: 65
2.8: 103
4.8: 227
5.5: 133
6.3: 150
8.6: 57
9.1: 53
9.25: 151
15.23: 68
15.24: 44
15.24 ff.: 234
15.25: 44, 53
15.25 ff.: 101
15.27: 53
15.28: 267, 273, 286 f.
16.17: 68
16.22: 158

2 Corinthians

1.14: 133
4.14: 53

6.18: 296
7.6: 68
8.9: 57
10.10: 68

Galatians

4.26: 221 f.

Ephesians

1.10: 143
1.20: 53
1.20 f.: 100
1.20 ff.: 150, 174
1.22 f.: 150
2.5: 65
2.6: 150
5.5: 44
5.23: 65
6.12: 224

Philippians

1.6: 133
1.10: 133
1.26: 68
2.5 ff.: 141
2.6: 57
2.9: 278 f.
2.10 f.: 53
2.11: 86
2.16: 133
3.20: 65
4.1: 151

Colossians

1.13: 44
2.14 f.: 100
3.1: 53
3.17: 159

1 Thessalonians

2.19: 53, 68, 151
3.13: 53, 68, 132
4.15: 68
4.15 f.: 53
4.15 ff.: 69
5.2: 133
5.23: 53, 68

2 Thessalonians
1.7: 53, 132
2.1: 53, 68
2.2: 133
2.8: 68 f.

1 Timothy
1.1: 65
1.17: 42, 297
2.3: 65
2.5 f.: 311
3.16: 104, 135
4.10: 65
6.2: 71
6.14: 68
6.15: 42, 141
6.16: 185

2 Timothy
1.9: 65
1.10: 65, 68
2.5: 151
2.8: 91
4.1: 44, 68
4.8: 68
4.18: 44

Titus
1.3: 65
2.10: 65
2.11: 68
2.11 ff.: 63
2.13: 62, 65
3.4: 65, 68, 70
3.4 ff.: 63
3.6: 65

Hebrews
1: 85
1.3: 53
1.3 ff.: 141
1.8: 44, 102
1.8 f.: 57
1.10 ff.: 56 f.
1.10–12: 54, 84
1.13: 53

2.5: 141
2.7: 104, 278
2.9: 104
2.14: 185
3.1: 112
3.1 ff.: 66
4.14: 135, 185
5.6: 53
7.1: 308
7.1 ff.: 135
7.17: 53
8.1 f.: 135
8.5: 135, 138
10.13: 53
12.2: 208
12.22: 221 f.
13.20: 54, 88

1 Peter
1.10 f.: 114
1.12: 104
2.5: 150
2.6 ff.: 83
2.9: 119, 226 f.
3.22: 54
4.11: 185
5.8: 177
5.11: 185

2 Peter
1.1: 65
1.11: 44, 65
1.16: 68
2.20: 65
3.2: 65
3.10: 133
3.12: 133
3.18: 65

1 John
2.28: 68
4.14: 65

James
1.12: 151
5.7 f.: 68

Jude
4: 158
14: 132
25: 65, 185

Revelation
1.4: 297
1.5: 141, 182, 108
1.6: 150, 154, 185
1.8: 296 f.
1.13: 152
1.13 ff.: 140
1.14: 297
1.17: 297
2.10: 147, 151, 154
2.26 f.: 88
2.27: 102
3.4 f.: 147, 152
3.11: 147, 151
3.18: 147, 152
3.21: 54, 147, 150 f.
4: 137, 147
4 f.: 138 f., 166, 168
4.1 ff.: 125
4.4: 147, 151 f., 154
4.8: 139, 157, 296 f.
4.11: 157
5: 137 f.
5.1: 54
5.1 ff.: 95
5.5: 91, 140
5.7: 54
5.10: 150
5.12 f.: 140
5.13: 140, 185
6.2: 154
6.11: 147, 152
6.16: 140
7.9: 147, 152
7.9 f.: 140
7.9–17: 137
7.11: 176
7.13 f.: 147, 152
7.15: 140
7.17: 140

8.1-4: 137
11.15: 44
11.15-19: 137
11.16: 147
11.17: 44, 139, 157, 269 f.
12.5: 88, 102, 140, 146
12.5 ff.: 224
12.7-9: 224
13.1 ff.: 176
13.5 ff.: 176
14.1-5: 137
14.14: 140, 151, 154
15.2-8: 137
15.3: 157, 296
15.3 f.: 139
15.5: 42
16.7: 157, 296
16.14: 296
17-19: 62
17.14: 42, 54, 141
19.1-10: 137
19.6: 44, 157, 296
19.12: 140, 151
19.15: 88, 102, 296
19.15 f.: 88
19.16: 42, 54, 141
20.4: 147, 150
21-22: 222
21.6: 297
21.22: 296
22.1: 140 f.
22.3: 140 f.
22.13: 297
22.16: 91, 94
22.20: 158

OT Apocrypha and Pseudepigrapha

APOCALYPSE OF ABRAHAM

17 f.: 125

ASCENSION OF ISAIAH

3: 143
4: 143, 152, 176
7: 142
8: 142
9: 60, 142 f., 152
10: 60, 142 f.
11: 143, 147

2 BARUCH

29.5: 128
30.1: 128
39.7: 128
72.2: 128

1 ENOCH

1.9: 132
38.2: 127
39.12-40.10: 125
45.3: 128
48.2: 128
48.7: 65
51.3: 128
55.4: 128, 250
61.8: 128
62: 128, 250
63: 250
67 f.: 250
69.27-29: 128
69.29: 127 f., 132
90.22-25: 250

3 ENOCH

5.14-6.3: 129
10.3-6: 129
12.1-4: 131
45: 126
48 C. 8: 129
48 (D).6-9: 105

4 EZRA:
7.28: 128

JUBILEES

11.2 ff.: 245
16.18: 150

3 MACCABEES

2.9: 67
3.12-30: 71

3.17: 68
5.8: 67
5.51: 67
6.2: 157

ODES OF SOLOMON

1.1-3: 151
7.16 f.: 226

SIBYLLINE ORACLES

6.16: 94
7.31: 94
7.324 ff.: 226
8.248: 89
8.254: 94, 102

PSALMS OF SOLOMON

3.6: 65
8.33: 65
16.4: 65
16.17: 65
17.24: 87
17.32: 48, 86
18.7: 48, 86

TESTAMENT OF LEVI

4: 310
4.1: 309 f.
5.1: 138
8: 108, 135, 148
8.2-10: 130
8.11: 68
8.14 f.: 68, 108
8.15: 69
14: 48

TESTAMENT OF JUDAH

22.2: 68
24.1-6: 94

TESTAMENT OF BENJAMIN

9: 48

NT Apocrypha and Pseudepigrapha

Gospel of Bartholomew
IV.61: 161
IV.64: 161

Gospel of the Hebrews
Fragm.: 114

Gospel of Nicodemus (Acts of Pilate)
Greek 5 (21): 104
Lat. A 5 (21): 104
Lat. B 7 (23): 104

Gospel of Peter
(4.)13: 58

Gospel of Thomas
Log. 2: 149

Epistle of the Apostles
3: 143
13: 143
14: 143
38: 153

Acts of John
22: 161
98: 81
108–115: 161
109: 81
112: 161

Acts (Martyrdom) of Paul
2 f.: 180 f.

Acts of Peter (Vercelli Acts)
20: 81
39: 161

Acts of Philip
144 (38): 161

Acts of Thomas
10: 161
39: 309
45 (42): 309
47 f. (44 f.): 161
48 (45): 310
49 (46): 309
54: 161
60 f.: 161
78: 309 f.
107: 161
125: 309 f.
144: 161
150: 309
158: 152
167: 161

Apocalypse of Paul
24: 153
29: 153

Apocalypse of Peter
Fragments: 104, 141, 152

Qumran Texts

1QS 9.11: 108
1QSa 2.12–20: 108
Dam. 8.5 ff.: 226
  12.23: 108
  14.19: 108
  19.10: 108

Josephus

Ant. III.5.2: 68
  III.8.5: 68
  IX.4.3: 68
  XIII.10.7: 107
  XVIII.8.6: 68
De bell. Iud. 2.8: 107

Philo

Agr. 41: 218
  43–49: 218
49: 248
50 f.: 193, 199, 218
51: 200
66: 218
82 ff.: 201
Cherub. 24: 200
  36: 207
Decal. 53: 200
  60: 200
Fuga 100 f.: 201
  101: 200
  108: 193
Gig. 52: 193
Heres. 99: 200
  301: 200 f., 207
Jos. 2 f.: 218
Leg. alleg. II.99: 201
  II.102: 210
  III.79 f.: 214
  III.81 f.: 193
  III.118: 200, 207
  III.134: 200
  III.150: 208
  III.224: 200, 207
Legat. 44: 218
  356: 43
Migr. 67: 207
  102: 193
  174: 208
Mut. 116: 193, 199
  151 f.: 214
Opif. 46: 200
  88: 200
  143: 192
Plant. 60: 208
Post. 67–69: 199
  68: 193
  127–129: 214
Prob. lib. 30 f.: 218
Prov. fragm. 2: 192, 213, 255
Praem. 54–56: 216
QE II.42: 192
  II.105: 216
Sacr. 51: 207
  104 f.: 199
Sobr. 56 f.: 214

Somn. II.243 f.: 214
  II.269 f.: 201
Spec. leg. I.12: 248
  I.14: 200
  III.189: 192
  IV.92: 208
  IV.184: 255
  IV.186: 193
  IV.187 f.: 254
Virt. 54: 216
  58: 218
Vita M. I.26: 208
  I.60–62: 218
  I.148–163: 216
  II.1–8: 216
  II.31: 216
  II.292: 216

Rabbinic Literature

Mishna b Sanh. 4.3: 168
  38b: 134
Bereshith R. 97: 325
Shemoth R. 2: 88
  30: 166
Horajoth 11.6 ff.: 115
Naso R. 12.15: 131

Ecclesiastical Authors and Anonymi

ACTS AND PASSIONS OF MARTYRS
of Agape, Eirene, Chione and Companions 7: 181
of Apollonius 8 f.: 175, 254
  47b: 182
of Carpus, Papylus and Agathonice 7: 182
of Coratus: 249
of Cyprian 6: 182
of Dasius 12: 181
of Felix of Thibiuca: 181
of Irenaeus, 6: 182
of Marcellus 5: 182
of Martha 148 f., 181
of Maximus 3: 182
of Pionius 23: 182
of Polycarp 8.2: 60, 178
  9.3: 178
  14.1: 59, 159
  17.3: 179
  19.2: 67, 72, 196, 211
  19.3: 58
  21: 181
of Martyrs of Scilli 5 f.: 182
  17: 182
of Mar Simon and Companions: 181
of Theodor 9: 182

ST. AMBROSE
Epist. 20.23: 328
De excess. fratr. Satyr. 1.12: 312
Exp. on Lk. 2.44: 220
  on Lk. 3.13: 110
De fide 1.4: 220
  3.17: 171
  4.1: 306
  5.2: 311
  5.12: 287
  5.14: 305
  5.19: 311
De myst. 36: 223
De Sancto Spir. 3.22: 304
Sermo c. Auxent. 36: 328

APOSTOLIC CONSTITUTIONS
II.26.5: 171
II.27.4: 323
II.44.3: 171
III.10.3: 323
IV.13: 321
V.20.11: 321
VI.1–3: 321 ff.
VI.2.1 f.: 322
VI.18.4: 305
VI.26.2: 305
VI.30.9: 171
VII.16: 321
VII.41.6: 272
VII.42.3: 274
VII.47.3: 274
VIII: 158
VIII.12.7: 274
VII.12.49: 274
VIII.15.9: 274
VIII.46.8: 323

ARGUMENTUM IN Ps. 109 (110): 237

ARIAN FRAGMENT 1: 274
  3: 270
  4: 274
  8: 274

ARIAN TRACT IN LK.: 270 f.

ARISTIDES
Apol. 15.1: 309

ST. ATHANASIUS
Apol. ad Const. 10: 324
  12: 324
  35: 324
De decr. Nic. syn. 30.3: 299
Epist. ad Afros. episc. 8: 299
Epist. ad Marc. 6: 282
Epist. 2 ad Serap. 2 f.: 299
Exp. Fidei 1: 299
Hist. Arian. 32.4: 317
  34.1: 324
De incarn. 25: 279
De incarn. et c. Arian. 3: 310
  20: 286
  22: 310 f.
Orat. 1 c. Arian. 38: 310
  41: 278 f., 310
  43 f.: 310
  46: 310
  46: 280
Orat. 2 c. Arian. 11: 277, 282
  13 f.: 280
  17: 277
  23: 299, 305
Orat. 3 c. Arian. 4: 299

Orat. c. Gent. 43: 276
In Ps. 2.6: 282
In Ps. 2.7: 289, 324
In Ps. 71 (72).1: 291
In Ps. 109 (110): 283
De synod. 3.2: 318
    10: 324
    22 f.: 271
    25: 272
    49.2: 299
    49.5: 277
Vita Antonii 81: 324
Ps.-Ath., 1 C. Apollin. 20: 238
    2 C. Apollin. 3: 238
Ps.-Ath., Orat. 4 c. Arian.
    11: 289
    52: 289

St. Augustine
Confess. XI.13.15: 300
De Gen. ad litt. IV.2: 300

Barnabas, Epistle of
4.13: 208
5.5: 61
5.12: 88
7.2: 61
8.5: 99
12.10: 92, 101
12.11: 86
14.9 :113
18.2: 208
21.9: 103

St. Basil
De Spir. Sancto 18.45: 268, 329

St. Clement, Epistle of
16.2: 61, 102
19.2: 71
36.5: 101
43.6: 59
47.7: 59
48.2 f.: 105

59–61: 59, 159
59.3: 71
59.3 f.: 159
60.4: 298
61.3: 159

2 Clement
20.5: 58, 208

Clement of Alexandria
Protr. 100.4: 207, 209 f.
    116.1–4: 217 f.
    118.4: 207
    121.1: 221
Paed. I.9.84: 298
    I.52.2 f.: 217
    I.54.2: 207, 209
    I.54.3: 197
    I.65. 2 f.: 210
    I.65.3: 197
    I.84.1–85.2: 217
    III.7.39: 298
    III.99.1: 196
    III.101.1: 223
    III.101.3: 196 f., 219, 223
Strom. I.156.3: 218
    I.158 f.: 214
    I.158–168: 217
    I.165.1: 213
    I.167.3: 198, 217
    I.168.4: 209, 214
    I.169.1 f.: 218
    II.18.1–19.4: 214
    II.20.1: 213
    II.21.1–5: 217
    IV.66.1: 167
    V.4.4: 298
    V.5.29: 253
    V.52.5: 201
    VI.18.167: 20
    VI.106.2: 167
    VI.107.2: 167
    VII.7.7: 197
    VII.9.1: 197
    VII.16.5: 197
    VII.42.7: 218

    VII.100.1: 210
Exc. ex Theod. 4.2: 197

Pseudo-Clementines
Epist. Clem. 14.1 f.: 207
Hom. 2.16: 254
    3.19: 244 f., 247, 253, 255
    3.24: 245
    3.52: 243
    3.61 f.: 246, 248, 253
    3.70: 170
    8.10: 254
    8.21 f.: 244 f.
    9.2 f.: 244 ff., 248, 252 f.
    9.5: 245
    10.3: 254
    10.12: 248
    10.15: 248
    18.4: 250
    20.2: 245
Rec. 1.21: 245
    1.38: 243 f.
    1.45 f.: 117
    1.47: 117, 254
    1.48: 244
    1.69: 243
    2.32: 244
    2.41 f.: 251
    2.44: 251
    3.52: 246
    5.19: 248
    5.22: 248

Contra Varimadum 1.53: 311

St. Cyprian
De bono pat. 7: 154 f.
Cath. eccl. unit. 27: 155
De dominic. orat. 13: 155
Epist. 10.4 f.: 154
    15.1: 184
    31.5: 184
    55.20: 154
    58.4: 154
    58.8: 154
    76.1: 154

Ad Fortunatum 11: 178
Ad Quir. 1.21: 86
  2.11 ff.: 95
  2.29: 282, 291
  2.30: 290
  3.17: 178

St. Cyril of Alexandria
In Ps. 2.6: 285
In Ps. 2.7: 290
In Ps. 96 (97).1: 292

St. Cyril of Jerusalem
Cat. 10.11: 110
Cat. 15.2: 272

Dialogue between Athanasius and Zacchaeus
  46: 81, 111
  49: 81
  58: 111
  79 f.: 89

Dialogue between Timothy and Aquila: 289

Didache
Title: 59
4.13: 59
6.2: 59
9.3 f.: 159
9.5: 59
10.2 ff.: 159
10.6.: 158, 164
11.2: 59
12.1: 59
14.1: 59
15.4: 59
16.1: 59
16.7 f.: 59

Didascalia
II.11.1: 167
II.18.2: 167
II.20.1: 167
II.20.9: 168
II.24.4: 168

II.25.9: 168
II.26: 167
II.28.6: 168
II.34: 321
II.34.4 f.: 167
II.44.3: 168
II.57.2 ff.: 168
VI.23.8: 171

Didymus
In Ps. 23 (24).10: 306
De Trin. 3.23: 312

Diognetus, Epistle to
5 f.: 174
7.4: 44
9.2: 70
9.6: 58

St. Epiphanius
Ancor. 118.10: 272
Haer. XXX.18.4: 243
  LIX.34.5 ff.: 82
  LXXII.3.1: 307
  LXXVII.13.5: 110

Eunomius
Apol. 27: 272, 287

Eusebius of Caesarea
Contra Marc. I.1.22: 233, 267
  I.4: 274
  II.1.3: 233, 267
  II.3.39: 233, 267
  II.4.22: 233, 267
Dem. ev. IV.1.4: 264
  IV.2.1: 264
  IV.7.2: 264
  IV.15: 119 f.
  V.19.3: 265 f.
Eccl. theol. I.13.2: 264
  I.20.43: 238
  II.7.1: 268
  II.7.16: 268
  II.23.3: 268

III.15.5: 264
III.16.3: 267, 286
HE I.2.3: 265 f.
  I.2.11: 265 f.
  I.3: 21, 110, 119 f.
  I.6.7 ff.: 115
  II.23.12 f.: 52
  III.20.1–6: 43, 174
  III.27.1 f.: 238
  IV.3.2: 58
  IV.18.1: 79
  IV.18.4: 249
  V.20.1: 249
  V.28: 79, 162 f., 238
  VI.17: 238
  VII.27.2: 163
  VII.30: 163
  VIII.1.1. ff.: 21
  IX.9.12: 21
  X.4: 19 f., 22, 265 f.
Laus C. 3.6: 264 ff.
  5: 318
  6.4: 264
  7: 318
  7.9: 264
  11: 318
  11.2: 264
  12.1 ff.: 263
  12.16: 264
Mart. Pal.: 249
Praep. ev. VII.15.2: 265 ff.
  VIII.14.2 f.: 192, 213, 255
In Ps. 22 (23): 89
In Ps. 71 (72).1: 289, 291
Theoph. 1.3: 264
  1.4 f.: 264
  1.22 f.: 263 f.
  1.34: 264
  1.37: 126
  1.38: 263
  1.41 ff.: 263
  2.13: 264
  2.83: 264
  2.97: 264
  3.1: 264
  3.38: 264

3.61: 264
Vita Const. 4.48: 318
    4.69: 12

St. Gregory of Nazianzus
Orat. 30.4: 286, 307

Gregory of Nyssa
Hom. in 1 Cor. 15.28:

Hermas
Vis. III.1.4–8: 169
    III.3.5: 298
Sim. VIII.2.1: 153
    VIII.3.6: 153

St. Hilary
C. Const. 6: 178
De synod. 29 ff.: 272 f.
    33: 272
De Trin. 11.29: 287
    11.39: 287
Tract. in Ps. 22.6: 282
    30: 290

Hippolytus
De Antichr. 6: 177
    25: 176
    59: 207
Ap. Trad. I.3.6: 159
    I.4.4: 159
    I.4.13: 159
    V.2: 120 f.
Comm. on the Blessings
    52.6–9: 110
    72.8–11: 110
    126 f.: 110
    143–145: 110
On David and Goliath
    16.5: 97
Comm. on Ps. 22 (23): 89
Comm. on S. of S. 3.1: 228
    8.2. ff.: 203
    22: 204
Fragm. 1 in Ezek.: 204
Comm. on Dan. 4.9: 176

Ref. V.7.32: 89
    V.8.18 ff.: 148
    V.26.15 f.: 105
    V.26.15 ff.: 129, 148
    VI.19.6: 251
    VI.34.3 ff.: 222
    IX.15: 309
Ps.-Hippolytus, Paschal Homily 63: 162

St. Ignatius
Eph. pref.: 58
    1.1: 58
    7.2: 58
    17.1: 208
    18.2: 58, 92
    19.1: 208
    19.3: 58
    20.2: 92
Magn. pref.: 58
    1.3: 208
    3.1: 166
    6.1: 165, 169
Philad. 6.2: 208
    9.2: 58, 68, 98
Polyc. 8.3: 58
Rom. 3.3: 58
    7.1: 208
    7.3: 92
Smyrn. 1.1: 92
    7.1: 58
    8.1 f.: 165 f.
    10.1: 58
Trall. 2.1: 166
    3.1: 165
    4.2: 208
    7.1: 58
    9.1: 92
(Interpolated version:)
Eph. 6: 171
Magn. 4: 172
Philad. 4: 172, 322
    9: 82
Smyrn. 8: 172, 322
    8.2: 274
    9: 171 f.

Trall. 5: 172
    7: 172
Ps.-Ign. ad Philipp. 7.1: 305
Ps.-Ign. ad Tars. 2.1: 305
    5.1: 305

St. Irenaeus
Adv. haer. I.23.3: 185, 251
    I.28.1: 79
    II.6.2: 309
    II.22.4: 208
    III.6.1: 85, 101
    III.8.1: 175
    III.9.2: 94, 220
    III.9.3: 116
    III.10.3: 86
    III.10.6: 101
    III.11.8: 195
    III.12.5: 208
    III.12.9: 99
    III.16.2: 309
    III.16.3: 266
    III.16.6: 194, 208
    III.17.1: 116
    III.19.2: 309
    III.21.3: 185
    IV.3: 56, 225
    IV.6.2: 79
    IV.10.2: 97
    IV.11.3: 221
    IV.20.11: 140
    IV.21.2 f.: 96
    IV.24.1: 208
    IV.25.1: 208
    IV.33.11: 88
    IV.33.13: 105, 195, 235, 292
    IV.34.4: 102
    IV.39.2: 230
    V.30.3: 185
Dem. 9: 86
    44 f.: 85
    47 f.: 58, 116
    49: 94, 97, 116, 288
    56: 266
    57: 97

71: 86
85 f.: 101 f., 105
Fragm.: 265

St. Jerome

Comm. on Isa. 11.2: 114
Tract. in Ps. 96.1: 292
Tract. in Ps. 98.1: 292

St. John Chrysostom

Comm. on Isa. 6: 225
Ecloga 21: De imperio: 323, 329
Expos. 2 in Ps. 121: 329
Hom. de Anna 2.4: 329
Hom. de stat. 3.2: 329
In illud: Vidi dominum hom. 4.4 f.: 329
  5.2: 323
  6: 327
  19: 327
Hom. 67 in Matt.: 223
Hom. in 2 Cor. 3.5: 106
Ps.-Chrysostom In Ps. 96.1: 285, 292

St. Justin Martyr

Apol. 6: 114
  11.1 f.: 174
  12.7: 208
  12.9: 112
  17: 175
  32: 97
  32.1 ff.: 96
  32.2: 221
  32.4: 93
  32.12 f.: 94
  33.5: 309
  33.7: 66
  34.1: 88, 93
  35.2: 99
  35.11: 98, 221
  39.1–3: 102
  40.11–19: 88, 281
  41.1–4: 99

45.1 ff.: 101
45.5: 102
51.7: 103
54.5: 96
55.5: 86
63: 230
63.5: 112 f.
63.14: 112
App. (2 Apol.) 2: 179
Dial. 12.2: 113
  14.4: 208
  14.8: 98
  24.1: 162
  29.1: 103
  30.3: 100
  32.1: 98
  32.1–6: 101
  33.1 f.: 95, 101
  34.1: 95
  34.2: 81, 265, 290
  34.2–4: 291
  36.2–6: 95
  36.3 f.: 103
  36.5: 101
  36.5 f.: 105
  46.1: 98
  47.5: 70
  49: 114
  49.8: 100
  50.3–5: 88
  52: 115
  52.1–4: 98
  52.2: 115
  52.2 f.: 96
  52.3 f.: 115
  53.2: 223
  53.3: 98
  53.6: 88
  54.2: 93
  56: 85, 112
  56.14 f.: 84 f., 101
  56.17: 102
  58.10: 112
  60.4: 112
  61.1: 81, 265
  62.5: 265

63.4: 102
63.5: 58
64.4: 91
64.6: 290
68.5 f.: 93
73.1–4: 99 f.
75.1–3: 112 f.
76.1: 93
76.3: 266
76.7: 58
78.1: 88, 93, 98
83.1: 101
83.1–4: 95
83.2 ff.: 102
83.4: 100
85.1–4: 103
86: 82, 85, 113
86 f.: 111
86.2–4: 111
86.3: 81
86.3–6: 113 f.
87: 114 f.
87.1 f.: 114
87.1–6: 113
87.4: 116
88.8: 288
96.1: 81, 111
97.4: 96
100.4: 81
106.4: 94, 195
109.1–3: 102
110.2: 102
113.1: 112
113.5: 109
117: 20
118.1: 101, 109
118.2: 93
120.3: 96
122.6: 97, 288
126.1: 81, 266
127.5: 101, 103
128.1: 58
137.2: 93
141.3: 115

Ps.-Justin, Cohort. ad Graec. 17: 249

LACTANTIUS
Div. inst. 4.25: 266
    7.19.5: 266
De mort. persec. 48.11: 20

LETTER OF THE ARIMINIUM SYNOD: 324

LETTER OF THE LUCIFERIANS: 320

LUCIFER OF CALARIS
De non parc. 8: 323

MARCELLUS OF ANCYRA:
Fragm. 19: 307
    31: 307
    60: 307
    96: 274
    111: 233 f.
    112: 234, 239
    113: 233 f.
    114: 234
    115: 234, 239
    117: 233 f., 236, 307
    127: 236

MAXIMINUS
Contra Judaeos: 220

MELITO OF SARDIS
De bapt., fragm.: 203
De fide, fragm.: 195 f., 202, 209, 165

METHODIUS
De creatis 9: 304
De resurr. II.10.4–6: 204
Symp. III.6.63 f.: 210
    IV.6.107: 210

NOVATIAN
De Trin. 11: 266
    18: 266
    26: 85, 289

ST. OPTATUS
De schism. Donat. 3.3: 320

ORIGEN
C. Celsum 5.45: 305
De princ. IV.1.1 f.: 20
Comm. on S. of S., Prol.: 226, 228 f.
    2: 89, 229
Comm. on Matt. 12.20: 221, 282
    16.12: 92
    16.4: 224
    16.14–19: 221
    16.19: 223
    Comm. ser. 39: 20
    Comm. ser. 111: 225
    Comm. ser. 125: 224
    Comm. ser. 130: 282
Comm. on Jn. 1.21 ff.: 81
    1.28: 89, 291
    1.29: 289 f.
    1.38: 100
    6.39: 282
    6.42: 226
    6.56: 223
    10.28: 226
    10.29: 221, 223 f.
    10.33: 222
    13.58: 282
    32.25: 278
Hom. on Num. 1.4: 227
    12.2: 226 f.
    28.4: 227
Hom. on Josh. 9.10: 21
Hom. on Judg. 6.3: 227
Hom. on S. of S.: 1.2: 230
    1.5: 229
    1.10: 229
    2.2 f.: 229 f.
    2.9: 229
Hom. on Ezek. 1.7: 266
In Ps. 2.7: 289
Cat. fragm. 29 f.: 220

PAMPHILUS
Apol. pro Orig. 1: 219
    5: 163

PAPYRI
Copt. mag.: 297
Greek: 308

PAUL OF SAMOSATA
Fragm.: 238 f.

ST. PETER CHRYSOLOGUS
Sermo 59: 106

PHYSIOLOGUS: 104, 144

ST. POLYCARP
Phil., pref.: 58
    1.1 f.: 59
    2.1: 59
    6.2 f.: 59
    11.2: 59
    12.2: 59

SOCRATES
HE 2.10: 271 f.
    2.18: 272

SOZOMENUS
HE III.5.9: 273

TATIAN
Orat. ad Graec. 14.1: 249

TERTULLIAN
Adv. Jud. 3.9: 102
    7: 97
    7.6 f.: 20
    9.14: 79
    9.23: 112
    10.11: 86
    12.1: 288
    14.12: 97
Adv. Marc. III.16.5: 112
    III.19.1 f.: 99
    III.20.3: 96, 288
    III.20.6 ff.: 92

III.21.3: 102
IV.1.4: 102
IV.22.8: 288
IV.36.9 ff.: 92
V.4.3: 102
V.8.4: 94
V.9.6: 101
V.9.6 ff.: 96, 290
Adv. Prax. 3: 250
  7.2: 289
  11: 85
  11.3: 289
Adv. Valent. 11.2: 169
Apolog. 33.3–34.2: 179
  37.4 f.: 20
De carne Chr. 14: 92
De corona 12.4: 175
  14.3 f.: 155
  15: 154
De exhort. cast. 12: 184
De fuga 10.1: 184
  12.9 f.: 175
De idol. 15.3: 175
De praescr. haer. 36.1: 169
Scorp. 14.2: 175
Ps.-Tert., Carmen adversus Marc. V.202: 300

THEODORE OF MOPSUESTIA
In Ps. 2.6: 285
In Ps. 2.7: 290

THEODORET OF CYRUS
HE I.4.46: 240
In Ps. 2.6: 285, 312
In Ps. 2.7: 290
In Ps. 71.1: 291
In Ps. 96.1: 292

In Ps. 98.1: 292
In Ps. 109 (110).1: 312

THEOPHILUS OF ANTIOCH
Ad Autolyc. 1.6: 301

TREASURE CAVE: 117 f.

Classical Authors

ARCHYTAS
Fragm.: 193, 206, 209

ARISTOTLE
Metaphysics XII: 248
Ps.-Arist., De mundo 398a: 191
  400b 6 ff.: 194, 206, 208

CICERO
De rep. 3.33: 184
De senect. 73: 184

DIO CHRYSOSTOM
Orat. 1.11 ff.: 200
  1.22: 255
  2.71: 200
  3.41–50: 200
  4.24 f.: 194
  4.62: 200
  12.27: 208
  12.34: 206
  36.31 f.: 208
  36.39: 204
  36.50: 206
  37.42–46: 254

DIOTOGENES
Fragm.: 192 f., 206, 209, 213, 216, 254 f.

ECPHANTUS
Fragm.: 199 f., 252 f., 255

HOMER
Iliad II.204: 248 f.

PLATO
Gorgias 67: 206
Leges 12.10: 206
Phaedr. 246a ff.: 201
Polit. 275a f.: 199
  302a: 206
Rep. 416a: 199
  440d: 199
  488a–e: 206

PLINY THE YOUNGER
Epist. 10.96.7: 162

PLOTINUS
Enn. V.5.3: 192

PLUTARCH
Ad princ. iner. 780 f.: 253

STHENIDAS
Fragm.: 254 f.

STOIC FRAGMENTS: 214

SUETONIUS
Vita Caes., Domitianus 13.2: 43

VERGIL
Fourth Eclogue: 63

www.ingramcontent.com/pod-product-compliance
Lightning Source LLC
Chambersburg PA
CBHW071145300426
44113CB00009B/1087